S0-BCZ-083

Rick Steves®

GREECE
ATHENS & THE
PELOPONNESE

Rick Steves with Cameron Hewitt and Gene Openshaw

CONTENTS

Welcome to Rick Steves' Europe

Travel is intensified living—maximum thrills per minute and one of the last great sources of legal adventure. Travel is freedom. It's recess, and we need it.

I discovered a passion for European travel as a teen and have been sharing it ever since—through my bus tours, public television and radio shows, and travel guidebooks. Over the years, I've taught millions of travelers how to best enjoy Europe's blockbuster sights—and experience "Back Door" discoveries that most tourists miss.

This book offers a balanced mix of Greek cities and villages, ancient sites and Byzantine churches, and great museums and relaxing beaches. It's selective: Rather than listing dozens of historic attractions, I recommend only the best ones. And it's in-depth: My self-guided museum tours and city walks provide insight into Greece's vibrant history and today's living, breathing culture.

I advocate traveling simply and smartly. Take advantage of my money- and time-saving tips on sightseeing, transportation, and more. Try local, characteristic alternatives to expensive hotels and restaurants. In many ways, spending more money only builds a thicker wall between you and what you traveled so far to see.

We visit Greece to experience it—to become temporary locals. Thoughtful travel engages us with the world, as we learn to appreciate other cultures and new ways to measure quality of life.

Judging by the positive feedback I receive from readers, this book will help you enjoy a fun, affordable, and rewarding vacation—whether it's your first trip or your tenth.

Kalo taxidi! Happy travels!

Rick Steves

GREECE

Slip a coaster under that rickety table leg, take a sip of ouzo, and watch the sun dip into the sea. You've arrived in Greece.

Greece offers sunshine, whitewashed houses with bright-blue shutters, delicious food, and a relaxed lifestyle. And, as the cradle of Western civilization, it has some of the world's greatest ancient monuments.

The ancient Greeks—who reached their golden age apex in Athens in the fifth century BC—have had an unmatched impact on European and American culture: democracy and mathematics, medicine and literature, theater and astronomy, mythology and philosophy. All of these—and more—were developed by a bunch of tunic-clad Greeks in a village huddled at the base of the Acropolis.

Today the capital of Athens is the teeming home of 3.75 million people—about one-third of the country's population of 11 million. Athens is a fascinating mix of ancient ruins and an old center with modern upgrades—world-class museums, fun pedestrian zones ringing the Acropolis, fine public transport, and a state-of-the-art airport.

By day, tour the Acropolis, the Agora, and the history-packed museums. Light a candle alongside black-clad widows at an icon-filled church. Haggle with a sandal maker at a busy market stall, or have coffee with locals in an old town café. At night, join the pan-European party of eating, drinking, and dancing in open-air tavernas, especially in the colorful Thissio and rickety-chic Psyrri neighborhoods.

Athens is a great city to see, and worth a few days to

*Athens' market square—
Monastiraki—with an
Acropolis backdrop; a stroll
through the Ancient Agora*

explore. Centrally located, it's also the perfect launchpad for
farther-flung Greek destinations. Commune with ancient
spirits at the center of the world: the oracle near the mountain
hamlet of Delphi. Take a vacation from your busy vacation on
one of the best and easiest-to-reach Greek islands, traffic-free
Hydra. Other top isle getaways are the whitewashed village-
island of Mykonos and the ridge-topping crescent of Santorini,
cradling a volcano's flooded crater.

An hour's drive west of Athens, the peninsula known as the
Peloponnese hangs from the rest of the Greek mainland by the
narrow Isthmus of Corinth. This stark, mountainous landscape
is dotted with the ruins of Mycenaean palaces, ancient temples,
frescoed Byzantine churches, and medieval hilltop castles
built by the Crusaders and the Venetians. At Mycenae, visit
the hub of a civilization that dominated Greece from 1600 to
1200 BC. Hike up the stone rows of the world's best-preserved
ancient theater at Epidavros. Run a lap at Olympia, site of the
first Olympic Games. To round things out, enjoy the stunning
landscapes of the wild Mani Peninsula and the engaging old
Venetian towns of Monemvasia (a fortified, village-topped
giant rock hovering just offshore) and Nafplio (the first capital
of independent Greece).

Greece is easy on travelers. Tourism makes up 20 percent
of the country's GDP, and the people are welcoming and

A Feast of Greek Pleasures

Greece's friendly people, mouth-watering food and drink, and joyful music and folk dances meld into a lesson in good living for travelers.

When I'm in Greece, I eat as the Greeks do. Around 9 p.m., I head to a taverna and order a medley of *meze* plates (Greek tapas) to share family-style. The selection, while predictable, never gets old for me: garlic dip, fava bean dip, *tzatziki* dip (made from yogurt, cucumber, and mint), or all three on a single serving platter; fried eggplant or zucchini; Greek salad; and big grilled peppers—red or green—stuffed with feta cheese.

Most of my meals also include something from the sea, such as grilled calamari or octopus, sardines, or a plate of fried small fish (three inch), smaller fish (two inch), or very small fish (one inch). With three-inch fish, I leave the head and tail on the plate (and try not to wonder about the once inky, now dry black guts). With the smaller fish, I leave nothing but a line of greasy fingerprints on the fringe of my paper tablecloth.

In Athens, I enjoy visiting the Central Market, where many locals come to do their weekly grocery shopping. It's a living, breathing, smelly barrage on all the senses. You'll see dripping-fresh meat, livestock in all stages of dismemberment, and the still-wriggling catch of the day. The fruit and vegetable stalls, just outside the market, are flanked by shops selling feta from the barrel and countless varieties of olives.

My favorite stop at the market is an ouzo bar. These bars, in the middle of the fish market, offer a memorable setting for a drink and snack. And it's cheap. About €3 gets you an ouzo (anise-flavored liquor) and a little ▶▶▶

The quintessential Greek salad; succulent octopus salad; fresh chickens winging it at Central Market

▶▶▶ *meze* plate to enjoy at the bar while taking in the action.

As you wander about, you'll often hear Greek music playing—it's best when it's live. In many towns on weekend summer evenings, you're likely to come across musicians sitting around an outdoor table playing traditional folk music on their bouzouki (a long-necked mandolin). When the weather cools down, they move inside to tavernas to entertain the late-night crowds.

Greeks love to dance, especially when celebrating events like weddings and baptisms, but any good music is reason enough. Popular dances include the graceful *kalamatianos* circle dance and the *syrtaki,* done with arms outstretched or thrown across one another's shoulders as immortalized by Anthony Quinn in the film *Zorba the Greek.* A few dancers might get carried away, "applaud" by throwing plates or flowers, and then dance on the tables into the wee hours.

Greeks tend to show hospitality with drinks—often ouzo. You don't drink ouzo straight; instead, you add ice or water, which turns the ouzo from clear to milky white. When Greeks really want to show hospitality, the drink is *tsipouro.* Like Italian grappa, this brandy-like firewater is about 40 percent alcohol and makes ouzo seem like kid stuff. The last time I had it, I had a hard time holding my camera steady as I took "going local" to a very tasty extreme.

But that's part of the appeal of this place. When in Greece, sometimes it's best to put down the camera, ditch the plans, and join in the fun. ▪

Dancers in traditional garb; folk music in Nafplio; embracing the Greek way of life—opa!

accommodating. Greeks strive to demonstrate *filotimo* ("love of honor"), roughly translated as being open and friendly and doing the right thing. Social faux pas made by unwitting foreigners are easily overlooked by Greeks.

You'll find two Greeces: traditional/old/rural and modern/young/urban. In the countryside, you'll see men on donkeys, women wearing headscarves, and families harvesting olives by hand. In bigger cities like Athens, it's a concrete world of honking horns and buzzing mobile phones. Well-dressed, educated Greeks listen to hip-hop music and Instagram their vacations. As the rural exodus continues, cities are now home to a majority of Greeks.

Despite modern changes, many Greek men and women play traditional roles. Women generally run the home; fewer women join the workforce than in other European countries. Men like to hang out at coffee shops, playing backgammon, watching sports on TV, and arguing over politics.

The Greek Orthodox Church—a rallying point for Greeks during centuries of foreign occupation—remains part of every-day life. Ninety-five percent of all Greeks declare themselves Orthodox, even if they rarely go to church.

Orthodox elements appear everywhere. Icon shrines dot the highways. Orthodox priests—with their Old Testament beards, black robes, cake-shaped hats, and families in tow—mingle with parishioners on street corners. Greeks routinely

Timeless Greece: Jesus in a Greek Orthodox church, locals in black in a whitewashed town

The appealing town and island of Mykonos; grilling souvlaki for a feast-day celebration

pop into churches to light a candle, asking for favors. Even the young celebrate feast days with their families and make the sign of the cross when passing a church.

Greeks are family-oriented, with large extended families. Kids live at home until they're married, and then they might just move into a flat upstairs in the same apartment building. The "family" extends to the large diaspora of emigrants. Three million Greek-Americans (including George Stephanopoulos, Pete Sampras, and Tina Fey) keep ties to the home country through their Orthodox faith and their festive celebratory traditions.

On warm summer nights, families spill into the streets to greet their neighbors on the evening stroll. For entertainment, they go out to eat, where they order large amounts and share it family-style. And when the music plays, it's time to dance.

Culturally rich, Greece has given the world the Olympic Games, tall tales of gods (such as Zeus, Apollo, and Aphrodite), and exciting heroes (Achilles, Odysseus, and Hercules). From Socrates to souvlaki, Greece has a classical past and a hang-loose present.

It's easy to surrender to the Greek way of living. With its long history, incomparable sights, and simple lifestyle, Greece has a timeless appeal.

Greece's Top Destinations

Opa! Over its 3,000 years of history, Greece has created more sights than you have time to see. To help you plan your trip, this overview categorizes the country's top destinations into must-see places (for everyone) and worth-it places (for those with extra time or special interests). I've also suggested a minimum number of days to allow per destination.

MUST-SEE DESTINATIONS

These three places—Greece's bustling capital, a pleasant port town, and a sleepy island—give you the essential Greek experience in an easy-to-manage package.

▲▲▲Athens (allow 2-3 days)

Greece's capital features the ancient world's most magnificent sight—the Parthenon atop the Acropolis hill—plus excellent museums (Acropolis and Archaeological), the Ancient Agora, an atmospheric old town, the lively Central Market, and funky neighborhoods bursting with avant-garde nightlife.

▲▲▲Nafplio (2 days, including day trips)

Strategic Nafplio, on the Peloponnese, was Greece's first capital. Today it's just a cozy port with an elegant old town, energetic street life, and a cliff-topping fortress offering dramatic sea-and-mountain views. A good home base, it's handy to the ancient sites of Mycenae and Epidavros.

▲▲▲Hydra (2 days)

The small island of Hydra—an idyllic and relaxing getaway—is an easy ferry ride from Athens or the Peloponnese. Hydra has a picturesque harbor, casual beaches, and enticing coastal trails. It's wonderfully traffic-free, unless you count the donkeys.

Evening fun in Athens' Psyrri neighborhood; burro on the traffic-free island of Hydra; one of the island's beaches; hilltop castle in Nafplio

(Clockwise from top) Ancient Epidavros theater; statuary from Olympia; refreshing Kardamyli; Lion Gate in Mycenae; (opposite) ghost town on the Mani Peninsula

WORTH-IT DESTINATIONS

You can weave any of these destinations—rated ▲ or ▲▲—
into your itinerary. It's easy to add some destinations based on
proximity (if you're going to Nafplio, Epidavros is nearly next-
door), but some out-of-the-way places can merit the journey,
depending on your time and interests.

▲Epidavros (half-day)
At 2,300 years old, this is the best-preserved theater of the
ancient world, with unbelievable acoustics. Open to sightseers
by day, it's used for performances on summer weekend nights.

▲Mycenae (half-day)
Long before Athens' golden age (450-400 BC), the mighty
Mycenaeans built this now-ruined mountaintop fortress, dating from roughly 1300 BC. The grand Lion Gate and massive
beehive tomb impressed even the golden-age Greeks and still
wow tourists today.

▲▲Olympia (1 day)
Birthplace of the Olympic Games, this famous site has
evocative temple ruins, a still-functional stadium (and original
starting line), an intimate museum of ancient masterpieces,
and a town nearby.

▲Kardamyli (1 day)
The cozy, unspoiled beach town is a fun hangout and a good
jumping-off point for the Mani Peninsula. Stroll the town, pop
into food shops, relax on the pebbly beach, and hike up to old
fortifications.

▲Mani Peninsula (1 day)
Easiest for drivers, this remote, rustic region has seaside

villages, eerie ghost towns, Byzantine churches, spectacular caves (Pyrgos Dirou), stark ridges, and jagged coastlines.

▲Monemvasia (1 day)

An old fortress town, dating from Venetian and Byzantine times, caps a gigantic rock peninsula jutting out into the sea. The modern town on the mainland offers million-dollar views of the monolith.

▲▲Delphi (1 day)

These dramatic mountainside ruins, near the town of Delphi, are draped with the Sanctuary of Apollo, where ancients came to consult the oracle. A great museum displays statues and treasures found on-site.

▲▲Mykonos (1-2 days)

This quintessential, popular island has a postcard-perfect whitewashed village, old-time windmills, and pulsating night-life. Temple ruins on nearby Delos, reachable by ferry, mark the fabled birthplace of Apollo and Artemis.

▲▲Santorini (1-2 days)

This stunningly situated, romantic island—actually the lip of a volcano's flooded crater—is renowned for cliff-clinging white villages, blue-domed churches, volcanic-sand beaches, and spectacular sunsets.

Rocky Monemvasia looming at twilight; a Santorini village spilling down the hill

Planning Your Trip

To plan your trip, you'll need to design your itinerary—choosing where and when to go, how you'll travel, and how many days to spend at each destination. For my best general advice on sightseeing, accommodations, restaurants, and more, see the Practicalities chapter.

DESIGNING AN ITINERARY

As you read this book and learn your options…

Choose your top destinations.

My recommended itinerary (see page 18) gives you an idea of how much you can reasonably see in two weeks, but you can adapt it to fit your own interests and time frame.

Athens has the country's best museums, ancient sites, shopping, and nightlife.

Drivers enjoy road-tripping, especially on the wide-open Peloponnese, which offers tempting sights without crowds—the monolithic Monemvasia, the beach village of Kardamyli, the remote Mani Peninsula—and wherever you go, ancient ruins are nearby. Explorers may want to linger.

Historians zero in on the ancient sites—the best are in Athens, Delphi, Epidavros, Mycenae, and Olympia. Hikers and nature lovers make tracks for the Peloponnese destinations of Nafplio, Kardamyli, and Monemvasia, and the islands of Hydra and Santorini. Nearly every hike in Greece comes with grand panoramic views.

If basking appeals, unroll your towel on one of the islands. Little, low-key Hydra is easy to reach and enjoy. Picturesque

Athens and the Peloponnese in Two Weeks by Car

Outside of Athens, this region is best visited by car. If you'd rather get around by bus, you'll see less in the same amount of time (or you can add more days to your itinerary to see it all)—see page 21.

Day	Plan	Sleep
1	Arrive in Athens	Athens
2	Sightsee Athens	Athens
3	More time in Athens	Athens
4	Boat to Hydra	Hydra
5	Relax on Hydra	Hydra
6	Boat back to Athens, pick up rental car, drive to Delphi	Delphi
7	Sightsee Delphi, drive to Olympia	Olympia
8	Sightsee Olympia, drive to Kardamyli	Kardamyli
9	Relax in Kardamyli	Kardamyli
10	Mani Peninsula loop drive, on to Monemvasia	Monemvasia
11	Sightsee Monemvasia	Monemvasia
12	See Mycenae en route to Nafplio	Nafplio
13	Nafplio, side-trip to Epidavros	Nafplio
14	Return to Athens, drop off rental car	Athens
15	Fly home, or continue to Mykonos and/or Santorini by plane or boat	

Mykonos offers more nightlife and a quick ferry to ancient Delos. Santorini has the best mix of beaches, sights, and stunning natural scenery. Photographers want to go everywhere.

Decide when to go.

Tourist season is roughly Easter through October. Peak season is summer, when Athens is packed with tourists, and hotel prices can be high. July and August are the hottest.

The best time to visit is late spring (May) and fall (Sept-Oct). It's pleasant, with comfortable weather, no rain, and smaller crowds (except during holiday weekends).

Winter (late Oct through mid-March) is colder, with some rainfall. Sights may close during lunch, TI offices keep shorter hours, and some tourist activities vanish altogether. Hotel rates

are soft; look for bargains. Avoid the islands in winter, when many hotels and restaurants close, and bad weather can delay or cancel ferries.

For weather specifics, see the climate chart in the appendix.

Connect the dots.

Link your destinations into a logical route. Determine which cities you'll fly into and out of. Begin your search for transatlantic flights at Kayak.com.

Decide if you'll travel by car or bus (Greece lacks a a robust rail system). A car is great for exploring the mainland and the Peloponnese, but is useless in Athens (rent when leaving Athens). Outside of Athens, buses get you to popular destinations

such as Delphi, but can be sparse and frustrating elsewhere. If you travel by bus, allow extra time.

To determine approximate travel times between destinations, study the driving map in the Practicalities chapter or check Google Maps. To connect Athens and the Greek islands, take a ferry or a flight.

Write out a day-by-day itinerary.

Figure out how many destinations you can comfortably fit in your time frame. Don't overdo it—few travelers wish they'd hurried more. Allow enough days per stop (see estimates in "Greece's Top Destinations," earlier). Minimize one-night stands. It can be worth taking an afternoon drive or bus ride to settle into a town for two consecutive nights—and gain a full uninterrupted day for sightseeing. Include sufficient time for transportation; whether you travel by bus or car, it'll take you at least a half-day to get between most destinations.

To get over jet lag, consider starting your trip in a more laid-back destination, such as Hydra or the other islands, before tackling Athens.

Check if any holidays or festivals fall during your trip—these attract crowds and can close sights (for the latest, visit Greece's tourist website, www.visitgreece.gr).

Give yourself some slack. Every trip, and every traveler, needs downtime for doing laundry, picnic shopping, people-watching, and so on. Pace yourself. Assume you will return.

Athens and the Peloponnese in Two Weeks by Bus and Boat

Day	Plan	Sleep
1	Arrive in Athens	Athens
2	Sightsee Athens	Athens
3	More time in Athens	Athens
4	Morning in Athens, afternoon bus to Delphi	Delphi
5	Sightsee Delphi	Delphi
6	Morning bus to Athens, then boat to Hydra	Hydra
7	Relax on Hydra	Hydra
8	Morning boat back to Athens, then bus to Olympia	Olympia
9	Sightsee Olympia	Olympia
10	Morning bus to Nafplio	Nafplio
11	Day trip to Mycenae	Nafplio
12	Day trip to Epidavros	Nafplio
13	Bus to Athens	Athens
14	Fly home, or continue to Mykonos and/or Santorini by plane or boat	

Notes: Research and consider bus connections carefully (usually easier to do in person than online); these can be limited and complicated, especially on the Peloponnese.

With limited time, you could see Delphi either as a day trip on Day 4 (return to Athens for the night) or as a single overnight (bus from Athens to Delphi on the morning of Day 4, spend the night in Delphi, then bus to Athens and boat to Hydra on Day 5).

If you've seen enough ancient sites, you could skip Olympia (which is time-consuming to reach by bus), and visit the very different town-and-giant-rock of Monemvasia (also time-consuming by bus, but worthwhile if it appeals to you), or easier, enjoy more beach time on Hydra.

Without a car, the easiest connection from Hydra to the Peloponnese is via Athens, but adventurous travelers could tackle the cheaper and shorter—though more complicated—boat-taxi-bus connection to Nafplio instead; for tips, see page 257.

This bus itinerary leaves out the hardest-to-reach destinations: Kardamyli/Mani Peninsula (best by car or with a hired local driver) and Monemvasia. With an extra week and a bunch of patience, you could include all of my recommended destinations.

Crowds leaving the Acropolis in late afternoon—a smart time to visit; arriving at the island of Hydra; beach sunset on Mykonos; Hydra ferry

Trip Costs Per Person

Run a reality check on your dream trip. You'll have major transportation costs in addition to daily expenses.

Flight: A round-trip flight from the US to Athens costs about $900-1,500, depending on where you fly from and when.

Public Transportation: For a two-week trip, figure on per-person costs of $150 by public transit (boat to Hydra, bus to everything else).

Car Rental: Allow roughly $350-500 per week (booked well in advance), not including tolls, gas, parking, and insurance. If you need the car for three weeks or more, leasing can be cheaper.

AVERAGE DAILY EXPENSES PER PERSON

$145
Applies to cities and popular islands, less on Peloponnese

Lodging
Based on two people splitting the cost of a $140 double room with breakfast.
★★★★★
$70

Meals
$15 for lunch, $20 for dinner
$35

Sights and Entertainment
This daily average works for most people.
$30

City Transit
Buses, Metro
$10

Budget Tips

To cut your daily expenses, take advantage of the deals you'll find throughout Greece and mentioned in this book.

In Athens, you'll save money buying the Acropolis combo-ticket, which covers a number of ancient sites (buy in advance online to save time). City transit passes (for multiple rides or all-day usage) decrease your cost per ride.

Some businesses—especially hotels—offer discounts to my readers (look for the RS% symbol in the listings in this book).

Reserve your rooms directly with the hotel. Some hotels offer a discount if you pay in cash and/or stay three or more nights (check online or ask).

Rooms can cost less outside ▶▶▶

Rick Steves Greece

▶▶▶ of tourist season (Easter-October). And even seniors can sleep cheaply in hostels (most have private rooms) for about $30 per person. Or check Airbnb-type sites for deals.

It's no hardship to eat inexpensively in Greece. You can get tasty, affordable meals at souvlaki stands, Greek fast-food shops, tavernas, cafeterias, and bakeries that sell sandwiches.

Cultivate the art of picnicking in atmospheric settings.

When you splurge, choose an experience you'll always remember, such as a walking tour, a food tour, or even a private tour with a guide who introduces you to a city or ancient site. Minimize souvenir shopping; focus instead on collecting wonderful memories. ■

Guide at an Athens museum; tasty samples at a Central Market shop; inviting view bar in Hydra

BEFORE YOU GO

You'll have a smoother trip if you tackle a few things ahead
of time. For more details on these topics, see the Practicalities chapter and RickSteves.com, which has helpful travel-tip
articles and videos.

Make sure your travel documents are valid. If your passport expires within six months of your return date, you need
to renew it (allow 12-plus weeks). Be aware of entry requirements; you may need to register with the European Travel
Information and Authorization System (ETIAS; quick and
easy process, https://travel-europe.europa.eu/etias_en). Get
passport and country-specific travel info at Travel.State.gov.

Arrange your transportation. Book your international flights. Overall, Google Flights is the best place to start
searching for flights. Figure out your transportation options:
It's worth thinking about renting a car, buying boat tickets
online, or booking flights to the islands. (You can wing it once
you're there, but tickets may cost more or be sold out.) Drivers:
Consider bringing an International Driving Permit (sold at
AAA offices in the US, www.aaa.com) along with your license.

Book rooms well in advance, especially if your trip falls
during peak season or any major holidays or festivals, or if
you're hoping to land a particular hotel on Mykonos or Santorini, where perennial visitors often book their favorite rooms
months ahead.

Hire local guides in advance. Reserve ahead by email;
popular guides can get booked up.

Consider travel insurance. Compare the cost of insurance
to the cost of your potential loss. Check whether your existing

insurance (health, homeowners, or renters) covers you and your possessions overseas.

Reserve ahead for key sights. By the time you visit, a timed-entry ticket may be required for the Acropolis. Check the latest at HHTicket.gr.

Call your bank. Alert your bank that you'll be using your debit and credit cards in Europe. Ask about transaction fees, and, if you don't already have one, get a "contactless" credit card (request your card PIN too). You don't need to bring euros for your trip; you can withdraw euros from cash machines in Europe.

Use your smartphone smartly. Sign up for an international service plan to reduce your costs, or rely on Wi-Fi in Europe instead. Download any apps you'll want on the road, such as maps, translators, transit schedules, and Rick Steves Audio Europe (see sidebar).

Pack light. You'll walk with your luggage more than you think. I travel for weeks with a single carry-on bag and a day pack. Use the packing checklist in the appendix as a guide.

Rick's Free Video Clips and Audio Tours

Travel smarter with these free, fun resources:

Rick Steves Classroom Europe, a powerful tool for teachers, is also useful for travelers. This video library contains about 500 short clips excerpted from my public television series. Enjoy these videos as you sort through options for your trip and to better understand what you'll see in Europe. Check it out at Classroom.RickSteves.com (just enter a topic to find everything I've filmed on a subject).

Rick Steves Audio Europe, a free app, makes it easy to download my audio tours and listen to them offline as you travel. For this book (look for the 🎧), these audio tours include my Athens City Walk and tours of the Acropolis, Ancient Agora, and National Archaeological Museum. The app also offers interviews (organized by country) from my public radio show with experts from Europe and around the globe. Find it in your app store or at RickSteves.com/AudioEurope.

Travel Smart

If you have a positive attitude, equip yourself with good information (this book), and expect to travel smart, you will.

Read—and reread—this book. To have an "A" trip, be an "A" student. Note opening hours of sights, closed days, crowd-beating tips, and whether reservations are required or advisable. Check the latest at RickSteves.com/update.

Be your own tour guide. As you travel, get up-to-date info on sights, reserve tickets and tours, reconfirm hotels and travel arrangements, and check transit connections. Visit local tourist information offices (TIs). Upon arrival in a new town, lay the groundwork for a smooth departure; confirm the road, bus, or boat you'll take when you leave.

Outsmart thieves. Pickpockets abound in crowded places where tourists congregate. Treat commotions as smoke-screens for theft. Keep your cash, credit cards, and passport secure in a money belt tucked under your clothes; carry only a day's spending money in your front pocket or wallet. Don't set valuable items down on counters or café tabletops, where they can be quickly stolen or easily forgotten.

Minimize potential loss. Keep expensive gear to a minimum. Bring copies or take photos of important documents (passport and cards) to aid in replacement if they're lost or stolen. Back up photos and files frequently.

Beat the summer heat. If you wilt easily, choose a hotel with air-conditioning, start your day early, take a midday siesta, and resume your sightseeing later. Churches offer a cool haven (though dress modestly—no bare shoulders or shorts). Take frequent breaks for ice cream or iced coffee.

Guard your time and energy. Taking a taxi can be a good value if it saves you a long wait for a cheap bus or an exhausting walk across town. To avoid long lines in Athens, follow my crowd-beating tips, such as sightseeing early or late, and buying your Acropolis ticket or combo-ticket online in advance (may be required by the time you visit).

Be flexible. Even if you have a well-planned itinerary, expect changes, strikes, closures, sore feet, bad weather, and so on. Your Plan B could turn out to be even better.

Attempt the language. Many Greeks—especially in the tourist trade and in cities—speak English, but if you learn some Greek, even just a few pleasantries, you'll get more smiles and make more friends. Apps such as Google Translate work for on-the-go translation help, but you can get a head start by practicing the survival phrases near the end of this book.

Connect with the culture. Interacting with locals carbonates your experience. Enjoy the friendliness of the Greek people. Ask questions; most locals are happy to point you in their idea of the right direction. Set up your own quest for the best baklava (or ouzo), finest temple, or craziest myth. When an opportunity pops up, make it a habit to say "yes."

Greece...here you come!

ATHENS

Αθήνα

ORIENTATION TO ATHENS

Though sprawling and congested, Athens has a compact, enjoyable core capped by the famous Acropolis—the world's top ancient site. In this historic town, you'll walk in the footsteps of the great minds that created democracy, philosophy, theater, and more...even as you're dodging motorcycles on "pedestrianized" streets. Romantics can't help but get goose bumps as they kick around the same pebbles that once stuck in Socrates' sandals, with the floodlit Parthenon forever floating ethereally overhead.

Many tourists visit Athens without ever venturing beyond the Plaka (Old Town) and the ancient zone. With limited time, this is not a bad plan, as greater Athens offers few sights (other than the excellent National Archaeological Museum). But for a more authentic taste of the city, check out the trendy Psyrri district—right next door to the Plaka—with its dilapidated-chic hipster dining and nightlife scene.

Because of its prominent position on the tourist trail—and the irrepressible Greek spirit of hospitality—the city is user-friendly. It seems that virtually all Athenians speak English, major landmarks are well-signed, and most street signs are in both Greek and English.

ATHENS: A VERBAL MAP

Most of Athens is a noisy, polluted modern sprawl: characterless, poorly planned, and hastily erected concrete suburbs that house the area's rapidly expanding population. The construction of the Metro and other

Athens Landmarks

Area	Description	Pronounced (Greek Name)
Syntagma	Main square	SEEN-dag-mah
Plaka	Old town	PLAH-kah
Adrianou	Old town's main street	ah-dree-ah-NOO
Akropoli	Acropolis	ah-KROH-poh-lee
Dionysiou Areopagitou / Apostolou Pavlou	Pedestrian walkways near Acropolis	dee-oo-nee-SEE-oo ah-reh-oh-pah-GEE-too / ah-poh-STOH-loo PAW-loo
Archaea Agora	Ancient market	ar-HEH-ah ah-goh-RAH
Monastiraki	Market district	moh-nah-stee-RAH-kee
Psyrri	Nightlife district	psee-REE
Thissio	Western dining district	thee-SEE-oh
Makrigianni / Koukaki	Southern residential and hotel districts	mah-kree-YAH-nee / koo-KAH-kee
Kolonaki	Wealthy museum, shopping, and residential area	koh-loh-NAH-kee
Exarchia	Edgy student district	ex-AR-hee-yah
Piraeus	Athens' port	pee-reh-AHS

infrastructure for the 2004 Olympics was, in many ways, the first time urban planners had ever attempted to tie the city together and treat it as a united entity.

But most visitors barely see that part of Athens. Almost everything of importance to tourists is within a few blocks of the Acropolis, in the Plaka, Monastiraki, Syntagma, and Psyrri neighborhoods. As you explore this city-within-a-city on foot, you'll realize just how small it is.

A good map is a necessity for enjoying Athens on foot. The free map you'll find at hotels and the TI works great. Get a good map and use it.

Athens by Neighborhood

The Athens you'll be spending your time in includes the following districts:

The Plaka (PLAH-kah, Πλάκα): This neighborhood at the foot of the Acropolis is the core of the tourist's Athens. One of the

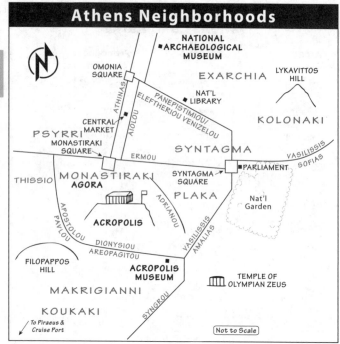

Athens Neighborhoods

NATIONAL ARCHAEOLOGICAL MUSEUM

OMONIA SQUARE

EXARCHIA

LYKAVITTOS HILL

ATHINAS

PANEPISTIMIOU/ ELEFTHERIOU VENIZELOU

NAT'L LIBRARY

AIOLOU

CENTRAL MARKET

KOLONAKI

PSYRRI

MONASTIRAKI SQUARE

SYNTAGMA

ERMOU

VASILISSIS SOFIAS

THISSIO

MONASTIRAKI

AGORA

SYNTAGMA SQUARE

PARLIAMENT

PLAKA

ADRIANOU

Nat'l Garden

ACROPOLIS

APOSTOLOU PAVLOU

DIONYSIOU AREOPAGITOU

VASILISSIS AMALIAS

FILOPAPPOS HILL

ACROPOLIS MUSEUM

TEMPLE OF OLYMPIAN ZEUS

MAKRIGIANNI

KOUKAKI

SYNGROU

To Piraeus & Cruise Port

Not to Scale

only parts of town that's atmospheric and Old World-feeling, it's also the most crassly touristic. Its streets are lined with souvenir shops, tourist-oriented tavernas, a smattering of small museums, ancient Greek and Roman ruins, and pooped tourists. The Plaka's narrow, winding streets can be confusing at first, but you can't get too lost with a monument the size of the Acropolis looming overhead to keep you oriented. Think of the Plaka as Athens with training wheels for tourists. While some visitors enjoy the Plaka, others find it obnoxious.

Monastiraki (moh-nah-stee-RAH-kee, Μοναστηρακι): This area ("Little Monastery") borders the Plaka to the northwest, surrounding the square of the same name. It's known for its handy Metro stop (where line 1/green meets line 3/blue), seedy flea market, and souvlaki stands. The Ancient Agora is nearby (roughly between Monastiraki and Thissio).

Psyrri (psee-REE, Ψυρρή): Just north of Monastiraki, once-dumpy Psyrri is now a thriving dining and nightlife district. Along its northern edge is the bustling Central Market. Don't be put off by the crumbling, graffiti-slathered buildings of Psyrri...this is one of central Athens' most appealing areas to explore, and for now, locals still outnumber tourists here.

Syntagma (SEEN-dag-mah, Σύνταγμα): Centered on Ath-

ORIENTATION

Greek Words and English Spellings

Any given Greek name—for streets, sights, businesses, and more—can be transliterated many different ways in English. Throughout this book, I've used the English spelling you're most likely to see locally, but you will definitely notice variations. If you see a name that looks (or sounds) similar to one in this book, it's likely the same place. For example, the Ψυρρή district might appear as Psyrri, Psyrrí, Psyri, Psirri, Psiri, and so on.

Most major streets in Athens are labeled in Greek in signs and on maps, followed by the transliteration in English. The word ΟΔος *(odos)* means "street," Λεωφόρος *(leoforos)* is "avenue," and Πλατεια *(plateia)* is "square."

If a name used in this book appears locally only in Greek, I've included that spelling to aid your navigation.

---

ens' main square, Syntagma ("Constitution") Square, this urban-feeling zone melts into the Plaka to the south. While the Plaka is dominated by tourist shops, Syntagma is where local urbanites do their shopping. Syntagma is bounded to the east by the Parliament building and the vast National Garden.

Thissio (thee-SEE-oh, Θησείο): West of the Ancient Agora, Thissio is an upscale, local-feeling residential neighborhood with lots of outdoor cafés and restaurants. It's easily accessible thanks to the handy "Acropolis Loop" pedestrian walkway bordering the base of the Acropolis.

Makrigianni (mah-kree-YAH-nee, Μακρυγιάννη) and **Koukaki** (koo-KAH-kee, Κουκάκι): Tucked just behind (south of) the Acropolis, these overlapping urban neighborhoods with characterless apartment blocks are so nondescript that many locals just call Makrigianni the "south Plaka." If you want to escape the crowds of the Plaka, this area—with hotels and restaurants within easy walking distance of the ancient sites—makes a good home base.

Kolonaki (koh-loh-NAH-kee, Κολωνάκι): Just north and east of the Parliament/Syntagma Square, this upscale diplomatic quarter is home to several good museums, high-end shops, and a yuppie dining zone. It's huddled under the tall, pointy Lykavittos Hill, which challenges the Acropolis for domination of the skyline.

Exarchia (ex-AR-hee-yah, Εξάρχεια): Just beyond Kolonaki is this graffiti-slathered, rough-and-funky student zone. A visit here is a fascinating but not-for-everyone glimpse into Athens counterculture.

Major Streets: Various major streets define the tourist's Athens. The base of the Acropolis is partially encircled by a broad traffic-free walkway, named **Dionysiou Areopagitou** (Διονυσίου Αρεοπαγίτου) to the south and **Apostolou Pavlou** (Αποστόλου Παύλου) to the west; for simplicity, I call these the "**Acropolis Loop.**" Touristy **Adrianou** street (Αδριανού) curves through the Plaka a few blocks away from the Acropolis' base. Partly pedestrianized **Ermou** street (Ερμού) runs west from Syntagma Square, defining the Plaka, Monastiraki, and Thissio to the south and Psyrri to the north. Where Ermou meets Monastiraki, **Athinas** street (Αθηνάς) heads north to Omonia Square. Running parallel to Athinas, heading north to the Central Market area, **Aiolou** street (Αιόλου) is mostly traffic-free and lined with shops and affordable eateries; the trendy **St. Irene/Agia Irini Square** (Άγια Ειρήνη) marks its southern end.

The tourist zone is hemmed in on the east by a series of major highways: The north-south **Vasilissis Amalias** avenue (Βασιλίσσης Αμαλίας) runs between the National Garden and the Plaka/Syntagma area. To the south, it jogs around the Temple of Olympian Zeus and becomes **Syngrou** avenue (Συγγρού). To the north, at the Parliament, it forks: The eastward branch, **Vasilissis Sofias** (Βασιλίσσης Σοφίας), heads past some fine museums to Kolonaki; the northbound branch, **Panepistimiou** (usually signed by its official name, **Eleftheriou Venizelou,** Ελευθερίου Βενιζέλου), angles northwest past the library and university buildings to Omonia Square.

PLANNING YOUR TIME

Although Athens is a massive city, its main sights can be seen quickly. The top sights—the Acropolis, Ancient Agora, Acropolis Museum, and National Archaeological Museum—deserve about two hours apiece. Two days total is plenty of time for the casual tourist to see the city's main attractions and have a little time left over for exploring (or to add more museums).

Day 1: In the morning, follow my Athens City Walk, then grab a souvlaki at Monastiraki. After lunch, as the crowds subside, visit the ancient biggies: First tour the Ancient Agora, then hike up to the Acropolis (book online in advance). Be the last person off the Acropolis. Stroll down the Dionysiou Areopagitou pedestrian boulevard, then promenade to dinner—in Thissio, Monastiraki, Psyrri, or the Plaka.

Day 2: Spend the morning visiting the Acropolis Museum and exploring the Plaka. For lunch, graze your way through my Psyrri and Central Market Walk. Then head to the National Archaeological Museum. Explore a different neighborhood for dinner.

Day 3: Museum lovers will want more time to visit other archaeological sites, museums, and galleries. The city has many "also-ran" museums that reward patient sightseers. I'd suggest heading

Daily Reminder

Sunday: Most sights are open, but the Central Market is closed. The Monastiraki flea market is best to visit today. An elaborate changing of the guard—including a marching band—usually takes place at 11:00 in front of the Parliament building. State-run sights and museums, including the Acropolis, are free on the first Sunday of the month during off-season (Nov-March). While most stores are closed, tourist shops in the Plaka stay open.

Monday: Most sights are open but the Benaki Museum of Islamic Art is closed. The Keramikos Cemetery Museum is closed on Mondays off-season (Nov-March) and the Acropolis Museum closes early (16:00).

Tuesday: Many museums and galleries are closed, including the Benaki Museum of Greek History and Culture, Benaki Museum of Islamic Art, Museum of Cycladic Art, Museum of the City of Athens, Museum of Greek Folk Musical Instruments, and the National Gallery.

Wednesday: The Benaki Museum of Islamic Art is closed.

Thursday: All major sights are open.

Friday: All major sights are open.

Saturday: The Jewish Museum of Greece is closed.

Evening Sightseeing: Many sights are open late in summer, often until 20:00. On Thursday year-round, the Museum of Cycladic Art is open until 20:00 and the Benaki Museum of Greek History and Culture is open until 23:30. The Acropolis Museum is open until 22:00 on Friday year-round.

toward Kolonaki to enjoy your choice of the Benaki Museum of Greek History and Culture, Museum of Cycladic Art, Byzantine and Christian Museum, or the National Gallery.

A third (or fourth) day could also be used for the long but satisfying side trip by bus to Delphi or a quick getaway by boat to the isle of Hydra. But these sights—and many others—are better as an overnight stop.

Overview

TOURIST INFORMATION

The Greek National Tourist Organization (EOT), with its main branch near the Acropolis Museum, covers Athens and the rest of the country. Although their advice can be hit-or-miss, it's worth a stop to pick up their free city map and *City Break* booklet. They also have information on museums, entertainment options, bus and train connections, and a handy WC (Mon-Sat 8:00-21:00, Sun

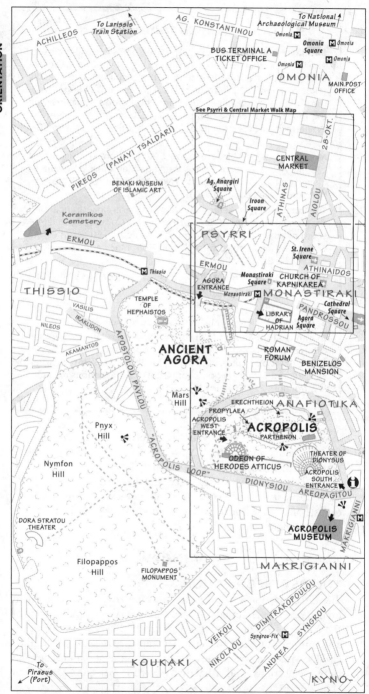

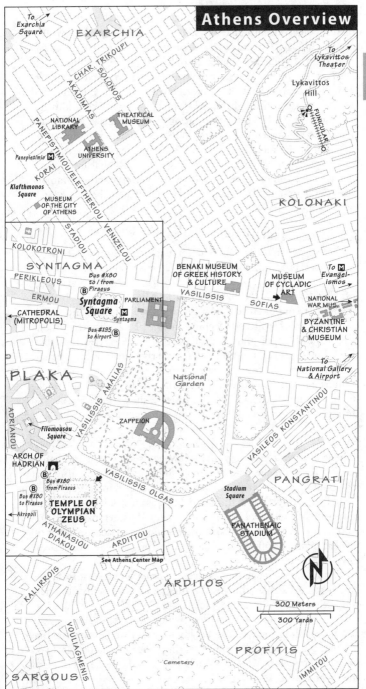

Athens Overview

To Exarchia Square

EXARCHIA

To Lykavittos Theater

Lykavittos Hill

CHAR TRIKOUPI

SOLONOS

AKADIMIAS

PANEPISTIMIOU

THEATRICAL MUSEUM

NATIONAL LIBRARY

ATHENS UNIVERSITY

FINICULAR

Panepistimio Ⓜ

KORAI

MIOU/ELEFTHERIOU VENIZELOU

KOLONAKI

Klafthmonos Square

MUSEUM OF THE CITY OF ATHENS

STADIOU

KOLOKOTRONI

SYNTAGMA

BENAKI MUSEUM OF GREEK HISTORY & CULTURE

MUSEUM OF CYCLADIC ART

To Ⓜ Evangel-ismos

PERIKLEOUS

Bus #X80 to / from Piraeus

VASILISSIS

SOFIAS

NATIONAL WAR MUS.

ERMOU

Ⓑ

PARLIAMENT

Syntagma Square

Ⓜ Syntagma

BYZANTINE & CHRISTIAN MUSEUM

CATHEDRAL (MITROPOLIS)

Ⓑ Bus #X95 to Airport

To National Gallery & Airport

PLAKA

VASILISSIS AMALIAS

National Garden

VASILEOS KONSTANTINOU

ADRIANOU

ZAPPEION

Filomousou Square

ARCH OF HADRIAN

Ⓑ Bus #X80 from Piraeus

VASILISSIS OLGAS

PANGRATI

Ⓑ Bus #X80 to Piraeus

← Akropoli

TEMPLE OF OLYMPIAN ZEUS

Stadium Square

PANATHENAIC STADIUM

ATHANASIOU DIAKOU

ARDITTOU

See Athens Center Map

KALLIRROIS

ARDITOS

Ⓝ

300 Meters

300 Yards

VOULIAGMENIS

PROFITIS

IMMITOU

SARGOUS

Cemetery

9:00-18:00, shorter hours off-season; on pedestrian street leading to Acropolis Museum at Dionysiou Areopagitou 18, Metro: Akropoli; +30 210 331 0392, www.visitgreece.gr, info@visitgreece.gr).

Helpful Websites: A great resource for anyone visiting Greece is **Matt Barrett's Athens Survival Guide** (www.athensguide.com). Matt, who splits his time between North Carolina and Greece, splashes through his adopted hometown like a kid in a wading pool, enthusiastically sharing his discoveries and observations on his generous website. While his practical information isn't always the most up to date, his perspectives and advice are top-notch. Matt covers emerging neighborhoods that few visitors venture into, and offers offbeat angles on the city and recommendations for untouristy restaurants. He also blogs about his latest impressions of the city.

ARRIVAL IN ATHENS

For information on arriving in (or departing from) Athens by plane, boat, bus, train, or car, see the Athens Connections chapter.

GETTING AROUND ATHENS

The tourist core of Athens is surprisingly walkable. Many travelers—on a short visit and sleeping in the Plaka—find they don't need to take public transit at all, once they're settled into their hotel. For short rides in the center, it's easy to flag down a yellow taxi (or hail one by using Uber). On a longer visit, it's smart to get comfortable with public transportation, which is useful for reaching the National Archaeological Museum, the port of Piraeus, and the airport.

By Taxi

Athens is a great taxi town. Its yellow taxis are cheap and handy (€3.50 minimum charge covers most short rides in town; after that it's about €1/km—tariff 1 on the meter, plus surcharges: €1.20 from Piraeus ports and train and bus stations, €4 from the airport—already included in airport flat rate). Between midnight and 5:00 in the morning or outside the city limits, prices are about 50 percent higher (tariff 2). Taxis have a fixed price of €38 from downtown to the airport.

Hotels and restaurants can call to order a taxi ("radio-taxi"), but there's a €2-4 surcharge. Warning: Cabbies may try to cheat you with a higher surcharge. Hold firm.

A good option is to use **Uber,** which operates in Athens only as a taxi-hailing service. You book your ride through the app like normal, but a taxi picks you up. Using Uber here inoculates you from any taxi fare rip-offs: You'll pay just the honest fare, and there's no calling surcharge.

By Public Transportation

For information on all of Athens' public transportation, see www.oasa.gr. Pick up a map locally, or refer to the "Athens Public Transportation" map at the back of this book. Beware of pickpockets when taking public transit.

Note that the tickets described next—except for the tourist ticket—do *not* cover journeys to the airport (see the Athens Connections chapter for information on getting to and from the airport).

Tickets: Athens' buses, trams, and Metro use the same ticketing system. A **basic ticket** (€1.20) is good for 90 minutes on all public transit and covers transfers. The **multiride** passes are available as paper tickets with 2, 5, or 11 rides (appears as "10+1" on ticket machines). They offer a slight per-ride discount, and do not expire—but cannot be shared between people.

If planning more than three rides in a day, consider the **24-hour ticket** (€4.10); for a longer visit using lots of public transit, you might get your money's worth with a **five-day ticket** (€8.20).

If starting and finishing at the airport, consider the **three-day tourist ticket** (€20), which includes a round-trip airport transfer on the Metro or Express bus #X95 as well as unlimited in-city travel on all Metro lines, the suburban railway *(Proastiakos)*, the tram, and the bus.

You can buy tickets at machines, staffed ticket windows (at some Metro stations), and some newsstands. When using the Metro, scan your ticket at the turnstile each time you start and end a journey. For buses, scan your ticket as you board. Those riding without a ticket (or with an unscanned ticket) are subject to stiff fines.

Metro

The Metro is the most straightforward way to get around Athens. Just look for signs with a blue M in a green circle. The Metro—

mostly built, renovated, or expanded for the 2004 Olympics—is slick and user-friendly. Signs are in both Greek and English, as are announcements inside subway cars, and electronic reader boards on the platforms show which exits have escalators going up or down. Trains run every few minutes on weekdays, and slightly less frequently on weekends (5:30-24:00, later on Fri-Sat, www.stasy.gr).

The Metro lines are color-coded and numbered. Use the end-of-the-line stops to figure out which direction you need to go.

Line 1 (green) runs from the port of Piraeus in the southwest to Kifissia in the northern suburbs. Because this is an older line—officially called ISAP (Η.Σ.Α.Π.) or electrical train *(elektrikos)* rather than "Metro"—it is slower than the other two lines. Key stops include **Piraeus** (boats to the islands), **Thissio** (enjoyable neighborhood with good restaurants and nightlife), **Monastiraki** (city center), **Omonia** (15-minute walk from National

Archaeological Museum), and **Victoria** (10-minute walk from National Archaeological Museum). You can transfer to line 2 at Omonia and to line 3 at Monastiraki (sometimes labeled "Monastirion").

Line 2 (red) runs from Anthoupoli in the northwest to Helliniko (Elliniko) in the southeast. Important stops include **Larissa Station** (train station), **Omonia** (National Archaeological Museum), **Syntagma** (city center), **Akropoli** (Acropolis and Makrigianni/Koukaki hotel neighborhood), and **Syngrou-Fix** (Makrigianni/Koukaki hotels). Transfer to line 1 at Omonia and to line 3 at Syntagma.

Line 3 (blue)—probably the most useful for tourists—takes you from the port of **Piraeus** to the airport in 55 minutes. Important stops in between are **Keramikos** (near Keramikos Cemetery), **Monastiraki** (city center), **Syntagma** (city center), **Evangelismos** (Kolonaki neighborhood, with Byzantine and Christian Museum and National War Museum), and the **airport** (requires a separate ticket). Transfer to line 1 at Monastiraki and to line 2 at Syntagma.

Underground Bonus: Because so much of ancient Athens was unearthed while the Metro tunnels were dug, you'll find displays from antiquity at many stations (especially at Akropoli, Syntagma, and Monastiraki). Stations without ancient treats to share do their best with modern art.

Bus

Public buses can help connect the dots between Metro stops, though the city center is so walkable that most visitors never ride one. In general, I'd avoid Athens' slow and overcrowded buses (taxis and UberTaxi are cheap and easy), but there are a few exceptions: Buses **#2, #4, #5,** and **#11** run from Syntagma north up the busy Eleftheriou Venizelou corridor, bearing right on 28 Oktovriou and stopping near the National Archaeological Museum (at the Polytechneio stop). From near Monastiraki (on Athinas street), bus **#035** also gets you to the National Archaeological Museum. Express bus **#X80** links the cruise terminals to Dionysiou Areopagitou (near the Acropolis Museum). Three special airport buses (€6 each) are also helpful: express bus **#X95** to Syntagma Square, express bus **#X96** to Piraeus, and express bus **#X93** to both bus terminals (bus info: www.oasa.gr).

Tram

The **Athens Coastal Tram** is slow and essentially worthless to tourists. It starts at Syntagma and runs 18 miles through the neighborhoods of Neos Kosmos and Nea Smyrni, emerging at the sea near Paleo Faliro. From there it splits: One branch heads north, to the modern stadium and Olympic coastal complex in Neo Faliro (SEF/Σ.Ε.Φ.); the other runs south, past the marinas and beaches to the Voulas neighborhood (www.stasy.gr).

The city also has various **suburban rail lines,** but you're unlikely to need them.

By Private Car with Driver

These companies offer tours from Athens and airport transfers for individuals and small groups as well as excursions from the cruise port: **George's Taxi,** run by George Kokkotos and his sons, has a solid reputation (for 4 people or fewer, call Nikolas at +30 693 220 5887; for larger groups, call Billy at +30 697 443 0678; www.georgestaxi.com, info@georgestaxi.com). **Tune In Tours** car service, run by Christos Dorzioti, has cars and minivans in Athens and Olympia (+30 210 653 7209, mobile +30 697 320 1213, www.tuneintours.com, info@tuneintours.com). **AthensTourTaxi** is another good and reliable service (+30 697 025 8817, www. athenstourtaxi.com, atsathens@gmail.com; Konstantinos and his father, Panagiotis).

HELPFUL HINTS

Theft Alert: Be wary of pickpockets, especially in crowds. Avoid carrying a wallet in your back pocket, and hold purses or small day bags in front, particularly at the following locations: Monastiraki flea market, Central Market, changing of the guard at the Tomb of the Unknown Soldier, major public transit routes (such as the Metro between the city and Piraeus or the airport), at the port, and on the main streets through the Plaka.

Emergency Help: The Tourist Police have a 24-hour help line in English and other languages for emergencies (171 or 1571). Their office, east of the Central Market in Psyrri, is open 24 hours daily (Dragatsaniou 4, +30 210 322 2230).

Slippery Streets Alert: Athens (and other Greek towns) have marble-like streets and red pavement tiles that can be very slick, especially when it rains. Watch your step.

Check Open Hours Locally: Unexpected staffing shortages, budget cuts, and other circumstances can cause the hours for sights in Greece to change without much notice. I've listed the posted hours, but it's smart to check locally for the most up-to-date information.

Free Sights: The National Garden and all of Athens' churches have no entry fee. Sights and museums run by the state, including the Acropolis, are free on national holidays and on the first Sunday of the month in off-season (Nov-March).

Laundry: A full-service launderette in the heart of the Plaka will wash, dry, and fold your clothes (same-day service if you drop off by noon; Mon and Wed 8:00-17:00, Tue and Thu-Fri until 20:00, closed Sat-Sun; Apollonos 17, +30 210 323 2226). **Easywash** has self-service locations across the city (all open daily until midnight), including one in the Plaka (Vlachou Angelou 8, +30 697 860 4401, www.easywashathens.gr). For both locations, see the map on page 183. There's also a self-service launderette in the Makrigianni neighborhood, close to the Acropolis Museum (daily 7:00-24:00, Veikou 3A—see map on page 188, +30 210 923 5811, www.athenslaunderette.gr).

Tours in Athens

∩ To sightsee on your own, download my series of free audio tours that illuminate some of Athens' top sights and neighborhoods, including the Acropolis, the Agora, the National Archaeological Museum, and my Athens City Walk (see sidebar on page 26).

ON WHEELS
Bus Tours
Various companies offer half-day, bus-plus-walking tours of Athens that include a guided visit to the Acropolis (about €65). Longer tours also include a guided tour of the Acropolis Museum (about €80).

Some companies also offer a night city tour that finishes with dinner and folk dancing at a taverna (about €70) as well as longer excursions, such as a 90-mile round-trip afternoon drive down the coast to Cape Sounion and the Temple of Poseidon (€50, not worth the time if visiting ancient sites elsewhere in Greece) or a 100-mile round-trip journey to ancient Corinth (including the Corinth Canal; €65, 4-6 hours). These buses pick up passengers at various points around town and near most hotels.

The most established operations include the well-regarded **Hop In** (modern comfy buses, narration usually English only, +30 210 428 5500, www.hopin.gr), **CHAT Tours** (+30 210 607 2000, www.chat-tours.com), **Key Tours** (+30 210 923 3166, www.keytours.gr), and **G.O. Tours** (+30 210 921 9555, www.gotours.com.gr). It's convenient to book tours through your hotel; most act as a booking agent for at least one tour company. While hotels do snare a commission, some offer discounts to their guests.

Athens and Beyond: Some companies also offer day-long tours to Delphi and to Mycenae, Nafplio, and Epidavros (either tour around €100 with lunch, €85 without), two-day tours to the monasteries of Meteora (from €200), and more. **Tune In Tours** offers day trips with smaller groups from Athens to the Peloponnese and mainland, as well as airport transfers and customized private tours of Athens (English-speaking drivers, reasonable rates, +30 697 320 1213, www.tuneintours.com, info@tuneintours.com; charming guides Christos and Niki).

Hop-On, Hop-Off Bus Tours
Several hop-on, hop-off bus companies offer 1.5-hour loops and 24-hour tickets for €16-25, including **CitySightseeing Athens** (red buses, www.citysightseeing.gr), **Athens Open Tour** (yellow buses, www.athensopentour.com), and the cheaper **Open Top Bus** (blue buses, www.sightsofathens.gr). The main stop is on Syntagma Square, though you can hop on and buy your ticket at any stop— look for signs around town. Because most of the major sights in Athens are within easy walking distance of the Plaka, I'd use this only if I wanted an overview of the city or had extra time to get to the outlying sights.

Tourist Trains
These goofy little trains can go where big buses can't, and can be useful for people with limited mobility. The **Athens Happy Train** offers hop-on, hop-off privileges at a few strategic stops (€5, about 2/hour 9:00-23:00, 40-minute loop; catch it at the bottom of Syntagma Square or at Monastiraki Square; +30 698 991 9091, www.athenshappytrain.com).

ON FOOT
Walking Tours
Athens Walking Tours offers several walks, including just the Acropolis (€35, daily at 11:30, 1.5 hours), the Acropolis and City Tour (€47 plus entry fees, daily at 9:30, 3.5 hours), and their combo Acropolis, City Tour, and Acropolis Museum Tour (€67 plus entry fees, daily at 9:30, 5.5 hours). Reserve all tours in advance (+30 210 884 7269, mobile +30 694 585 9662, www.athenswalkingtours.gr,

Despina). They also offer a food tour, wine-tasting tour, and cooking lesson with dinner.

Context Athens' "intellectual by design" walking tours are geared for serious learners and led by "docents" (historians, architects, and academics) rather than by guides. They cover ancient sites and museums and offer themed walks with topics ranging from food to architecture to the Byzantine era (www.contexttravel.com/city/athens, info@contexttravel.com).

Alternative Athens delves into the Greek capital's contemporary side, with a less strict focus on weighty history. They run excellent food tours, as well as walks focusing on street art, Greek designers, Athens' neighborhoods, and Greek mythology (+30 211 012 6544, www.alternativeathens.com).

Food Tours

A good way to experience Greek culture is through its cuisine. Several companies offer culinary walking tours around Athens (see page 194 for a rundown).

Local Guides

A good private guide can bring Athens' sights to life. While there's some variation, most charge around €55-60 per hour and have a 3-hour minimum (but will negotiate a lower rate for longer gigs). I've enjoyed working with each of these guides: **Faye Georgiou** (+30 697 768 5503, fayegeorgiou@yahoo.gr); **Dora Mavrommati** (+30 694 689 9300, mavrom.dor@gmail.com); **Danae Kousouri** (+30 697 353 3219, danaekousouri@gmail.com); **Niki Vlachou** (+30 697 242 6085, www.olympictours.gr, niki@olympictours.gr); **Angelos Kokkaliaris** (+30 697 412 7127, www.athenswalkingguide.com, angelo@athenswalkingguide.com); **Anastasia Gaitanou** (+30 694 446 3109, anastasia2570@yahoo.com); and **Effie Perperi** (+30 697 739 6659, effieperperi@gmail.com).

SIGHTS IN ATHENS

Athens offers numerous world-class museums and ancient sites. If you're feeling a bit pressured about your Athens sightseeing priorities, consider this: Of all the archaeological sites here, only the Acropolis and the Agora matter. Of all the museums, the National Museum of Archaeology and the Acropolis Museum are the most important (if a bit redundant). Of the remaining museums, those in the Kolonaki district (Benaki Museum of Greek History and Culture, Museum of Cycladic Art, Byzantine and Christian Museum, and National Gallery) are the best, depending on your interests. Beyond these turnstile sights, take my two walks (Athens City Walk and Psyrri and Central Market Walk), and you'll get an "A" and have time for recess.

I've arranged Athens' sights in this chapter by neighborhood for handy sightseeing. You'll notice that some of Athens' most important sights have the shortest listings and are marked with a 📖. That's because they are covered in much more detail in one of my self-guided walks or tours. A 🎧 means the walk or tour is available as a free audio tour (via my Rick Steves Audio Europe app—see page 26). Some walks and tours are available in both formats—take your pick.

For general tips on sightseeing, see the Practicalities chapter. Be aware that hours at some sights may vary from those listed in this book. Check locally before planning your day.

ACROPOLIS AND NEARBY

A broad pedestrian boulevard that I call the "Acropolis Loop" strings together the Acropolis (and Theater of Dionysus), Mars Hill, Acropolis Museum, and the Ancient Agora. A pair of other ancient sites (Arch of Hadrian and Temple of Olympian Zeus) are within a few minutes' walk of the Acropolis Museum.

▲▲▲Acropolis

Arguably the most important ancient site in the Western world, the Acropolis (which means "high city" in Greek) rises gleaming like a beacon above the sprawl of

modern Athens. This is where, circa 450 BC, the Athenian ruler Pericles spared no expense in transforming a site laid waste by an earlier war with Persia into a complex of lavishly decorated temples to honor the city's patron goddess, Athena. The mighty Parthenon, the most famous temple on the planet, and three other major monuments built during this golden age—the Erechtheion, Propylaea, and Temple of Athena Nike—survive in remarkably good condition given the battering they've taken over the centuries. By the time you visit, a timed-entry ticket may be required. Check HHTicket.gr as soon as you know which day you plan to visit.

Your Acropolis ticket also includes access to the scant remains of the **Theater of Dionysus,** scattered southeast of the Acropolis, just above the Dionysiou Areopagitou walkway (and only possible to visit in conjunction with your Acropolis entrance).

Cost and Hours: €20, €10 off-season (Nov-March), covered by Acropolis combo-ticket; daily 8:00-20:00 (last entry likely earlier), Sept until 19:00, Oct until 18:00, Nov-March until 17:00, hours subject to change—check online before planning your visit; two entries: main entrance at western end of the Acropolis, and the south entrance at the base of the Acropolis next to the Acropolis Museum; +30 210 321 4172. Book a timed-entry ticket or combo-ticket online in advance at www.etickets.tap.gr.

📖 See the Acropolis Tour chapter or 🎧 download my free audio tour.

▲▲"Acropolis Loop"
(a.k.a. Dionysiou Areopagitou and Apostolou Pavlou)

Strolling this wide, well-manicured, delightfully traffic-free pedestrian boulevard bordering the Acropolis to the south and west is a delight. It's composed of two streets with tongue-twisting names—Dionysiou Areopagitou and Apostolou Pavlou (think of them as Dionysus Street and Apostle Paul's Street); for simplicity, I refer to them collec-

Acropolis Tickets

The big decision: get the Acropolis-only ticket or the combo-ticket? A **basic Acropolis ticket** costs €20 (€10 Nov-March) and covers entry to the Acropolis, as well as access to sights on the north and south slopes, including the Theater of Dionysus. But if you plan to visit Athens' other major ancient sites, the €30 **Acropolis combo-ticket** is the better deal, as it covers not only the Acropolis and Theater of Dionysus, but also the Ancient Agora (€10), Roman Forum (€8), Temple of Olympian Zeus (€8), Library of Hadrian (€6), and Keramikos Cemetery (€8; individual entry prices are cut in half for all of these sights in winter; no winter discount on combo-ticket). The combo-ticket is valid for five days.

These sights are always free for kids under 5 and half-price for ages 5 to 25. They're free on national holidays, and on the first Sunday of the month from November through March.

By the time you visit, a timed-entry ticket to the Acropolis may be required, even for those with a combo-ticket. It's smart to buy the combo-ticket online in advance and make your Acropolis reservation at the same time. For both, go to HHTicket.gr: Select "region of Attica," then "Acropolis and Slopes." From there select your date, time, and single or combo-ticket, then pay. You'll receive an email with your digital ticket.

tively as the "Acropolis Loop." One of the city's many big upgrades from hosting the 2004 Olympics, this walkway immediately became a favorite local hangout, with vendors, al fresco cafés, and frequent special events enlivening its cobbles.

Dionysiou Areopagitou, wide and touristy, starts from the Acropolis Museum and runs along the southern base of the Acropolis. It was named for Dionysus the Areopagite, first bishop and patron saint of Athens and a member of the ancient Roman-era senate that met atop Mars Hill (described next). The other section, **Apostolou Pavlou**—quieter, narrower, and tree-lined—curls around the western end of the Acropolis and the Ancient Agora. It feels more local and has the best concentration of outdoor eateries. When the pollution and racket of Athens start to wear you down, take a walk here; in the early evening especially, with the Acropolis glowing above you, there's magic to be had. This section was named for the Apostle Paul, who presented himself before Dionysus the Areopagite at Mars Hill.

Where Apostolou Pavlou meets the Thissio Metro stop (see the "Athens Overview" map on page 37), you can head west on Ermou—a similarly enjoyable pedestrianized boulevard—to reach Keramikos Cemetery. If you head east on Ermou (with traffic), you'll come to Syntagma Square. Or, if you want to encircle the

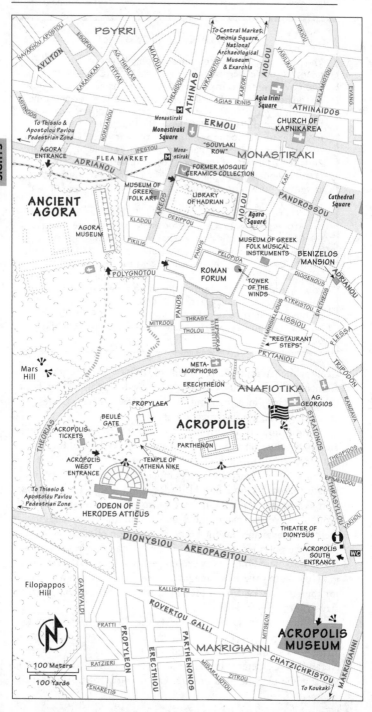

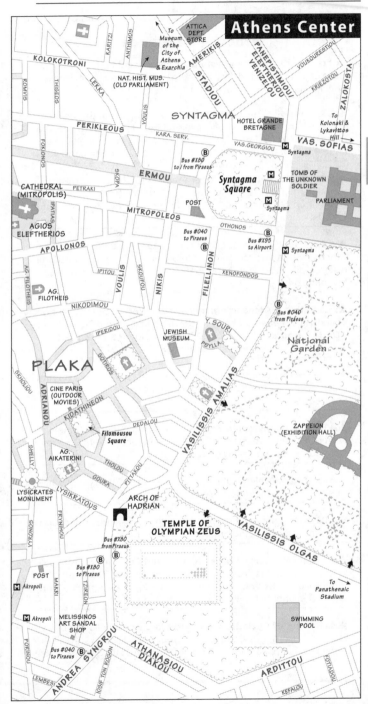

SIGHTS

Athens at a Glance

Sights generally keep consistent morning opening hours but can close earlier than listed. Many closing times depend on the sunset. Check locally.

▲▲▲**Acropolis** The most important ancient site in the Western world, where Athenians built their architectural masterpiece, the Parthenon. **Hours:** Daily 8:00-20:00 (last entry likely earlier), Sept until 19:00, Oct until 18:00, Nov-March until 17:00. See page 46.

▲▲▲**Acropolis Museum** Modern temple for ancient art. **Hours:** Mon 9:00-16:00, Tue-Thu and Sat-Sun until 20:00, Fri until 22:00; Nov-March Mon-Thu 9:00-17:00, Fri until 22:00, Sat-Sun until 20:00. See page 52.

▲▲▲**Ancient Agora** Social and commercial center of ancient Athens, with a well-preserved temple and an intimate museum. **Hours:** Daily 8:00-20:00, Oct until 18:00, Nov-March until 17:00. See page 54.

▲▲▲**National Archaeological Museum** World's best collection of ancient Greek art, displayed chronologically from 7000 BC to AD 500. **Hours:** Wed-Mon 8:00-20:00, Nov-March 8:30-15:30; Tue 13:00-20:00 year-round. See page 62.

▲▲**"Acropolis Loop"** Traffic-free pedestrian walkways ringing much of the Acropolis with vendors, cafés, and special events. See page 46.

▲▲**Temple of Olympian Zeus** Remains of the largest temple in ancient Greece. **Hours:** Daily 8:00-20:00, Oct until 18:00, Nov-March until 15:00. See page 53.

▲▲**Anafiotika** Delightful neighborhood draped across the hillside north of the Acropolis. See page 55.

▲▲**Psyrri** Vibrant neighborhood near the center, great for eating, exploring, and escaping other tourists. See page 61.

▲▲**Benaki Museum of Greek History and Culture** Exquisite collection of artifacts from the ancient, Byzantine, Ottoman, and modern eras. **Hours:** Wed-Mon 10:00-18:00 except Thu until 23:30, Sun until 16:00, closed Tue. See page 64.

▲▲**Museum of Cycladic Art** World's largest compilation of Cycladic art, from 4,000 years ago. **Hours:** Wed-Mon 10:00-17:00 except Thu until 20:00, Sun from 11:00, closed Tue. See page 65.

▲▲**Byzantine and Christian Museum** Fascinating look at the Byzantines, who put their own stamp on Greek and Roman culture. **Hours:** Daily 8:00-20:00 except Tue from 13:00. See page 66.

▲▲**National Gallery** Great art by this nation's top artists from around 1850 to the present. **Hours:** Wed-Mon 10:00-18:00, closed Tue. See page 69.

▲**Mars Hill** Historic spot—with a classic view of the Acropolis—where the Apostle Paul preached to the Athenians. See page 52.

▲**Thissio** Good neighborhood for food and drink, often accompanied by fine views of the Acropolis. See page 54.

▲**Roman Forum and Tower of the Winds** Ancient Roman marketplace with wondrously intact tower. **Hours:** Daily 8:00-20:00, until 15:00 off-season. See page 56.

▲**Church of Kapnikarea** Small 11th-century Byzantine church with symbols of Greek Orthodox faith. **Hours:** Likely open daily 8:30-13:30 plus Tue and Thu-Fri 17:00-19:30. See page 57.

▲**Church of Agios Eleftherios** Tiny Byzantine church decorated with a millennia of Christian bric-a-brac. **Hours:** Likely open daily 8:30-13:30 & 17:00-19:30. See page 58.

▲**Syntagma Square** Famous public space with a popular changing-of-the-guard ceremony five minutes before the top of each hour. See page 58.

▲**Ermou Street** Pleasant traffic-free pedestrian street brimming with international chain stores and fun people-watching. See page 59.

▲**Panathenaic (a.k.a. "Olympic") Stadium** Gleaming marble stadium restored to its second-century AD condition. **Hours:** Daily 8:00-19:00, Nov-Feb until 17:00. See page 60.

▲**Central Market** A fun and aromatic sensory adventure, with a mind-boggling assortment of food and local color. Hours: Mon-Sat 7:00-15:00, closed Sun. See page 62.

▲**Museum of the City of Athens** Former royal residence with exhibits about the city's 19th- and 20th-century history. **Hours:** Mon and Wed-Fri 9:00-16:00, Sat-Sun 10:00-15:00, closed Tue. See page 63.

base of the Acropolis, head east on Adrianou, the pedestrian street you'll hit just before the Thissio Metro stop, and stroll through the Plaka on your way back to Dionysiou Areopagitou.

▲Mars Hill (Areopagus)

The knobby, windswept hill crawling with tourists in front of the Acropolis is Mars Hill, also known as Areopagus (from *Areios Pagos,* "Ares Hill," referring to the Greek version of Mars). While the views from the Acropolis are more striking, rugged Mars Hill (near the Acropolis' main entrance, at the western end) makes a pleasant perch. As you're climbing Mars Hill, be warned: The stone stairs (and the top of the rock) have

been polished to a slippery shine by history, and can be treacherous even when dry. Watch your step and use the metal staircase.

This hill has an interesting history. After Rome conquered Athens in 86 BC, the Roman overlords wisely decided to extend citizenship to any free man born here. (The feisty Greeks were less likely to rise up against a state that had made them citizens.) Whereas Rome called the shots on major issues, minor matters of local governance were determined on this hill by a gathering of leaders. During this time, the Apostle Paul—the first great Christian missionary and author of about half of the New Testament— preached to the Athenians here on Mars Hill. Paul looked out over the Agora and started talking about an altar he'd seen—presumably in the Agora (though archaeologists can't confirm)—to the "Unknown God." (A plaque embedded in the rock near the stairs contains the Greek text of Paul's speech.) Although the Athenians were famously open-minded, Paul encountered a skeptical audience and only netted a couple of converts (including Dionysus the Areopagite—the namesake of the pedestrian drag behind the Acropolis). Paul moved on to Corinth, where he enjoyed a better reception.

▲▲▲Acropolis Museum

This museum is a modern-day temple to the Acropolis. Located at the foot of Athens' famous ancient hill, it contains relics from the Acropolis, including statues of young men and women, gods and goddesses, reliefs that once adorned the hilltop temples, and five of the six original Caryatids (lady-columns) that once held up the roof of the Erechtheion temple. But the highlight is a life-size re-creation of the frieze that once wound all the way around the outside of the Parthenon, blending original pieces with copies of

panels housed in the British Museum and other collections. Completed in 2009, the stunning glass building is a work of art in itself. The top floor sits slightly askew, like a graduation cap, mimicking the orientation of the Parthenon. The glass walls are designed not only to flood the place with natural light, but also to disappear into the background so that the architecture plays second fiddle to the real stars: the statuary and the views of the Acropolis.

Cost and Hours: €10, €5 off-season (you can buy tickets on the museum website to avoid the ticket-buying line, but not the security line); Mon 9:00-16:00, Tue-Thu and Sat-Sun until 20:00, Fri until 22:00; Nov-March Mon-Thu 9:00-17:00, Fri until 22:00, Sat-Sun until 20:00. The museum faces the south side of the Acropolis from across the broad Dionysiou Areopagitou pedestrian drag, and is right at the Akropoli Metro stop; +30 210 900 0900, www.theacropolismuseum.gr.

📖 See the Acropolis Museum Tour chapter.

▲Arch of Hadrian

This stoic triumphal arch stands at the edge of the new suburb of ancient Athens built by the Roman Emperor Hadrian in the second century AD. Now it overlooks a busy highway at the edge of the tourist zone (just a few steps up Dionysiou Areopagitou from the Acropolis Museum).

📖 For more on the Arch of Hadrian, see page 88 of the Athens City Walk chapter.

▲▲Temple of Olympian Zeus

Started by an overambitious tyrant in the sixth century BC, this giant temple (behind the Arch of Hadrian) was not completed until Hadrian took over seven centuries later. Now 15 of the original 104 Corinthian columns stand evocatively over a ruined base in a field. You can get a good view of the temple ruins for free by peeking through the fence by the Arch of Hadrian, but if

you have the Acropolis combo-ticket, consider dropping in for a closer look.

Cost and Hours: €8, covered by Acropolis combo-ticket; daily 8:00-20:00, Oct until 18:00, Nov-March until 15:00; Vasilissis Olgas 1, Metro: Akropoli; +30 210 922 6330, http://odysseus. culture.gr.

📖 For more about the temple, see page 88 of the Athens City Walk chapter.

ANCIENT AGORA AND BEYOND

These sights are listed in geographic order, starting with the Agora and fanning out from there (mostly to the west—see the "Athens Overview" map on page 37). You can walk to the cemetery and the Gazi district via the wide, pedestrianized Ermou street.

▲▲▲Ancient Agora: Athens' Market

If the Acropolis was golden age Athens' "uptown," then the Ancient Agora was "downtown." Although literally and figuratively overshadowed by the impressive Acropolis, the Agora was for eight centuries the true meeting place of the city—a hive of commerce, politics, and everyday bustle. Everybody who was anybody in ancient Athens spent time here, from Socrates and Plato to a visiting missionary named Paul. Built upon, forgotten, and ignored for centuries, the Agora was excavated in the 1930s. Now it's a center of archaeological study and one of the city's top tourist attractions. A visit here lets you ponder its sparse remains, wander through a modest museum in a rebuilt stoa (the Agora Museum), admire its beautifully preserved Temple of Hephaistos, and imagine sharing this hallowed space with the great minds of the ancient world.

Cost and Hours: €10, covered by Acropolis combo-ticket; daily 8:00-20:00, Oct until 18:00, Nov-March until 17:00; Agora Museum generally has the same hours; main entrance on Adrianou—from the Monastiraki Metro stop, walk a block south (uphill, toward the Acropolis); +30 210 321 0180, info: search "Agora" at http://odysseus.culture.gr.

📖 See the Ancient Agora Tour chapter or 🎧 download my free audio tour.

▲Thissio

This pleasant zone, around the far side of the Acropolis (just follow the main pedestrian drag), has a relaxed vibe and a thriving passel of cafés and restaurants with Acropolis views, plus an appealing open-air cinema (see Nightlife in Athens). If you stroll around the

"Acropolis Loop," you'll wander right past Thissio. Consider stopping off for a meal, a drink, or just to poke around.

Benaki Museum of Islamic Art

Sometimes it seems the Greeks would rather just forget the Ottoman chapter of their past...but when you're talking about nearly 400 years, that's difficult to do. If you're intrigued by what Greeks consider a low point in their history, pay a visit to this branch of the Benaki Museum (listing for main branch, Benaki Museum of Greek History and Culture, appears later in this chapter). The 8,000-piece collection, displayed in two renovated Neoclassical buildings, includes beautifully painted ceramics, a rare 14th-century astrolabe, and part of a marble room from a 17th-century Cairo mansion.

Cost and Hours: €9; Thu-Sun 10:00-18:00, closed Mon-Wed; northeast of Keramikos Cemetery at Agion Asomaton 22, at the corner with Dipilou, Metro: Thissio, +30 210 325 1311, www.benaki.gr.

Keramikos Cemetery

Named for the ceramics workshops that used to surround it, this is a vast place to wander among marble tombstones from the seventh century BC onward. While the sprawling cemetery provides more exercise than excitement—and requires a good imagination to take on much meaning—the small, modern museum is a delight. With a wealth of artifacts found right here, it explains the evolution of ancient burial rituals one age at a time.

Cost and Hours: €8, covered by Acropolis combo-ticket; daily 8:00-20:00, Oct until 18:00, Nov-March until 15:00 and closed Mon; Ermou 148, Metro stops: Thissio or Keramikos, +30 210 346 3552.

THE PLAKA, MONASTIRAKI, AND SYNTAGMA

The following sights are scattered around the center of Athens, within the roughly triangular area formed by the Plaka, Monastiraki, and Syntagma neighborhoods.

☐ Most of these sights are covered in more detail in the Athens City Walk chapter.

Between the Plaka and Monastiraki Square
▲▲Anafiotika

Clinging to the northern slope of the Acropolis (just above the Plaka), this improbable Greek-island-on-a-hillside feels a world apart from the endless sprawl of concrete and moped-choked streets that stretch from its base. You could call it a well-established squatter community settled in a national archaeological site. For a break from the big city, escape here for an enjoyable stroll.

▲Roman Forum (a.k.a. "Roman Agora") and Tower of the Winds

After the Romans conquered Athens in 86 BC, they quickly filled in the original Agora with monumental buildings. Then, they ex-

panded 100 yards east to build their own version of an agora—an open space or forum—where people came to do business. Today it's a pile of ruins, watched over by the marvelously intact Tower of the Winds. Panels circling the top of the tower depict the eight winds that shape Athenian weather. You can see virtu-

ally the entire site for free from the hillside (see description on page 91). But going inside yields a closer look (the entry gate is at the west end near the tallest standing colonnade).

Cost and Hours: €8, covered by Acropolis combo-ticket; daily 8:00-20:00, until 15:00 off-season; corner of Pelopida and Aiolou streets, Metro: Monastiraki, +30 210 324 5220.

Visiting the Roman Forum: You'll enter through four colossal Doric columns, part of a **gateway** built by Emperor Augustus (c. 11 BC). The inscription in Greek says it was generously financed by his adoptive father, Julius Caesar, and dedicated to Athens' favorite goddess, Athena. You'll emerge into a vast open-air **courtyard** where Romans and Athenians gathered to shop and schmooze. The courtyard was surrounded by rows of columns, creating a shaded arcade housing businesses. On the right side was a bubbling fountain.

The 40-foot-tall, octagonal **Tower of the Winds** was an observatory, with a weathervane on top, sundials on its sides, and a clock powered by water within. Inside is a big round (and still-not-fully-understood) stone in the pavement with markings like a clock dial. The holes indicate that some device was mounted on top—perhaps a set of metal gears. As water flowed down from the Acropolis it was channeled into the narrow groove you see here. The water powered the gears, which turned the hands of the clock to show the time of day. Additional hands (turning at much slower speeds) could show the day of the year, the month of the zodiac, and so on.

To the right of the Tower of the Winds is a gray-stone-paved area with broken columns—all that remains of the Agora's other monumental entrance. The two arches nearby may have marked the offices of the market's quality-control inspectors. To the left of the Tower is a rectangular area surrounded by a ditch. It has a surviving stone bench with two toilet-seat holes in it, making it clear what this once was: the Agora's **public restroom.**

Library of Hadrian

About a block from the Roman Forum, down Aiolou street (enter at the four Doric columns), is an area of Roman ruins containing what's left of the Library of Hadrian (erected AD 131-132). Like at the Roman Forum, you can essentially see it all from outside. Notice the round Roman arch, standing proudly in the center as if to remind all that Greece was incapable of constructing something like this, and therefore could never be as grand as Rome. Wandering the grounds, you can view the scant remains of the only Roman mosaic floor I've seen in Athens, but little more.

Cost and Hours: €6, covered by Acropolis combo-ticket; daily 8:00-20:00, shorter hours off-season; across from Agora Square, Metro: Monastiraki, +30 210 324 5220.

Museum of Greek Folk Musical Instruments

If you're interested in things musical, this museum is cute and cheap to enter. On its three floors, you can listen to recordings of different instruments and styles of music, and examine instruments dating from the 18th century to today. The main floor shows off drums, flutes, and bagpipes. Upstairs are stringed instruments—fiddles, violins, mandolins, and so on. And downstairs are bells, the boards hammered by Orthodox priests to announce worship services, and other percussion instruments. Throughout, photos, video clips, and paintings illustrate the instruments being played.

Cost and Hours: €3; Wed-Mon 8:30-15:30, closed Tue; near Roman Forum at Diogenous 1, Metro: Monastiraki, +30 210 325 0198.

Churches in the Center

▲Church of Kapnikarea

Sitting unassumingly in the middle of Ermou street, this small 11th-century Byzantine church offers a convenient look at the Greek Orthodox faith.

Cost and Hours: Free, likely open daily 8:30-13:30 plus Tue and Thu-Fri 17:00-19:30.

SIGHTS

Cathedral (Mitropolis)

Dating from the mid-19th century, this is the big head church of Athens—and therefore of all of Greece. The cathedral, with a beautifully restored interior, is the centerpiece of a reverent neighborhood, with a pair of statues out front honoring great heroes of the Church; surrounding streets lined with religious-paraphernalia shops (and black-cloaked, long-bearded priests); and the cute little Church of Agios Eleftherios (described next).

Cost and Hours: Free, likely open daily 8:00-19:00, closed 13:00-16:30 off-season, Plateia Mitropoleos.

▲Church of Agios Eleftherios

This tiny church, huddled in the shadow of the cathedral, has a delightful hodgepodge of ancient and early Christian monuments embedded in its facade. Like so many Byzantine churches, it was partly built (in the late 12th century) with fragments of earlier buildings, monuments, and even tombstones...a hodgepodge of millennia-old bits and pieces.

Cost and Hours: Free, likely open daily 8:30-13:30 & 17:00-19:30, Plateia Mitropoleos.

Benizelos Mansion

Two blocks south of the cathedral, this reconstructed mansion is noteworthy because it's the only surviving house of its type from the 18th century left in Athens, and one of the few anywhere in southern Greece. It's typical of the *konaki*-type house built throughout the Ottoman Empire at the time, with a high wall for privacy, courtyards, and an upper floor where people lived. A few panels in English describe how the different rooms were used, but this sleepy sight is interesting mostly for its unique glimpse into Athens' Ottoman period.

Cost and Hours: Free; hours sporadic but likely Tue-Thu 10:00-13:00, Sun until 16:00, closed Mon and Fri-Sat; Adrianou 96, +30 21 0324 8861, https://archontiko-mpenizelon.gr.

Syntagma Square and Nearby

▲Syntagma Square (Plateia Syntagmatos)

The "Times Square" of Athens is named for Greece's historic 1843 constitution, prompted by demonstrations right on this square. A major transit hub, the square is watched over by Neoclassical masterpieces such as the Hotel Grande Bretagne and the Parliament building.

Parliament

The former palace of King Otto is now a house of democracy. In front, colorfully costumed evzone guards stand at attention at the

Tomb of the Unknown Soldier and periodically do a ceremonial changing of the guard to the delight of tourists (guards change five minutes before the top of each hour, less elaborate crossing of the guard around :25 after, full ceremony with marching band Sundays at 11:00—get there early as they may start a bit before 11:00).

▲Ermou Street

This pedestrianized thoroughfare, connecting Syntagma Square with Monastiraki (and on to Thissio and Keramikos Cemetery), is packed with international chain stores. It's enjoyable for people-watching and is refreshingly traffic-free in an otherwise congested area.

Jewish Museum of Greece

Many Jewish communities trace their roots back to medieval Spain's Sephardic diaspora and, before that, to classical Greece. (Before the Nazis invaded, Greece had 78,000 Jews; more than 85 percent of them perished in the Holocaust.) This interesting collection of more than 8,000 Jewish artifacts—thoughtfully displayed on four floors of a modern building—traces the history of Greek Jews since the second century BC. Downstairs from the entry, you can visit a replica synagogue with worship items. Then spiral up through the split-level space (borrowing English descriptions in each room) to see exhibits on Jewish holidays, history, Zionism, the Nazi occupation and Holocaust, and traditional dress—all laced with the personal stories of Greek Jews.

Cost and Hours: €6; Mon-Fri 9:00-14:30, Sun 10:00-14:00, closed Sat; Nikis 39, at the corner with Kidathineon—ring bell to get inside; Metro: Syntagma, +30 210 322 5582, www.jewishmuseum.gr.

SOUTHEAST OF SYNTAGMA

The busy avenue called Vasilissis Amalias rumbles south of Syntagma Square, where you'll find the following sights. Note that the Arch of Hadrian and the Temple of Olympian Zeus (both described earlier) are just south of the National Garden and Zappeion.

National Garden

Extending south from the parliament, the National Garden is a wonderfully cool retreat from the traffic-clogged streets of central Athens. Covering an area of around 40 acres, it was planted in 1839 as the palace garden, created for the pleasure of Queen Amalia. Opened to the public in 1923, the garden has many pleasant paths, a café, WCs, scattered picturesque ancient columns, a playground, and several zoo-type exhibits of animals.

Cost and Hours: Free, open daily from dawn to dusk.

Zappeion

At the southern end of the National Garden stands the grand mansion called the Zappeion, surrounded by formal gardens of its own.

To most Athenians, the Zappeion is best known as the site of the outdoor Aegli Cinema in summer (behind the building, on the right as you face the colonnaded main entry; for details, see the Nightlife in Athens chapter). But the building is more than just a backdrop. During Ottoman rule, much of the Greek elite, intelligentsia, and aristocracy fled the country. They returned after independence and built grand mansions such as this. Finished in 1888, it was designed by the Danish architect Theophilus Hansen, who was known (along with his brother Christian) for his Neoclassical designs. The financing was provided by the Zappas brothers, Evangelos and Konstantinos, two of the prime movers in the campaign to revive the Olympic Games. This mansion housed the International Olympic Committee during the first modern Olympics in 1896 and served as a media center during the 2004 Olympics. Today the Zappeion is a conference and exhibition center.

Cost and Hours: Gardens free and always open, building only open during exhibitions for a fee; Vasilissis Amalias, Metro: Akropoli or Evangelismos.

▲Panathenaic (a.k.a. "Olympic") Stadium

In your travels through Greece, you may see several ruined ancient stadiums (including the ones in Olympia and Delphi). Here's your chance to see one intact.

Cost and Hours: €10, includes audioguide; daily 8:00-19:00, Nov-Feb until 17:00; kiosk near the entrance sells Olympic memorabilia; southeast of the Zappeion off Vasileos Konstantinou, Metro: Akropoli or Evangelismos, +30 210 752 2985, www.panathenaicstadium.gr.

Visiting the Stadium: Enter the stadium, take a seat, and look around to appreciate its rich history and gleaming marble.

This place has many names. Officially it's the Panathenaic Stadium, built in the fourth century BC to host the Panathenaic Games. Sometimes it's referred to as the Roman Stadium, because it was rebuilt by the great Roman benefactor Herodes Atticus in the second century AD, using the same prized Pentelic marble that was used in the Parthenon. This magnificent material  gives the place its most popular name: Kalimarmaro ("Beautiful Marble") Stadium.

The stadium was restored to its Roman condition in preparation for the first modern Olympics in 1896. It saw Olympic action again in 2004. Today, it's occasionally used for ceremonies and concerts. As in ancient times, around 50,000 spectators fill the stadium for big events.

Take a lap around the track, pose on the podium, and visit the modest permanent exhibit, showcasing the various torches, vintage posters, and other memorabilia commemorating the modern games. Head to the top row for a commanding view of the Acropolis and Parthenon.

NORTH OF THE CENTER
Several worthwhile sights are north of the Athens central core.

Above Monastiraki Square
Athinas street leads north from Monastiraki Square to Omonia Square (see the "Athens Overview" map on page 37). Walking this grand street offers a great chance to feel the pulse of modern workaday Athens, with shops tumbling onto broad sidewalks, striking squares, nine-to-fivers out having a smoke, and lots of urban energy. ▢ This area is covered in delicious detail in the Psyrri and Central Market Walk chapter.

Farther up Athinas street, past Omonia Square, is the superb National Archaeological Museum.

▲▲Psyrri
This funky district, just north of the Ancient Agora, offers a real-world alternative to the tourist-clogged, artificial-feeling Plaka. While parts are outwardly grungy and run-down, Psyrri has blossomed with a fun range of eateries, cafés, and clubs, with every-

thing from dives to exclusive dance halls to crank-'em-out chain restaurants (for recommendations on where to eat, see the Eating in Athens chapter). It's especially lively at night.

▲Central Market

Take a vibrant, fragrant stroll through the modern-day version of the Ancient Agora. It's a living, breathing, and smelly barrage on all the senses. You'll see dripping-fresh meat, livestock in all stages of dismemberment, still-wriggling fish, exotic nuts, and sticky figs. It may not be Europe's most charming market, but it offers a lively contrast to Athens' ancient sites. The entire market square is a delight to explore, with a dizzying variety of great street food and a carnival of people-watching (open Mon-Sat 7:00-15:00, closed Sun, on Athinas between Sofokleous and Evripidou, between Metro stops Omonia and Monastiraki).

▲▲▲National Archaeological Museum

This museum is the single best place on earth to see ancient Greek artifacts. Strolling through the chronologically displayed collec-

tion—from 7000 BC to AD 500—is like watching a time-lapse movie of the evolution of art. You'll go from the stylized figurines of the Cycladic Islands, to the golden artifacts of the Mycenaeans (including the so-called Mask of Agamemnon), to the stiff, stoic kouros statues of the Archaic age. Then, with the arrival of the Severe style (epitomized by the *Artemision Bronze*), the art loosens up and comes to life. As Greece enters the Classical Period, the *Bronze Statue of a Youth* is balanced and lifelike. The dramatic *Artemision Jockey* hints at the unbridled exuberance of Hellenism, which is taken to its extreme in the *Statue of a Fighting Gaul*. Rounding out the collection are Roman statuary, colorful wall paintings from Thira (today's Santorini), room upon room of ceramics, and what may be the world's first computer (known as the Antikythera mechanism, some 2,000 years old).

Cost and Hours: €12, €6 off-season, €15 combo-ticket includes Byzantine and Christian Museum; Wed-Mon 8:00-20:00, Nov-March 8:30-15:30, Tue 13:00-20:00 year-round; 28 Oktovriou (a.k.a. Patission) #44—see page 150 for transit options; +30 213 214 4800, www.namuseum.gr.

📖 See the National Archaeological Museum Tour chapter or download 🎧 my free audio tour.

Exarchia

For an edgier taste of Athens, explore Exarchia—long the heart and soul of Athens' feisty love of freedom and its non-conformist spirit.

Wedged between the National Technical University, Omonia Square, and Lykavittos Hill, Exarchia is populated mostly by students and counterculture idealists. The neighborhood, slathered in graffiti, is defiant, artsy, and vibrant.

SIGHTS

The handiest way to visit Exarchia is to take a taxi to its central Exarchia Square and explore on foot (or book a walking tour focusing on the district's boisterous street art; see the listing for Alternative Athens on page 194). You might ask your cabbie for a 10-minute impromptu graffiti tour of the neighborhood before jumping out at the square.

Exarchia Square feels like the community hub—find its centerpiece, a circa-1920 statue of cupids that's generally covered in spray paint. Youth activities and political banners contribute to the folk/artsy/radical vibe. Next, walk uphill and then to the right. The Art Deco "Blue Apartment" flat (top corner of the square) was a Modernist mecca in the 1920s—the heartbeat of this scene where only dead fish go with the flow. At the top end of the square, pop into the Vox Occupied Community Center (an art center, bar, and open-air theater). Then, just wander the nearby streets. Because of the cheap rent and abundance of students (three universities are nearby), the streets are lined with cafés, bars, art centers, and bookstores. Each evening, Exarchia is a thriving festival of alternative lifestyles. And, if there's a demonstration happening down at Syntagma Square, it's just a quick scooter ride away.

North of Syntagma Square

Just a few blocks up from Syntagma Square and the traffic-free Ermou street thoroughfare are more museums, including the National Historical Museum (in the Old Parliament building), the Numismatic Museum (coins), and this place:

▲Museum of the City of Athens

Housed in the former residence of King Otto and Queen Amalia (where they lived from 1836 to 1843), this museum combines an elegant interior with a charming overview of Athens beyond ancient times. Come here if you want to learn more about the 19th- and early-20th-century history of the city.

SIGHTS

Cost and Hours: €5; Mon and Wed-Fri 9:00-16:00, Sat-Sun 10:00-15:00, closed Tue; Paparigopoulou 5, Metro: Panepistimio, +30 210 323 1397, www.athenscitymuseum.gr. The recommended Black Duck Garden bar/restaurant shares the museum's courtyard, but is independently run (see listing on page 195).

Visiting the Museum: The ground floor has two highlights. In the first room (to the right as you enter) is a giant panoramic late-17th-century painting of Louis XIV's ambassador and his party with Athens in the background. The work shows a small village occupied by Ottomans (with prickly minarets rising from the roof-tops), before the Parthenon was partially destroyed (it's the only painting depicting an intact Athens and Parthenon).

In the next room, a large model shows Athens circa 1842, just as it was emerging as the capital of Greece. A touchscreen computer lets you choose various locations on the model, read more about those sights, virtually circle around them, and watch videos.

Upstairs are lavishly decorated rooms and exhibits that emphasize King Otto's role in the fledgling Greek state following the Ottoman defeat. Throughout the place you'll see idyllic paintings of Athens as it was a century and a half ago: a red-roofed village at the foot of the Acropolis populated by Greek shepherds in traditional costume. Stepping back outside into the smog and noise after your visit, you'll wish you had a time machine.

THE KOLONAKI MUSEUM STRIP, EAST OF SYNTAGMA SQUARE

The district called Kolonaki, once the terrain of high-society bigwigs eager to live close to the Royal Palace (now the parliament), is today's diplomatic quarter. Lining the major boulevard called Vasilissis Sofias are many embassies, a thriving scene with high-end shops, and some of Athens' top museums. These are listed in the order you'd reach them, heading east from the parliament (see the "Athens Overview" map on page 37).

▲▲Benaki Museum of Greek History and Culture

This exquisite collection takes you on a fascinating walk through the ages. And, as it's housed in a gorgeous Neoclassical mansion, it gives a peek at how Athens' upper crust lived a century ago. The mind-boggling array of artifacts—which could keep a museum lover busy for hours—is crammed into 36 galleries on four floors, covering seemingly every era of history: antiquity, Byzantine, Ottoman, and modern. The private collection nicely complements the many state-run museums in town. Each item is labeled in English, and it's all air-conditioned. The Benaki gift shop is a fine place to buy jewelry (replicas of museum pieces).

Cost and Hours: €12; Wed-Mon 10:00-18:00 except Thu

until 23:30, Sun until 16:00, closed Tue; classy terrace café where some of today's high society hang out, across from back corner of National Garden at Koumbari 1, Metro: Syntagma, +30 210 367 1000, www.benaki.gr.

Visiting the Museum: The first exhibit (on the ground floor, rooms 1-12) kicks things off by saying, "Around 7000 BC, the greatest 'revolution' in human experience took place: the change from the hunting-and-gathering economy of the Paleolithic Age to the farming economy of the Neolithic Age..." You'll see fine painted vases, gold wreaths of myrtle leaves worn on heads 2,300 years ago, and evocative Byzantine icons and jewelry. Look for Byzantine icon art, including two pieces by Domenikos Theotokopoulos before he became El Greco (in a glass case in the center of Room 11).

Upstairs (from room 12), the first floor picks up where most Athens museums leave off: the period of Ottoman and Venetian occupation. Here you'll find traditional costumes, furniture, household items, farm implements, and entire rooms finely carved from wood and lovingly transplanted from Northern Greece. In Rooms 22 and 23, a fascinating exhibit shows Greece through the eyes of foreign visitors, who came here in the 18th and 19th centuries (back when Athens was still a village, spiny with Ottoman minarets) to see the same ruins you're enjoying today.

Climb up through smaller rooms (from room 25) to the enticing terrace café and exhibit hall (which may have temporary exhibits). On the top floor, Romantic art finally brings you into the 20th century.

▲▲Museum of Cycladic Art

This modern, cozy, and enjoyable museum shows off the largest exhibit of Cycladic art anywhere, collected by one of Greece's richest shipping families (the Goulandris clan). You can see Cycladic art elsewhere in Athens (such as in the National Archaeological Museum), but it's displayed and described most invitingly here. While the first floor up is all Cycladic, there are four floors—each with a fine exhibit. Note that the museum's entrance is a few steps up the side street (Neophytou Douka). A pleasant café is near the gift shop on the ground floor.

Cost and Hours: €12; Wed-Mon 10:00-17:00 except Thu until 20:00, Sun from 11:00, closed Tue; Neophytou Douka 4, Metro: Evangelismos, +30 210 722 8321, www.cycladic.gr.

Visiting the Museum: You'll climb the same marble staircase from the first to the fourth floor as the exhibit unfolds one floor at a time.

The **first floor** focuses on art from the Cycladic Islands, which surround the isle of Delos, off the coast southeast of Athens. The Aegean city-states here—predating Athens' golden age by 2,000 years—were populated by a mysterious people who left no written record. But they did leave behind an ample collection of fertility figurines. These come in different sizes but follow the same general pattern: skinny, standing ramrod-straight, with large alien-like heads. Some have exaggerated breasts and hips, giving them a violin-like silhouette. Others (likely symbolizing pregnancy) appear to be clutching their midsections with both arms. These items give an insight into the matriarchal cultures of the Cycladic Islands. With their astonishing simplicity, the figurines appear almost abstract, as if Modigliani or Picasso had sculpted them.

While that first floor is the headliner, don't miss three more floors of exhibits upstairs: ancient Greek art, Cypriot antiquities, and scenes from daily life in antiquity. The highlight—for some, even better than the Cycladic art itself—is the engrossing **top-floor exhibit** that explains ancient Greek lifestyles. With the help of artistic renderings, this exhibit displays the collection in use. Artifacts, engaging illustrations, and vivid English descriptions resurrect a fun cross-section of the fascinating and sometimes bizarre practices of the ancients: weddings, athletics, agora culture, warfare, and various female- and male-only activities (such as the male-bonding/dining ritual called the symposium). Listen for the music that accompanies the exhibit—historians' best guess at what the ancients listened to. A 12-minute movie at the end dramatizes events in the life of "Leon," a fictional young man of ancient Greece. Another movie (on a monitor to the left) demonstrates burial rituals (for the dearly departed Leon), many of which are still practiced by Orthodox Christians in Greece today.

▲▲Byzantine and Christian Museum

This excellent museum displays key artifacts from the Byzantine era—the 1,000-year period (c. AD 330-1453) that came after Greece's ancient glory days. While the rest of Europe fragmented into fiefdoms, Byzantium ruled large swaths of the eastern Mediterranean, with Athens as a key city. And, as the empire's dominant language and culture were Greek, today's Greeks proudly consider the Byzantine Empire "theirs." In  this museum, you'll see bits of 2,000-year-old rubble, medieval tableware, exquisite gold religious objects, and lots and lots of icons. The museum's handy café/restaurant is on a breezy terrace overlooking a park.

Cost and Hours: €8, €15 combo-ticket includes National Archaeological Museum; daily 8:00-20:00 except Tue from 13:00; Vasilissis Sofias 22, Metro: Evangelismos, +30 213 213 9517, www. byzantinemuseum.gr.

Self-Guided Tour: In the peaceful courtyard, buy your ticket in the building straight ahead, then enter the permanent collection in the building to the left. The museum's layout can be confusing, as the "rooms" flow into each other without clear divisions. Use my tour to get a thematic overview, then browse freely among the many interesting and beautiful objects.

The first few rooms show how the Byzantine Empire grew from its Roman roots.

Entryway: Three maps show snapshots of the Byzantine world: First (AD 337-565), it was huge, when it was synonymous with the Roman Empire. When Rome fell, its eastern half (called Byzantium) carried on as the largest realm in Europe (1056). By the end of the Byzantine era (1453), the empire was smaller still, with only two major cities—Constantinople and Athens.

• *Now step into Room I.1.*

Rooms I.1-4: The statuettes and reliefs in **Room I.1** show how pagan Rome became Christian Byzantium. A pagan shepherd became the Bible's "Good Shepherd;" the myth of Orpheus with his lyre symbolized the goodness of Creation; and ancient philosophers became wise Jesus.

Continue down the first set of stairs into **Room I.2.** In secular life, ancient Roman knowhow continued on into medieval times, with high-quality Byzantine jewelry, ceramics, glassware, coins, and good luck charms *(eulogiai)*. Descend the next steps to **Room I.3** to find column fragments and a mosaic floor (depicting animals and ancient laurel wreaths) that suggest how the same structural elements of the Roman basilica (or assembly hall) evolved into the Christian basilica (or church).

In **Room I.4,** stone fragments like these, from ruined ancient temples, were recycled to build Christian churches, while the Parthenon was repurposed as Athens' cathedral.

• *Descend the final staircase to a series of rooms on medieval Byzantium (c. AD 500-1200), starting in...*

Room II.2: With the fall of Rome, the Byzantine world (as the museum plaque says) entered an "Age of Crisis," marked by invaders from the north and east sweeping across Europe. The few broken stone fragments displayed here attest to how little art survived.

• *To the left is the section called...*

Room II.1: While Western Europe struggled to pick up the pieces after Rome fell, the Byzantine world was held together by strong emperors and the "eastern pope," the Orthodox patriarch.

See their symbols of authority: chain-mail armor, the long scroll of a patriarchal decree, coins with imperial insignia, and signet rings.
• *Continue ahead into the large Room II.3.*

Rooms II.3-II.9: In **II.3 and II.4,** you'll see how the Christian faith in Eastern Europe was evolving into what we now call Orthodox, with its distinct imagery and rituals. On display are uniquely Orthodox painted icons: of Mary-and-the-Babe, Jesus-as-Pantocrator ("All Powerful"), and a double-sided icon that was paraded atop a pole during services. Byzantines preferred to depict their saints as stiff, stylized figures on gold backgrounds, to avoid worshipping the "graven images" prohibited in the Bible. Orthodox Christians also developed the altar screen (iconostasis) that shielded the church's inner sanctum (see the interestingly carved marble slabs from such a screen).

The room to the right **(II.5)** shows how Athenian churches (such as the well-known Church of Kapnikarea—described in the next chapter) developed their own unique style, featuring wall frescoes like these, and topped with a Pantocrator in the dome (like the one at the end of the room).

Breeze quickly through Rooms **II.6-9,** with artifacts from Byzantium's declining years (c. 1200-1400). By the 13th century, Venetian merchants (the "Latins") were asserting their power in the Byzantine trading empire. Still, the cities of Constantinople and Athens remained more civilized than parts of the medieval west, as attested by the collection of finely worked carved reliefs and ceramics. Byzantine painting techniques were spreading west, and Byzantine knowledge was passed along in illuminated manuscripts and books.
• *Now enter a large hall with lots of big colorful icons.*

Rooms IV.1-4: Browse **Room IV.1-2** to its far left end. The paintings are bigger, brighter, and more realistic, with hints of 3-D background. There are dramatic, heart-racing scenes of saints slaying dragons and chariots of fire. Unlike the stiff, flat icons of an earlier age, now saints pose with the relaxed gravitas of ancient statues. It's clear that, with the arrival of the Venetians, there was cross-pollination between Byzantine icon-makers (in Crete, Ionia, and Athens) and the budding Renaissance painters of Italy.

Then, overnight, the Byzantine Empire came to an end. Make a U-turn to the right at the far end of the hall, into Room **IV.3.** In 1453, the Ottoman Turks conquered Constantinople, and went on to capture most of the territory that once belonged to Byzantium. In Greece, Christians (called *Romioi*) carried on their faith under Islamic rule (1453-1832). They developed the rich worship regalia still used today—icons, miters, silver vessels, and gold-embroidered vestments.

In the far left corner, step into the darkened **Room IV.4.** The printed book helped shape a common Greek identity ("the New Hellenism"), spurring the desire to be free of Ottoman rule and create the modern democratic nation of Greece.

• *Finally, return back upstairs to...*

Room IV.5: The final displays bring Byzantium up to modern times, mainly in its legacy to religious art. The flat simplified techniques of Byzantine art have even influenced modern abstract painters—a timeless style that's, well, iconic.

National War Museum

This imposing three-story museum is a living lecture on Greek warfare, from Alexander the Great to today. The overtly patriotic exhibit, old-school and staffed by soldiers, stirs the souls of Greeks and history buffs.

Cost and Hours: €6; Tue-Sun 9:00-19:00, closed Mon; Rizari 2 at Vasilissis Sofias, Metro: Evangelismos, +30 210 725 2975, www.warmuseum.gr.

Visiting the Museum: Start by riding the elevator upstairs to the first floor. Here you'll get a quick chronological review of Greek military history, including replicas of ancient artifacts you'll see for real in other museums—fine history lessons in early war technology. On display are maps of various campaigns, and models of fortified towns you may see later in your travels through Greece (like Monemvasia and Mystras), plus amazing video clips of World War I that help visually reconstruct the story.

The mezzanine level focuses on the Greek experience in the 20th century, including World War II (Nazi occupation, resistance, and liberation), and Cyprus. Back on the ground floor you'll parade past military uniforms, browse an armory of old weapons, and (outside) ogle modern military machines—tanks, fighter jets, and more (visible from the street, even when the museum is closed).

▲▲National Gallery

Athens' striking and newly renovated National Gallery is to Greece what the Orsay Museum is to France: a gathering of the great art of this nation's top artists from about 1850 until today.

The finest of Greek paintings are beautifully displayed and described in chronological order on three floors, connected by a central marble staircase. Walking through the ages—from Conservative/Realist to Impressionist and into the 20th century—you'll notice artistic trends spreading from Western Europe to Greece, but with a 20-year delay. The exhibits are well described in English throughout, with a focus on the dance between Western Europe and Greece. (While you'll likely not recognize a single name, it seems many of the great Greek artists studied in Paris.) The cultural challenge: for Greece to be part of the West yet remain true to its own heritage. While there is a bottom floor dedicated to a few works by the European masters, the reason to visit this gallery is to enjoy the best collection of Greek paintings anywhere.

Cost and Hours: €10; Wed-Mon 10:00-18:00, closed Tue; just beyond the National War Museum at Vasileos Konstantinou 50—a 10-minute walk behind the Parliament; Metro: Evangelismos, +30 214 408 6201, www.nationalgallery.gr.

ATHENS CITY WALK

From Syntagma Square to Monastiraki Square

Athens is a bustling metropolis of nearly four million people, home to one out of every three Greeks. While the city seems to sprawl endlessly as a concrete mess, the heart and soul of Athens is engaging and refreshingly compact. This walk takes you through the striking contrasts of the city center—from chaotic, traffic-clogged urban zones, to sleepy streets with bearded priests shopping for a new robe or chalice, to peaceful, barely-wide-enough-for-a-donkey back lanes that twist their way up toward the Acropolis.

The walk begins at Syntagma Square, meanders through the fascinating old Plaka district, and finishes at lively Monastiraki Square (near the Ancient Agora, markets, good restaurants, and a handy Metro stop). This sightseeing spine will help you get a once-over-lightly look at Athens, which you can use as a springboard for diving into the city's various colorful sights and neighborhoods.

Along the way, we'll weave through the rich tapestry of Athens' 2,500-year story—from the grandiose ruins of the ancient world, to mysteriously medieval Orthodox churches, to the lively places where today's Athenians go about their timeless existence.

Orientation

Length of This Walk: Allow plenty of time. This three-part walk takes two hours without stops or detours. But if you explore and dip into sights here and there—pausing to ponder a dimly lit Orthodox church, or doing some window (or actual) shopping—it can enjoyably eat up a half-day or more. This walk is also easy to break up—stop after Part 2 and return for Part 3 later.

When to Go: Do this walk early in your visit, as it can help you get your bearings in this potentially confusing city. Morning is best, since many churches close for an afternoon break, and other sights—including the Acropolis—are too crowded to enjoy by midmorning.

Getting There: The walk begins at Syntagma Square, just northeast of the Plaka tourist zone. It's a short walk from my recommended Plaka hotels; if you're staying away from the city center, get here by taxi or Metro (stop: Syntagma).

Churches: Athens' churches are free but keep irregular hours—generally daily 8:30-13:30 and some evenings (17:00-19:30). If you want to buy candles at churches (as the locals do), be sure to have a few small coins.

Cathedral: Free, likely open daily 8:00-19:00, closed 13:00-16:30 off-season.

Temple of Olympian Zeus: €8, covered by Acropolis combo-ticket (see sidebar on page 47); daily 8:00-20:00, Oct until 18:00, Nov-March until 15:00.

Roman Forum: €8, covered by Acropolis combo-ticket, daily 8:00-20:00, until 15:00 off-season.

Library of Hadrian: €6, covered by Acropolis combo-ticket, daily 8:00-20:00, shorter hours off-season.

Tours: ∩ Download my free Athens City Walk audio tour.

Dress Code: To enter churches, a modest dress code—no bare shoulders or shorts—is encouraged.

Starring: Athens' top squares, churches, and Roman ruins, connected by bustling urban streets that are alternately choked with cars and mopeds, or thronged by pedestrians, vendors... and fellow tourists.

The Walk Begins

This lengthy walk has three parts: The first introduces modern Athens, centered on Syntagma Square and the Ermou shopping street. The second part focuses on Athens' Greek Orthodox faith, with visits to three interesting churches. And the third part is a wander through the old core of Athens, including the charming-but-touristy Plaka, the mellow Greek-village-on-a-hillside of Anafiotika, and some impressive ancient monuments.

In a sense, we'll be walking back in time—from bustling modern Athens, through its mystical medieval period, to the place where the city was born: the Acropolis.

PART 1: MODERN ATHENS

This first part of the walk lets you feel the pulse of a modern capital.
• *Start at Syntagma Square. From the leafy park at the center of the square, climb to the top of the stairs and stand across the street from the big Greek Parliament building.*

❶ Syntagma Square (Plateia Syntagmatos)

Here in Syntagma Square (SEEN-dag-mah) you're in the heart of this great capital, and in many ways the heart of the entire Greek nation. Here is where the nation is governed. It's where citizens gather for angry demonstrations and national celebrations—the "Times Square" of Greece. Surrounding the square are posh hotels, major banks, and the Greek Parliament. Around the edges, the streets are choked with buses, cars, taxis, and mopeds. And in the fountain-dotted square, Athenians go about their business: hustling off to work, handing out leaflets, feeding pigeons, listening to street musicians, or just enjoying a park bench in the shade.

From here, sightseeing options spin off through the city like spokes on a wheel. Face the Parliament building (east) and get oriented. To the left is the head of Vasilissis Sofias avenue, lined with embassies and museums, including the Benaki Museum of Greek History and Culture, Museum of Cycladic Art, Byzantine and Christian Museum, National War Museum, and National Gallery. This boulevard leads to the ritzy Kolonaki quarter, with its high-end shopping promenades and funicular up to the top of Lykavittos Hill.

Extending behind and to the right of the Parliament building is the National Garden, Athens' "Central Park." Here you'll find the Zappeion mansion-turned-conference-hall (with a fine summer outdoor cinema nearby) and, beyond the greenery, the evocative, ancient Panathenaic Stadium.

This area is also one of Athens' prime transit hubs, with many bus stops and the city's busiest Metro station beneath your feet.

Behind you, at the west end of the square, stretches the traffic-free shopping street called Ermou, which heads to the Plaka neighborhood and Monastiraki Square. (We'll be heading that way soon.)

Syntagma Square is a breezy oasis, shaded with a variety of trees: cypress, plane, palm, orange, and laurel. Breathe deeply and

CITY WALK

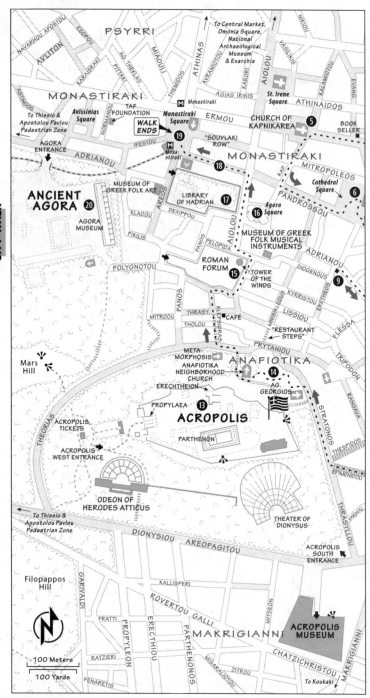

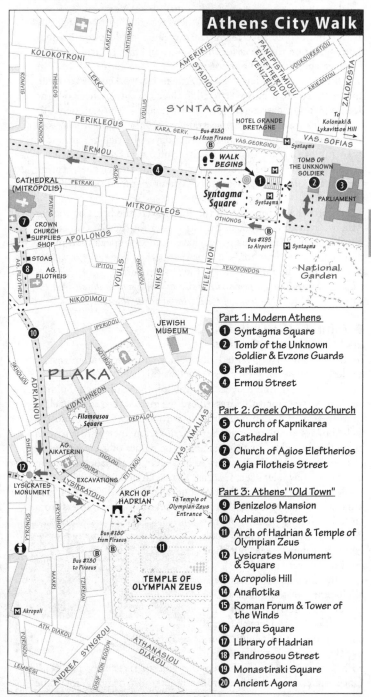

CITY WALK

Athens City Walk

Part 1: Modern Athens
1. Syntagma Square
2. Tomb of the Unknown Soldier & Evzone Guards
3. Parliament
4. Ermou Street

Part 2: Greek Orthodox Church
5. Church of Kapnikarea
6. Cathedral
7. Church of Agios Eleftherios
8. Agia Filotheis Street

Part 3: Athens' "Old Town"
9. Benizelos Mansion
10. Adrianou Street
11. Arch of Hadrian & Temple of Olympian Zeus
12. Lysicrates Monument & Square
13. Acropolis Hill
14. Anafiotika
15. Roman Forum & Tower of the Winds
16. Agora Square
17. Library of Hadrian
18. Pandrossou Street
19. Monastiraki Square
20. Ancient Agora

ponder the fact that until 1990, Athens was the most polluted city in Europe. People advertising facial creams would put a mannequin outside on the street for three hours and film it turning black. The message: You need our cream.

But over the last few decades, Athens has worked hard to clean up its act. Traffic is now restricted in the city center. Check out the license plates of passenger cars. Only cars with even-numbered license plates are allowed in on certain days of the week—those with odd numbers are allowed on the other days. The rich get around it by owning two cars. The city has instituted other green policies—more pedestrian zones, better public transit, and cleaner heating fuel. Thanks to this, 21st-century Athens is a much more livable place.

While the Acropolis and the Agora were the heart of ancient Athens, Syntagma has been the city center for the last two centuries. Whenever the Greek people have needed to speak their mind, they've gathered here to do it. For that part of Athens' story, turn your attention to our next stop—the Parliament.

• *Using the crosswalk (one on either side of Syntagma Square), cross the busy street. Directly in front of the Parliament you'll see the...*

❷ Tomb of the Unknown Soldier and the Evzone Guards

In the nation that invented democracy, nothing epitomizes its modern struggle for self-rule so much as this spot.

Here you'll find Greece's Tomb of the Unknown Soldier, guarded by the fancifully dressed evzone guards. The tomb itself is simple—a marble slab marked only with a cross. Carved into the wall above is an image of a fallen warrior from ancient times, with helmet and shield. On either side are the names of great battles in Greek history since 1821. (They're in the Greek alphabet, but I can make out a few—let's see, Cyprus, Korea, Crete.)

The much-photographed evzone, clad in traditional pleated kilts, white britches, and shoes with pom-poms, are soldiers from an elite infantry unit of the Greek army. They may look goofy to a non-Greek, but their families are very proud.

The soldiers do a ceremonial changing of the guard at five minutes before the top of each hour. There's also a less elaborate crossing on the half-hour. During the ceremonies, they march

with a slow-motion, high-stepping gait to their new positions. Once there, they stand ramrod straight, just begging for some clown to pose at their side. Try getting one to smile. ("Hey, Demetrios. Nice pom-poms.") A full changing-of-the-guard ceremony, complete with marching band, takes place most Sundays at 11:00.

The guards remind Greeks of the crucial moment when modern Greece was born. The year was 1821. After nearly four centuries under the thumb of the Ottoman Turks, the Greeks rose up. They were led by ragtag bands of mountain guerrilla fighters. Their uniforms were modeled after ancient warriors, complete with Mycenaean pom-poms. Today's evzone guards proudly wear the same outfit. In fact, their winter skirts have exactly 400 pleats...one for each year of Ottoman occupation (and don't you forget it).

The Greek War of Independence became a kind of cause célèbre throughout Europe. Even the English poet Lord Byron donned a uniform like this and died fighting for Greek freedom. Finally, in 1829, the rebels drove the Ottomans out. However, no sooner had they driven out the Ottomans, when they got...an Otto.

• *For the rest of the story, take a step back for a view of the...*

❸ Parliament

Although this grand building now houses Greek democracy, it began life as a palace for an authoritarian king. After Greece gained its independence, the first government was so weak (with a capital in far-off Nafplio) that Europe's powers-that-be installed an outsider to rule as king.

In 1832, Prince Otto of Bavaria, just 17 years old, became King Otto of Greece. He moved the capital to Athens and built himself a magnificent royal palace—today's Parliament building.

However, the Greeks, having just freed themselves from Ottoman rule, chafed under this dictatorial Bavarian monarch. On September 3, 1843, angry rioters gathered in the square to protest. Wisely, King Otto stepped onto the balcony of this building, quieted the mob, and gave them exactly what they wanted—a democratic constitution. Modern Athens was born, and the square was dubbed "Syntagma"—the Greek word for constitution.

It was King Otto who shaped the look of modern Athens. His architects (imported from Bavaria) created a grand European capital in the Neoclassical style. Broad new boulevards were blasted through, punctuated with vast squares like Syntagma. Otto revived elements from the classical world—things like the Greek columns and triangular pediments you see on the Parliament building.

The Story of Athens

On this walk, we'll encounter 2,500 years of Athens' history.

Athens emerged as a major city around 500 BC. But when Persia invaded (480 BC), Athens was burned to the ground. The Athenians rallied, united their fellow Greeks, drove the Persians out...and the Greek golden age began.

From 450 to 400 BC, Athens reigned supreme. Its population was about 100,000. The Acropolis and the Agora marked the center of town. Athens' high culture set the tone for Western civilization. By the time of the conqueror Alexander the Great (c. 333 BC), Greek culture had spread throughout the known world, with Athens as the capital of this vast "Hellenistic" empire.

When the Romans arrived (146 BC), they made Athens their regional capital, erecting even greater temples, theaters, and forums. But as the Roman Empire declined, so did Athens. A horrendous barbarian invasion in the third century BC left the city in ashes. And as Christianity became established, many great pagan sanctuaries and schools were closed.

When Rome fell in 476 AD, Greece came under the sway of the Byzantine Empire—that is, the eastern half of the empire that didn't fall. For the next thousand years, Athens was ruled from far-off Constantinople (modern Istanbul). Now Eastern Orthodox, Athens was soon dotted with impressive Orthodox churches filled with glorious mosaics.

In 1453, Constantinople fell to the Ottoman Turks, and Athens came under the rule of Muslim sultans. The Parthenon became a mosque, Greek Christians assumed a low profile, and the city became a rural backwater. Its population shrank to just 2,000, a cluster of red-tiled homes in the shadow of the Acropolis—today's Plaka. Athens hit rock bottom.

Then in 1821, Athens' rebirth began. The Greeks rose up, evicted the Ottomans, and demanded self-rule. They rebuilt Athens in the Neoclassical style, with broad boulevards and a new city center at Syntagma Square.

The city grew even more after World War I, when thousands of refugees poured in, and Athens' population doubled almost overnight. After World War II, starving Greek peasants from the countryside flooded Athens looking for work. In the last half of the 20th century, Athens' population exploded from one million to nearly four million.

Authorities scrambled to make the growing city livable. For years, there was lots of ugly urban sprawl and cheap housing. But the 2004 Olympic Games brought major improvements in infrastructure, public transportation, green policies, and an overall beautification program. Today, the city is a major European cultural capital and attractive tourist destination. More than one in three Greeks proudly call greater Athens home.

This set the tone for buildings like the opulent **Hotel Grande Bretagne** (to the right as you face Syntagma Square). All over town, you'll see pastel-colored buildings highlighted in white trim. The rectangular windows, flanked by white Greek half-columns, are fronted by balconies, and topped with cornices. Many of the buildings themselves are also framed at the top with cornices. As you continue this walk, you'll see a few surviving Neoclassical buildings, as well as modern buildings mimicking their geometric symmetry.

Today, the Parliament building is where 300 elected representatives tend to the business of state for the Greek nation. (Or, as more cynical locals would say, tend to the business of setting themselves up for cushy, post-political lives.)

• *One of the grandest of Otto's new streets was the one that spilled directly out the bottom of Syntagma Square. And that's where we're headed next—Ermou street.*

To get there, cross back to Syntagma Square and head to the bottom of the square where you'll find the start of the traffic-free boulevard called...

❹ Ermou Street

This pedestrian mall called Ermou (air-MOO) is the modern city's main axis. As you stroll, you'll see a mix of modern and traditional, global and local.

There are lots of international clothing chain stores—some well-known in America, others more local, some housed in elegant Neoclassical mansions with ironwork balconies. Talented street performers provide an entertaining soundtrack. All of Athens walks along here: businesspeople buying a daily paper, teenagers cruising the mall, hawkers selling lottery tickets, Orthodox priests stroking their beards. You'll see old men twirling worry beads and young activists gathering signatures. Street vendors sweep up their illegal wares and scurry off when they see the police. You may even see a few 20th-century relics, like pay telephones.

Keep an eye out for people selling local snacks—including pretzel-like sesame rings (called *koulouri*) and roasted ears of corn. At #13 (two blocks down on the left) is Gregory's, the popular "Greek Starbucks" coffee chain with its distinctive green logo.

As you continue down Ermou street, think of how much Athens has changed in the last two centuries. In 1800, this neighbor-

The Eastern Orthodox Church

In the fourth century AD, the Roman Empire split in half, dividing Europe down the middle. Over the centuries, Western Christians gravitated toward the pope in Rome as their spiritual head, while Easterners turned to the patriarch in Constantinople (Istanbul). Each group developed slightly different beliefs and ways of worship. In 1054, the Great Schism between the pope and the patriarch made that division between Roman Catholicism and Eastern Orthodox official.

Orthodox Christian—whose name in Greek means "right faith" (orthos dogma)—claim to follow the earliest Christian practices. The church is less hierarchical, so rather than having one all-powerful pope and headquarters (like the Vatican), there are about a dozen regional branches—Greek Orthodox, Russian Orthodox, Serbian Orthodox, and so on. The Greek constitution recognizes Orthodox Christianity as the "prevailing" religion of Greece. The archbishop of Athens is Greece's "pope."

Orthodox churches have their own worship rituals. As you enter any Greek Orthodox church, you can join in the standard routine: Drop a coin in the wooden box, pick up a candle, say a prayer, light the candle, and place it in the candelabra. Make the sign of the cross and kiss the icon.

Rather than a table-like altar, Orthodox churches come with an altar screen (the iconostasis) covered with curtains. A typical iconostasis has four icons, or pictures of saints: Jesus and John the Baptist to the right, Mary and a local saint to the left.

This iconostasis divides the lay community from the priests— the material world from the spiritual one. Following Old Testament Judeo-Christian tradition, the Bible is kept on the altar behind the iconostasis. The spiritual heavy lifting takes place behind the iconostasis, where the priests symbolically turn bread and wine into the body and blood of Jesus. Then they open the doors or curtains and serve the Eucharist to their faithful flock—spooning the wine from a chalice while holding a cloth under each chin so as not to drop any on the floor.

The church has few pews. Worshippers stand through the service as a sign of respect (though some older parishioners sit on the seats along the walls). Traditionally, women stand on the

hood was a run-down village of dirt alleyways. Then streets like Ermou were bulldozed through as part of the city's revival. But the turbulent 20th century turned the once-chic street into all that was once so terrible about Athens: ugly modern buildings, tacky neon signs, double-parked trucks, and noisy traffic. When Ermou was first pedestrianized in 2000, merchants were upset. Now they love the ambience of this people-friendly shopping zone.

About a block before the church up ahead, look for the little **book wagon** carrying on a long tradition (probably on the right).

left side, men on the right (equal distance from the altar, to represent that all are equal before God).

The Orthodox faith tends to use a Greek cross, with four equal arms (like a plus sign), which focuses on God's perfection. The longer Latin cross used by Catholics more literally evokes the Crucifixion, emphasizing Jesus' death and sacrifice. This also extends to the floor plans of church buildings: Many Orthodox churches have Greek-cross floor plans rather than the elongated nave-and-transept designs that are common in Western Europe.

Orthodox icons (golden paintings of saints) are not intended to be lifelike. Packed with intricate symbolism and often cast

against a shimmering golden background, they're meant to remind viewers of the metaphysical nature of Jesus and the saints rather than their physical form, which is considered irrelevant. You'll almost never see statues, which are thought to overemphasize the physical world—and, to Orthodox people, feel a little too close to the forbidden worship of graven images.

Most Eastern Orthodox churches have at least one mosaic or painting of Christ in a standard pose—as Pantocrator, a Greek word meaning "All Powerful." The image, so familiar to Orthodox Christians, shows Christ as King of the Universe, facing directly out, with penetrating eyes. Behind his head is a halo divided by a cross—a symbol for the Crucifixion, hinting of the Resurrection and salvation that follow.

Orthodox services generally involve lots of chanting—a dialogue between the priest and the congregation. The church is filled with the evocative aroma of incense, heightening the ambience. While Catholic and Protestant services tend to be more about teaching religious tenets, Orthodox services are about creating a religious experience. Each of these ritual elements does its part to help the worshipper transcend the physical world and enter into communion with the spiritual one.

CITY WALK

They sell colorful, old-fashioned books, including alphabet books (labeled Αλφabhtapio, *alphabetario*), which have been reprinted for nostalgic older Greeks. The English word "alphabet" comes from the first two Greek letters (alpha, beta).

• *Ermou street leads straight to our next stop—a little brick church stranded in the middle of the road amid all this commercial bustle. You can't miss it.*

CITY WALK

PART 2: THE GREEK ORTHODOX CHURCH

This part of our walk introduces you to the Orthodox faith of Greece, including stops at three different churches. The first of our churches is one of Athens' oldest—from medieval times, when Greece was part of the Byzantine Empire (AD 323-1453).

❺ Church of Kapnikarea

Built around the year 1000, this is a classic Orthodox church in the Byzantine style. It's square and topped with a central dome—quite

different from Western churches that are long and narrow—with windows of slender columns supporting tall arches. The walls are made of brick and mortar, with large blocks scavenged from earlier buildings incorporated into it.

Make your way to the entrance. Over the door is a mosaic of Mary and baby Jesus on a gold background. Though modern, this maintains the traditional rigid style of so many icons.

Inside the Church: If the church is open, step inside. You're welcome to visit, as long as you're modestly dressed, keep your voice low, and don't take photos.

In the narrow entryway, notice the bank of candles, and observe the standard routine. Worshippers light candles, place them in the candelabra, make the sign of the cross, and (traditionally, at least) kiss the icon—you might even see lipstick smudges on the protective glass. The icon gets changed with a different saint according to the church calendar. Also notice the candle-recycling box on the ground behind the candelabra.

Explore deeper into the main part of the church. Find the typical Orthodox features: The nave is basically square and symmetrical, with four equal arms radiating out from the dome. The decoration includes frescoes on the walls, icons here and there, a wooden pulpit, a few hanging lamps, and a handful of chairs (in Greek Orthodox tradition, worshippers stand—women on the left side, men on the right).

The focus of the church is the white-marble partition—the iconostasis. During the service, the priest goes through the iconostasis' doorway, into the inner sanctum, to prepare the eucharist. Notice the four typical icons: Jesus and John the Baptist to the right of the door, and Mary-and-babe to the left, along with a local saint.

Now, look up into the central dome. Looking back at you from heaven is Jesus, as Pantocrator ("All Powerful"). He surveys the universe with his penetrating gaze, raises his hand, and gives it his blessing.

• *From this humble chapel, let's head to the most important church in the Greek Orthodox world. Walk toward the Acropolis, slightly downhill on Kapnikareas street (to the left as you come down Ermou street). After two blocks turn left on traffic-free Pandrossou street, which leads to the...*

❻ Cathedral (Mitropolis)

This is the "Greek Vatican"—the home church of the archbishop who presides over the country's 10 million Orthodox Christians.

It's the city's cathedral, or (in Greek), its "metropolitan" church. It's probably flying the blue-and-white Greek flag, because it's the national church.

Though the structure is relatively modern (built in 1842), it has many typical Byzantine-style fea-

tures, like tall windows, horseshoe arches, and a glittering mosaic of the Annunciation.

Inside the Church: You'll find the same features found in all Orthodox churches but on a grander scale, including candles at the entrance, iconostasis with four icons, Pantocrator in the dome, and so on. Notice the balconies. In past times, this was where women worshipped. But in 1954, Greek women got the vote, and now they worship alongside the men.

On Cathedral Square: Out front stands a statue of a man with a staff, giving a blessing. This is the honored **Archbishop Dam-askinos** (1891-1949), who presided here in the early 20th century. During the Nazi occupation of Greece, he was one of the rare Christian leaders who spoke out on behalf of persecuted Jews. The Nazis threatened to put Damaskinos before a firing squad. The feisty archbishop joked that they should hang him instead, in good Orthodox tradition. After the war, he served as Greece's caretaker prime minister, helping bring stability to the war-torn country. Athens' Jewish community erected this statue as a show of thanks.

The statue depicts many typical Orthodox features. Damaskinos wears the distinctive hat of an Orthodox archbishop—a kind of fez with cloth hanging down the sides. He carries a staff and blesses with his right hand. Look closely at the hand—he's touching his thumb to his ring finger. This is the traditional Orthodox sign of the cross. The gesture forms the letters of the alphabet that spell out the Greek name of Jesus. Try it yourself. Touch your thumb to the tip of your ring finger. Now, your pinkie forms the letter I; your slightly crossed index and middle fingers are an X; and your thumb and ring finger make a double-C. These four letters— I, C, X, C—are short for...Jesus Christ. Very clever. So, if you were an Orthodox priest, you'd hold your fingers like this and wave your arm three times, tracing the shape of a cross, and chanting "the Father, the Son, and the Holy Spirit."

Notice Damaskinos' necklace. It's the double-headed eagle of the Byzantine Empire, when Orthodoxy became the state religion. The two heads demonstrated how the Byzantine emperor ruled both East and West, as well as both the secular and the spiritual worlds. The Byzantine Empire ruled parts of the Eastern Mediter-

ranean for a thousand years, with Athens as one of its premier cities. But then everything changed.

For that, find the statue at the far end of the square—behind Damaskino to the left, farthest from the cathedral. The statue of a warrior holding a sword is **Emperor Constantine XI,** the final ruler of that great Byzantine Empire. In 1453, Emperor Constantine was toppled from power and the great city of Constantinople was conquered by the Ottoman Turks. Almost overnight, Muslims controlled Athens, and Orthodox Christians had to lay low for the next four centuries.

• *That's when our next stop came into play in Athens' long history. Head for the small church along the right side of the cathedral. It's the...*

❼ Church of Agios Eleftherios

When the Ottomans took control, they evicted Athens' archbishops from their previous cathedral—the Parthenon, which at that time was used as a church. With the Parthenon now a mosque, the archbishop moved here, to this humble church with a venerable history.

Built in the 12th and 13th centuries, it's dedicated to a popular saint *(agios)*. The little church is still referred to as "the old cathedral," since it actually was once the cathedral. (If you go inside, you'll find a mostly bare space with features we've seen before: iconostasis, icons, Pantocrator, and so on.)

Check out the facade. The church is a jigsaw puzzle of reused stones scavenged from earlier monuments, some of them extremely old. Over the door, the lintel has crosses, lions, and rosettes. A little higher up is a row of carved panels featuring more crosses, griffins and eagles, sphinxes, eagles eating snakes, and ancient floral designs. These date from the second century AD. They were once part of a calendar of pagan Athenian festivals that stood in the Ancient Agora. Even higher, there's a frieze from before the time of Christ, depicting toga-clad men in an ancient parade.

Notice the wide variety of crosses. The Maltese cross has four V-shaped arms. It was popular with Crusaders who passed through here on their way to Jerusalem. The Latin cross has a long base and shorter crossbar, symbolic of the Crucifixion. The one with two crossbars is the Patriarchal Cross, popular with archbishops. The Greek cross has four equal arms, symbolic of God's perfection.

Circle the church (counterclockwise) to find more ancient stones and symbols, both Christian and pagan. You'll find more crosses, geometrical patterns, an eagle carrying off a rabbit, a lion chomping on a gazelle, Christ chained to a column, Grecian urns, an anchor cross (symbolizing security), and a couple of robed saints. There are even old tombstones.

This combination of pagan and Christian elements testifies to Athens' long history, incorporating diverse cultural traditions.

• *We're at ground zero of the Greek Orthodox faith. Let's check out a few nearby sights that show off the Orthodox church of today.*

Make your way directly behind the Church of Agios Eleftherios, where there's a row of shops. These shops are along a street called...

❽ Agia Filotheis Street

This neighborhood is a hive of activity for Orthodox clerics. It's home to many stores selling all kinds of religious objects. The Orthodox religion comes with its own unique religious paraphernalia, from robes to incense burners, candelabras to icons. **Crown Church Supplies** (at #5) is a family-run business that's been tailoring robes for Orthodox priests since 1907.

Turn right and explore more of Agia Filotheis street. Cross Apollonos street and go another 30 yards to #15 Agia Filotheis street, on the left. Explore these **stoas** (mini malls) with several workshops of local artisans who make religious objects. You may see painters at work creating or restoring icons. Or tailors fashioning bishops' robes. Or metalworkers creating gold lamps and chalices exquisitely worked in elaborate repoussé design.

In this neighborhood, keep an eye out for Orthodox priests. They dress all in black, wear beards, and don those fez-like hats. While they look like celibate monks, most are husbands and fathers. Married priests are welcome, as long as they marry before becoming priests. They're generally well-educated pillars of the community, serving as counselors and spiritual guides to the cosmopolitan populace.

A little farther along (on the left) is the cute little **Church of Agia Filotheis,** named for one of the patron saints of Athens. This garden church is a popular place for weddings. A few steps farther (at #19, on the left) is an impressive marble building with a golden double eagle on the facade and busts of bishops out front. Note the heightened security. This is the official **residence of the archbishop** of Athens.

• *At this point, our walk focuses on...*

PART 3: ATHENS' "OLD TOWN" (THE PLAKA AND ANAFIOTIKA)

This part of our walk explores the atmospheric twisty lanes of old Athens. Before the city grew into a modern metropolis, it consisted of ramshackle homes huddling at the base of Acropolis hill. Here we'll find some of Athens' oldest monuments, dating back to ancient times. These days, the neighborhood called the Plaka is both atmospheric and very touristy.

• *Continue up Agia Filotheis street a few more yards until you reach a tight five-way intersection. Make a hard right, slightly downhill on Adrianou street (labeled* Αδριανού*). After about 100 yards, where Adrianou meets Apollonos street (*Απολλωνς*), on the left you'll find the...*

❾ Benizelos Mansion

Other than the marble columns and tumbled stone blocks of antiquity, and the Neoclassical palaces of the 19th century, not much from the rest of Athens' history remains visible. A few churches like those we just saw, a repurposed Ottoman mosque or two...and this house, which belonged to the Benizelos family and was built in the 18th century. If it's open (sporadic, but generally Tue-Thu 10:00-13:00, Sun until 16:00), pop into the courtyard. (If it's closed, you can look through the windows on the street-facing wall.)

The house is an example of a *konaki*, a style of residence once common across Greece. The ground floor, constructed of stone, was for storing grain, wine, and olive oil; there was even a medieval olive press here. The upper floor, with refined woodwork, was where people lived. In the middle of the arcaded hallway is the elegant main sitting room, and on either side are two rooms accessed through a wooden partition screen: one for summer, and one for winter (with a fireplace).

Behind the house there's another, larger courtyard. The property was once much bigger, and included a garden and a few other buildings. These were luxury digs in the day: Only the richest families lived like this, and this mansion is the only one of its kind left in town.

• *Now head back the way you came on Adrianou, uphill and into the scrum of souvenir stands and tourists.*

⑩ Adrianou Street

Touristy Adrianou street is the main pedestrian drag of the Plaka, cutting through the neighborhood. We'll walk about 200 yards up to where it dead ends.

As you walk, you'll be running the full gauntlet of Greek souvenirs—sea sponges, olive oil, icons, carpets, jewelry, sandals, cheap Greek statues, and tacky T-shirts that say "Got Ouzo?" There are also plenty of cafés seemingly designed for tired tourists.

And what's with all the worry beads for sale? They range from cheap glass beads to authentic hand-cut amber. Greeks traditionally fondle and twirl these strings of beads. Worry beads may be based on religious beads used to keep track of prayers, like Catholics use the rosary or Muslims use prayer beads. But today's worry beads have no religious overtones—they're used to relieve anxiety and get focused. Traditionally, only men used worry beads, but they're becoming increasingly popular among Greek women.

• *Window-shop your way gently uphill until you reach the T-intersection with Lysikratous street.*

We now turn our attention to some of Athens' oldest monuments, from the ancient days when it was one of the greatest cities on earth. (To get in an ancient mood, check out the excavation site amid the trees nearby, showing the level of the street 2,000 years ago.)

Looking left, down Lysikratous street, you can see our next stop—the Arch of Hadrian. (If your fuel gauge is running low, you could skip the Arch of Hadrian and the Temple of Olympian Zeus, and jump ahead to the Lysicrates Monument, which is just a few steps to your right.)

• To continue the walk, head down Lysikratous street, cross busy Vasilis-sis Amalias avenue (crosswalk nearby), and approach the...

⓫ Arch of Hadrian and Temple of Olympian Zeus

In 146 BC, Athens came under the control of the growing Roman Empire. But the Romans—who loved Greek culture, architecture, and statues—only made the city greater.

Athens' best benefactor was the great Greco-phile Emperor Hadrian (or, as he was known in Greece, Adrianou). He built an enormous planned neighborhood known as—what else?—Hadrianopolis.

The **Arch of Hadrian**—a classic triumphal arch in the Roman style—marked the entrance to the emperor's planned community. The arch was once brilliant white, made of the same Pentelic marble as the Parthenon. It's now stained by exhaust from some of Athens' worst traffic. The arch is topped with Corinthian columns, with their leafy capitals. Corinthian was the Greek style preferred by the Romans. Hadrian built the arch in 132 AD to mark the line between Greek Athens and the new Roman city. An inscription on the west side (facing Vasilissis Amalias) reads, "This is Athens, ancient city of Theseus." The opposite frieze says, "This is the city of Hadrian, and not of Theseus." This arch must have been a big deal for Hadrian, as the emperor himself came here to celebrate the inauguration.

Now look past the arch to see the huge—and I mean huge—Corinthian columns. These are all that remain of the **Temple of Olympian Zeus** (entrance is a 5-minute walk to the left, circling the fence clockwise—but you can see basically everything from here). This was the largest temple in ancient Greece and took almost 700 years to complete. It was begun in the sixth century BC by the Greeks, then lay abandoned, half-built, for centuries. Finally, Hadrian finished the job in 131 AD.

Did I mention the temple was huge? Those Corinthian columns are a towering 56 feet high. Compare that with the 34-foot-high columns of the puny Parthenon. The finished temple was 360 feet long by 145 feet wide. It was the size of a football field, or more than twice the square footage of the Parthenon.

The Temple of Olympian Zeus had 104 columns—two rows of 20 columns on each of the long sides and three rows of eight columns along each end. Only 15 columns remain standing. The fallen column you see—like a tipped-over stack of bottle caps—was knocked over by a storm in 1852. This over-the-top temple was dedicated to Zeus, who lived on Mount Olympus. The temple contained two enormous statues: one of the ruler of the gods—Zeus—and an equally colossal statue of the ruler of the Greeks...Hadrian.

• *Let's delve even deeper into Athens' past, as we make our way to the Acropolis.*

Backtrack up Lysikratous street to where we were earlier, at the T-intersection. Just uphill from that intersection, Lysikratous street spills out into a small, leafy square with the Acropolis rising above it. In the square is a round, white monument.

⓬ Lysicrates Monument and Square

The elegant marble Lysicrates monument has Corinthian columns that support a dome topped with a (rather damaged) statue. Check

out the frieze around the top portion. You may be able to see that it represents Dionysus turning pirates into dolphins.

The monument is the sole survivor of many such monuments that once lined this street. This was the ancient "Street of the Tripods," so-called because the monuments came with bronze tripods alongside. These three-legged stands (like those you'll see in the museums) held trophies—things like ornamental vases and cauldrons. Here on this street, the ancient "Oscars" were awarded to winners of theatrical competitions staged at the nearby Theater of Dionysus. The Lysicrates Monument honors one of the winners—the winning choral team from the year 334 BC. Excavations around the monument have uncovered the foundations of other monuments, which are now reburied under a layer of red sand, awaiting further study.

Now stroll the square itself. Shaded by trees, this is a pleasant place to take a break before we climb the hill. Have a coffee at one of the café tables, or try a frappé—an iced coffee with foam. Or you can grab a cold drink from a store and sit for free on the benches under the trees.

• *When you're ready to move on, find the Epimenidou staircase on the left side of the square, and start climbing. At the top of the stairs, the street leads left to the south entrance gate and Acropolis Museum, but for now we'll turn right to continue around the lower flanks of...*

⓭ Acropolis Hill

As you walk (past olive trees), you're treading the same paths followed by humans since the beginning of recorded time. From cave dwellers to modern man, Athenians have lived on, around, or in the shadow of this hill. The Acropolis—or "high city"—has been the heart of Athens since the Neolithic era, around 7000 BC. The sheer plateau was a natural fortress—faced with 100-foot cliffs, and fed by permanent springs.

Acropolis hill is a limestone ridge that's flat on top. Its footprint covers seven acres. The Mycenaeans built the first palaces on top (around 1400 BC), and their Greek descendants built temples to their patron goddess Athena (around 800 BC). When the Persians destroyed all of the Acropolis' temples (480 BC), it left a blank canvas. The resilient Greeks built the Parthenon, ushering in the golden age. And for 2,500 years, the grand structures atop this hill have inspired the Western world.

• *At the small **Church of St. George of the Rock** (Agios Georgios), there's a fork in the road. Go uphill, along the left fork. You'll soon be immersed in a maze of tiny, whitewashed houses. This charming "village" is the neighborhood called...*

⑭ Anafiotika

As you enter the narrow lanes, don't worry about getting lost. Just keep following signs that point to *Acropolis*—even if the path seems impossibly narrow. You'll eventually emerge on the other side.

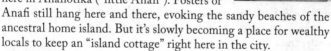

The tiny homes cling to the hillside, built into and around the Acropolis' craggy outcroppings. This neighborhood of Anafiotika was built by people from the tiny Cycladic island of Anafi, who came to Athens looking for work after Greece gained its independence from the Ottomans. (Many stoneworkers and builders hired to construct the modern city of Athens built these higgledy-piggledy residences after-hours.) Some descendants of the original islanders still live here in Anafiotika ("little Anafi"). Posters of Anafi still hang here and there, evoking the sandy beaches of the ancestral home island. But it's slowly becoming a place for wealthy locals to keep an "island cottage" right here in the city.

Keep heading generally left and uphill, following *Acropolis* signs when you see them. Weave through narrow paths, lined with flowers and dotted with cats, dozing peacefully in the sunshine or slithering luxuriously past your legs. In this delightful spot, nestled beneath the walls of the Acropolis, the big city seems a world away. Notice the male fig trees—they're the ones with no fruit, so they keep away flies and mosquitoes. Smell the chicken-manure fertilizer, peek into delicate little yards, and enjoy the blue doors and maroon shutters. It's a transplanted Cycladic Island world.

As you gaze out over the rooftops of modern Athens below, keep an eye out for **views of Lykavittos Hill,** the cone-shaped mound in the distance. It's the highest hill in Athens, topped with a tiny white church at just over 900 feet above sea level. By comparison, the Acropolis is only 490 feet tall. The Lykavittos summit, which can be reached by a funicular, has a restaurant and view terrace. Although it looms high over the cityscape, Lykavittos Hill will always be overshadowed by the hill you're climbing now.

From the Acropolis—Athens' oldest sight—our walk starts making its way back to the modern world.

• *Follow the* Acropolis *signs, through the narrow walkways, until you emerge from the maze of houses at a T-intersection with a wider, cobbled lane. Turn right (downhill) and continue on the cobbled lane past the neighborhood church tucked around the corner to the right. After 50 yards, turn left on a wider road (Theorias), and walk toward the small stone Church of the Metamorphosis. (Note: To reach the Acropolis main entrance from here, you would continue along this road as it bends left around the hill. For now, though, let's continue our walk.)*

Just before the church (near the sign for the Athens University History Museum), turn right down the steep, narrow staircase called Klepsidras. Go 100 yards down the stairs (past cute homes, interesting graffiti, the free little museum, and the recommended Klepsidra Café), until the staircase dead-ends at a railing overlooking some ruins.

⓫ Roman Forum and Tower of the Winds

The rows of columns framing this rectangular former piazza were built by the Romans. The Romans loved the city of Athens and made it even more beau-

tiful. This square was the commercial center, or forum, of Roman Athens. The columns supported a covered porch providing shade for shoppers browsing the many stores fronting the square. Picture this place filled with Roman bureaucrats and Greek locals. The forum—or open-air piazza— was a feature found in every city Rome conquered. Here, it was dotted with Greek-style buildings and statues. Like Americans in Paris, Romans relished living in sophisticated Athens, sprinkling their Latin conversations with Greek phrases as they discussed the plays of Sophocles and Aristophanes. It's possible to enter the Roman Forum for a closer look at the rubble—the entrance is on the west end—but you can see just about everything from here (for more on what's inside, see page 56).

Now, take a few steps to the right for a closer look at the octagonal, domed **Tower of the Winds.** Built in the first century BC, this building was an ingenious combination of clock, weather station, and guide to the planets. The tower was once capped with a weathervane in the form of a bronze Triton—half-man, half-fish. Bronze rods (no longer visible) protruded from the walls and acted as sundials to indicate the time. And when the sun wasn't shining, people told time using the tower's sophisticated water clock inside, powered by water piped in from springs on the Acropolis. Much later, under Ottoman rule, dervishes used the tower as a place for their whirling worship and prayer.

Look closely at the tower's carved reliefs. They depict the traditional eight winds of the world as winged angels, who fly in, bringing the weather. Find the weather-angel holding the curved rudder of a ship—he's the wind who brings good sailing weather. The next relief (to the right) shows an angel turning an urn upside down, spilling out rain.

To see more reliefs, circle the Tower counterclockwise, as we make our way downhill to our next destination. As you turn the corner, find the old bearded man wrapping his cloak up tight against the cold weather. On the Tower's right side is an angel with a robe full of fruit, bringing the abundance of summer. Next (as you continue circling counterclockwise), an angel with a round shield is about to dump out hailstones. Finally (at the downhill side of the Tower), find the north wind, wearing a heavy robe and blowing on a conch shell to usher in winter.

From this vantage point, you can look through the fence into the Roman Forum. Find some rectangular ruins surrounded by a wider rectangular ditch—the ancient forum's public restroom.

• *By now you should be at the downhill side of the Tower of the Winds. Facing the Tower, turn 180 degrees, and find the start of narrow Aiolou (Αιολoy) street. Head downhill on Aiolou street one block, where it opens up into the leafy, restaurant-filled...*

⑯ Agora Square (Plateia Agoras)

This square is the touristy center of the Plaka. Starting from here, you have your choice of restaurants, where you can dine with Brits on holiday or have a beer with a group of Aussies. The Plaka can be both atmospheric and crassly touristic. Its streets are lined with souvenirs, tacky tavernas, a smattering of small museums, ancient ruins, and exhausted tourists. The narrow, winding streets can be confusing at first, but you can't get too lost with a monument the size of the Acropolis looming overhead. Think of the Plaka as Athens with training wheels for tourists, then dare to explore beyond it.

On the left side of the square you'll see the second-century AD ruins of the ❶ **Library of Hadrian,** built by that Greek-loving Roman emperor, Hadrian, for the good of his beloved Athens. Four lone columns sit atop apse-like foundations. The ruins around it are all that's left of a big rectangular complex that once boasted 100 marble columns. It was a huge cultural center, with a library, lecture halls, garden, and art gallery. Notice how the excavated stones rest neatly in stacks awaiting funding for reconstruction.

• *We're on the home stretch now. Continue downhill alongside the ruins one block, and turn left onto* ❶ *Pandrossou street—a narrow lane choked with souvenir shops. Expert pickpockets work this crowded lane—be careful. Wade through the knee-deep tacky tourist souvenirs. Several shops supply fans of the "Round Goddess"—a.k.a. soccer—with t-shirts and jerseys. Continue until you spill out into Monastiraki Square.*

❶ Monastiraki Square Spin-Tour

We've made it from Syntagma Square—the center of urban Athens—to the city's *other* main square, Monastiraki Square, the gateway to the touristy Old Town. To get oriented to Monastiraki Square, stand in the center, face the small church with the cross on top (which is north), and pan clockwise.

The name Monastiraki ("Little Monastery") refers to this square, the surrounding neighborhood, the flea-market action nearby...and the cute **Church of the Virgin** in the square's center (12th-century Byzantine, mostly restored with a much more modern bell tower).

Beyond the church (straight ahead from the end of the square), **Athinas street** veers left to the Central Market, Omonia Square, and (after about a mile) the National Archaeological Museum.

Just to the right (behind the little church) is the head of **Ermou street**—the bustling shopping drag we walked down earlier. If you turned right and walked straight up Ermou, you'd be back at Syntagma Square in 10 minutes.

Next (on the right, in front of the little church) comes Mitropo-

leos street—Athens' **"Souvlaki Row."**
Clogged with outdoor tables, this atmospheric lane is home to a string of restaurants
that serve sausage-shaped, skewered meat—
grilled up spicy and tasty. The place on the
corner—Bairaktaris (Μπαϊρaktapho)—is
the best known, its walls lined with photos
of famous politicians and artists who come
here for souvlaki and pose with the owner.
But the other joint here—Taverna Thanasis—has a better reputation for their souvlaki
(and prices). You can sit at the tables, or, for
a really cheap meal, order a souvlaki to go.
(For details, see the Eating in Athens chap-
ter.) A few blocks farther down Mitropoleos is the cathedral we
visited earlier.

Continue spinning clockwise. Just past Pandrossou street
(where you entered the square), you'll see a **former mosque** (look for
the Arabic script under the por-
tico and over the wooden door).
Known as the Tzami (from the
Turkish word for "mosque"),
this was a place of worship when
Athens was under Ottoman rule
(15th-19th centuries).

To the right of the mosque,
behind the fence along Areos
street, you might glimpse some
huge Corinthian columns. This is the opposite end of the **Library
of Hadrian** complex we saw earlier. Areos street stretches up toward the Acropolis. If you were to walk a block up this street, then
turn right on Adrianou, you'd reach the ⓴ **Ancient Agora**—one
of Athens' top ancient attractions (􀀀 see the Ancient Agora Tour
chapter and 🎧 my free Agora audio tour). Beyond the Agora are the
delightful Thissio neighborhood and ancient Keramikos Cemetery.

As you continue panning clockwise, next comes the pretty yellow building that houses the **Monastiraki Metro station.** This was
Athens' original, 19th-century train station—Neoclassical with a
dash of Byzantium. This bustling Metro stop is now the intersection of two lines: the old line 1 (green, with connections to the
port of Piraeus, the Thissio neighborhood, and Victoria—near the
National Archaeological Museum) and the modern line 3 (blue,
with connections to Syntagma Square and the airport). **Excavations** for the station revealed an ancient aqueduct, which confined
Athens' Eridanos River to a canal. The river had been a main axis
of the town since the eighth century BC. In the second century

AD, Hadrian and his engineers put a roof over it, turning it into a more efficient sewer. Inside (ticket required), you can still see an exposed bit of ancient Athens—Roman brick and classic Roman engineering—and a cool mural showing the treasure trove archaeologists uncovered with the excavations. The stands in front of the station sell seasonal fruit and are popular with commuters.

Just right of the station, Ifestou street leads downhill into the **flea market** (antiques, jewelry, cheap clothing, and so on). If locals need a screw for an old lamp, they know they'll find it here.

Keep panning clockwise. Just beyond busy Ermou street (behind the A for Athens hotel—which has a rooftop bar popular for its views) is the happening ❹ **Psyrri** district. For years a run-down slum, this zone is being gentrified by twentysomethings with a grungy sense of style. Packed with cutting-edge bars, boutique hotels, restaurants, cafés, and nightclubs, it may seem foreboding and ramshackle, but it's actually fun to explore. Wander through by day to get your bearings, then head back at night when it's buzzing with activity.

This walk has taken us through 2,500 years of Athens' history—though in reverse order. We started in modern Athens, at Syntagma Square and Ermou street. Next, we saw medieval Athens—Orthodox churches and the winding streets of the Plaka. Then, we saw ancient ruins—both Greek and Roman. And, we've ended on a bustling square where Athens—both old and new—comes together. Explore and enjoy this global capital—the springboard of so much Western civilization, and the place that more than one in three Greeks call home.

• *Our walk is over. If you've worked up an appetite, savor a spicy souvlaki on "Souvlaki Row" or eat your way through the local and colorful Psyrri neighborhood.* 📖 *My Psyrri and Central Market Walk begins right here.*

CITY WALK

ANCIENT AGORA TOUR

Αρχαία Αγορά

While the Acropolis was the ceremonial showpiece, the Agora was the real heart of ancient Athens. For some 800 years (c. 600 BC-AD 300), it was the place where people came to shop, businessmen struck deals, laws were passed, worshippers venerated the gods, and theaters hummed with nightlife.

Agora means "gathering place," but you could call this space by any of the names we typically give to the busiest part of a city—downtown, main square, forum, piazza, marketplace, commons, and so on. It was a lively place where the pace never let up—much like modern Athens.

Little survives from the Classical-era Agora. Other than one very well-preserved temple and a rebuilt stoa, it's a field of humble ruins. But that makes it a quiet, uncrowded spot to wander and get a feel for the ancients. Nestled in the shadow of the Acropolis, it's an ideal prelude to your visit there.

Orientation

Cost: €10, covered by €30 Acropolis combo-ticket; see sidebar on page 47).

Hours: Daily 8:00-20:00, Oct until 18:00, Nov-March until 17:00. The Agora Museum inside generally has the same hours.

Information: +30 210 321 0180, http://odysseus.culture.gr.

Getting There: From the Monastiraki Metro stop, walk a block south (uphill, toward the Acropolis). Turn right on Adrianou street, and follow the pedestrian-only, café-lined street along the railroad tracks for about 200 yards. The Agora entrance is on your left, across from a small, yellow church. The entrance can be hard to spot: It's where a path crosses over the railroad tracks (look for a small, pale-yellow sign that says *Ministry of Culture—Ancient Agora*).

Visitor Information: Panels with printed descriptions of the ruins are scattered helpfully throughout the site.

Tours: ⋒ Download my free Ancient Agora audio tour.

Length of this Tour: Allow 1.5 hours.

Services: Water fountains are at the entrance and inside the Stoa of Attalos. The only WCs on the site are inside the Stoa of Attalos, at its northernmost end.

Eating: Picnicking is not allowed in the Agora. Loads of cafés and tavernas line busy Adrianou street near the entrance, and more good eateries front the Apostolou Pavlou pedestrian walkway that hems in the western edge of the Agora, in the district called Thissio.

Starring: A well-preserved temple, a rebuilt stoa with a nice museum, some monumental statues, and the ruins of the civilization that built the Western world.

The Tour Begins

Entering the site from Adrianou street, belly up to the **illustration** at the top of the ramp that shows the Athenian Agora at the peak of

its size. Face the Acropolis (to the south) and look out over the expanse of ruins and trees. This overgrown field was once the center of Athenian life.

Get oriented. You're standing near #26 on the illustration. At your feet runs the Panathenaic Way (#21), the Agora's main street, then and now. The long column-lined building to the left is the reconstructed Stoa of Attalos (#13). To your right (though likely obscured by trees) is the Temple of Hephaistos (#20). Directly ahead of you (through more trees) are the remains of the Odeon of Agrippa (#12).

In the distance, the Agora's far end is bordered by hills. From left to right are the Acropolis (#1), the Areopagus ("Hill of Ares," or Mars Hill, #2), and Pnyx Hill (#3).

The place where you're standing was near the Altar of the Twelve Gods, which was once considered the geographical center of Athens, from which distances were measured. You've arrived at ground zero of ancient Athens.

On this self-guided walk, we'll go up the Panathenaic Way to the Stoa of Attalos, turn right and cross the Agora to the Temple

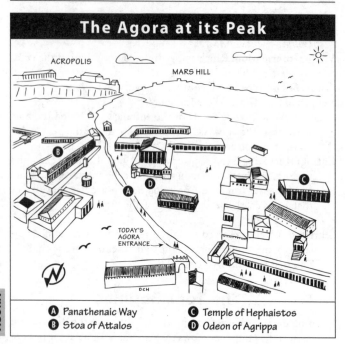

The Agora at its Peak

ACROPOLIS

MARS HILL

TODAY'S
AGORA
ENTRANCE →

DCH

A Panathenaic Way
B Stoa of Attalos
C Temple of Hephaistos
D Odeon of Agrippa

AGORA

of Hephaistos, then return to the Odeon. We'll end by heading up the Panathenaic Way again toward the Acropolis.

• *Walk to the bottom of the ramp at your left to the path that was once Athens' main street. Find a shady spot to ponder ancient Athenian life in its heyday.*

❶ The Panathenaic Way—the Agora in its Prime

Imagine walking through the Agora along its main drag in ancient times.

On your left stood the Stoa of Attalos, which looked much like this modern reconstruction today. On your right was the Agora's main square, surrounded by gleaming, white-marble buildings. Everywhere you looked there were temples, government buildings, and theaters, all fronted with columns and topped with red-tile roofs. The place was studded with trees and dotted with statues, fountains, and altars. The streets were lined with wooden market stalls where merchants sold produce, pottery, and trinkets.

The Agora buzzed with people, day and night. Imagine men and women dressed in their simple tunics—men's tunics extending to their knees and women's to their ankles. They came to shop—to buy groceries, clothes, painted plates and pitchers, or to get their wagon wheel fixed. If you needed a zoning permit for your business, you came to the courthouse. Worshippers gave offerings to

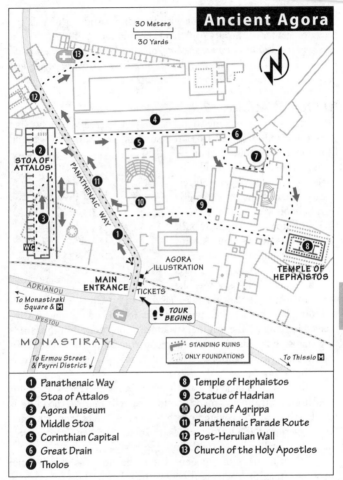

Ancient Agora

30 Meters
30 Yards

STOA OF ATTALOS

PANATHENAIC WAY

WC

AGORA ILLUSTRATION

MAIN ENTRANCE

TICKETS

TOUR BEGINS

ADRIANOU
To Monastiraki Square & M

IFESTOU

MONASTIRAKI

To Ermou Street & Psyrri District ↓

To Thissio M

TEMPLE OF HEPHAISTOS

AGORA

STANDING RUINS
ONLY FOUNDATIONS

❶ Panathenaic Way
❷ Stoa of Attalos
❸ Agora Museum
❹ Middle Stoa
❺ Corinthian Capital
❻ Great Drain
❼ Tholos
❽ Temple of Hephaistos
❾ Statue of Hadrian
❿ Odeon of Agrippa
⓫ Panathenaic Parade Route
⓬ Post-Herulian Wall
⓭ Church of the Holy Apostles

the gods at any number of temples and altars. At night, people came for plays and concerts. The tavernas rocked.

The Panathenaic Way started at the main city gate, cut diagonally through the Agora's main square, and wound its way up to the Acropolis—two-thirds of a mile in all. This was the city's main north-south road, and here in the Agora it intersected with the main east-west road to the busy port of Piraeus. Though some stretches were paved, most of it (then as now) was just packed gravel.

All roads led to the Agora. This was the place for speeches, political announcements, celebrations, and demonstrations. On holidays, the parade ran right up this street. At any time, this was the place to be—to run into eccentric characters like Socrates or

Diogenes, or just to hang out with friends. In short, this was the buzzing center of the city of Athens, population 100,000.

• *Now turn your attention to the long, colonnaded building on your left. The entrance is at the far (south) end. Step onto its shaded porch, look down the long rows of columns, and admire the...*

❼ Stoa of Attalos

This stoa was an ancient shopping mall. Covered walkways like this protected shoppers from the sun and the rain. The ground floor once had about 20 shops—today, those rooms hold the museum. Upstairs were offices, which today house the American School.

The stoa was originally built around 150 BC by King Attalos II of Pergamon (in modern-day Turkey). Though he was not a Greek, Attalos was—like so many other ancient people—fascinated by Greek culture. This building was his way of saying thanks for the education he'd received in Athens. The original structure is long gone, but the building that stands today is a faithful reconstruction, built in the 1950s by the American School of Classical Studies, which helped excavate the Agora.

This stoa is typical of many others in ancient Athens. It stands two stories tall and was made of white Pentelic marble, the same as the Parthenon. The covered porch is about 400 feet long. It's lined with one row of 45 Doric columns (the outer layer) and another row of 22 Ionic columns—a typical mixing of styles.

Like the malls of our generation, the stoa was also a social magnet. Imagine ancient Greeks—their hard labor being done by enslaved people—lounging here, just enjoying the shade of the portico.

The statues on display in the arcade once populated the Agora—gods, heroes, athletes, and ceremonial *stele*. For example, on the wall near the fifth Ionic column, find the impressive sculpt-ed head of a bearded man with a full head of hair. This Head of a Triton (c. 150 AD) once deco-rated the Odeon of Agrippa, which we'll see later.

• *About halfway down the arcade you'll find the entrance to the Agora Museum (included with your ticket).*

❸ Agora Museum

The Agora itself is mostly ruins, but the excellent little museum displays some choice rubble that helps bring the place back to life. Start in the corner, with a photo from 1952 showing this spot before the stoa was reconstructed—just a long platform.

This long hall is laid out chronologically, letting you trace the history of the Agora through artifacts (mainly pottery) found here. Follow the collection by the numbers found in the display cases' upper-right corner. The cases are rather confusingly labeled but easy to find.

• *The first cases chart the rise of the Agora from a tiny settlement to the center of enlightened golden age Athens.*

Case #1 (center of the room): This reclining female figure dates from the Agora's first inhabitants, way back around 4,000 BC, who found a home in this rectangular-shaped valley in the protective shadow of the Acropolis.

#8 (right wall): These tomb offerings came from the next settlers: the Mycenaeans (c. 1600-1200 BC), who built atop the Acropolis and used the Agora as a cemetery.

#9 (right): This handsome vase (with its intricate patterns, symmetrical designs, and stick figures) is, not surprisingly, from the Geometric period (1100-700 BC). Its presence indicates that the Agora now had permanent residents and pottery workshops.

#3 (center): As Athens grew, the pottery got more sophisticated, depicting increasingly realistic humans and animals. During this Archaic era (700-480 BC) the Agora expanded, got its first monumental buildings, and hosted its first Panathenaic parade.

#26 (right): Yes, it's just what it looks like—a baby's commode. It dates from the time when the Agora was still largely a residential neighborhood, rather than the all-commercial "downtown" it would become.

#4 (center): This bust of Nike (which means Victory) celebrates Athens' triumph over Persia, when it rebuilt the Agora, ushered in the golden age (roughly 450-400 BC), and established a flourishing democracy.

• *The next several displays are devoted to one of Athens' greatest inventions—democracy.*

#30 (right): The pottery shards with names painted on them were voter ballots (called *ostrakon*) used to vote out—or ostracize—corrupt tyrants. On the two shards, #37 and #17, read the Greek names—Themistocles and Aristides (ΘΕΜΙΣΘΟΚΛΕΣ ΝΕΟΚΛΕΟΣ and ΑΡΙΣΣΤΕΙΔΕΣ). During the golden age, these men were famous rivals, in both politics and romance. Both served Athens honorably and both were also exiled in political power struggles.

#31 (right): This contraption is an early voting machine called the *kleroterion*. It was used to select city council members. It was done randomly, to make sure each citizen fulfilled their civic duty—kind of like jury duty. Citizens put their name in the slots, then black and white balls went into the tube (on the left) to randomly select who would serve. Now look below the machine—you'll see actual bronze ballots from the fourth century.

#32 (right): The *klepsydra* ("water thief") was a water clock used to time speeches at council meetings. It took six minutes for the 1.7 gallons to drain out. A gifted orator truly was good to the last drop...but not a second longer.

#67 (left): The bronze shield was captured from defeated Spartans in the tide-turning Battle of Sphacteria, which gave Athens the upper hand in the Peloponnesian War. The victory was only temporary, and Athens drained itself in those wars with Sparta.

Just to the left of case #67 is the "Stele of Democracy." A relief carving shows Lady Democracy crowning a man representing the Athenian people. The inscription proclaims that all tyranny is outlawed. Note the monument's date: from around 336 BC, the year Alexander the Great took control of Greece and began spreading Greek culture throughout the known world.

• *The final exhibits date from the Agora's later years, when it was the center of a large, multicultural, cosmopolitan Hellenistic world.*

#66 (left): These marble "herm" heads of prominent men stood atop columns that were placed at major intersections. They warded off evil spirits and were signposts, with the latest news and directions attached.

#34 and **#35** (right): Pottery was a popular export product for the sea-trading Greeks. The sophisticated Athenians set the trends—from black figures painted on a red background (case #34) to red on black (case #35).

#5 (center): In the middle of the room is a case of coins. These drachms and tetradrachms feature Athena with her helmet. In golden age times, a drachm was roughly a day's wage. The ancients put coins like these in the mouth of a deceased person as payment to carry the soul safely across the River Styx. Coin #7, a four-drachm piece, features the owl as on Greece's €1 coin today.

#60-61 (left) and **#42** (right): What are these objects? It's exactly what you think—ancient barbecue grills. Those long-ago people weren't really so different from you and me.

#58 and **#56** (left): These sculpture heads date from the Agora's next great era, the Romans. The Romans loved Greek culture and expanded the Agora, leaving many of the ruins seen today. As these busts show, the Romans were more honest than the Greeks when it came to portraying people with less-than-ideal features.

#55 (far end): After the decline of Rome, the Agora suffered, but—as these fine, intricately patterned pieces of Byzantine pottery attest—it still shone on. Athens remained an important regional capital in the enlightened Byzantine Empire ruled from Constantinople (modern-day Istanbul). The Agora was a vital neighborhood of Athens until 1204, when invading Venetians sacked and looted it, and the Agora was abandoned...leaving all these artifacts in the rubble, waiting for archaeologists to retrieve them and build this museum.

• *Exit this room and turn right into the arcade for a WC and water fountain. To reach the stoa's upper floor (with a few more exhibits, statues, and Agora views), turn left and to go the end of the arcade, where you'll find the stairway leading up to the second level.*

From here in the open-air **upper stoa,** you have great views down into the Agora and across to the Temple of Hephaistos. Along the wall you'll find a changing exhibit, and hiding behind it, storage cases with shelf upon shelf of pottery shards, all of them dug up right here in the Agora. The models show the Agora from various eras, helping you mentally resurrect the rubble and comprehend the changes that occurred over the centuries. Halfway down the hall, focus on the model of the Agora at its peak of grandeur, under the Romans, in the second century AD. It was sure something. Find the Stoa of Attalos on one side, the Temple of Hephaistos on the other, and the Odeon of Agrippa in between. Now find the long, low building behind the *odeon.* This was another stoa—the Middle Stoa. That's where we're headed next.

• *Go back downstairs, return to the spot where we first entered, and head across the Panathenaic Way. Continue straight (west) along the lane and across the middle of the Agora. You're walking alongside the vast ruins (on your left) of what once was the...*

AGORA

The Agora in Action

Think of all the people, famous and not, who've walked the very paths you do. It's where they shopped and schmoozed. Where they invented democracy. Citizens gathered here by the thousands to listen to speeches and cast votes to ostracize their tyrants. The Agora is where the earliest plays were performed—originally in the open air—as the Greeks pioneered modern theater.

The roving philosopher **Socrates** (469-399 BC) spent much of his life simply hanging out in the Agora, questioning passersby, and urging people to "know thyself." Socrates discussed the meaning of piety, as recorded by Plato in the dialogue called the Euthyphro. "The lover of inquiry," said Socrates, "must follow his beloved wherever it may lead him." Shortly after, Socrates was tried and condemned to death here for "corrupting the youth"...by encouraging them to question Athenian piety.

Plato, Socrates' disciple and chronicler of his words, spent time teaching in the Agora, as did Plato's disciple **Aristotle.** (Their schools—Plato's Academy and Aristotle's Lyceum—were located elsewhere in Athens.)

The great statesman **Pericles**—whose Funeral Oration over the Greek dead from the first year of the Peloponnesian War is a famous expression of Athenian ideals—must have spent time here, since he oversaw the rebuilding program after the Persian invasion.

When Athens triumphed over Sparta in one battle during the Peloponnesian War (425 BC), **General Cleon** displayed the

❹ Middle Stoa

This long set of ruins—about 500 feet long by 60 feet wide—stretches clear across the Agora. It served as a big mall of shops and offices for busy Athens. It looked something like the reconstructed Stoa of Attalos that we just saw, except this was only one story tall. You can probably make out two long lines of stubby column fragments from the columns that supported the roof. You'll also find a few stone steps, and the reddish-colored blocks (near the far end) from the foundation.

Remember that, during the golden age, this central part of the Agora was just an open field, a "gathering place." But as Athens grew and expanded, so did its commercial center. The Middle Stoa (180 BC) was one of several grand buildings that began to fill shields of captured prisoners in the Agora. This action mocked the Spartans for their surrender, since brave Spartans were always supposed to die with their shields on.

Diogenes the Cynic lived as a homeless person in the Agora and shocked the Athenians with his anti-materialist and free lifestyle. He lived in a wooden tub (in disregard for material comfort), masturbated openly (to prove how simply one's desires could be satisfied), and wandered the Agora with a lighted lamp in daylight (looking for one honest man in the corrupt city). According to legend, Alexander the Great was intrigued by this humble philosopher who shunned materialism. One day he stood before him and said, "Diogenes, I will give you whatever you want. What would you like?" History's first hippie looked at the most powerful man on earth and replied, "Please get out of my sunshine."

The playwright **Aristophanes** set scenes in the Agora, the tragedian **Sophocles** spent time here, and many classic Greek plays got their big debut here at the "Broadway" of ancient Greece.

The **Apostle Paul** stopped in Athens on his way to Corinth in AD 49 (Acts 17:17). He debated with the pagan philosophers in the "marketplace"—likely the Agora. And he decried the Athenians' altars to pagan gods when he preached from Mars Hill, overlooking the Agora.

In short, the Agora was always at the heart of every key point in Greek history. Here the Athenians mobilized to confront the onslaught of the Persians. It's where they greeted the coming of Alexander the Great and tolerated the conquering Romans. As Athens declined, the Athenians faced off here against invaders, from the Herulians to the Slavs. And even as the Agora slowly fell into ruin, for centuries thereafter, every famous European who visited Athens made a point to tour the Agora and ponder these inspiring ruins.

AGORA

the space. Eventually it became jam-packed with big marble buildings—the maze of ruins you see today.

• *Midway down the lane (near the wooden section of the path), you'll come across a huge capital of a column.*

❺ Corinthian Capital

This capital once stood here atop a colossal column. Carved in the fourth century BC, this is one of the earliest examples of the style known as Corinthian. The Corinthian order featured slender, fluted columns topped with leafy capitals like this. The style was actually rarely used by Greeks, but it became wildly popular with the Romans. When the Romans occupied Athens, they incorporated older Greek capitals like this one into their massive theater. You can see the ruins of that theater (Odeon of Agrippa) as you look toward the Agora entrance.

• *But we're getting ahead of ourselves. Continue westward across the Agora. Near the end of the Middle Stoa, you'll see a gray wellhead—still in its original spot and worn by the grooves of ropes.*

Just beyond the well to the right, you'll spy a round platform—the tholos. Make your way there—after passing the wooden bridge and turning left, you'll cross over a ditch that was once part of the...

❻ Great Drain

This ditch was part of Athens' impressive waterworks system. It was dug in the fifth century BC and still functions today. The ditch captures rainwater runoff from the southern hills and channels it through the Agora. At this point, two main collection ditches meet and join. If you look closely, you can see exposed parts of the stone-lined ditch. The well we just saw was also part of this water system.

From here you have good views of the Acropolis. The towering but empty pedestal of the Monument of Agrippa (on the hill's right end) marks the entrance to the Acropolis. To the left of that is the Erechtheion temple. To the right of the Acropolis is craggy Mars Hill, where the Apostle Paul famously preached. The long ridgeline farther to the right is Pnyx Hill. This wide, gentle slope is where Athenian citizens gathered by the thousands to debate policy when the Agora was too small.

• *But the real center of Greek democracy is just a few steps away. It's that round footprint with a stubby column in its center. This is the...*

❼ *Tholos*

This rotunda-shaped building housed Athens' rulers. It was built around 465 BC, right at the dawn of the golden age and of Athenian democracy. About 60 feet across, this round structure was originally ringed with six Ionic columns and topped with a cone-shaped roof.

The *tholos* was the center of Athenian government. It was the headquarters, offices, and meeting hall for the city's 50 ministers. They also lived and ate here, since the law required that at least a third of these ministers be on the premises at all times. The *tholos* housed the official weights and measures. By law, any shopper in the Agora could stop in here and use these to check whether a butcher or tailor was shortchanging them.

The 50 ministers were selected from the 500 ministers who met next door in the *bouleuterion* (council house). They, in turn, were elected by the foundation of Athenian democracy—the thousands of free adult male citizens.

The *tholos* was also a kind of temple to democratic rule. The altar in the middle—where the broken column is now—once held a flame that was always kept burning. This represented the hearth of the extended "family" that was Athens.

• *Our next stop is the big temple atop the ridge. To reach it, climb the stairs to the left and go through the trees, pausing along the way at a* ***viewpoint*** *with a chart. (This is an ideal spot to take a seat, view the entire Agora, and read the sidebar on "The Agora in Action.") Then continue to the...*

❽ Temple of Hephaistos

One of the best preserved and most typical of all Greek temples, this is textbook golden age architecture. Started in 450 BC—just

before the Parthenon—it was built at Athens' peak as part of the massive reconstruction of the Agora after invading Persians destroyed the city (480 BC). But the temple wasn't completed and dedicated until 415 BC, as work stalled when the Greeks

started erecting the great buildings of the Acropolis.

This is a classic peristyle temple (like the Parthenon), meaning that the building is surrounded by columns. Also like the Parthenon, it's made of Pentelic marble in the Doric style, part of Pericles' vision of harking back to Athens' austere, solid roots. But the Temple of Hephaistos is only about half the size of the grand Parthenon and has fewer carvings.

Priests would enter from here at the Agora-facing entrance, through the six columns, beneath the covered portico (note the coffered ceiling), and into an alcove ringed by three walls (called the *pronaos* or "pre-temple") before reaching the central hall *(cella).* There they'd worship a large bronze statue of Hephaistos, the blacksmith god, and one of Athena, patroness of Athens and of arts and crafts. According to legend, Hephaistos hit on Athena, she spurned him, he spilled his semen on the ground...and Athens was born. Appropriately, the temple of these crafty gods was originally surrounded by metalworking and pottery workshops.

The carved reliefs are typical of the Greek love of the "contest," depicting legendary battles between heroes, animals, gods, and mythological beasts. The metopes above the outer entrance show 10 scenes from the Labors of Hercules. They're interspersed with panels of three vertical lines, meant to imitate the humble-but-virtuous look of early Greek dwellings made of wood.

Looking between the six columns, you'll see the inner frieze, with its scenes of Theseus battling Athens' oppressors. (The great mythological hero would eventually slay the bull-headed Minotaur.) These decorations led Athenians to mistakenly believe that the temple once held the remains of Theseus—and to this day, they call it the Theseion.

Take a few steps to the right to view the temple's long side. Like most temples, it was built atop a platform. The temple has six columns on each end and 13 on the long sides (counting the corners twice). The columns are Doric—with no base and a simple capital—though these columns are fluted (with vertical stripes), which is not as common. The columns were made by stacking seven column drums. The four carvings (metopes)

above the columns also depict Theseus' battles. The rest of the metopes are blank—possibly because they were never finished, but maybe because they once held painted frescoes.

If you venture to the temple's rear entrance, you'll find a fine frieze of the mythological battle when centaurs crashed a wedding of the mortal Lapith tribe. On the temple's other long side, you can make out bullet holes on the crossbeam, a painful reminder of Greece's 1940s civil war.

The temple is remarkably well preserved. It remained an important place of worship when the Romans arrived, was converted into a church (and given a roof) in the Christian era, and even stayed open under the Muslim Ottomans.

• *We now turn to sights from the Roman period—perhaps the greatest era of the Agora's history. Wind your way down the hill (northeast) to the middle of the Agora and find the headless...*

❾ Statue of Hadrian

The Roman Emperor Hadrian ruled Athens around 120 AD, when Rome was at its peak and Athens was a vital part of the Europe-wide empire. The statue shows Hadrian wearing the typical Roman military uniform, complete with a breastplate and leather skirt. Where Hadrian's belly button would be, find the tiny insignia on the armor. It shows Romulus and Remus, the legendary founders of Rome being suckled by the she-wolf who raised them. Now look who's standing atop the she-wolf—it's Athena.

This symbolized Hadrian's vision—that by conquering Greece,

Rome actually saved and supported that great civilization. Hadrian was a true Grecophile and great benefactor of Athens. In fact, if this statue still had its head, you'd see that Hadrian was the first Roman emperor to wear a Greek-style beard. Hadrian was nicknamed Graecula ("The Little Greek") for his love of Greek philosophy, literature, and the handsome teenager Antinous.

Hadrian personally traveled to Athens, where he financed major construction projects. If you walk through Athens, you can still see remains of Hadrian's Arch, the Library of Hadrian, the Temple of Olympian Zeus, and an entire planned neighborhood called Hadrianopolis. Athens' main street through the Plaka is called Adrianou—"Hadrian's" street.

• *It was under Roman rule that the Agora got one of its best-known structures. Continue on, heading straight down the lane (to the left of Hadrian), and you'll pass three giants on four pedestals, which once guarded the...*

AGORA

❿ Odeon of Agrippa

The Odeon of Agrippa was an ancient theater and concert venue. It was once fronted by a line of six colossal statues, which func-

tioned as columns. Of these, only three survive, along with an empty pedestal. The head of a fourth statue is preserved in the Stoa of Attalos—we saw that earlier. Of the statues that remain here, two are meant to be Tritons, with fish tails, while the other monster has the tail of a snake.

The *odeon* was the centerpiece of the Agora during the Roman era. A plaque explains the history of this building: If you recall, during the golden age, the center of the Agora was nothing but open space. But when the Romans conquered, they started filling it in with monumental buildings. The *odeon* was first built under Caesar Augustus (15 BC). It was a popular place, both for the theater-loving Greeks and their Greek-culture-loving Roman masters.

The theater stood two stories tall and was built into the natural slope of the hill. Originally, the main entrance was on the opposite side, near the Middle Stoa (which we saw earlier). Patrons would enter through monumental columns with Corinthian capitals. As they entered from that end, they were at the top row, looking down at the stage, ringed with 20 rows of seats. The place could seat a thousand spectators. Overhead, the glorious roof spanned 82 feet, with no internal support columns. In its heyday, Athenians might have enjoyed lute concerts, poetry readings, and plays by Aristophanes, Euripides, and Sophocles. The less-sophisticated Romans probably flocked here for more lowbrow entertainment.

The giant statues came later. Around 150 AD, the theater's roof collapsed. By now, the center of Athens was moving away from the Agora, and there were already larger theaters elsewhere. So the *odeon* was rebuilt as a smaller lecture hall of only 500 seats. The entrance was moved to this end, with the six colossal statues standing guard.

• *Continue to the main road, where you'll see we've made a loop. Turn right and head toward the Acropolis, walking once again on the Panathenaic Way. This street was on the...*

⓫ Panathenaic Parade Route

Even as the importance of the Agora declined in later years, the Panathenaic Way remained Athens' traditional main street. From

earliest memory, Greeks had trod this path whenever they entered Athens on their way to the holy Acropolis to worship the gods. And whenever Athenians had big events, this was naturally the parade route.

Every year in the middle of summer, the city hosted the Panathenaic Festival (a grander version, the Great Panathenaic Festival, happened every four years). This celebrated the birthday of the goddess Athena and, therefore, of the city itself. The crowning event was when the Athenians marched up to the Acropolis to give honor to the statue of Athena atop the hill.

The parade started at the city's main gate (located near today's Keramikos Metro stop). Thousands participated—old and young, men and women, soldiers and poets. They banged on tambourines and danced in the streets. Some rode on horseback, others walked. The Panathenaic Way was lined with bleachers full of spectators. At the heart of the parade was a float on wheels, carrying the ceremonial wool robe specially woven as a gift for Athena. The parade wound its way through the Agora and up the Acropolis, where the new dress was presented to Athena.

For nearly 800 years, glorious events like this graced the Agora. But Athens' glory days were coming to an end.

• *Continue up the Panathenaic Way, past the Stoa of Attalos. Along the left-hand side of the Panathenaic Way are several crude walls and column fragments.*

⓬ Post-Herulian Wall

This wall marks the beginning of the end of Classical Athens.

In AD 267, the Herulians (a Germanic people) sailed down from the Black Sea and utterly devastated Athens. The crumbling Roman Empire was help-

less to protect its provinces. The Herulians burned most of the Agora's buildings to the ground, including the Odeon of Agrippa, leaving the place in ashes.

As soon as the Herulians left, the surviving Athenians began hastily throwing up this wall to keep future invaders at bay. They used anything they could find: rocks, broken columns, statues, frieze fragments, you name it—all thrown together without mortar. They cobbled together a wall 30 feet high and 10 feet thick. Archaeologists recognize pieces scavenged from destroyed buildings, such as the Stoa of Attalos and the Odeon of Agrippa.

Despite this wall, the Agora never really recovered. A few major buildings were rebuilt, notably a university to preserve the knowledge of Socrates, Plato, Aristotle, and company. But the last great Roman Emperor, Justinian, closed that pagan school in AD 529.

Then came more invasions, mainly the Slavs in 580 AD. Athens dwindled, and its few residents settled in other parts of the city. By 700, the Agora had become a virtual ghost town, now located outside the city walls, exposed to bandits and invaders. It was cannibalized by the Athenians themselves as a quarry for precut stones—it's no wonder so little survives today.

• *After the invaders came...the Christians. On the right is the...*

⓭ Church of the Holy Apostles

This charming little church with the lantern-like dome marks the Agora's revival. It was built around the year 1000, while Athens was under the protection of the Byzantine Empire, ruled from Constantinople. Athens slowly recovered from centuries of invasions and neglect. Like many Christian churches of the period, this one was built atop the ruins of a pagan religious site. In ancient times, this had been a nymphaeum, or temple atop a sacred spring. The new church commemorated St. Paul, who likely converted pagans to Christianity here in the Agora.

This early church was the prototype for later Athenian churches. It has a central dome, with four equal arms radiating out, forming a Greek cross. The windows have the tall horseshoe-shaped arches typical of the Byzantine style. The church was built of large, rectangular blocks of ashlar stone.

Circle around to the entrance (with its jutting entrance hall that unfortunately spoils the original four equal arms). If it's open, pop in; notice that the windows are in flower and diamond shapes. The church contains some interesting 18th-century frescoes in the Byzantine style and an icon on the altar. The marble altar screen has some pieces missing, leaving wide-open spaces—these frames once held icons. Now stand in the center of the church and look up. At the top of the dome is Christ Pantocrator ("All Powerful"). Images like this must have given Athenians a sense of security in troubled times, knowing their god was overseeing everything.

• *End your tour by looking back over the Agora and modern Athens.*

Legacy of the Agora

When Athens came under the control of the Ottomans in the 15th century, the Agora experienced something of a revival. Under the Muslims, Christian churches like the Holy Apostles were tolerated...but taxed. (The decorative pattern of bricks ringing the eaves, shaped like Arabic letters, were added under an Ottoman-era renovation.)

By the 18th century, the Agora had become a flourishing residential district of houses and churches. In the early 20th century, outdoor movies were shown in the Agora.

Then in the 1930s, Greece got serious about preserving its classical heritage. They forced everyone out and demolished everything, except the historic Church of the Holy Apostles, and excavations began.

As the ancient Agora has become a museum, its former city-center functions have moved elsewhere in Athens. The government center is now at Syntagma Square. The marketplace is Athens'

Central Market. Nightlife has shifted to the Plaka, Psyrri, and elsewhere. Monastiraki Square has become one of the new urban hubs. And what's replaced the Panathenaic Way as the city's main arterial? I guess that would be the Metro system.

Looking out from this vantage point, realize that the city of Athens has been continuously inhabited for nearly 3,000 years. It was this city that set the tone for all Western civilization to follow. And the cradle of it all was this small patch of land where the people of Athens gathered—the Agora.

ACROPOLIS TOUR

Ακρόπολη

Even in this age of superlatives, it's hard to overstate the historic and artistic importance of the Acropolis. Crowned by the mighty Parthenon, the Acropolis ("high city") rises above the sprawl of modern Athens, a lasting testament to ancient Athens' glorious golden age in the fifth century BC.

On this tour we'll hike up through the Propylaea gate, ogle the famous Caryatid statues at the Erechtheion, and admire the perfect proportions of the Parthenon. Climbing Acropolis Hill and rambling its ruins, you'll feel like you've journeyed back in time to the birthplace of Western civilization. And it all comes with breathtaking, as-far-as-the-eye-can-see views over the rooftops of Athens—one of Europe's most sprawling cities.

Orientation

Cost: €20 for Acropolis-only ticket; €30 for Acropolis combo-ticket, which covers Athens' other major ancient sites (see page 47). In the off-season (Nov-March), it's €10 for the Acropolis-only ticket and free the first Sun of each month. By the time you visit, timed-entry tickets may be required (even for those with a combo-ticket); see below.

Hours: Daily 8:00-20:00 (last entry likely earlier), Sept until 19:00, Oct until 18:00, Nov-March until 17:00. Be aware that hours are subject to change; check locally before planning your day.

Information: +30 210 321 4172, for general info search "Acropolis" at http://odysseus.culture.gr, for online tickets go to HHTicket.gr.

Advance Tickets: By the time you visit, a timed-entry ticket may be required. Check the ticket website above as soon as you know which day you plan to visit. Time slots are available at the top of each hour. Plan to arrive 30 minutes before your reserved time.

The place is miserably packed with tour groups from 10:00 to about 12:30 (and fewer time slots are available). On some days, as many as 6,000 cruise passengers converge on the Acropolis in a single morning. Even buying a timed-entry ticket doesn't ensure a speedy entry: The worst lines are caused by the bottleneck of people trying to squeeze into the site through the Propylaea gate. Try to book a ticket for the cool morning hours, right when it opens, or late in the day—as the sun goes down, the white Parthenon stone gleams a creamy golden brown, and it's suddenly peaceful.

Strategies for Your Visit: The Acropolis has two entrances; both work well, but you'll see different things on the way in, depending on which one you use.

The **west entrance** (where this tour begins) is near Mars Hill (to the right as you face the Acropolis from the Plaka). To get there from the Plaka, just fix your eyes on the Acropolis, start walking uphill veering right, and find the roads that funnel you there. To reach the west entrance from south of the Acropolis, head up the path that splits off from Dionysiou Areopagitou street.

The **south entrance,** at the base of the Acropolis and next to the Acropolis Museum, can be less crowded (near Metro: Akropoli). From this entrance, you'll climb a steep-but-shady tree-lined path and pick up our tour at the first stop. You can see the Theater of Dionysus (described near the end of this chapter) on the way up, and Mars Hill (listed in the Sights in Athens chapter) at the end of the visit.

If you want to visit the Acropolis Museum afterward, consider this plan: Start at the west entrance, climb Mars Hill, then tour the Acropolis. On your way out, follow the path to the south entrance, stopping at the Theater of Dionysus. The Acropolis Museum entrance is across the street from the south entrance gate.

Note that there's no way to reach the Acropolis without a lot of climbing (though wheelchair users can take an elevator—see later). Figure a 10- to 20-minute hike from the base of the Acropolis up to the hilltop archaeological site.

Visitor Information: Supplement the tour in this chapter with the free information brochure (ask for it on-site) and info plaques posted throughout.

Tours: For a live **guide,** consider making advance arrangements with one of my recommended local guides (see page 44). You

ACROPOLIS

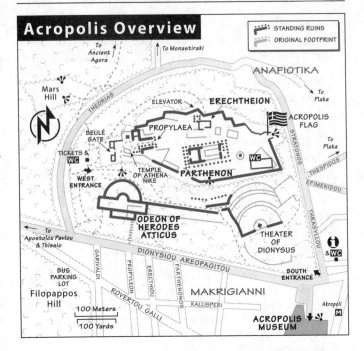

ACROPOLIS

can hire your own tour guide at the entrance, but I wouldn't—the guides here tend to be rude and overpriced.

🎧 Download my free Acropolis **audio tour.** This sight is particularly suited to an audio tour, as it allows your eyes to enjoy the wonders of the Acropolis while your ears learn its story.

Length of This Tour: Allow two hours. Visitors with more time can precede this tour with the Ancient Agora Tour (see the previous chapter).

Baggage Check: Backpacks are allowed; baby strollers are not. There's a checkroom just below the west ticket booth near Mars Hill.

Services: There are WCs up to the right from the west ticket booths, and more WCs and drinking fountains atop the Acropolis in the former museum building (behind the Parthenon). Picnicking is not allowed on the premises.

Also near the west ticket booths are a drinking fountain and machines selling cheap bottles of cold water.

Flanking the south entrance are cafés, shops, and newsstands selling food, water, and souvenirs; the Athens TI is also nearby, with good information and free WCs.

Wheelchair Accessibility: People with wheelchairs can take the elevator that ascends the Acropolis (from the west ticket booth, go around the left side of the hilltop).

Plan Ahead: Wear sensible shoes—Acropolis paths are steep and uneven. In summer, it gets very hot on top, so take a hat, sunscreen, sunglasses, and a bottle of water.

Starring: The Parthenon and other monuments from the golden age, plus great views of Athens and beyond.

BACKGROUND

The Acropolis has been the heart of Athens since the beginning of recorded time. This limestone plateau, faced with sheer, 100-foot cliffs and fed by permanent springs, was a natural fortress. The Mycenaeans (c. 1400 BC) ruled the area from their palace on this hilltop, and Athena—the patron goddess of the city—was worshipped here from around 800 BC on.

But everything changed in 480 BC when Persia invaded Greece for the second time. As the Persians approached, the Athenians evacuated the city, abandoning it to be looted and vandalized. All the temples atop the Acropolis were burned to the ground. The Athenians fought back at sea, winning an improbable naval victory at the Battle of Salamis. The Persians were driven out of Greece, and Athens found itself suddenly victorious. Cash poured into Athens from the other Greek city-states, which were eager to be allied with the winning side.

By 450 BC, Athens was at the peak of its power and the treasury was flush with money...but in the city center, the Acropolis still lay empty, a vast blank canvas. Athens' leader at the time, Pericles, was ambitious and farsighted. He funneled Athens' newfound wealth into a massive rebuilding program. Led by the visionary architect/sculptor Pheidias (490-430 BC), the Athenians transformed the Acropolis into a complex of supersized, ornate temples worthy of the city's protector, Athena.

The four major monuments—the Parthenon, Erechtheion,

Propylaea, and Temple of Athena Nike—were built as a coherent ensemble (c. 450-400 BC). Unlike most ancient sites, which have layer upon layer of ruins from different periods, the Acropolis we see today was started and finished within two generations—a snapshot of the golden age set in stone.

The Tour Begins

• *Our route starts at the **west entrance**, near Mars Hill. (If you enter via the south entrance, just follow the path up, where you'll join this tour at the first stop—you can see Mars Hill after the visit.)*

Before entering, check out the huge, craggy boulder of **Mars Hill** (a.k.a. Areopagus), just downhill (toward the Agora) from the

ticket booth. Consider climbing this rock for great views of the Acropolis' ancient entry gate, the Propylaea, and the Ancient Agora. Mars Hill's bare, polished rock is extremely slippery—a metal staircase to the left helps somewhat. (For more on Mars Hill and its role in Christian history, see page 52.)

Before you show your ticket and enter the Acropolis site, make sure you have everything you'll need for your visit. Once inside, there are no services except WCs and water fountains.

• *Enter the site and start climbing the paths that wind up the hill, following signs on this one-way tourist route (bearing to the right). Before you reach the summit, peel off to the right for a...*

❶ View of the Odeon of Herodes Atticus

This large, 5,000-seat amphitheater built during the Roman era is still used today for performances. From this perch you get a good

look at the stage setup. The three-quarter-circle floor was the stage. There, musicians and actors performed in the Greek style. Rising behind it are the overgrown remnants of a raised stage and a stage wall for the backdrop (which were not used in traditional Greek theater, but were common for Roman-style spectacles). Originally, the theater had a wood-and-tile roof as well.

The *odeon* was built in 161 AD by Herodes Atticus, a wealthy landowner, in memory of his wife. Herodes was a Greek with Roman citizenship. He was a legendary orator and a friend of Emperor Hadrian. This amphitheater is the most famous of the many impressive buildings Herodes financed around the country. Greeks know it's technically an *odeon*, namely a theater used mainly for songs ("odes") rather than drama.

In the 1950s, the ruined theater was reconstructed. Now on many summer nights it hosts music, dance, and theatrical performances under the stars.

• *Back on the path, bear left and continue uphill to the grand entrance gate of the Acropolis: the Propylaea. Stand at the foot of the (very) steep marble staircase, facing up toward the big Doric columns.*

As you face the Propylaea, to your left is a tall, grayish stone pedestal with nothing on it: the Monument of Agrippa. On your right, atop the wall, is the Temple of Athena Nike. Behind you stands a doorway in a wall, known as the Beulé Gate.

❷ Propylaea

The entrance to the Acropolis couldn't be through just any old gate; it had to be the grandest gate ever built. Ancient visitors would

stand here, catching their breath before the final push to the summit, and admire these gleaming columns and steep steps that almost fill your field of vision. Imagine the psychological impact this awe-inspiring, colonnaded entryway to the sacred rock must have had on ancient Athenians.

The Propylaea (pro-PEE-leh-ah) is U-shaped, with a large central hallway (the six Doric columns), flanked by side wings that reach out to embrace the visitor. The central building looked like a mini Parthenon, with Doric columns topped by a triangular pediment. Originally, the Propylaea was painted bright colors.

The left wing of the Propylaea was the Pinakotheke, or "painting gallery." In ancient times this space contained artwork and housed visiting dignitaries and VIPs.

The buildings of the Acropolis were all constructed within about a 50-year span, and they were intended to complement one another. The Propylaea was built in five short years (437-432 BC, by Mnesicles). Both buildings are Doric (with Ionic touches) and are aligned east-west, with columns of similar width-to-height ratios. In other words, the Propylaea welcomed the visitor with an

The Acropolis

1. View of Odeon of Herodes Atticus
2. Propylaea (Entrance Gate)
3. Temple of Athena Nike
4. Monument of Agrippa
5. Beulé Gate
6. Passing Through the Propylaea
7. Surveying the Acropolis
8. Statue of Athena Promachos
9. View of the Parthenon
10. West End Sculpture
11. North Side
12. East End & Entrance
13. Erechtheion: Porch of the Caryatids
14. Erechtheion: East End
15. Viewpoint with Greek Flag
16. More Views of Athens

STANDING RUINS
ORIGINAL FOOTPRINT

appropriately grand first taste of the Acropolis they were about to enter.

• *Before ascending, notice the monuments flanking the entryway. To the right of the Propylaea, look up high atop the block wall to find the...*

❸ Temple of Athena Nike

This little temple—nearly square, 11 feet tall, with four columns at both ends—had delightful proportions. Where the Parthenon and

Propylaea are sturdy Doric, this temple pioneered the Ionic style in Athens, with elegant scroll-topped columns. The Temple of Athena Nike (NEEK-ee) was started a few years after the Propylaea was finished (c. 427-421/415 BC). It was designed by Callicrates, one of the architects of the Parthenon.

The Acropolis was mainly dedicated to the goddess Athena, patron of the city. At this temple, she was worshiped for bring-

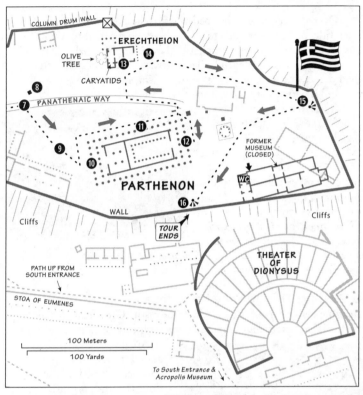

ing the Athenians victory ("Nike"). A statue of Athena inside the temple celebrated the turning-point victory over the Persians at the Battle of Plataea in 479 BC. It was also meant to help ensure future victory over the Spartans in the ongoing Peloponnesian War. The statue was never given wings, because Athenians wanted Athena to stay and protect their city—hence the place became known as the Temple of Wingless Athena.

• *To the left (as you face the Propylaea) is a gray-stone pedestal, the...*

❹ Monument of Agrippa

The pedestal—even without anything on it—reaches as high as the Temple of Athena Nike. It's 25 feet tall, made of gray marble with yellow veins. Several statues have graced this prime location. Originally, it held a bronze statue of a four-horse chariot. The driver was the race champion at the Olympic Games held in 178 BC.

Over the centuries, this pedestal has supported many egos. Each ruler of Athens wanted to put his mark on the mighty Acropolis. When Rome occupied the city, Marc Antony placed a statue of himself and his girlfriend Cleopatra atop the pedestal. After their defeat, the Roman general Agrippa (son-in-law of Augustus) replaced it with a statue of himself (in 27 BC).

It was the Romans who expanded the Propylaea by building the structure at the base of the stairs—the ❺ **Beulé Gate.** This ceremonial doorway became the official entrance to the Acropolis, making the Propylaea entry even grander.

• *Climb the steps (or today's switchback ramps for visitors). Partway up, try to pull off to one side—out of the steady tourist torrent—to take a closer look inside the Propylaea.*

❻ Passing Through the Propylaea

Imagine being part of the grand parade of the Great Panathenaic Festival, held every four years. The procession started a mile away,

at Athens' city gate, then passed through the Agora, up past Mars Hill, and through the Propylaea. Men on horseback, musicians, dignitaries, and maidens carrying gifts for the gods all ascended these stairs. In those days, there was a ramp in the middle of the staircase, which narrowed as they ascended, funneling them into the central passageway. There were five doorways into the Propylaea, one between each of the six columns.

The Propylaea passageway had a roof. The marble-tile ceiling, now partially restored, was painted sky blue and studded with stars. Floral designs decorated other parts of the building. The interior columns are Ionic, a bit thinner than the Doric columns of the exterior. You'll pass by some big column drums with square holes in the center, where iron pins once held the drums in place. Greek columns were not usually made from a single piece

ACROPOLIS

of stone, but from sections—"column drums"—stacked on top of one another.

• *The Propylaea and its monuments are certainly impressive. But this is just the opening act. Pass through the Propylaea. As you emerge out the other end, you're on top of the Acropolis. There it is—the Parthenon! Just like in the books (except for the scaffolding). Pause and take it all in.*

❼ Surveying the Acropolis

The "Acropolis rock" is a mostly flat limestone ridge covering seven acres, scattered with ruins. There's the Parthenon ahead to the right. To the left of that, with the six lady-columns (Caryatids), is the Erechtheion. The Panathenaic Way ran between them. The processional street and the buildings were aligned east-west, like the hill.

Ancient visitors standing here would have come face-to-face with an imposing statue of Athena, 30 feet tall, carrying a shield and a spear. This ❽ **statue of Athena Promachos** once stood between the Propylaea and the Erechtheion. Today there's just a field of rubble, with the statue's former location marked by three stones forming a low wall.

The Athena Promachos was one of three well-known statues of Athena on the Acropolis. As the patron goddess of the city, Athena was worshipped for her wisdom, her purity, and her strength. Here she appeared in "strength" mode, as a "Frontline Soldier" *(promachos)*, armed and ready for battle. The bronze statue was cast by Pheidias, the man in charge of the overall design of the Acropolis. It was so tall that the shining tip of Athena's spear was visible from ships at sea, 30 miles away. The statue was taken to Constantinople in ancient times and was most likely destroyed in the Middle Ages.

• *Move a little closer for the classic view of the world's most famous temple. If you're tired, I've installed a handy white marble bench for you to take a load off while you take in the...*

❾ View of the Parthenon

The Parthenon is the hill's showstopper—the finest temple in the ancient world, standing on the highest point of the Acropolis, 490 feet above sea level. The Parthenon is now largely in ruins, partly from the ravages of time, but mostly from a freak accident in 1687 (see the "After the Golden Age" sidebar, later).

Imagine how awesome the Parthenon must have looked when

it was completed nearly 2,500 years ago. It's the largest Doric temple in Greece—228 feet long and 101 feet wide. Its footprint covers more than 23,000 square feet.

At each end were eight fluted **Doric columns.** Along each side were 17 columns, for a total of 46. In addition, there were 23 inner columns in the Doric style, plus 4 in the Ionic style.

The outer columns are 34 feet high and 6 feet in diameter. In its heyday, the temple was decorated with statues and carved reliefs, all painted in vivid colors. It's considered Greece's greatest Doric temple (though not its purest textbook example because it incorporates Ionic columns and sculpture).

The Parthenon served the cult of Athena the Virgin, with a statue of the goddess inside. It also served as the Fort Knox-like treasury of Athens. The west end is the classic view that greets visitors—but the building's main entrance was at the other end.

This awe-inspiring temple was completed in less than a decade—from around 450 to 440 BC. The sculptural decoration took a few more years. The project's overall "look" was supervised by the master sculptor-architect Pheidias. The construction was handled by well-known architects Ictinus and Callicrates. The two main sculptors were Agoracritos and Alcamenes.

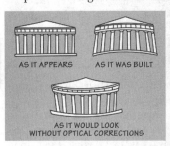

AS IT APPEARS   AS IT WAS BUILT

AS IT WOULD LOOK
WITHOUT OPTICAL CORRECTIONS

It's big, sure. But what makes the Parthenon truly exceptional is that the architects used a whole bagful of **optical illusions** to give the building an ever-so-subtle feeling of balance, strength, and harmonious beauty.

For example, look at the temple's steps. Architects know that a long, flat baseline on a building looks to the human eye like it's sagging, and that parallel columns appear to bend away from each other. To create a building that looked harmonious, the Parthenon's ancient architects compensated. The base of the Parthenon actually arches several inches upward in the middle to counteract the "sagging" illusion.

Now check out the columns. They tilt ever so slightly inward (one of the reasons why the Parthenon has withstood earthquakes so well). If you extended the columns upward several miles, they'd eventually touch. Also, the corner columns are thicker than the rest

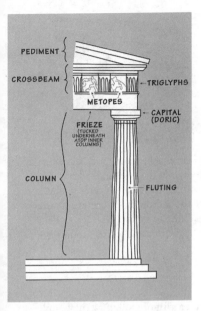

to make them appear the same size. And all of the columns bulge imperceptibly halfway up, giving the subconscious impression of stout, barrel-chested men bearing the weight of the roof. For a building that seems at first to be all about right angles, the Parthenon is amazingly short on straight lines. (For more on Greek columns, see page 503.)

All these clever refinements form a powerful subconscious impression on the viewer that brings an otherwise-boring architectural box to life. It's amazing to think that all this was planned and implemented in stone so long ago. (For more on Greek temples, see page 499.)

⑩ West End Sculpture

The statues and carved reliefs that once decorated the Parthenon are now mostly eroded or missing. The cream of the crop, sometimes called the "Elgin Marbles," are in the British Museum in London. (For details, see the "After the Golden Age" sidebar, later.) A few pieces are in Athens' Acropolis Museum.

But try to imagine this grand temple in its prime. Originally, the Parthenon's sculptures were all painted in bright colors, and the building looked much livelier than today's stately gray ruin.

Look up at the crossbeam atop the eight columns, decorated with panels of relief carvings called **metopes.** These depict Athenians battling that legendary race of female warriors, the Amazons. Originally there were 92 Doric-style metopes in high relief, mostly designed by Pheidias himself.

The crossbeams once supported a triangular pediment (now gone). This area was once filled in with statues, showing Athena with her olive tree competing with Poseidon and his trident to be Athens' patron god. Today just one statue remains (and it's a reconstruction).

Move closer and look between the eight columns. Inside, there's another row of eight columns, supporting a covered entrance porch. Look up above the inner columns. Decorating those crossbeams are more relief carvings—the "frieze." Originally, a 525-foot-long **frieze** of panels circled the entire building. It showed the Pana-

ACROPOLIS

thenaic parade—women, men on horseback, musicians, sacrificial animals being led to the slaughter—while the gods looked on.

If you're having trouble envisioning all this, you can see many of these sculptures in the flesh at the Acropolis Museum, at the base of the hill. The museum was built to house Greece's collection...and to try to entice the rest back from museums around the world.

• *Continue along the long left (north) side of the Parthenon.*

⓫ North Side

This view of the Parthenon gives you a glimpse into how the temple was constructed.

Look between the columns—you can see remnants of the interior walls. These were built with thousands of rectangular blocks. The temple interior consisted of an entry hall and a *cella*. The *cella* was the inner sanctum, where Athena was worshipped. The roof was made of wooden beams—now long gone. The roof tiles were made of ultra-white, translucent marble from the island of Paros, so the interior actually glowed.

Now concentrate on the columns that surround the Parthenon. These formed an open-air porch around the inner sanctum. The columns are in the Doric style—stout, lightly fluted, with no base. The capitals on top of the columns are simple, consisting of a plate topped with a square slab. The capitals alone weigh 12 tons.

The Parthenon's builders used only the very finest materials. The white Pentelic marble came from Mount Pentelikon, 10 miles away. Unlike the grand structures of the Egyptians (pyramids) and the Romans (Colosseum), the Parthenon was built not by enslaved people but by free men who drew a salary (though it's possible that slaves worked at the quarries).

The Parthenon was constructed from 100,000 tons of marble. Imagine the engineering problems of quarrying and transporting all that stone. Most likely the **column drums** (5-10 tons each) were cut at the quarry and rolled here. To hoist the drums in place, the builders used four-poster cranes (and Greek mathematics), centering the drums with a cedar peg in the middle. The drums were held together by metal pins that were coated in lead to prevent corrosion, then fitted into a square hole cut in the center of the drum.

Remember that the Parthenon is intentionally off-kilter in places for aesthetic effect. Each piece was sized and cut for a specific location. The Parthenon's stones are so well-crafted that they fit together within a fraction of an inch. The total cost to build the Parthenon (in today's money) has been estimated at more than a billion dollars.

• *If you see cranes and scaffolding here, it's part of a heroic effort to shore up the structure against the ravages of pollution (see the sidebar). Continue on to the...*

⓬ East End and Entrance

This end was the original entrance to the temple. Over the doorway, the triangular pediment depicted the central event in Athenian history—the **birth of Athena,** their patron goddess. Today, the pediment barely survives, and the original statues of the gods are partly in the British Museum. Originally, the gods were gathered at a banquet (see a copy of the reclining Dionysus

at the far left—looking so drunk he's afraid to come down). Zeus got a headache and asked Hephaistos to relieve it. As the other gods looked on in astonishment, Hephaistos split Zeus' head open, and—at the peak of the pediment—out rose Athena. The now-missing statues were surprisingly realistic and three-dimensional, with perfect anatomy and bulging muscles showing through transparent robes.

Imagine this spot during the age of Pericles and Socrates, on the big day—the **Panathenaic Festival:**

The Parthenon is gleaming white, adorned with painted statues. It sits on a grassy field. The parade gathers here at the entrance. Musicians play flutes, girls dance, and riders rein in their restless steeds. On open-air altars, the priests make an offering to Athena—100 oxen, the ultimate sacrificial gift to the gods.

A select few are allowed to go inside. They proceed up the steps, through the majestic columns, and into the *cella.* It's cavernous—100 feet long, 60 feet wide, and four stories tall, with a pool in the middle. At the far end of the room towers an enormous 40-foot tall statue of **Athena Parthenos** (Athena the Virgin), wearing a soldier's helmet, with a shield by her side. Athena's left hand

ACROPOLIS

Acropolis Now: The Renovation Project

The scaffolding, cranes, and modern construction materials you see here are part of an ongoing renovation project. The challenge is to save what's left of the Parthenon from the modern menaces of acid rain and pollution, which have already caused irreversible damage. Funded by Greece and the EU, the project began in 1976, which means that they've been

at it more than four times as long as it took to build the Parthenon in the first place.

The project first involves cataloging every single stone of the Parthenon—blocks, drums, capitals, bits of rock, and pieces lying on the ground or in museums around the world. Next, archaeologists hope to put it back together, like a giant 70,000-piece jigsaw puzzle. Along the way, they're fixing previous restorations that were either inaccurate or problematic. For example, earlier restorers used uncoated iron and steel rods to hold things together. As weather fluctuations caused the metal to expand, the stone was damaged. This time around, restorers are using titanium rods.

Whenever possible, the restorers use original materials. But you'll also see big blocks of new marble lying on the ground—freshly cut from the same Pentelic quarries that supplied the original stone. The new marble is being used to re-

place damaged and missing pieces. Many of the columns have light-colored "patches" where the restorers have installed the new stone, cut to fit exactly. Though it looks much whiter, in time the newly cut marble will age to match the rest of the Parthenon.

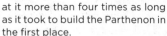

When complete, the renovated Parthenon won't look like a fully restored building—just a shored-up version of the ruin we see today. If you want to see what the Parthenon temple looked like in its heyday, there's a full-scale replica open to visitors...in Nashville, Tennessee.

holds a spear. Her other hand has a small statue of Nike—she literally holds Victory in the palm of her hand.

The statue was the work of the master Pheidias himself (c. 440 BC). It was made of wood, then plated with ivory for skin and a ton of gold for her garments. No one knows exactly when or how the statue vanished.

During the Panathenaic parade, the citizens of Athens would approach the statue of Athena and present the goddess with a newly woven robe. In return, Athena would ensure the continuing success of the great city of Athens.

• *Our next stop is the Erechtheion, the temple across the street. (But perhaps most important right now is the modern brown-brick building nearby, with WCs and a drinking fountain.)*

Approach the Erechtheion. Start by enjoying the porch supported by six statues.

⓮ Erechtheion: Porch of the Caryatids

Though overshadowed by the more impressive Parthenon, the Erechtheion was perhaps more prestigious. It stood on one of the

oldest sites on the hill, where the Mycenaeans had built their palace centuries before. (Those huge ruined stones scattered in front of the Erechtheion are all that's left of the Mycenaean palace.)

The temple's most famous feature is the **Porch of the Caryatids.** An inspired piece of architecture, this balcony has six beautiful maidens functioning as columns that support the roof. Each of the **lady-columns** has a base beneath her feet, pleated robes as the fluting, a fruit-basket hat as the capital, and—in the back—locks of hair as buttresses. Both feminine and functional, they pose gracefully, exposing a hint of leg. The Caryatids were modeled on and named after the women of Karyai, near Sparta, famous for their upright posture and noble character. (These are faithful copies of the originals. Five of the originals are on display in the Acropolis Museum.)

Near the porch—below and to the left—notice the **olive tree.** Greece has 140 million of these trees. Though this particular tree is not ancient, there's been an olive tree on this spot for thousands of years. It marks the sacred place where, according to legend, Athena first planted one. Olive trees have been called "the gift of Athena to Athens."

• *Let's view the Erechtheion from a different angle. Walk to the right, to*

ACROPOLIS

the east end of the structure. Find a spot where you can look through the six columns and get a sense of what the temple was like inside.

⓮ Erechtheion: East End

This unique, two-story temple fits nicely into the slope of the hill. The east end (with the six Ionic columns) was the upper-level entrance. The lower entrance was on the north side (to your right, 10 feet lower), where you can see six more Ionic columns. By the way, it's those columns that are the "face of the Acropolis" that Athenians see from the Plaka below.

The Erechtheion was constructed around 410 BC. The architect, Mnesicles, was the same man who did the Propylaea. Whereas the Propylaea and the Parthenon are both sturdy Doric style, the Erechtheion is elegant Ionic. The columns are thinner, more deeply fluted, and topped with a scroll-like capital. In its day, the Erechtheion was a stunning building of white Pentelic marble, with black trim and painted columns.

Now look inside the temple. You can make out that the inner worship hall, the *cella,* is divided in two by walls (more on that in a minute). The Erechtheion also once held a life-size statue of Athena made of olive wood depicting her as **Athena Polias,** Protector of the City. Dating from about 900 BC, this statue was much older and more venerable than either of Pheidias' colossal statues. It supposedly dropped from the sky as a gift

from Athena herself. It was so revered that, when the Persians invaded, Pericles took the statue for safekeeping as the Athenians evacuated their city.

The Erechtheion is supposedly the spot where Athena and Poseidon fought it out for naming rights to the city. Poseidon threw his trident, which opened a gash in the earth to bring forth the gift of water. It left a diagonal crack still visible in the pavement of the lower, north entrance. (Cynics say it was lightning.) Athena won the contest by stabbing a rock with her spear. This sprouted the blessed olive tree that stood near the Porch of the Caryatids. The twin *cella*s of the Erechtheion allowed the worship of both gods—

Athena and Poseidon. They're side by side to show that they were still friends.

• *Look to the right (beyond the Plaka-facing porch). The modern **elevator** carries people with limited mobility up to the Acropolis. The north wall of the Acropolis has a retaining wall built from **column drums** from remains of a half-finished temple destroyed when Persia invaded in 480 BC. The Athenians rebuilt as fast as they could with the scattered material to fortify the city against Sparta.*

Turn 180 degrees and walk to the far end of the Acropolis. There you'll find an observation platform with a giant Greek flag.

⓯ Viewpoint with Greek Flag

The Greek flag's blue-and-white stripes symbolize the nine syllables of the Greek phrase for "Freedom or Death." That phrase took

on new meaning when the Nazis entered Athens in April 1941. According to an oft-repeated (but unverified) story, the Nazis confronted a Greek soldier who was guarding this flag and ordered him to remove it. He calmly took it down, wrapped himself in it—and jumped to his death. A month later, two heroic teenagers, Manolis Glezos and Apostolos Santas, scaled the wall, took down the Nazi flag, and raised the Greek flag. This was one of the first well-known acts of resistance against the Nazis, and the boys' bravery is honored by a plaque near the base of the steps. To this day, Greeks can see this flag from just about anywhere in Athens and think of their hard-won independence.

From this observation deck, you have a great **view of Athens.** The Ancient Agora spreads below the Acropolis, and the sprawl of modern Athens whitewashes the surrounding hills. In 1830, the population of Athens' core was about 5,000. By 1900, it was 600,000, and during the 1920s, with the influx of Greeks from Turkey, the population surged to 1.5 million. The city's expansion could barely keep up with its exploding population. With the boom times in the 1950s and 1980s, the city grew to nearly four million. Pan around. From this perch you're looking at the homes of one out of every three Greeks.

Looking down on the **Plaka,** find (looking left to right) the Ancient Agora, with its Temple of Hephaistos. Next comes the Roman Forum (the four columns) with its round, white, domed Temple of the Winds monument. The **Anafiotika** neighborhood

ACROPOLIS

After the Golden Age: The Acropolis Through History

Classical: The Parthenon and the rest of the Acropolis buildings survived through classical times largely intact, despite Herulian looting (AD 267). As the Roman Empire declined, precious items were carried off, including the 40-foot Athena statue from the Parthenon.

Christian: The Christian emperor Theodosius II (Theodosius the Great) labored to outlaw pagan worship and to close temples and other religious sites. After nearly a thousand years as Athena's temple, the Parthenon became a Christian church (fifth century AD). It remained Christian for the next thousand years, first as the Byzantine Orthodox Church of Holy Wisdom, then as Mother Mary of Athens (11th century), and at the end as a Roman Catholic cathedral of Notre Dame (dedicated to Mary in 1205 by Frankish Crusaders). Throughout medieval times it was an important stop on the pilgrimage circuit.

The Parthenon's exterior was preserved after its conversion to a church, but pagan sculptures and decorations were removed (or renamed), and the interior was decorated with colorful Christian frescoes. The west end of the building became the main entrance, and the interior was reconfigured with an apse at the east end.

Muslim: In 1456, the Turks arrived and converted the Parthenon into a mosque, adding a minaret. The Propylaea gateway was used as a palace for the Turkish ruler of Athens. The Turks had no respect for the sacred history of the Acropolis—they even tore down stones just to get the lead clamps that held them in place in order to make bullets. (The exasperated Greeks even offered them bullets to stop destroying the temple.) The Turks also used the Parthenon to store gunpowder, unfortunately leading to the

clings to the Acropolis hillside directly below us. About eight blocks beyond that, find the dome of the cathedral.

Farther in the distance, **Lykavittos Hill,** Athens' highest point, is crowned with the Chapel of St. George (and an expensive view restaurant; cable car up the hill). Looking still farther in the distance, you'll see

greatest catastrophe in the Acropolis' long history. It happened in...

1687: A Venetian army laid siege to the Acropolis. The Venetians didn't care about ancient architecture. As far as they were concerned, it was a lucky hit of mortar fire that triggered the massive explosion that ripped the center out of the Parthenon, rattled the Propylaea and the other buildings, and wiped out the Turkish defenders. Pieces of the Parthenon lay scattered on the ground, many of them gathered up as souvenirs by soldiers.

Lord Elgin: In 1801, Lord Elgin, the British ambassador to the Ottomans in Constantinople, got "permission" from the sultan to

gather sculptures from the Parthenon, buy them from locals, and even saw them off the building (Greeks scoff at the idea that "permission" granted by an occupying power should carry any weight). He carted half of them to London, where the marbles (formerly known as the "Elgin Marbles") are displayed in the British Museum to this day, despite repeated requests for their return. Although a few original frieze, metope, and pediment carvings still adorn the Parthenon, most of the sculptures are on display in museums, including the nearby Acropolis Museum.

From Independence to the Present: In the 19th century, newly independent Greece tore down the Parthenon's minaret and the other post-Classical buildings atop the Acropolis, turning it into an archaeological zone. Since then the site has been excavated and has undergone several renovations. Today, the Acropolis strikes wonder in the hearts of visitors, just as it has for centuries.

lighter-colored bits on the mountains behind—these are **Pentelic quarries,** the source of the marble used to build (and now restore) the monuments of the Acropolis.

As you continue panning to the right, you'll spot the beige Neoclassical **Parliament** building, marking Syntagma Square; the **National Garden** is behind and to the right of it. In the garden is the yellow **Zappeion,** an exhibition hall. The green area in the far distance contains the 60,000-seat, marble **Panathenaic Stadium**—an ancient venue (on the site where golden age Athens held its games), which was rehabbed in 1896 to help revive the modern Olympics.

• *Complete your visual tour of Athens at the south edge of the Acropolis. To reach the viewpoint, walk back toward the Parthenon, going past it to the left to the cliff-top wall.*

⑯ More Views of Athens

Look to the left. In the near distance are the huge columns of the **Temple of Olympian Zeus.** Begun in the sixth century BC, it

wasn't finished until the time of the Roman emperor Hadrian, 700 years later. It was the biggest temple in all of Greece, with 104 Corinthian pillars housing a 40-foot seated statue of Zeus, a replica of the famous one created by Pheidias in Olympia. This area was part of Hadrian's "new Athens," a planned community in his day, complete with the triumphal **Arch of Hadrian** near the temple.

The **Theater of Dionysus,** with its illustrious history, lies in ruins at your feet. It's fair to say that this is where our culture's great tradition of theater was born. During Athens' golden age, Sophocles and others watched their plays performed here. Originally just grass with a circular dirt area as the stage, the theater was eventually expanded, and stone seating added, to accommodate 17,000 patrons in about 330 BC, during the time of Alexander the Great. During Roman times, a raised stage was added, and the theater was connected to the Odeon of Herodes Atticus by a long, covered stoa, creating an ensemble of inviting venues. Today, plans are afoot to restore the theater to its former greatness. It's free to visit the theater with your Acropolis ticket (it's accessible only from inside the Acropolis site—see the end of the tour for directions).

Beyond the theater is the wonderful **Acropolis Museum,** a black-and-gray modern glass building with three rectangular floors stacked at irregular angles atop each other. The top floor, which houses replicas and some originals of the Parthenon's art, is angled to match the orientation of that great temple.

Looking right, you see **Filopappos Hill**—the green, tree-dotted hill topped with a marble funerary monument to a popular Roman senator, Philopappos, who died in the early second century. This hill is where the Venetians launched the infamous mortar attack of 1687 that destroyed the Parthenon. Today, a theater here hosts popular folk-dancing performances (described in the Nightlife in Athens chapter).

Farther in the distance, you get a glimpse of the turquoise waters of the **Aegean** (the only island visible is Aegina). While the
Persians were burning the Acropolis to the ground, the Athenians
watched from their ships as they prepared to defeat their foes in
the history-changing Battle of Salamis. In the distance, far to the
right, is the port of Piraeus. Today Piraeus is the main departure
point for boats to the islands, but it's also the ancient port from
which Athenian ships sailed and returned with the wealth that
made this city so great.

• Our tour is finished. Enjoy a few final moments with the Acropolis
before you leave.

The Acropolis exits are back the way you came—through the Propylaea. From here, you can exit either on the west side (go through the Beulé
Gate) or to the south (go back toward the Odeon of Herodes Atticus, turn
left, and walk downhill along the path).

Exit from the west side if you want to visit **Mars Hill** on the way
out. Or passing Mars Hill, you can head to the **Plaka** and **Ancient
Agora** (follow the roads winding downhill) or the **Acropolis Museum**
(turn left on the pedestrian boulevard, walk down to Dionysiou Areopagitou street, and turn left).

To reach the **Theater of Dionysus**, head toward the south entrance.
You'll reach the theater and eventually the south entrance, with the
Acropolis Museum across the street.

ACROPOLIS

ACROPOLIS MUSEUM TOUR

Μουσείο Ακρόπολης

Athens' Acropolis Museum is a custom-built showcase for sculptures from the Acropolis, starring its greatest temple, the Parthenon.

We'll start with broken fragments from the Acropolis' earliest temples, then focus on the great works of the Acropolis' glory years—roughly 500 to 400 BC. These sculptures are surprisingly lively, dramatic, and realistic. We'll see graceful maidens bearing gifts, superheroes battling monsters, and stately robed women who doubled as temple columns. Finally, on the top floor, is the museum's star attraction: an entire floor dedicated to the Parthenon's sculptures, laid out in the exact dimensions of the Parthenon itself.

Be aware that many statues here—though original and very historic—are pretty ruined and less impressive than, say, the Parthenon sculptures ("Elgin Marbles") in London's British Museum. But the Acropolis Museum more than makes up for that with high-quality copies, its Parthenon-replica layout, and nifty modern displays that bring the ruins to life.

The museum is a sort of 21st-century Trojan horse, intended to pressure the British to return the Parthenon sculptures. For years, the Brits claimed that Greece couldn't give those ancient treasures a suitable home. But now Athens can proudly say, "Oh really?"

The museum works equally well either before you visit the Acropolis (to help you visualize the ruins you'll see) or afterward (to see the statues close-up after you've seen where they once stood). There's a convenient entrance/exit that connects the two sights. (And this book's description of the Acropolis might help you as you tour the Acropolis Museum—see the previous chapter.)

With its striking exterior and irreplaceable Acropolis statues, the Acropolis Museum is a bold symbol of today's Athens.

Orientation

Cost: €10, €5 off-season. You can buy tickets on the museum website to avoid the ticket-buying line (but not the security line).

Hours: Mon 9:00-16:00, Tue-Thu and Sat-Sun until 20:00, Fri until 22:00; Nov-March Mon-Thu 9:00-17:00, Fri until 22:00, Sat-Sun until 20:00.

Information: +30 210 900 0900, www.theacropolismuseum.gr.

Getting There: It's the gigantic, can't-miss-it modern building—the main entrance faces the south side of the Acropolis from across the broad Dionysiou Areopagitou pedestrian drag. The museum is next to the Akropoli Metro stop on Makrigianni, a street lined with restaurants.

Visitor Information: Pick up a free map (in Greek) at the information desk when you enter. Museum guards can answer questions, and a 13-minute video plays continuously in the upper atrium (level 3). The bookstore sells *The Short Guide* (well worth €3).

Baggage Check: There's a free bag check at the counter near the turnstiles at the base of the ramp (required for big bags).

Length of This Tour: Allow 1.5 hours.

Services: Wheelchairs and strollers are available. A gift shop is on the ground floor and level 2 has a bookstore.

Eating: Choose from the ground-floor **café** or the **restaurant** on level 2. Since the menu is the same and pricey in both places, you may as well enjoy the smashing Acropolis views from the restaurant upstairs. You can even visit the restaurant without a museum ticket—just request a guest pass at the ticket desk. For a fast and cheap bite, I like the **souvlaki joint** 100 yards away at the Akropoli metro station entry.

Starring: Greek national pride, a helpful overview of the Acropolis' history, marble masterpieces from one of the most influential archaeological sites in human history—and high hopes that more will eventually join the collection.

The Tour Begins

The eye-catching, glassy building—designed by Swiss-born, New York-based architect Bernard Tschumi—gives a postmodern jolt to Athens' concrete cityscape. Its lower level is aligned with ancient foundations beneath it, while the top floor sits askew, mirroring the nearby Parthenon. The glass walls allow visitors to enjoy the artifacts inside while gazing out at the Acropolis itself.

• *Enter on the ground floor (level 0) and buy your ticket.*

LEVEL 0

Browse a few introductory displays (about the Acropolis' evolution from 1200 BC to AD 1500) and look through the glass floor at the sixth-century BC excavation site—two-story houses and even evidence of plumbing. Then stow your coat and bag and go through the turnstiles onto a wide ramp.

❶ The Ramp

Look through the ramp's glass floor at more of the ancient ruins excavated beneath the museum. These were houses and shops of

a once-lively neighborhood here at the base of the Acropolis (the excavation is included with your ticket and is worth a quick look at the end of your visit—look for an access ramp at the museum entrance). As no one actually lived on top of the Acropolis, which was reserved for the temples of the gods, ancient Athe-

nians settled either down here or over by the Agora. The artifacts you see here, found on the hill's slopes, symbolize the transition from the everyday world below to the sacred realm above.

Case #5 (on the left), with ancient vases painted with wedding scenes, makes it clear that the Acropolis was a popular place to get married.

Case #6 (on the left) showcases vases and figurines used as offerings; as Athenians ascended the hill to worship the gods, they brought these objects to bribe the gods to answer their prayers.

They might stop at the **Sanctuary of Dionysus** (also described on the left), which had a theater built into the slope of the Acropolis just uphill from today's museum. Devotees of Dionysus would drink wine while watching performers sing ecstatic songs or recite poems.

The square stone **treasure box** (offering box; just before the stairs, on the right) is where worshippers of Aphrodite would drop in a silver drachma to ensure a good love life.

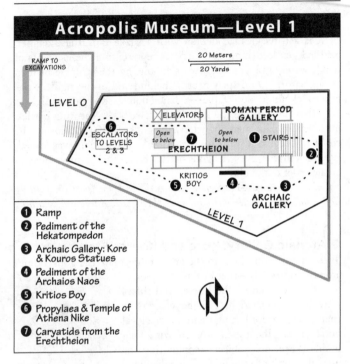

Acropolis Museum—Level 1

20 Meters
20 Yards

RAMP TO
EXCAVATIONS

LEVEL 0

ELEVATORS

ROMAN PERIOD
GALLERY

ESCALATORS
TO LEVELS
2 & 3

Open
to below

Open
to below

STAIRS

ERECHTHEION

KRITIOS
BOY

LEVEL 1

ARCHAIC
GALLERY

❶ Ramp
❷ Pediment of the
Hekatompedon
❸ Archaic Gallery: Kore
& Kouros Statues
❹ Pediment of the
Archaios Naos
❺ Kritios Boy
❻ Propylaea & Temple of
Athena Nike
❼ Caryatids from the
Erechtheion

• *Let's ascend to the sacred realm of the gods. Climb the stairs at the end of the ramp. Straight ahead is a collection of statues in a triangular frame.*

LEVEL 1

This floor has statues from the Acropolis' first temples, a century before the Parthenon. The Acropolis has two layers of history: before the Persian sacking in 480 BC (Archaic) and after (golden age or Classical). The Archaic statues survived because they were buried under later Acropolis buildings before being excavated in the 1800s. Today you'll see no Archaic-period construction on the Acropolis...only the Classical remains of what was rebuilt after 480 BC.

❷ Pediment of the Hekatompedon

This triangular set of statues adorned the entrance to the first great temple on the Acropolis (from 570 BC). It was called the Hekatompedon ("100-foot-long") for its legendary size. The temple was dedicated to Athena, the patron of the city of Athens, and it stood in the Acropolis' prime location—right where the Parthenon is today.

On the far left, bearded Hercules wrestles with the dragon-tailed sea monster Triton (still colorful with sixth-century BC paint). In the (very damaged) center, two lions kill a bull. To the right is a three-headed demon with a snake tail. These dapper, bearded gentle-demons hold objects representing the elements of wind, water, and fire—perhaps symbolizing the struggle of man versus nature. On display nearby (behind and to the right) is another Hekatompedon statue—a mama lion feasting on a bull.

These statues are the first of many we'll see featuring battles: between animals, men, monsters, and gods. The Greeks loved "the contest," because it was through struggle that wisdom was forged. In Greek myths, even the gods battled each other as they strove to create order out of chaos.

• Let's see more non-Parthenon statues. Turn right (past the feasting lion) and enter a gallery flooded with daylight and columns spanning the room.

❸ Archaic Gallery: Kore and Kouros Statues

These statues were gifts to the gods, to decorate the gods' homes atop the Acropolis—that is, their temples.

Browse around. The **horses and riders** were likely donated by rich benefactors to thank the gods for letting them win the local horse races. The robed women with long braids **(kore)** hold objects representing the gifts they bring to the gods. The naked men **(kouros)** may represent athletes, or gods, or a deceased ancestor. What they all have in common is that they're stiff and unrealistic, standing at attention with generic faces and mysterious smiles.

This was the style of the Archaic era (c. 700-480 BC) that preceded the Greek golden age: Men are generally naked (showing off buff and toned bodies); the bearded dudes are adults, and boys are beardless; and women are modestly clothed, with braided hair and pleated robes—essentially columns with breasts. Though these statues were once painted (some still show traces), they are a far cry from the lively golden age wonders we'll see from the Parthenon.

• Of all the statues on the Acropolis, the most important were of the goddess most dear to Athenians—Athena. Halfway down the gallery, on the right, find a large statue of Athena, a robed woman carrying a snake. She's one statue of several in the triangular...

❹ Pediment of the Archaios Naos

Athena, dressed in an ankle-length cloak, strides forward, brandishing a snake as she attacks a giant, who sprawls backward onto his bum. In this "Battle of the Gods and Giants," it was Athena, the goddess of wisdom, who wielded rational thought to overcome brute force.

And thanks to Athena, the city of Athens came to dominate its Greek neighbors. In gratitude, the Athenians began building a grand new temple to Athena to replace the Hekatompedon. These statues decorated the entrance.

But then came the event that changed Greece's history forever. When the Persians invaded Greece for the second time (in 480 BC), they looted Athens and burned the Acropolis' temples to the ground. It was a horrible tragedy, but it left the hilltop a blank canvas. And when Athens rebounded, they were determined to rebuild the Acropolis better than ever as a symbol of rebirth. The centerpiece would be a brand-new temple to Athena—the Parthenon.

• *Continue another 20 steps to the middle of the room, where the* ❺ *Kritios Boy (c. 480 BC) seems to be stepping gracefully from Archaic stiffness into Greece's golden age. From this point on, we'll be viewing artifacts from those golden age buildings you can actually see today atop the Acropolis—the Propylaea, Erechtheion, and Parthenon.*

Continue to the end of the hall and circle clockwise around the escalators. Find displays featuring the Propylaea, the grand entrance to the newly rebuilt Acropolis.

❻ Propylaea and Temple of Athena Nike

The **model of the Propylaea** shows how this entrance gate once looked—a grand, steep staircase that led the visitor up, up, up, and then through majestic columns, to emerge atop the Acropolis. (Tourists go through the same gate today.)

As you climbed, you'd pass by the **Temple of Athena Nike** (the empty platform standing just in front, on the right side), built to honor the fierce goddess who brought Athens *Nike* (Victory). Ruins from that temple are displayed a few steps to the left of the model. (Everything described in the next two paragraphs is within 10 yards of this model.)

This U-shaped set of reliefs (c. 410 BC) formed the balustrade ringing the temple. See how naturally the winged goddess Nike goes about her business: adjusting her sandal, leading a bull to sacrifice, ascending a staircase, and so on. (By the way, Nike survived the destruction of pagan images in the Christian era because they mistook winged Nikes for angels.)

Displayed nearby (in glass cases in the wall) are more chunks of the Temple of Athena Nike. You'll see toes gripping rocks, windblown robes, and realistically twisted bodies—exuberant, life-filled carvings signaling Athens' emergence from the Persian War.

• *Near the Propylaea model (on this level, behind the escalator) is something you won't want to miss. Standing all on their own, as if starring in their own revue on a beautifully lit stage, are the...*

❼ Caryatids from the Erechtheion

Here stand five of the original six lady-columns that once supported the roof of the prestigious Erechtheion temple. (The six on the Acropolis today are copies; the other original is in London's British Museum.) While the Parthenon was the Acropolis' showstopper, the cute little Erechtheion (see the **model** back near the escalators) was actually Athens' holiest temple, as it marked the exact spot where legend says Athens was born.

These remarkable lady-columns wear robes pleated like fluted columns. Their hair is braided behind them. Eyes straight forward, they step out gracefully, swaying their hips naturally while balancing the crossbeams atop their heads. The six statues form a harmonious ensemble, yet each is unique. They were the finishing touch on the architect Mnesicles' final temple, and they sum up the balance and serenity of the golden age.

Despite their elegant appearance, these sculptures were structurally functional. Each has a column for legs, a capital-like hat, and buttressing locks of hair. The Caryatids were modeled on the famously upright women of Karyai, near Sparta, and now any female statue used as a column is called a "caryatid."

Time and the elements have ravaged these maidens. As recently as the 17th century (see the engravings), they had fragile arms holding ritual bowls for libations. Until the 1950s (before modern smog), their worn-down faces had crisp noses and mouths. In a half-century of Industrial Age pollution, they experienced more destruction than in the previous 2,000 years. But their future looks brighter now that they've been brought

indoors out of the acidic air, cleaned up with a laser, and safely preserved for future generations. (For more on the Caryatids in their original location, see page 129.)

• *Now let's head upstairs for the grand finale—the Parthenon sculptures.*

*Ride the escalators up. Pause on **level 2** to take note of the restaurant and terrace with grand Acropolis views. If you need a break, this level has a peaceful and cushy lounge. Then continue up the escalators to the top floor.*

LEVEL 3: THE PARTHENON

This floor features the collection of Parthenon structures, laid out the way they were on the original Parthenon. In fact, this floor has roughly the same dimensions as the Parthenon—228 feet long and 101 feet wide. The escalators deposit you "inside" this virtual Parthenon, in the temple's *cella*—the inner sanctum.

• *Start by getting acquainted with the Parthenon through the exhibits here in the* cella.

❽ Parthenon Exhibits

The **video** in the small theater reconstructs the Parthenon before your eyes, letting you see where today's puzzle pieces fit into the overall structure. It also covers the Parthenon's 2,500-year history—including a not-so-subtle jab at how Lord Elgin got the marbles and made off with them to England.

The **model of the Parthenon** in its prime also shows the surviving sculptures in their original locations. Learn the terminology: The triangular ensemble over the two ends are the pediment sculptures. Beneath that is a row of relief panels running around the building, called the metopes. There was another similar row of relief panels, called the frieze, located under the eaves above the inner row of columns (but unfortunately this model lacks the detail to show it; see the diagram on page 125).

The **model of the east pediment** (the one to the left as you face the escalator) shows the statues you'd see above the Parthenon's main entrance. In the center, at the very peak of the triangle, a tiny winged angel (Nike) is about to place the olive wreath of victory on Athena (carrying a shield). This was the crowning moment of the legendary event that put Athens on the map—the birth of Athena. Zeus (seated on his throne) allowed Athena, the goddess of wisdom, to rise from his brain fully grown and fully armed to inaugurate the golden age of Athens. The other gods at this Olympian banquet—naked men and clothed women—are astounded by Athena's sudden appearance and recoil in amazement.

The drama and realism of these statues was incredible. Find powerful Poseidon (seated to the right with his trident), Apollo (with his lyre), and Aphrodite (reclining farther right). At the far left, Helios' four horses bring the sunrise, while four more (far

ACROPOLIS MUSEUM

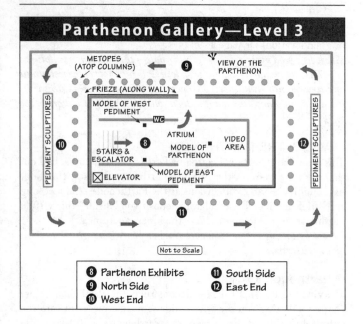

Parthenon Gallery—Level 3

METOPES (ATOP COLUMNS)
VIEW OF THE PARTHENON
❾

FRIEZE (ALONG WALL)

MODEL OF WEST PEDIMENT
WC
ATRIUM
VIDEO AREA

PEDIMENT SCULPTURES
❿

❽
MODEL OF PARTHENON

STAIRS & ESCALATOR
⊠ ELEVATOR
MODEL OF EAST PEDIMENT

PEDIMENT SCULPTURES
⓬

⓫

Not to Scale

❽ Parthenon Exhibits   ⓫ South Side
❾ North Side   ⓬ East End
❿ West End

right) bring sunset. Next to the sunrise horses (on the left), find Dionysus, just kicking back and chilling with another cup of wine. Try to remember how impressive these sculptures were in their prime, because—as you'll soon see—what remains today is mostly just fragments.

The **model of the west pediment** (on the opposite wall) shows Athena (with spear, shield, and spiky crown) competing with Poseidon for Athens' favor by giving gifts to the city. Athena won by presenting an olive tree (behind the two of them), which sprouted next to the Parthenon. A big, heavenly audience looks on. Had Poseidon bested Athena, you'd be in Poseidonia today instead of Athens.

Above the escalator, you may want to grab a stool and watch the 10-minute **video** to learn about the 1801 plundering of the Acropolis by Lord Elgin and the English—the story of the sculptures formerly known as the "Elgin Marbles."

• Now let's go see the actual sculptures—the pediments, metopes, and frieze—that once decorated the exterior of the Parthenon. We'll tour the floor counterclockwise. Facing the big video screen, turn left and enter the huge outer gallery that rings the cella. (You'll be in the north gallery.) Step up to the window for a stunning **view of the Parthenon**—the temple that these sculptures once adorned. Now turn around and take in what remains.

ACROPOLIS MUSEUM

Parthenon Sculptures

This floor is cleverly designed to re-create the dimensions of the Parthenon. The stainless-steel columns mark the location of each marble column. The re-lief panels you see once ringed the Parthenon. The metopes (displayed higher up) formed a continuous band around the Parthenon's exterior. The frieze (mounted lower) also ran around the Parthenon's exterior, but inside the columned arcade. In their heyday, all these panels were originally painted in realistic colors.

The darker-brown panels are originals. The white plaster ones are copies of the originals in other museums, mainly the British Museum. Even with copies, you'll notice there are a few gaps here and there, because some pieces have been lost forever and scholars don't know what was represented there.

We're lucky the Parthenon sculptures have survived as well as they did. First, they were exposed to 2,000 years of the elements. Then, in 1687, the Parthenon was accidentally blasted to smithereens during a battle with the Ottomans. In 1801, Lord Elgin took the best of the shattered pieces back to London. Today, of the original marble frieze, the museum owns only 32 feet. These panels were already so acid-worn that Lord Elgin didn't bother taking them.

Despite all the damage, keep this in mind as you tour the floor: Everything we know about the statues that adorned that great temple has been re-created in this one perfect space.

• *Remember, we'll be touring the floor counterclockwise, starting here on the...*

❾ North Side

Start with the museum's highlight—a life-size replica of the 525-foot **frieze** that once wrapped all the way around the outside of the Parthenon. It depicts the big parade of the Great Panathenaic Festival held every four years, when citizens climbed up the Acropolis to the Parthenon to celebrate the birth of their city.

The parade is in full swing. Chariots lumber in. Parade marshals stand by, supervising the affair. Men lead animals such as lambs and oxen to be sacrificed to the gods. At the heart of the procession are elegant maidens dressed in pleated robes. They shuffle along, carrying gifts for the gods on their shoulders, such as incense burners and jars of wine to pour out an offering. (There was one more gift for the gods that was the whole purpose of the parade—we'll come to that at the end.)

All the participants are heading in the same direction—uphill. Notice how, although the horses gallop and rear back spiritedly, the men's gazes remain steady and form a harmonious line around the Parthenon.

Now turn to the **metopes** (higher and closer). Though pretty worn, these depict scenes of epic Greek contests—men battling monsters, gods battling giants, and superheroes of legend. Remember, the Greeks loved competition of all sorts, as it reflected the dynamic built into the cosmos. The panels on this side of the Parthenon depicted the epic struggles of the Trojan War. Find the lovely Helen who started it all, the brave Greek warrior Odysseus who wandered at war's end, and the hero on the losing team, Aeneas (five panels).

• *Head counterclockwise around the floor, turning the corner to the Parthenon's...*

❿ West End

The sculptures here once decorated one of the Parthenon's two entrances. This was the temple's back door (though it's the iconic view that greets today's visitors).

The triangular **pediment** that once sat over the entrance (but which is now displayed on the ground) is pretty fragmentary and hard to make out. It once showed Athena in the center competing with Poseidon for Athens' affection (described earlier, under "Parthenon Exhibits").

The **metopes** are also pretty weathered (but at least they're originals). They depict another evenly matched contest—this time between Greek men and the legendary Amazons (on horseback).

The **frieze** picks up where we left off—the Panathenaic parade. Here, we have some of the museum's best scenes: Muscular horses with bulging veins are posed in every which way. Their riders' cloaks billow in the breeze as they gallop up the Acropolis. Some panels have holes drilled in them, where gleaming bronze reins were fitted to heighten the festive look. In the middle of the parade, one guy has to buck the one-way flow, stopping to tie his shoe. Climb the little platform for a close-up view of the best-preserved panel.

• *Turn the corner to the other long side.*

⓫ South Side

The **metopes** here are some of the museum's finest. This is the legendary battle between men (the Lapiths) and half-horse centaurs. Follow the story, working right-to-left (starting at the far end of the hall): The centaurs have crashed a party (first three panels) to carry off the pleated-robed Lapith women. The Lapith men fight back (next six panels), but it's clear the centaurs are winning. Note the high-quality original metope (displayed on the ground for closer inspection—southwest corner) where a centaur has a man in a headlock and reaches back, hoping to deliver the final blow. But the Lapiths rally (final two panels) and start to get the upper hand. For the Greeks, this contest symbolized how rational men had to constantly do battle to control their animalistic urges.

Now turn to the **frieze,** which seems to be picking up steam as we build to the parade's climax. It's a true celebration involving all

of Athens: men on horseback, musicians, animals, priests, and dignitaries, all joining together on this festive anniversary of the birth of their great city. They're all headed to the Parthenon to present gifts to Athena.

• *The parade congregated around the Parthenon's entrance. Let's join them there. Continue around the bend to the east end, with some of the Parthenon's most famous statues.*

⑫ East End

These sculptures adorned the Parthenon's main entrance. Take a seat and see how the sculptures—pediment, frieze, and metopes—all culminate thematically here.

The **metopes** (though heavily damaged) illustrated the most primary myth in the Greek world: when the Olympian gods defeated the brutish Giants, thus creating the world of mortal men.

The **pediment** depicted the most important myth for the Athenians: the birth of Athena. (It's heavily damaged, with many gaps. Mentally fill them in with the model we saw in the entrance hallway on this floor, earlier.) The peak of the triangle (now missing) once showed Athena springing from Zeus' head while the other gods reacted in astonishment. Of the pieces and copies here, you can make out Dionysus (reclining on the left), Aphrodite (lounging on the right), and the chess-set horse heads. The other figure is Hebe, the cupbearer of the gods, who seems to be hurrying to give Dionysus a refill.

For the Athenians, the most important of the gods was Athena, and the Panathenaic parade was all about honoring her.

And so, the **frieze** depicts the culmination of the Panathenaic parade: when they arrive at the Parthenon and present their gifts. The most precious gift was a new robe (the *peplos*), woven by Athens' young girls. Find the robe in the central panel, where a man and a girl neatly fold the robe for presentation. Nearby, the gods look on approvingly, seated on their thrones. Athena, to the right, turns her back, apparently bored with the tiresome annual ritual.

In real life, the parade would congregate at the Parthenon entrance. Then a few chosen citizens would enter the temple and head to the inner sanctum *(cella)*, where there was a 40-foot-tall wooden statue of Athena. They'd present the new robe to her, giving her thanks. Athena must have been pleased, as she made Athens the greatest city the Western world has known.

• *Finish your tour by strolling around the gallery again, reviewing the art, gazing out the windows, and taking a moment to...*

Ponder the Parthenon

There's the Parthenon itself, perched on the adjacent hilltop. Let the museum disappear around you, leaving you to enjoy the art and

the temple it once decorated. The Parthenon is one of the most influential works humankind has ever created. For 2,500 years it's inspired generations of architects, sculptors, painters, engineers, and visitors from around the globe. Here in the Acropolis Museum, you can experience the power of this cultural landmark.

The people of Athens relish the Acropolis Museum. They grow taller with every visit, knowing that Greece finally has a suitable place to preserve and share the best of its artistic heritage.

• *On your way down, stop by the restaurant on level 2 for its exterior terrace and the awesome view of the Acropolis, and consider touring the ancient excavations beneath the museum—accessed via a ramp back at the museum entrance (scan your ticket for entry).*

ACROPOLIS MUSEUM

NATIONAL ARCHAEOLOGICAL MUSEUM TOUR

Εθνικό Αρχαιολογικό Μουσείο

The National Archaeological Museum is far and away the top ancient Greek art collection anywhere. Ancient Greece set the tone for all Western art that followed, and this museum lets you trace its evolution—taking you in air-conditioned comfort from 7000 BC to AD 500 through beautifully displayed and described exhibits on one floor. You'll see the rise and fall of Greece's various civilizations: the Minoans, the Mycenaeans, those of Archaic Greece, the Classical Age and Alexander the Great, and the Romans who came from the west. You can also watch Greek sculpture evolve, from prehistoric Barbie dolls, to stiff Egyptian style, to the *David*-like balance of the golden age, to wet T-shirt, buckin'-bronco Hellenistic, and finally, to the influence of the Romans. Walk once around fast for a time-lapse effect, then go around again for a closer look.

This museum is tired, pretty old-school, and slated for a major renovation (which will mean several years of closure). But until then, it's still a great way to either start or finish off your sightseeing through Greece. It's especially worth visiting if you're traveling beyond Athens, because it displays artifacts found all around Greece, including Mycenae, Epidavros, Santorini,

and Olympia—and the treasures displayed here are generally better than those remaining at the sites themselves. The sheer beauty of the statues, vases, and paintings helps bring the country's dusty ruins to life.

Orientation

Cost: €12, €6 off-season, €15 combo-ticket includes entry to the Byzantine and Christian Museum.

Hours: Wed-Mon 8:00-20:00, Nov-March 8:30-15:30, Tue 13:00-20:00 year-round.

Information: +30 213 214 4800, www.namuseum.gr.

Getting There: The only major Athens sight outside the city center, the museum is a mile north of the Plaka at 28 Oktovriou (a.k.a. Patission) #44. Your best bet is to take a **taxi,** which costs about €4 from the Plaka. By **Metro,** use the Omonia stop (as you exit, follow signs to *28 Oktovriou/28 October street,* and walk seven blocks to the museum—about 15 minutes). You can also hop a **bus:** A short walk north of Monastiraki is the Voreu (Βορεου, "North") stop, where you can catch bus #035; ride it to the Patission (Πατησιων) stop, a block in front of the museum. Or, from Syntagma Square (near the corner of the National Garden), catch bus #2, #4, #5, or #11 to Polytechneio (Πολυτεχνειο). Or you could **walk:** It's a straight shot up partly pedestrianized, partly smog-choked Aiolou.

Tours: ∩ Download my free National Archaeological Museum audio tour.

Length of This Tour: Allow, at the very least, two hours for this tour; more if you want to dig deeper into this world-class museum.

Baggage Check: Free and required, except for small purses. It's outside and to the right of the main entrance.

Services: A museum shop, WCs, and an inviting café surround a shady and restful courtyard in the lower level. To get there from the main entrance lobby, take the stairs down behind the ticket desk.

No-no's: Although photography is allowed, goofy poses in front of statues are not. The Greek museum board considers this disrespectful of the ancient culture and is very serious about it—you may hear "No posing!" from stern guards if they catch someone trying to match Zeus' thunderbolt-throwing pose.

Eating: The **$$$ Museum Garden** café in the park in front of the building is pricey, but the generous portions are shareable, and it stays open after the museum closes (nice outdoor tables, or spacious indoor seating).

Starring: The gold Mask of Agamemnon, stately kouros and kore statues, the perfectly posed *Artemision Bronze,* the horse and jockey of Artemision, and the whole range of Greek art.

The Tour Begins

The collection is delightfully chronological. To sweep through Greek history, simply visit the numbered rooms in order. From the entrance lobby (Rooms 1-2), start with the rooms directly in front of you (Rooms 3-6), containing prehistoric and Mycenaean artifacts. Then circle clockwise around the building's perimeter (Rooms 7-33) to see the evolution of classical Greek statuary. Keep track of your ticket—you'll need it to enter or reenter some rooms.

Use the following self-guided tour for an overview, then browse to your heart's content, using the excellent information posted in each room.

• *From the entrance lobby, go straight ahead into the large central hall (Room 4). This first area—Rooms 3-6—is dedicated to prehistory (7000-1050 BC). Start in the small side room to the right, Room 6. In the display case directly to the right as you enter, you'll find stiff marble figures with large heads, known as...*

❶ Cycladic Figurines

Goddess, corpse, fertility figure, good-luck amulet, spirit guide, beloved ancestor, or Neolithic porn? No one knows for sure the

purpose of these female figurines, which are older than the Egyptian pyramids. Although these statuettes were made only in the Cycladic Islands, well-traveled ones have been found all over Greece. The earliest Greeks may have worshipped a Great

Mother earth goddess long before Zeus and company (variously called Gaia, Ge, and other names), but it's not clear what connection she had, if any, with these statuettes. The ladies are always naked, usually with folded arms. The figures evolved over the years from flat-chested, to violin-shaped, to skinny. There is evidence that the eyes, lips, and ears were originally painted on.

The **map** (straight across from the entry) shows the circle (or "cycle") of the Cycladic Islands, with the sacred island of Delos, near Mykonos, in the center. As these islands were in close proximity, there was plenty of trade between them. In the glass case to the right of the map are two interesting figurines. One plays the harp, the other a flute—proof that humans have been making music for at least 5,000 years.

Elsewhere in the long Cycladic Hall, you'll find more figurines, painted vases, and tools such as knives and spears made of

National Archaeological Museum

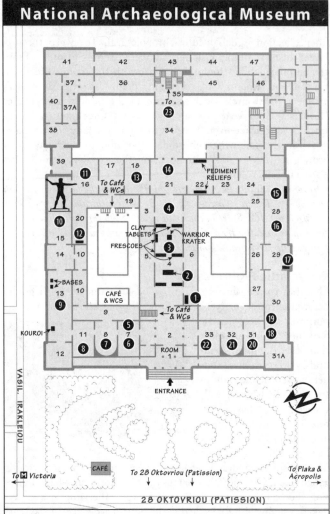

1. Cycladic Figurines
2. Mask of Agamemnon, Etc.
3. More Mycenaean Artifacts
4. Vapheio Cups
5. Dipylon Vase
6. Kore Statue, c. 650 BC
7. Kouros from Sounion
8. Kore Statue, c. 550 BC
9. More Kouroi & Bases
10. Artemision Bronze
11. Attic Funerary Monuments
12. Athena Varvakeion
13. Funeral Steles
14. Artemision Jockey
15. Grave Relief of a Horse
16. Bronze Statue of a Youth
17. Philosopher Portrait Head
18. Fighting Gaul
19. Aphrodite, Pan & Eros
20. Emperor Augustus
21. Sleeping Maenad & Antinous
22. Various Busts
23. Upstairs to Wall Paintings

ARCH. MUSEUM

worked obsidian. Finely worked objects like these were popular export items in the peaceful, trade-oriented, artistic Cycladic world. Notice the impressively painted bathtub on the left. And you'll see carved marble bowls so thin and delicate that light shines through, along with bronze blades, tweezers, needles, and curious "frying pan" grave offerings. All are from around 2500 BC, roughly 1,000 years before the rise of the first great civilization on Greece's mainland—Mycenae.

• *To see the golden treasures of Mycenae, return to the long central hall (Room 4), which is divided into four sections. Here you'll find the...*

❷ Mask of Agamemnon and Other Mycenaean Treasures

Room 4 displays artifacts found in the ruins of the ancient fortress-city of Mycenae, 80 miles west of Athens. You're surrounded by 30 pounds of gold pounded into decorative funerary objects—swords, daggers, armor, and jewelry—all found buried alongside 19 bodies in a circle of Mycenaean graves. Many items were discovered in the cemetery that archaeologists call "Grave Circle A." (For more on the history of this site, see the Mycenae chapter.) The objects' intricately hammered detail and the elaborate funeral arrangements point to the sophistication of this early culture.

In the glass case facing the entry door is the so-called **Mask of Agamemnon** (c. 1550 BC). Made of beaten gold and showing a man's bearded face, this famous mask was tied over the face of a dead man—note the tiny earholes for the string.

The Mycenaeans dominated southern Greece a thousand years before the golden age (1600-1200 BC). They appear in the misty era of Homer's (fanciful) legends of the Trojan War, and in the 19th century, the ruins of the real-life Troy (in western Turkey) were unearthed. The archaeologist Heinrich Schliemann (the Indiana Johann of his era) suggested that the Mycenaeans were the Greeks who'd conquered Troy (which may be true). So, Schliemann next excavated Mycenae and found this remarkable trove. He went on to declare this funeral mask to be that of the legendary Greek King Agamemnon, who conquered the Trojans. (Unfortunately, that part can't be true, because the mask predates the fall of Troy around c. 1300 BC.)

Explore more artifacts nearby. On the wall to the left of the mask, find the sheet of gold foil that once wrapped dead babies for burial. On the back side of the Mask of Agamemnon case, there's

ARCH. MUSEUM

a knife and sheath with a warrior-versus-lions scene. Unlike the peaceful Cycladians, the warlike Mycenaeans turned their artistic skills to making weapons.

• *In the next section of Room 4, you'll find...*

❸ More Mycenaean Artifacts

A **model of the Acropolis of Mycenae** (left side) shows the dramatic hilltop citadel where many of these objects were unearthed. Find the famous Lion Gate entrance (#1 on the model), the round cemetery known as Grave Circle A (#2), and the king's royal palace crowning the hill (#8). Midway through Room 4, look for brightly colored **frescoes,** done in the style of the Mycenaeans' sophisticated neighbors, the Minoans (and featuring the Minoan sport of bull-jumping). At the end of this area, on the left, **clay tablets** show the Mycenaean written language known as Linear B, which has a syllabic script (in which marks stand for syllables) that was cracked only in the 1950s.

In the central display case is Schliemann's favorite find— a painted two-handled vase known as the **House of the Warrior Krater** (#1426). A woman (far left) waves goodbye to a line of warriors heading off to war, with their fancy armor and duffle bags hanging from their spears. This 3,000-year-old scene of Mycenaean soldiers is timeless, with countless echoes across the generations.

• *Continue to the last section of Room 4. In the center, a glass case displays the...*

❹ Vapheio Cups

These gold cups (c. 1600-1550 BC), found with other precious items in a Mycenaean tomb, are metalwork masterpieces. The intricate worked detail on #1 shows a charging bull sending a guy head over heels. On #2 you'll see a bull and a cow making eyes at each other, while the hind leg of another bull gets tied up by one good-looking cowboy. These realistic, joyous scenes are the product of the two civilizations that made 15th-century BC

Greece the wonder of Europe—the Mycenaeans and the Minoan culture of Crete.

Near where you entered this section, note the light and flexible bone helmet (14th-13th century BC). Made from many pieces of boar tusk, a helmet such as this was a prized possession.

For four centuries (c. 1600-1200 BC), the warlike Mycenaeans dominated Greece. They were rich enough to hire accomplished Minoan artisans to paint their frescoes and decorate their cups. Then, suddenly—whether from invasion, famine, internal strife, or natural disaster—the Mycenaeans disappeared from history's radar screen. It plunged Greece into the 500-year ancient Dark Ages (c. 1200-700 BC). Little survives from that chaotic time, so let's pick up the thread of history as Greece began to recover a few centuries later.

• *Backtrack to the entrance lobby, then turn right, and begin circling clockwise around the perimeter of the building, starting in Room 7. After scanning your ticket again to enter this room, look for the tall vase on your right.*

❺ Dipylon Vase

This monumental ocher-and-black vase (c. 750 BC), as tall as a person, is painted with a funeral scene. Vases such as this marked

the graves of well-off Greeks; the belly-handled shape of this one tells us it likely honored a woman (men's graves were typically marked by pedestalled vases).

In the center, the deceased lies on a funeral bier, flanked by a line of mourners who pull their hair in grief. It's far from realistic. The triangular torsos, square arms, circular heads, and bands of geometric patterns epitomize the style of what's known as the Geometric Period (9th-8th century BC). A few realistic notes pop through, such as the raw emotions of the mourners and some grazing antelope and ibex (on the neck of the vase). Note the one little child in attendance. Discovered in Athens' Keramikos Cemetery, the vase gets its name from the nearby Dipylon Gate, the ancient city's renowned main entrance.

This (relatively) sophisticated vase demonstrates that, after centuries of tumult and war, the Greeks were beginning to settle down. They were establishing cities and expanding abroad (as seen on the map nearby). They were developing a written language and achieving the social stability that could afford to generate art. Next came large-scale statues in stone.

ARCH. MUSEUM

• *In Rooms 7-14 you'll get a look at some of these giant statues, including the early Greek statues called...*

Kore and Kouros

Some of the earliest surviving examples of post-Mycenaean Greek art (c. 700-480 BC) are these life-size and larger-than-life statues

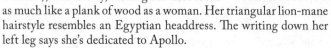

of clothed young women (kore/korai) and naked young men (kouros/kouroi). Influenced by ancient statues of Egyptian pharaohs, they're big and stiff, with triangular faces and arms at their sides. But as you walk through the next few rooms, you'll see the statues become increasingly more realistic and natural in their movements, with more personality.

• *Start with the statue facing the vase in the middle of Room 7, a...*

❻ **Kore** (c. 650 BC): With hands at her sides and dressed in a full-length robe (called a chiton), this skinny, rectangular kore looks as much like a plank of wood as a woman. Her triangular lion-mane hairstyle resembles an Egyptian headdress. The writing down her left leg says she's dedicated to Apollo.

• *In the next room (Room 8), your eyes go right to a very nice pair of knees that belong to a...*

❼ **Kouros from Sounion** (c. 600 BC): A typical kouros from the Archaic period, this young naked man has braided dreadlocks and a stable forward-facing pose, and is stepping forward slightly with his left leg. His fists are clenched at his sides, and his scarred face obscures an Archaic smile—a placid smile that suggests the inner secret of happiness. His anatomy is strongly geometrical and stylized, with almond-shaped eyes, oval pecs, an arched rib cage, cylindrical thighs, trapezoidal knees, and a too-perfect symmetry. While less plank-like than earlier statues, he's still much flatter than an actual person. The overdeveloped muscles (look at those quads!) and narrow waist resemble those of an athletic teenager.

Rather than strict realism, kouros statues capture a geometric ideal. The proportions of the body parts follow strict rules—for example, most of the later kouros statues are precisely seven "heads" tall. Although this kouros steps forward slightly, his hips remain even (think about it—the hips of a real person would shift forward on one side).

The Four Stages of Greek Sculpture

Archaic (c. 700-480 BC): Rigid statues with stylized anatomy, facing forward, with braided hair and mysterious smiles (see photo).

Severe (c. 480-460 BC): More re-alistic and balanced statues (with no smiles), capturing a serious no-bility. Works from this transitional period are sometimes described as Early Classical.

Classical (c. 460-323 BC): Real-istic statues of idealized beauty with poses that strike a balance between movement and stillness, with understated emotion. (With-in this period, the golden age was roughly 450-400 BC.)

Hellenistic (c. 323-30 BC): Pho-torealistic (even ugly) humans engaged in dramatic, emotional struggles, captured in snapshot poses that can be wildly unbalanced.

The Greeks were obsessed with the human body—remember, these statues were of (idealized) humans, not gods. Standing naked and alone, these statues represented a microcosm of the rational order of nature.

Statues were painted in vivid, lifelike colors. But the rough surface lacks the translucent sheen of Classical Age statues, be-cause Archaic chisels were not yet strong enough for the detail work without cracking the marble.

Kouros statues were everywhere, presented as gifts to a god at a sanctuary or to honor the dead in a cemetery. This one was dedi-cated to Poseidon at the entrance to the temple at Sounion. As a funeral figure, a kouros symbolized the deceased in his prime of youth and happiness, for-ever young.

• *Continue into the next room (Room 11). On the left, holding a flower, is a...*

❽ Kore (c. 550 BC): Where a male kouros was naked and either life-size or larger than life (emphasizing masculine power), a female kore was often slightly smaller than life and modestly clothed, capturing feminine

ARCH. MUSEUM

grace (males were commonly naked in public, but women never were). This petite kore stands with feet together, wearing a pleated chiton belted at the waist. Her hair is braided and held in place with a diadem (a wreath-like headdress), and she wears a necklace. Her right hand tugs at her dress, indicating motion (a nice trick if the artist lacks the skill to actually show it), while her left hand holds a flower. Like most ancient statues, she was painted in lifelike colors, including her skin. Her dress was red—you can still see traces of the paint—adorned with flower designs and a band of swastikas down the front. (In ancient times—before German archaeologist Schliemann's writings popularized it and Hitler appropriated it—the swastika was a harmless good-luck symbol representing the rays of the sun.) This kore, like all the statues in the room, has that distinct Archaic smile (or smirk, as the Greeks describe it). Browse around. Study the body types—the graceful, *Avatar*-like builds, those mysterious smirks, and the rigid hairdos.

• *The next room—a long hall labeled* Room 13—*has...*

❾ More Kouroi: These statues, from the late Archaic period (around 500 BC), once decorated the tombs of hero athletes—per-

haps famous Olympians. Notice that these young men are slightly more relaxed and realistic, with better-formed thighs and bent elbows.

Farther down Room 13 (left side), find the two square marble **Bases for Funerary Kouroi.** These were pedestals for kouros statues of the deceased. The carved reliefs are yet another baby step in the artistic march toward realism. On the first base, the relief shows wrestlers and other athletes, with remarkably realistic twisting poses. Around the right side, notice the dog-and-cat fight. The second base features a field hockey-like game, each scene reflecting the vigor of the deceased man in his prime.

During the Archaic period, Greece was prospering, growing, expanding, trading, and colonizing the Mediterranean. The smiles on the statues capture the bliss of a people settling down and living at peace. But in 480 BC, Persia invaded, and those smiles soon vanished.

• *Pass through Room 14 and into Room 15, which is dominated by one of the jewels of the collection, the...*

❿ Artemision Bronze (of Zeus or Poseidon)

This statue was discovered amid a shipwreck off Cape Artemision (north of Athens) in 1928. The weapon was never found, so no one

ARCH. MUSEUM

knows for sure if this is Zeus or Poseidon. The god steps forward, raises his arm, sights along his other arm at the distant target, and prepares to hurl his thunderbolt (if it's Zeus) or his trident (if it's Poseidon).

The god stands 6'10" and has a physique like mine. His hair is curly and tied at the back, and his now-hollow eyes once shone white

with inset bone. He plants his left foot and pushes off with the right. Although every limb moves in a different direction, the whole effect is one of balance. The statue's dimensions are a study in Greek geometry. His head is one Greek foot high, and he's six heads tall (or one Greek fathom). The whole figure has an "X" shape that would fit into a perfect circle, with his navel at the center and his fingertips touching the rim. Although the bronze statue—cast with the "lost wax" technique (explained later, under *"Artemision Jockey"*)—is fully three-dimensional, it's most impressive from the front. (Later Greek statues, from the Hellenistic era, seem fully alive from every angle, including the three-quarter view.)

This Zeus/Poseidon, from c. 460 BC, is an example of the transition into the Classical style, as sculpture evolved beyond the so-called Severe style (480-460 BC). (The famous charioteer of Delphi, pictured on page 382, is textbook Severe: far more lifelike than a kouros, but still frontal and unmoving.) Historically, the Severe/Early Classical Period covers the time when Greece battled the Persians and emerged victorious—the era when ordinary men had also just shaken off tyrants and taken control of their own destiny through democracy. The Greeks were entering the dawn of the golden age. During this time of horrific war, the Greeks made art that was serious (no more Archaic smiles) and unadorned, and that expressed the noble strength and heroism of the individuals who had carried them through tough times. The statues are anatomically realistic, celebrating the human form.

With his movements frozen, as if Zeus/Poseidon were posing for a painting, we can examine the wonder of the physical body. He's natural yet ideal, twisting yet balanced, moving while at rest. (Later Greek sculptures would improve upon this, with figures that look almost as if they've been caught mid-motion with the click of a camera.) With his geometrical perfection and godlike air, the figure sums up all that is best about the art of the ancient world.

We're entering the golden age.

• *Continue into Room 16, filled with big marble vases labeled* ⑪ **Attic**

ARCH. MUSEUM

Funerary Monuments. *These grave markers take the shape of the ceramic urns used for the ashes of cremated bodies. Vase #4485 is particularly touching: A grieving family looks on as Hermes (with his winged sandals) leads a young woman to the underworld.*

Continue into Room 17, then turn right into Room 19. (Note that the WCs and café are out the door ahead of you.) Turn right in Room 19, then hook left into Room 20. At the far end of this room is item #129, the...

⑫ Athena Varvakeion

This marble statue, known as the *Athena Varvakeion* (c. AD 250), is considered the most faithful copy of the great *Athena Parthe-*

nos (438 BC) by Pheidias. It's essentially a one-twelfth-size replica of the 40-foot statue that once stood in the Parthenon. Although a miniature copy of the glorious original, it provides a good introduction to Greek art at its golden age pinnacle. Athena stands dressed in flowing robes, holding a small figure of Nike (goddess of victory) in her right hand and a shield in her left. Athena's helmet sprouts plumes with winged horses and a sphinx. To give a sense of scale of the original, the tiny Nike in Athena's hand was six feet tall in the Parthenon statue. Athena is covered in snakes. She wears a snake belt and bracelet; coiled snakes decorate her breastplate; and a snake is curled up inside her shield, representing the goddess' connection to her half-snake son, who was born out of the earth and considered to be one of the ancestors of the Athenians. The snake-headed Medusa (whom Athena helped Perseus slay) adorns the center of her chest.

• *Backtrack to Room 17, turn right, and continue circling the museum clockwise into Room 18, which has...*

⑬ Funeral *Stele*s

The tombstones that fill this room, all from the fifth century BC, are more good examples of golden age Greek art. With a mastery of the body, artists show poignant scenes of farewell, as loved ones bid a sad goodbye to the dead, who are seated. The tombstone in the center of the room depicts a rich woman pondering which treasure from her jewel box to take with her into eternity. On the left wall, a woman who died in childbirth looks at her baby, held by a servant as it reaches for its dead mother. Other scenes include a beautiful young woman, who died in her prime, gazing into a mirror. Servants are shown taking part in the sad event, as if part of the family.

Though shallow reliefs, these works are effectively three-di-mensional. There's a timeless melancholy in the room, a sense that no matter who you are—or how rich—when you go, you go alone... and shrouds have no pockets.

• *Pass into Room 21, a large central hall. We'll take a temporary break from the chronological sequence to see statues dating from the second cen-tury BC, when Greece was ruled by Rome. The hall is dominated by the...*

⓮ Artemision Jockey

In this bronze statue (c. 140 BC), the horse is racing in full stride, as a young jockey hangs on for dear life. The statue was recovered in

pieces from the seafloor off Cape Artemision. Missing were the reins the jockey once held in his left hand and the whip he used with his right to spur the horse to go even faster—maybe too fast, judging by the look on his face.

Greeks loved their horse races, and this statue may celebrate a victory at one of the Panhellenic Games. The jockey is dressed in a traditional short tunic and has inlaid eyes. His features indicate that he was prob-ably ethnically part Ethiopian.

The statue, like other ancient bronzes, was made not by ham-mering sheets of metal, but with the classic "lost wax" technique. The artist would first make a rough version of the statue from clay, cover it with a layer of wax, and then cover that with another layer of clay to make a form-fitting mold. When heated in a furnace to harden the mold, the wax would melt—or be "lost"—leaving a nar-row space between the clay model and the mold. The artist would then pour molten bronze into the space, let it cool, break the mold, and—*voilà!*—end up with a hollow bronze statue. This particular statue was cast in pieces, which were then welded together. After the cast was removed, the artist added a few surface details and polished it smooth. Notice the delightful detail on the rider's spurs, which were lashed to his bare feet.

Stylistically, we've gone from stiff Archaic, to restrained Se-vere, to balanced Classical...to this wonderful example of the un-bridled emotion of Hellenism. It doesn't sit primly, but dominates its space.

The **other statues** in the room are second-century BC Roman copies of fifth-century BC Greek originals. Thanks to excellent copies like the ones in this room, we know what many (otherwise lost) golden age Greek masterpieces looked like. (By the way, when the Romans tried to re-create a bronze statue in marble, they often added extra support. So, if you see a tree trunk buttressing some statue, it's likely a Roman copy.)

• *But, with the Romans, we're getting ahead of ourselves. To pick up where we left off (in the golden age), head straight past the jockey into Room 22 (with pediment reliefs). Then pass through a couple of rooms displaying funeral monuments until you reach the long Room 28, where you'll come face-to-face with a large...*

⓫ Grave Relief of a Horse

The spirited horse steps lively and whinnies while an Ethiopian boy struggles with the bridle and tries to calm him with food. The realistic detail of the horse's muscles and veins is astonishing, offset by the panther-skin blanket. The horse's head pops out of the relief, becoming fully three-dimensional. The boy's pose is slightly off-balance, anticipating the "unposed poses" of later Hellenism (this relief is from the late fourth century BC). We sense the emotions of both the overmatched boy and the nervous horse. We also see a balance between the horse and boy, with the two figures creating a natural scene together rather than standing alone.

• *Farther down Room 28 stands the impressive, slightly larger-than-life-size...*

⓬ Bronze Statue of a Youth

Scholars can't decide whether this statue (c. 340-330 BC) is reaching out to give someone an apple or demonstrating a split-finger fastball. He may be Perseus, holding up the head of Medusa, but he's most likely the mythical Paris, awarding a golden apple to the winner of a beauty contest between goddesses (sparking jealousies that started the Trojan War). Imagine how striking this statue would have been in its original full shine, before the bronze darkened with age.

The figure is caught mid-step as he reaches out, gazing intently at the person he's giving the object to. Split this youth vertically down the middle to see the *contrapposto* (or "counter-poise") stance of so many Classical statues. His left foot is stable, while the right moves slightly, causing his hips to shift. Meanwhile, his right arm is tense while the left hangs loose. These subtle, contrary motions are in perfect balance around the statue's vertical axis.

In the Classical Age, statues reached their peak of natural realism and balanced grace. During the following Hellenistic Period, sculptors added to that realism, injecting motion and drama. Statues are fully three-dimensional (and Hellenistic statues even more so, as they have no "front": You have to walk around them to see the whole picture). Their poses are less rigid than those in the Archaic period and less overtly heroic than those of the Severe. The beauty of the face, the perfection of the muscles, the balance of elegant grace and brute power—these represent the full ripeness of the art of this age.

• *Continue into the small Room 29. To the left of the next doorway, find a black bronze head in a glass case. Look into the wild and cynical inlaid eyes of this...*

⑰ Head from a Statue of a Philosopher

This philosopher was a Cynic, part of a movement of nonmaterialist nonconformists founded in the fourth century BC by Diogenes.

The term "cynic" aptly describes these guys with unkempt hair who questioned their society's obsessions with wealth and status. The statue's aged, bearded face captures the personality of a distinct individual and is considered a portrait of a real-life person.

From c. 240 BC, it's typical of the Hellenistic Period, the time after the Macedonian Alexander the Great conquered Greece and spread Greek culture across the Mediterranean world. Hellenistic Greek society celebrated individualism and everyday people like this. Rather than Photoshop out their eccentricities, they presented their subjects warts and all. For the first time in history, we see human beings in all their gritty human glory: with wrinkles, male-pattern baldness, saggy boobs, and middle-age spread, all captured in less-than-noble poses.

The glass case to the left shows other parts of his body. The statue likely shipped in pieces (like an Ikea self-assembly kit) for practical purposes.

This statue, like a number of the museum's statues, was found by archaeologists on the seabed off the coast of Greece. Where the wreck off Cape Artemision gave us Zeus/Poseidon and the bronze horse, another wreck (off the Greek mainland's southern tip) yielded this statue and the bronze youth (depicting Paris/Perseus).

ARCH. MUSEUM

• *Continue into the long Room 30 and head to the far end to find the...*

⓲ Statue of a Fighting Gaul

Having been wounded in the thigh (note the hole), this soldier has fallen to one knee and reaches up to fend off the next blow. The style of his helmet indicates that he's not a Greek, but a Gaul (from ancient France). The artist catches the exact moment when the tide of battle is about to turn. The face of this Fighting Gaul says he's afraid he may become the Dying Gaul.

The statue (c. 100 BC) sums up many of the features of Hellenistic art: He's frozen in motion in a wild, unbalanced pose that dramatizes his inner thoughts. The diagonal pose runs up his left leg and out his head and outstretched arm. Rather than a noble, idealized god, this is an ordinary soldier caught in an extreme moment. His arms flail, his muscles strain, his eyes bulge, and he cries out in pain. This statue may have been paired with others in a theatrical mini-drama that heightened emotion. Hellenism shows us the thrill of victory, and—in this case—the agony of defeat.

• *To the right in the same room, on the other side of the doorway, is a...*

⓳ Statue of Aphrodite, Pan, and Eros

In this playful marble ensemble (c. 100 BC) from the sacred island of Delos, Aphrodite is about to whack Pan with her sandal. Strik-

ing a classic *contrapposto* pose (with most of her weight on one foot), Aphrodite is more revealing than modest, her voluptuous body polished smooth. There's a bit of whimsy here, as Aphrodite seems to be saying, "Don't! Stop!"...but may instead be saying, "Don't stop." The actions of the (literally) horny Pan can also be interpreted in two ways: His left arm is forceful, but his right is gentle—holding her more like a dance partner. Eros, like an omnipresent Tinkerbell, comes to Aphrodite's aid—or does he? He has the power to save her if she wants help, but with a hand on Pan's horn and a wink, Eros seems to say, "OK, Pan, this is your chance. Come on, man, go for it." Pan can't believe his luck. This marble is finer than those used in earlier statues, and it has been polished to a sheen with an emery stone. As you walk around this delightful statue, enjoy the detail, from the pudgy baby feet and the remnants of red paint on the sandal to the way the figures all work together in a cohesive vignette.

• *Now, enter Room 31 to see a...*

⑳ Statue of the Emperor Augustus

This statue of Augustus (c. 12-10 BC) introduces us to the next great era of ancient Greece—as a part of the vast Roman Em-

pire. Augustus, the adopted son of Julius Caesar, was the founder of the Roman Empire and its first emperor. This is the only known statue of him on horseback, although it is missing its lower half. He holds the (missing) reins in his left hand and raises his right hand in a gesture of blessing or of oration—an expression of the emperor's power.

Although Greece was conquered by Rome, Greek culture ultimately "conquered" the Romans. The Romans were great warriors, engineers, and administrators, but they had an inferiority complex when it came to art. Grecophile Romans imported Greek statues and cranked out high-quality copies to beautify their villas. (Even today, most "Greek" statues in Europe are actually Roman copies.) As Augustus remade the city of Rome, he used Greek-style columns and crossbeams—a veneer of sophistication on buildings erected with no-nonsense, brick-and-concrete Roman-arch engineering. It's largely thanks to the Romans and their respect for Greek culture that so much of this ancient art survives today.

• *For more Roman-era art, step into Room 32 and find a portrait of a beautiful woman asleep on a rock.*

㉑ Sleeping Maenad (and Friends)

In the center of the room is a marble statue (c. AD 120) featuring a sleeping Maenad, a female follower of the god Dionysus. This Roman copy was made during the reign of Emperor Hadrian. Like a sleeping beauty, this slumbering Maenad lies exposed atop a rock on a soft skin of a panther. As if being mooned by the Maenad, a bust of the emperor himself stands on the nearby wall. (He politely averts his eyes.)

Nearby, find a bust of **Hadrian.** This Roman emperor was a Grecophile in two senses—he not only loved Greek culture, but he also had a hunky young Greek boyfriend named Antinous. To Hadrian's left is a fine portrait bust (labeled simply "male portrait")

ARCH. MUSEUM

that may depict **Antinous** (or is it Channing Tatum?). Look into his disarmingly beautiful eyes. After the young man drowned in the Nile in AD 130, the depressed Hadrian had him deified and commissioned statues of him throughout the empire.

• *Although Greece flourished under the Romans, their time was coming to an end. Continue into Room 33 to see...*

⓶ Busts from the Late Roman Empire

These busts (AD 300-500) capture the generic features and somber expressions of the late Roman Empire. As Rome decayed and fell to invaders, ancient culture and artwork went into steep decline. The empire shifted its capital eastward to Constantinople (modern Istanbul). For the next thousand years, the Byzantine Empire, which included Greece, lived on as a Christian, Greek-speaking enclave, while Western Europe fragmented into various

smaller realms. During that time, ancient Greek culture was buried under centuries of rubble. Then, during the Renaissance (c. 1300), there was a renewed interest in the glory of ancient Greece. Gradually, Greek sites were unearthed, its statues cleaned up and repaired, and Greek culture once again was revived in all its inspirational glory.

• *Exit into the entrance lobby and take a breath. You've seen the core of this museum and its highlights. If you have an appetite for more, consider one more stop: some colorful frescoes as old as Stonehenge but as fresh as today.*

To get there, return to the boy on the horse. Behind the horse (in Rooms 34-35), find the grand ⓸ *staircase. Climb to the top of the stairs, continue straight into Room 48, and go to the far end of the room to see...*

Cycladic Wall Paintings

These magnificent paintings are a product of the first great Greek civilization: the Minoans. These murals once decorated the walls of homes at Akrotiri on the island of Santorini (Thira). When the island's volcano blew in a massive, bigger-than-Krakatoa eruption (c. 1630 BC), it preserved these frescoes in a thick blanket of ash.

Akrotiri's people shared an artistic tradition with the Minoans (centered on the isle of Crete). Unlike most early peoples, they were not fighters but traders, and their industriousness made them rich. Their homes and palaces were unfortified, featuring elaborate furniture (like the bed in the next room, cast in plaster from a hole in the ash). The walls were decorated with colorful frescoes like these, which celebrate life in rolling springtime landscapes and everyday scenes.

Two boys, perhaps a prince and his servant, box (notice their mostly shaved heads). An antelope buck turns to make eyes at a doe.

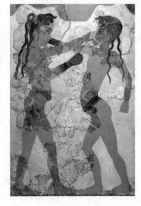

Flirting swallows soar over hillsides of lilies. The frescoes are vivid, featuring primary colors of red, yellow, and blue, with thick black outlines. Some parts were painted while the plaster was still wet, so the pigments were absorbed, resulting in the glowing translucent effect that distinguishes these paintings. Remember that most early cultures used art only as propaganda for a king, to commemorate a famous battle, or to represent a god. But the Aegeans were among the first to love beauty for its own sake. That love of beauty became part of the legacy of ancient Greece.

• *Whew! Our tour is over. There's lots more to see in the museum, though—science and tech buffs in particular may want to seek out the* **Antikythera mechanism,** *known as the world's first computer (in rooms 38 and 39).*

ARCH. MUSEUM

PSYRRI & CENTRAL MARKET WALK

Until recently, the Psyrri neighborhood was a grimy area of workshops and cottage industries—a hotbed of poets, musicians, revolutionaries, and troublemakers. Now it's one of central Athens' trendiest areas. Cosmetically, it still isn't the prettiest place—it's filled with pungent odors, crumbling buildings, and graffiti. But if you take time to explore, you'll find Psyrri (psee-REE) is a great place to simply hang out.

On our walk, we'll see this neighborhood in transition. There are traditional bakeries and craftspeople from the neighborhood's past. But we'll also find cutting-edge art galleries, excellent restaurants, creative boutiques, fun tavernas, and a welcoming atmosphere. Our walk culminates at the huge Central Market, home to spice vendors, truck farmers, butchers, and locals shopping for the evening meal.

The walk starts on Athens' central square, Monastiraki, and ends on a pleasant pedestrian street that's a straight shot back to the center, near the starting point. This stroll is light on history, but heavy on local life and sampling Athenian goodies. It's a nice change of pace from this book's heavy-hitting historical walks.

Orientation

Length of This Walk: Allow just over an hour—more if you stop for snacks and meals.

When to Go: Ideally, do the walk on an empty stomach, around lunchtime, when the market is thriving and you have plenty of room to fill up on snacks. Note that the Central Market shuts down around 15:00 and is closed all day Sunday, and a couple of the coffee shops and bakeries mentioned in this walk close around 17:00. The walk can also be interesting in the early evening, just as the nightlife scene is livening up.

Getting There: The walk begins at Monastiraki Square, with its own Metro stop (and at the end of my "Athens City Walk").

Street Art: We'll see some impressive street art on this walk; for a more in-depth look at this art form, consider Alternative Athens' street-art tour (see page 44).

Starring: Funky graffiti, fragrant market stalls, and delectable Athenian snacks.

The Walk Begins

PSYRRI

Begin on Monastiraki Square. While this is a hub both for transit and high-power sightseeing, we're going to turn our back on those and...explore.

• *With the Acropolis and the yellow Metro station behind you, set your sights on the A for Athens hotel. Cross busy Ermou street and head up the lane on the left side of the hotel (the street is labeled* Μιαουλη/*Miaouli). Walk one short block up this street, to the Y-intersection. Stand on the stairs to your right (at a Metro entrance) and take in the buildings around you. You've plunged into a world of wild graffiti, also known as...*

❶ Street Art

The graffiti around you—some artistic, some ugly and crude—is the perfect introduction to this gentrifying neighborhood.

Let's be honest: Athens is not the most architecturally stimulating city, and many buildings are run down. This street of ugly concrete buildings looks like Psyrri 20 years ago, when many Athenians welcomed the colorful graffiti as a kind of urban beautification. For the 2004 Olympics, the city commissioned street artists to aid in dressing up the city. That move helped employ local artists and spur this neighborhood's renewal. Since then, graffiti has become something of a tradition. Artists use these blank walls as a canvas to express their frustrations and dreams.

A fine example of high-class street art is on the wall above the elevator at the top of the stairs, next to the Metro entrance.

This abstract mural—titled *Colorful Warrior*—was done by one of Athens' most respected street artists, Vangelis Choursoglou

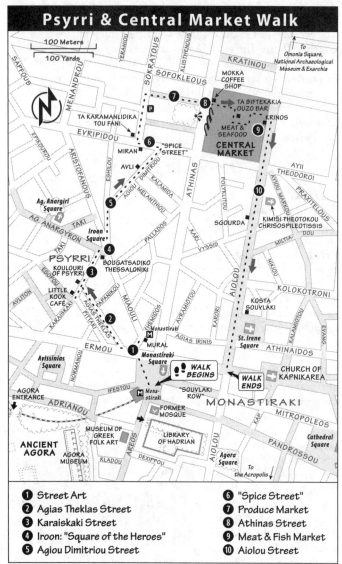

Psyrri & Central Market Walk

① Street Art
② Agias Theklas Street
③ Karaiskaki Street
④ Iroon: "Square of the Heroes"
⑤ Agiou Dimitriou Street
⑥ "Spice Street"
⑦ Produce Market
⑧ Athinas Street
⑨ Meat & Fish Market
⑩ Aiolou Street

(who goes by the street name "Woozy"). Woozy's portfolio includes murals in London, Nicaragua, and Shenzhen, China. In Athens, city authorities grant permits to certain artists, like Woozy. Unauthorized graffiti is officially illegal, but artists are rarely charged, and most do their work clandestinely, late at night.

This walk passes lots of street art—everything from basic tagging by vandals, to slogans from rival soccer fans, to beautiful murals. Much of it was created by alumni of the Athens School of Fine Arts.

• *Backtrack to busy Ermou street. Turn right, walk one block, then angle right up Agias Theklas street.*

❷ Agias Theklas

Humble Psyrri has always been the home of hardworking crafts-people and small factories (in contrast to central business hub Syn-

tagma and the touristy Plaka). As you stroll into the heart of the neighbor-hood, notice the architec-tural mix: once-attractive historic buildings—some run-down, some lovingly restored—and eyesore midcentury concrete for which there's little hope. You can see why graffiti might be considered an improvement.

Continuing along this street, look for slices of local life: little hardware stores overflowing into the streets and grocery stores ca-tering to the neighborhood. With its hip cachet and proximity to downtown, Psyrri is becoming a hotspot for Airbnb rentals. Locals worry that it's only a matter of time before long-time shops (and colorful resident characters) are priced out. Stay tuned.

Two-thirds of the way down the block, a cramped little park-ing lot on the right makes the perfect "canvas" for an ever-changing series of big, wild paintings.

It was in an apartment on this street where English poet Lord Byron stayed in 1810. Back then, Psyrri was a hotbed of revolution-aries like Byron fighting for Greek independence. That noncon-formist atmosphere still lives on in Psyrri today. Byron resided at the home of the Makri family, where he befriended their 12-year-old daughter—who inspired him to pen the poem, "Maid of Ath-ens, ere we part / Give, oh give me back my heart!"

• *Continue to the T-intersection with...*

❸ Karaiskaki Street

Detour a half-block left to the **Little Kook** café (can't miss it, at #17—it looks like a candy store vomited), which captures the creative spirit of to-day's Psyrri. This fairy tale-themed coffee and tea

house sprawls through several surrounding buildings. Ogle the café's creative window displays, which change with the seasons: During autumn, they have Halloween-themed decor; in December, it's Christmas; in summers past they've had a circus theme. A giant dragon perches on top of the main building guarding his territory below. Around the corner, Pittaki Lane is equally colorful and photo-op perfect. You could pause here for a break in the Kook's fanciful interior, with elaborate, multitiered cakes to match...or continue the walk (more tempting and more authentically Athenian snacks await). Pace yourself.

Head back up the way you came on Karaiskaki. On the left is **Koulouri of Psyrri** (marked *Κουλουρι Του Ψυρρη*). *Koulouri*

are the little sesame-encrusted dough rings sold cheaply at carts all over Athens. This bakery supplies most of those carts (notice the row of delivery scooters parked out front). Step into the shop and buy one—you won't find any fresher. Two rings cost about a euro, and they have a cooler of drinks.

Athenians eat *koulouri* a variety of ways: plain, as a sandwich, or dipped in honey (honey + sesame = a taste kind of like peanut butter). The name comes from the Greek word for "zero" (inspired by its shape). *Koulouri* date back to early Christian times but were introduced in Athens in the 1920s, when the Greco-Turkish War brought a million Greek refugees from Turkey to Athens, along with their beloved *koulouri* and other foods we'll encounter on our walk.

• *Continue up Karaiskaki street another block, where you emerge into Psyrri's main square.*

❹ Iroon: "Square of the Heroes"

This lively square—filled with al fresco café tables and tourists— is entertaining day and night. The space is called "Square of the Heroes" for the Greek freedom fighters who settled here in the 1830s following independence from the Ottomans. The streets nearby are named for Greek heroes. And the name Psyrri itself

comes from an early resident named Psiris, who built a church here in what's now the epicenter of the neighborhood named for him.

The square gives a sense of how much this genteel neighborhood has changed over the years...and how much it hasn't. It began life in Ottoman times (1700s) as a typical neighborhood of twisting narrow lanes. Even today, as you can see, Psyrri's streets spin off from this central square at all angles, like wings on a pinwheel. The neighborhood's central location attracted diplomats, aristocrats, scholars from the nearby university, immigrants from the isle of Naxos, and, after the War of Independence, those aforementioned "heroes."

After independence, as Athens expanded and modernized into grid-plan neighborhoods like Syntagma, Psyrri remained quiet and residential. Meanwhile, the local mafia moved in. These strong-arm Koutsavakides—who wore long moustaches, pointed boots, and walked with an exaggerated limp—took over Psyrri. Residents who could afford to fled elsewhere, and by the time the government cracked down, Psyrri was a slum. It remained that way—the humble home of sandal makers and factory workers—until the late 1990s.

That's when artists, designers, and alternative-lifestyle enthusiasts discovered Psyrri, taking advantage of its cheap rents and marvelous location. For the 2004 Olympics, Psyrri was targeted for redevelopment, with rezoning laws designed to lure restaurants and nightclubs. Gentrification quickly followed, and now Psyrri is back where it was two centuries ago: one of the city's most in-demand areas.

Look up, to where a giant **mural** laughs down over this leafy square. One of the neighborhood's first (from 2004), this is the work of Alexandros Vasmoulakis, another respected Athenian street artist.

Ready for another snack? At the bottom of the square (on the right) **Bougatsadiko Thessaloniki** (labeled *Μπουγατσάδικο*) spe-

cializes in a delicate pastry called *bougatsa*. Step inside to see if a baker is at work: They roll out a sheet of super-elastic dough, then pull, prod, and toss it like an oversized pizza crust until it's as thin as the skin of a balloon. Then the baker folds it over several

times, fills it with custard, and pops it in the oven. Ask for a portion at the counter—it's especially good when it's ʰʊɪ. *Bougatsa* is a specialty of the northern city of Thessaloniki—so this shop's name is a mark of quality.

• *To continue our walk, exit the square at the upper-right corner. (For a full meal in this area, see my recommendations on page 197). Pass under the leafy canopy. At the fork just after that, bear right, up...*

❺ Agiou Dimitriou Street

Enjoy this quieter, more local-feeling part of Psyrri. The painfully hip atmosphere is slowly mellowing to workaday.

On the left, at #12, is a little hole-in-the-wall shop selling distractions for Greek men: worry beads, pocketknives, shaving gear, pipes, and dice and backgammon boards. Right next to that is the easy-to-miss door (marked *αυλή*) leading to the recommended **Avli** restaurant. Hidden in a courtyard, its name is simply, "Courtyard." This is a good, untouristy alternative to many Psyrri tavernas.

Farther along, humble storefronts sell textiles and fake flowers, and a few little "everything" shops spill out into the street. Your transition from trendy Psyrri to the real world is nearly complete. Carry on.

• *At the end of Agiou Dimitriou street you run directly into a city-block-sized complex of buildings housing vendors—all part of the...*

Central Market

Athens' Central Market (Varvakios Agora/Βαρβάκειος Αγορά) isn't cute or idyllic, like a small-town French *halles,* and it's not a tourist trap, like Barcelona's La Boqueria. The Central Market is refreshingly real: a thriving marketplace where workaday Athenians stock up on ingredients. A walk through the market is a treat for all the senses—sights, smells, and sounds. This walk will help you navigate and appreciate its many parts. I'll also

point out some distinctively local restaurants and treats to enjoy while you're here.

• *Let's start by circling the Market's perimeter clockwise, taking in some of the vendors along the way. Turn left onto Evripidou street, which is also known as...*

❻ Spice Street

Different parts of the Central Market specialize in different products. As you can tell from the first whiff, Evripidou is all about spices. You'll pass three spice shops in row. Step into the first one at #37 (Χατζηγεωργίου) and inhale. Intoxicating!

These spice sellers are the great-great-grandchildren of those ethnic-Greek refugees from the Greco-Turkish war of the 1920s, who arrived bringing a pungent whiff of exotic Istanbul bazaars.

Check out the variety of products. You'll see bushels of rice, grains, nuts, and dried fruits. Keep an eye out for bunches of partially dried flowering herbs tied up with string—this is Greek mountain tea, an herbal mixture revered for its healing properties. You'll also see classic Greek oregano, thyme, basil, and the precious Greek red saffron.

Walk a few doors down and stop at the venerable **Miran** deli. Display cases and café tables (often used by food tours) sit under

hanging salamis and other meats. The big slabs coated in bright-red spices are *pastourma*, a salted-and-dried meat with a powerful rub of paprika, cumin, fenugreek, garlic, and other spices. You might already know it by its English name—pastrami. But here, the pastrami meat is commonly camel—another aspect of Middle Eastern cuisine that caught on in 1920s Athens. (By the way, you're walking on sidewalks broken by grooves intended to help visually-impaired people. I've encountered grooved sidewalks like these across Europe but have yet to see someone use them—making them a well-meaning but expensive waste of money.)

Diagonal from Miran (ahead, at the opposite corner) is another deli, called **Ta Karamanlidika tou Fani** (Τα Καραμανλίδικα

του Φάνη), serving some explosively flavorful *pastourma* dishes. It's also a full-service restaurant—recommended for lunch or dinner.

Greek delis, Turkish spices, and even a few Asian groceries...it's a reminder that Athens re-

mains, as it always has been, a cultural melting pot.

• *Take a right here (at the deli/restaurant), onto Sokratous street. Head up the street about 100 yards, past more shops and a parking-garage en-*

*trance. Turn right into an open square recently remodeled to house fruit
and vegetable vendors. This is the Central Market's...*

❼ Produce Market

Known as Anoikti Agora (Open Market), this is part of the largest open-air market in Greece. It's a festive scene (even if it's un-

ceremoniously wedged next to a
big parking garage). This strip
explodes with fresh fruits and
veggies—whatever's in season.

You'll also encounter pet
shops, pots and pans, heaps
of nuts and dried fruits, and a
dozen different kinds of olives
and feta sold from the barrel.
And you'll see bushels of le-

gumes—lentils, chickpeas, beans, and so on. Legumes are a staple
of Greek cooking, the traditional source of vegetable protein in a
hardscrabble land. In fact, Greece's national dish is not souvlaki,
Greek salad *(horiatiki),* or baklava, but a bean soup called *fasolada.*
• *At the end of the produce market, you'll reach busy...*

❽ Athinas Street

One of the main thoroughfares of central Athens, this street connects Monastiraki (a 10-minute walk to your right) with the transportation hub called Omonia (10 minutes to the left). Directly
across the street is the yellow, Neoclassical entrance to the covered
part of the Central Market. Before crossing, pause to orient yourself: The facade heralds the covered market built in the 19th century to accommodate the city's growth spurt and to clear out vendors
from archaeological sites. The fish section is in the middle (under
the three open arches), while meat can be found for sale all around.

Halfway through the covered market, dead
ahead on the left, is a row of small restaurants (open long after the bars close since
their tripe soup is considered good medicine
for sobering up). We'll enter, explore, and
leave on the opposite side. But first, I need
a coffee.

A few steps to the left of the market entrance is the recommended **Mokka Coffee
Shop** (at Athinas 44, with a coffee-bean retail outlet next door).

Regarded as one of Athens' best, this
coffee house offers both espresso-style lattes
and macchiatos and more traditional Greek

coffee—an unfiltered preparation that's similar to Turkish coffee (but milder, as the beans are roasted at a lower temperature). This is listed on the menu as "*ibrik* single" or "*ibrik* double"—named for the little copper pitcher they prepare it in. (While *ibrik* is the old Arabic word, modern Greeks call this a *briki*.)

Take a seat (near the cashier and a tray of hot sand) and the waiter will come by. If you order an *ibrik*, tell them how much sugar you want, as that's part of the preparation. First, they put the very fine grounds, cold water, and sugar into the *briki*. Then they nestle the *briki* into the hot sand to heat it. Greeks know a quality coffee by the rich, velvety, light-brown foam that forms at the top.

When your coffee arrives, here's the technique: Pour it from the little pitcher into your cup. Then wait a few minutes to let the grounds settle to the bottom. Then sip it slowly to avoid the highly caffeinated "mud" at the bottom. Greeks claim that because it's unfiltered, more healthy nutrients stay in your brew, compared to filtered coffee.

While you sip, think of the way that simple rituals—like drinking coffee—can become cultural cornerstones. Traditionally the coffee house was where Greek men would gather to gossip and grouse, while clacking their worry beads and playing backgammon. Meanwhile, women would invite each other over for coffee in their homes. Then they'd swirl the leftover grounds around in the cup and read fortunes. Many Greeks worry about the loss of these cultural institutions that were once sacred. Which reminds me of one more bit of etiquette here at Mokka—don't mention Starbucks.

• *Now that you can't sit still, you might as well explore the adjacent...*

❾ Meat and Fish Market

Opened in 1886, the Central Market's meat and fish hall is a vivid parade of proteins. Vegetarians may want to skip this part.

Take a few steps up the main corridor into the gut of the market. Counters are piled high with beef, pork, chicken, lamb, and goat. Notice the livestock proudly pictured on the signs above some of the stalls. Little delivery scooters nudge their way past pedestrians.

About halfway up this main drag (on the right, high up) is the sign for Δημοτική Ψαραγορά (Municipal Fish Market). Turn right up this little lane. On your left is the recommended **Ta Biftekakia Ouzo Bar**—a great spot to sample another Greek specialty, the anise-flavored liquor ouzo.

(It's marked by a big red *A* and the sign *Μπυρα-Ουζο-Τσιπουρο*, advertising the holy triumvirate of cheap Greek booze: beer, ouzo, and grappa-like *tsipouro* brandy.) Kostas sells cheap glasses of ouzo and little plates of bar snacks to enjoy while observing the market bustle.

Just beyond is the **fish market.** Watch your step here—the floors are wet and slippery. Turn left and make your way past the display tables, piled high with big fish (red mullet, sea bream, sea bass), small fish (sardines, anchovies, smelt), fish steaks (mostly from swordfish, tuna, or bonito), mussels, shrimp, Mediterranean lobster (clawless), squid (calamari), the similar cuttlefish, and octopus.

The waters of the Aegean are overfished, and supply struggles to meet demand—especially in the tourist season. Much of the seafood served in Greek restaurants is frozen and imported. If you see *kat* or just a *k* on a menu, it means frozen *(katepsygmenos)*. When Athenians want fresh, they head to tavernas in the seafront suburbs, such as Piraeus (and, farther out, Anavyssos).

At the end of the first stretch of fish, jog right a bit to return to the meat market. In the passage, you'll pass displays showcasing the **"fifth quarter"** of hard-to-sell meat: hooves, tripe, liver, and other organs. You may also see barrels of snails—a cheap source of protein during times of hardship, when locals developed a taste for the little critters that persists today. Venture left past all the guts. Popping out of the market, turn right and right again onto the pedestrian mall, Aiolou street. (Doughnuts are about 30 yards ahead on the right.)

⓫ Aiolou Street

Quieter than the parallel Athinas drag, Aiolou is emerging as one of downtown Athens' most appealing streets. From here, we'll stroll 10 minutes gently downhill to Ermou street and back to Monastiraki where we started.

For a fun treat, stop by **Krinos Greek Donuts** (Κρίνος, at #87), a venerable shop where locals have been indulging their sweet tooth since 1923. Step inside for a plate of *loukoumades*—piping-hot doughnuts, fresh out of the industrial fryer. The English menus at the tables explain your options. The classic: drizzled with syrup, walnuts, and cinnamon. Order at the counter in back to eat in, or at the window on the street to take your doughnuts to go. (A single order is six doughnuts—enough for two. Eating in is better as you can slop up all the sweet sauce.)

Continue down Aiolou street as the Psyrri neighborhood gives way to Monastiraki. This pleasant, pedestrianized street bustles

with interesting stores, designer coffee shops, occasional street musicians, and lots of lunch-focused restaurants for busy urbanites. A block down on the left is the petite, gorgeously restored **Kimisi Theotokou Chrisospileotissis church,** with icon and candle kiosks out front (just before the larger church of Agia Paraskevi). It's free to step into the beautiful, serene interior.

Farther along, on the right, just before the intersection with Vyssis street, you'll pass the **Sgourda** dish-ware company (outfitting Athenian homes since 1870). Continue straight, down the middle lane, through the odd-angled intersection. The next block has some quick-and-cheap lunch spots (see the Eating in Athens chapter).

Farther downhill are more trendy eateries and the little **square of St. Irene**—the epicenter of hip, young locals, day or night (plus the recommended **Kosta** souvlaki stand). The square used to be known as the square of the flower vendors; these days only one remains open, and it's still loyally frequented by Athenians.

• *We're on the final stretch. Hitting Ermou street, you're back in the heart of Athens. Monastiraki Square, where we began our walk, is a block to the right. Cathedral Square is one block past Ermou and a couple of blocks to the left, on Mitropoleos. And the Acropolis is straight up. Enjoy!*

SLEEPING IN ATHENS

Athens' central core (the Plaka, Syntagma, and Monastiraki) includes big, fancy, business-class hotels, but small, inexpensive guesthouses are relatively scarce and overbooked. For more options, expand your search beyond the old center. The lively Psyrri district is worth considering, as it's close to the center, stuffed with enticing food options—from tavernas to a thriving market—and near many major sights. I've also found a few gems in the Makrigianni and Koukaki neighborhoods, behind the Acropolis and a short walk from the Plaka action. These offer a less touristy experience and slightly lower prices.

The accommodations listed here cluster around the €110-150 range but include everything from €40 bunks to deluxe doubles at €350 and up. In general, temper your expectations. Athenian buildings are often cheaply constructed, with well-worn public spaces and temperamental plumbing and elevators. A welcoming front-desk staff can help compensate, but be ready for hiccups. Any hotel charging less than about €100 may include a few quirks. Spending just €20-30 extra is enough to buy you a much higher degree of comfort. If you're even a little high maintenance (be honest), consider splurging here. If you want an Acropolis-view room, you'll usually pay more. Budget travelers: Don't be sucked in by *very* cheap, too-good-to-be-true deals (most of those hotels are in sleazy districts around Omonia Square, or down in the coastal suburbs of Glyfada and Voula).

Athens is a noisy city, and Athenians like to stay out late. This, combined with flimsy hotel construction and heavy traffic on city streets, can make things challenging for light sleepers. I've tried to recommend places in quieter areas, but finding a peaceful corner isn't always possible (be ready to use earplugs).

For some travelers, short-term, Airbnb-type rentals can be a good alternative; search for places in my recommended hotel neighborhoods. You can often find a well-equipped, spacious, centrally located apartment for less than the cost of a midrange hotel room. Given the hit-or-miss quality of Athenian hotels, a carefully chosen apartment can be an excellent value.

I rank accommodations from $ budget to $$$$ splurge. For the best deal, contact smaller hotels directly by phone or email. When you book direct, the owner avoids a commission and may be able to offer a discount. Book well in advance for peak season or if your trip coincides with a major holiday or festival (see the appendix).

For details on reservations, short-term rentals, and more, see the "Sleeping" section in the Practicalities chapter.

HOTELS IN THE CENTER

Sleeping in the central Plaka, Syntagma, and Monastiraki area offers proximity to the sights (you'll rarely need public transportation). It can be more congested and more touristy than outlying neighborhoods, but in general, the pluses of sleeping in this zone outweigh the minuses.

Boutique and Business Class

$$$$ **Central Hotel** has 84 cookie-cutter rooms, sleek public spaces, and an anonymous business-class vibe. The several classes of rooms are priced based on whether they have balconies and/or views. If you stick with the cheaper rooms, it's a good value at the low end of this price range (elevator, swanky rooftop terrace with bar and restaurant, Apollonos 21, +30 210 323 4357, www.centralhotel.gr, reservation@centralhotel.gr).

$$$$ **InnAthens** feels urban and urbane. It sits at the edge of the Plaka—a bit less convenient than the others I list here—with 37 industrial-mod rooms ringing an atrium, and a recommended wine bar on the premises (elevator, Souri 3 at intersection with busy Filellinon, +30 210 325 8555, www.innathens.com, info@innathens.com).

$$$$ **Hotel Plaka,** buried on an urban street in the busy heart of town, has a rooftop bar/restaurant and 67 modern rooms (some with Acropolis views) with updated bathrooms. Its classy management adds some nice touches, such as a staff member on hand at breakfast to answer travel questions (RS%, elevator, at the corner of Mitropoleos and Kapnikarea, reservation +30 210 322

SLEEPING

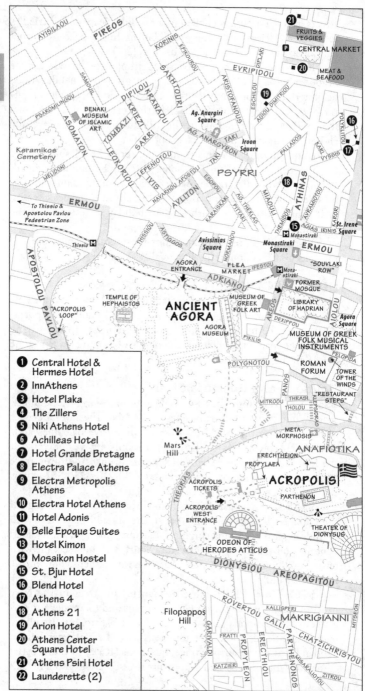

1 Central Hotel & Hermes Hotel

2 InnAthens

3 Hotel Plaka

4 The Zillers

5 Niki Athens Hotel

6 Achilleas Hotel

7 Hotel Grande Bretagne

8 Electra Palace Athens

9 Electra Metropolis Athens

10 Electra Hotel Athens

11 Hotel Adonis

12 Belle Epoque Suites

13 Hotel Kimon

14 Mosaikon Hostel

15 St. Bjur Hotel

16 Blend Hotel

17 Athens 4

18 Athens 21

19 Arion Hotel

20 Athens Center Square Hotel

21 Athens Psiri Hotel

22 Launderette (2)

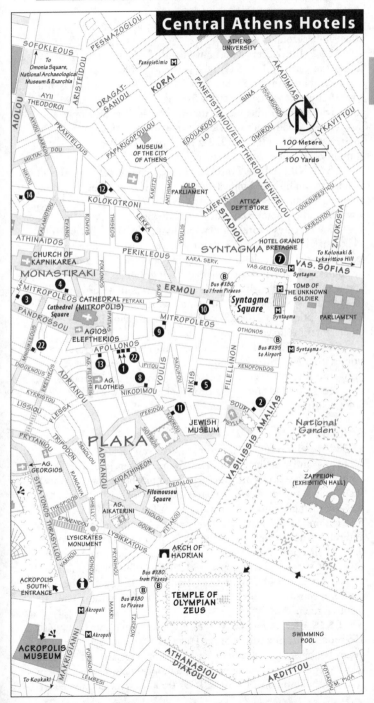

Central Athens Hotels

2706, reception +30 210 322 2096, www.plakahotel.gr, plaka@athenshotelsgroup.com).

$$$$ The Zillers is a conveniently located boutique hotel facing the cathedral. It feels posh—with marble, hardwood, and a classic spiral staircase—but still friendly. Six of the 10 rooms have Acropolis views; streetside rooms are more expensive and come with some traffic and church-bell noise. The rooftop breakfast terrace becomes an excellent, *haute cuisine* restaurant at night (Mitropoleos 54, +30 210 322 2278, www.thezillersathenshotel.com, info@thezillersathenshotel.com).

$$$$ Niki Athens Hotel has a classy, movie-set vibe. The 23 rooms are smallish and industrial-mod in style, and there's a good, attached vegan restaurant (elevator, Nikis 27, +30 210 322 0913, www.nikiathenshotel.com, info@nikihotel.gr).

$$$ Hermes Hotel, professionally run by the folks at Hotel Plaka, has lower rates and a slightly more appealing location on a less-trafficked street closer to Syntagma. Some of its 45 rooms have balconies, and guests share a pleasant lounge, a kids' activity room, and a rooftop patio with a peek at the Acropolis (RS%, possible to add child's cot, elevator, Apollonos 19, reservation +30 210 322 2706, reception +30 210 323 5514, www.hermeshotel.gr, hermes@athenshotelsgroup.com).

$$$ Achilleas Hotel is tranquil considering its central location, with a fern-themed lobby on a relatively quiet street. Straddling the line between business and boutique, its 35 rooms are splashed with bold colors (elevator, Lekka 21, +30 210 323 3197, www.achilleashotel.gr, achilleas@tourhotel.gr).

Splurges

$$$$ Hotel Grande Bretagne, a five-star splurge with 320 sprawling and elegantly furnished rooms, is considered the best hotel in Greece and ranks among the grand hotels of the world. It's *the* place to stay if you have royal blood—or wish you did and feel like being treated like royalty for a few days. Built in 1862 to accommodate visiting heads of state, it became a hotel in 1874 and retains its 19th-century elegance as part of Marriott's top-tier luxury collection (breakfast extra, elevator, overlooking Syntagma Square at Vassileos Georgiou 1, +30 210 333 0000, www.marriott.com, reservations.gb@luxurycollection.com). If you'd rather just eat here, consider their recommended rooftop restaurant, the GB Roof Garden.

$$$$ Electra Palace Athens is a luxury five-star hotel with 155 rooms in a quiet corner of the Plaka, not far from Syntagma. It's pricey but plush, if a bit snooty, with top-notch service and elegance (elevator, garden patio, indoor pool, Acropolis-view outdoor pool in summer, Nikodimou 18, +30 210 337 0000, www.electrahotels.gr, epconcierge@electrahotels.gr). Nearby, the same company operates two similarly equipped hotels: **$$$$ Electra Metropolis Athens**, with 216 rooms in the busy heart of Syntagma near the cathedral (Acropolis-view roof garden, Mitropoleos 15, +30 214 100 6200) and **$$$$ Electra Hotel Athens**, at #5 on the busy pedestrian Ermou street (+30 210 337 8000).

Affordable Downtown Sleeps

$$ Hotel Adonis, in the heart of the Plaka on the quiet, traffic-free upper reaches of Kodrou, is a thoughtfully managed budget option. Most of the 26 rooms are no-frills, though a couple on the fourth floor have good views of the Acropolis, as does the rooftop bar (RS%, includes breakfast on roof terrace—which also opens at night for drinks and snacks, elevator, Kodrou 3, +30 210 324 9737, www.hotel-adonis.gr, info@hotel-adonis.gr, owner Spiros, assisted by Nikos).

$$ Belle Epoque Suites is a minimalist boutique hotel, friendly and funky but with no lobby. The 17 smallish rooms are a bit retro, a bit modern; some have balconies, and there's a rooftop garden and attached café (elevator, Praxitelous 7, +30 210 700 0314, www.belleepoquesuites.com, info@belleepoquesuites.com).

$$ Hotel Kimon rents 15 rooms over a jolly, suitcase-themed lobby. Its location—in the Plaka, near the cathedral—is handy, the atmosphere is artsy, and the price is right (cheaper "economy" rooms are simpler and very affordable, no breakfast, no elevator, top-floor terrace with a corner that looks up at the Acropolis, Apollonos 27, +30 210 331 4658, www.kimonhotelathens.com, info@kimonhotelathens.com).

Hostel: Top-of-the line as hostels go, **$ Mosaikon** has cool and modern bunk rooms, with en suite bathrooms and individual, key-card lockers. This isn't a party place, but the rooftop terrace and attached café are good for hanging out. It also offers nice though pricey **$$$** doubles and lofts (elevator, Kolokotroni 61, +30 210 323 5000, www.mosaikon.gr, info@mosaikon.gr).

IN AND NEAR PSYRRI

This hip area of Athens is a melting pot of in-the-know restaurants, buzzing nightlife, and newer boutique hotels. While most of the hotels have an interchangeable "modern" decor, and you aren't likely to find luxurious balconies or extravagant rooftops with sweeping views, sleeping here puts you in the middle of all the action, steps away from the sights, with contemporary Athens at your doorstep.

Closer to the Center

$$$ St. Bjur is an airy, fresh hotel with 16 decent-sized rooms perched above busy Athinas, half a block from Monastiraki Square. It's a good value for a central location, with its own all-day Brunch Factory restaurant (breakfast extra, elevator, Athinas 11, +30 210 321 5208, www.stbjur.gr, info@stbjur.gr).

$$$ Blend Hotel offers a sleek, contemporary respite in 24 varied rooms and suites and a prime location along the spine of Psyrri's popular Aiolou street (Vyssis 2, +30 210 322 1552, www.blendhotel.gr, askmeanything@blendhotel.gr).

$$$ Athens 4, housed in a design-forward former textile factory, oozes accessible chic, from its 23 uniquely styled rooms to its minimalist facade and public areas (Polyklitou 4, +30 201 322 4524, www.athens4.com, reservations@athens4.com).

$$ Athens 21 has no particular flair, but what it does it does well, namely provide a clean, well-run refuge smack dab amid all the action. The 19 rooms are straightforward and a good value, though may come with some street noise (elevator, breakfast extra, Athinas 21, +30 210 325 0408, www.athens21.gr, info@athens21.gr).

Near the Central Market

The area around the market is typically quiet after dark.

$$$ Arion Hotel is a reliable option with 51 spacious business-style rooms and a roof terrace between Iroon Square and the market. It doesn't have much personality, but it's reasonably polished compared to its scruffy surroundings (elevator, Agiou Dimitriou 18, +30 210 324 0415, www.arionhotel.gr, arion@tourhotel.gr).

$$ Athens Center Square Hotel, part of the Plaka and Hermes Hotel group, is slightly less expensive than its downtown sister properties—mostly because of its location, overlooking the somewhat seedy market square. Its 54 rooms are functional, minimalist, and colorfully painted, and the roof garden has Acropolis views (RS%, elevator, just off Athinas street overlooking the produce market at Aristogitonos 15, reservation +30 210 322 2706, reception +30 210 321 1770, www.athenscentersquarehotel.gr, acs@athenshotelsgroup.com).

$ Athens Psiri Hotel is a good budget choice for this part of town. It's on a busy street and its immediate surroundings aren't so charming, but you're a stone's throw from all that's hip. The 25 rooms are surprisingly spacious for this price range—request a quieter room at the back (elevator, no breakfast, Sofokleus 32, +30 210 523 4329, www.athenspsirihotel.com, info@athenspsirihotel.com).

MAKRIGIANNI AND KOUKAKI, BEHIND THE ACROPOLIS

With the Acropolis Museum standing boldly as their gateway, the adjoining residential areas of Makrigianni and Koukaki, just south of the Acropolis, feel typically Athenian urban. (Some locals call Makrigianni the "south Plaka.") Full of six-story concrete apartment buildings, hole-in-the-wall grocery stores, and corner cafés, these neighborhoods let you feel like a temporary Athenian while still providing relatively easy access to major sights. Most can be reached by a longish walk—figure 5-10 minutes to the edge of the Plaka (which involves passing a gauntlet of aggressively touristy eateries near the Acropolis Museum), then another 10 minutes to Monastiraki. These hotels are all located between the Akropoli and Syngrou-Fix Metro stops. Be aware that to reach most points of interest from these stops, you'll change Metro lines at Syntagma.

$$$$ Hotel Hera is a tempting splurge, with 38 plush rooms above a classy lobby. With helpful service, lots of thoughtful little touches, an air of elegance, and a handy location near the Acropolis end of this neighborhood, it's a fine value (elevator, rooftop Acropolis-view restaurant, Falirou 9, +30 210 923 6682, www.herahotel.gr, info@herahotel.gr).

$$$ Acropolis View doesn't look like much from the outside and the lobby is stuck in the 1980s, but the selling point is in the name: many of the 32 rooms have nice views over green Filopappos Hill or the city. Breakfast is served on the roof terrace, gazing toward the Parthenon (elevator, Webster 10, +30 210 921 7303, www.acropolisviewhotel.gr, av_hotel@otenet.gr).

$$ Acropolis Stay has a generic name but a personal touch. This is a little collection of apartments, attentively managed by Vasilis and team. The 10 comfy rooms vary in size, but all are efficiently designed and come with kitchenettes (breakfast extra, Spirou Donta 3, +30 210 921 0222, www.acropolistay.gr, info@acropolistay.gr).

$ Marble House Pension is a small, family-run place hiding at the end of a little cul-de-sac, a few minutes' walk past my other listings in this area. The 16 cozy rooms—most with small balconies—are simple but well cared for, and (true to its name) it's deco-

SLEEPING

Makrigianni & Koukaki Hotels & Restaurants

Accommodations
1. Hotel Hera
2. Acropolis View
3. Acropolis Stay
4. Marble House Pension
5. Athens Backpackers Hostel

Eateries
6. Strofi Athenian Restaurant
7. Mani Mani
8. Balcony Restaurant & Launderette
9. Acropolis Museum Restaurant
10. To Kati Allo Restaurant
11. Souvlaki Stand

rated with real marble. If you don't mind the more remote location, it's an excellent deal (cheaper rooms with shared bath, reserve with credit card but pay in cash, breakfast extra, air-con extra, 3 floors with no elevator, closed Dec-Feb; 5-minute walk from Syngrou-Fix Metro at Zinni 35a—from Zinni street take the alley to the left of the tidy Catholic church, +30 210 923 4058, www.marblehouse.gr, info@marblehouse.gr; Christos with mom Nancy and retired-but-present dad Thanos). They also rent a beautifully appointed modern apartment next door.

Hostel: The best place in town for backpacker bonding, ¢ **Athens Backpackers** is youthful and fun-loving with two bars, including one on the rooftop. Well-run by gregarious Aussies, it offers good bunks, laundry, and an opportunity to meet up with other travelers (Makri 12, +30 210 922 4044, www.backpackers.gr, info@backpackers.gr).

EATING IN ATHENS

Greek food is just plain good. And Athens, the melting pot of Greece (and the Balkans), is one of the best places to experience the cuisine, thanks to a stunning variety of tasty and affordable eateries.

I've listed these restaurants by neighborhood. You probably won't be able to resist dining in the touristy Plaka at least once—it's fun, folkloric, and full of clichés (beware the tourist traps). But don't be afraid to venture elsewhere. For a trendy and youthful local scene, target Psyrri—just beyond the tourist zone. For those staying near the Acropolis Museum in Makrigianni or Koukaki, I've listed a couple of convenient options (including my two favorite elegant restaurants in all of Athens).

I rank eateries from **$** budget to **$$$$** splurge. For more advice on eating in Greece, including ordering, tipping, and Greek cuisine and beverages, see the "Eating" section of the Practicalities chapter.

EATING TIPS

Restaurants: Locals and tourists alike fill tavernas, *mezedopolios* (eateries selling small *meze*—Greek tapas), *ouzeries* (bars selling ouzo liquor and pub grub), and other traditional eateries dishing up the basics. Greeks like to eat late—around 21:00 or later. Restaurants in Athens tend to stay open until midnight or even past that.

Smoking: Though smoking is not allowed in indoor spaces, don't be surprised to find that some restaurants and bars don't enforce the law.

Budget Snacks: To save money and time, try one of Greece's street-food specialties. Options include souvlaki (meat-on-a-skewer meal), savory pie (filled with meat, cheese, or vegetables), *koulouri* (bread rings), *loukoumades* (Greek doughnuts), and more.

Food Tours: To learn about local eating traditions and sample lots of Greek cuisine, join a food tour; for recommendations, see the sidebar later in this chapter.

📖 For a do-it-yourself approach, see the Psyrri and Central Market Walk chapter and follow my self-guided walk through the Psyrri neighborhood, which hits several eating spots and leads you through the Central Market action.

TOURISTY MEALS IN THE PLAKA

Diners—Greeks and tourists alike—flock to the Plaka. In this neighborhood, the ambience is better than the food. I've avoided the obvious, touristy joints on the main pedestrian drag—with shards of broken plates in the cobbles and obnoxious touts out front luring diners with a desperate spiel—in favor of more authentic-feeling eateries huddled on the quieter hillside just above. Eat at one of my recommendations, or simply choose  the place that appeals to you with live music, a pleasant square, or a great view of an ancient monument. Prices are pretty consistent and painless, and the quality is acceptable.

At the top of the Plaka, stepped lanes are lined with eateries featuring interchangeable food, delightful outdoor seating, and noisy tourists. Many of these places have live music and/or rooftop gardens.

$$ Scholarhio Ouzeri Kouklis, at the intersection of Tripodon and Epicharmou streets, serves only small plates. While jammed with tourists, it's fun, inexpensive, and ideal for small groups wanting to try a variety of traditional *meze* (local tapas) and drink good, homemade booze on an airy perch at the top of the Plaka. Since 1935, the Kouklis family has been making ouzo liquor and feeding people here—maintaining that 1930s atmosphere. Drinks are cheap, and the stress-free €17 meal deals (including dessert and a drink) are worth considering. Many wait for a spot to open up on the lively front terrace, but you can instead climb to the upstairs dining room with its romantic balconies for two (daily 11:30-24:00, Tripodon 14, +30 210 324 7605, www.scholarhio.gr).

EATING

If the scene here is a bit too intense or touristic, the neighboring **To Kafeneio** (immediately across the lane and downhill at Epicharmou 1) also offers a fun and characteristic variety of *meze* plates.

$$$ Xenios Zeus (Ξένιος Ζευς) sits proudly at the top of the Mnisikleous steps, offering traditional, home-cooked Greek food inside or out on a terrace overlooking Athens' rooftops. Greeks actually eat here (daily 10:30-24:00, closed Nov-March, Mnisikleous 37, +30 210 324 9514, www.xenioszeus.com.gr). They promise a free bottle of ouzo to diners with this book (be sure to ask).

$$ Klepsidra Café is parked on a picturesque corner high in the Plaka (a block directly above the Roman Agora) with an authentic "old Plaka" ambience, tiny tables littering the ramshackle steps, and a somewhat younger and more local crowd. Friendly George and his team serve light bites—a few traditional dishes, savory pies, *meze,* and salads, plus good desserts, traditional coffee, and booze (daily 9:00-24:00, Thrasivoulou 9, +30 210 321 2493).

$$$ Palia Taverna tou Psara (Old Fisherman's Tavern) is a big, slick, impersonal, pricey eatery. It's the kind of place where a rowdy, rollicking group of a hundred can slam down a dish-'em-up Greek meal. While often dominated by tour groups, it can be enjoyable. There's live folk music on weekends (daily 12:00-24:00, Eretheos 16, +30 210 321 8734, www.psaras-taverna.gr).

$$ Vryssaki Art Café is a delightful 19th-century home on the corner of a quiet lane on the back side of the Agora (a long block before the Roman Forum entrance). Their cozy courtyard offers an inviting refuge from the crowds or you can enjoy drinks and light bites on the balcony (wraps, toasts, sandwiches; daily 10:00-24:00, Vrysakiou 17, +30 210 321 0179, www.vryssaki.gr).

NEAR SYNTAGMA SQUARE

These options are in the gritty urban streets near Syntagma Square and the Plaka—an area that's more residential and pleasantly less touristic.

$$$$ Aneton, with an esteemed chef, serves beautifully presented modern Greek cuisine in an intimate and romantic setting. It's dressy but not pretentious (the name means "comfortable") with

EATING

1 Scholarhio Ouzeri Kouklis
2 To Kafeneio
3 Xenios Zeus
4 Klepsidra Café
5 Palia Taverna tou Psara
6 Vryssaki Art Café
7 "Souvlaki Row":
   Bairaktaris Restaurant
   & Taverna Thanasis
8 Aneton
9 2Mazi Restaurant
   Wine Bar
10 Athinaikon Restaurant
11 Tzitzikas Kai Mermigas
12 Avocado Vegetarian Café
13 Kimolia Art Café
14 Black Duck Garden
15 GB Roof Garden Restaurant
16 Oineas Restaurant
17 O Nikitas
18 Avli
19 Ta Karamanlidika tou Fani
20 Diporto
21 Athanaton Stoa Eateries
22 Ta Biftekakia Ouzo Bar
23 Epirus Tavern
24 Tylixto
25 Kosta Souvlaki
26 Feyrouz
27 Falafellas
28 Krinos Greek Doughnuts
29 To Thissio Eateries
30 Mikel Coffee

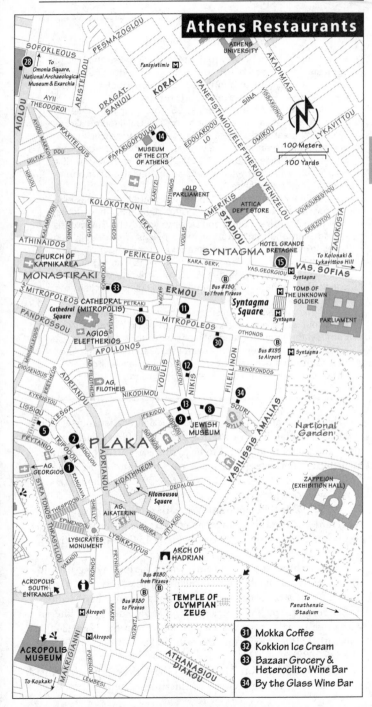

EATING

Athens Restaurants

31 Mokka Coffee

32 Kokkion Ice Cream

33 Bazaar Grocery & Heteroclito Wine Bar

34 By the Glass Wine Bar

Food Tours

Food tours are a great way to get to know Greeks, who love to cook and love to eat. With a tour, you'll learn a lot about Greek history and culture through food, plus you'll get to sample classic dishes. Here are a few good choices:

Alternative Athens offers a 3.5-hour tour that includes a Greek coffee, a walk through the Central Market, Greek sweets, a meat-and-cheese shop, a specialty grocery store, and a chance to sample some typical *meze* (€60/person, Mon-Sat at 10:00, none on Sun, +30 211 012 6544, mobile +30 694 840 5242, www.alternativeathens.com; they also offer home-cooked meal experiences).

Culinary Backstreets' longer tours are for people who are passionate about food. They offer several 5.5-hour tours, including Backstreet Plaka and Downtown Athens. The groups are smaller, and you'll stop at more places (from family-run holes-in-the-wall to trendier eateries), linger longer at stops, and eat more unique food—a lot more of it. You won't want to eat for the rest of the day ($135/person; tour times vary—check their schedule, 2-7 people, www.culinarybackstreets.com).

Many more small businesses and guides run creative food-tour experiences—search online. For example, EatWith.com is a thriving international website for food tours. Browse for offerings in Athens with several stops to munch and learn before sitting down to a characteristic taverna meal (generally about €50/person, up to 10 people per group).

---

six tables inside and six out. With a selection of first courses that make for a fun family-style sharing meal, great Greek wines by the glass, and a staff that is eager to help, this is a worthwhile splurge. Their bitter chocolate ganache can send two into orbit (Mon-Sat 12:00-24:00, closed Sun, +30 210 806 6700, Navarchou Nikodimou 3, www.aneton.gr).

$$$$ 2Mazi Restaurant Wine Bar fills a tranquil, leafy courtyard—which I prefer over their forgettable inside tables—and serves quality modern Greek dishes (daily 13:00-24:00, Nikis 48, +30 210 322 2839, www.2mazi.gr).

$$$ Athinaikon Restaurant, with a heritage going back to the 1930s, is a venerable businessman's favorite, serving a variety of traditional *meze* plates and Greek, Italian, and other Mediterranean recipes. You'll dine in a no-nonsense art-deco/mod interior with professional service and a local crowd (Mon-Sat 12:00-24:00, Sun until 22:00, a block from the cathedral at Mitropoleos 34, +30 210 325 2688).

$$$ Tzitzikas Kai Mermigas (The Cricket and the Ant) serves modern, regional Greek cuisine from a fun and accessible

menu. Choose between indoor seating surrounded by vintage grocery ads, or grab a sidewalk table in a bustling urban zone (daily
12:30-24:00, Mitropoleos 12, +30 210 324 7607).

$$$ Avocado Vegetarian Café (at the 4 Seasons Organic
Food Market) is a good bet if you need an eatery with a passion
for organic farming and nothing with eyeballs. The menu includes
pastas, pizzas, veggie burgers, and sandwiches, as well as lots of
energy juices (Mon-Sat 12:00-22:00, Sun until 17:00, Nikis 30,
+30 210 323 7878).

$$ Kimolia (Κιμωλία) **Art Café** is a cute little pastel place at
the edge of the Plaka. Katerina and Nikos have only a small menu
of fresh sandwiches and drinks. But the relaxing vibe, friendly service, and piano in the back make it a nice place to take a break
(daily 10:00-24:00, Iperidou 5, +30 211 184 8446).

$$$$ Black Duck Garden—a cozy urban oasis tucked into
the courtyard of the Museum of the City of Athens—is a mansion
with a tranquil courtyard and garden to slip away from the tourist
crowd. The short, Mediterranean-focused menu is all about quality.
At night, the garden is lit with candles and hanging lanterns for a
casual yet romantic feel. It's popular with the local art community
(daily 10:00-24:00, may be closed in winter, Ioannou Paparigopoulou 5, +30 210 325 2396).

$$$$ (and up) GB Roof Garden Restaurant at the Hotel
Grande Bretagne is posh as can be. It's pure fancy-hotel-restaurant
elegance—in a rooftop garden with spectacular Acropolis views
that stretch all the way to the sea. To splurge on fine Greek and
Mediterranean cuisine with a rooftop view, this is a good choice
(daily 13:00-24:00, reservations required for dinner, smart casual
dress code after 18:00, on Syntagma Square, +30 210 333 0766,
www.gbroofgarden.gr). For upscale bar food or a pricey beer or
cocktail with a view, drop by their swanky lounge.

"SOUVLAKI ROW" NEAR MONASTIRAKI

The junction of Monastiraki Square and Mitropoleos street is souvlaki heaven.

$$ Bairaktaris Restaurant (Μπαϊρακταρησ), facing the big
Monastiraki Square, dominates the scene with food to go or to sit
down and dine. For a souvlaki pita sandwich (or wrap) to go, just
pay at the outdoor cashier, take your receipt to the window, and
within moments you'll have a €3 lunch to enjoy (you'll see public
benches on the square). To eat at the restaurant, grab an outdoor
spot facing the square, on the pedestrian street, or inside the char-
acteristic, fun-loving dining hall. The sit-down menu (with big-
ger portions and higher prices) features shaved gyro meats, kebabs,
hearty Greek salads, and a few other standard Greek dishes plus
wine, beer, and ouzo (open daily until very late, live music daily,

EATING

Souvlaki: A Quick and Cheap Meal

My favorite fast-food meal in Greece is souvlaki (the Greek equivalent to our hot dog). It's quick, cheap, filling, and oh so Greek. The terminology can be tricky:

Souvlaki is usually pork or chicken grilled on a little skewer (as its name means). When you get it to go, the meat is wrapped in a wonderful greasy pita pocket with lettuce, tomato, onions, and *tzatziki* (cucumber-yogurt-garlic sauce), then tucked into a paper cone. If you like yours spicy, grab the shaker and sprinkle on some red pepper (or ask the vendor to season it for you). A souvlaki is often bulked up with doughy French fries (which you can decline).

The **gyro** *(yee-roh)* is a virtually identical type of sandwich made from a hunk of meat cooked on a spinning vertical rotisserie (also called a gyro, meaning "turn"). The meat—usually pork, chicken, lamb, or a combination—is shaved into a steamy, tasty pile and then wrapped in a pita with the usual accompaniments.

The **kebab**—your third "meat on a spindle" option—is also sold at many souvlaki stands. This is basically a long, skinny, uncased sausage made of minced meat, pierced by a souvlaki spindle, and grilled. It's served the same way as a souvlaki or a gyro: wrapped in pita with tomatoes, onions, and *tzatziki.*

Souvlaki Tips: Even with the rise of international fast-food places, the traditional **souvlaki stand** seems as ubiquitous as ever. A souvlaki stand typically sells several variations on the theme: a big portion on a plate, or a smaller portion wrapped in a pita.

In touristy **restaurants,** the challenge can be to get a cheap sandwich or wrap rather than a €12 souvlaki plate. A souvlaki plate is a huge meal, but you can also make a full meal with a single souvlaki, gyro, or kebab and a shared Greek salad. Whether you get it to go or to dine in, a wrap should cost about €3.

Mitropoleos 71). The souvlaki plate (around €10) can feed two or even three. They don't say so on the menu, but they serve half portions of this plate for half-price if you ask.

$$ Taverna Thanasis, filling the smaller, charming square behind Bairaktaris, is huge and more of a local favorite. Greek meat-lovers come here for their special kebab. Unlike Bairaktaris, they serve cheap souvlaki wraps at your table (long hours daily, +30 21 0324 4705, Mitropoleos 69).

PSYRRI AND THE CENTRAL MARKET

The mix of trendy and crusty gives this fun area just north of Monastiraki a unique charm. While I've listed a few restaurants to consider, the scene is ever-changing with countless creative little eateries and a different vibe each night—you might just wander and see what feels best. For more on this area, see the Psyrri and Central Market Walk chapter.

Iroon Square

Iroon Square is the lively hub of Psyrii action—just right for a touristy, folksy Greek dining experience in a jumble of places eager to take your money. Each of the square's surrounding streets has a unique and ever-evolving character with memorable places to eat.

$$$ Oineas Restaurant is understated and popular with locals for its tasty classic Greek dishes (Mon-Fri 16:00-24:00, Sat-Sun from 13:00, two blocks from Iroon Square at Aisopou 9, +30 210 321 5614).

$$ O Nikitas (Ο Νικήτας), just a block from the tourist kitsch, sits on a peaceful square, serving mainly *meze* plates and good food to a local crowd (daily 12:00-19:00, Thu-Sat until 22:00 in season, across from a cute church at Agion Anargyron 19, +30 210 325 2591). Their *bifteki* (fancy hamburger patty) is a fave.

$$ Avli (Αυλή; Courtyard) is for the adventurous. Step through its speakeasy door into a long, skinny, and thriving courtyard with a thicket of tiny tables, the clack of worry beads, and Greeks wondering, "How did that tourist find this place?" They have a simple menu with small plates perfect for ordering family-style and sharing. If you leave the table, a cat may take your seat. This is a good spot to try the old pine-flavored *retsina* wine (Wed-Mon 12:00-24:00, closed Tue, Agiou Dimitriou 12—look for the small doorway labeled *αυλή*, no reservations).

On Sokratous Street, near the Produce Market

These are great finds for adventurous diners, or those looking to do as the Athenians do.

$$$ Ta Karamanlidika tou Fani (Τα Καραμανλίδικα Του Φάνη), my favorite in this area for a serious meal, offers a nice change of pace from the typical Psyrri tavernas. It's a quality meat-and-cheese shop that doubles as a restaurant. With its mix of authentic Anatolian flavors, aged cheese, and cured meats, it's a tasty reminder that many Greek Turks settled here in Athens in the 1920s—bringing their cuisine with them. Several dishes include *pastourma*—meat coated in delicious herbs and spices, similar to pastrami. Friendly Maria and her gang offer a fun and enticing menu with a variety of tasty small plates and a popular meat-and-cheese taster plate with *tsipouro* (grappa-like brandy). The dining area is bigger than it looks (Mon-Sat 12:00-23:00, closed Sun, Sokratous 1, reservations smart, +30 210 325 4184, www.karamanlidika.gr).

$$ Diporto, in business since 1887, feels like a time warp. Difficult to find and true to its name, it has two doors (both painted a drab brown) leading down almost dangerously into its unfinished-cellar space lined with wooden casks of wine. They have just a few dishes—all simmering in pots on the rustic stove. Service and ambience are basically nonexistent in this dive, but local old-timers—who crowd around a few rickety, shared tables—appreciate the cooking (no English spoken...or needed; Mon-Sat 8:00-19:00, closed Sun; Sokratous 9—across from the parking-garage entrance at the produce market, +30 210 321 1463).

In the Central Market

Athanaton Stoa, a tiny lane within the covered Central Market (on the side farthest from the Acropolis) has a string of enticing little **$$** restaurants that are comfy and characteristic amidst all the bloody chaos. (I enjoyed Taverna Aris.) These places stay open until after the bars close, as they're a favorite with drunks ready to sober up. Other market options include:

$ Ta Biftekakia Ouzo Bar, in the thick of the market and run by helpful Kostas, is great for a drink and snack. Pay about €3-4 for an ouzo and little *meze* plate to enjoy while you observe the action (on a side aisle, midway down the Central Market fish section; Mon-Sat 8:00-16:00—sometimes later, closed Sun). It's easy to miss—look for the big *A* sign or the sign advertising Μπυρα-Ουζο-Τσιπουρο—beer, ouzo, *tsipouro*.

$$ Epirus Tavern (Οινομαγειρείο Η Ήπειρος) is the place for a lowbrow, stick-to-your-ribs meal. This place (quiet and spacious even though it's in the market) is known for its meat soups, particularly those made with tripe. Survey what's cooking at the counter and point (Mon-Sat 6:00-19:30, closed Sun; from the grand entry, it's in the far-right corner at Filopimenos 4, +30 210 324 0773).

On Aiolou Street

The pedestrianized lane called Aiolou, which runs north from near

Monastiraki to the Central Market, is a virtual food circus of fast and affordable options, all **$**. Here are a few to consider, listed in the order you'd reach them walking north to the market:

Tylixto, at Aiolou 19C, is a hit for anything tucked in a pita (the restaurant's name means "wrapped"). With small tables right in the flow of the pedestrians, you'll munch a cheap meal amid a people parade.

Kosta Souvlaki (ΚΩΣΤΑ), about a block north of Ermou (opposite Aiolou 29 on a sweet square facing the Church of St. Irene)

is a local favorite that's been serving up good souvlaki pitas since the 1940s. This is a classic place: no gyro slices or kebabs...just traditional skewer-roasted souvlaki wraps. You can get yours to go or grab a rustic little table on the square (Mon-Sat 9:00-18:00, closed Sun).

Feyrouz, across from Aiolou 50 and 20 steps down the lane, is a sweet and gentle little family-run spot where earnest and English-speaking Savvas serves gracefully spicy Turkish/Syrian/ Greek street food (like pizzas) with paper plates and simple tables inside and out. It's best for lunch or a light dinner (Mon-Sat 12:00-22:00, closed Sun, +30 213 031 8060). For dessert, don't miss the baklava-type Levantine treats sold by the family's sister in a place just across the lane.

Falafellas, at Aiolou 51, is a popular hole-in-the-wall spot selling falafel sandwiches to locals who recognize the quality (and need nowhere to sit).

Krinos Greek Doughnuts (Κρίνος), just outside the market at Aiolou 87, is famed for its *loukoumades*—fried Greek doughnuts. Get them to go or enjoy inside at a once-venerable meeting place. You'll pay a few euros for a sharable portion of six doughnuts in a small box (to go, buy at window facing the street) or on a plate (inside, buy at counter in the back). They're most enjoyable seated so you can cut them to bits and smash them into the classic honey, walnuts, and cinnamon syrup (as locals remember doing with their grandparents here) along with a nice coffee or tea (Mon-Sat 9:00-19:30, closed Sun, +30 210 321 6852).

THISSIO

This pleasant neighborhood just west of the center is easy to reach from downtown and significantly quieter—plus it comes with ogle-worthy views of the Acropolis. It's good for an evening stroll (see the Nightlife in Athens chapter) or a bite to eat. Browse along the

Apostolou Pavlou strip and find the combination of menu and view that most appeals. Or look deeper in the neighborhood for these two places, where you trade better food for no panorama.

$$$ Merceri, at the less touristy end of the Iraklidon promenade, boasts a vaguely Art Deco dining room and accolades for chefs Melina and Maria. The menu is short, varied, and carnivorous, combining Greek flavors with international influences such as salmon sushi served with cheese from the island of Naxos (Wed-Mon 12:00-24:00, closed Tue, Iraklidon 21, +30 210 341 7511).

$$ To Kousoulo (ΤΟ ΚΟΥΣΟΥΛΟ) offers no culinary discoveries, but they do the Greek standards well, portions are generous, and the streetside terrace is inviting (daily 9:00-24:00, corner of Amfiktionos and Iraklidon, +30 211 412 2239).

MAKRIGIANNI AND KOUKAKI

The area around the Acropolis Museum—where this neighborhood meets the Plaka—is home to a trendy and touristy row of restaurants, cafés, and ice-cream shops along pedestrian Makrigianni street. While there are countless hardworking and appealing eateries along these streets, the following restaurants are worth serious consideration. For locations, see the map on page 188.

$$$$ Strofi Athenian Restaurant is my choice in Athens for white-tablecloth, elegantly modern, rooftop-Acropolis-view dining. Niko Bletsos and his staff offer attentive service, gorgeously presented plates, and classic Greek cuisine—especially lamb. And though they have a fine air-conditioned interior, the rooftop is comfortable regardless of how hot or cool the evening. For a flood-lit Acropolis view, you'll be glad you made reservations (Tue-Sun 12:00-24:00, closed Mon, about 100 yards down Propyleon street off Dionysiou Areopagitou at Rovertou Galli 25, +30 210 921 4130, www.strofi.gr).

$$$ Mani Mani (Μάνη Μάνη) offers a touch of class for reasonable prices, with cuisine and ingredients from the Mani Peninsula. The dining is indoors only, and the food, like the decor, is thoughtfully updated. As this is justifiably popular, reservations are smart (daily 14:00-23:00 in summer, shorter hours off-season, go upstairs at Falirou 10, +30 210 921 8180, www.manimani.com.gr).

$$$ Balcony Restaurant is upscale but unpretentious in the heart of the neighborhood. With a forgettable dining room and a homey terrace high above the traffic, they serve creative and modern Greek/Mediterranean cuisine accompanied by a good wine list (Mon-Fri 16:30-24:00, Sat-Sun from 13:00, Veikou 1, +30 211 411 8437).

The **$$$ Acropolis Museum Restaurant** is sleek and modern with dressy tables (inside and out), an amazing Acropolis view terrace, and a good lunch and dinner menu. No museum ticket is required: Simply enter the museum, pick up a free restaurant ticket, and catch the elevator before the turnstile. Special dinners are served on Friday and Saturday until midnight (service can be slow—perhaps that's why breakfast is served until noon; open same hours as museum: Mon 9:00-16:00, Tue-Thu and Sat-Sun until 20:00, Fri until 22:00; shorter hours Nov-March; +30 210 900 0915).

$$ To Kati Allo Restaurant (Το Κάτι Άλλο Ψησταριά), immediately under the far side of the Acropolis Museum, is the quintessential neighborhood hole-in-the-wall. It's old-fashioned and a bit forlorn, yet strangely appealing and reasonably priced amid all the trendy, Starbucky places on the nearby boulevard. Run by English-speaking Kostas, it offers both sidewalk seating and inside tables with air-conditioned comfort. The blackboard menu features a short list of choices, but I'd go straight to the counter displaying what's on for the day and explore your options directly with Kostas (daily 11:00-24:00, off Makrigianni street at Chatzichristou 12, +30 210 922 3071).

$ Souvlaki at the Akropoli Metro station is an efficient and busy joint cranking out souvlaki, gyros, and salads with a few simple tables on the plaza just steps away from the entrance to the Akropoli Metro stop. Service is speedy, the menu is very clear, the wraps are cheap and filling, and the people-watching is entertaining (daily 11:00-24:00, across the street from the Acropolis Museum, Athanasiou Diakou 1).

COFFEE, ICE CREAM, AND WINE BARS
Chilled Treats and a Rare Central Grocery Store

Cold Coffee With a Straw? Greeks love their coffee cold. You have options: A Greek *frappé* is instant coffee (Nescafe) and water mixed with evaporated milk and sugar to taste, poured over ice, and served with a straw. A *freddo* is a double shot (usually) of espresso blended with ice. Without milk it's a *freddo espresso*. With milk it's a *freddo cappuccino* and comes with a creamy foam top.

For good local coffee for half the price of Starbucks, you'll find handy branches of the local chains **Gregory's** (Γρηγόρης), **Everest,** and **Coffee Island** all over town. They have all the typical coffee drinks you'd find at home, plus cold coffee drinks like *frappé* and *freddo*, which locals love to drink in summer. The **Mikel Coffee** chain is a bit pricier and posher (one handy location is near Syntagma Square at Mitropoleos 3). For the location of Mikel and the next three listings, see the "Athens Restaurants" map earlier in this chapter.

For Greek coffee made the traditional way (heated in a tray of hot sand), visit **Mokka,** at the entrance to the Central Market (daily 7:30-15:30, Athinas 44, +30 210 321 6892; see page 176 for a full description).

Kokkion Ice Cream serves up decadent, mouth-watering flavors of gourmet ice cream and sorbet made with fresh, local ingredients and a nod to traditional Greek tastes (daily 8:00-24:00, just north of Monastiraki Square at Protogenous 2).

Bazaar Grocery Store, just behind the cathedral (and next to recommended Heteroclito wine bar—see the next section) is a convenient little supermarket with premade sandwiches in the back (Mon-Sat 8:00-21:00, closed Sun, Petraki 30).

Wine Bars (with Light Bites)

These places focus on wine and small plates to go with it. For locations, see the "Athens Restaurants" map earlier in this chapter.

By the Glass wine bar is a relaxed, jazz-cool place where you can enjoy a bar stool—or find a quiet table inside or out on a breezy arcade—and learn from the server about Greek wines. Their menu includes countless wines by the glass plus plates of mixed Greek cheeses and meats, salads, and other upscale nibbles (daily 13:00-24:00, between the Plaka and National Garden at Souri 3, inside the InnAthens hotel, +30 210 323 2560). In summer their

tables spill into the shady square across the street.

Heteroclito is a sophisticated-but-unpretentious, urban-feeling wine bar buried in the tight streets near Syntagma Square. They serve carefully curated Greek wines by the glass, along with a short list of accompanying finger food. Inside and upstairs is comfy, and outside is great for people-watching (Mon-Sat 12:30-24:00, Sun from 18:00, Fokionos 2 at corner with Petraki—facing the back of the cathedral, +30 201 323 9406).

SHOPPING IN ATHENS

Most shops catering to tourists are open long hours daily (souvenir stores in the Plaka can be open past midnight). Those serving locals are open roughly 9:00 to 20:00 on weekdays, have shorter hours on Saturday, and are closed on Sunday. Afternoon breaks are common, and some places close early a few nights a week.

For details on getting a VAT (Value-Added Tax) refund on your purchases, see the Practicalities chapter.

WHERE TO SHOP
Popular Shopping Streets

The main streets of the Plaka—especially **Adrianou** and **Pandrossou**—are crammed with crass tourist-trap shops selling cheap plaster replicas of ancient artifacts, along with calendars, magnets, playing cards, postcards, and profane T-shirts. Competition is fierce, so there's room to bargain, especially if you're buying several items. If you're determined to shop here, look for typical Grecian clothing (white cotton dresses and flowing blouses), sandals, or cosmetics (olive-based soaps, lotions, and beauty products). While still touristy, these products are at least more authentic than kitschy trinkets. For a list of more tasteful shops nearby, see "Higher-End Souvenirs," later.

For midrange shopping at mostly international chain stores, stroll the pedestrianized **Ermou street** between Syntagma Square and Monastiraki. You'll find more local flavor at Greek shops such as **Kem** (handbags; Kornarou 1, just off Ermou), **Heroes** (unique Greek-themed jewelry and accessories, handmade by Athens native Eugenia Kokkala-Mela; Aiolou 9, just off Ermou), and the clothing stores **Regalinas** (Ermou 37) and **Bill Cost** (Ermou 14).

While tourists and big-money Athenians strut their stuff on

SHOPPING

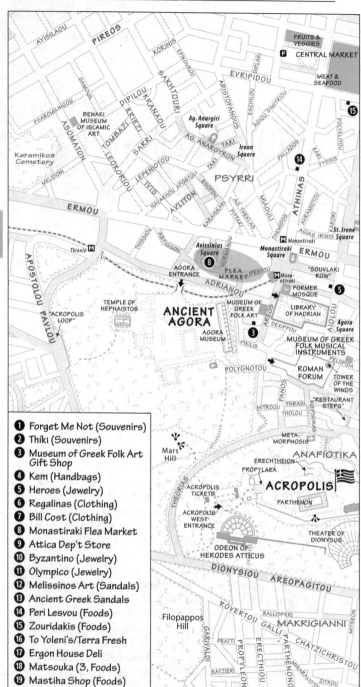

1 Forget Me Not (Souvenirs)
2 Thíki (Souvenirs)
3 Museum of Greek Folk Art Gift Shop
4 Kem (Handbags)
5 Heroes (Jewelry)
6 Regalinas (Clothing)
7 Bill Cost (Clothing)
8 Monastiraki Flea Market
9 Attica Dep't Store
10 Byzantino (Jewelry)
11 Olympico (Jewelry)
12 Melissinos Art (Sandals)
13 Ancient Greek Sandals
14 Peri Lesvou (Foods)
15 Zouridakis (Foods)
16 To Yoleni's/Terra Fresh
17 Ergon House Deli
18 Matsouka (3, Foods)
19 Mastiha Shop (Foods)

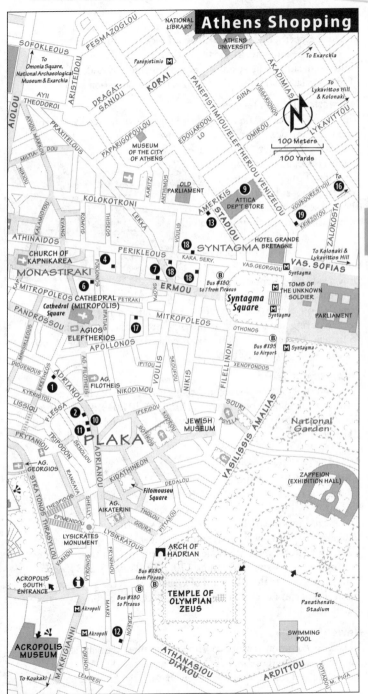

SHOPPING

Ermou, many locals prefer the more authentic shops on the streets just to the north, such as **Perikleous, Lekka,** and **Kolokotroni.**

For top-end international boutiques (like Prada and Louis Vuitton), head for the swanky **Kolonaki** neighborhood, just north of Syntagma Square—particularly posh Voukourestiou street.

Monastiraki Flea Market

This famous flea market stretches west of Monastiraki Square, along Ifestou street and its side streets. It's a fun place for tourists and pickpockets to browse but isn't ideal for buying quality gifts. You'll see plenty of souvenir shops, but the heart of the market is Avissinias Square, filled with antique shops selling furniture, household items, jewelry, dusty books, knickknacks, and stuff that might raise eyebrows at the airport. There's

something going on every day, but the market is best and most crowded on Sundays, when store owners lay out the stuff they've been scouting for all week. If buying here, make sure to bargain (Sun flea market open 8:00-15:00, packed with locals by 10:00, Metro: Monastiraki or Thissio).

Department Store

The largest department store in Athens is **Attica,** which has a cafeteria on the top floor but no views (Mon-Fri 10:00-21:00, Sat until 20:00, closed Sun, near Syntagma Square at Panepistimiou 9, +30 211 990 0000).

WHAT TO BUY

Higher-End Souvenirs

Check out these shops for a thoughtfully curated selection of artsy souvenirs. **Forget Me Not** sells ceramics, housewares, fun T-shirts, and locally produced clothing and beachwear (Adrianou 100, +30 210 325 3740, www.forgetmenotathens.gr). **Thíki** has totes, T-shirts, pillowcases, and stationery featuring famous Greek quotes and evil-eye designs (Adrianou 120, +30 210 323 5234, www.thikigreece.com). The **Museum of Greek Folk Art**'s gift shop also offers a range of tasteful items inspired by their museum collection (Adrianou 45).

Jewelry

The most common jewelry motifs are the olive branch, seashells, and the Greek evil eye *(mati)*. Serious buyers say that Athens is the best place in Greece to purchase jewelry, particularly at the **shops** along Adrianou. The choices are much better than you'll find else-where, and—if you know how to haggle—so are the prices. The best advice is to take your time, and don't be afraid to walk away. The sales staff gets paid on commission, and they hate to lose a potential customer. Most stores have similar selections, which they buy from factory wholesalers. If feeling shy about bargaining, ask "Do you have any discounts?" to start the conversation.

For something more specialized (with high prices), visit **Byz-antino,** which creates pricey handmade replicas of museum pieces, along with some original designs (daily 11:00-21:00, Adrianou 120, +30 210 324 6605, https://byzantino.com, run by Kosta).

Olympico also creates their own modern pieces in the Greek style, along with museum copies (daily 11:00-22:00, shorter hours off-season, Adrianou 122, +30 210 324 8697, www.olympicojewlery.com, George).

The gift shop at the **Benaki Museum of Greek History and Culture** (described on page 64) is also popular for its jewelry.

Handmade Sandals

The best place to buy real leather sandals is **Melissinos Art,** the famous "poet sandal maker" of Athens. Pantelis Melissinos, who's also a poet, painter, and playwright, is the third generation in his craft. His father, Stavros, was also a master sandal maker, and the shop has been an Athens landmark since 1920. In the windows, you'll see photos of celebrities who have worn Melissinos sandals over the decades, from Jackie O. to John Lennon. Supposedly, when the Beatles came to the shop in 1968, they asked Stavros why he didn't ask for their autographs. He asked why, in turn, they hadn't asked for his, adding, "I will be around long after the Beatles."

At this shop, you'll find an assortment of styles in basic shades of tan for about €50 per pair. They can also customize a pair for you. The price goes up if you want leather or beading in various colors, and you'll have to wait a day or two (Tue-Sat 10:00-17:00, Mon from 12:00, closed Sun; two blocks down Athanasiou Diakou from the Akropoli metro station in Makrigianni at Tzireon 16; +30 210 321 9247, www.melissinos-art.com).

For a more contemporary, fashion-forward pair of sandals, try the **Ancient Greek Sandals** boutique near Syntagma Square. Their all-natural, handmade sandals marry traditional design with modern style, and run €150-200 a pair (Mon-Sat 10:00-20:00, closed Sun; Kolokotroni 1, +30 210 323 0938, www.ancient-greek-sandals.com).

Religious Items

Icons and other Greek Orthodox objects can make good souve-nirs. For the best selection, visit the shops near the cathedral,

SHOPPING

Worry Beads

As you travel through Greece, you may notice Greek men spinning, stroking, and generally fidgeting with their worry beads. Greeks use these beaded strings to soothe themselves and get focused—especially during hard times. Loosely based on prayer beads, but today a secular hobby, worry beads make for a fun Greek souvenir. You'll see them sold all over central Athens.

Many major faiths employ some version of stringed beads as a worship aid, typically to help keep track of prayers while calming and focusing the mind. Think of the Catholic rosary, Muslim prayer beads, and the long, knotted rope belts worn by medieval monks. Hindus and Buddhists also make use of beads. Greeks—likely inspired by Muslims during the nearly 400 years of Ottoman rule—adopted the habit, but it no longer carries any religious connotations.

The most typical type of worry bead is the *komboloï*, a loop with an odd number of beads (it can be any number, as long as it's odd). The top of the loop may have a fixed "main bead" (or two), also called the "priest." The *begleri* version—popular since the 1950s—is a single string with an even number of beads (so it can be comfortably balanced in the hand).

The beads are made from a variety of materials. The basic tourist version is a cheap "starter set" made from synthetic materials, similar to marbles. You'll pay more for organic materials, which are considered more pleasant to touch: precious stones, bones, horn, wood, coral, mother-of-pearl, seeds, and more. The most prized worry beads are made of amber. Most valuable are the hand-cut amber beads, which are very soft and fragile; machine-cut amber is processed to be stronger.

When buying, try several different strings to find one that fits well in your hand; tune in to the smoothness of the beads and the sound they make when clacking together.

There is no "right" or "wrong" way to use your worry beads—everyone finds a routine that works for them. Some flip or spin the beads in their hands, while others sit quietly and count the beads over and over. There are as many ways to use worry beads as there are Greeks. Their seemingly nervous habit appears to have the opposite effect—defusing stress and calming the nerves.

along Agia Filotheis street (most are closed Sat-Sun, described on page 85).

Specialty Foods

All over Athens you'll see specialty food stores selling locally produced goods such as olive oil, wine and liqueurs, mustards, and sweets like boxed baklava, *halva* (a confection usually made from sesame paste), *loukoumi* (a.k.a. Greek delight), and jars of "spoon sweets" (jam-like spreads).

The best place to shop for these is where the locals do—near the Central Market. Specialty grocers and spice shops cluster around Athinas and Evripidou streets, including **Peri Lesvou,** which sells items produced on the island of Lesbos (closed Sun, Athinas 27, +30 210 323 3227) and **Zouridakis,** featuring products from Crete (closed Sun, Evripidou 25, +30 210 321 1109).

Yoleni's/Terra Fresh is two stores under one roof. This top-end, all-purpose Greek grocery store is in the posh Kolonaki area, about a 10-minute walk from Syntagma Square. The shelves are stocked with high-end wine, olive oil, liqueur, honey, and other temptations. There's also a café with sandwiches and salads, a wine bar, a steak house, and a venue for cooking classes (long hours daily, Solonos 9, +30 212 222 3622).

Ergon House Deli is stocked with artisanal products—both Greek and international—worthy of an upper-fork picnic or to bring home as souvenirs. Order off the menu to enjoy a meal under the airy glass atrium (flanked by an herb wall), or grab a loaf of freshly baked bread and a snack for lunch on the go (cooking classes available, open daily 7:00-24:00, Mitropoleos 23, +30 210 109 090, https://house.ergonfoods.com).

For chocolate and other Greek goods, check out **Matsouka** (ΜΑΤΣΟΥΚΑ) and its offshoots, around the corner from Syntagma Square (with other branches around the city). Their main branch (at Karageorgi Servias 10) sells nuts, candies, dried fruit, honey, olive oil, and other goodies. Around the corner at Nikis 4 is another shop with spices, chocolates, and more; and a half-block away (at the corner of Karageorgi Servias and Voulis) is their top-end chocolate shop, selling pricey Greek, French, and Belgian pralines. Even if you're not buying, step inside and take a deep whiff. Notice the case of fancy desserts. Greeks bring these to a home when they're invited for a visit instead of, say, a bottle of wine (all Matsouka shops open daily 8:00-23:00).

Also near Syntagma Square, **Mastiha Shop** specializes in (and is named for) a unique Greek treat—a sweet resin produced only by trees on a particular part of Chios island. *Mastica* has been revered since ancient times for its medicinal properties in treating stomach ailments. These days, this shop uses the distinctively flavorful substance for products from cookies and liqueurs to essential oils and preserves. *Mastica* is also commonly used in chewing gum (look for the EΛMA brand, sold at newsstands all over Greece) and as a sweet treat for kids, who dip a spoon in a jar of *mastica* syrup and eat it like a lollipop. Drop in for some free samples (closed Sun, a block above Syntagma Square at Panepistimiou 6, +30 210 363 2750).

NIGHTLIFE IN ATHENS

Athens is a thriving city...and the Athenians know how to have a good time after hours. I've provided some ideas for how to spend an evening, from folk performances to outdoor movies, enjoying rooftop cocktails, or simply strolling around and finding a scene that appeals to you.

Athens is most inviting from May through October (aside from miserably hot August), when al fresco activities such as outdoor cinema, festivals (including the Athens & Epidavros Festival), folk-dancing shows at Dora Stratou Theater, and outdoor sidewalk cafés and bars are in full swing.

In the heat of summer, some clubs close down to relocate to outdoor venues on the coast. In the winter, your options are limited to indoor venues (concerts and other performances). But folk musicians, who tend to spend their summers in small towns and islands, hibernate in Athens in winter—offering ample opportunities to hear traditional music. A number of tavernas feature live music and dancing locals year-round, providing a wonderful setting for a late dinner.

Events Listings: Athens has a constantly rotating schedule of cultural activities, such as concerts to suit every audience. For local events, look for publications such as the English-language version of the daily newspaper *Kathimerini* (www.ekathimerini.com).

PERFORMANCES
Festivals
Athens' biggest party is the **Athens & Epidavros Festival,** held every June and July. The festival's highlights are its world-class performances of dance, music, and theater at the ancient Odeon of Herodes Atticus, nestled spectacularly below the floodlit Acropolis. Outdoor performances at other venues enliven the already

NIGHTLIFE

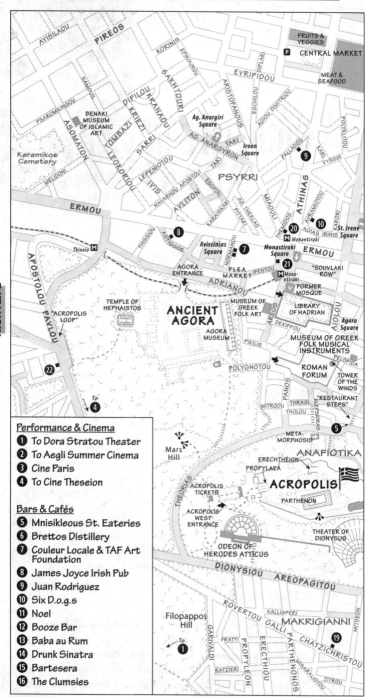

Performance & Cinema
1. To Dora Stratou Theater
2. To Aegli Summer Cinema
3. Cine Paris
4. To Cine Theseion

Bars & Cafés
5. Mnisikleous St. Eateries
6. Brettos Distillery
7. Couleur Locale & TAF Art Foundation
8. James Joyce Irish Pub
9. Juan Rodriguez
10. Six D.o.g.s
11. Noel
12. Booze Bar
13. Baba au Rum
14. Drunk Sinatra
15. Bartesera
16. The Clumsies

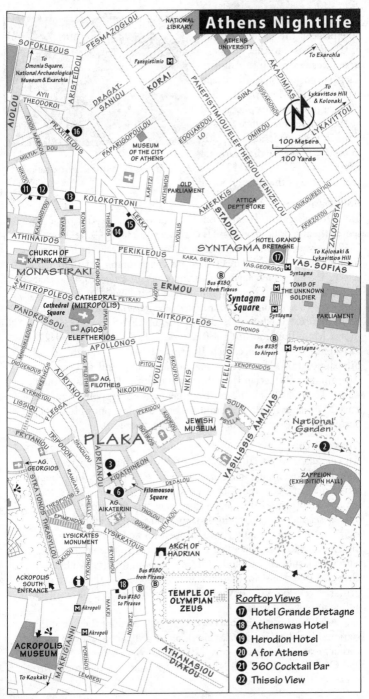

Athens Nightlife

NIGHTLIFE

100 Meters
100 Yards

Rooftop Views
17 Hotel Grande Bretagne
18 Athenswas Hotel
19 Herodion Hotel
20 A for Athens
21 360 Cocktail Bar
22 Thissio View

hopping city. Performances also take place at the famous Theater of Epidavros on the Peloponnese (these extend into August). Tickets go on sale from late April to early May. You can buy them online, over the phone, and at the festival box office (closed Sun, in the arcade at Panepistimiou 39, opposite the National  Library, +30 210 893 8112, http://aefestival.gr). Same-day tickets are also sold at the theater box office.

Folk Dancing

The **Dora Stratou Theater** on Filopappos Hill is the place to see authentic folk dancing. The theater company—the best in Greece—was originally formed to record and preserve the country's many traditional dances. Performances rotate, but their repertoire includes such favorites as the graceful *kalamatianos* circle dance, the *syrtaki* (famously immortalized by Anthony Quinn in *Zorba the Greek*), and the dramatic solo *zimbetikos* (€15, 1.5-hour performances run June-late Sept, generally Fri-Sun at 21:30, no shows Mon-Thu, morning +30 210 324 4395, evening +30 210 921 4650, www.grdance.org). The theater is on the south side of Filopappos Hill. If you're taking the Metro, get off at Petralona (10-minute walk) rather than the farther Akropoli stop (20-minute walk). To walk to the theater from below the Acropolis, figure at least 20 minutes (entirely around the base of Filopappos Hill, signposted from western end of Dionysiou Areopagitou).

Outdoor Cinema

Athens has a wonderful tradition of outdoor movies. Screenings take place most nights in summer (around €10, roughly June-Sept, sometimes in May and Oct depending on weather; shows start around 20:00 or 21:00, depending on when the sun sets; many offer a second, later showing). Drinks are served at these "theaters," which are actually compact open-air courtyards with folding chairs. Movies typically are shown in their original language, with Greek subtitles (though children's movies might be dubbed in Greek). Of Athens' many outdoor-cinema venues, these are particularly well-known, convenient, and atmospheric. Call or check online to see what's playing.

Aegli Summer Cinema is a cool, classic outdoor theater in the National Garden (at the Zappeion), playing the latest blockbusters with a great sound system (+30 210 336 9369).

Cine Paris, in the Plaka, shows movies on the roof with

Acropolis views (overlooking Filomousou Square at Kidathineon 22, +30 210 322 2071, www.cineparis.gr).

Cine Theseion, along the Apostolou Pavlou pedestrian drag in the Thissio neighborhood, enjoys grand floodlit Acropolis views from some of its seats—one of the reasons it was voted the "best outdoor cinema in the world." It shows both classic and current movies (Apostolou Pavlou 7, +30 210 347 0980 or +33 210 342 0864, www.cine-thisio.gr).

Other Outdoor Venues

The rebuilt ancient theater at the foot of the Acropolis, the **Odeon of Herodes Atticus** occasionally hosts concerts under the stars. The theater atop **Lykavittos Hill** is another outdoor favorite (currently under renovation but may reopen by the time you visit—check locally). Both of these are used in summer for the Athens & Epidavros Festival.

STROLLING AFTER DARK
Apostolou Pavlou Promenade and Thissio Neighborhood

A peaceful pedestrian lane circles the Acropolis, providing locals and visitors alike a delightful place for an evening stroll. This promenade is what I call the "Acropolis Loop" (consisting of Dionysiou Areopagitou to the south and Apostolou Pavlou to the west).

The promenade cuts through the Thissio district, just beyond the Agora, where the tables and couches of clubs and cocktail bars clog the pedestrian lanes under the Acropolis. More upscale than the Plaka, Thissio gives you an easy escape from the tired tourism of that zone. Thissio is basically composed of three or four streets running into Apostolou Pavlou (part of the "Acropolis Loop"). Iraklidon street is a tight lane with people socializing at café tables squeezed under trees. Akamantos street, while still colorful, is a bit more sedate. Backgammon boards chatter, TVs blare the latest sporting events, and young Athenians sip their iced coffees en masse. As the sun sets and the floodlit temples of the Acropolis ornament the horizon, you understand why this quiet and breezy corner is such a hit with locals enjoying an evening out.

Come here just to stroll through a fine café scene, enjoy dinner or a drink and some great people-watching, or see a movie under the stars (at Cine Theseion, listed earlier).

To reach Thissio, walk the pedestrian lane around the Acropolis from either end. It makes a wonderful destination after the more peaceful stretch from the Acropolis Museum (Metro: Akropoli). Or ride the Metro to Thissio, then follow the crowds uphill along the broad Apostolou Pavlou walkway toward the Acropolis. For more details about this main drag, see page 46.

BARS, CAFÉS, AND LATE-NIGHT SPOTS

Athens abounds with bars and cafés serving drinks in lively and atmospheric settings (including on rooftops boasting grand views). I've listed a few good areas to explore. Note that although bars are supposed to be nonsmoking, many places don't adhere to this rule. Expect to leave most bars smelling of smoke.

In the Center

Plaka: Although the Plaka is jammed full of tourists and few locals, it couldn't be more central or user-friendly, with live traditional music spilling out of seemingly every other taverna. One pleasant area to explore is the stepped lane called **Mnisikleous** (some of my restaurant recommendations in this area have live music; see the Eating in Athens chapter).

Brettos—the oldest distillery in Athens, dating from 1909—is a popular stop for tourists and locals wanting to taste various shots and wines by the glass. While buried in the Plaka kitsch, it seems a world apart once you step inside and grab a stool under huge old casks and lit-up bottles of colorful liquors (daily 10:00-24:00, just off Adrianou at Kydathineon 41, +30 210 323 2100).

For drinks, I also enjoy the following wine bars: **By the Glass** (near the National Garden) and **Heteroclito** (near the cathedral). Both serve good food (for full descriptions, see the end of the Eating in Athens chapter).

Monastiraki: Right on Monastiraki Square, several rooftop bars offer some of the best views of the city. **Couleur Locale,** tucked inside the Monastiraki flea market, is one popular perch (see "Rooftop Bars," later).

Next door to Couleur Locale, the **TAF Art Foundation** is a hidden garden café and bar in one of Athens' oldest houses. Nine families once lived around this communal courtyard, where you can relax with a coffee by day or join artsy Athenians for drinks after dark (daily 10:30-24:00, Normanou 5, +30 210 323 8757).

Adrianou Street: This street just north of the Agora has a line of inviting restaurants and cafés with outdoor seating—some with spectacular Acropolis views and all good for a drink. For something completely un-Greek, head a few blocks away to **James Joyce Irish Pub** to drink a pint of your favorite Irish brew (Astiggos 12, +30 210 323 5055).

Psyrri

Northeast of Monastiraki Square, the center of this seedy-chic district is Iroon Square, with several cute bar/cafés spilling into the square under a jolly mural. Nearby

Lepeniotou and Esopou streets are fun for their creatively decorated places. ⚏ You can get your bearings by doing my Psyrri and Central Market Walk. For dining recommendations, see the Eating in Athens chapter.

Juan Rodriguez, a block off Athinas, is a noisy Art Deco/ Roaring '20s-style bar packed with locals—it's often "standing-room" only (Pallados 3, +30 210 322 4496).

Near St. Irene Square: The square surrounding the Church of St. Irene, across busy Athinas street just east of Psyrri, offers one of the most delightful wine-and-coffee scenes in the center. Day or night you'll find the place filled with locals enjoying stylish, modern bar/cafés and classy ambience. The streets that peel off from the square are largely traffic-free and lined with more inviting places. Consider **Six D.o.g.s** bar, hiding down some stairs in a nondescript alley, with a sunken courtyard and seating on multilevel terraces (tropical cocktails, Avramioutou 6, +30 210 321 0510).

Around Kolokotroni and Praxitelous Streets

These lively streets, north of Syntagma and Monastiraki, offer a mix of open-air courtyards, high-end cocktails, contemporary charm, and classic dive-bar atmosphere.

On and near Kolokotroni: On a lively square lined with outdoor tables, **Noel** is busy and festive year-round (Kolokotroni 59, +30 211 215 9534). Next door, **Booze Bar** is a time-warp, '90s-era dive with chess boards, vinyl picnic furniture, and lots of decorative chickens (Kolokotroni 57, +30 211 405 3733). **Baba au Rum,** wedged on a tiny street nearby, serves seriously good cocktails (Klitiou 6, +30 211 710 9140).

Across from a branch of the city college, **Drunk Sinatra** is where retro chic meets burlesque (Thiseos 16, +30 210-331-3733). Around the corner, **Bartesera** occupies a traditional Athenian arcade and offers a standard cocktail menu, a covered patio, and Konstantinos the dog (Kolokotroni 25, +30 210 322 09805).

Closer to Syntagma Square, several bars pepper the streets around the Old Parliament building (just off Stadiou). This area offers a quieter, darker feel, and serves a more professional clientele. The recommended **Black Duck Garden** restaurant is a good option here (by the Museum of the City of Athens—see listing on page 195).

On Praxitelous: There's a good reason **The Clumsies** tops all the "best of" lists. Its creatively crafted cocktails are works of liquid art, the space is contemporary casual, and the atmosphere is just loud enough to let loose without having to shout. If you're overwhelmed by the menu, try the cocktail sampler (four half-size cocktails-€20, open daily 18:00-22:00, brunch menu until 18:00, above-average bar food, Praxitelous 30, +30 210 323 2682).

Rooftop Bars

A touristy-yet-appealing way to spend an evening is at one of Athens' many rooftop bars, all with views of floodlit monuments.

Plaka/Syntagma: For a great view and overpriced cocktails, visit the recommended rooftop restaurant and bar of the **Hotel Grande Bretagne,** across the street from Syntagma Square. There are also several rooftop bars at hotels near the Acropolis Museum, including the Sense Restaurant, on top of the **Athenswas Hotel** (Dionysiou Areopagitou 5), and the Point α Bar at the **Herodion Hotel** (Rovertou Galli 4). You'll be in the company of other tourists, and views are less impressive, as you're looking at the backside of the Acropolis, but these spots are convenient to some of my recommended accommodations in Makrigianni and Koukaki.

Monastiraki: The rooftop of the **A for Athens** hotel is popular with both locals and tourists who come to gawk at its views. Thanks to its prime spot on Monastiraki Square, it offers a dramatic vantage point of the Acropolis looming above the city. If this place is too crowded, try the **360 Cocktail Bar** on the same square (but with less impressive panoramas).

Next door to the Monastiraki flea market, **Couleur Locale** (listed earlier, under "In the Center") has a getaway rooftop bar and third-floor terrace—both with good coffee, fancy cocktails, Acropolis views, and a hip, indoor greenhouse ambience (daily 10:00-late, also a restaurant, Normanou 3, +30 216 700 4917).

Thissio: If strolling the pedestrian promenade through Thissio, consider a stop at the **Thissio View** restaurant and bar (Apostolou Pavlou 25).

ATHENS CONNECTIONS

Athens is the transportation hub for all of Greece. Because the tourist core of Athens is so compact, and with good public transportation, don't rent a car until you are ready to leave the city—you absolutely do *not* want to drive in Athens traffic. If you're venturing to landlocked destinations beyond Athens, the best option for the rest of your trip is to travel by car. Buses can get you just about anywhere for a reasonable fare, but connections to remote areas can be long and complicated, and straightforward schedule information is hard to come by (note that most of my recommended sights beyond Athens do not have train service). Boats and planes work well for reaching the islands.

For a map of Athens transit, see the back of this book. For specifics on transportation beyond Athens, see the "Connections" sections in each of the destination chapters in this book. And for general information on transportation by plane, boat, bus, and car, see the Practicalities chapter.

By Plane

ELEFTHERIOS VENIZELOS INTERNATIONAL AIRPORT

Athens' airport is at Spata, 17 miles east of downtown (airport code: ATH, +30 210 353 0000—press 2 for English, www.aia.gr). This slick, user-friendly airport has two sections: B gates (serving European/Schengen countries—no passport control) and A gates (serving other destinations, including the US). Both sections feed into the same main terminal building (with a common baggage claim, ATMs, shops, car-rental counters, information desks, and additional services). On floor 2 (above entrance/exit #3) is a mini museum of Greek artifacts dug up from the area around the airport.

Getting from the Airport to Downtown

Your best route into the city depends on where you want to go: If you're headed to Syntagma Square, the bus is generally better (cheapest, frequent, and scenic—but slow). For Monastiraki, Psyrri, or the Makrigianni area south of the Plaka, the Metro is more direct—and isn't susceptible to traffic jams. Electronic boards in the baggage and arrivals halls show upcoming bus and train departures.

By Bus: Buses wait outside exit #5. Express bus #X95 costs €5.50 and operates 24 hours daily between the airport and Syntagma Square (3-5/hour, roughly 1 hour depending on traffic; +30 210 820 2900, www.oasa.gr). The downtown bus stop is on Othonos street, along the side of Syntagma Square; get off after the bus takes a 180-degree turn around a big square filled with palm trees.

By Metro: Line 3/blue zips you downtown in 45 minutes for €9 (2/hour, direction: Dimotiko Theatro, daily 6:30-23:30; €18 for 2 people, €27 for 3, half-price for people under 18 or over 65, ticket good for 90 minutes on other Athens transit; the €20 three-day tourist ticket, which includes round-trip airport transfer by Metro or bus as well as unlimited in-city travel on all public transit, is only worthwhile if you plan on returning to the airport within 72 hours).

To reach the Metro from the airport arrivals hall, go through exit #3, cross the street, go up the escalator, and cross the skybridge to the rail terminal. Buy tickets at the machines or ticket window, and follow signs down to the platforms. In downtown Athens, this train stops at Syntagma (where you can transfer to line 2/red) and Monastiraki (transfer to line 1/green).

To return to the airport by Metro, you can catch a train from Syntagma (2/hour, 5:30-24:00). Keep in mind that some Metro trains terminate at Doukissis Plakentias. If so, just hop off and wait—another train that continues to the airport should come along soon.

By Taxi or Uber: A well-marked taxi stand outside exit #3 offers fixed-price transfers that include all fees and tolls (€40 to central Athens, covers up to 4 people, fare increases to €55 or more between 24:00 and 5:00). If you are comfortable using Uber back home, you can also use it in Athens to get to and from the airport. In Athens, Uber operates as UberTaxi. You'll book your ride through the app, but a taxi will pick you up. Rates to and from the airport are fixed, so Uber won't save you money on this route. I use it for the convenience and familiarity.

By Car Service: A variety of private services offer airport transfers for approximately the same cost as a taxi, but often with a nicer car and more personal and professional service. Most hotels have a service they like to work with, or you can book on your own (reserve at least a day before). Or consider one of the private drivers listed on page 41.

Getting from the Airport to Other Transit Points

To reach the **port of Piraeus,** you can take express bus #X96 (€6, runs 24 hours daily, 2-4/hour, 1-1.5 hours depending on traffic; leaves from outside airport exit #5, stops at Piraeus' Karaiskaki Square, then at the Metro station; +30 210 820 2900, www.oasa. gr). Or, take Metro line 3/blue from the airport to the port (€9, 55 minutes). A taxi from the airport to the port costs about €50.

Express bus #X93 goes directly to **bus terminals A and B** (same price and frequency as #X96, above).

By Boat

ATHENS' PORT: PIRAEUS

Piraeus, a city six miles southwest of central Athens, has been the port of Athens since an-cient times. Today it's also the main port for services to the Greek islands, mak-ing it the busiest passenger port in the Mediterranean. While the port is vast, most of it is used for ferry traffic; all cruise ships moor at one end.

Orientation to Piraeus

All ferries, hydrofoils, catamarans, and cruise ships use Piraeus' Great Harbor (Megas Limin). To the east are two smaller harbors used for private yachts: Limin Zeas and the picturesque Mikroli-mano, or "Small Harbor."

The Great Harbor area is ringed by busy streets. At the north-east corner is the hub of most activity: the Metro station, housed inside a big yellow Neoclassical building with white trim (some-times labeled "Electric Railway Station" on maps). Trainspotters with time to kill can visit the free and good little electric-railway museum inside. Next door to the Metro station is the suburban train station. Just south of the Metro station is Karaiskaki Square, which juts out into the harbor. Cheap eateries, flophouse hotels, and dozens of travel agencies round out the dreary scene. The port does have several grungy waiting areas and WCs (between gates

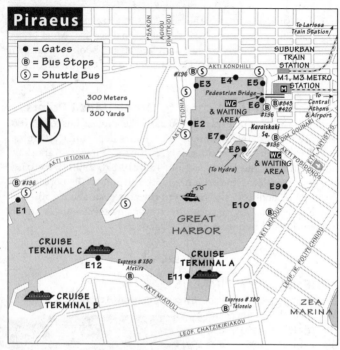

E5 and E6, and between E8 and E9), but trust me, killing several hours in Piraeus waiting for a ferry is a traveler's hell you'd prefer to avoid.

Gates: Twelve "gates" (docks) wrap around the harbor for about three miles, numbered in clockwise order. Big electronic display boards show gate numbers and times for upcoming departures. Gate assignments depend on both the destination and the company operating the line, but you can generally expect the following:

- **E1:** Dodecanese Islands (Rhodes)
- **E2:** Crete; North Aegean Islands (Samos, Ikaria, Chios, Mytilene)
- **E3:** Crete and Kithira (vehicle entrance)
- **E4:** Kithira (vehicle exit)
- **E5:** Bus Terminal (pedestrian entrance)
- **E6:** Cyclades (including **Mykonos** and **Santorini**), pedestrian walkway to Metro
- **E7:** Cyclades (including high-speed boats to **Mykonos** and **Santorini**)
- **E8:** Saronic Gulf Islands (Argosaronikos in Greek, including **Hydra,** Spetses, Paros, and Ermioni)
- **E9:** Cyclades (including **Mykonos** and **Santorini**), Samos, Ikaria

E10:   Vehicle exit from E9

E11:   Cruise Terminal A

E12:   Cruise Terminals B and C

These departure gates could change—carefully check your ticket for the gate number, and ask a local if you're unsure.

Information: Official tourist information is in short supply here, although temporary TI kiosks may pop up near the cruise terminals when ships arrive. Your best sources of information are the many travel agencies scattered around the area; all have a line on current boats, where they leave from, and how to get tickets. The port police, with several offices clearly marked in English, can be helpful (+30 210 451 1001). You can also call the Piraeus Port Authority's cruise and ferry terminal line at +30 210 455 0110. The port authority website is www.olp.gr.

Baggage Storage: You can leave bags at an office about 50 yards south of the Metro station. Look for the *Baggage Locker* sign on the main harbor road, nearest the cross street Kapodistriou (daily 6:00-22:00).

Getting from Piraeus to the Islands

For the lowdown on Greece's ferry network, including tips on looking up schedules and buying tickets, see page 553 of the Practicalities chapter. Know ahead of time from which gate your ferry leaves.

Arriving at the Piraeus Metro station, you'll step out into a little square. Head for the busy road, cross at the crosswalk, and enter the port area. Straight ahead are gates E6 and E7. Gates with higher numbers are to your left; those with lower numbers are to your right. (For example, Hydra-bound boats usually depart from gate E8, to your left on the far end of the tree-filled park toward gate E9.) If your boat leaves from gates E1 or E2 on the north side of the port, look for a free shuttle bus just inside the port gate at E5.

From Piraeus by Boat to: Hydra (6-8/day June-Sept, 4/day Oct-May, 1.5-2 hours), **Mykonos** (3-4/day in high season, 2.5 hours via fast boat, 5.5 hours on slow boat; off-season likely 1 slow boat daily), **Santorini** (4-5/day in high season, 5 hours via fast boat, 8 hours by slow boat; off-season likely 1 slow boat daily). The frequency and durations listed here are approximate; schedules can change from season to season, and sailings can be canceled on short notice—confirm everything locally. See page 553 of the Practicalities chapter for tips on finding the most up-to-date schedules.

Getting from Piraeus Ferry Terminals to Athens

By Train: Metro line 1/green conveniently links Piraeus with downtown Athens (€1.20, good for 90 minutes including transfers, departs about every 10-15 minutes between 6:00 and 24:00). The Metro station is in a big, yellow Neoclassical building near gate

E6. Buy your ticket from a machine, validate it, and hop on the train. In about 20 minutes, the Metro reaches the city-center Monastiraki stop, near the Plaka and many recommended hotels and sights. (For Syntagma, Akropoli, and Syngrou-Fix Metro stops, ride one more stop to Omonia to transfer to line 2/red.) Warning: The Metro line between Piraeus and downtown Athens teems with pickpockets—watch your valuables and wear a money belt.

A **suburban train** also connects Piraeus' train station with Athens, but there's no reason to take it (less frequent, more transfers).

By Taxi: A taxi between Piraeus and downtown Athens should cost about €20, and can take anywhere from 20-40 minutes, depending on traffic and on your starting/ending point at Piraeus. Uber works well, and is often cheaper. The app works as it does at home, but instead of a nondescript car, you'll get a taxi.

By Bus to Bus Terminal A (Kifissou): For long-distance buses to the Peloponnese, you'll need to connect through Athens. To reach Athens' Bus Terminal A (Kifissou), take bus #420 (2-3/hour, catch bus at stop across the street from Gate E6).

Getting from Piraeus Cruise Terminals to Athens

Piraeus has three cruise terminals at two different docks. The main terminal—Terminal A ("Miaoulis")—is at dock E11. Farther out, dock E12 has two terminal buildings: Terminal B ("Themistocles") and Terminal C ("Alkimos"). For more details, see my *Rick Steves Mediterranean Cruise Ports* guidebook.

Getting to Athens: You can either hire a **taxi** (these wait outside the cruise terminals; €25 is a fair fare to downtown), summon an **Uber** (see "By Taxi or Uber," earlier), or arrange in advance for a **private car and driver** (try one of my recommended drivers listed on page 41).

If you don't want to hire a taxi or driver, the easiest option is to pay for an all-day **hop-on, hop-off bus tour,** which stops at all the major sights in Athens (€16-25; for more info on the various hop-on, hop-off companies, see page 43). Catch these from outside each cruise terminal.

For a cheaper, public-transit option, **express bus #X80** is most direct. This designed-for-cruisers route takes you from outside the cruise terminals into Athens, stopping at Dionysiou Areopagitou (near the Acropolis Museum) and Syntagma Square (2/hour when cruise ships are in town, 1 hour). Or you can do a bus-plus-Metro combo: Ride local **bus #843** to the Piraeus Metro station (bus stop: Stathmos ISAP/ΣΤΑΘΜΟΣ Η.Σ.Α.Π.), then hop the **Metro** (line 1/green) into downtown Athens. For any bus, you'll need to buy a ticket before you board—either at a newsstand kiosk or at a small ticket kiosk (usually located near a stop), and remember to scan it once you've boarded. For Terminal A, use bus stop Teloneio (ΤΕΛΩΝΕΙΟ); for Terminals B and C, it's Afetira (ΑΦΕΤΗΡΙΑ).

Getting from Piraeus to the Airport

From Piraeus, you can reach the airport by **taxi** (around €50), Metro line 3/blue (€9, 55 minutes), or by **bus** #X96, which goes directly to the airport (€6, runs 24 hours daily, 2-4/hour depending on time of day, 1-1.5 hours depending on traffic). In Piraeus, bus #X96 stops directly in front of the Metro station (Stathmos ISAP/ΣΤΑΘΜΟΣ Η.Σ.Α.Π. stop), and along the top of Karaiskaki Square (Plateia Karaiskaki/ΠΛ. ΚΑΡΑΙΣΚΑΚΗ stop, between gates E7 and E8).

By Bus

Athens has two major intercity bus stations—both far from downtown, and neither conveniently reached by Metro. Buses serving the south, including the Peloponnese, use the bus station called Kifissou, or "Terminal A." Most buses serving the north, including Delphi, use the station called Liossion, or "Terminal B."

Although most destinations in this book are served by at least one daily direct bus from Athens, connecting between destinations outside of Athens can involve several changes. All Greek buses are operated by ΚΤΕΛ (KTEL) but there's no useful general website or phone number (each region has its own website for its own schedules; some are better than others). For example, for bus service to destinations like Nafplio and Epidavros, check the schedules and general bus information at www.ktelargolida.gr.

TERMINAL A (KIFISSOU)

This bus station is about three miles northwest of the city center. Getting here on public transit is a pain involving a Metro-plus-bus connection (Metro to Omonia then bus #051) or a bus-plus-longish-walk (bus #12 from Syntagma Square to the Papathanasiou/ΠΑΠΑΘΑΝΑΣΙΟΥ stop, then 10 minutes by foot). It's easier to take a taxi (pay no more than €15 from central Athens). Buses from here head to southwest Greece.

In the station's vast ticket hall (follow signs to ΕΚΔΟΤΗΡΙΑ), the counters are divided by which region they serve; if you aren't sure which one you need, ask at the information desk near the main door. Beyond the ticket hall are a cafeteria, a restaurant, and a supermarket, and the door out to the buses. This immense bus barn is crammed with well-labeled bus stalls, which are organized—like the ticket windows—by region. Taxis wait out in front of the ticket hall, as well as under the canopy between the ticket hall and the bus stalls (Terminal A info +30 210 512 4910).

There's also a ticket office for Terminal A a couple of blocks from Omonia Square at 59 Sokratous street—much closer to the city center (see map on page 37, look for ΕΚΔΟΤΗΡΙΑ sign; Mon-Fri 7:00-17:00, Sat 7:30-15:30, closed Sun, +30 210 523 7889).

By Bus from Terminal A to: Nafplio (roughly hourly direct, 2.5 hours), **Epidavros** (2-3/day, 2.5 hours), **Mycenae** (go to Nafplio first, then 2-3/day, none on Sun, 45 minutes), **Olympia** (8/day, 5.5 hours, change in Pyrgos), **Monemvasia** (4-5/day, 6 hours), **Kardamyli** (1/day direct, more with change in Kalamata, 5-6 hours).

TERMINAL B (LIOSSION)

Smaller, more manageable, and a bit closer to the city center, Liossion (lee-oh-SEE-yohn) is in northwest Athens, a 15-minute, €8 taxi ride from the Plaka. You can also take the Metro to Attiki and then take any bus going north on Liossion street about a mile to Praktoria. Buses from here head northwest (Terminal B info +30 210 831 7186).

By Bus from Terminal B to: Delphi (4-5/day, 3 hours).

By Train

Greek trains are of limited usefulness to travelers sticking to the destinations described in this book. That may change, as the Greek train system has recently been privatized; however, it remains unclear when service will be expanded.

Though essentially useless if connecting south, trains do serve areas north of Athens well (such as Thessaloniki). If you do take the train from Athens, you'll most likely use **Larissa Station,** just north of downtown (on Metro line 2/red). For now, the few trains are operated by Greek Railways (www.hellenictrain.gr). For more extensive travels beyond Greece, you can study your options at www.ricksteves.com/rail.

By Car

RENTING A CAR

Syngrou avenue is Athens' "rental-car lane," with all the established, predictable big companies (and piles of little ones) competing for your business. Syngrou is an easy walk from the Plaka and recommended hotels in Makrigianni and Koukaki. Budget travelers can often negotiate deals by checking with a few rental places and haggling. Or consider local company **Swift/Escape,** run by Elias, who can help you drive out of central Athens to avoid the stress of city-center driving (one-day rental: €40-60 depending on size of car; three-day rental: from €118 for compact; extra charge to drop car outside of Athens; open Mon-Sat 9:00-19:00, until 17:00 in winter, open Sun and after hours by request; at 43 Syngrou avenue, +30 210 924 7006 or +30 693 667 4476, www.greektravel. com/swift, elimano95@gmail.com).

ROUTE TIPS FOR DRIVERS

Avoid driving in Athens as much as possible—traffic is stressful, and parking is a headache. Before you leave Athens, get detailed directions from your rental agency on how to get back to their office and drop off your car.

Here's your strategy for getting out of the city: If you're heading north, such as to **Delphi,** aim for expressway 1 northbound (toward Lamia; see specific directions on page 386). To head for the **Peloponnese,** go westbound on expressway 6, which feeds into expressway 8 to Corinth (the gateway to the Peloponnese). The handy E-75 expressway (a.k.a. Kifissou avenue), which runs north-south just west of downtown Athens, offers an easy connection to either of these.

Assuming you pick up your car on or near Syngrou avenue, and traffic isn't that heavy, the best bet (with the fewest traffic lights and turns) is usually to simply head south on Syngrou. As you approach the water, the road forks; follow signs toward *Piraeus* on the left. After the merge, get into the right lane and be ready to hop on E-75 northbound. Then watch for your exit: for the Peloponnese, keep left toward Korinthos (Corinth) and merge onto expressway 8; for Delphi, continue straight north to expressway 1.

CONNECTIONS

THE
PELOPONNESE
Πελοπόννησος

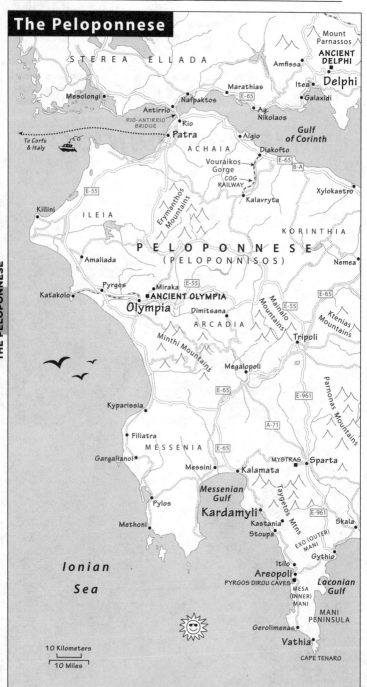

THE PELOPONNESE

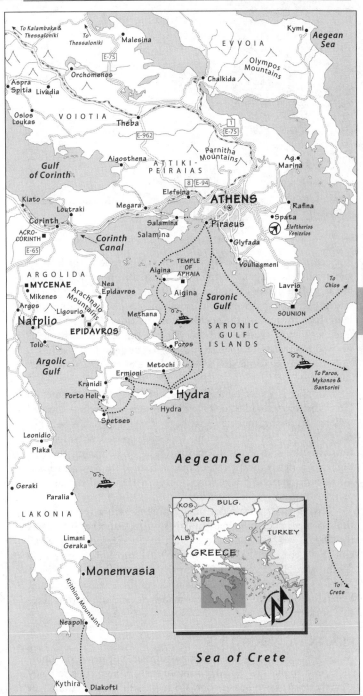

NAFPLIO

Ναύπλιο

The charming Peloponnesian port town of Nafplio is small, cozy, and strollable. Elegant Nafplio is a must-see on any Greek visit because of its historical importance, its accessibility from Athens (an easy 2.5-hour drive or bus ride), and its handy location as a home base for touring the ancient sites of Epidavros and Mycenae (each a short drive away and described in the next two chapters). Nafplio has great pensions, appealing restaurants, fine beaches, a thriving evening scene, and a good balance of real life and tourist convenience.

Nafplio is understandably proud of its special footnotes in Greek history. Thanks to its highly strategic position—nestled under cliffs at the apex of a vast bay—it changed hands between the Ottomans and the Venetians time and again. But Nafplio ultimately distinguished itself in the 1820s by becoming the first capital of a newly independent Greece, headed by President Ioannis Kapodistrias. Although those glory days have faded, the town retains a certain genteel panache.

Owing to its prestigious past, Nafplio's harbor is guarded by three castles: one on a small island (Bourtzi), another just above the Old Town (ancient Akronafplia), and a third capping a tall cliff above the city (Palamidi Fortress). All three are wonderfully floodlit at night. If you're not up for the climb to Palamidi, explore Nafplio's narrow and atmospheric back streets, lined with elegant Venetian houses and Neoclassical mansions, and dip into its likeable museums.

PLANNING YOUR TIME

Nafplio is light on sightseeing opportunities, but heavy on ambience. Two nights and one day is more than enough time to enjoy everything the town has to offer. With one full day in Nafplio, get

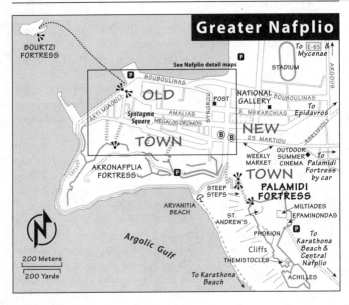

Greater Nafplio

BOURTZI FORTRESS

To E-65 & Mycenae

STADIUM

See Nafplio detail maps

BOUBOULINAS

OLD

POST

NATIONAL GALLERY

BOUBOULINAS

To Epidavros

S. MERARCHIAS

AKTI MIAOULI

Syntagma Square

AMALIAS

MEGALOS DROMOS

SYNGROU

ARGOUS

ASKLIPIOU

TOWN

NEW

25 MARTIOU

WEEKLY MARKET

OUTDOOR SUMMER CINEMA

TOWN

To Palamidi Fortress by car

AKRONAFPLIA FORTRESS

PALAMIDI FORTRESS

STEEP STEPS

MILTIADES

EPAMINONDAS

ARVANITIA BEACH

ST. ANDREW'S

PHOKION

Cliffs

THEMISTOCLES

To Karathona Beach & Central Nafplio

ACHILLES

200 Meters

200 Yards

Argolic Gulf

To Karathona Beach

an early start and do the arduous hike up to the Palamidi Fortress in the morning, when the pathway is mostly shaded, and before the worst heat of the day (to save time and sweat, you can also drive or taxi there). Then get your bearings in the Old Town by following my self-guided walk, and visit any museums that appeal to you. In the afternoon, hit the beach.

Nafplio also serves as an ideal launch pad for visiting two of the Peloponnese's best ancient sites (each about a 30-minute drive and covered in the next two chapters): the best-preserved ancient theater anywhere, at **Epidavros;** and the older-than-old hilltop fortress of **Mycenae.** It's worth adding a day to your Nafplio stay to fit these in. If you have a **car,** you can see both (and drive up to the Palamidi Fortress) in a full day; for an even more efficient plan, consider squeezing them in on your way into or out of town (for example, notice that Mycenae is between Nafplio and the major E-65 expressway to the north). These sites are also reachable by **bus.** While it may be possible to do them both by bus on the same day, for a more relaxed approach consider two full days in Nafplio, spending a half-day at each site, and two half-days in town.

Orientation to Nafplio

Because everything of interest is concentrated in the peninsular Old Town, Nafplio feels smaller than its population of 15,000. The mostly traffic-free Old Town is squeezed between the hilltop Akronafplia fortress and the broad seafront walkways of Bouboulinas

NAFPLIO

and Akti Miaouli; the core of this area has atmospherically tight pedestrian lanes bursting with restaurants and shops. Syntagma Square (Plateia Syntagmatos) is the centerpiece of the Old Town. From here, traffic-free Vasileos Konstantinou—called "Big Street" (Megalos Dromos) by locals—runs east to Syngrou street, which separates the Old Town from the New Town. The tranquil upper part of the Old Town, with some of my favorite accommodations, is connected by stepped lanes.

TOURIST INFORMATION

Nafplio's TI is just inside Town Hall, on Town Hall Square (Mon-Fri 9:00-15:00, Sun 9:00-12:00, closed Sat, +30 2752 024 444). Check locally to confirm opening hours for sights and museums in this chapter. If side-tripping out to Epidavros or Mycenae in the off-season, call ahead to double-check opening times.

Note that the town's name can be spelled in a number of ways in English: Nafplio, Nauplio, Navplio, Naufplio, Nauvplio, and so on—and all these variations may also appear with an "n" at the end (Nafplion, etc.).

ARRIVAL IN NAFPLIO

By Car: Parking is free, easy, and central along the port, which runs in front of the Old Town (look for the big lots). If you're staying higher up, ask your hotel about more convenient parking (for example, near the abandoned Hotel Xenia on the road up to the Akronafplia fortress).

By Bus: The main bus station and KTEL bus-company office (ΚΤΕΛ in Greek) are conveniently located on Syngrou street, right where the Old Town meets the New; from here all my recommended accommodations are within a 10-minute walk. Buy tickets for local trips (including Mycenae and Epidavros) directly from the driver. For long-distance buses—to Athens, for example—buy your ticket in the office. Note some buses also arrive and depart from a second stop, just around the corner on Plapouta street (ask in the office which stop your bus will use).

HELPFUL HINTS

Market Days: A market featuring local products like honey, wine, and olives takes over the street called 25 Martiou on Wednesdays and Saturdays until 14:00.

Festivals: Nafplio hosts a classical music festival in late June with a mix of Greek and international performers playing at the Palamidi Fortress and the St. Spyridon and St. George churches (details at TI). The town is also a good base for seeing drama and music performances at the famous Theater of Epidavros during the Athens & Epidavros Festival (weekends in July-Aug; see page 211). The local bus company operates special buses to the festival.

Bookstores: For local guidebooks, maps, and more, check **Nafplia Bookstore,** where they also sell English paperbacks and stamps (long hours daily, 25 Terzaki street, +30 2752 024 682). On Syntagma Square, next to the National Bank building, **Odyssey** sells a few maps, guidebooks, and English books stuffed between rows of toys and tacky souvenirs (long hours daily, tel. +30 2752 0-23 430).

Travel Agency and Car Rental: Conveniently located near the bus station, **Stavropoulos Tours** can help you book flights and boat tickets to anywhere in Greece (handy for trips within the Aegean Islands or to Hydra) and provides bus information (Mon-Sat 9:00-14:00 & 18:00-21:30, closed Sun, 24 Plapouta street, +30 2752 025 915, mobile +30 694 454 5691, www. stavropoulostours.gr, helpful Theodore). Several **car-rental** places are nearby (across from the Land Gate on Syngrou street).

Hop-On, Hop-Off Bus: Nafplio City Tour operates both a little tourist train and an open-top bus that zip around town. Their main advantage is a cheap way to get to Palamidi Fortress if you don't want to hoof it (departs from the square called Friends of the Greeks/Plateia Filellino, roughly hourly April-Sept, weekends only off-season; €4 for the train, €8 for the bus; +30 210 417 6144, www.nafpliocitytour.gr).

Local Guide: Charming Nafplio native **Patty Staikou** enjoys sharing her town and nearby ancient sites Epidavros, Mycenae, Nemea, and others (about €60/hour, can meet you at the sites, mobile +30 697 778 3315, staipatt@yahoo.gr).

Nafplio Walk

This self-guided walk, which takes about 1.5 hours, will give you a feel for Nafplio's pleasant Old Town.

• *We'll begin on the harborfront square opposite the fortified island, marked by a sturdy obelisk.*

❶ Square of the Friends of the Greeks (Plateia Filellinon)

This space is named for the French soldiers who died while fighting for Greek independence in 1821. On the memorial ❷ **obelisk,** a Classical-style

Nafplio

Walk

❶ Square of the Friends of the Greeks
❷ Obelisk
❸ Akti Miaouli Promenade
❹ Bouboulinas Promenade
❺ Church of St. Mary Above All Saints
❻ Antica Gelateria di Roma
❼ Syntagma Square
❽ Archaeological Museum
❾ National Bank of Greece
❿ "Big Street"
⓫ Soutsou Shops
⓬ Town Hall Square
⓭ To National Gallery
⓮ St. George Square
⓯ Church of St. Spyridon
⓰ Staikopoulou Street

Other

⓱ Karonis Wine Shop
⓲ Bookstore (2)
⓳ Travel Agency
⓴ Tourist Train/Bus Departure Point

Boats to Bourtzi Fortress

WALK BEGINS

Square of the Friends of the Greeks

50 Meters
50 Yards

AKTI MIAOULI PROMENADE

To Arvanitia Beach

FARMAKOPOULOU

MINIATI

ETHNIKIS ʼANTISTASEOS

30 NOEMVRIOU

FORMER MOSQUE

ZIGOMALA

ELEVATOR TO PALACE HOTEL

Cliffs

NAFPLIA PALACE HOTEL

AKRONAFPLIA FORTRESS

medallion shows brothers in arms: Hellas and Gallia (Greeks and French). On the other side is the French inscription.

You might see a cruise ship docked here on the **waterfront.** The port was deepened a few years back to accommodate a busy cruise industry (bigger ships, however, still drop anchor around the bend).

Plenty of Nafplio bars, cafés, restaurants, and tavernas face the harbor. The embankment called ❸ **Akti Miaouli** promenades to the left with a long line of sedate al fresco tables. (These places are mostly worth it for the view.) The promenade becomes a scenic shoreline path that continues all the way around the point to Arvanitia Beach, where a road returns to town up and over the saddle between the two fortresses.

The ❹ **Bouboulinas** promenade heads in the other direction (to the right, as you face the water)—first passing fish tavernas and then a string of bars.

From the harbor, you can also see the three Venetian forts of Nafplio and another across the

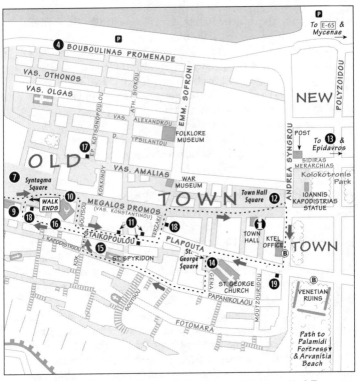

bay. The mighty little fortress island just offshore, called **Bourtzi,** was built during the first Venetian occupation (15th century) to protect the harbor. Most of what you see today is an 18th-century reconstruction from the second Venetian occupation. A shuttle boat departs from here to visit the island. It's a fun little trip, but there's little to see beyond a pleasant city view.

Capping the hill high above is the **Palamidi Fortress** (highest, to the left). Locals claim that the Palamidi Fortress, built in just three years (1711-1714), is the best-preserved Venetian fort in the Mediterranean. It can be reached by climbing nearly a thousand stone stairs...or by paying for a taxi. (I taxi up and walk down.) The view is rewarding, but the building itself is a bulky, impressive, empty shell. Below the Palamidi Fortress and to the right is Nafplio's ancient acropolis, the **Akronafplia fortress,** built upon the remains of an ancient fort. The big stones at the base of its wall date from the third century BC. (For more on visiting Bourtzi, Palamidi, and Akronafplia, see "Nafplio's Three Venetian Fortresses," later.)

Across the bay, dramatically capping a hill beyond the island fort of Bourtzi, is a **fourth Venetian fort.** This 300-year-old fort was built upon the ancient Acropolis of Argos (which dates from the Mycenaean Age, about 1500 BC).

With all this defensive investment, you can imagine how much Venice valued this strategic city as a trade and naval station. Today, locals still call the bay Porto Catena. That's Italian for "Chain Port," as chains once were strung from the island fort to the mainland in order to control ship traffic.

• *With your back to the water, walk up the street to the right of Hotel Grande Bretagne (Farmakopoulou). After a block, on the first corner (left), is a popular* gelateria. *Resist temptation for just a minute and first head across the small square to the...*

❺ Church of St. Mary Above All Saints

This church has a proud history: It originally dates from the 15th century; today's building is from the 18th century; and just a few years ago, they peeled back, then reapplied, all the plaster. The priest at this church is particularly active, keeping it open late into the evening (long after many other Nafplio churches have closed). Outside the door he posts a daily message—a thought to ponder or a suggested prayer.

Step inside—it's generally open. The flat ceiling with the painted Trinity in three circular panels shows a Venetian influence—most Greek Orthodox churches of this period are domed. The more typical iconostasis, a wall of Greek Orthodox icons, separates worshippers from priests. As is standard in Greek churches, the icon in the center changes with the season. In the front left corner you might find Q-tips and little plastic baggies for taking home priest-blessed oil. ("If you believe, then it heals.") A glass case in the same corner shows off relics (mostly bones of saints) and little treasures (such as the Ostrich Egg, painted in Russia and symbolic of the Resurrection). There are a few more museum cases on the right. If you're so moved, drop in a coin for a candle (near the entry) and light up a prayer. Notice the heavy-duty venting for the busy candle trays and the icon above the candles featuring the saint-protected city of Nafplio.

The mural just outside the church (on the wall, to the right of the door as you leave) is something of a nationalistic history of Greece in a nutshell. Follow it, starting with Adam and Eve to the golden age of ancient Greece (featuring Socrates, Plato, Aristotle, and others), the founding of Christianity and the Greek church, the building of the monasteries at Meteora, the Ottoman occupation (see the Greek priest being hanged by a Turk), independence (with a banner that says "democracy" in Greek), World Wars I and II (find the Nazi with a gun and a Greek resistance hero mightily perched on a rock), and finally, the Greek version of heaven, which looks like Meteora.

• *Now dip into...*

❻ Antica Gelateria di Roma

Greece has great honey-dripping desserts, but nobody does ice cream like the Italians. This recommended ice-cream parlor is run by Marcello and family, who offer a taste of Italy: gelato, fruit-based *sorbetto*, and other treats such as biscotti, *limoncello,* and cappuccino (and air-conditioning). This popular, fun-loving place is one holdover from the Venetian occupation that no local will complain about.

• *Gelato in hand, exit Marcello's; go left behind the church and into the big square.*

❼ Syntagma Square (Plateia Syntagmatos)

Like the main square in Athens, Nafplio's central plaza is dubbed "Constitution Square," celebrating the 1843 document that es-

tablished a constitutional monarchy for Greece. Nafplio was one of the first towns liberated from the Ottoman Turks (1822) and became the new country's first capital. The square is a delightful mix of architectural styles, revealing the many layers of local history.

Survey this scene in a counterclockwise spin-tour, starting on your immediate right. The big building flying the Greek flag was originally the Venetian arsenal. Of course, wherever Venice ruled, you'll find its symbol: the winged lion of its patron saint, Mark (over the door). The building is stout with heavily barred windows because it once stored gunpowder and weapons. Today it houses the town's ❽ **Archaeological Museum** (described later, under "Sights in Nafplio").

Just to the left of the museum is a domed former **mosque.** In 1825, with the Muslim Ottomans expelled, this building was taken over and renovated to house independent Greece's first parliament. (Now it serves as a conference center.)

The big ❾ **National Bank of Greece** hearkens back to the very earliest Greek civilizations, with its dark-red columns that taper toward the base, as if they were tree trunks stood on their heads

(shaped and painted just like the ones in the circa-1500 BC Minoan palaces on Crete). In front of the bank stands another Venetian winged lion from the old fortress. The second former **mosque** fronting this square (see red-tile domes at the far end) was converted after independence into Greece's first primary school; today it's a gallery and theater. To the left, look up past the popular cafés and restaurants to appreciate the square's series of stately Neoclassical buildings. The square is a popular hangout for parents enjoying coffee while their kids run wild—future soccer stars-in-training.

• *Head across the square and walk down the pedestrian street (opposite the side you entered).*

❿ The "Big Street" (Megalos Dromos)

Nafplio's main drag, connecting the main square with Town Hall Square, is named for King Constantine (Vasileos Konstantinou). Locals know it as Megalos Dromos (Big Street).

The town is something of a shoppers' paradise—many streets are crammed with shops selling everything from the usual tacky tourist trinkets to expensive jewelry, all aimed at the fat wallets of Athenian weekenders. This is a fine scene in the early evening when everyone's out strolling.

• *Turn right at the first corner up the narrow alley (Soutsou), then turn left onto touristy Stai-kopoulou. At the end of the next block, a trio of shops are worth browsing.*

⓫ Soutsou Shops

The **Worry Bead** shop on the left (at #25) features a remarkable selection. The cheapest, synthetic sets cost about €8; the priciest, which can cost hundreds of euros, are antique or made of amber (for more information on worry beads, see page 208). The **Komboloï Museum** upstairs shows off a few small rooms of the owner's vast worry-bead collection, while a handful of English labels explain how variations on worry beads are used by many different faiths (€2, generally open 9:30-20:00). A few doors farther down (at #29) you'll find the artisan **Olive Tree** shop (look for the *Ελιά* sign), where father-and-son duo Thomas and Lefteris are hard at work creating handmade olive-wood crafts (generally daily 10:30-23:00). Finally, across the street (at #52) is a **sandal-maker's shop** (Σανδαλοποιείο, daily 10:00-23:00). This is *the* place to buy traditional Greek sandals—or to simply appreciate the country's number one fashion staple.

• *At the next intersection, turn left and walk one block back down to the "Big Street." Turn right onto Megalos Dromos and follow it until you emerge into...*

⑫ Town Hall Square

A statue marks the one-time location of the palace of **King Otto** (Όθων), the first head of state of post-Ottoman Greece. The great powers—England, France, and Russia—insisted that the newly independent Greeks have a monarchy, so Otto was imported from Bavaria. He wasn't here for long, though: An enthusiastic student of classical history, Otto was charmed by the idea of reviving the greatness of ancient Athens and moved the capital to Athens after just one year. (The palace that once stood here burned down in 1929.)

Otto, looking plenty regal, gazes toward the New Town. Fifty yards in front of Otto (on the right) is the Neoclassical first high school of Greece—today's Town Hall, and home to the TI. The monument in front celebrates a local hero from the war against the Ottomans. Until recently this square was named Three Admirals Square—remembering those three great European powers that helped the Greeks overthrow their Ottoman rulers in the 1820s.

• *At the far end of Town Hall Square, you hit the busy...*

Syngrou Street and the New Town

This thoroughfare (sometimes spelled Siggrou or Syggrou) separates the Old Town from the New. Out of respect for the three-story-tall Old Town, no new building is allowed to exceed that height—even in the New Town.

In the square across the street, a statue honors **Ioannis Kapodistrias,** the president of Greece's short-lived republic (back when Nafplio was the capital). He faces the Old Town...and

Otto, who stepped in when the president's reign was cut tragically short. (We'll get the whole story later.)

Just behind Kapodistrias is the family-friendly **Kolokotronis Park.** For a cheap and fast meal, consider grabbing a bite at one of the gyro and souvlaki eateries surrounding the park (order and pay at the bar, then find a bench in the park). Goody's (on the left, by the post office) is a branch of the popular Greek hamburger chain.

A few minutes' walk straight ahead, past the end of the park, is the ⓭ **National Gallery,** which shows off evocative artwork from the Greek War of Independence (described later, under "Sights in Nafplio").

Facing Ioannis, head south (right) on Syngrou street. The commotion at the end of the block surrounds Nafplio's tiny but busy **bus station.**

At the next corner we'll turn right. But first, just behind the row of buses, you'll see the ruined remains of Nafplio's **Land Gate,** part of the city's 18th-century Venetian fortifications. Take a little loop from here through the gate and study the amazing Venetian stone defensive work around and above you.

• *Return to the corner, and head back into the Old Town on Plapouta street. Walk to...*

⓮ St. George Square

The focal point of the square, Nafplio's *mitropolis* (equivalent to a Catholic cathedral), is dedicated to St. George and was the neighborhood church for King Otto (whose palace was once on Town Hall Square, which we walked through earlier). Step into the church's dark interior (noticing the clever double-hinge system that prevents the doors from slamming) to see a gigantic chandelier hovering overhead.

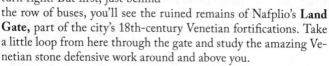

Back outside, surveying St. George Square, you get a feel for an old Nafplio neighborhood. Like most of the Old Town, well-worn Neoclassical buildings date from the boom that followed the city's rise to prominence when it was Greece's first capital. During the 1820s and 1830s, Nafplio became a haven to refugees from other lands still threatened by the Ottomans.

• *Walk a block slightly uphill (toward the fortress) and turn right on Papanikolaou street.*

Upper Streets of the Old Town

Strolling this quiet lane, note that the Neoclassical grid-planned town is to your right, while the higgledy-piggledy Ottoman town climbs the hillside (with winding and evocative lanes and stepped alleys) on your left. Consider as you walk how Greece's struggling economy leaves so many buildings with such potential in abandoned shambles.

Straight ahead (100 yards away) stands the white bell tower marking the ⓕ **Church of St. Spyridon** and its square. Facing the square (on the left, hiding in a niche in the wall, near the steps) is the first of several 18th-century Turkish fountains you'll see. When the Ottomans controlled Greece, they still used the Arabic script you see here, rather than the Latin alphabet used for modern Turkish. This panel names the guy who paid for the fountain, and tells when he had it built (1734-1735) and why (to provide water for his horses). Other fountains have similar tributes, verses from the Quran, or jaunty greetings.

Continue straight along the side of the church to another **Ottoman fountain** (on the left)—with its characteristic decor of cypress trees and flowers.

Between here and the door of the church (on the right) is the spot marking the rough equivalent—to the Greeks—of Ford's Theater (where Lincoln was assassinated). A plaque on the wall commemorates the story: Ioannis Kapodistrias was elected the first president of independent Greece in 1828. But just three years later, in 1831, he was shot and stabbed in this spot by Mani landowners who feared his promises of land reform. This led to chaos, less democratic idealism, and the arrival of Greece's imported Bavarian royalty (King Otto, whom we met earlier).

If it's open, pop into the church to see a painting (at the back) depicting the assassination. Across from the church is a collapsing *hamam*, a Turkish bath from the 18th century.

• *At the next corner (Kokkinou street), turn right and climb down the slippery marble steps to Staikopoulou street (where we saw the Soutsou shops, earlier). This time we'll take it left, back to Syntagma Square.*

ⓖ Staikopoulou Street

This bustling pedestrian drag is lined with grill restaurants (the harborfront is better for fish) and their happy hustlers, and another fine Ottoman fountain (on the right after a block).

A couple of blocks down, head right and back into Syntagma Square. Find the tiny black cube in the center and sit on it. Apart from being a handy meeting point for the town's kids and a stand for the community Christmas tree, it means absolutely nothing.

• *Our walk is over. From here you can enjoy the rest of the city. In addition to the museums we've already passed, a few more sights—including a folklore museum and a war museum—are within a few blocks. Adventurers may want to head to any of Nafplio's Venetian forts. Or, if you're ready to relax, hit the beach.*

Sights in Nafplio

MUSEUMS

▲Nafplio Archaeological Museum

Nafplio's top museum is small but gives a concise overview of prehistoric Greece and the Mycenaean civilization. Visit here for a great warm-up before you go to Mycenae.

Cost and Hours: €6, includes lengthy audioguide; generally Wed-Mon 8:30-15:30, closed Tue; at the bottom of Syntagma Square, +30 2752 027 502, http://odysseus.culture.gr.

Visiting the Museum: The museum occupies the top two floors of the grand Venetian arsenal on the main square.

The little collection (starting on the ground floor, well-described in English) was excavated from nearby tombs. While nothing here is from Mycenae itself, many of the artifacts date from the same late Bronze Age (c. 1500 BC)—a reminder that the region is rich in late Bronze Age sites. The display runs in chronological order, with Stone Age tools suddenly giving way to a dolphin fresco inspired by the Minoan civilization on Crete. Eye-catching jewelry includes a bull-shaped crystal bead (look for the magnifying glass inside a glass case) and strings of gold beads.

The star of the museum stands in the center: the "Dendra Panoply," a 15th-century BC suit of bronze armor that was discovered in a Mycenaean chamber tomb. Also found at the site (and displayed here) is a helmet made from boar tusks. Experts consider this the oldest surviving suit of armor in all of Europe.

The second floor displays artifacts from the Age of Homer to the Roman occupation. Particularly striking are the ceremonial terra-cotta masks along one wall. Dating from the seventh century BC, these likely were designed to scare off evil spirits. Check out the display of rare glasswork from the first century AD—somehow these pieces have survived two millennia without getting smashed.

▲National Gallery
(Alexandros Soutzos Museum, Nafplio Annex)

Housed in a grandly restored Neoclassical mansion, this museum's permanent collection, displayed upstairs, is devoted to Romantic artwork (mostly paintings) stemming from the inspirational Greek War of Independence (1821-1829), which led to Nafplio's status as the first capital of independent Greece. The small, manageable collection is arranged thematically. The English descriptions here are worth reading, as they explain the historical underpinnings for the art, illuminating common themes such as the dying hero, naval battles, and the hardships of war. The art itself might not be technically masterful, but the patriotism shimmering beneath it is stirring even to non-Greeks.

Cost and Hours: €5, free on Mon; open Mon and Wed-Sat 10:00-15:00, Wed and Fri also 17:00-20:00, Sun 10:00-14:00, closed Tue; a 5-minute walk into the New Town from the post office along a major road called Sidiras Merarchias, at #23, +30 2752 021 915, http://odysseus.culture.gr.

Papantoniou Museum of Peloponnese Folklore

Dedicated to Peloponnesian culture, this modern exhibit fills two floors with clothing, furniture, and jewelry that trace the cultural history of Nafplio and the surrounding region. While not particularly engaging, the interesting collection—which ranges from colorful and traditional costumes, to stiff urban suits, to formal gowns, to looms and spinning wheels—is well-displayed.

Cost and Hours: €5, Mon-Sat 9:00-14:30, Sun 9:30-15:00, fun gift shop with Greek crafts, Vasileos Alexandrou 1, +30 2752 028 379, www.pli.gr.

War Museum (Nafplio Branch)

This small exhibit, operated and staffed by the Greek armed forces, is best left to ardent Greek patriots and military buffs; for most others it's not worth the small admission fee. It displays old illustrations and photos of various conflicts (some providing a peek into Nafplio's past cityscape), plus weapons and uniforms (with some English descriptions) housed in what was Greece's first military school. The top floor, dedicated to the modern era, displays WWII-era political cartoons from the Greek perspective.

Cost and Hours: €3, daily 9:00-19:00, off-season until 17:00 and closed Mon, on Amalias, +30 2752 025 591.

NAFPLIO'S THREE VENETIAN FORTRESSES

In the days when Venice was the economic ruler of Europe (15th-18th centuries), the Venetians fortified Nafplio with a trio of stout fortresses. These attempted—but ultimately failed—to fend off Ottoman invasion. Conquered by the Ottomans in 1715, Nafplio remained in Turkish hands until the Greeks retook the city in 1822. Today all three parts of the Venetian fortifications are open to visitors (with nothing to see but stones and views). These are listed in order from lowest to highest.

Bourtzi

This heavily fortified island—just offshore from Nafplio's waterfront—offers a pleasant vantage point (pictured above), offering fine views back on the city. Locals are working to build a museum chronicling the island's interesting history, from Ottoman origins and Venetian expansions to its roles as an active fort during the Greek revolution and a grand 1930s hotel. But until it's complete, there's not much to do here.

Cost and Hours: Boats depart from the bottom of the square called Friends of the Greeks/Plateia Filellinon, €5 round-trip, won't run with fewer than four people, schedule can be sporadic—check sign on promenade for next departure, once on island it's free to enter the fortress, +30 697 201 5296.

Akronafplia

Nafplio's ancient acropolis, capping the low hill just behind the

Old Town, is fairly easy to reach (a manageable but sometimes-steep 10- to 15-minute uphill hike—from the Old Town, just find your way up on any of a number of narrow stepped lanes, then bear left to reach the main road that leads up into the eastern end of the fortress). The earliest surviving parts of this fortress date back to the third century BC, but the Venetians brought it up to then-modern standards in the 15th century. Up top, there's little to see aside from a few ruins (free to enter and explore anytime). The top of the parklike hill is flanked by two hotels: At the east end (toward Palamidi) stands the deserted and decaying Hotel Xenia; and at the west end (below a little heliport at the end of the road), the top-of-the-top Nafplia Palace hotel entices you to enjoy a drink from its terrace café. You can avoid the hike up by riding the elevator from the top of the Old Town to this hotel (see "Nafplio Walk" map).

▲▲Palamidi Fortress

This imposing hilltop fortress, built by the Venetians between 1711 and 1714, is the best-preserved of its kind in Greece. Palamidi towers over the Old Town, protected to the west by steep cliffs that plunge 650 feet to the sea. From its highest ramparts, you can spot several Aegean islands and look deep into the mountainous interior of the Peloponnesian Peninsula.

Cost and Hours: €8, €4 off-season, daily 8:30-sunset (or earlier), +30 2752 028 036.

Getting There: You can reach the fortress the old-fashioned way: by **climbing** the looooong flight of 999 steps that leads up

from the road to Akronafplia fortress (near the top end of Polyzoidou street and the bus stop, just outside the Old Town). The toughest part of the climb is the heat; bring water, wear good shoes, and go first thing in the morning, when the path is mostly in shade. (If you get a late start, do the Palamidi hike in the early evening, though call first to confirm the closing time.)

To avoid the climb, you can catch a **taxi** to the top for about €10 one-way (and perhaps take the steps down). Or check if the **hop-on, hop-off bus** or **tourist train** are running (see "Helpful Hints," earlier). If you have a car, you can **drive** to the top and park for free: Follow signs east of town for the beach at *Karathona/Καραθωνα*, and after ascending the hill, watch for the turnoff on the right up to *Palamidi/ Παλαμηδη*.

Services: WCs are just outside St. Andrew's Bastion, near the ticket kiosk for hill climbers, and in the parking lot.

Visiting the Fortress: The fortress is actually a collection of fortresses or bastions within its exterior walls. Notice how the various bastions could defend themselves against each other if attackers breached the outer walls or one of the bastions was taken. You can navigate by following the handy signs and info posts you'll see throughout. St. Andrew's Bastion is the main bastion to visit. I'd study this one and then just explore the other bastions with a sense of fun and wonder.

St. Andrew's Bastion (Agios Andreas) is the best preserved and offers great views over the rooftops of old Nafplio. Inside, find the small church. Behind it, under the first archway, is a tiny entrance leading to the cell of the miserable little Kolokotronis Prison (you'll need to crouch and scramble to get inside). While untrue, Greeks love the legend that the Greek hero Theodoros Kolokotronis was imprisoned here by his political  opponents after playing a key role in liberating Greece from Ottoman rule. Back outside, scamper up the giant vaults, which form an angled approach up to the ramparts. Imagine that the entire vault structure functioned as a cistern. Enjoy the views.

ACTIVITIES
Beaches
When ready for some beach time or a swim you have three good choices in and near Nafplio (all free, with easy parking and showers): Arvanitia (in town), Karathona (2 miles away via a scenic walk), and Tolo (6 miles away, with good bus connections).

Arvanitia Beach, on the backside of the peninsula, is a 10-minute walk from the Old Town (walk over the saddle between the two forts or along the pedestrian path leading from the

Old Town and around the peninsula). It's a small, pebbly beach with clear, deep water. Crowded in summer, it's popular with the young crowd and has a bar and a free open-air gym workout zone in the parking lot.

Karathona Beach is for more serious beach-going. This half-mile-long sandy beach with shallow water is popular with families, dotted with beachfront tavernas, and lined with palm trees. From Nafplio's Arvanitia Beach you can walk there in 45 minutes along an unpaved seafront lane.

Tolo Beach, the best beach of all with nice sand and shallow water, is farther away (6 miles from Nafplio, hourly buses from bus station). You'll find plenty of services (hotels, restaurants, rental paddle boats, and a small town of shops and cafés). While at Tolo, consider visiting the nearby ancient site at **Asini,** less than a mile away on a rocky promontory jutting into the sea. There isn't much left of the 3,000-year-old acropolis, but interpretive panels do a good job of explaining its history, and the setting is impressive.

Walking
One of the great delights of a Nafplio visit is taking a stroll along the waterfront. Locals are understandably proud of their tree-lined, peaceful, and scenic walking and jogging lane that circles the peninsula from the town center to Arvanitia Beach and Karathona Beach. The first part (to Arvanitia Beach) is a stone-paved path; after that you'll follow an unpaved trail. Start on the promenade nearest the island fort and walk out onto the spit, and then continue around the peninsula to Arvanitia Beach. For a longer walk, continue another two miles from Arvanitia to Karathona Beach, passing beneath the Palamidi Fortress on the way. While you can circle back to the town center from Karathona Beach via the New Town, most people prefer to retrace their steps along the waterfront. Energetic walkers can also make a loop to Karathona via the Palamidi Fortress.

Wine Tasting at the Karonis Wine Shop
Dimitri Karonis specializes in Greek wines and ouzo, and gives serious wine shoppers an informative wine tasting (Καρωνη, Mon-Sat 8:30-14:00 & 18:00-21:30, also most Sun 12:00-14:00 & 18:45-21:30 in summer; closed Sun off-season; near Syntagma Square at Amalias 5, call or email ahead to arrange a more in-depth tasting for €10-12, +30 2752 024 446, karonisd@otenet.gr).

SIGHTS NEAR NAFPLIO
These ancient attractions are both within a half-hour drive of Nafplio (in different directions) and covered in the next two chapters. If you have time to do only one, go for Mycenae; it has more to see.

NAFPLIO

▲▲▲Epidavros

This ancient site, 23 miles (by car) east of Nafplio, has an underwhelming museum, forgettable ruins...and the most magnificent theater of the ancient world. It was built nearly 2,500 years ago to seat 15,000. Today it's kept busy reviving the greatest plays of antiquity. You can catch musical and dramatic performances here in summer. Try to see Epidavros either early or late in the day; the theater's marvelous acoustics are best enjoyed in near-solitude.

▲▲▲Mycenae

This was the capital of the Mycenaeans, who won the Trojan War and dominated Greece 1,000 years before the Acropolis and other golden age Greek sights. The Classical Greeks marveled at the huge stones and workmanship of the Mycenaean ruins. Visitors today

can still gape at the Lion Gate; peer into a cool, ancient cistern; and explore the giant *tholos* tomb called the Treasury of Atreus. The tomb, built in the 15th century BC, is like a huge underground igloo, with a vast subterranean dome of cleverly arranged stones.

Nightlife in Nafplio

NAFPLIO

Nafplio enjoys a thriving after-hours scene with several nightlife microclimates—the age of the clientele varies every few blocks. I enjoy simply joining the evening strolling scene at all these places. For the best sunset stroll, head down the promenade Akti Miaouli and then out on the spit to the tiny lighthouse. Poke around to find the café or bar that appeals to you most for a pre- or post-dinner drink. Note that there are no true dance clubs in Nafplio, which has a strict noise ordinance: no loud music in the Old Town after 23:00. (Instead, huge seasonal outdoor clubs sprout along the roads leading out of town.) A few zones to consider:

Akti Miaouli Promenade: The upper crust enjoys the cafés lining the promenade Akti Miaouli. Prices are higher, but the water views (with the illuminated island fortress) could be worth the expense. At its farthest southern end is a lively playground and a fun, youthful place for drinks. This promenade leads to the breakwater spit and then to the path leading both romantically and scenically around the peninsula.

Bouboulinas Promenade and Beyond: Beyond the fish restaurants are several café/bars—once *the* place to be seen, they now provide a peaceful setting for a drink. A block beyond the Bouboulinas promenade is a stretch of teen-friendly fast-food places, described later under "Eating in Nafplio."

Syntagma Square and Nearby: People of all ages seem to enjoy the floodlit marble drawing-room vibe of Syntagma Square. Cafés and restaurants with ample, atmospheric al fresco seating surround a relaxed open area with people at play. From Syntagma, the neighboring streets are home to several popular café/bars. To find them, just follow the noise.

Arvanitia Beach: Blublanc Beach Bar comes out of hibernation every summer at Arvanitia Beach, transforming it from a popular swimming spot by day into a dance party at night (May-Sept, +30 2752 096 031).

Cinema: The local cinema (at Kolokotronis Park) plays movies in their original languages with Greek subtitles. In summer, the theater moves nearby (continue walking along 25 Martiou for 10 minutes) into the open air.

Sleeping in Nafplio

Nafplio enjoys an abundance of excellent accommodations. Because this is a chic getaway for wealthy Athenians, many of the best beds are in well-run, boutique-ish little pensions. (Some of the smaller pensions are run by skeleton staff, so don't expect 24-hour reception; let them know what time you'll arrive so they can greet you.) The many options allow hotel seekers to be picky.

It's boom or bust in Nafplio. At the busiest times (June, July, especially Aug, and weekends year-round), hotels are full and prices go up; outside these times, hoteliers are lean and hungry, and rates become soft. Don't be afraid to ask for a deal, especially if you're staying more than a couple of nights. If your hotel doesn't include breakfast, most cafés in town sell a basic breakfast for €7-8.

Most of these accommodations are uphill from the heart of the Old Town. The good news: They provide fresh breezes, have almost no mosquitoes, and offer a quiet retreat from the bustling

Accommodations
1. Ippoliti Hotel
2. Aetoma Hotel
3. Amymone Guesthouse, Adiandi Hotel & Amymone Suites
4. Pension Marianna
5. Amfitriti Palazzo
6. Byron Hotel
7. Hotel Leto Nuevo
8. Aethra Boutique Rooms
9. Pension Rigas
10. Pension Filyra
11. Pension Anapli

Eateries & Other
12. Mezedopoleio O Noulis
13. Kastro Karima
14. I Gonia tou Kavalari
15. Alaloum Restaurant (2)
16. Wild Duck
17. Aiolos Taverna
18. To Omorfo Tavernaki
19. Bounos Psarosavouras
20. Trattoria La Gratella
21. Mitato Souvlaki
22. Gyro Grill, Pizza Alpha & Mandaloun
23. Trendy Grill Strip
24. Supermarket
25. Antica Gelateria di Roma & Pergamonto

Map labels: Boats to Bourtzi Fortress · OBELISK · Square of the Friends of the Greeks · AKTI MIAOULI PROMENADE · FARMAKOPOULOU · ANTISTASEOS · 50 Meters · 50 Yards · MINIATI · To Arvanitia Beach · To P · CHURCH OF ST. MARY ABOVE ALL SAINTS · ETHNIKIS · ARCH. MUS. · 30 NOEMVRIOU · FORMER MOSQUE · ZIGOMALA · Cliffs · AKRONAFPLIA FORTRESS

NAFPLIO

old center. The bad news: You'll climb a few flights of stairs to reach your room.

$$$$ Ippoliti Hotel (Ιππολύτι) is a classy business-hotel splurge, with 19 elegantly decorated, hardwood-floor rooms with antique touches. In summer, breakfast is served on the patio beside the small swimming pool (elevator, small gym, near the waterfront at Ilia Miniati 9, at corner with Aristidou, +30 2752 096 088, http://ippoliti.gr, ippoliti@ippoliti.gr).

$$$ Aetoma Hotel is a family-run gem offering five individually styled rooms with high ceilings, balconies, and lots of natural light in the house where owner Panagiota was born. She and her son, Akis, now invite travelers to share in the history of their home (Spiridonos 2, +30 2752 027 373, www.aetoma.gr, stay@aetoma.gr).

$$$ Amymone Guesthouse (Αμυμώνη), and the slightly more expensive **Adiandi Hotel** (Αδιάντη) and **Amymone Suites,** are a trio of super-stylish, trendy boutique hotels a few doors apart along one of Nafplio's most inviting restaurant lanes. The guesthouse and hotel boast anything-but-cookie-cutter rooms, all with different color schemes and decor. At the suites, rooms are breezy-

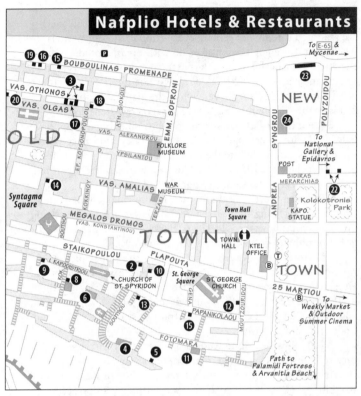

Nafplio Hotels & Restaurants

chic with natural woods and reclaimed furnishings. The very central location can come with more noise than my other listings, and each building has lots of stairs with no elevator. All three share an owner and the same phone number (+30 2752 022 073) but have independent websites (Amymone Guesthouse, 9 rooms, Othonos 39, www.amymone.gr, info@amymone.gr; Adiandi Hotel, 7 rooms, Othonos 31, www.hotel-adiandi.com, info@hotel-adiandi.com; Amymone Suites, 7 rooms, Othonos 18, www. amymone-suites.gr, info@amymone-suites.gr).

$$$ **Pension Marianna** is my choice for the most welcoming place in town. The friendly Zotos brothers—Petros, Panos, and Takis—offer genuine hospitality, fair rates, and comfortable rooms in their stony little paradise. It's scenically situated just under the lower Akronafplia wall, well worth the steep climb up the stairs from the Old

Town. The 26 rooms—some with views and/or little balconies—are scattered throughout several levels. Atop it all is an airy terrace where you can enjoy breakfast made with organic products from their nearby farm (RS%, breakfast extra, family rooms, no elevator, Potamianou 9, +30 2752 024 256, www.hotelmarianna.gr, info@hotelmarianna.gr). Park above town at the giant, abandoned Hotel Xenia at the Akronafplia fortress and walk a few steps down.

$$ Amfitriti Palazzo's seven plush rooms, highest up, have balconies with sweeping views and fun classy-mod decor, with some rooms built right into the rock (family room, top of the hill—just under the old wall, +30 2752 096 250, www.amfitriti-pension.gr, info@amfitriti-pension.gr, Aggeliki and family).

$$ Byron Hotel is a traditional, family-run standby with 18 simple, older-feeling rooms (some with views) in a scenic setting up some stairs above the Old Town (Platonos 2, +30 2752 022 351, www.byronhotel.gr, byronhotel@otenet.gr, Aris).

$$ Hotel Leto Nuevo is partway up the slopes of the Akronafplia fortress. Its 18 boutiquish rooms all have sea views and either a bathtub or rain shower; ask about elusive and popular room #121, which is higher up (discount without breakfast, Zigomala 28, +30 2752 028 093, www.letohotelnafplio.gr, scale707@gmail.com, Sofia and her son Vasilis).

$$ Aethra Boutique Rooms has 10 rooms with contemporary style in a renovated old mansion, higher up along some stairs (lovely garden area, rooftop view terrace, corner of Zigomala and Kokkinou, +30 2752 025 253, www.aethra.gr, info@aethra.gr, Katia and Litsa).

$$ Pension Rigas is a gem with six cozy, charmingly rustic rooms in a refurbished old building with exposed stone and beams, hardwood floors, high ceilings, and lots of character. Its comfy lobby and small patio area provide a convivial space for guests to share travel stories (Kapodistriou 8, +30 2752 023 611, https://pensionrigas.inn.fan, rigaspension@hotmail.com, run by friendly Australian Lena).

$ Pension Filyra (Φιλύρα) has six tastefully and colorfully decorated rooms at a nice price in a few buildings in the heart of the Old Town (no breakfast, Aggelou Terzaki 29, +30 2752 096 096, www.pensionfilyra.gr, pensionfilyra@gmail.com, Rania).

$ Pension Anapli is on the budget end, but cute, with nine colorful, dressed-up rooms with iron-frame beds (Fotomara 21, +30 2752 024 585, www.pensionanapli.gr, info@pensionanapli.gr).

Eating in Nafplio

Nafplio is bursting with tempting eateries. Because most cater to Athenians on weekend breaks and aim to please repeat customers, prices can be a bit high. In two high-profile restaurant zones—the tavernas along Staikopoulou street (just above Syntagma Square) and the fish restaurants on Bouboulinas street (along the waterfront)—waiters compete desperately for the passing tourist trade. While I'd avoid the places on Staikopoulou, if you want seafood, the Bouboulinas fish joints are the best in town. I've focused most of my coverage on the tight pedestrian lanes between these two areas, toward the water from Syntagma Square, where values are good and ambience is excellent. Several places offer live traditional Greek music (generally weekends in summer after 20:30 or 21:00; get details from your hotel).

RESTAURANTS

$$$ Mezedopoleio O Noulis (Ο Νουλησ)—run by Noulis, the man with the mighty moustache shown on the sign—serves up an inviting range of *meze* (appetizers). Three or four *meze* constitute a tasty meal for two people. This authentic-feeling place offers a rare chance to sample *saganaki flambé* (fried cheese flambéed with Metaxa brandy). As Noulis is temperamental and likes to do it all himself, don't come here if you're in a hurry (Mon-Sat 13:00-15:00 & 19:00-23:00, closed Sun; Oct-mid-May Tue-Sun 13:00-16:00, closed Mon; no reservations, Moutzouridou 22, +30 2752 025 541).

$$$ Kastro Karima, on a quiet street near the Church of St. Spyridon, serves simple but tasty dishes at reasonable prices, including a variety of traditional spreads. Choose between sidewalk tables or the stony-chic interior (Tue-Sun 13:00-24:00, closed Mon, Papanikolaou 32, +30 2752 025 279).

$$ I Gonia tou Kavalari (Η Γωνια του Καβαλαρη, "Kavalari's Corner"), nestled behind Syntagma Square, is an easygoing rustic eatery with live music twice a week and a tempting tapas-style menu of inexpensive *meze* (Tue-Sun 12:00-late, closed Mon, Amalias 2, +30 2752 500 180).

$$$ Alaloum Restaurant (Αλαλούμ) serves big portions of Greek and Mediterranean dishes, including a famous "mother-in-law's salad." Sharing is encouraged (sit inside or out, Wed-Mon 12:00-24:00, closed Tue and for two weeks in June, Papanikolaou 42, +30 2752 028 213). A second location at Bouboulinas 63 serves the same menu with a different view (daily 12:00-late).

$$$$ Wild Duck, on the fishy Bouboulinas drag, is more creative than your average taverna. Call it "Mediterranean with Greek influences," featuring pasta, risotto, seafood, and meat, plus interesting combinations like octopus served with hummus (Mon-

NAFPLIO

Fri 17:00-23:30, Sat-Sun from 9:00, Bouboulinas 67, +30 2752 028 562).

Tavernas on Olgas Street: The lane called Olgas, tucked away in a grid of streets just two blocks up from the waterfront, is filled with charming, family-run tavernas serving Greek classics to happy tourists. At any of these, you can choose between a cozy, rustic interior or outdoor tables. Window-shop along here and consider these two good options: **$$ Aiolos** (good mixed-grill platters, drunken chicken, *saganaki,* and *sousamotiro*—fried cheese with sesame seeds, Olgas 30, +30 2752 026 828) or **$$ To Omorfo Tavernaki** (Το Όμορφο Ταβερνάκι), literally "The Beautiful Little Tavern" (traditional home-style Greek dishes, Kotsonopoulou 1, +30 2752 025 944, Tsioli family).

$$$ Fish Restaurants on Bouboulinas: As you stroll the harborfront, you'll soon come upon the fishy aromas and aggressive come-ons of the town's best seafood eateries (all open daily, roughly 12:00-24:00). Wherever you choose to dine, part of the fun is the strolling scene. Seafood here is typically priced by the kilogram or half-kilogram (figure about 300-400 grams for a typical portion—around €20-30 for a seafood entrée, or about €10-20 for a meat dish). **Bounos Psarosavouras** gets a thumbs-up from locals for its consistent quality (daily 12:00-24:00, Bouboulinas 77, +30 2752 027 704).

Italian: Your best bet if you're craving Italian, **$$$ Trattoria La Gratella** serves tasty and reasonably priced pizza, pasta, and *secondi* with a bright and modern interior and nice outdoor tables (June-Nov daily 13:00-24:00, Olgas 44, +30 2752 028 350).

CHEAP GYRO PITA AND SOUVLAKI JOINTS

Each of these places serves souvlaki and gyro pita sandwiches and more for a quick, inexpensive meal. You can sit inside or out on the sidewalk, or get takeaway.

$$ Mitato Souvlaki is an inviting little joint that does both meat and veggie gyros, just steps off the main square (daily 11:00-23:00, off Syntagma Square behind National Bank building at Staikopoulou 14, +30 2752 021 159).

Dining in Kolokotronis Park: Several cheap family- and student-style diners line the park (along Sidiras Merarchias street, just beyond Town Hall Square), all with noisy indoor seating and peaceful options in the park. **$ Gyro Grill** offers perhaps the cheapest hot dinner in town. **$$ Pizza Alpha** and **$ Mandaloun** (good Lebanese) are a few doors down.

"Trendy Grill Strip": This thriving strip of eateries is where high-school kids take their dates (facing the harbor and parking, just east of the Bouboulinas promenade). Along with **$$ Trendy**—the busiest souvlaki joint in town—**$$ Pizza Scuola** is popular.

Picnics: The **supermarket** at the corner of Syngrou and Flessa, between the post office and the "Trendy Grill Strip," is the most convenient of several supermarkets in town (Mon-Fri 8:00-21:00, Sat until 20:00, closed Sun).

DESSERT
Antica Gelateria di Roma is known for its mouthwatering array of *gelati* (dairy-based ice cream) and *sorbetti* (fruit-based sorbet) made fresh on the premises daily by Italian gelato master Marcello Raffo, his wife Monica, and his sister Claudia. The Raffos also offer other Italian snacks and drinks (daily 9:00-late, Farmakopoulou 3, at corner with Kominou, +30 2752 023 520).

Pergamonto (Περγαμοντο), next door to the gelateria, does fresh-from-the-deep-fryer *loukoumades* (Greek doughnuts), with a range of toppings. I say go traditional, with honey or cinnamon and sugar (generally daily 15:00-24:00, Komninou 1, +30 2752 024 570).

Nafplio Connections

BY BUS
The tiny KTEL bus station is convenient and central, and has schedules in English. Their website has an English option and sells tickets (www.ktelargolida.gr). While the ticket agent can give information, confirm your plans (and transfers) with your driver or other passengers.

Direct buses go to **Athens** (nearly hourly, 2.5 hours), **Epidavros** (2-3/day, 1/day late on Sun, possibly 1/day Oct-April, 45 minutes), and **Mycenae** (1-2/day, none Sun, 45 minutes). For details see those chapters.

Journeys to other Peloponnesian destinations likely require a change in Tripoli and multiple transfers; get an early start and be prepared for frustrations and delays: **Tripoli** (2/day, 1.5 hours), **Monemvasia** (may be possible from Tripoli—check locally; generally 1/day, 4.5 hours), **Olympia** (2/day, 5 hours, change in Tripoli). For these destinations, check carefully in person with an agent at the KTEL office, or the nearby Stavropoulos travel agency (see "Helpful Hints," earlier in this chapter).

BY TAXI
To cut some time off the trip to the ancient sites, you can take a taxi to **Mycenae** or **Epidavros** (€70 round-trip for either one, with one-hour wait; bargain hard for the best price).

NAFPLIO

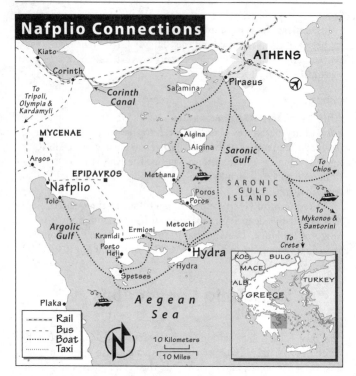

Nafplio Connections

Kiato

Corinth

To Tripoli, Olympia & Kardamyli

MYCENAE

Argos

EPIDAVROS

Nafplio

Tolo

Argolic Gulf

Kranidi

Porto Heli

Plaka

Corinth Canal

Salamina

Methana

Ermioni

Metochi

Spetses

ATHENS

Piraeus

Aigina
Aigina

Saronic Gulf

SARONIC GULF ISLANDS

Poros
Poros

Hydra

Hydra

Aegean Sea

To Chios

To Mykonos & Santorini

To Crete

KOS   BULG.

MACE.

ALB.   TURKEY

GREECE

Rail
Bus
Boat
Taxi

10 Kilometers

10 Miles

N

BY BOAT

To reach long-distance boats connecting to **Hydra** and the other islands in the nearby Saronic Gulf, you'll first need to get to the ports of Tolo, Ermioni, or Metochi. For specifics on ferry connections from these ports to Hydra, see page 415.

Getting to the Ports: Infrequent excursion boats (2-3/week April-Oct) to Hydra operated by Pegasus Tours leave from the port at **Tolo,** a short drive or bus ride (20 minutes) from Nafplio. These boats usually leave fairly early in the morning; Pegasus runs a bus from Nafplio to the port, or you'll need to take a taxi (€30 one-way).

Hellenic Seaways ferries leave from farther away in **Ermioni** (a.k.a. Hermioni), about 1.5 hours southeast of Nafplio. Buses that are supposedly going to Ermioni usually go instead to Kranidi, a larger town about six miles from Ermioni's port (2/day Mon-Fri, Sat-Sun may be 1/day in summer, 2 hours; this Nafplio-Kranidi bus connection may require a transfer at the town of Ligourio—pay careful attention so as not to miss the change). From Kranidi, it's about a €20 taxi ride to the dock at Ermioni (try to split the fare with other Ermioni-bound travelers).

NAFPLIO

Passenger ferries leave from even farther away in **Metochi,** which is best reached by car (allow 2 hours).

ROUTE TIPS FOR DRIVERS

Nafplio is a quick and easy drive from Athens—about 2 hours, much of it on toll highways. (When asked about the poor little road connecting the city to the toll highway, locals explain it's intentional...to keep the Athenians out.) To reach **Monemvasia** from Nafplio (3-4 hours), it's fastest to use the A-71 toll road between Megalopoli and Sparta (*Sparti* on road signs). If you're not in a hurry, consider taking the scenic route described on page 354.

EPIDAVROS

Επίδαυρος

Nestled in a leafy valley some 20 miles east of Nafplio, Epidavros was once the most famous healing center in the ancient Greek world. It was like an ancient Lourdes, a place of hope where the sick came to be treated by doctor-priests acting on behalf of Asklepios, the god of medicine.

The site began as a temple to Apollo, god of light, who was worshipped here in Mycenaean times. By the fourth century BC, Apollo had been replaced by his son, Asklepios (who was said to have been born here). Because pilgrims prayed to Asklepios for health, a sanctuary was needed, with a temple, altars, and statues to the gods. The sanctuary reached the height of its popularity in the fourth and third centuries BC, when it boasted medical facilities, housing for the sick, mineral baths, a stadium for athletic competitions, and a theater.

These days the famous theater is Epidavros' star attraction. It's the finest and best-preserved of all of Greece's ancient theaters—and that's saying something in a country with 132 of them. Epidavros also has some (far) less interesting sights. The once-great sanctuary is now little more than a lonely field of rubble. The small Archaeological Museum displays a few crumbled fragments of statuary. But the theater alone makes Epidavros worth the side trip.

GETTING THERE

By Car: From **Nafplio** it's a 30-minute **drive** to the east, along winding roads. There's plenty of free parking at the site.

Head east out of Nafplio, and watch for, then follow signs pointing to *Ancient Theater*. If you're connecting Epidavros and Mycenae (see next chapter; allow an hour), you can avoid driving all the way back into Nafplio by watching for signs to either site.

Be aware that names on signs can vary. Confusingly, many

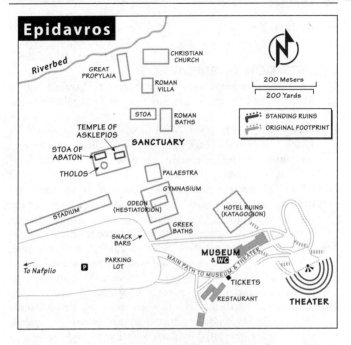

Epidavros

- Riverbed
- GREAT PROPYLAIA
- CHRISTIAN CHURCH
- ROMAN VILLA
- STOA
- ROMAN BATHS
- TEMPLE OF ASKLEPIOS
- SANCTUARY
- STOA OF ABATON
- THOLOS
- PALAESTRA
- GYMNASIUM
- STADIUM
- ODEON (HESTIATORION)
- GREEK BATHS
- HOTEL RUINS (KATAGOGION)
- SNACK BARS
- MUSEUM & WC
- PARKING LOT
- To Nafplio
- MAIN PATH TO MUSEUM & THEATER
- TICKETS
- RESTAURANT
- THEATER

- 200 Meters
- 200 Yards
- STANDING RUINS
- ORIGINAL FOOTPRINT

locations in this area carry the name Epidavros/Επιδαυρος. Don't be distracted by signs to Nea ("New") Epidavros/Νεα Επιδαυρος, or Palea ("Old") Epidavros/Παλαιά Επιδαυρος, which will route you to a modern coastal town far from the theater. Also be aware that Epidavros can be spelled "Epidaurus" in English.

By Bus: From **Nafplio,** buses run to Epidavros (Mon-Sat 2-3/day—buses usually leave Nafplio around 10:30, 12:30, and 14:30; 1/day late on Sun; possibly 1/day Oct-April; 45 minutes). Return buses from Epidavros to Nafplio typically leave in the afternoon (Mon-Sat 2-3/day, last bus usually around 18:00; 1/day late on Sun). Confirm bus schedules locally.

In summer, it may be possible to see both Epidavros and Mycenae in one long day from Nafplio by bus: Take the 9:30 bus from Nafplio to Mycenae, spend about 90 minutes at the site, and return to Nafplio on the 12:00 bus; then catch the 14:30 bus to Epidavros, tour the site, and return to Nafplio on the last bus, arriving back in the city in the early evening. (This wouldn't work on Sun, when there are no buses to Mycenae.) Taking the bus to Epidavros first and then to Mycenae doesn't work (it gives you less than an hour at Epidavros and only 30 minutes at Mycenae).

From **Athens,** buses head to Nafplio, then continue on to Epidavros (2-3/day, 2.5 hours, may require transfer in Nafplio—ask when you buy your ticket).

EPIDAVROS

By Taxi: You can get to Epidavros by taxi from Nafplio (€70 round-trip with one-hour wait).

ORIENTATION TO EPIDAVROS

Cost: €12 (€6 off-season) includes the theater, the Archaeological Museum, and the rest of the Sanctuary of Epidavros archaeological site.

Hours: Daily May-Oct 8:00-20:00 (in theory), off-season until 17:00. +30 2753 022 009, http://odysseus.culture.gr. Off-season and during holidays, sights can close suddenly: Check locally before planning your day.

Length of This Tour: Unfortunately, Epidavros is not really "on the way" to anything else. Budget two to three hours for the round-trip excursion from Nafplio. You can see the entire site in an hour, but it's delightful to linger at the theater.

Services: There's not much here. A simple café/restaurant is along the lane between the parking and ticket office, and food shacks in the parking lot sell slushies and snacks. WCs are near the parking lot, and more are near the museum.

Performances: The theater is still used today for performances on summer weekends during the annual Athens & Epidavros Festival (generally July-Aug Fri-Sat at around 21:00; ideally buy tickets the day before, schedule at www.aefestival.gr). Special buses run from Athens and Nafplio on performance nights.

Starring: The most intact (and most spectacularly situated) theater from ancient Greece.

◗ SELF-GUIDED TOUR

From the parking lot, follow signs up the lane to the ticket desk. Buy your ticket and enter. The theater, sanctuary, and museum are all a couple minutes' walk from one another. The stunning theater is 90 percent of the experience: Climb the seats, take some photos, try out the acoustics—and that's it. Then zip through the little museum and wander the grounds beyond.

• *From the entry gate, go straight and climb the stairs on the right up to the theater. Enter the theater, stand in the center of the circular "orchestra," and take it all in. (I've marked your spot with a weathered marble stump, where fellow theatergoers might be posing, singing, or speaking.)*

Theater of Epidavros (c. 300 BC)

This magnificent sight is built into the side of a tree-covered hill. The perfect symmetry of its two tiers of seating stands as a tribute to Greek mathematics. It's easy to locate the main elements of a typical Greek theater: the round **orchestra,** the smaller **stage** area *(skene),* and the **seating** *(kavea).*

The audience sat in the bleacher-like seats (made of limestone blocks) that were set into the hillside, wrapping partially around the performers. Together, the lower rows and 21 upper rows (added by the Romans, c. 50 BC) seated up to 15,000. The spectators looked down on the orchestra, a circular area 70 feet across where the group of actors known as the chorus sang and danced. Behind the orchestra are the rectangular foundations of the *skene* (which is often covered with a modern stage). The *skene* had a raised stage where actors performed, a back wall for scenery, dressing rooms in the back, and various doorways and ramps where actors could make dramatic entrances and exits. The *skene* was not very tall, so spectators in the upper seats could look over it during the performance, taking in the view of the valley below.

The ancient acoustical engineering is remarkable. The acoustics are superb—from the orchestra, whisper to your partner on the top row. (The center stone marks where an altar to Dionysus, the god of wine and theater, once stood.)

Picture a typical performance of a Greek tragedy here at this theater. Before the show began, spectators filed in the same way tourists do today, through the passageway between the seating and the *skene*. The performance began with a sober monologue by a lone actor, setting the scene. Next, the chorus members entered in a solemn parade, singing as they took their place in the orchestra circle. Then the story unfolded through dialogue on the stage, interspersed with songs by the chorus members. At play's end, the chorus sang a song summing up the moral of the play, then paraded out the way they came.

The chorus—a group of three to 50 singers—was a key part of Greek plays. They commented on the action through songs, accompanied by flute or lyre (small harp), and danced around in the orchestra (literally, "dancing space").

For about seven centuries (c. 300 BC-AD 400), the theater at Epidavros hosted song contests and plays, until the Christian Emperor Theo-

dosius II closed the sanctuary in the fifth century. Over time, the theater became buried in dirt, preserving it until it was unearthed in almost original condition in 1881. Today it is once again a working theater.

Even if you're not here for one of the theater's official performances, you can still enjoy the show: Tourists often take turns performing monologues, reciting poems, or just clapping to try out

Greek Theater

The Greeks invented modern theater, and many plays written 2,500 years ago are still performed today.

In prehistoric times, songs, poems, and rituals were performed to honor Dionysus, the god of wine and revelry. By the sixth century BC, these fertility rites developed into song competitions between choruses of men who sang hymns about Dionysus, heroes, and gods. The contests were held at religious festivals as a form of worship.

Later, Athenian playwrights (such as Thespis, the first "thespian") introduced spoken monologues that alternated with the chorus' songs. Over time, these monologues became dialogues between several actors that became as important as the chorus. Plays evolved from Dionysian hymns to stories of Dionysus to stories of all sorts—myths of gods and heroes, and comedies about contemporary events. By the golden age (c. 450-400 BC), Athens was the center of theater's prime, premiering plays by Sophocles, Euripides, and Aristophanes.

Greek plays fall into three categories. Tragedies, the oldest and most prestigious, feature gods and legends—and usually end with the hero dying. Comedies are satires about contemporary people and events. "Satyr plays" spoof the seriousness of tragedies—for example, Oedipus with a massive strap-on phallus.

Greek drama, like Greek art and philosophy, put human beings at center stage. The theaters were built into hillsides, giving the audience a glimpse of human emotions against the awesome backdrop of nature. The plays showed mortals wrestling with how to find their place in a cosmos ruled by the gods and Fate.

EPIDAVROS

the acoustics. If there's an actor inside you, speak up. Try reciting any of the ancient Greek passages presented in the sidebar.

When you've finished your turn on stage, climb the stairs to the seats to join the spectators. From up here can you fully appreciate the incredible acoustics—not to mention the remarkable scale and intactness of the place. No matter how high you climb, you can hear every word of the naturally amplified performances down below...all while enjoying the backdrop of sweeping mountains and olive groves.

• *Walk down the stairs across from the theater to find the...*

Archaeological Museum

The exhibits in this dusty little old-school museum come with English descriptions. The first room (of three) displays various *stele*s (in-

scribed stone tablets). Some of these document successful cases where patients were healed here by the god Asklepios. Others are rules governing the hospital. The only people to be excluded from the sanctuary were the terminally ill and pregnant women (both

were considered too high-risk—their deaths would sully the sanctuary's reputation). The room also holds a case displaying some medical instruments that'll make you glad you were born after the invention of anesthetics. (You can see small pots for measuring dosages.)

The second room has many (headless) statues of gods who were invoked in the healing process—most of them textbook examples of that wonderfully relaxed *contrapposto* (S-shaped) stance that was revived centuries later by Renaissance sculptors (find the statue striking the sassiest pose). The columns and cornice on display were part of the sanctuary's impressive entryway (propylaea).

The star of the final room is an extremely well-preserved capital from a Corinthian column. The builders of the temple buried

it on the site, perhaps as an offering to the gods. Archaeologists who dug it up in the 19th century were astonished at its condition; it may have been the prototype for all the capitals in the temple complex. The room also displays two replicas of small, square reliefs (left wall) showing the god Asklepios on his throne. Asklepios is often depicted

Greek Monologues

To get you into the theatrical mood, here are a few (condensed) passages from some famous Greek plays.

Oedipus Rex **(or** *Oedipus Tyrannus***), by Sophocles**

A man unwittingly kills his father, sleeps with his mother, and watches his wife commit suicide. When he learns the truth, he blinds himself in shame and sorrow:

> "With what eyes could I ever behold again my honored
> father or my unhappy mother, both destroyed by
> me?
> This punishment is worse than death, and so it should be.
> I wish I could be deaf as well as blind, to shut out all sorrow.
> My friends, come bury me, hide me from every eye,
> cast me into the deepest ocean and let me die.
> Anything so I can shake off this hated life.
> Come friends, do not be afraid to touch me, polluted as I am.
> For no one will suffer for my sins—no one but me."

Antigone, **by Sophocles**

The heroine Antigone defies the king in order to give her brother a proper burial. Here she faces her punishment:

> "O tomb, my bridal chamber, where I go most miserably,
> before my time on earth is spent!
> What law of heaven have I broken?!
> Why should I ever beseech the gods again,

as a kindly, bearded man, carrying a staff with a snake wound around it, the forerunner of today's medical symbol.

• *Outside, follow the path up the stairs to the left as you leave the museum (and only WC within the site) to the sprawling field of ruins called the...*

Sanctuary of Epidavros

While Epidavros' theater is stunning, the ruins of the sanctuary itself (in a huge open field between the theater and parking lot) are a distant also-ran compared with those at other great ancient sites, such as Delphi and Olympia. The various ruins are well-described in English, but precious little survives—orient yourself using one of the numerous maps and wander. Walking from the museum to the far end of the site, you'll first pass the

hotel overlooking the ruins (at the top of the short staircase). Con-

if I am to be punished for doing nothing but good.
If I am guilty, I accept my sin.
But if it is my accusers that are wrong,
I pray that they do not suffer any more than the evils they
have inflicted upon me."

Plutus, **by Aristophanes**

In this comedy, a man befriends a blind beggar who is actually
Plutus, the god of wealth, in disguise. He helps Plutus regain his
sight by bringing him to Epidavros. (If the monologue lacks some
of Aristophanes' famed side-splitting humor, maybe it's because
I left out the bit about cutting a huge fart in the presence of the
god Asklepios.)

"Having arrived at the Temple of Asklepios, we first led
our patient to the sea to purify him. Back at the temple, we gave offerings of bread and wheat cake, then
bedded down. During the night, the god Asklepios
appeared, sitting on the bed. He took a clean rag and
wiped Plutus' eyelids. He then whistled, and two huge
snakes came rushing from the temple and licked the patient's eyelids. As quick as you could drain 10 shots of
wine, Plutus stood up—he could see! Asklepios disappeared with the snakes, and, as dawn broke, we clapped
our hands with joy and gave praise and thanks to the
mighty god."

tinuing along the path are the baths, dining hall, stadium, circular
temple, dormitory, and foundations of the Temple of Asklepios—
in that order.

Considering that the sanctuary was a kind of healing resort
with a mix of doctors and priests to serve the visitors or patients,
it needed a **hotel** *(katagogion)*. Only the footprint of a 160-room,
luxury two-floor spa hotel survives. You can see the stone foundations (the wood-and-tile superstructure is long gone) and thresholds with hinge holes.

Logically there would
be a **bathhouse** and **restaurant** *(hestiatorion)*
for so many important
guests. The scant remains
of those are seen next.
Beyond them stretches a
fine **stadium**. Every four
years, Epidavros' 6,000-
seat stadium was used for

the Festival of Asklepios (similar to other ancient Greek athletic competitions).

Archaeologists are reconstructing one important building beyond the stadium—the circular building, or *tholos*, had a labyrinth in its basement. Some believe the sick would go here to meditate with snakes. Exactly why and what happened is still a mystery.

The sick would then spend the night in the **stoa of Abaton** (the large dormitory building just beyond the *tholos*). Here they would likely pray for a miracle while meditating on the experience they had with the snakes. Perhaps they hoped to be visited in a dream by Asklepios, who could give them the secret to their cure. Stories of the miracles people experienced here spread far and wide, making Epidavros very popular.

Like a square memorial, just to the right is the covered foundation of the **Temple of Asklepios**—the center of this sacred complex.

When you've had enough, retrace your steps past the museum to find the exit.

MYCENAE

Μυκήνες

Mycenae—a fortress city atop a hill—was the hub of a mighty civilization that dominated the Greek world between 1600 and 1200 BC, a thousand years before Athens' golden age. The Mycenaeans were as distant and mysterious to ancient Greeks as Plato and Socrates are to us today. Ancient Greek tourists visited the dramatic ruins of Mycenae and concluded that the Mycenaeans must have been the heroes who'd won the Trojan War, as related in Homer's epic poems, the *Iliad* and the *Odyssey.* They thought of the Mycenaeans as their ancestors, the first "Greeks."

Following the same ancient sandal-steps as the ancient Greeks, today's visitors continue to enjoy Mycenae's majestic setting of mountains, valleys, and the distant sea. Exploring this still-impressive hilltop, you'll discover the famous Lion Gate, a fine little museum, an enormous domed burial chamber...and distant echoes of the Trojan War.

When it comes to unraveling the mystery of the Mycenaeans, modern historians—armed with only the slimmest written record—are still trying to sort out fact from legend. They don't know exactly who the Mycenaeans were, where they came from, or what happened to them. Here are the sketchy (and oft-disputed) details:

Around 1600 BC, a Bronze Age civilization originating in Asia Minor developed an empire of autonomous city-states that covered the southern half of mainland Greece and a few islands. Their capital was the city of Mycenae, which also gave its name to the people and the era. From contact with the sophisticated Minoan people on the isle of Crete, the militaristic Mycenaeans borrowed elements of religion and the arts.

Sometime around the year 1200 BC, the aggressive Mycenaeans likely launched an attack on Troy, a rich city on the northwest coast of Asia Minor (present-day Turkey). After a long siege, Troy fell, and the Mycenaeans became the undisputed rulers of the Aegean. Then, just as suddenly, the Mycenaeans mysteriously disappeared, and their empire crumbled. Whether the Mycenaeans fell victim to a sudden invasion by the Dorians (a Greek tribe), an attack of the mysterious tribes later dubbed the "Sea People," a drought, or internal rebellion—no one knows. Whatever the reason, by 1100 BC, Mycenae was abandoned and burned, and Greece plunged into four centuries known as the Middle Ages.

Nearly three millennia later, in 1876, German archaeologist Heinrich Schliemann excavated this site and put it back on the archaeologists' (and tourists') map. Today a visit to Mycenae is a trip back into prehistory to see some of the oldest remains of a complex civilization in Europe—a thousand years older than Athens' Acropolis.

GETTING THERE

By Car: Mycenae is 18 miles north of Nafplio (follow signs to Athens, on the way to the major E-65 expressway). From the modern town of Mycenae/Μυκήνες (near the larger town of Fichti/Φιχτι), the ruins are about two miles north, dramatically perched atop a hill. If you're connecting Mycenae and Epidavros by car (allow 60 minutes), you can avoid driving all the way back into Nafplio by watching carefully for signs to either site. At Mycenae, drivers can use the free parking lot near the entrance to the ruins and museum; if it's full, park along the road leading to the lot.

By Bus: Buses run from Nafplio directly to ancient Mycenae (check schedule locally but generally Mon-Sat 1-2/day—likely at 9:30 and 14:00; no buses on Sun; possibly fewer buses Oct-April, 45 minutes). The timing for the return trip can make taking a bus a pain: You'll have either about half an hour to see the site (not enough) or 2.5 hours (too much for some people). For advice about connecting Mycenae and Epidavros in one bus-based day trip from Nafplio, see page 261. If you do take the bus, confirm that your bus goes to the archaeological site; other buses take you only as far as Fichti, two miles away (a €5 cab ride).

By Taxi: You can take a taxi to Mycenae from Nafplio (about €50-70 round-trip with time to sightsee). It's best to arrange your return in advance, but to get a return taxi from Mycenae on the spot, call +30 694 643 1726.

MYCENAE

ORIENTATION TO MYCENAE

Cost: €12 (€6 off-season) ticket includes archaeological site, museum, and Treasury of Atreus up the road.

Hours: Roughly April-Oct daily 8:00-20:00, closes an hour or two earlier in fall, Nov-March daily until 15:30. Mycenae's hours can change without notice—ask your hotel or call ahead; +30 2751 076 585, http://odysseus.culture.gr.

Services: WCs are just above the museum, but none are on the actual site. A stand in the parking lot sells basic snacks.

Planning Your Time: Decide whether to see the museum first (to help reconstruct the ruins) or the site first (to get the lay of the land). To complement the information in this self-guided tour, read the chapter on Athens' National Archaeological Museum, where many Mycenaean artifacts are displayed (see page 149).

Length of This Tour: Allow an hour for the site, a half-hour for the museum, and a half-hour for the Treasury of Atreus.

Pronunciation: Mycenae is pronounced my-SEE-nee by English-speakers; Greeks call the town Mykenes/Μυκήνες (mee-KEE-nehs), also spelled Mikenes. The ancient people are known as the Mycenaeans (my-seh-NEE-uhns).

Starring: The hilltop fortress at the center of the most ancient, powerful, and enigmatic of ancient Greek civilizations.

❍ SELF-GUIDED TOUR

The three main sightseeing areas at Mycenae are a few minutes' walk from one another. The **archaeological ruins** consist of the walled city of Mycenae atop the hill called the acropolis. Here you'll find the famous Lion Gate entrance, Grave Circle A (which yielded precious artifacts), and the ruins of the palace. Below the site is the **museum,** housing artifacts that were found here. Finally, as impressive as anything here is the **Treasury of Atreus**—a huge domed tomb located about 300 yards downhill from the main site (along the main road). A handful of other ruins and tombs are scattered around the area, but stick to these three to start your visit.

Note that some of the ruins (confusingly) have different names—for example, the Treasury of Atreus is also known as the Tomb of Agamemnon.

• *Buy your ticket for the archaeological site and enter, climbing the ramp up the acropolis.*

Archaeological Site

• *You'll enter the fortified complex through the...*

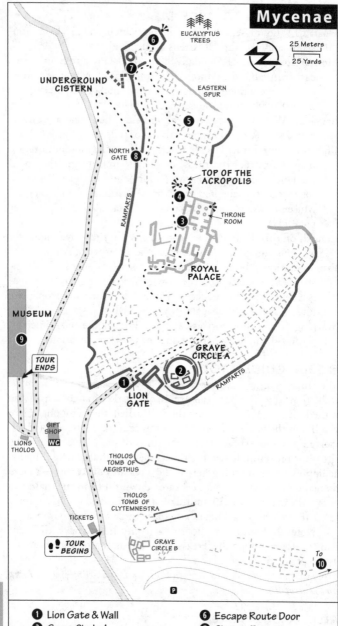

Mycenae

25 Meters
25 Yards

EUCALYPTUS TREES

UNDERGROUND CISTERN

EASTERN SPUR

TOP OF THE ACROPOLIS

THRONE ROOM

NORTH GATE

RAMPARTS

ROYAL PALACE

MUSEUM

TOUR ENDS

GRAVE CIRCLE A

RAMPARTS

LION GATE

GIFT SHOP
WC

LIONS THOLOS

THOLOS TOMB OF AEGISTHUS

THOLOS TOMB OF CLYTEMNESTRA

TICKETS

TOUR BEGINS

GRAVE CIRCLE B

To ⑩

P

1 Lion Gate & Wall
2 Grave Circle A
3 Royal Palace & Throne Room
4 Top of the Acropolis
5 Houses & Storerooms Ruins

6 Escape Route Door
7 Cistern Entrance
8 North Gate
9 Museum
10 To Treasury of Atreus

MYCENAE

❶ Lion Gate and Wall

The grand Lion Gate (c. 1300 BC) guards the entrance to this fortress city on a hill. Above the doorway, two lionesses flank a

column, symbolically protecting it the way the Mycenaean kings once protected the city. The lions' missing heads may have once turned outward, greeting visitors. The heads were made of stone or possibly of gold (anything made of a precious material like that would have been plundered long ago).

The lions form a triangle above the massive lintel (the crossbeam above the door). Mycenaean architects used the weak corbelled arch, less sturdy than the rounded Roman arch developed later. A simple horizontal stone spans the door, while heavy stones above it inch in to bridge the gap. The lintel is slightly arched to distribute the weight to the sides and add to its strength.

Apart from its rather fragile technology, Mycenaean architecture is really massive. The lintel weighs 18 tons—as much as a WWII B-17 bomber. The exterior walls that girdle the base of the hill (c. 1300 BC) were about 40 feet high, 20 feet thick, and 3,000 feet long. They were built with an estimated 14,000 boulders weighing 5 to 10 tons each. Marveling at the enormous scale, Classical-era Greeks figured the legendary Perseus (who slew the Medusa) must have built the city with the help of the giant one-eyed Cyclopes, and dubbed the style "cyclopean." In reality, the Myce-

naeans probably lifted these big stones into place the same way the Egyptians built the pyramids—by building ramps and rolling the stones up on logs drawn by oxen or horses.

Pass through the gate. Carved into the stone are **postholes** that held the wooden door. Just as you emerge, look left to see a square **niche** in the wall—this could have been a small shrine where statues of the gods who guarded the gates were displayed, or just a simple closet. Poke your head in to study the stonework.

• Head up the ramp. About 30 yards ahead, you'll see (below and on the right) a circular wall that encloses rectangular graves. Walk a bit higher up the path and look down for the best view.

❷ Grave Circle A (c. 1550 BC)

Judging from what was dug up in this round cluster of graves, My-cenaean royalty were buried here. The rectangular holes are called shaft graves, which were cut into the rock up to 20 feet deep. There are six such shaft graves here, each of which contained several bodies (19 total—9 women, 8 men, and 2 children). The bodies were found embalmed and lying on their backs along with their most precious belongings, with their heads facing east—toward  the rising sun—indicating a belief in an afterlife. Gravestones atop the graves (like the one displayed in the museum) were decorated with a spiral, possibly a symbol of continuous existence.

In 1876 these graves were unearthed by the famed German archaeologist Heinrich Schliemann. Schliemann had recently dis-covered the long-lost city of Troy, finally giving some historical credibility to Homer's tales. He next turned his attention to My-cenae, the legendary home of Agamemnon. In Grave Circle A, he found a treasure trove of gold swords, spears, engraved cups, and ritual objects buried with the dead—30 pounds in all, confirming Homer's description of Mycenae as a city "rich in gold."

The prize discovery was a gold mask showing the face of a bearded man. Masks like this were tied onto the faces of the de-ceased. This one was obviously for an important warrior chief-tain. Schliemann was convinced the mask proved that Homer's tales of the Trojan War were true, and he dubbed it the "Mask of Agamemnon." This mask and other artifacts are now in the Na-tional Archaeological Museum in Athens.

Could it really be the Mask of Agamemnon? No. Not only is it unlikely that Agamemnon ever really existed, but the mask is from the 16th century BC—at least 300 years before the legendary king supposedly burned Troy.

The Mycenaeans practiced several different types of burial: interred in a pit (for the poorest), encased in a ceramic jar called a cist grave (for wealthier folks), laid in a shaft grave (for royalty), or placed in an elaborate domed chamber called a *tholos* (like the Treasury of Atreus, which we'll visit at the end of this tour).

• *Continue to climb up the paths, zigzagging past the ruins of former houses and shops, to the top of the acropolis. At these highest levels, you have been walking through the foundations of the former...*

MYCENAE

Mycenae and Troy: Fact or Fiction?

Several sites at Mycenae bear legendary names—Agamemnon's Palace, the Tomb of Clytemnestra, the Tomb of Agamemnon, and so on. Although these fanciful names have no basis in fact,

real-life Mycenae does sound very similar to the legends found in writings attributed to the poet Homer (c. 850 BC) and other ancient scribes.

The tales of the Trojan War are set during the time when the Mycenaeans dominated the Greek world and had the power to conquer Troy. They tell of the abduction of the beautiful Helen (who had "the face that launched a thousand ships") by Paris, a prince of Troy. Outraged at the loss of his bride, Menelaus, king of Sparta, convinced his brother Agamemnon, king of Mycenae, to lead the Greeks in an attack on Troy. But the winds were not favorable for launching the fleet. An oracle told Agamemnon that he had to sacrifice his daughter to get underway, so he lied to his wife, Clytemnestra, and ordered the priests to kill their daughter.

After the sacrifice, the Greek ships finally made it to Troy. When a long siege failed to defeat the Trojans, Odysseus suggested tricking the enemy by building a wooden idol (the famous Trojan horse), leaving it outside the city walls, and pretending to withdraw. The Trojans took the bait, brought the horse inside, and were met with an unpleasant surprise: the greatest warriors of Greece emerging from inside the horse to complete the conquest of Troy. The famous heroes of the Trojan War include Achilles and Ajax on the Greek side, and Paris' brother Hector—all of whom died by the war's end.

Homer's *Odyssey* tells of the homeward journey of Odysseus, who survived the war only to wander for 10 years, thwarted by the god Poseidon, before finally reaching home. Agamemnon's fate is also told in the epic. After sacking Troy, Agamemnon returned to Mycenae with his Trojan concubine, where he was murdered by his wife (who was still brooding over her daughter's sacrifice and not very happy about the new competition). Not that Clytemnestra was a dutiful spouse—her new lover helped her murder Agamemnon and the concubine.

Metaphorically, Agamemnon's tragic story matches that of the historical Mycenaeans—no sooner had they returned home victorious from Troy than their own homes were destroyed. These legends of ancient Mycenae were passed down through oral tradition for centuries until, long after the fall of both Troy and Mycenae, they were preserved for posterity in Homer's *Iliad* and *Odyssey* as well as other ancient epics.

❸ Royal Palace and Throne Room (Megaron)

Kings ruled the Mycenaeans from this palace, which consisted of a line of several rectangular rooms (about all that remains today are the outlines of the rooms).

Imagine entering the palace and walking through a series of rooms. You'd start in an open-air courtyard—that's the biggest flat rectangle to the far right, paved with concrete. Then you'd enter the palace itself, passing between two columns (see the remaining round bases) onto a covered porch. Next, at the far end of the porch, was a small anteroom. Finally, you'd spill into the main hall—the throne room—at the east end. This great hall, or *megaron*, contains the outlines of a round hearth (not visible), which is where a fire burned. Here you could make burnt offerings to the gods. The four remaining bases around the hearth once held four inverted columns that supported the roof, which had a sunroof-type hole to let out the smoke. Against the south wall to the right (facing the gorge) sat the king on his throne—the very center of power of the Mycenaean Empire. The walls and floors were brightly painted with a pattern of linked spirals.

The same type of palace was found in every Mycenaean city, and later became the standard layout of the Greek temple—courtyard, colonnaded porch, small room *(pronaos),* and main hall with its sacred *cella* area toward the back, where only the priest could go.
• *While we're on the top of the acropolis, check out the view and imagine the city/fortress at its peak.*

❹ Top of the Acropolis: Mycenae the Fortress-City

Mycenae was a combination citadel, palace, home for up to 60,000 people, and administrative capital of the extended empire of My-

cenaean cities. But first and foremost, it was a fortress, occupying a superb natural defensive position guarding a major crossroads in Greece. The hill is flanked by steep ravines. To the south there are spacious views across the fertile plains of Argos to the Argolic Gulf, giving the inhabitants ample time to prepare for any attack by sea. The cone-shaped hill in the distance ringed with walls near the top was the fortress of Argos. The port of Mycenae controlled trade on the road from Corinth to Nafplio, and sea trade from Nafplio to points beyond.

In case of siege, Mycenae could rely on natural springs located on the mountainside to the east (facing the gorge, look left up the small canyon—near the eucalyptus trees, a little above acropolis level, with a patch of exposed reddish hillside behind it). The water was channeled through clay pipes underground to a cistern dug inside the acropolis.

• *Facing the distant bay, find the Acropolis of Argos in the distance, and imagine the torches and bronze plates once used to reflect and flash messages across long distances. Now, work your way eastward (farther away from the entrance, and a bit downhill), noticing natural defenses provided by cliffs on the right, before descending to the...*

Cistern and Other Sights at the East End

The ruins at this end were once mostly ❺ **houses, storerooms, and workshops.** At the far eastern end, you'll see the doorway in the wall (now covered with a gate). This was an ❻ **escape route** out the back.

Find the gaping cave-like opening of the ❼ **cistern,** where (slippery!) steps lead down. The cistern stored water from springs within the hillside, in case of siege or drought.

• *Head back toward the entrance—but bear to the right, following the north (outer) wall. Walk down the stairs and look for a gate on the right.*

This ❽ **North Gate,** smaller than the Lion Gate, has a similar rectangular cross-beam shape and heavy lintel. The wooden door is a reconstruction of the original, fit into the original holes cut in the lintel stone. Next to the North Gate is a niche in the wall (similar to the one at the Lion Gate) to display guardian gods.

• *From here you can explore your way along the ramparts back to the Lion Gate. Or, if you're ready to move on, exit through the North Gate and bear left/downhill along the serpentine path to the museum, the modern building on the hillside below.*

❾ Museum

Whereas the ruins give a sense of the engineering sophistication of these people, the museum emphasizes their artistic, religious, literary, and cultural sides. You'll see various funeral objects from the graves, plus everyday objects that show influences from the Egyptian, Minoan, and Hittite cultures.

• *Follow the one-way, counterclockwise route through the collection, beginning in the...*

Entrance Hall

The model of the Mycenae acropolis in the center of the room helps you visualize the city as it once was. Otherwise, the information posted here is pretty dull (on one side, a description of myths relating to this city; on the other, a dry history of the excavation).

• *From the entrance hall, move into the next room, on your right, where you'll find...*

Religious Symbols

This room shows off religious items found in temples. Snakes were believed to have sacred connections and were used for bridging the worlds of the living and the dead. The mysterious two-foot-tall figurines were likely used by priests in rituals to scare away evil. Pottery items found in homes were simply practical in an age without plastic storage. Notice the well-preserved elegant designs and colors that were baked into the clay.

• *Descend to the lower level to see...*

Funeral Objects

This room is filled with items found in tombs from about 1500 BC. In the octagonal case, you'll see reproductions of the famous Mask

of Agamemnon and other golden items (such as crowns and medallions). These objects were discovered here in graves. (The originals are now in Athens' National Archaeological Museum.) On the wall behind the mask is a highly decorated funeral *stele* (gravestone) from Grave Circle B.

Diagrams below the artifacts show where each object on display was found in relation to the skeleton of the deceased. Back then, you *could* take it with you. Those with the means were sure to pack along jewelry, tools, kitchen utensils, even children's toys and sippy cups. The miniature furniture was necessary for packing light. Tiny figurines may have represented the Goddess Earth. Notice the small baby coffin (a clay box with a lid, immediately left of the entry door).

• *As you continue into the next room, notice (on your left) a big clay urn used as a coffin for burial, with a band of spiral designs across the middle.*

Many funeral objects (such as this urn) were engraved with a spiral pattern—possibly a symbol of the never-ending path of life.

Mycenaean Writing and Everyday Objects

In the case partitioning the room are fragments of clay tablets inscribed in the Mycenaean written language known to scholars as Linear B. Each character represented a syllable. These fragments concern distinct subjects, including "Religion," "Lists of Names," "Products," inventories, and so on. Very few written documents survived from the Mycenaean era—no literature or history or stories—so we know very little of the Mycenaeans' inner thoughts.

On the other side of the partition, a glass case displays sealstones, used to put a person's mark in wax or clay on a sealed document or box, to ensure it reached the intended recipient unopened. The Mycenaeans led an active trading life, and every businessman would have had one of these. The red one on top, in the center (#14), has the symbol from the Lion Gate on it.

To the left a large map shows the vast Mycenaean trading world. The Mycenaeans were seafarers, bringing back gold from Egypt, lapis lazuli from Afghanistan, amber from Scandinavia, ivory from Syria, jewelry from Spain, and more. Near the door, the display on "Women of the Mycenaean World" makes it clear they had plenty of toiletry and jewelry items: combs, tweezers, mirrors, beads, pendants, and so on.

• *Leaving the museum, take the ramp back up to the parking lot. (Just below the WC next to the museum, on your right, is the broken but interesting* **Tholos Tomb of the Lions.**) *At the parking lot, continue to the last area, one of the highlights of Mycenae: the tomb known as the* **Treasury of Atreus.** *It's located about 300 yards south of the ruins, along the road back toward the modern town of Mycenae. You can walk there in less than 10 minutes. Or, if you have a car, stop at the Treasury on your way out of the site—there's a small parking lot there. Show your entry ticket once more and follow the crowds gradually uphill to get to the...*

⑩ Treasury of Atreus (a.k.a. Tomb of Agamemnon, 13th century BC)

Mycenae's royalty were buried in massive beehive-shaped underground chambers called *tholoi*, which replaced shaft graves (like the ones at Grave Circle A) beginning in the 15th century BC.

The entryway to this *tholos* itself is on a grand "cyclopean" scale—110 feet long and 20 feet wide. Imagine entering in a funeral procession carrying the body of the king. The walls rise at a diagonal up to the entrance, giving the illusion of swallowing you up as you enter.

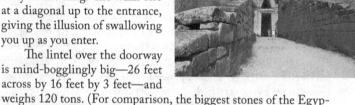

The lintel over the doorway is mind-bogglingly big—26 feet across by 16 feet by 3 feet—and weighs 120 tons. (For comparison, the biggest stones of the Egyptian pyramids were 30 tons.) Notice before entering the hints of doorway hinges and ornamental pillars that once stood here.

Step inside and hear the 3,300-year-old echoes of this domed room. The round chamber is 47 feet in diameter and 42 feet tall, with an igloo-style dome made of 33 rings of corbelled (gradually projecting) stones, each weighing about 5 tons. The dome was decorated with bronze ornaments (you can see a few small nail holes where they were attached in the fifth row of stones up). The soot on the dome is from the campfires of fairly recent shepherds.

Kings were elaborately buried in the center of the room along with their swords, jewels, and personal possessions. There is also a side chamber (the door to the right), which has a purpose that can only be speculative. At some point grave robbers got in, and modern archaeologists have not found any bodies or treasures.

So why didn't the dome collapse? The weight of the dome is distributed by two triangular niches—one over the main lintel, and one over the side doorway. Notice how the main lintel has a crack on the interior side. That crack is to the side of the doorway, right where the triangular niche spills all the weight of the dome onto it. Without this arch, the lintel would have cracked in the center and the dome would have collapsed. Look carefully at the smaller triangle above the smaller side-door arch to find its little crack (on the left). Again, without the arch, the weight over the door would have caused the lintel to break—and you wouldn't be standing here marveling at 3,300-year-old Mycenaean engineering.

• Our tour's over. While only about 10 percent of the site has been excavated, I've Mycenae-n enough.

OLYMPIA

Αρχαία Ολυμπία

A visit to Olympia—most famous as the site of the original Olympic Games—offers one of your best opportunities for a hands-on experience with antiquity. Take your mark at the original starting line in the 2,500-year-old Olympic Stadium. Visit the Temple of Zeus, former site of a gigantic statue of Zeus that was one of the Seven Wonders of the Ancient World. Ponder the temple's once-majestic columns—toppled like towers of checkers by an earthquake—which are as evocative as anything from ancient times. Take a close look at the Archaeological Museum's gold-medal-quality statues and artifacts. And don't forget to step back and enjoy the setting itself. Despite the crowds that pour through here, Olympia remains a magical place, with ruins nestled among lush, shady groves of pine trees.

The modern-day town of Olympia (pop. 13,000) is a tidy, pleasant, working-class community catering to the needs of the thousands of tourists who flock here year-round to visit the site. For drivers, a day and single overnight are enough time here; for those using public transportation, limited bus connections might require a two-night stay.

Patra (sometimes spelled Patras), the port for boats bringing travelers to Greece from Italy, is described at the end of this chapter.

Orientation to Olympia

The Sanctuary of Olympia sits in the fertile valley of the Alphios River in the western Peloponnese, 12 miles southeast of the regional capital of Pyrgos. The archaeological site curves along the southeastern edge of the tidy modern village of Archaia (Ancient) Olympia. The town's layout is basically a low-lying, easy-to-manage grid, five streets wide by eight streets long. The main road (called Praxitelous Kondyli) runs from Pyrgos in the north and leads right into a parking lot (and bus stop) at the south end of town. From here the museum and site are due east, over the Kladeos River.

Tourist Information: There's no TI, but your hotelier should be able to answer most questions. You can also check local guide Niki Vlachou's **Olympia Travel Guide** website, which contains updated information on sights—opening times, entry fees, discounts, etc.—and a detailed interactive area map (www.olympiatravelguide. com). She'll also answer questions from my readers free of charge (see her listing below, under "Helpful Hints").

ARRIVAL IN OLYMPIA

For driving directions into and out of Olympia, as well as options for reaching Olympia from the cruise-ship port of Katakolo, see "Olympia Connections," later.

By Bus: The bus drops you off just before the retail strip on the main street, a quick walk from the well-signed sights.

By Car: Parking is free and easy. It's fine to park on the streets in town. The best parking lots are near the Archaeological Museum, behind the main road next to the train station (see "Olympia Town" map). Avoid the bus lot near the Museum of the History of the Olympic Games in Antiquity, where you may get a ticket.

HELPFUL HINTS

Services: Olympia's main street has wide sidewalks, countless gift shops, and ample hotels, eateries, minimarkets, ATMs, and other tourist services.

Taxis: There's a taxi stand in town a block off the main street on the shady, angled side street called Georgiou Douma (+30 2624 022 555).

Local Guide: Unlike many other popular ancient sites, the Sanctuary of Olympia is not surrounded by hopeful guides-for-hire. Consider making advance reservations with fantastic local guide **Niki Vlachou** (reasonable and negotiable rates; in addition to guiding at Olympia, Niki can arrange transportation, wine tastings, olive-press visits, cooking classes, and meals in local homes; +30 697 242 6085, www.olympictours.gr, niki@ olympictours.gr).

Sights in Olympia

There are two main parts to your Olympia visit: the Sanctuary of Olympia archaeological site and the Archaeological Museum. With time and interest, a quick stop at the smaller Museum of the History of the Olympic Games in Antiquity is worthwhile.

OLYMPIA

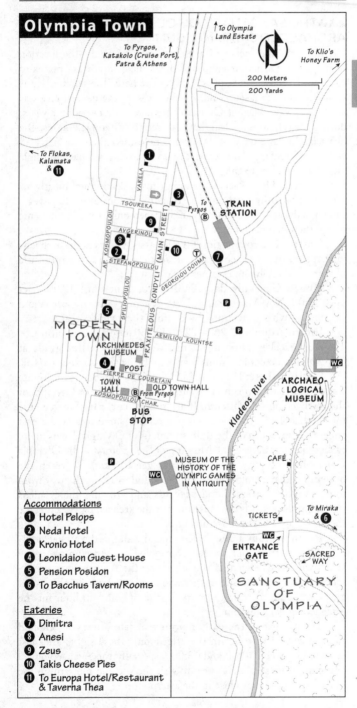

Olympia Town

To Olympia
Land Estate

To Klio's
Honey Farm

To Pyrgos,
Katakolo (Cruise Port),
Patra & Athens

200 Meters

200 Yards

To Flokas,
Kalamata
& ⓫

VARELA

❶

➡

❸

To Pyrgos
Ⓑ

TRAIN
STATION

TSOUREKA

AP. KOSMOPOULOU

AVGERINOU

❾

❽

❷

STEFANOPOULOU

KONDYLI (MAIN STREET)

❿

Ⓣ

❼

GEORGIOU DOUMA

SPILIOPOULOU

PRAXITELOUS

Ⓟ

Ⓟ

❺

MODERN
TOWN

AEMILIOU KOUNTSE

ARCHIMEDES
MUSEUM

Kladeos River

ARCHAEO-
LOGICAL
MUSEUM

❹

POST

PIERRE DE COUBETAIN

WC

TOWN
HALL

OLD TOWN HALL

Ⓑ From Pyrgos

KOSMOPOULOU

CHAR.

BUS
STOP

Ⓟ

WC

MUSEUM OF THE
HISTORY OF THE
OLYMPIC GAMES
IN ANTIQUITY

CAFÉ

To Miraka
& ❻

TICKETS

WC

ENTRANCE
GATE

SACRED
WAY

SANCTUARY
OF
OLYMPIA

Accommodations
❶ Hotel Pelops
❷ Neda Hotel
❸ Kronio Hotel
❹ Leonidaion Guest House
❺ Pension Posidon
❻ To Bacchus Tavern/Rooms

Eateries
❼ Dimitra
❽ Anesi
❾ Zeus
❿ Takis Cheese Pies
⓫ To Europa Hotel/Restaurant
 & Taverna Thea

▲▲▲THE SANCTUARY OF OLYMPIA AND ARCHAEOLOGICAL MUSEUM

Olympia was the mecca of ancient Greek religion—the location of its greatest sanctuary and one of its most important places of worship. In those times, people didn't live here: The sanctuary was set aside as a monastery and pilgrimage site; the nearest city was 30 miles away. Ancient Greeks came here only every four years, during the religious festival that featured the Olympic Games. The heart of the sanctuary was a sacred enclosure called the Altis—a walled-off, rectangular area that housed two big temples, multiple altars, and statues to the gods.

Whereas Delphi served as a pilgrimage destination mostly for groups of wealthy men on a particular mission, every four years Olympia drew 40,000 ordinary dudes (men only) for a Panhellenic party: the Olympic Games.

Cost: A €12 combo-ticket (€6 off-season) covers the archaeological site, the Archaeological Museum, and the Museum of the History of the Olympic Games in Antiquity.

Hours: Generally daily 8:00-20:00, Sept until 19:00, Oct until 18:00, Nov-March 8:00-15:00. Schedules vary by season and can change without warning, so confirm these times locally.

Information: +30 2624 022 742, http://odysseus.culture.gr. The free, excellent, and interactive visual/audio **online guide** at http://olympiacommongrounds.gr helps bring the sanctuary to life.

Getting There: If staying in Olympia, it's an easy five-minute **walk** from the town center to either the Sanctuary of Olympia or the Archaeological Museum. If arriving by **car,** park for free near the Archaeological Museum at one of two small lots at the east edge of town, south of the train station (see "Olympia Town" map, earlier; don't park near the Museum of the History of the Olympic Games in Antiquity, where you may get a ticket). To reach the museum and site from the parking lots, follow the path away from town, walking several hundred yards and crossing the Kladeos River. Up the stairs is the museum. For the archaeological site, take the path opposite the museum entry.

Planning Your Time: I recommend walking the archaeological site first, then touring the Archaeological Museum to reconstruct what you've seen. If you're passing the Archaeological Museum en route to the site anyway, you can buy your combo-ticket at the museum. Allow 1.5 hours for the site, and an hour for the Archaeological Museum.

Try to visit in the early morning or late afternoon (though the site can be very hot in the afternoon). These sights are most crowded between 10:00 and 13:00 (especially the Archaeological Museum). Off-season, it's best to visit the site and museum in the morning in case they close in the afternoon.

If arriving late in the day, you can use your combo-ticket to tour one place in the late afternoon and the other parts the next morning (one entry per place).

If you have all day for sightseeing, first hit the small Museum of the History of the Olympic Games in Antiquity, which provides background on the ancient games that'll help enliven your visit to the site (allow about a half-hour for this museum).

Services: There are WCs near the archaeological site (follow the signs). The museum has a shop and WCs (outside, to the right as you face the entrance), but no café or food (no food is allowed inside the site, though you can—and should—bring a water bottle). There's a café with snacks and sandwiches midway on the path between the site and the museum. The kiosk next to the ticket booth at the site sells guidebooks to the site and museum.

Sanctuary of Olympia (The Site)

This center of ancient Greek religion dedicated to Zeus hosted the Olympic Games for more than a thousand years (c. 776 BC-AD 393). As you wander among these sporting arenas, temples, and statues, contemplate how the 100-meter dash was much more than a mere running race to the people of this civilization: It was a spiritual exercise that unified Greeks and expressed the most cherished values of Western civilization.

❍ Self-Guided Tour

Buy your tickets at the booth, use the WCs across the way if you need to, then head to the entrance gate. Inside, walk straight ahead (passing an orientation board) down into the ancient world of Olympia. This main path is called the Sacred Way.

• *As you walk into the site, look to your left (through the trees) to catch glimpses of...*

❶ Kronos Hill

This hill was sacred to the ancient Greeks, who believed it to be the birthplace of Zeus—and the place where, as a clever baby, he es-

caped his father, Kronos, who'd tried to eat him. Zeus later overthrew Kronos and went on to lead the pantheon of gods. (Other versions of the myth place this event on Mt. Olympus, in northern Greece, where the gods eventually made their home.)

• *The Sacred Way leads down into a wide field scattered with ruins. To the left of the path was an enclosed area filled with various temples and*

OLYMPIA

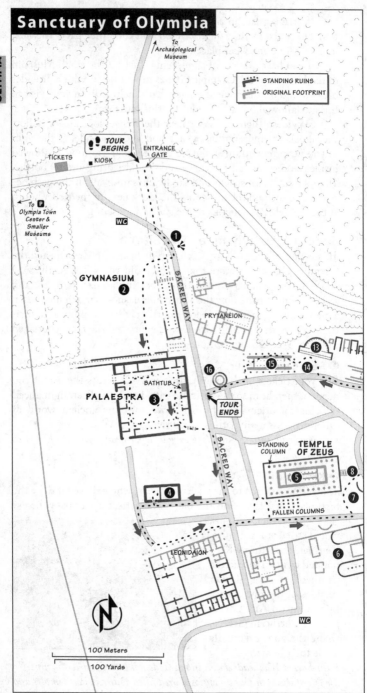

Sanctuary of Olympia

To Archaeological Museum

STANDING RUINS
ORIGINAL FOOTPRINT

TICKETS

TOUR BEGINS

KIOSK

ENTRANCE GATE

To P
Olympia Town
Center &
Smaller
Museums

WC

GYMNASIUM 2

SACRED WAY

1

PRYTANEION

13

15

14

PALAESTRA 3

BATHTUB

16

TOUR ENDS

SACRED WAY

STANDING COLUMN

TEMPLE OF ZEUS

5

8

7

4

FALLEN COLUMNS

6

LEONIDAION

WC

N

100 Meters

100 Yards

OLYMPIA

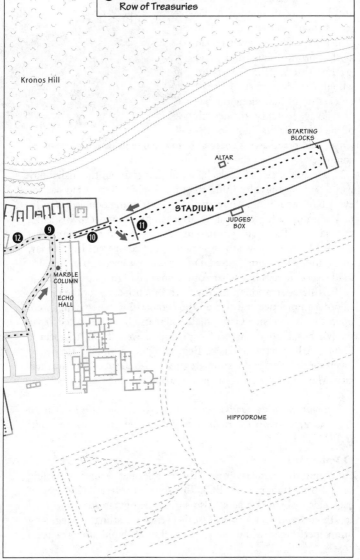

1 View of Kronos Hill
2 Gymnasium
3 Palaestra
4 Workshop of Pheidias
5 Temple of Zeus
6 Bouleuterion
7 Pedestal of Nike
8 Winner's Circle
9 Bases of Zanes & Row of Treasuries
10 Krypti
11 Stadium & Finish Line
12 Metroon & the Altar of Zeus
13 Nymphaeum
14 Altar of Hera
15 Temple of Hera
16 Philippeion

Kronos Hill

STARTING BLOCKS

ALTAR

STADIUM

JUDGES' BOX

MARBLE COLUMN

ECHO HALL

HIPPODROME

altars; to the right were buildings for the athletes, who trained and lived in a complex of buildings similar to today's Olympic Village.

Head to the right along the small path just before the two long rows of stubby columns. They mark the eastern edge of what was once the...

❷ Gymnasium

This was the largest building in the whole sanctuary, built in the fourth century BC. The truncated Doric columns once supported a covered arcade, one of four arcades that surrounded a big rectangular courtyard. Here athletes trained for events such as the sprint, discus throw, and javelin throw. The courtyard (about the size of six football fields, side-by-side along the Sacred Way) matched the length of the Olympic Stadium, so athletes could practice in a space akin to the one in which they would compete.

Because ancient Greeks believed that training the male body was as important as training the mind, sports were a big part of every boy's education. Moreover, athletic training doubled as military training (a key element in citizenship)—so most towns had a gymnasium. The word "gymnasium" comes from the Greek *gymnos* (naked), which is how athletes trained and competed. Even today, the term "gymnasium" is used in many European countries (including Greece) to describe what Americans call high school.

Athletes arrived in a nearby town a month early for the Games in order to practice and size up the competition. The Games were open to any freeborn Greek male (men and boys competed separately), but a good share of competitors were from aristocratic homes. Athletes trained hard. Beginning in childhood, they were given special diets and training regimens, often subsidized by their city. Many became professionals, touring the circuit of major festivals.

• *At the far end of the gymnasium ruins, a small set of stairs leads down to a square space ringed by twin rows of taller, more intact columns. This is the...*

❸ Palaestra

Adjoining the gymnasium was this smaller but similar "wrestling school" (built around 300 BC). This square courtyard (216 feet on each side—about one acre), also surrounded by arcades, was used by athletes to train for smaller-scale events: wrestling, boxing, long jump (performed while carrying weights, to build strength), and

OLYMPIA

The Ancient Olympic Games

The Olympic Games were athletic contests held every four years as a way of honoring Zeus, the king of the gods. They were the culmination of a pilgrimage, as Greeks gathered to worship Zeus, the Games' patron.

The exact origins of the Games are lost to time, but they likely grew from a local religious festival first held at the Sanctuary of Olympia in about 1150 BC. According to one legend, the festival was founded by Pelops, namesake of the Peloponnese; a rival legend credits Hercules. Sporting events became part of the festivities. A harmonious, healthy body was a "temple" that celebrated its creator by performing at its peak.

The first Olympic Games at which results were recorded are traditionally dated at 776 BC. The Games grew rapidly, attracting athletes from throughout the Greek world to compete in an ever-growing number of events (eventually taking up to five days). They reached their height of popularity around 400 BC. Of the four major Greek games (including those at Delphi, Corinth, and Nemea), Olympia was the first, biggest, and most prestigious.

Besides honoring Zeus and providing entertainment, the Games served a political purpose: to develop a Panhellenic ("all-Greek") identity among scattered city-states and far-flung colonies. Every four years, wars between bickering Greeks were halted with a one-month "sacred truce" so that athletes and fans could travel safely to Olympia. Leading citizens from all corners would assemble here, including many second- and third-generation Greeks who'd grown up in colonies in Italy, France, or Africa. Olympia was geographically central, and for the length of the festivities, it was the symbolic heart of Greece.

This went on for 1,169 years, finally concluding in AD 393. Olympia today lives on in the spirit of the modern Olympic Games, revived in Athens in 1896. Every other year, athletes from around the world gather and compete in contests that challenge the human spirit and, it's hoped, foster a sense of common experience. Whether we're cheering on an American swimmer, a Chinese gymnast, or a Jamaican sprinter to go faster, longer, and better than any human has before, the Games bring the world together for a few weeks, much as they united the Greek world in this tranquil pine grove so many centuries ago.

pankration, a kind of ancient "ultimate fighting" with only two rules: no biting and no eye-gouging.

Picture athletes in the courtyard working out. They were always naked, except for a layer of olive oil and dust for a bit of protection against scrapes and the sun. Sometimes they exercised in time with a flute player to coordinate their movements and to keep up the pace. Trainers and spectators could watch from the shade of the colonnades. Notice that the columns are smooth (missing their fluting) on the lower part of the inside face. This way, when it rained, athletes could exercise under the arcade (or take a breather by leaning up against a

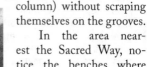

column) without scraping themselves on the grooves.

In the area nearest the Sacred Way, notice the benches where athletes were taught and people gathered for conversation. You can still see the bathtubs that athletes used to wash off their oil-dust coating. (They also used a stick-like tool to scrape off the oily grime.)

Besides being training facilities, *palaestrae* (found in almost every city) were also a kind of health club where men gathered to chat.

• *Exit the* palaestra *on the left to continue down the Sacred Way, then take the next right. Climb the stairs at the far end, and peek into the ruined brick building that was once the...*

❹ Workshop of Pheidias

In this building, the great sculptor Pheidias (c. 490-430 BC) created the 40-foot statue of Zeus (c. 435 BC) that once stood in

the Temple of Zeus across the street (for details on how he constructed it, see the sidebar). The workshop was built with the same dimensions as the temple's *cella* (inner room) so that Pheidias could create the statue with the setting in mind. Pheidias arrived here having recently completed his other masterpiece, the colossal *Athena Parthenos* for the Parthenon in Athens. According to ancient accounts, his colossal Zeus outdid even that great work.

How do we know this building was Pheidias' place? Because archaeologists found sculptors' tools and molds for pouring metals, as well as a cup with Pheidias' name on it (all now displayed in the museum). After the last ancient Games were held, this workshop was turned into a Christian church (fourth century AD—notice the semicircular part at the end facing east, which was added as an altar; see "Olympia's Legacy," later).

• *Head out of the workshop, then loop around back and to the left, past a large, open, rubble-strewn field (to the right) with dozens of thigh-high Ionic capitals. This was the site of the massive* **Leonidaion,** *a luxury, four-star hotel—boasting 145 rooms, private baths, and a central pool— built in the fourth century BC to house dignitaries and famous athletes during the Games.*

Cross the Sacred Way, head up the ramp/stairs, then veer left toward Olympia's main sight, marked by a single standing column.

❺ Temple of Zeus

The center of ancient Olympia—both physically and symbolically—was the massive temple dedicated to Zeus, king of the gods and patron of the Games. It was the first of the golden age temples, one of the biggest (not much smaller than the Parthenon) and the purest example of the Doric style.

The temple was built in the fifth century BC (470-455 BC), stood for a thousand years, and then crumbled into the evocative ruin we see today, still lying where it fell in the sixth century AD.

Stand in front of the rubble field strewn with big gray blocks, two-ton column drums, and fallen 12-ton capitals. They're made not of marble but of cheaper local limestone. Look closely and you

can see the seashell fossils in this porous (and not terribly durable) sedimentary rock. Most of the temple was made of limestone, then covered with a marble-powder stucco to make it glisten as brightly as if it were made of pure marble. The pediments and some

OLYMPIA

Statue of Zeus

Imagine yourself as a visitor to the Temple of Zeus in ancient times. You'd enter from the east end (the end opposite the Sacred Way). Peering to the far side of the temple, you'd see the monumental statue of Zeus sitting 40 feet high on a golden throne. The statue gleamed gold and white, with colored highlights. In his right hand Zeus held a winged statue of Nike (goddess of victory), and in his left hand was a scepter topped with an eagle. Zeus completely filled the space. His head almost touched the ceiling (which was higher than the exterior columns), and his arms almost touched the sides, making the colossal statue appear even bigger. A cistern of olive oil on the temple floor reflected golden hues onto the statue.

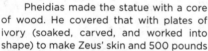

Pheidias made the statue with a core of wood. He covered that with plates of ivory (soaked, carved, and worked into shape) to make Zeus' skin and 500 pounds of gold plates for the clothes and the throne. (Such statues, when decorated with gold and ivory—as many religious statues in ancient Greece were—are called "chryselephantine.") Pheidias' assistants painted the throne with scenes of the gods.

The statue was considered by ancient people as one of the Seven Wonders—a list of tourist musts that also included the Colossus of Rhodes and the pyramids of Egypt. We know the general outlines of the statue because it appeared on coins of the day.

We also know that the statue stood for 900 years, but no one knows what became of it. It may have been melted down by Christians or destroyed in the earthquakes that toppled the temple. Others think the pieces were carried off to Constantinople and accidentally burned in that city's catastrophic fire of AD 476.

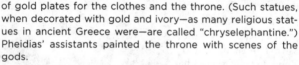

other decorations were made of expensive white marble from the isle of Paros.

An olive tree near the temple's southwest corner (to your left) marks the spot of the original tree (planted by Hercules, legends say) from which the winners' wreaths were made. Then as now, olives were vital to Greece, providing food, preservatives, fuel, perfumes...and lubrication for athletes.

You're standing near the back (west) end of the temple, near its most sacred part: the *cella*, where Pheidias' statue of Zeus stood. The interior of the temple is closed indefinitely; to get a good look you'll have to head back to the path that runs along what was once the south porch of the temple—the side facing away from Kronos Hill.

As you walk around the temple, try to reconstruct it in your mind. It was huge—about half an acre—and stood six stories tall. The lone standing column is actually a reconstruction (of original pieces, cleaned and restacked), but it gives you a sense of the scale: It's 34 feet tall, 7 feet thick, and weighs 9 tons. This was one of 34 massive Doric columns that surrounded the temple: 6 on each end and 13 along the sides (making this a typical peripteral/peristyle temple, like Athens' Parthenon and Temple of Hephaistos in the Ancient Agora).

The columns originally supported a triangular pediment at each end (now in the Archaeological Museum), carved with scenes

of the battle of the Lapiths and centaurs (west end) and Pelops and the chariot race (east end, which was the main entrance).

Along the south side of the temple, you'll see five huge fallen columns, with their drums lined up in a row like dominos. To the right of the path (across from the fallen columns) are the ruins of the ❻ **Bouleuterion,** the council chamber where, by stepping on castrated bulls' balls, athletes took an oath not to cheat. As this was a religious event, and because physical training was a part of moral education, the oaths and personal honor were held sacred.

Continue down the path to the front (east) end of the temple

and duck off the path to the left to find the 29-foot-tall, white-marble, triangular ❼ **Pedestal of Nike.** It's missing its top, but it once held a famous statue (now in the museum) of the goddess Nike, the personification of victory.

She looked down upon the ❽ **Winner's Circle,** here at the main entrance to the temple, where Olympic victors were announced and crowned. As thousands gathered in the courtyard below, priests called the name of the winner, who scaled the steps to the cheers of the crowd. The winner was crowned with a wreath of olive (not laurel) branches, awarded a statue in his honor—and nothing more. There were no awards for second and third place and no gold, silver, or bronze medals—those are inventions of the modern Olympics. However, winners were usually showered with gifts and perks from their proud hometowns: free food for life, tax exemptions, theater tickets, naming rights for gymnasiums, statues, pictures on ancient Wheaties boxes, and so on.

In the courtyard you can see pedestals that once held statues of winners, who were considered to be demigods. The inscriptions listed the winner's name, the date, the event won, his hometown, and the names of his proud parents.

With the main entrance of the Temple of Zeus at your back, walk toward the tall **marble column** off to your left. This column was built in 270 BC to honor Egyptian King Ptolemy II, the son of one of Alexander the Great's generals. After an eight-year modern-day restoration, the column now reaches its original height, allowing visitors to better visualize the scale of Olympia's monuments. It stands in front of the ruins of the **Echo Hall,** a long gallery where winners were announced as if into a microphone—the sound echoed seven times.

• *From the column, walk toward the low wall at the base of Kronos Hill. The foot of the hill is lined with a row of pedestals, called the...*

❾ Bases of Zanes and Row of Treasuries

These 16 pedestals once held bronze statues of Zeus (plural "Zanes"). At the ancient Olympic Games, as at the modern ones, it was an honor just to compete and there was no shame in not finishing first. Quitters and cheaters were another story. The Zeus statues that once lined this path were paid for with fines levied on cheaters, whose names and ill deeds were inscribed in the bases. As people entered the stadium (to the right), they'd spit on the names on the bases. Offenses ranged from doping (using forbidden herbs) or bribing opponents, to failing to train in advance of the Games or quitting out of cowardice. Drinking animal blood—the Red Bull of the day—was forbidden. Official urine tasters tested for this ancient equivalent of steroids.

Just behind the statues (and a few feet higher in elevation) is a terrace that once held a row of treasuries. These small buildings housed expensive offerings to the gods. Many were sponsored by colonies as a way for Greeks living abroad to stay in touch with their cultural roots.

• *Turn right and pass under the arch of the...*

OLYMPIA

❿ Krypti

As you enter the stadium through this tunnel, imagine yourself as an athlete who has trained for years and traveled for days, carrying the hopes of your hometown on your shoulders...and now finally about to compete. Built around 300 BC, this tunnel once had a vaulted ceiling; along the walls are niches that functioned as equipment lockers. Just like today's NFL players, Olympia's athletes psyched themselves up for the big contest by shouting as they ran through this tunnel, then emerging into the stadium to the roar of the crowd.

• *On your mark, get set, go. Follow the Krypti as it leads into the...*

⓫ Stadium

Line up on that original marble-paved starting line from the ancient Olympic Games and imagine the scene. The place was filled with 45,000 spectators—men, boys, and girls—who sat on the man-made banks on either side of the track. One lone adult woman was allowed in: a priestess of the goddess Demeter Chamyne, whose altar rose above the sea of testosterone from the

north (left) bank (still visible today).

The stadium (built in the fifth century BC) held no seats except those for the judges, who sat in a special box (visible on the south bank, to your right). The Hellanodikai (Judges of the Greeks) kept things on track. Elected from local noble families and carefully trained over 10 months for just a few days of Games, these referees were widely respected for their impartiality.

The stadium track is 192 meters (640 feet) from start to finish line. The Greek word *stadion* literally means a course that is 600 traditional Olympic feet long, supposedly first marked out by Hercules. The line at the near (west) end marked the finish, where all races ended. (Some started at this end as well, depending on how many laps in the race, but most started at the far end.) The racers ran straight up and back on a clay surface, not around the track. There were 20 starting blocks (all still visible today), each with two

grooves—one for each foot (athletes competed barefoot). Wooden starting gates (similar to those used in horse races today) made sure no one could jump the gun.

The first Games featured just one event, a sprint race over one length of the stadium, or one *stadion*. Imagine running this distance in 19.3 seconds, as Usain Bolt of Jamaica did at the 2012 Olympic Games. Over time, more events were added. There were races of two *stadia* (that is, up and back, like today's 400-meter event), 24 *stadia* (similar to today's 5K race), and a race in which athletes competed in full armor, including shields.

At the height of the Games (c. 400 BC), there were 13 events held over five days, most here in the stadium. Besides footraces, you'd see events such as the discus, javelin, boxing, wrestling, long jump, *pankration* (a wrestling/boxing/martial arts mix), and the pentathlon. (The decathlon is a modern invention.) During the 2004 Games in Athens, the shot-put competition was held in this stadium. South of the stadium was the hippodrome, or horse-racing track, where riding and chariot races took place.

Compare this stadium and the events held here with the gladiatorial contests in ancient Rome several centuries later: In the far more massive Colosseum, the sensationalistic events weren't about honor, athletic glory, or shared humanity, but a bloody fight to the death, staged to remind the citizens of the power of the state. Good thing it's the Greek games we now emulate.

• *Backtrack through the tunnel and continue straight past the pedestals for the Zeus statues. You'll bump into some rectangular foundations, the ruins of the...*

⑫ Metroon and the Altar of Zeus

The **Metroon** (mid-fourth century BC) was a temple dedicated to the mother of the gods, Rhea (also known as Cybele). The site also honored the mother-goddess of the earth, worshipped as Gaia.

Somewhere near here once stood the Altar of Zeus, though no one knows exactly where—nothing remains today. At this altar the ancient Olympians slaughtered and burned animals in sacrifice to

Zeus on a daily basis. For special festivals, they'd sacrifice 100 cattle (a "hecatomb"), cook them on the altar, throw offerings into the flames, and feast on the flesh, leaving a pile of ashes 25 feet high.

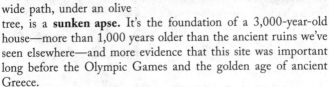

In the middle of the wide path, under an olive tree, is a **sunken apse.** It's the foundation of a 3,000-year-old house—more than 1,000 years older than the ancient ruins we've seen elsewhere—and more evidence that this site was important long before the Olympic Games and the golden age of ancient Greece.

• *To the right are the ruins of a semicircular structure built into the hillside, the...*

⑬ Nymphaeum

This was once a spectacular curved fountain lined with two tiers of statues of emperors, some of which are now in the Archaeological Museum. The foun-

tain provided an oasis in the heat and functioned as an aqueduct, channeling water throughout the Sanctuary of Olympia. It was built toward the end of the sanctuary's life (around AD 150) by the wealthy Roman Herodes Atticus (who also financed construction of the famous theater at the base of the Acropolis in Athens—the Odeon of Herodes Atticus).

When the Romans conquered Greece in the second century BC, they became fans of Greek culture, including the Olympics. The Romans repaired neglected buildings and built new structures such as this one. But they also changed (some say perverted) the nature of the Games, transforming them from a Greek religious ritual to a secular Roman spectacle. Rome opened the Games to any citizen of the empire, broadening their appeal at the cost of their Greekness.

Rome's notorious Emperor Nero—a big fan of the Olympics—attended the Games in the mid–first century AD. He built a villa nearby, started music contests associated with the Games, and entered the competition as a charioteer. But when he fell off his chariot, Nero ordered the race stopped and proclaimed himself the winner.

• *Directly in front of the Nymphaeum are the rectangular foundations of what was once the...*

⓮ Altar of Hera

These humble foundations provide a bridge across millennia, linking the original Olympics to today's modern Games. Since 1936, this has been where athletes light the ceremonial Olympic torch (for both the summer and winter Games). A few months before the modern Games begin, local women dress up in priestess garb and solemnly proceed here from the Temple of Hera. A curved, cauldron-shaped mirror is used to focus the rays of the sun, igniting a flame. The women then carry the flame into the stadium, where runners light a torch and begin the long relay to the next city to host the Games, wherever in the world that may be.

• *Fifteen yards farther along are the four standing Doric columns that mark the well-preserved...*

⓯ Temple of Hera

First built in 650 BC, this is the oldest structure on the site and one of Greece's first monumental temples. The temple originally honored both Hera and her husband Zeus, before the Temple of Zeus was built.

The temple was long but not tall, giving it an intimate feel. Its length-to-width ratio (and number of columns: 6 on the short sides, 16 on the long ones) is 3:8, which was considered particularly harmonious and aesthetically pleasing, as well as astronomically significant (the ancients synchronized the lunar and solar calendars by making the year three months longer every eight years).

The temple was originally made of wood. Over time, the wooden columns were replaced with stone columns, resulting in a virtual catalog of the various periods of the Doric style. The columns are made from the same shell-bearing limestone as most of the site's buildings, also originally covered in marble stucco.

Inside, a large statue of Hera once sat on a throne with Zeus standing beside her. Hera's priestesses wove a new dress for the statue every four years. The temple also housed a famous statue of Hermes and was topped with the Disk of the Sun (both are now in the museum).

Although women did not compete in the Olympics, unmarried women did compete in the Heraean Games, dedicated to Hera. The Heraean Games were also held here every four years, though not in the same years as the Olympics. Wearing dresses that left one shoulder and breast exposed, the young women raced on foot (running five-sixths of a *stadion*, or 160 meters/525 feet). Like the men, the winners received olive wreaths and fame, as well as a painted portrait displayed on a column of the Temple of Hera.
• *Walking out the back of Hera's temple, you'll reach our last stop: a round temple with three reconstructed Ionic columns. This was the...*

⑯ Philippeion

The construction of the Philippeion marked a new era in Greece: the Hellenistic era. (Compare these gracefully slender Ionic columns to the earlier, stouter Doric columns of the Temple of Hera—in the centuries between when they were built, Greek ideals of proportion had shifted away from sturdiness and strength to a preference for elegant beauty.)

Philip of Macedon built this monument to mark his triumph over the Greeks. The Macedonians spoke Greek and had many similar customs, but they were a kingdom (not a democracy), and the Greeks viewed them as foreigners. Philip conquered Greece around 340 BC, thus uniting the country—by force—while bringing its Classical Age to an end.

The temple—the first major building visitors saw upon entering the sacred site—originally had 18 Ionic columns of limestone and marble stucco (though today it appears dark, as the gleaming stucco is long gone). Inside stood statues of Philip and his family, including his son, the man who would bring Greece to its next phase of glory: Alexander the Great.

Just north of the Philippeion, bordering the Sacred Way and difficult to make out, are the scant remains of the Prytaneion, the building that once housed the eternal Olympic flame.

Olympia's Legacy

After the Classical Age, the Games continued, but not in their original form. First came Alexander and a new era of more secular values. Next came the Romans, who preserved the Games but also commercialized them and opened them up to non-Greeks. The

Games went from being a somber celebration of Hellenic culture to being a bombastic spectacle. The lofty ideals for which the games were once known had evaporated—along with their prestige. As Rome/Greece's infrastructure decayed, so did the Games. A series of third-century earthquakes and the turmoil of the Herulian invasion (in AD 267) kept the crowds away. As Greece became Christian, the pagan sanctuary became politically incorrect.

The last ancient Games (the 293rd) were held in AD 393. A year later, they were abolished by the ultra-Christian emperor Theodosius I as part of a general purge of pagan festivals. The final blow was delivered in 426, when Theodosius II ordered the temples set ablaze. The remaining buildings were adopted by a small early Christian community, that turned Pheidias' workshop into their church. They were forced to abandon the area after it was hit by a combination of earthquakes (in 522 and 551) and catastrophic floods and mudslides. Over the centuries, two rivers proceeded to bury the area under 25 feet of silt, thus preserving the remaining buildings until archaeologists started excavations in 1875. They finally finished digging everything out in 1972.

• *The Archaeological Museum is 200 yards to the north and well-signed.*

Archaeological Museum

Many of Olympia's greatest works of art and artifacts have been removed from the site and are now displayed, and well-described in English, in this compact and manageable museum.

❯ **Self-Guided Tour:** The museum has a prescribed route to follow for your visit. This tour takes you past the highlights, but there's much more to see if you have time.

• *From the ticket desk, go left through the first room with pre-historic artifacts, then straight into the larger, longer room. Amid a mishmash collection of helmets, shields, and other armor, you'll see several...*

❶ Tripods: These cauldrons-with-legs were used as gifts to the gods and to victorious athletes. For religious rituals, tripods were used to pour liquid libations, to hold sacred objects, or to burn incense or sacrificial offerings. As ceremonial gifts to the gods, tripods were placed atop and around temples. And as gifts to athletes, they were a source of valuable bronze (which could easily be melted down into some other form), making for a nice "cash" prize.

• *Along the right wall is an assortment of cool-looking...*

❷ Griffins: Because Greeks considered the lion the king of the beasts, and the eagle the top bird, the half-lion-half-eagle grif-

Olympia Archaeological Museum

MAIN HALL

BULL

ENTRANCE

SHOP & WC

1. Tripods
2. Griffins
3. Disk of the Sun
4. Zeus & Ganymede
5. Nike of Paeonius
6. Bronze Helmet of Miltiades
7. Temple of Zeus: West Pediment
8. Temple of Zeus: East Pediment
9. Workshop of Pheidias
10. Hermes of Praxiteles
11. Nymphaeum Statues
12. Site Model

fin was a popular symbol of power for the ancient Greeks, even if no such animal actually existed.

• *At the end of this hall you'll find the...*

❸ **Disk of the Sun:** This terra-cotta disk—seven-and-a-half feet across and once painted in bright colors—was the central roof decoration (called an *acroterion*) that perched atop the peak of the roof of the Temple of Hera. It stood as a sun- or star-like icon meant to ward off bad juju and symbolize Hera's shining glory.

• *Go past the sun disk and into the next room, which features large, decorated terra-cotta **pediments**—a reminder that these temples were not the plain-white marble we imagine them today. Make a right into another long room. On your left as you enter, have a look at the...*

❹ **Statue of Zeus Carrying Off Ganymede:** See Zeus' sly

look as he carries off the beautiful Trojan boy Ganymede to be his cup-bearer and lover. The terra-cotta statue was likely an *acroterion* (rooftop decoration) placed atop one of the treasury houses.

• *Just ahead on your left you'll see a statue rising and floating on her pedestal. She's the...*

❺ **Nike of Paeonius:** This statue of Victory (c. 421 BC) once stood atop the triangular Pedestal of Nike next to the Temple of Zeus. Victory holds her billowing robe in her outstretched left hand and a palm leaf in her right as she floats down from Mt. Olympus to proclaim the triumph of the Messenians (the Greek-speaking people from southwest Peloponnese) over Sparta.

The statue, made of flawless pure-white marble from the island of Paros, is the work of the Greek sculptor Paeonius. It was damaged in the earthquakes of AD 522 and 551, and today, Nike's wings are completely missing. But they once stretched behind and above her, making the statue 10 feet tall. (She's about seven feet today.) With its triangular base, the whole monument to Victory would have been an imposing 36 feet tall, rising above the courtyard where Olympic winners were crowned.

• *In the glass case to the right as you face Nike are two bronze helmets. The battered green one (#2) is the...*

❻ **Bronze Helmet of Miltiades:** In September of 490 BC, a huge force of invading Persians faced off against the outnum-

bered Greeks on the flat plain of Marathon, north of Athens. Although most of the Athenian generals wanted to wait for reinforcements, Miltiades convinced them to attack. The Greeks sprinted across the plain, into the very heart of the Persians— a bold move that surprised and routed the enemy. According to legend, a runner carried the good news to Athens. He raced 26.2 miles from Marathon to Athens, announced "Hurray, we won!"... and dropped dead on the spot.

The legend inspired the 26.2-mile race called the marathon— but the marathon was not an Olympic event in ancient times. It was a creation for the first modern Games, revived in Athens in 1896.

• *Next, the route takes you into the museum's largest hall. On the left wall are...*

OLYMPIA

❼ Statues from the West Pediment of the Temple of Zeus:
These statues fit snugly into the 85-foot-long pediment that stood

over the back side of the
temple (facing the Sacred
Way). Study the scene de-
picting the battle of the
Lapiths and centaurs: The
centaurs have crashed a
human wedding party
in order to carry off the
women. See one dramatic
scene of a woman and her
horse-man abductor just left of center. The Lapith men fight back.
In the center, a 10-foot-tall Apollo stands calmly looking on. Fresh
from their victory in the Persian Wars, the Greeks were particularly fond of any symbol of their struggles they had waged.

The statues from the West Pediment are gorgeous examples
of the height of golden age sculpture: Notice the harmony of the
poses and how they capture motion at the perfect moment without
seeming melodramatic. The bodies, clearly visible under clothing,
convey all the action, while the faces (in the statues that still have
them) are stoic.

• On the opposite side of the hall are...

❽ Statues from the East Pediment of the Temple of Zeus:
Olympic victors stood beneath this pediment—the temple's main

entrance—as they received
their olive wreaths. The
statues tell the story of
King **Pelops,** the legendary founder of the Games.
A 10-foot-tall Zeus in the
center is flanked by two
competing chariot teams.
Pelops (at Zeus' left hand,
with the fragmented legs)
prepares to race King Oenomaus (at Zeus' right) for the hand of
the king's daughter Hippodamia (standing beside Pelops). The
king, aware of a prophecy predicting that he would be murdered
by his son-in-law, killed 13 previous suitors after defeating them
in chariot races. But Pelops wins this race by sabotaging the king's
wheels (that may be what the crouching figure is up to behind the
king's chariot), causing the king to be dragged to his death by his
horses (just like that chariot race in *Ben-Hur*). Pelops becomes king
and goes on to unify the Peloponnesian people with a festival: the
Olympic Games.

OLYMPIA

As some of the first sculpture of the golden age (made after the Persian invasion of 480 BC), these figures show the realism and relaxed poses of the new age (note that they're missing those telltale Archaic-era smiles). But they are still done in the Severe style—the sculptural counterpart to stoic Doric architecture—with impassive faces and understated emotion, quite different from the exuberant West Pediment, made years later. Still, notice how refined the technique is—the horses, for example, effectively convey depth and movement. But seen from the side, it's striking how flat the sculpture really is.

• *Retrace your steps into the hall with the Nike statue, then make a right into the next room with the Zeus statue painting...*

❾ **Workshop of Pheidias Room:** The poster shows Pheidias' great statue of Zeus, and a model reconstructs the workshop where he created it. In the display case directly to the left as you enter, find exhibit #10, the clay cup of Pheidias. The inscription on the bottom (hence the mirror) reads, "I belong to Pheidias." The adjacent case holds clay molds that were likely used for making the folds of Zeus' robe. The case in the opposite corner contains lead and bronze tools used by ancient sculptors to make the statues we've seen all day.

• *The room hiding behind the Zeus poster contains...*

❿ **Hermes of Praxiteles:** This seven-foot-tall statue (340-330 BC), discovered in the Temple of Hera, is possibly a rare original by the great sculptor Praxiteles. Although little is known of this fourth-century sculptor, Praxiteles was recognized in his day as the master of realistic anatomy and the first to sculpt nude women. If this statue looks familiar, that's because his works influenced generations of Greek and Roman sculptors, who made countless copies.

Hermes leans against a tree trunk, relaxed. He carries a baby—the recently orphaned Dionysus—who reaches for a (missing) object that Hermes is distracting him with. Experts guess the child was probably groping for a bunch of grapes, which would have hinted at Dionysus' future role as the debauched god of wine and hedonism.

Circle the statue counterclockwise and watch Hermes' face take on the many shades of thoughtfulness. From the front he appears serene. From the right (toward the baby), he seems sad. But from the left (toward his outstretched arm), there's the hint of a smile. (And from the back, nice cheeks!)

The statue has some of Praxiteles' textbook features. The body has the distinctive S-curve of Classical sculpture (head tilted one way, torso the other, legs another). Hermes rests his arm on the tree stump, over which his robe is draped. And the figure is interesting from all angles, not just the front. Praxiteles could make hard, white, translucent marble appear as supple, sensual, and sexual as human flesh.

• *Return to the Pheidias room, then make a left, continuing until you come to a statue of a bull, from the Roman-era Nymphaeum fountain.*

⓫ Nymphaeum Statues: The grand semicircular fountain near the Temple of Hera had two tiers of statues, including Roman emperors and the family of the statue's benefactor, Herodes Atticus. Here you can see some of the surviving statues, as well as a **bull** (in the center of the room) that stood in the middle of the fountain. The bull's inscriptions explain the fountain's ori-

gins. Compared to the energetic statues we just saw from the west pediment of the Temple of Zeus, these stately statues are static and lackluster.

The next (smaller) room holds more Roman-era statues, from the Metroon and the Temple of Hera.

• *The route leads back to the main entrance foyer, where to the right you'll find an interesting...*

⓬ Model of the Site, Reconstructed: This model shows Olympia as it appeared at the height of its glory. You can see the original placement of some of the artifacts we just viewed in the museum: On the Temple of Zeus, notice the pediments, topped with statues and tripods. Southeast of the temple is the Pedestal of Nike, supporting the statue of Nike. Find Pheidias' workshop and the Temple of Hera, topped with the Disk of the Sun.

• *With that, you've seen the core of Olympia's archaeological collection. For more on the Games themselves, consider checking out the Museum of the History of the Olympic Games in Antiquity.*

OLYMPIA

OTHER SIGHTS IN OLYMPIA
▲▲Museum of the History of the Olympic Games in Antiquity

Most people are familiar with the modern-day Olympics, but the games played by those early Olympians were a very different opera-

tion. Perched on a low hill across the river from the Sanctuary of Olympia archaeological site (above the south parking lot), this collection offers a handy "Ancient Olympics 101" lesson that helps bring the events to life and nicely complements the other attractions in Olympia. If you can spare the 30-45 minutes it takes to see this museum, stop here first to get your imagination in gear before seeing the ancient site.

The rooms around the perimeter of the building tell the story of the original Games. You'll learn about the various religious elements of the celebration and how women participated in sports, see the awards and honors for the victors, and admire a beautiful mosaic floor (c. AD 200) depicting some of the events. The main central hall focuses on the athletic contests themselves, displaying ancient discuses, javelin heads, halters (weights used in the long jump), and large shields that were carried by fully armor-clad runners in some particularly exhausting footraces.

Cost and Hours: Covered by Sanctuary of Olympia combo-ticket; daily 8:00-20:00; Nov-March Mon 10:00-17:00, Tue-Sun 8:00-15:00; WCs outside building.

Archimedes Museum

Located on the main drag in Olympia town, the Archimedes Museum is most appealing to engineering nuts, but its interactive exhibits can be fun for anyone. This museum shows off replicas of ancient Greek technologies such as the Archimedes screw, the crane used to build the Parthenon, the Antikythera mechanism (ancient computer thought to have been used in astronomy), and the pantograph (the original photocopier). The models (and museum) were created by mechanical engineer and author Konstantinos Kotsanas, who has dedicated his life to understanding and recreating ancient Greek technology.

Cost and Hours: Free, donations accepted, daily 9:30-20:30, off-season until 15:30, +30 693 183 1530, https://archimedesmuseum.gr.

Olympia Land Estate

Five minutes outside town, the Liarommatis family runs a small winery and olive grove welcoming visitors for a tour and tasting. After a short introduction to the farm—25 acres of olive trees and 100 acres of vineyards—and explanation of the harvest, you'll see the modern winery, learn about the production process, and visit the farmhouse for a relaxed-yet-informative tasting paired with light snacks. By the end, you'll be surprised to discover how easy it is to master the names of each Greek grape.

Cost and Hours: €15, Mon-Sat 10:00-15:00, closed Sun, in the village of Koskina, friendly Amanda speaks English, +30 2624 023 021, www.olympiagi.gr. Drop-ins are welcome but may need to wait for a tour to begin; to reserve a tour time, call ahead or make a reservation on their website.

Klio's Honey Farm

What makes this rustic and low-key sight worth visiting is the enthusiasm of its proprietor, Klio. A veteran professional beekeeper, she'll charm you with her presentation on the history and intricacies of raising bees. Getting there is fun, too: After a 15-minute walk from the center of town on a dirt road past clucking chickens, you'll find the little farm that belongs to Klio's grandmother. Enjoy Klio's stories and try some local treats, including fresh-from-the-hives honey. You may even get to meet some more members of this friendly Greek family.

Cost and Hours: €10 for an hour-long visit; Mon-Sat 10:30-18:00, closed Sun, reduced hours off-season; best to call ahead, +30 6977 714 530, www.klioshoneyfarm.com.

Sleeping in Olympia

Olympia's impressive archaeological site and museum—and the town's inconvenient location far from other attractions—make spending the night here almost obligatory. Fortunately, there are enough good options to make it worthwhile, including one real gem (Hotel Pelops). If you have a car, consider sleeping above Olympia in the more charming village of Miraka.

IN OLYMPIA

For locations, see the "Olympia Town" map, earlier.

$$ Hotel Pelops is Olympia's top option, with 18 comfortable rooms—try this place first. Run by the warm, welcoming Spiliopoulos clan—father Theodoros, Aussie mom Suzanna, and children Alkis, Kris, and Sally—the hotel oozes hospitality. They're generous with travel advice and include free tea and coffee in each room. On the wall of the breakfast room, look for the four Olympic torches that family members have carried in the official relay: Tokyo 1964, Mexico City 1968, Athens 2004, and Rio 2016 (elevator, cooking classes extra—arrange well in advance, Varela 2, +30 2624 022 543, www.hotelpelops.gr, hotelpelops@gmail.com).

$$ Neda Hotel has 44 rooms that are a bit overpriced and in need of modernization. But there are two reasons to consider staying here: It's the only place in town with a swimming pool (decent size, surrounded by chaises, café tables, and a small bar), and its top-floor dining room, where the buffet breakfast is served, has outdoor seating and lovely views of Olympia (elevator, Karamanli 1, +30 2624 022 563, www.hotelneda.gr, info@hotelneda.gr, Tyligadas family).

$ Kronio Hotel, run by friendly Panagiotis Asteris, rents 24 straightforward rooms along the main street; most have balconies and bathtubs (elevator, Tsoureka 1, +30 2624 022 188, www. hotelkronio.gr, hotelkronio@hotmail.com).

$ Leonidaion Guest House leans trendy, with a minimalist aesthetic and old-school-cool terrazzo floors. Most of the seven rooms have balconies, and the top-floor suite enjoys a sweeping view over the countryside. Owner Damiano is an excellent ambassador for this part of Greece (corner of Spiliopoulou and Pierre De Coubertin, +30 2624 023 507, www.leonidaion.gr, info@ leonidaion.gr).

¢ Pension Posidon is a good budget option, with 10 simple but clean rooms in a homey, flower-bedecked house just two blocks above the main street (most rooms have balconies, breakfast extra, rooftop patio, Stefanopoulou 9, +30 2624 022 567, mobile +30 697 321 6726, www.pensionposidon.gr, info@pensionposidon.gr, Liagouras family).

NEAR OLYMPIA, IN MIRAKA

The village of Miraka, which sits on a hill above Olympia, is the site of the ancient settlement of Pissa (Archea Pissa/Αρχαια Πισα). Today it offers an authentic-feeling Old-World village experience and a scenic perch with fine views over the olive groves in the valley below.

$$ Bacchus Tavern (also a recommended restaurant) rents 11 modern, comfortable rooms in a traditional village a 10-minute drive above Olympia. This is a luxurious-feeling retreat from the drabness of modern Olympia (family rooms, apartment, inviting terrace and swimming pool, +30 2624 022 298, mobile +30 693 714 4800, www.bacchustavern.gr, bacchuspension@gmail.com, Kostas and Achilleas).

Getting There: From Olympia's town center, take the main road out of town toward Pyrgos, then turn right toward Tripoli and twist uphill on the modern highway. After the fourth tunnel, exit to the left and curve around to reach Miraka. Bacchus Tavern is on the right as you enter town (look for the parking lot).

Eating in Olympia

Because its restaurants cater to one-nighters, Olympia has no interest in creating return visitors—making its in-town cuisine scene pretty dismal. For something more special, it's worth the drive (or taxi ride) to one of the more interesting places in the hills above town. See the "Olympia Town" map, earlier, for locations.

IN THE TOWN CENTER

The shady, angled side street called Georgiou Douma is lined with touristy places serving mediocre food—but if you're attracted to the area's convenient location and leafy scene, try **$$$$ Dimitra** (ΔHMHTPA), close to the train station. It's higher-end, Greek-meets-international fusion and a better bet than most of the places along this strip (open daily for dinner, weekends only off-season, +30 2624 029 183).

$$ Anesi, located just outside the tourist zone, has zero atmosphere but is the local favorite for grilled meat (open daily for lunch and dinner, closed Nov-Dec, one block off main street at corner of Avgerinou and Spiliopoulou, +30 2624 022 644).

$ Zeus is a popular café-bar and does reliable lighter meals or a grab-and-go lunch (daily 8:00-24:00, on the corner of the main street and Avgerinou, +30 2624 023 913).

$ Fresh Cheese Pies: Takis opens at 7:00 and closes when he runs out of his freshly baked pies, made with handmade dough and various fillings (along the main street, look for the sign that says *Homemade*).

IN THE HILLS ABOVE OLYMPIA

The area's best dining experiences are up in the hills above town, where locals head to enjoy the food and views. The two places to the west are a five-minute ride out of town—you could walk to either of these (20-30 minutes each way), but I'd drive or spring for a taxi. Bacchus, to the east, is far beyond walking distance.

West of Town

$$$ Europa Hotel's elegant garden restaurant on the hills overlooking Olympia is a 20-minute uphill hike or a 5-minute drive/taxi ride (it's well-signed; from middle of town, follow the small road behind Hotel Hercules). Brothers Nikos and Alkis practice their culinary art on fresh products from the hotel's farm. The "farm dish" consists of layers of Talagani cheese and roasted vegetables—a refreshing break from traditional Greek salad; the grilled meats and fish are savory and satisfying. Drink in the magnificent terrace dotted with olive trees, rose bushes, and grapevine arbors—in the fall, some of those grapes might come to your table as dessert (open daily for dinner starting at 19:00, 1 Drouva, +30 2624 022 650).

$$ **Taverna Thea** (Θεα), a few more minutes farther into the hills, is a homier (and cheaper) alternative to dining at the Europa Hotel. Greek Andreas and Swedish Erika proudly serve a standard menu plus some regional specialties to happy locals, who usually gather in the garden terrace after dark, and in-the-know tourists who enjoy the balcony views earlier in the evening (fresh fish specialties; Mon-Sat 19:00-24:00, Sun from 13:00; +30 2624 023 264). From the middle of town, follow signs to Europa Hotel (listed above); near the top of the hill, take the fork to the right, following *Krestena, Floka,* and/or *theatre*/Θεατρο signs, then stay on the same road as it crests the hill, while looking for the Ταβερνα sign on the left, across the street from the taverna itself.

East of Town

$$$ **Bacchus Tavern,** with a striking setting and pleasant decor that mingles new and old, is the best eatery in the area. The Zapantis family is proud of their traditional, homemade Greek cuisine with creative flair. Olympians favor their lamb baked in oregano and olive oil. Ask owner Kostas how he once used water from the swimming pool to save his tavern from wildfires (affordable fixed-price meals, good vegetarian options, daily 12:30-24:00, Fri-Sun only in Jan-Feb, +30 2624 022 298). For driving directions, see the Bacchus Tavern hotel listing, earlier.

Olympia Connections

BY BUS

For all connections, you'll transfer first in **Pyrgos** to the west (about hourly Mon-Fri, 7/day Sat-Sun, last bus leaves Olympia at 22:15, 35 minutes).

From Pyrgos you can connect to **Athens** (7-8/day, 4.5 hours), **Patra** (up to 7/day, 2 hours, some onward connections to **Delphi**), **Kalamata** (1-2/day, 2.5 hours, onward connections to **Kardamyli, Sparta,** and **Monemvasia**), and **Tripoli** (2-3/day, 3 hours, some onward connections to **Nafplio**). For the Pyrgos bus station, call +30 2621 020 600. For schedules, see the KTEL website for this region (www.ktelileias.gr; click "Εισιτήρια Online" for schedules in English).

BY CRUISE SHIP

Cruise ships stop at the village of Katakolo (kah-TAH-koh-loh), about 18 miles west of Olympia. Along the waterfront is a pedestrian promenade with several restaurants. This is a good place to try seafood and spend time before reboarding your ship.

Getting to Olympia from Katakolo

By Big Bus: Big bus tours run from Katakolo's main street to Olympia (€10-15 round-trip; ask how much time you'll have in Olympia—it's generally between 1.5 and 3 hours, and you'll want at least 2). The agency that runs the bus understands how much you don't want to miss your boat—and all but guarantees you won't. But note that you may have to wait up to 30 minutes in Katakolo until they collect enough passengers to make the trip worthwhile.

By Tour: Olympic Traveller offers various packages combining round-trip transport to Olympia with a 2.5-hour guided tour of the site and museum, likely with recommended local guide Niki Vlachou (€70-110/person, groups never larger than 25, +30 697 320 1213, www.olympictraveller.com, info@olympictraveller.com). For €30 you can skip the guided tour in Olympia, but enjoy a narrated ride, quick pick-up times (they won't dally at the port waiting for the bus to fill up), and guaranteed on-time return to your cruise ship.

By Taxi: Taxis descend upon the dock, hoping to pick up passengers; round-trip fare for a two-hour visit costs €120 (talk to a few drivers to find a good match). For the best prices and service, book in advance. Consider **Takis Tsaparas** (+30 694 543 4913, www.taxikatakolon.gr).

By Rental Car: There's only one game in town if you want to rent a car: **Dias Travel Agency** (from €45/day plus gas, best to book ahead, +30 2621 041 727, www.rentacarkatakolo.gr). The route to Olympia is an easy 30-minute drive that bypasses any towns; ask the rental agent for directions.

By Train: While there is train service between Katakolo and Olympia, it's unpredictable—use one of the more reliable options above instead.

Wine Tasting and a Beach: If you don't want to visit Olympia, one option is to ride the hop-on, hop-off tourist train, which stops at Mercouri winery and at rocky Agioas Andreas Beach, where you'll find a few restaurant/beach bars. Catch it in Katakolo in the square next to the church at the end of the promenade (€8, roughly every 40 minutes, last train 2 hours before cruise ships leave, Katakolo Train Tours, +30 694 777 8842).

ROUTE TIPS FOR DRIVERS

Olympia is situated in the hilly interior of the Peloponnese, connected to the outside world by one main highway, called E-55. You can take this west to **Pyrgos** (30 minutes), where E-55 forks: Take it north to **Patra** (2 hours from Olympia) and **Delphi** (4 hours from

Olympia—see Delphi's "Route Tips for Drivers" on page 386); or south to **Kalamata** (2 hours) and on to **Kardamyli** (2.5 hours from Olympia). Or, from Olympia, you can take E-55 east on its twisty route to **Tripoli** (2 hours), then get on the major E-65/A-7 expressway to zip to **Nafplio** (3.5 hours from Olympia) or **Athens** (4 hours from Olympia).

Patra

The big port city of Patra (Πάτρα, sometimes spelled Patras in English, pop. 170,000) is many visitors' first taste of Greece, as it's the hub for boats arriving from Italy (and from the Ionian Islands, such as Corfu). While it's not a place to linger, Patra has rejuvenated its main thoroughfare to become a fairly enjoyable place to spend a little time waiting for your boat or bus.

Patra sprawls along its harborfront, which is traced by the busy road called Othonos Amalias. The city's transit points line up along here (from north to south, as you'll reach them with the sea on your right): the North Port Terminal for some local ferries, a ragtag main bus station, the low-profile train station, and the South Port Terminal where ferries from Italy dock. See www.patrasinfo.com for more information on the town.

Visiting Patra: Patra has several enjoyable pedestrian zones that bustle with a lively, engaging chaos you'll find only in a Mediterranean port town. Stretching west from the bus station, the pedestrianized Riga Fereou (two blocks inland from Othonos Amalias) is where locals spend their time eating, drinking coffee, and shopping. Riga Fereou intersects with another pedestrian zone, called Agiou Nikolaou. Both streets are lined with al fresco cafés, restaurants, and shops—and are fine places to feel the pulse of urban Greece.

Patra has several worthwhile sights. The **archaeological museum,** housed in a modern building on the north side of town, displays artifacts from the city and surrounding area, and focuses on themes of private life, public life, and cemeteries (about 1.5 miles from city center—best to take a taxi or drive, +30 2613 616 100). The town **castle,** built by the Emperor Justinian in the sixth century, is reachable from a staircase at the top of Agiou Nikolaou (+30 2610 623 390). Near the castle, the impressively restored **ancient *odeon*** (theater) dates from Roman times (+30 2610 276 207). And along the waterfront, south of the main transit zone, the vast **Church of Agios Andreas** is the city's *mitropolis* (like a cathedral). You'll also find decent **public beaches** northeast of the marina.

Sleeping in Patra: If you're stuck here overnight, these options are handy: **$$ Maison Grecque** (boutique hotel in a historic family mansion, 25is Martiou 116, +30 2610 241 212, www.mghotels.gr)

or **$ Galaxy City Center** (more generically business-style, Agiou Nikolaou 9, +30 2610 275 981, www.galaxyhotel.com.gr).

Patra Connections: You can sail by **boat** from Patra to several towns in Italy, including Bari, Ancona, Brindisi, and Venice; many boats stop at the Greek island of Corfu en route (check Superfast Ferries—www.superfast.com, Grimaldi Lines—www.grimaldi-lines.com, Minoan Lines—www.minoan.gr, and ANEK Lines—www.anek.gr). **Buses** connect Patra directly to Athens and Pyrgos (with onward connections to Olympia); see www.patrasinfo.com for more information.

OLYMPIA

KARDAMYLI
& THE MANI
PENINSULA

Καρδαμύλη • Μάνη

The Mani Peninsula is the southernmost tip of mainland Greece (and of the entire European continent, east of Spain)—and it really does feel like the end of the road. Sealed off from the rest of Greece by a thick ring of mountains, the peninsula has seen its population ebb and flow throughout history with tides of refugees fleeing whatever crises were gripping the rest of Greece. The only part of Greece that never completely fell to the Ottoman invaders, the Mani became the cradle of the 1821 revolution that finally brought independence to the Greeks.

In the Mani, travelers discover a timeless region of rustic villages and untrampled beaches. A day's drive around this desolate, rural peninsula offers dramatic mountain scenery and bloody history all tied up in a hardscrabble and evocative package—making hedonism on the Mani coast feel all the more hedonistic. At the end of the day, you can retire to charming Kardamyli.

PLANNING YOUR TIME

Two nights and a full day is a minimum for this area. Sleep in Kardamyli. With one day, first take my self-guided walk of Kardamyli to get your bearings, then head up to Old Kardamyli. In the afternoon, go for a hike or hit the beach. With a second day and a car, drive the Mani Peninsula. To really be on vacation, add more nights. Those with three days here can do the driving tour at a more leisurely pace, saving the Pyrgos Dirou Caves and the detour to Kastania for a separate side-trip from Kardamyli. Or instead of returning to Kardamyli, you can head from the Mani loop directly to Monemvasia.

Kardamyli

The village of Kardamyli (kar-dah-MEE-lee) is the gateway to the Mani Peninsula and its best home base. It's an atypical resort

that delicately mixes chic hotels and conscientious travelers with real-world Greece. Relax and tune in to the pace of country life. On Kardamyli's humble main drag, locals-only mom-and-pop shops mingle with trendy tourist boutiques.

Little Kardamyli is one of the oldest city names in Greek history. In the *Iliad,* Homer described "well-peopled" Kardamyli as one of seven cities presented to the Greek hero Achilles to persuade him to return to the siege of Troy. Achilles' son Pyrrhus sailed to Kardamyli, then walked to Sparta to claim the hand of Ermioni. And the legendary Gemini twins—Castor and Pollux—are said to be buried here.

Kardamyli is wedged between the sparkling pebble beaches of the Messenian Gulf and towering Mount Profitas Ilias (7,895

feet)—the Peloponnese's highest peak, which is snowcapped from November to early May. Between the sea and the distant mountaintop, dramatic hills and cliffs are topped with scenic villages, churches, and ruined towers. As throughout the rest of the Mani, in the sixth century AD Kardamyli's residents fled from pirates into these hills—returning to sea level only in the 18th century, after the construction of Old Kardamyli's defensive tower house made it safe.

Visitors can enjoy hiking into the hills, learning about the region's rough-and-tumble history at Old Kardamyli, swimming at the town's Ritsa Beach, and driving deeper into the Mani Peninsula, but the real charm of Kardamyli is its low-key ambience—the place works like a stun gun on your momentum. I could stay here for days, just eating well and hanging out. It's the kind of place where travelers plan their day around the sunset.

Orientation to Kardamyli

Tiny Kardamyli—with just 230 year-round residents—swells with far more visitors in the summer months. The town is compact, gathered around a convenient central spine (the main road running south from Kalamata). Kardamyli is small enough to feel like a cozy village, but big enough to serve the needs of its many visitors—with small grocery stores, ATMs, and more.

Tourist Information: Because Kardamyli has no TI, hoteliers pick up the slack, sometimes offering free hiking maps and usually eager to direct visitors to the best restaurants and activities. The helpful official town website has lots of good information, including accommodations (www.kardamili-greece.com).

Arrival in Kardamyli: For specifics on driving into town, see "Route Tips for Drivers," later.

Kardamyli Walk

You could walk from one end of Kardamyli to the other in 10 minutes, but you'd miss the point. Slow down—and keep an eye out for intriguing pockets of traditional Greek village culture. This leisurely self-guided stroll lasts about an hour.

• Start at the beginning of town, by the...

Village Church

The modern Church of St. Mary, with its thriving congregation, is the heart of this town. Notice the loudspeakers outside, which allow overflow crowds to take part in the service on very important days, such as Easter. Kardamyli takes its Easter celebration very seriously: On Good Friday, a processional passes through the town and the priest blesses each house. At midnight on Holy Saturday, everyone turns off their lights and comes  to this main square. The priest emerges from the church with a candle, passing its flame through the candle-carrying crowd, who then take the light home with them...gradually illuminating the entire town. And then the fireworks begin.

Before we head into the middle of town, walk a few yards up the main street, away from the church and the main square, and look on the right for a wooden wall painted olive green (before the two grocery stores). This is the **Botana Herb Shop,** a celebration of what grows in the hills above Kardamyli. Welcoming owner Yian-

KARDAMYLI & MANI PENINSULA

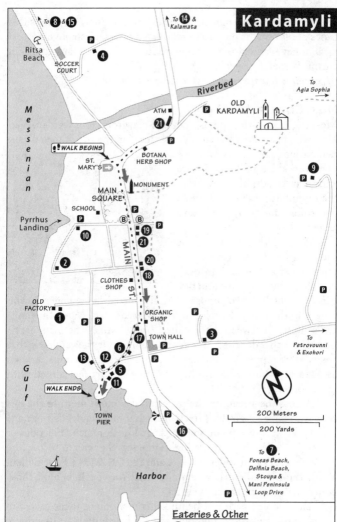

Kardamyli

To 8 & 15
Ritsa Beach
SOCCER COURT
To 14 & Kalamata
Riverbed
To Agia Sophia
OLD KARDAMYLI
ATM
21
Messenian
WALK BEGINS
ST. MARY'S
BOTANA HERB SHOP
MAIN SQUARE
MONUMENT
9
SCHOOL
Pyrrhus Landing
10
B B
19
21
2
20
18
CLOTHES SHOP
OLD FACTORY
1
ORGANIC SHOP
3
17
TOWN HALL
To Petrovounni & Exohori
6
13
12
5
WALK ENDS
11
TOWN PIER
16
Gulf
200 Meters
200 Yards
To 7,
Foneas Beach,
Delfinia Beach,
Stoupa &
Mani Peninsula
Loop Drive
Harbor

Accommodations

1 Hotel Anniska
2 Hotel Liakoto
3 Hotel Esperides
4 Antonia's Apartments
5 Marina Studios & Gorgones Rooms (Les Sirenes)
6 Olympia Koymanakou Rooms
7 To Kalamitsi Hotel
8 To Melitsina Village Hotel
9 Vardia Hotel

Eateries & Other

10 Psaras Restaurant
11 Harilaos Restaurant
12 Tikla Cuzina & Wine Bar
13 Aquarella Café & Cocktail Bar
14 To Kastro Taverna
15 To Elies Restaurant
16 Taverna Dioskouroi
17 Lola Frozen Yogurt
18 Androuvista Café
19 Maistros Café
20 Souvlaki Shop
21 Groceries (2)

nis Dimitreas, a walking encyclopedia on local foraging, offers free tastes of his organic produce—marinated olives, fresh olive oil, and local honey—and also sells homemade herbal teas, soaps, and skin creams (generally open daily).

• *Extending toward town from the church is the leafy...*

Main Square

Most of the year, this spot is a popular playground for Kardamylian kids, who play under the eucalyptus trees (on the site of the ancient gymnasium). But on New Year's Day, a local club fills the square with truckloads of snow from the mountains, turning it into a playground for giddy grown-ups as well.

Walk to the far end of the square. In the little park is the town water spigot and an odd-ball collection of **monuments.** Find the busts of two almost comically medal-laden generals who fought in the Greek Revolution and Macedonian Wars. The modern sculpture between them, called *Unity,* evokes the many fortified towers that dot the Mani Peninsula. Despite the vendettas that frequently cropped up among the peninsula's inhabitants, known as Maniots, those who live here today generally feel united with one another.

Across the street, on the pedestal, is a **monument to the heroes** who have fought for Greek unity and independence since antiquity. Next to the palm branch is the Greek motto "Freedom or Death." While two wars are highlighted in the wreath below (the 1821 Greek War of Independence and the 1912-1913 First Balkan War), the monument is a reminder that the ideals behind those conflicts date back to the ancients.

The cobbled path just behind this monument takes hikers to the restored ruins and museum of **Old Kardamyli** (a 10-minute trek, described later under "Sights in Kardamyli").

Back across the street at the end of the square, look down to the **waterfront.** The primary school (with a small playground) sits just behind the square. The school has a number of Albanian kids, because as a couple of generations of Kardamyli's young people moved to Athens in search of work, Albanian workers migrated here to do stonework and other manual-labor jobs. And more recently, Greeks who are struggling economically have been unable to afford a family.

Now look in the opposite direction, up at the **hillsides.** From here you can see two of the most popular nearby hiking destinations:

On the left is a little hilltop church, and to the right is the village of Petrovouni. An enjoyable three-hour loop covers both (described later, under "Hiking").

• *Across from the end of the park begins the commercial zone of...*

Kardamyli's Main Street

The next few blocks reveal a fascinating blend of traditional Greek village lifestyles side-by-side with pleasantly low-key tourism. In most Greek towns with such a fine seaside setting, the beaches are lined with concrete high-rise hotels, and the main streets are a

cavalcade of tacky T-shirt shops. But the people of Kardamyli are determined to keep their town real—a hard-fought local law prohibits new construction over a certain height (ruling out big resorts), and the town has made long-term sustainability a priority over short-term profit. (It also helps that the beach has

pebbles instead of sand, which keeps away the party crowds.) Its residents have created a smart little self-sustaining circle: The town keeps its soul even as it profits from visitors...allowing it to attract the caliber of travelers who appreciate Kardamyli for what it is.

Take a walk down the main street for examples of both faces of Kardamyli. Notice that nearly all of the buildings are traditionally built, using stone from this area. Even newer buildings (such as the café right at the start of the street) match the old style. As you stroll you'll see:

Noeas (on the left, with the green awning): A tempting bakery/pastry shop.

Maistros Café (on the left, with breakfast and backgammon): This is Kardamyli's closest thing to a place where the "old boys" hang out.

The **pharmacy** (left, after the handy little supermarket): Pop inside to see how tastefully it's been renovated.

Psaltiras Wine Bar and Olive Oil Shop (left): Nicos Psaltiras speaks English and loves to share his quality local products.

2407 Kardamili Mountain Shop (left): Named for the height in meters of the tallest mountain in the Peloponnese, this is the go-to place for outdoor equipment, bike rentals, and advice on walks and treks. See the chalkboard outside, or 2407m.com, for their weekly schedule of excursions and tours.

Souvlaki Shop (left): Here you'll find local-style "fast food" dished up by shepherds serving their own freshly butchered meat.

Androuvista Café (left): This delightful little café bakes its much-loved walnut cake daily.

Blauel Olive Shop (right): This shop is a pioneer in organic olive-oil production. Stop in and try some tasty samples.

The **butcher** (left): Peek inside to see a classic butcher block and a row of hooks with tools and smocks. Local shepherds produce lots of goats.

Bio Organic Shop (left): Pop in for homegrown goodies—and possibly some samples of olive oils and honeys.

Lola Frozen Yogurt (right, just off the main street): Try this fun stop for homemade ice cream, tempting cakes, and a peaceful courtyard out back.

Farther down Main Street are the **Town Hall** and a **hardware store** (supplying out-of-towners working on their fixer-upper retirement/vacation properties). But we'll hang a right down the cobbled lane, past a **real estate office** (one of a few in town for visitors dreaming of a vacation home here).

• *You're walking toward the water, and getting a little taste of...*

Kardamyli's Back Streets

As you step off the main drag, notice how civilization seems to melt away as the town's back streets quickly turn into cobbles, gravel, or red dirt.

Meandering past small shops down the road to the sea, you'll see some signs advertising **rooms** (Δωμάτια, *dhomatia*) for visitors—a great value for cheap sleeps. If you look like you need a roof over your head tonight, someone might offer you a room as you pass.

• *Continue down to the water, walk out on to the concrete pier, and look around at...*

Kardamyli's Waterfront

Not so long ago, no roads connected Kardamyli to the rest of civilization. This pier was the main way into and out of the area, providing a link to the big city of Kalamata and bustling with trade and passengers. The old smokestack (behind your right shoulder as you face the water) marks the site of a once-thriving olive-oil factory. The oil was shipped from this pier. The factory has been deserted since the 1950s when—in true Maniot fashion—a rival company from Kalamata bought it in order to close it and become the region's sole olive-oil producer. Much of the original equipment is rusty but intact, though not open to visitors. There's talk of turning it into a museum.

Between the 1950s and the 1970s, an ever-improving network of roads made this port obsolete. Today only one professional fisherman works out of Kardamyli. He brings his catch right here to the pier to sell to locals, tourists, and restaurateurs. To the left, a set of concrete steps leads around a watery curve to a rocky alcove where there may be a handful of swimmers. The small harbor across the bay has only a few boats. Even without its traditional industries, Kardamyli still thrives, and most of its traditional lifestyles remain intact...thanks in part to respectful visitors like you.

Above the harbor the Mirginos Tower completes the ring of fortifications that starts at the other end of town at Old Kardamyli. The little island offshore (Miropi) holds the barely visible ruins of an old church.

• *Our walk is finished—time to take a deep breath of sea air, relax, and soak in the slow pace of Kardamyli life. There are a couple of relaxing bars with fine sea views within a few steps.*

Sights in Kardamyli

Old Kardamyli

The fortified compound of Old Kardamyli perches just above today's modern town. On the ancient Mani Peninsula, "old" is relative—this settlement, marked by a fortified tower, was established by the first families to return to flat ground at the end of the 17th century (they had been forced into the hills in the Middle Ages by pirates). After sitting in ruins for centuries, the

complex has been partially restored and converted into a little museum about the Mani Peninsula and its traditional architecture. It's worth the short hike through an olive grove to poke around the tiny, fortified cluster and visit the museum.

The trail to Old Kardamyli begins just behind the monument to the heroes along the main street. From here it's an up-and-down 10-minute walk—just follow the cobbled path, lined with lampposts, which leads through an up-close slice of traditional village life and an olive grove. As you approach the site, make a right after the little bridge. Behind the ruined building on the right (under a eucalyptus tree near the final lamppost) is an old cistern once used to draw and carry water back home. Continue on straight and curl around the right side of Old Kardamyli to hike up into the complex. Standing inside the fortified complex, imagine the stark reality of life within these walls, where a church, olive press, iron smith, garden, and cistern were the necessities for the frightened community to survive.

Passing through the archway, on the right you'll see the **Church of St. Spyridon** (circa 1750). Though it's not open to visitors, the exterior is interesting for its bell tower and its typical-in-Greece use of fragments of older buildings in its construction (such as the 3,500-year-old Mycenaean-age sill, wall chunks plundered by the Venetians, and Byzantine marble frames that surround the door and windows). Over the window and door, notice the crowned double-headed eagle, a symbol of the Byzantine Empire and the Orthodox Christian Church.

Now head toward the tower complex itself. The **Mourtzinos Tower** was built by the powerful Troupakis family at the begin-

ning of the 18th century. It's named after the leader of the Troupakis clan, who was known for his scowling face *(mourtzinos)* during the War of Independence.

Attached to the tower, the former **Troupakis residence** now houses a multilevel museum (€3, Wed-Mon 9:00-16:00, until 20:00 in summer, closed Tue and Nov-March). Poke into all the little doors to see exhibits about the Maniots' terraces, cisterns, beekeeping, agricultural production, salt pans, and quarries. On the top floor you can learn about the different subregions of the Mani.

The cute little church just uphill from the complex, **Agios Nikolaos,** marks the beginning of a cobbled path that leads up,

up, up to the distant church on the hilltop (called Agia Sophia). High above on the bluff was the site of the acropolis of Homeric-era Kardamyli (from 1250 BC). You can do the whole strenuous loop up to the church, then walk around to the adjacent village of Petrovouni (see "Hiking," below). Or, for just a taste, hike about five minutes up the cobbled trail to find two graves burrowed into a rock (on the right, behind the green gate). These are supposedly the **graves of Castor and Pollux,** the "Gemini twins" of mythology. These brothers of Helen of Troy had different fathers. When Castor died, Pollux—who was immortal because he was fathered by Zeus—asked his dad to bond the brothers together in immortality. Zeus agreed and turned them into the Gemini constellation. These brothers, so famous for their affection for each other, remain in close proximity even in death: Notice the connecting passage at the back of the graves.

Beaches
Many visitors come to Kardamyli to enjoy the beach. Most simply head for nearby **Ritsa Beach,** a pleasant pebbly stretch that be-

gins just beyond the village church. You can swim anywhere along its length, but most beach bums prefer the far end, where the water gets deeper quicker (no showers).

Ritsa Beach is book-ended by twin restaurants with outdoor seating. Recommended **Elies,** at the far end, is everyone's favorite.

If you have a car and want to get out of town, you could day-trip to two more good sand/fine-gravel beaches that lie to the south, near the hamlet of Neo Proastio on the way to Stoupa: **Foneas Beach** (a cove flanked by picturesque big rocks) and **Delfinia Beach.** It's a short walk down from the road to access either. The resort town of **Stoupa** also has some good sandy beaches and a promenade perfect for strolling.

As elsewhere in Greece, water shoes are recommended to avoid stepping on spiny sea urchins. Locals claim that the water's warm enough for swimming year-round, except in March, when it's chilled by snowmelt runoff from the mountains.

Hiking
Hiking vies with beach fun as Kardamyli's biggest attraction. Especially in spring and fall, visitors head away from the sea to explore the network of color-coded trails that scramble up the surrounding hills. Many of these follow the ancient *kalderimi* (cobbled

paths) that once were the only way of traveling between villages. Ask your hotel for a map that explains the routes and codes; for serious hikes, buy a more detailed hiking map. As the hikes tend to be strenuous—uphill and over uneven terrain—wear good shoes and bring along water and snacks (some walks pass through villages where you can buy food and drinks, but don't count on it).

The most popular destinations sit on the hillsides just behind Kardamyli: the hilltop church of **Agia Sophia** and the village of **Petrovouni.** You can hike to either one or (with more time and stamina) do a loop trip that includes both. Consider this plan: Start by visiting Old Kardamyli, then continue past the small Agios Nikolaos church and the ancient graves of Castor and Pollux (described earlier). After about 30 minutes take the uphill stone pathway on your sharp right—the higher church of Agia Sophia is at the top of the ramp. Then, if your energy holds, follow the dirt path (to the left of the church as you face the sea) around to Petrovouni—this shortcut avoids a boring two-mile trek along the paved upper road. From there you can head back down into Kardamyli. The paths are very steep (there's about a 650-foot elevation gain from Kardamyli to Petrovouni), and the round-trip takes about 1.5 hours at a good pace with few breaks (follow the yellow-and-black trail markings). Other trips lead farther into the hills, to the remote village of **Exohori.** To avoid brutal heat in the summer, time your hike to finish by 10:00.

Sleeping in Kardamyli

Most of Kardamyli's accommodations cater to British, European, and Australian tourists who stay for a week or more. Rather than traditional hotels, you'll find mostly "apartments" with kitchenettes, along with simpler and cheaper rooms *(dhomatia).* While some places offer breakfast, most charge extra, assuming that you'll make your own in your kitchenette or get a pastry and a coffee at a bakery or café. If you want breakfast, be sure to tell your host the day before (they'll likely buy fresh bread for you in the morning).

IN THE TOWN
$$$ Hotel Anniska and **Hotel Liakoto** (Sunny Place) rent nicely appointed, resort-feeling apartments with kitchenettes. The Anniska has 22 apartments that share an inviting lounge and a delightful seaview terrace (breakfast extra, +30 2721 073 601). The Liakoto's 25 apartments cluster around a swimming-pool courtyard oasis, all with sea views that turn golden at sunset (breakfast extra and worth it, +30 2721 073 600). Both hotels are run by friendly British-Australian-Greek couple Ilia and Gerry (www.anniska-liakoto.com, info@anniska-liakoto.gr).

$$ Hotel Esperides has 19 rooms and apartments with kitchenettes, all surrounding a pleasant garden veranda just a few steps up from the main road. You'll enjoy a friendly welcome and lots of travel advice (breakfast extra, closed Nov-March,

arrange arrival time in advance because reception isn't open 24 hours, +30 2721 073 173, www.hotelesperides.gr, esperideshoteln@ gmail.com).

$$ Antonia's Apartments sit among the olive trees, just up from Ritsa Beach and a short walk from the town center (turn right after the first beach restaurant). Its two newer apartments in the tower house are stylishly furnished with thoughtful touches that put them several notches above the norm. The two older units, while more old-fashioned, are a bit bigger, with two separate bedrooms. All four apartments have seaview verandas (lending library, +30 2721 073 453, antoniasapartments@yahoo.gr, lovingly tended by knowledgeable Elias).

$ Marina Studios & Gorgones Rooms (Les Sirenes) are owned by the same family and occupy 10 rooms in the building above a busy restaurant. The rooms are simple, but all have kitchenettes and most have views or balconies overlooking Kardamyli's little harbor (good windows block out most of the dining noise, reserve via Booking.com, Gorgones: +30 693 233 4855, http://www.gorgonesrooms.gr/; Marina: +30 698 572 7177).

$ *Dhomatia:* You'll see signs advertising rooms (Δωματια) all over town. Though air-conditioning is a safe bet, rooms are generally quite simple, with kitchenettes but no breakfast. English can be limited, credit cards aren't accepted, and value can vary. If you're in a pinch, check out a few, pick the best, and don't be afraid to haggle. Try warm and welcoming **Olympia Koymanakou,** who rents five rooms on the cobbled lane just up the road from the harbor and speaks just enough English (shared kitchen, Paraleia street, +30 2721 073 623, mobile +30 693 479 2259).

JUST OUTSIDE KARDAMYLI

These enjoyable retreats sit a bit farther from Kardamyli's main street. While walkable, they're more practical if you have a car (especially the Kalamitsi).

$$$ Kalamitsi Hotel is an enclave hovering above its own bay, beach, and olive grove a two-minute drive down the road from Kardamyli (toward Areopoli, just around a big curve in the road). There are 17 rooms in the main building, plus 15 bungalows that bunny-hop across its plateau; the rooms aren't fancy, but it's a charming place (suites, breakfast extra, dinner available, +30 2721 073 131, www.kalamitsi-hotel.gr, info@kalamitsi-hotel.gr).

$$$ **Melitsina Village Hotel,** at the top of Ritsa beach, feels more resorty. This collection of stone buildings housing 23 sophisticated studios and apartments, most with kitchenettes and terraces, gives you that "get away from it all" vibe (+30 2721 073 334, www.melitsina.com, info@melitsina.com).

$$ **Vardia Hotel** is a stony retreat huddled on a hilltop just above town. All of its 18 studios and apartments have balconies overlooking town and the sea beyond, and a steep, rocky path leads from the hotel's view veranda directly to Old Kardamyli (breakfast extra, +30 2721 073 777, mobile +30 694 611 9741, www.vardia-hotel.gr, info@vardia-hotel.gr).

Eating in Kardamyli

Kardamyli prides itself on pleasing return visitors, who come here on holiday year after year. When you ask locals where to dine, they shrug and say, "Anywhere is good"...and you sense it's not just empty town boasting. As you dine, notice the dignified European visitors conversing quietly around you...and try to imitate them.

IN TOWN, NEAR THE SEA

These places all have sea views. The first one is near the top of the short main street; the next three are side-by-side overlooking the harbor. All have fine interiors if the weather is disagreeable. The first three are serious restaurants, while the last one is more of a bar that serves food.

$$ **Psaras Restaurant** (Ψαράς) overlooks Pyrrhus landing, an appropriate location given the fish-forward menu. Rustic wood tables under a covered patio and the sound of lapping waves make this a great spot for a memorable meal (daily 11:30-23:00, +30 2721 073 365).

$$$ **Harilaos Restaurant** is bright and elegant, boasts fine views over the harbor, and serves fresh fish and classic Greek dishes (daily 12:00-23:00, closed Nov-March, +30 2721 073 373).

$$$$ **Tikla Cuzina & Wine Bar,** with a stylish covered terrace and a stony-mod interior, aims to innovate on the Greek

standards—think roast lamb served with eggplant mousse (daily 13:00-24:00, from 17:00 in shoulder season, closed Nov-March, +30 2721 074 444).

$$ Aquarella Café and Cocktail Bar is youthful and hip, taking full advantage of its romantic seaside setting with sofas under trees and backgammon boards. Relax with drinks and snacks—there are even cigars on the menu. They also serve breakfast (open daily 8:00-24:00, +30 2721 075 010).

JUST OUTSIDE KARDAMYLI

$$ Kastro Taverna is a gourmet's delight and a splurge for your taste buds (but no pricier than most other restaurants in town). Sitting amid an olive grove just outside town toward Kalamata, it's a 15-minute walk or quick drive from the town center. The trek is worth it—the chef uses local products for his daily specials, including meat and produce from his farm in the hills above town. A highlight is the *keftedes* (meatballs) in a savory tomato sauce, but it's hard to go wrong with anything on the menu. Choose between the cozy fireplace interior and the broad veranda with distant sea views (Tue-Sun 19:00-23:00, closed Mon and mid-Oct-mid-March, +30 2721 073 951).

$$$ Elies (Ελιές), with what most locals consider the best lunch around, is a 15-minute walk up from the town center, on Ritsa Beach. Relax with beachgoers at pastel tables in the shade of olive trees and enjoy their excellent Greek cuisine. They serve simple, traditional Greek dishes for lunch from April through October and offer a fancier dinner menu in summer (daily 13:00-18:00, mid-June-mid-Sept until 23:00, +30 2721 073 140). Kids enjoy their playground.

$$$ Taverna Dioskouroi sits in a lovely setting on the headland overlooking Kardamyli's adorable little harbor, on the southern end of the village (daily specials, daily 13:00-22:00, on the right 200 yards south of the village, +30 2721 073 236).

OTHER OPTIONS

Breakfast: Consider these options if you're not eating breakfast at your hotel. Several places mentioned on my self-guided walk offer breakfast fare: **Lola Frozen Yogurt** (dainty setting, garden tables out back) has light bites and good coffee, **$$ Androuvista Café** serves walnut cake, a beloved local specialty, and **$$ Maistros Café,** on the main square, is an old-school cafeteria with local clientele and full array of breakfast options. Bohemian-chic **Aquarella** is also open mornings.

Picnics: There are two grocery stores at the entrance to town, and one on the main street just past the square (all open long hours daily). For a fast bite, the **souvlaki shop** on the main street is good (described earlier, on my self-guided walk).

Kardamyli Connections

Kardamyli's biggest disadvantage is its tricky-to-reach position on the far-flung Mani Peninsula. The nearest major city (with good bus connections to the rest of Greece) is Kalamata, about 24 twisty miles to the north. The bus schedule between Kalamata and Kardamyli changes frequently (generally 3-4/day Mon-Fri—first bus around 7:00, last at around 20:00; 2-3/day Sat-Sun, 1 hour; in Kardamyli, catch bus at main square). It's best to inquire about buses with your hotel, though you can also try the Kalamata bus station (+30 2721 028 581, www.ktelmessinias.gr).

You can also get to Kalamata by taxi for around €65—a handy option for catching early buses out of Kalamata off-season, when buses from Kardamyli to Kalamata might not run early enough. Ask your hotelier for help booking a taxi.

ROUTE TIPS FOR DRIVERS

The Mani Peninsula's mountains make driving slow going, but if you don't mind spending a few euros on tolls, A-7 allows you to bypass the town of Kalamata, shaving 30 minutes off your travel time. Cheapskates driving through Kalamata should follow signs reading *Port, Seafront,* or *Areopoli.* Once past the port, keep driving in the same direction, with the water on your right. The road to Kardamyli is badly signed—you might see directions in Greek for Καρδαμύλη (Kardamyli) or Μάνη (Mani)—but as long as you keep the water on your right, you'll end up on the highway.

Either way, heading south from Kalamata, you'll twist over a suddenly remote-feeling terrain of dramatic mountains and emerge overlooking a grand bay with views over Kardamyli.

After going through Kardamyli, the road continues south, passing near—or directly through—a string of scenic villages before climbing back up over mountains and around a dramatic bay to the regional capital of Areopoli.

From Areopoli you can head east to Gythio and then on to Monemvasia (about 2 hours total), or head south for a loop of the Mani on lesser roads (described next).

Mani Peninsula Drive

KARDAMYLI LOOP

The Mani Peninsula is where the rustic charm of Greece is most apparent. For many travelers, this peninsula is the rural slice of Greek coast-and-mountains that they came to this country to see. The region's dramatic history has left behind a landscape that's at once eerily stark and remarkably scenic. While mountains edged with abandoned terraces hint that farming was once more extensive, olives have been the only Mani export for the last two centuries. Empty, ghostly hill towns cling barnacle-like onto distant ridges, still fortified against centuries-old threats. Cisterns that once caught rainwater to sustain hardy communities are now mucky green puddles that would turn a goat's stomach. The farther south you go, the bleaker conditions become. And yet many Mani towns feature sumptuous old fresco-slathered churches...pockets of brightness that survive in this otherwise parched land.

This region is difficult to fully experience without a car. To really delve into this backcountry corner of Greece, follow this loop drive from Kardamyli.

PLANNING YOUR DRIVE

To hit all the places described here in one day, you'll need to get an early start and not linger too long in any one place. It takes about eight hours to drive the entire loop, pausing just long enough to stretch your legs and snap a few photos at each sight. You can also incorporate part or all of this drive on the way from Kardamyli to Monemvasia—figure on six to seven hours (less if you only hit the highlights as far as Pyrgos before heading east).

The major towns worth stopping at are Agios Nikolaos, Areopoli, and Gerolimenas. Any of these are a good place to grab lunch (whether picnic or sit-down)—most of the other settlements in this area are so small you might not be able to find anywhere to eat. For me, though, it's the tiny, remote spots that are most atmospheric; my favorites are **Kastania, Cape Tenaro,** and **Vathia.** Also worthwhile are the **Pyrgos Dirou Caves,** which you can visit at the beginning or end of the drive, as you'll pass by them on your return to Kardamyli (bear in mind what time they close). If you prefer a later start or a more relaxed day, you could skip Kastania or the cape (saving you about an hour each).

Along the way, you'll experience stunning coastal vistas equal to California's Big Sur or the French Riviera. But keep a firm grip on the wheel—the route is a string of hairpin curves, missing guardrails, and blind corners in ancient stone villages.

Sightseeing Tip: The light inside old churches can be very dim—if you have a flashlight, bring it along to illuminate the frescoes.

From Kardamyli to Kastania

Head south from Kardamyli on the main road. After a few miles you'll pass the attractive little resort town of **Stoupa.** While Kardamyli turns its back to the sea, Stoupa embraces it—with a fine sandy beach arcing right through its center. (Stoupa also works as a separate jaunt from Kardamyli.)

Just after Stoupa is the turnoff for our first stop, **Kastania** (Καστανεα). Note that Kastania is a time-consuming detour from the main road (allow 1.5 hours for the round-trip, including 30 minutes to walk around). If short on time, you might want to skip it or consider making it a separate side-trip from Kardamyli or a detour en route to Monemvasia.

• *To reach Kastania, look for the turnoff from the main road. You'll see a large blue road sign pointing left to a long list of destinations; the sign is near a prominent rocky hill and just before a tiny church on your right. Follow any signs to* Neochori, *which is en route to Kastania. Leaving the main road, head uphill, passing through what feels like the peninsula's version of modern "urban sprawl." Keep going, following the well-traveled blacktop through two other villages along the way.*

Kastania

Wedged in a gorge, the village of Kastania offers you a rare opportunity to explore a traditional, still-inhabited Mani village that's somewhat off the tourist track. It may feel sleepy today, but Kastania was once a local powerhouse. During the 19th-century Greek War of Independence, it boasted no

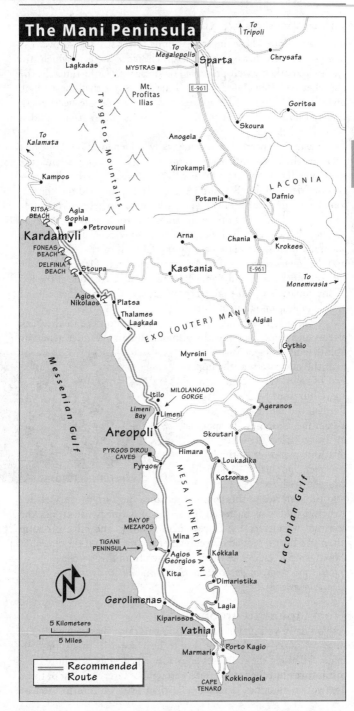

The Mani Peninsula

To Tripoli

To Megalopolis

Sparta

Lagkadas

MYSTRAS

Chrysafa

E-961

Mt. Profitas Ilias

Goritsa

To Kalamata

Skoura

Anogeia

Taygetos Mountains

Kampos

Xirokampi

LACONIA

RITSA BEACH

Agia Sophia

Petrovouni

Potamia

Dafnio

Kardamyli

FONEAS BEACH

Arna

Chania

Krokees

DELFINIA BEACH

Stoupa

Kastania

E-961

To Monemvasia

Agios Nikolaos

Platsa

Thalames

Lagkada

EXO (OUTER) MANI

Aigiai

Myrsini

Gythio

Messenian Gulf

Itilo

MILOLANGADO GORGE

Limeni Bay

Limeni

Ageranos

Areopoli

Skoutari

PYRGOS DIROU CAVES

Himara

Loukadika

Pyrgos

Kotronas

MESA (INNER) MANI

BAY OF MEZAPOS

Mina

TIGANI PENINSULA

Agios Georgios

Kokkala

Kita

Dimaristika

Laconian Gulf

Gerolimenas

Lagia

Kiparissos

Vathia

5 Kilometers

5 Miles

Marmari

Porto Kagio

CAPE TENARO

Kokkinogeia

Recommended Route

fewer than 400 "guns" (as Maniots called their menfolk), gathered under a warlord whose imposing family tower still stands over the town square. The town also had many churches, some of which still feature remarkably well-preserved old frescoes. (Unfortunately, the churches are often closed. If you come across one that doesn't look open, try the door. If it's locked and you see people nearby, ask if they know how to get inside—sometimes there's a key hidden somewhere close by.)

Kastania is nestled in a strategically hidden location: You don't even see the town until you're right on top of it. As you enter the town, you'll pass the first of many Byzantine churches on the left—this one dedicated to St. John (Agios Ioannis). Beyond the church, look for a round traffic mirror and park your car wherever you safely can nearby. To the right from the traffic mirror is what seems to be an alley. It's actually the link to the **main square.** Walk up into the square, which is watched over by the Church of the Assumption and the town's tower house (which you can climb if it's open). Poke into one of the very traditional cafés for a coffee. The one at the top of the square is a real time warp, where old-timers gather around simple tables, smoking and chatting.

Consider hiking uphill from the square to take in the back streets and some deep breaths of mountain air. Wander generally uphill, and along a rustic lane near the old cistern at the upper end of town you'll come across the **Church of St. Peter** (Agios Petros), the oldest of the town's Byzantine churches. It appears to be cobbled together using bits and pieces of antiquity. If it's open, go inside—it's richly adorned with frescoes that have  told Bible stories to this community since the 14th century. A destructive mold has hastened the aging of its precious art, but the spiritual wonder of the place remains intact. The olive-oil lamp often still burns, tended by a caretaker family. Even if the church is closed, stop to enjoy the views over town from this perch.

• *Return to your car, backtrack to the main road, and turn left (south). Continue driving...*

From Stoupa to Areopoli

As you drive you may notice rooftop **solar panels** attached to cy-lindrical tanks—an efficient way to heat water in this sunny climate. All along the route, set on roadside pedestals, are those little **miniature churches** you've seen throughout Greece. Most of these are "votive churches," erected as a thank-you gesture to God by someone who was spared in an accident. Little churches with a photograph of a person, however, are memorials to someone who lost their life on the highway.

Heading south, you'll pass another fine beach town, **Agios Nikolaos** (St. Nicholas). About a kilometer (half-mile) off the road, this is a little fishing port with wild rocks, a tiny bell tower, a scrawny lighthouse, a tough fleet of little fishing boats, inviting stay-a-while cafés, and harborfront restaurants selling fresh fish to stray travelers. The waterfront eatery **Vesuvius** has a ladder down to the sea from its terrace, so you can combine swimming, basking, and eating.

After Agios Nikolaos the road begins to curve up the mountain, passing through **Platsa** (with two interesting churches). If the church of St. John/Agios Ioannis is open, poke inside to see a ceiling fresco with Jesus surrounded by zodiac symbols—a reminder of the way early Christians incorporated pre-Christian mythology. On the far (south) end of town, the church of St. Nicholas/Agios Nikolaos sits abandoned behind an athletic field and is recognized as one of the region's oldest Byzantine churches, dating from the 10th century.

Higher up, the village of **Thalames**—its square shaded by a giant plane tree—is known for its olive-oil production (several shops on the square sell it). Then, in **Lagkada,** watch (on the left) for the remarkably well-preserved Byzantine Church of the Metamorphosis, lavishly decorated with terra-cotta designs.

As you ascend ever higher, notice how the landscape fades from green to brown. From here on out, the Mani becomes characteristically arid. You'll begin to see **terraces** etched into the mountainsides, a reminder of how hard Maniots had to work to earn a living from this inhospitable land. They'd scrape together whatever arable soil they could into these little patches to grow olive trees and wheat. Some of the larger stone walls surrounding the terraces demarcate property boundaries.

Soon you cross the "state line" that separates the Exo (Outer) Mani from the Mesa (Inner) Mani—its southern tip and most striking area.

As you reach the lip of the dramatic Milolangado Gorge, the town of **Itilo** (EE-tee-loh) comes into view. Like Kardamyli, this town was mentioned in Homer's *Iliad.* The fortifications on the southern side of the gorge belong to Kelefa Castle, built by the Ottomans in 1670 in a short-lived attempt to control the rebellious Maniots. Enjoy the views before heading down to Limeni Bay, where you'll pass the settlements of Neo (New) Itilo and **Limeni,** birthplace of the war hero Petros Mavromichalis, whom we'll meet shortly (see the sidebar for more about Petros). Fish lovers detour into Limeni for lunch at Takis Taverna—where local fishermen bring their best catch—overlooking the harbor, while adventure seekers enjoy hiking the 3.5 miles up from the bayside road into the gorge itself.

• *Continuing up the other side of the gorge, and then cresting the top, you'll shortly arrive in...*

Areopoli

Areopoli (ah-reh-OH-poh-lee)—named after Ares, the ancient god of war—is the de facto capital of the Inner Mani. Less charming but more lived-in than other Mani towns, Areopoli is the region's commercial center.

As you arrive from Itilo, turn right at the stop sign, veer left following the sign to *Diros Caves,* then turn right just past the supermarket and stone wall into a modern main square, **Plateia Athanaton** (where you should be able to find a place to park). Dominating the square is a statue of **Petros Mavromichalis** (1765-1848). This local-boy-done-good was selected to rule the region by the Ottoman overlords, who assumed they could corrupt him with money and power. But they underestimated his strong sense of Mani honor. On March 17, 1821, Mavromichalis gathered a ragtag Maniot army here in Areopoli and marched north to Kalamata, launching the War of Independence. Mavromichalis looks every inch a warrior, clutching a mighty curved sword, with a pistol tucked into his waistband.

The square hosts a lively market on Saturday mornings. At other times, everything else of interest is to be found about 500 yards west of here, around the old main square, **Plateia 17 Martiou.** If Mavromichalis jumped off his pedestal, marched toward the candy-colored cafés, and headed left, he'd reach the old center of town in five minutes: a stony fortified village settlement circling a stone church. Reaching the old town, circle the square counterclockwise (keeping the church on

your left) and find the life-size memorial plaque on the wall to your right. This is the spot where Petros mustered his men for the march to Kalamata. Just past the plaque, near the well, is a rustic bakery (Της Κυρά Μηλιάς) run by Milia, who makes bread and savory pies in a wood-fired oven. For an edible souvenir, survey the bags of cookies on the rack by the door. Continue rounding the church until you're facing the bell tower. Now step back and take it in: This is the 18th-century Church of Taxiarhes (Archangels), sporting an impressive four-story bell tower and dominating the square. The carvings above the main door show the archangels Gabriel and Michael, flanked by the saints Georgios and Dimitrios on horseback.

If you want more of a wander, keep the bell tower at your back and take the path straight in front, skirting around the ruins of the

war tower of Petros Mavromichalis. Follow this alley as it winds its way next to a church (on the left, just after the tower). At the end of the alley, jog left, then right. On this square are the Church of St. John and the Pikoulakis Tower—home to the two-room **Mani Byzantine Museum,** which has a few artifacts from the Christian history of this area (closed Tue).

• *Your next stop is the Pyrgos Dirou Caves, about six miles south of Areopoli. Follow the well-marked signs for* Diros Caves; *the turnoff is marked with a blue sign in the center of Pyrgos town. If you go past Pyrgos and reach the turnoff sign for* Γκλεζι, *you've gone too far—backtrack into Pyrgos. The cave entry is along a small bay, reached by a steep road that twists down to the water.*

(If you're skipping the caves, or saving them for the end of your drive, follow signs toward Kotronas/ Κότρωνας *just south of Areopoli—take the left turn at the fork—and pick up this tour at "Eastern Mani," later.)*

▲Pyrgos Dirou Caves (a.k.a. Diros Caves and Vlychada Cave)

These remarkable cave formations— discovered by locals in the 1870s and opened to the public in 1963—rank among Europe's best. The formations range from stout stalactites and stalag-

History of the Mani Peninsula

The Mani feels as wild as its history. The region was supposedly first developed around 200 BC by breakaway Spartans (from the famously warlike city to the north). Spartan stubbornness persisted in the Mani character for centuries—and made Maniots slow to adopt Christianity. In the 10th century, St. Nikon finally converted the Maniots, and a flurry of Byzantine church-building followed.

Most coastal Mani towns (including Kardamyli) were slowly deserted in the Middle Ages as marauding pirate ships forced people to flee into the hills. There they hid out in villages tucked in the folds of the mountains, far from the coast. (Later, in the 18th century, the construction of protective tower houses allowed Maniots to tentatively begin to return to their coastal settlements.)

Fertile land here was at an absolute premium and hotly contested. In the 17th and 18th centuries, this hostile corner of Greece was known to travelers as the "land of evil counsel" *(Kalavoulia)* because of its reputation for robbery and piracy—a more reliable way to survive than trying to eke out an honest living by farming. Maniots banded together in clans, whose leaders built the characteristic tower settlements *(kapitanias)* that are a feature of the region. Each *kapitania* controlled its own little city-state-let of land. Some larger towns were occupied by several rival *kapitanias*. Honor was prized even more than arable land, and each clan leader had a chip on his shoulder the size of a big slab of feta cheese. Vendettas and violent bickering between clans—about control of territory or sometimes simply respect—became epidemic. If Greece had a Tombstone and an OK Corral, this is where they'd be.

mites to delicate hair-like structures—many of them surprisingly colorful, thanks to reddish iron deposits.

Cost and Hours: €15; daily 9:00-17:00, Nov-April until 16:30; +30 2733 052 222.

Crowd-Beating Tips: Because this is a very popular attraction, you might be in for a wait during busy summer months (lines are worst from 12:00 to 14:00 and any time in August). Figure about an hour total to tour the caves (not counting time in line). Booking a ticket online can secure a place and help avoid a long wait: www.diros-caves.gr.

Visiting the Caves: Once you've bought your ticket and your group is called, you'll walk five minutes down to the cave entrance

When they weren't fighting each other, the Maniots banded together to fight off foreign invaders. Locals brag that the feisty Mani—still clinging to the stubborn militarism of the ancient Spartans—remained the only corner of Greece not fully under the thumb of the Ottoman Turks. During nearly four centuries of Turkish rule, the sultan struck a compromise to appoint more or less Ottoman-friendly Maniots as regional governors. After a failed Greek uprising against the Turks in the late 18th century, Greeks from all over the country flooded into the Mani to escape harsh Ottoman reprisals. As the population boomed, competition for the sparse natural resources grew even fiercer.

Perhaps not surprisingly, the hot tempers of the Maniots made the peninsula the crucible for Greek independence. On March 17, 1821, Maniot Petros Mavromichalis, the Ottoman-appointed governor *(bey)*, led a spirited rebellion against his Turkish superiors. Mavromichalis succeeded in taking Kalamata six days later, and the War of Independence was underway. What began in the remote hills of the Mani quickly engulfed the rest of Greece, and by 1829 the Ottomans were history and Greece was independent.

Looking around today at the barren landscape of the Mani Peninsula, which now barely supports 5,000 people, it's hard to believe that 200 years ago it sustained a population of almost 60,000. Over time that number was depleted by blood feuds, which raged into the early 20th century. The end of Ottoman rule in the early 19th century and the devastating Greek Civil War of the mid-20th century sparked population shifts out of the region, as Maniots sought easier lifestyles elsewhere in Greece, or set out for the promise of faraway lands, primarily America, the UK, and Australia. But these days, as the Mani emerges as a tourist destination, many Maniot emigrants are returning home—bringing back with them an array of accents from around the world.

for your appointed entry time (if the gate's open, you can also drive right down to the cave entrance after getting your ticket). The temperature in the caves is usually between 60 and 65 degrees Fahrenheit—you may want a sweater. (Be sure to pick up the English brochure, which says about as much as your Greek guide.)

After you've boarded a little boat, your guide poles you along underground canals, softly calling out (usually in Greek only) the creative names for each of the spectacular formations: "Hercules' columns," "palm forest," "golden rain," "crystal lily," and so on. Stalactites drip down directly overhead, and damp cave walls, beautifully lit, are inches away—you'll need to duck or bend from time to time as the boat glides through some of the narrower passageways. In some places the water beneath you is 100 feet deep...you're actually floating near the ceiling of a vast, flooded cavern. (Life preservers are provided.) Pinch yourself: This isn't a movie or a Disney ride, but the real deal. After your three-quarter-mile boat trip, you return to dry land and walk another quarter-mile for up-close views of more limestone formations.

Eastern Mani

To experience the Mani's most rugged and remote-feeling area, cross over the spine of the peninsula to the eastern coast. The few tourists you encounter melt away the farther south you drive, until it's just you, sheer limestone cliffs, fortified ghost towns, olive trees, and tumbling surf. Here the terrain seems even more desolate than what you've seen so far.

Yet as you explore the countryside you'll notice huge building projects, hotel developments springing up like mushrooms—including the luxury Tzokeika Traditional Settlement just north of Platsa at the beginning of this drive—and decadent private mansions. (Athenian big shots like to have a Mani escape.) The impressive stonework is generally done by Albanian workers. Mixed in are tiny 13th-century Byzantine churches clinging to the stark land like barnacles and lots of mobile "honey farms." Bee farmers chase the sage and thyme, setting up their hives where the pollen is best. The honey of the Mani is the most expensive and prized in Greece. With so much to see, drive carefully so you don't wind up the reason for another roadside shrine.

After taking the turn for **Kotronas**/Κότρωνας just south of Areopoli, head overland through stark scenery. Cresting the hills at **Himara**/Χιμαρα, you'll begin to glimpse the Mani's east coast. At **Loukadika**/Λουκαδικα, bear right (south) along the main road toward **Kokkala**/Κοκκαλα, and you'll soon find yourself traversing the top of a cliff above some of the best scenery on the Mani. Heading south you'll see more and more fortified towers climbing up the rocky hillsides. Imagine that each of these towers represents the many ruthless vendettas that were fought here.

Approaching **Dimaristika**/Διμαριστικα, notice the three tower settlements that dot the hill at three different levels. It's easy to imagine why the Ottomans never took this land—the villages could see them coming by ship from miles away and bombard them with cannonballs. And if the Ottomans managed to make landfall, they'd have to climb up, up, up to overtake the forts. It just wasn't worth the trouble.

The village of **Lagia**/Λαγια was supposedly the site of the last Mani vendetta, a scuffle in the 1930s. The town seems almost abandoned today, but most of these houses are owned by Maniots who now live in Athens and come back for the holidays. On the square (along the main road through town) is a monument honoring Panagiotis Vlahakos, a villager who died in a 1996 conflict over a small Aegean island (called Imia in Greek, or Kardak in Turkish) claimed by both Greece and Turkey. The Ottomans left this country close to two centuries ago, but Greek-Turkish relations are still raw.

• *Leaving Lagia, continue straight ahead. After about five minutes, you'll reach a fork. If you're ready to head back around to the western Mani coast, take the right turn (direction: Lagia—and skip down to the "Vathia" section of this tour). But to reach the most distant corner of mainland Greece, Cape Tenaro, bear left toward the long list of Greek names (including* Kokkinogeia/Κοκκινόγεια). *Switchback your way tightly down toward the sea, always following signs for* Kokkinogeia/Κοκκινόγεια; *if highway signs are missing, look for smaller hiking-route signs that mark the* Tenaro Archaeological Site *(not Porto Kagio). After cresting the small isthmus over to the west side of the cape, with both bays in front of you, you'll come to a poorly-marked fork just after a stone shed; bear right, then take a sharp left. You'll shortly pass near* Marmari/Μαρμαρι *(but not through it; it'll be below and to the right as you follow hikers' signs to take an uphill left fork). Then keep following signs to* Tenaro/Ταίναρο *and Sanctuary and Death Oracle, staying left. You'll come to the literal end of the road.*

Imagine the work it takes to eke out a subsistence living in this god-forsaken corner of Greece, spending your days digging up stones to build the fortified tower houses you see capping the hills.

Cape Tenaro (a.k.a. Cape Matapan): Greece's "Land's End"

Drive out to the tip of the rocky promontory known as the "Sanctuary of the Dead." As the farthest point of the known world, this was where the ancient Greeks believed that the souls of the deceased came to enter the underworld. An underwater cave here was thought to belong to Hades, god of the underworld. It was also the site of a temple and oracle devoted to Poseidon, the god  of the sea (marked today by a ruined Christian church). Visitors can still explore the scant unexcavated ruins of an ancient town that was called Tenaron (mentioned in the *Iliad*). An inviting restaurant also offers travelers a good opportunity for a break.

Just below the parking lot are the ruins of an early Christian church, likely constructed using giant blocks scavenged from the

temple upon which it sits. To visit the poorly marked ruins of Tenaron, walk down from the parking lot toward the water, then
bear right around the far side of the bay. You'll soon be able to
pick out the footprints of ancient Greek and Roman structures.

Hiding behind one of these low
walls, about a five-minute walk
around the tiny bay, is a surprisingly intact floor mosaic from a
Roman villa, just sitting out in
the open. If you've got time to
kill and are up for a longer hike,
trudge another 30 minutes out
to a lighthouse at the end of the
world. A busy shipping channel
lies just offshore; you can count the vessels heading east to Athens
or to ports to the west.

• *Retrace your tracks back to civilization. Reaching the first fork (unmarked, with the stone shed), turn left and head up the west coast of
the Mani (toward* Vathia/Βαθειά—*not the direction you came down
from). Soon you'll be treated to views of the classic Mani ghost town. The
pullout on the left, 100 yards before the town, offers the best view. Then
continue and park after you see the sign for the* Aspalathos *restaurant.
From there you can walk into the stony village. Circle it clockwise (a
former donkey mill is inside the first house on the left). Consider how a
settlement like this with no roads and only footpaths can't survive in the
modern age.*

Vathia

The most dramatic of all the Mani tower villages, Vathia is Ven-
detta-ville—it seems everyone here barricaded themselves in forts.

The more towers a town had, the
more dangerous it was—and it's
hard to imagine cramming more
towers into a single town than
they did in Vathia. Built on a
rocky spur and once famed for
its olive oil, Vathia was an extreme example of what can hap-
pen when neighbors don't get
along. The 80-some houses were
split north/south into two rival camps, which existed in a state of
near-permanent hostility. Now Vathia is mostly uninhabited.
Once-intimidating towers are now haunting ruins, held together
with boards and steel cables.

• *Driving north, you'll pass through the larger town of Kiparissos—
originally Kenipolis (New City), which was settled by those who left*

ancient Tenaron—then turn off when you see Γερολιμένας *(signs in Greek only) to reach the town center and port of...*

Gerolimenas

Gerolimenas (Γερολιμένας; yeh-roh-LEE-meh-nahs, roughly "sacred port"), nestled at the back of a deep sheltered bay, is a cute fishing town kept alive by tourism. The waterfront is lined with cafés and restaurants, and the water is good for a swim—making it an all-around enjoyable place to take a break and watch the surf.

• *Continue back out to the main road and turn left, toward* **Kita**. *This town was the setting for the Mani's final major feud in 1870, which raged for weeks until the Greek army arrived, artillery in tow, to enforce a truce.*

For one last little detour, hang a left turn at the village of Agios Georgios (toward Μέζαπος/Mezapos/Beach*), and go a bit more than a mile down to the...*

Bay of Mezapos

At the cove at Mezapos (MEH-zah-pohs), carved out of limestone by the surf, boats bob picturesquely in the protective harbor, watched over by an extremely sleepy hamlet. Mezapos was once a notorious haven for pirates. It's easy to see why if you look across the bay to see the long, naturally fortified peninsula aptly named Tigani (frying pan). This was once thought to be the site

of the Frankish castle of Maina (roughly, "clenched fist"), which some believe to be the namesake of the Mani.

• *Continuing north you'll first pass the village of Pyrgos—with the turnoff for the caves—then arrive back at Areopoli. From here retrace your route around Itilo Bay back to Kardamyli; or, if you're continuing onward, head east just beyond Areopoli to reach Monemvasia.*

MONEMVASIA

Μονεμβασία

Monemvasia (moh-nehm-vah-SEE-ah), a gigantic rock that juts improbably up from the blue-green deep just a few hundred yards offshore, is a time-warp to the medieval Peloponnese. Its little lower town hamlet hides on the seaward side of the giant rock, tethered to the mainland only by a skinny spit of land. This remarkably romantic walled town—with the remains of an even bigger upper town scattered along the peak high above—is a stony museum of Byzantine, Ottoman, and Venetian history dating back to the 13th century. Summiting Monemvasia is a key experience on any Peloponnesian visit.

Monemvasia means "single entry"—and the only way to get here is to cross the narrow causeway. At the mainland end of the causeway is the nondescript town of Gefyra (YEH-fee-rah), a smattering of hotels, restaurants, shops, and other modern amenities that offer a handy 21st-century base and springboard for exploring the Rock.

Heading to or from Monemvasia, consider a stop at Mystras, near Sparta. Although the town of Sparta has little of touristic interest, the site of Mystras has well-preserved Byzantine churches (dating from the 13th to 14th century) that evoke the grandeur of the Byzantine Empire before it fizzled out.

PLANNING YOUR TIME

It takes only a couple hours to see Monemvasia—a stroll through the lower town, a hike to the upper town, and you've done it all. Though doable as a day trip from Kardamyli or Nafplio (3 hours by car each way), I don't recommend it. Spending the night in Monemvasia (or mainland Gefyra) allows you to linger on the floodlit cobbles and makes the long trip down here more worthwhile.

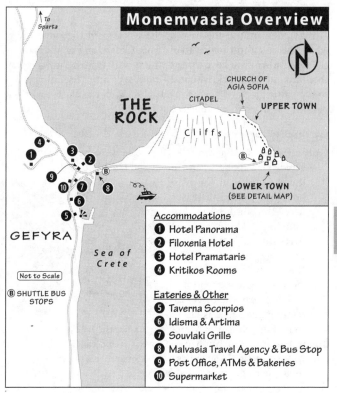

Monemvasia Overview

To Sparta

THE ROCK

CHURCH OF AGIA SOFIA

CITADEL

UPPER TOWN

Cliffs

LOWER TOWN
(SEE DETAIL MAP)

GEFYRA

Sea of Crete

Not to Scale

B SHUTTLE BUS STOPS

Accommodations
1 Hotel Panorama
2 Filoxenia Hotel
3 Hotel Pramataris
4 Kritikos Rooms

Eateries & Other
5 Taverna Scorpios
6 Idisma & Artima
7 Souvlaki Grills
8 Malvasia Travel Agency & Bus Stop
9 Post Office, ATMs & Bakeries
10 Supermarket

MONEMVASIA

Orientation to Monemvasia

Monemvasia is moored to the mainland at the village of Gefyra, where most of its services are located. The road into Gefyra from Sparta becomes the main street. Clustered where the road bends left toward the Rock you'll find the post office, a few ATMs, and a couple of bakeries; around the corner to the right, toward the water, is a supermarket. At the start of the causeway across from the shuttle bus stop, the Malvasia Travel Agency sells bus and shuttle tickets and serves as the town's bus stop.

After passing through Gefyra, the main road leads to the causeway across to the Rock (Vraxos). The hamlet of Monemvasia itself, which locals call To Kastro ("The Castle"), is out of sight around behind the Rock. To Kastro is divided into the lower town (with shops, hotels, and restaurants) and the ruins of the upper town high above. Only a dozen or so people actually live in Monemvasia, and it's fair to say every business there caters to tourists.

ARRIVAL IN MONEMVASIA

A road runs around the base of the Rock from the causeway to Monemvasia's lower town. To get from Gefyra on the mainland to the lower town, you have three options: walk (across the causeway, then around the Rock, about 20 minutes); drive (go all the way to the castle gate and then circle back to grab the closest roadside parking spot); or take a shuttle bus (see next).

HELPFUL HINTS

Gefyra-Monemvasia Shuttle Bus: Use this handy service to avoid the walk between Gefyra and old Monemvasia (2/hour, leaves Gefyra on the half-hour 8:00-24:00, off-season Mon-Thu until 14:00, Fri-Sun until 23:00, and departs the castle a few minutes later; €1.10 each way). Buy tickets at the **Malvasia Travel Agency** mentioned earlier or pay the driver directly if the office is closed (bus is signed *Kastro*, which means "castle").

Name Variation: In English the town's name can also be spelled Monemvassia, Monembasia, or Monembacia. During the Venetian period it was called Malvasia.

Addresses: Locals don't bother with street numbers, or even names—both Monemvasia and Gefyra are small enough that everyone knows where everything is. If you can't find something, just ask around.

Prepare for Sun: If climbing to the top of the Rock in the summer, go early or late, as it can be brutally hot at midday. Wear good shoes (the rocks are slippery even when dry), bring sun protection (there's very little shade up there), and carry water (there are no shops up top, but you can buy water at gift shops along the lower town's main drag).

Monemvasia Walk

There are only two things to see in Monemvasia: the walled lower town and the castle ruins of the upper town high above. This self-guided walk covers both.

Lower Town

Begin outside the 17th-century **main gate,** designed by the Ottomans who were occupying the town at the time (and who knew a thing or two about designing—and breaching—gates like this

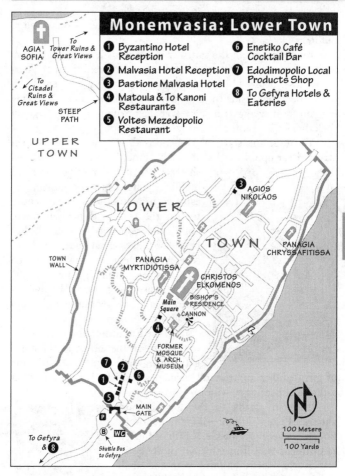

Monemvasia: Lower Town

1. Byzantino Hotel Reception
2. Malvasia Hotel Reception
3. Bastione Malvasia Hotel
4. Matoula & To Kanoni Restaurants
5. Voltes Mezedopolio Restaurant
6. Enetiko Café Cocktail Bar
7. Edodimopolio Local Products Shop
8. To Gefyra Hotels & Eateries

AGIA SOFIA

To Tower Ruins & Great Views

To Citadel Ruins & Great Views

STEEP PATH

UPPER TOWN

LOWER

TOWN

3 AGIOS NIKOLAOS

TOWN WALL

PANAGIA MYRTIDIOTISSA

PANAGIA CHRYSSAFITISSA

CHRISTOS ELKOMENOS

BISHOP'S RESIDENCE

Main Square

CANNON

4

FORMER MOSQUE & ARCH. MUSEUM

7 2
1 6
5

P

B WC

MAIN GATE

To Gefyra & 8

Shuttle Bus to Gefyra

100 Meters

100 Yards

MONEMVASIA

one). The only public WCs are downstairs to the right, in front of the gate.

Look up to the cliff and down to the sea, appreciating how successfully the crenellated wall protected this mighty little nugget of Byzantine power. There are only four entrances: two on this side, one on the opposite side, and one from the sea. Combine that with the ridiculously easy-to-defend little causeway (once equipped with a drawbridge) and the perfect bird's-eye view from the top of the Rock (ideal for spotting would-be in-

vaders from miles and miles away), and Monemvasia was a tough nut to crack.

Enter the gate. (The stairway inside leads left up to a terrace with a monument noting the fact that the 20th-century poet Yiannis Ritsos—beloved by Greeks but unknown abroad—spent much of his life here.) Inside the gate, notice that the road jogs, preventing you from even getting a peek at the town until you emerge on the other side—another defensive measure. And then...

You're at the start of Monemvasia's narrow, cobbled **main street.** Bear uphill (left) at the fork, through a gauntlet of tourist

shops, hotel offices (renting rooms in buildings scattered all over town), and cafés with inviting terraces stretching toward the sea. Elsewhere in town, doors and windows are small, but here—on what's always been the main commercial drag—the wide, arched windows come with big built-in counters for displaying wares. Enjoy this atmospheric lane, scouting cafés and restaurants for later.

At the **Edodimopolio local products shop** (on the left, near the entry gate), energetic Fotini stocks all sorts of gifty edibles and natural cosmetics, and she is happy to offer samples of her honey-wine and olive oil.

The lane leads to the town's **main square,** Plateia Dsami—literally "Mosque Square," a very rare-in-Greece tip of the hat to Ottoman rule. The namesake mosque still stands (the blocky building with the small red dome, on the right). In the middle of the square, notice two symbols of the town: a cannon (Monemvasia was nothing if not well defended) and a well. Monemvasia is honeycombed with cisterns for catching rainwater...the one thing that a city clinging to a rock floating in the sea needs to survive.

Walk to the edge of this square and survey the rooftops of the **lower town.** Notice a unique feature of Monemvasia houses: sharply angled rooflines, which allowed built-in tile gutters to carefully channel rainwater through pipes plumbed into the walls and ultimately into cellar cisterns. Houses are built of stone quarried from right here on the Rock—a very efficient way to get building materials. Whereas the stone walls of many houses are exposed today, historically most

walls were covered with plaster, which once gave the skyline Santorini-like soft edges.

Now turn around and face the Rock and the **upper town.** Notice the stoutly walled, zigzag-ging path that climbs the cliff face. Halfway up and a little to the right, between the square's bell tower and church, is a small cave (with a white entrance) burrowed into the cliff—a humble chapel reached by a precarious footpath. You can see from here that most of the upper town is in ruins...but it is fun to explore (described later).

Before leaving the square, do a little sightseeing. The old mosque—which has also served as a church, prison, and coffee shop—today hosts a modest **archaeological museum** (€3, Wed-Mon 8:30-15:30, closed Tue, +30 2732 061 403). The one-room display, though sparse, is well-presented and described clearly in English: pottery fragments, the stone chancel screen (iconostasis) from a long-gone Byzantine church, and an explanation of how many ancient architectural elements were scavenged to build early Christian churches.

Across from the mosque/museum is the whitewashed, 11th-century **Church of Christos Elkomenos** ("Christ in Pain"). In its

day, this was a very impor-tant Byzantine church. The Venetians substantially expanded the church: No-tice the elaborately carved lintel above the entrance, a sure sign of Venetian influence. The peacock relief above the lintel was added after independence (1820s), as was the bell tower. The church may be closed for recon-struction when you visit, but if it's open (generally daily 9:00-14:00 & 16:00-20:00), step into the tidy white interior. The twin plat-forms in the rear are said to be for the thrones used when the em-peror and empress visited from Constantinople. Hiding behind the marble iconostasis (peek behind the curtain) is a small reminder of the church's humble Byzantine origins: old amphitheater-like stone risers where bishops once stood.

The artistic highlight of the entire region is in a small chapel to the right: a precious icon of the Crucifixion dating from around

Monemvasia's History

Mighty Monemvasia, a Gibraltar-like rock with a Crusader-style stone town at its base, has ruins scattered all across its Masada-like plateau summit.

Monemvasia's upper town may have been founded in the sixth century AD by refugees fleeing Slavic raids into the Peloponnese. Gradually the settlement spread down the hill and,

thanks to its uniquely well-defended position, became a powerful town. It was a center of both trade and military importance, with the merchants living below and the nobility living above. In the declining days of the Byzantine Empire (1262-1460), when nearby Mystras was its ecclesiastical base, Monemvasia was its main city and one of the great commercial centers of the Byzantine world, with a thriving population in the tens of thousands. It was known for its Malvasia wine, a lightly fortified red that was prized at the royal courts of Europe. Over the next several centuries, highly strategic Monemvasia changed hands again and again—mostly back and forth between the Venetians and the Ottomans. While most of the buildings that survive today date from the second period of Venetian rule (1690-1715), foundations and architectural elements from each chapter survive.

By the 18th century, Monemvasia slipped into decline... until it was rediscovered by tourists in the 1970s. Today, Monemvasia is a leading destination both for international visitors and for wealthy Athenians who have converted its old houses into weekend retreats.

1300, the peak of the Byzantine Renaissance. As this is the world in which El Greco trained, you could consider it "proto-El Greco." The emotions portrayed were groundbreaking for the age (English description outside the door). This icon was stolen in the 1970s, making headlines across the country, and is displayed now only with high security (no photos are allowed). If you're so moved, drop a coin in the box, light a candle, and say a prayer.

Although it's a little town today, Monemvasia was once important enough to be a bishopric. Back outside, to the right as you face the church, notice the entrance to the bishop's former residence—with the Venetian coat of arms (the winged lion of St. Mark) above the door. You'll also see that the church is attached by an archway to a small chapel.

Descend through the archway to the right of the church. The steps lead down through steeply cobbled streets to the seawall. It's a maze, but to get there, make a hard right after the first set of steps, then head down farther until you make a right at the *Portello* sign. Take the next left, then continue straight. A gate (tiny and therefore easy to defend) at the center of the wall leads out to a rocky platform with ladders into the sea for swimmers (there's a handy shower here). Retracing your steps, the first left will take you up some rough stone stairs to the eastern ramparts directly above the gate. Facing the sea, turn left and follow the wall until you emerge in a large, open square with the whitewashed Church of Panagia Chryssafitissa and good views of upper Monemvasia.

As you explore the lower town's twisty lanes, keep in mind that the architecture of Monemvasia has been influenced by a variety of styles over the centuries: Byzantine, Venetian, and Ottoman. Wandering the streets, you may notice pointed archways or large lintels (stones over windows), which are distinctively Venetian; or occasional tulip-shaped windows (curling on top with a little peak in the middle), which are unmistakably Turkish. Observe the many arched passageways spanning narrow lanes—the only way a crowded, walled town could grow. Quite a few houses are still in ruins, but with Monemvasia's tourism on the rise, many are now  being excavated and rebuilt. Because the town is protected, restoration requires navigating a lot of red tape and painstaking attention to historical accuracy.

You'll see lots of little churches. In Byzantine times, ecclesiastical and political power overlapped, and building a church gave a wealthy family more prestige and power. Also, a trading town like this would have been home to communities from different lands—each with its own style of worship and particular church.

Each significant site around town is numbered and explained by posted information...but there's no need to get bogged down by those details. Just have fun with the perfect medieval streetscapes awaiting discovery around each turn.

When you're ready to climb the Rock, make your way to the top of town and huff up the steep path to the...

Upper Town

The ruins of the upper town (free and open 24 hours daily) are spread across a broad, rolling plateau at the summit of the Rock.

Unlike the well-preserved lower town, very little of the upper town has survived intact. The last weary resident left the plateau nearly a century ago, and it is now a wasteland of ruined old buildings, engulfed by shrubs and wildflowers that seem to sprout from the rocks. As you explore up here, watch your step—sudden cliffs, slippery rocks (dangerous even when dry, especially treacherous when wet), and open cisterns are genuine hazards.

Nearing the top of the trail, curl through yet another defensive gateway. The door here, with its metal casing, is likely 18th-century Ottoman—and is probably the best artifact surviving in the upper town. As you emerge onto the top, observe the collection of buildings to your right at the gate (with fine views onto the lower town from the tiny square) and the Church of Agia Sofia above you to the left. The best way to enjoy the top of the Rock is to let your

inner child take over for a king- or queen-of-the-castle scramble across the ramparts and ruins.

Follow the trail up to the 12th-century Byzantine **Church of Agia Sofia.** Thanks to recent erosion, the church hangs precariously (and scenically) close to the edge of a sheer cliff. Like so many buildings here, the church has elements from various eras of history: a Byzantine core (it retains its original octagonal design), Ottoman features (you can still see the prayer niche, or mihrab), and a triple-arched loggia grafted onto the front in the 16th century by the Vene-

tians. The interior was white-washed when it was converted into a mosque under Turkish rule, but fragments of original frescoes survive.

From here you can climb higher up the hill for good **views** back down onto the church. If you want to lengthen your hike, you can climb all the way to the **citadel,** the fortification at the peak of the Rock (visible from here). Or, for an easier walk, head downhill to the crenellated watchtower area out toward the sea; this **promontory** has the best views back up to the church.

As you explore, remember that this was regarded as the mightiest fortress in Byzantine Greece. Not surprisingly, it was never captured in battle—only by a protracted starve-'em-out siege. Monemvasia's Achilles' heel was its dependence on the mainland for food. Though some basic supplies were cultivated atop the Rock, they weren't enough to sustain the entire town for very long.

Back near the entrance gateway, consider heading right, along the wall (as you face the lower town and water), for good views back down onto the lower town. If you continue farther along this path, you'll reach an old Turkish house, and then the granddaddy of all the town's cisterns: a **cavernous vaulted hall.**

Our tour of the Rock is finished. When you're done enjoying the views and the evocative ruins, head back down the way you came up.

Evenings in Monemvasia

Monemvasia's **lower town** is touristy yet peaceful and romantic after dark, with several bars and cafés open late and plenty of rooftop seating. Everything of interest is along the main street or on the town square, though the back streets are worth a wander just for atmosphere. My choice for a drink is the **Enetiko Café Cocktail Bar** (about 100 yards in from the gate, with great cocktails, a relaxed vibe, and a view terrace). Evenings along the harborfront in mainland **Gefyra** can be delightful, too, with plenty of places for a drink or meal, and the best sunset views of the Rock.

At night the long walk between the mainland and the Rock—dodging cars in the dim light—could be nerve-racking for some. Consider taking advantage of the shuttle bus that goes on the half-hour until midnight in high season (see "Helpful Hints," earlier).

Sleeping in Monemvasia

Monemvasia accommodation is a choice between charm (sleeping on the Rock) and convenience (sleeping in Gefyra)—but you can't have both. For me, the magic of a night on the Rock is worth the hassle. Prices here are high in July and August, especially on weekends, when this is a popular retreat for Athenians. Off-season, you can usually get a good deal.

ON THE ROCK

Staying in Monemvasia's old lower town, romantic and appealing to many, is a lot of work because you can't park nearby. Various hotels rent rooms scattered through old buildings. All have decor that mixes new and old, with old-fashioned Monemvasia flourishes (such as low platform beds, tight bathrooms, head-banging archways, and stone shower enclosures without curtains). Keep in mind that Monemvasia is a honeycomb of cobblestone alleys and stairs. Luggage with wheels won't work here. If you stay on the Rock, be prepared to carry your luggage to your hotel (drivers may want to cram essentials into a day pack).

The first two "hotels" are actually a reception desk near the entry gate that manages mostly elegantly remodeled rooms scattered throughout the lower town, with a communal building for breakfast. Review their websites and compare what they offer. For locations see the "Monemvasia Lower Town" map, earlier.

$$$ Byzantino Hotel rents 20 tasteful, old-fashioned rooms in the lower town, some with sea views and balconies (breakfast at their café, +30 2732 061 351, www.hotelbyzantino.com, info@hotelbyzantino.com). Avoid the pricey rooms in their Lazareto Hotel, outside the lower town, just across the causeway from the mainland.

$$$ Malvasia Hotel is a collection of 25 rustic but atmospheric rooms around town in three different buildings (+30 2732 061 160, www.malvasiahotel-traditional.gr, malvasia@otenet.gr).

$$ Bastione Malvasia Hotel, with 22 rooms, is a hidden oasis away from the crowds at the far end of the Rock. The attached outdoor café patio is a gem and can make up for rooms that don't have sea views or balconies (+30 2732 063 008, www.bastionemalvasia.gr, info@bastionemalvasia.gr).

IN GEFYRA

Sleeping in the mainland town of Gefyra lacks the romance of a night in old Monemvasia, but it's less expensive and easier. The following listings are each a solid value if rooms on the Rock are booked up, or for those who'd rather trade atmosphere for the convenience of parking a few steps from their room. For locations see the "Monemvasia Overview" map, earlier.

$$ Hotel Panorama is well-run by friendly Angelos and Rena Panos. At the top of Gefyra, a 10-minute hike up from the main street, it's quiet and comes with great views. Its 27 motel-like rooms all have balconies; some have sea views (family rooms, no elevator, +30 2732 061 198, www.panoramahotel-monemvasia.gr, info@panoramahotel-monemvasia.gr).

$$ Filoxenia Hotel is a family-run place across from the beach. The 20 rooms are functional but fine, and all come with balconies (breakfast extra, elevator, +30 2732 061 716, www.filoxenia-monemvasia.gr, info@filoxenia-monemvasia.gr).

$$ Hotel Pramataris offers 20 modest but comfortable rooms. All rooms have balconies; most have views of the Rock (+30 2732 061 833, www.pramatarishotel.gr, hotelpr@gmail.com).

¢ Kritikos Rooms are an excellent value. Hard-working Eleni offers nine rooms, some with kitchenettes. Most have a balcony or terrace, and all are spotless (no breakfast, +30 6978 881 057, kritikos.rooms@gmail.com).

Eating in Monemvasia

ON THE ROCK

The first two eateries are along the main pedestrian artery of Monemvasia's lower town, just before the main square. For locations see the "Monemvasia Lower Town map," earlier.

$$$ Matoula (Ματούλα), with its delightful vine-shaded terrace looking out to sea, is the most appealing restaurant on the Rock. Amid all the pretense of this town, it serves good traditional Greek dishes at fine prices. Consider the daily specials and *barbounia* (red mullet) or ask owner Venetia about the daily specials (seafood splurges, daily 12:00-late, +30 2732 061 660).

$$$ To Kanoni ("The Cannon"), next door to Matoula, is another good choice, with a cozy interior and a scenic upper veranda (pricier seafood dishes, daily 8:00-23:00, +30 2732 061 387, say hi to Petros). I like the tables on the cool rooftop terrace, with a view down on the old square.

$$ Voltes Mezedopolio, a welcoming little place just inside the gate, is run by two hardworking brothers and makes a good stop to enjoy *meze* plates family-style. The restaurant has no view, but the atmosphere is friendly and the prices are very good (daily 18:00-23:00, +30 2732 061 919).

IN GEFYRA

A collection of interchangeable eateries cluster like barnacles at the Gefyra end of the causeway. In good weather, it's pointless to eat anywhere here without a view of the Rock. I like to walk along the water (on either side of the causeway) and survey the options. For locations see the "Monemvasia Overview" map, earlier.

At **$$ Taverna Scorpios,** Vasillis and Julie share the duties of cooking and taking good care of diners at rustic white tables under a blue canopy. It has a castaway ambience and my favorite views of the Rock (daily 12:00-24:00, +30 2732 062 090).

$$ Idisma & Artima (ΗΔΥΣΜΑ & ΑΡΤΥΜΑ), with its big people-watching windows and stylish interior, brings a bit of panache to scruffy Gefyra. It specializes in seafood, with a few meat dishes and some *meze* plates rounding out the menu (Mon-Fri 17:00-24:00, Sat-Sun from 12:00, +30 694 939 4088).

Fast Food and Picnics: For a quick snack, side-by-side **$ souvlaki grills** in the center a block from the causeway are equally good for souvlaki and gyros (eat in with the locals or take away). There are a few bakeries on Gefyra's main drag, and the supermarket around the corner will help you round out your moveable feast for the top of the Rock. While you can buy basic drinks and snacks in Monemvasia's lower town, there's no grocery store there—do your shopping in Gefyra.

Monemvasia Connections

By Bus: Monemvasia is not well-connected by bus and has no bus station. Buses stop across the street from the Malvasia Travel Agency, just before the causeway; you can buy tickets on the bus or at the travel agency (recommended a day in advance in busy times, +30 2732 061 752).

Four buses leave for **Sparta** each day (likely at 6:00, 7:15, 14:15, and 17:00; 2 hours); these continue on to **Tripoli** (4 hours total) and then **Athens** (6 hours total). You'll need to change in Sparta to reach just about anywhere else, such as **Areopoli** on the Mani Peninsula (3 hours from Sparta). You may be able to reach **Nafplio** from Tripoli (1.5 hours, confirm locally).

By Shared Taxi: Hotels can arrange a shared taxi to **Athens** (€50/person, 4 hours, departs early each morning).

ROUTE TIPS FOR DRIVERS

Monemvasia's a bit out of the way, but the trek is worth it. Allow 2.5 hours from **Kardamyli** (if you're doing the Mani loop en route, factor 6-7 hours, including stops; if heading direct, consider a pit stop in Gythio, a workaday port town with fine harborfront restaurants, about 1.5 hours from Monemvasia) or roughly 3 hours from **Nafplio** (on the fast road via the A-71, Sparta, and Tripoli). If you pass through Sparta, you can easily fit in a visit to the nearby Byzantine city and churches of Mystras (see next section).

You can speed on the highway for most of the route between Nafplio and Monemvasia, but you'd be missing one of the most stunning scenic drives in Greece: The coastal road between Nafplio and cute little Leonidio is very pretty, and the twisty cliffside uphill from (or downhill to) Leonidio is jaw-dropping. The mountain town of Kosmas is good for a quick break. Between Monemvasia and Kosmas, look for signs to Skala and Vrontamas. The route requires a little planning (as roads aren't well-marked) and isn't for the squeamish. Even with a GPS on board, you may want to ask your hotelier for route tips.

Sparta and Mystras

Located roughly between Kardamyli, Monemvasia, and Nafplio, the town of Sparta is near the site of Mystras, which is worth a stop. Its impressive Byzantine churches are fine examples of the empire's last golden age.

SPARTA

Sparta (Σπάρτη)—where mothers famously told their sons to "come home with your shield...or on it"—is a classic (and, I hope, thought-provoking) example of how little a militaristic society leaves as a legacy for the future.

The ancient Sparta that dominated Greek affairs in the sixth and fifth centuries BC isn't one visitors can experience: The various excavation sites around town go down no farther than the level of Roman Sparta, which was built on the foundations of the classical city from the first century BC.

One reason why so little remains is that the town was abandoned in the 13th century, and its buildings were dismantled for reuse in the construction of nearby Mystras. Sparta was reestablished in 1834 on the initiative of King Otto and his Bavarian court, whose classical education had given them a strong appreciation of Sparta's place in history. Otto ordered his planners to create a city of wide boulevards and parks; thanks to this grid system, Sparta is easier to navigate than many Greek cities.

Though there's nothing much to see here, if you're curious, aim for the **statue of Leonidas** in the center of town (up Palaeologou Avenue and past the main square). This is the ancient Spartan hero king, famous for his taunt before the Persians slaughtered him and his last 300 troops in 480 BC: "Come and get it." (Those words are on the statue's base.) In the median a block before the statue, a **monument** honors 27 centuries of hometown athletes—medalists in Olympic Games from 720 BC to AD 1996 (mostly for running and wrestling).

The **acropolis of ancient Sparta** is signposted from the statue of Leonidas. It's a pleasant 10-minute walk, but the ruins that lie scattered among the olive trees are actually Roman-era or later. The main feature of the excavations is an impressive Roman theater; however, much of its stone seating was removed and used in the defensive wall built around the city's acropolis in the fourth century AD.

MYSTRAS

Mystras (Μυστράς), four miles west of Sparta, is the most important Byzantine site in Greece. It was here, in the foothills of the Taygetos Mountains, that the Byzantine Empire enjoyed a final dazzling period of creative energy (1262-1460) before it was swallowed up by the Ottomans.

The main attractions in Mystras are its churches—regarded as some of the finest surviving examples of late Byzantine archi-

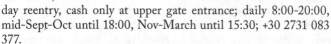

tecture in Greece. The extravagantly decorated frescoes were painted by the empire's greatest artists (although their names sadly went unrecorded). Because of ongoing restoration work, some of the churches may be closed when you visit.

Cost and Hours: €12, €6 off-season, ticket valid for same-day reentry, cash only at upper gate entrance; daily 8:00-20:00, mid-Sept-Oct until 18:00, Nov-March until 15:30; +30 2731 083 377.

Services: There's a good restaurant a block below the entrance and a cluster of options lining the town square below the site. If you have a car, consider driving to the next village, Pikoulianika, which has a handful of rustic tavernas, including Restaurant Chromata (open for dinner), offering good views over Mystras and Sparta (5 minutes from the upper gate—follow signs). The only WC in the site is before entering.

Prepare for Sun: If visiting Mystras in the summer, go early morning or late afternoon, as the heat can be fierce at midday.

There is almost no shade: Wear sunblock, a hat, and good walking shoes, and carry your own water.

With Limited Time: Lower Mystras has more to offer; if you're short on time or energy, concentrate your sightseeing there.

Background

The last rulers of the Byzantine Empire were the Palaiologos family—known as the "despots"—but they were not tyrants; the name comes from a subdivision of the Byzantine church called a "despotate." Under the Palaiologos family, Mystras became the Byzantine Empire's cultural and intellectual capital. It was home to many great artists and to the philosopher Plethon, who was responsible for the revival of Plato's teachings. Plethon and other scholars based here had a major impact on the Italian Renaissance, especially after he visited Florence in 1438.

After the fall of Constantinople to the Ottomans in 1453, the Byzantine emperors retreated here, and Mystras became the last outpost of their empire. But Mystras' golden age came to an end when the city surrendered to the Turks in 1460.

While Mystras is many centuries old, it was a thriving center until more modern times: Mystras had about 15,000 people living within its walls even during Muslim Ottoman rule (1460-1828). During that period, the sultan appointed the Orthodox patriarch, who was allowed to carry on if he didn't cause trouble. You'll see only one mosque in the entire site (built for the sultan's bureaucracy).

Then, with Greek independence in the early 1800s, the Ottomans were expelled. King Otto consolidated power in part by dissolving the Orthodox monasteries and nationalizing the Greek Orthodox Church. He shut down Mystras and turned the great city into a quarry, providing stone for the building of modern Sparta. (He dreamed of making Sparta and Athens twin cities for his new Greece.)

Visiting the Site

The gangly site stretches halfway up the mountain, with entrances at the bottom and top. Figure 2-3 hours to see the whole thing, including the castle at the tippy-top.

I'll assume you'll park at the main (lower) gate and visit the site by zigzagging uphill, and then retrace your steps back down to leave. To avoid backtracking (and an uphill walk) drivers can divide the visit into two segments: Park and start at the lower entrance, then drive about a mile up the road to the top for the rest of the site (showing your ticket to reenter). Tour groups start up top at the upper gate entrance and see Mystras as a long downhill walk—convenient if you can find a ride to the top entrance.

Here are the main stops from the bottom to the top.

Metropolis (Church of Agios Demetrios): The cathedral was built in 1270 and dedicated to St. Demetrios. Stepping into the courtyard, you see columns recycled from ancient Sparta, the bishop's residence, and a fountain built with a mishmash of ancient plunder. Inside the cathedral are more ancient columns. The double-headed eagle relief set into the floor in the center commemorates the coronation of the last Byzantine emperor, which took place here in 1449. (Since ancient times, the double-headed eagle has been the symbol of anyone considering himself the successor of the Roman emperor—from the Byzantines to Habsburgs to Holy Roman Emperors.)

Museum: From the courtyard, steps lead to a small museum (featuring old holy books, marbles, and artifacts from local graves).

Before leaving the courtyard, enjoy the uphill view of the rest of Mystras. The lower zone was for the common people and merchants (and this cathedral). The upper zone was for the nobility and ruling elite. The intact building directly above is the Palace of the Despots (described later). Imagine the despot surveying his realm from that perch.

Churches of Theodoros and Hodegetria: Beyond the Metropolis, a path slopes gently uphill to the right. This takes you to the churches of St. Theodoros and Hodegetria; the latter was part of the former Brontochion Monastery, nestled below a grove of tall cypress trees. It's worth the detour just to admire the frescoes and the magnificent, multiple red-tiled domes of the Hodegetria.

Convent and Church of Pantanassa: Opposite the Metropolis, a steep path leads up toward the imposing Church of Pantanassa. The only living part of Mystras, it's home to a small group of sweet, elderly, black-veiled nuns who live in a row of modest rooms (on the left as you enter the church's walled compound). They tend the flower gardens and produce linen embroidered with Byzantine motifs, sold in the small shop at the end of the row. (A sister told me they actually have my guides and me on their prayer list in thanks for the thoughtful visitors who come here with this book, or on our tours, and buy their handmade embroidery work. Please buy their delightful little souvenirs...I can use the prayers.) The church here is home to Mystras' best collection of frescoes and more columns and capitals plundered from ancient Sparta.

Monemvasia Gate: From the convent, continue uphill, following signs to the palace through the well-fortified gate. The gate provided the only access between the lower town and the upper town.

Palace of the Despots: The original palace is the closest wing of the building on the right, which was built by the Crusaders. Although the palace has been closed to the public for many years, it may have opened again by the time you visit. Check out the pointed Gothic arches of the top-

MONEMVASIA

floor windows—a favorite motif found at other Crusader castles around the Peloponnese. In the final decades of their rule, the Palaiologos despots built the second wing. Its massive central hall, which covers the entire second floor, served as their throne room. From here, drivers can choose to retrace their steps back to the exit and drive to the upper gate—saving more energy than time—or continue on foot.

Agios Nikolaos Church, Church of Agia Sofia, Top Entry, and Crusader Castle: The top part of the site is a long climb (not worth the sweat for many if it's hot). The Agios Nikolaos Church (which comes first) is most interesting and worth hiking up to see. It was built in the early 1600s during Ottoman rule. Near the top entry is the Church of Agia Sofia. High above, capping the mountain, stands the Crusader Castle, built in 1249, which offers a commanding view into a 400-yard-deep gorge and out across the Peloponnese.

BEYOND
ATHENS

DELPHI

Δελφοί

Perched high on the southern slopes of Mt. Parnassos, and overlooking the gleaming waters of the Gulf of Corinth, Delphi (Greeks pronounce it "thell-FEE" or "dell-FEE," not "DELL-fye") is without doubt the most spectacular of Greece's ancient sites.

Back then, Delphi was famous throughout the world as the home of a prophetess known as the oracle (a.k.a. the Pythia). As the mouthpiece of Apollo on earth, she told fortunes for pilgrims who came from far and wide seeking her advice on everything from affairs of state to wars to matrimonial problems. Delphi's fame grew, and its religious festivals blossomed into the Pythian Games, an athletic contest that was second only to the Olympics.

Today Delphi offers visitors several worthwhile sights. The archaeological site contains the ruins of the Sanctuary of Apollo. Next door is the great Archaeological Museum, where statues and treasures found on the site help bring the ruins to life. And a short walk from the site are still more ruins—including the Kastalian Spring and the photogenic Sanctuary of Athena, taking you back to Delphi's prehistoric origins.

PLANNING YOUR TIME

It's possible to visit Delphi as a long day trip from Athens, but it's more relaxed as an overnight stop, allowing you to enjoy the pleasant modern town and craggy mountainside setting (suitably awesome for the mysterious oracle). Though the town is crammed with tourists, it still feels laid-back, offering sweeping vistas of the valley below and the Gulf of Corinth in the distance. (It's hard to

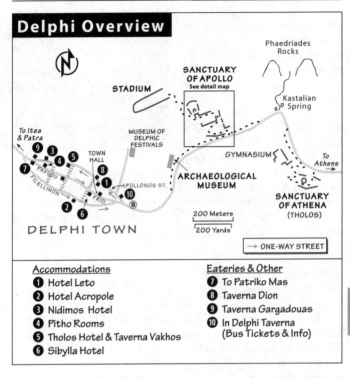

Delphi Overview

Phaedriades Rocks

STADIUM

SANCTUARY OF APOLLO
See detail map

Kastalian Spring

MUSEUM OF DELPHIC FESTIVALS

TOWN HALL

To Itea & Patra

GYMNASIUM

To Athens

ARCHAEOLOGICAL MUSEUM

APOLLONOS ST.

SANCTUARY OF ATHENA
(THOLOS)

200 Meters
200 Yards

DELPHI TOWN

→ ONE-WAY STREET

Accommodations
1 Hotel Leto
2 Hotel Acropole
3 Nidimos Hotel
4 Pitho Rooms
5 Tholos Hotel & Taverna Vakhos
6 Sibylla Hotel

Eateries & Other
7 To Patriko Mas
8 Taverna Dion
9 Taverna Gargadouas
10 In Delphi Taverna
(Bus Tickets & Info)

DELPHI

find a hotel or restaurant that doesn't boast grand views.) Especially after a stay in bustling Athens, Delphi is an appealing place to let your pulse slow.

Seeing Delphi's sights will take you two to three hours. If you've got a car, a good plan is to arrive by early afternoon, then spend the rest of the day at the archaeological sites and museum. In hot high summer, you may even be able to push the site visits into the early evening—check opening hours once you arrive. Alternatively, arrive in Delphi late in the day, enjoy dinner and a sunset, then see the sights the next morning before you head onward.

Orientation to Delphi

Visitors flock from all over Greece to walk the Sacred Way at Delphi. Many don't bother to spend the night. But the town, a half-mile west of the archaeological site and museum, is a charming place in its own right. Delphi, sometimes spelled Delfi or Delfoi in English (pop. 2,300), was custom-built to accommodate the hordes of tourists. The main street, Vasileos Pavlou-Friderikis, is a tight string of hotels, cafés, restaurants, and souvenir shops. Two other streets run roughly parallel to this main drag (Apollonos is one

block uphill/north, and Filellinon is one block downhill/
south), connected periodically
by steep stairways. The three
streets converge at the eastern
end of town.

TOURIST INFORMATION

Delphi has no TI. The Town
Hall office on the main drag
often posts current hours for the museum and archaeological site
(at Pavlou-Friderikis 12, on the sanctuary end of town). Its entryway has a model of the Sanctuary of Apollo in ancient times. Before you head out to the sanctuary, stop here to give it a good look;
compare it to the map later in this chapter to preview what you'll
see at the site.

ARRIVAL IN DELPHI

Delphi is three hours north of Athens and is reachable by bus or
by car.

By Bus: Buses to Delphi depart Athens 4-5 times a day from
Terminal B (check local schedules—you can get one at the Athens
TI or go to www.ktel-fokidas.gr; online tickets available). Most
buses have air-conditioning but no WC and make a café rest stop
en route. The drive takes you past Thiva (ancient Thebes) and has
nice views of Mt. Parnassos as you approach.

Buses drop you off at the sanctuary (east) end of town. It's
smart to buy your return ticket as soon as you arrive, because buses
can fill up. Buy tickets from the In Delphi taverna (signed Εν
Δελφοισ): From the stop, walk toward town past a storefront or
two, staying on the right (uphill) side of the road. The restaurant
doubles as the town's ersatz bus station; waiters sell bus tickets and
can tell you today's schedule. For more on buses back to Athens, see
"Delphi Connections" at the end of this chapter.

Many Athens-based companies offer convenient one-day
package tours to Delphi, which include transportation, a guided
tour, and lunch. Ask at your Athens hotel for details.

By Car: For tips on getting to Delphi by car, see "Route Tips
for Drivers" at the end of this chapter. Note that Delphi's town
streets are one-way. When arriving from the east, you'll go right at
the fork onto the uppermost of three streets, Apollonos. Parking is
limited at the site/museum; it's better to leave your car in town and
walk (10 minutes). Park anywhere where the street doesn't have a
double-yellow line.

Delphi: From Legend to History

Delphi's origins are lost in the mists of time and obscured by many different, sometimes conflicting, legends.

The ancients believed that Delphi was the center of the world. Its position was determined by Zeus himself, who released two eagles from the opposite ends of the world and noted where they met.

It was here that a prophetess (the sibyl) worshipped Gaia, the mother of the gods. A serpent (python) guarded the ravine of the Kastalian Spring. Apollo, the god of the sun and music, arrived in the guise of a dolphin (*delfini,* hence Delphi) and killed the snake. The sibyl's role was later taken on by an oracle priestess, the Pythia, and she and the place now served Apollo.

Historically speaking, the site was probably the home of a prophetess as early as Mycenaean times (1400 BC). The worship of Apollo grew, and the place gained fame for the oracle and for its religious festivals. Every four years, athletes and spectators gathered here to worship Apollo with music and athletic competitions: the Pythian Games, which soon rivaled the Olympics. The Sanctuary of Apollo reached the height of its prestige between the sixth and fourth centuries BC, by which time Delphi so dominated Greek life that no leader would make a major decision without first sending emissaries here to consult the oracle. The sanctuary was deemed too important to be under the control of any one city-state, so its autonomy was guaranteed by a federation of Greek cities.

Even when Greece was conquered by the Macedonians (Alexander the Great) and Romans, the sanctuary was preserved and the conquerors continued to consult the oracle. For a thousand years, Apollo spoke to mortals through his prophetess, until AD 394, when Christians shut down the pagan site.

DELPHI

HELPFUL HINTS

Unpredictable Hours: Don't count on the opening hours given here: They're likely to fluctuate. Check locally as you plan your day.

Services: The main drag, Pavlou-Friderikis, has just about everything you might need, including ATMs and several cafés and shops.

Local Guide: A great guide, **Penny Kolomvotsou** can resurrect the ruins at Delphi and tailor a tour to your particular interests (reasonable prices, great with families, mobile +30 694 464 4427, kpagona@hotmail.com). Penny can also arrange activities in Delphi such as hiking and pottery classes.

Weather: Delphi is in the mountains and can be considerably cooler and rainier than Athens. Check the forecast and dress accordingly, especially off-season.

Sights in Delphi

Delphi's most important sights are its archaeological site (with the Sanctuary of Apollo) and the adjacent Archaeological Museum. A short walk farther on are the other archaeological sites associated with the sanctuary (Kastalian Spring, the gymnasium, and the Sanctuary of Athena). The skippable Museum of Delphic Festivals is in Delphi town.

▲▲▲THE SANCTUARY OF APOLLO AND ARCHAEOLOGICAL MUSEUM

Ancient Delphi was not a city, but a sanctuary—a place of worship centered on the Temple of Apollo, where the oracle prophesied. Surrounding the temple is what remains of grand monuments built by grateful pilgrims. And the Pythian Games produced what are perhaps the best-preserved theater and stadium in Greece.

Planning Your Time: Allow 1.5-2 hours for the archaeological site (hiking to the stadium alone is nearly a half-hour round-trip) and another 45-60 minutes for the museum. You can do the archaeological site and the museum in either order, but it's worth stopping first at the museum to check the day's opening hours, posted on the wall just up the steps (before the ramp). Crowds and weather might help you decide. If it's hot or raining, do the museum first to hedge your bets for better conditions for the site. With all things being equal, I recommend doing the site first:

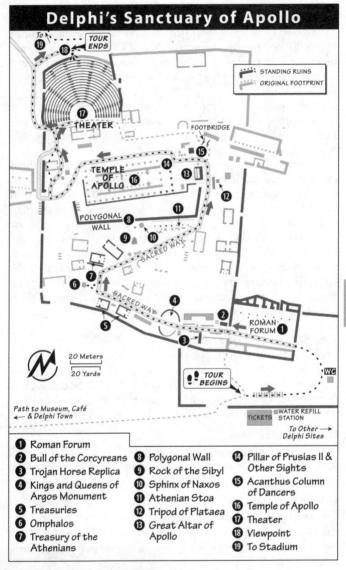

Delphi's Sanctuary of Apollo

STANDING RUINS
ORIGINAL FOOTPRINT

19 To...
TOUR ENDS
18

17 THEATER

FOOTBRIDGE

15

14

TEMPLE OF APOLLO
16 **13**

12

POLYGONAL WALL
8 **11**

9 **10**

SACRED WAY

7

6

SACRED WAY

4

5

2

ROMAN FORUM
1

3

20 Meters
20 Yards

TOUR BEGINS

WC

Path to Museum, Café
← & Delphi Town

TICKETS   WATER REFILL STATION

To Other →
Delphi Sites

1 Roman Forum
2 Bull of the Corcyreans
3 Trojan Horse Replica
4 Kings and Queens of Argos Monument
5 Treasuries
6 Omphalos
7 Treasury of the Athenians
8 Polygonal Wall
9 Rock of the Sibyl
10 Sphinx of Naxos
11 Athenian Stoa
12 Tripod of Plataea
13 Great Altar of Apollo
14 Pillar of Prusias II & Other Sights
15 Acanthus Column of Dancers
16 Temple of Apollo
17 Theater
18 Viewpoint
19 To Stadium

DELPHI

You'll have more energy for the climb (there's a 700-foot elevation gain from the entrance to the stadium), and later, when you tour the museum, you can more easily imagine the original context of the items on display.

To visit the other sights to the east of the Sanctuary of Apollo, allow another 30-45 minutes by foot (though you can view two of them, distantly, from in front of the site).

Cost: It's €12 to enter both the site and the museum.

Hours: In summer, both the site and the museum are open daily 8:00-18:00 or later (generally April-Oct). In winter, both are open daily at least 9:00-15:00 (generally Nov-March). Upon arrival in Delphi, confirm opening times either with your hotel or by stopping by the museum.

Information: +30 2265 082 313, http://odysseus.culture.gr.

Closures: Parts of the site—especially the path to the stadium, above the theater—can be closed after heavy rains (to keep visitors safe from possible rockslides).

Getting There: The archaeological site and museum are about a half-mile east of the modern town of Delphi. Parking is limited, so it's best to leave your car in town and walk (10 minutes). You'll reach the museum first; to reach the site, continue along the path past the museum.

Services: A WC and a simple café are outside the museum. At the site itself, you'll find only a water-refill station to the right of the ticket booth (you can bring a water bottle but no food inside the site). The sanctuary's WC is just above the entrance, up the first set of stairs, after you've scanned your ticket (inhaling the fumes there is not guaranteed to give you any prophetic visions).

The Sanctuary of Apollo

Looking up at the sheer rock face, you see the ruins clinging to a steep slope. From here you ascend a switchback trail that winds up, up, up: through the ruins to the Temple of Apollo, the theater, and the stadium, 700 feet up from the road. Every pilgrim who visited the oracle had to make this same steep climb.

◎ Self-Guided Tour

• *Start up the path, going to the right up a set of stairs (WCs at the top). After you double back on the switchback path, you enter a rectangular area with 10 gray columns, marking the...*

❶ Roman Forum

This small public space stood outside the sanctuary's main gate. The columns supported an arcade of shops (check out the illustration on the information plaque). Here pilgrims could pick up handy last-minute offerings—small statues of Apollo were popular—before proceeding to their date with the oracle. At festival times, crowds of pilgrims (all of them men) gathered here for parades up to the temple, theater, and stadium.

Gaze up at the hillside and picture the ruins as they were 2,000 years ago: gleaming white buildings with red roofs, golden statues atop columns, and the natural backdrop of these sheer gray-red rocks towering up 750 feet. It must have been an awe-inspiring sight for humble pilgrims, who'd traveled here to discover what fate the fickle gods had in store for them.

The men began their ascent to the oracle by walking through the original entrance gate, between 10-foot walls, entering the sanctuary on the street known as the Sacred Way.

• *A huge wall once enclosed the whole sanctuary, forming a rough rectangle, with the Temple of Apollo in the center. As you climb the five steps out of the forum, you're passing through a gate in the walls and beginning your walk along the...*

Sacred Way

The road is lined with ruins of once-glorious statues and monuments financed by satisfied pilgrims grateful for the oracle's advice. Immediately to the right is a pedestal of red-gray blocks, 17 feet long. This once held a huge bronze statue, the ❷ **Bull of the Corcyreans** (c. 580 BC), a gift from the inhabitants of Corfu to thank the oracle for directing them to a great catch of tuna fish.

A dozen or so steps farther along (left side) was an even bigger statue, a colossal bronze replica of the ❸ **Trojan Horse.**

Just beyond that (right side) is a semicircle 40 feet across, which was once lined with 10 statues of the legendary ❹ **Kings and Queens of Argos,** including Perseus, Danae, and Hercules.

Next comes a row of so-called ❺ **Treasuries** (left side), small buildings that housed precious gifts to the gods. These buildings and their contents were paid for by city-states and kings to thank the oracle and the gods for giving them success (especially in war). From the outside they looked like mini temples, with columns, pediments, statues, and friezes. Inside they held gold, jewels, bronze dinnerware, ivory statues, necklaces, and so on. The friezes and relief sculptures that once adorned the Sikyonian and Siphnian Treasuries are now in the museum.

• *At the corner where the path turns to go uphill is a cone-shaped stone called an...*

❻ Omphalos

The ancients believed that Delphi was the center of the world and marked that spot with a strange cone-shaped monument called an

DELPHI

omphalos (navel). The omphalos was also a symbolic tombstone for the python that Apollo slew.

Several omphalos stones were erected at different places around the sanctuary. The original was kept inside the Temple of Apollo. A copy graced the temple's entrance (it's now in the museum). Another copy stood here along the Sacred Way, where this modern replica is today.

As the center of the world, Delphi was also the starting point for history. From here the oracle could predict the course of human destiny.

• *Rounding the bend up the stairs, on the left you'll face the...*

❼ Treasury of the Athenians

The Athenians built this temple to commemorate their victory over the Persians (ancient Iranians) at the Battle of Marathon in

490 BC. The tiny inscriptions on the blocks honor Athenian citizens with praise and laurel-leaf wreaths, the symbol of victory at Delphi's Pythian Games. When the ruins were rebuilt (1904-1906), the restorers determined which block went where by matching up pieces of the inscriptions.

The structure's ceremonial entrance (east end) has two Doric columns of expensive marble from Paros. They support six metopes (reconstructed; the originals are in the museum) that feature the Greeks battling the legendary Amazon women—symbolizing the Greek victory over the Persians at Marathon.

• *Follow the path as it continues uphill. By now you have a great view to the left of the...*

❽ Polygonal Wall and Other Ancient Features

The retaining wall (sixth century BC) supports the terrace with the Temple of Apollo. It runs across the hillside for some 250 feet at heights of up to 12 feet. It has survived in almost perfect condition because of the way that the stones were fitted together (without mortar). This created a "living" wall, able to absorb the many earthquakes for which the region is renowned (earthquakes caused the other buildings here to crumble).

Near the wall, just above the Treasury of the Athenians, the 10-foot ❾ **Rock of the Sibyl** hearkens back to the murky prehistoric origins of this place as a sacred site. According to legend, the

oracle's predecessor—called the sibyl—sat atop this rock to deliver her prophecies, back when the area was sacred to Gaia, the mother of the gods.

Just behind that rock, near the stubby white column (walk up the path to get a better view), is a pile of rocks with a black slab pedestal. This was once a 35-foot-tall pillar holding the statue of the ❿ **Sphinx of Naxos** (c. 570-560 BC, now in the museum). Inhabitants of the isle of Naxos used their best marble for this gift to the oracle, guaranteeing them access to her advice even during busy times.

A few more steps up, the three white fluted Ionic columns along the wall belonged to the ⓫ **Athenian Stoa,** a 100-foot-long open-air porch. Here the Athenians displayed captured shields, ships' prows, and booty from their naval victory over Persia at the decisive Battle of Salamis (480 BC). It was the oracle of Delphi who gave Athens the key to victory. As the Persian army swarmed

over Greece, the oracle prophesied that the city of Athens would be saved by a "wooden wall." The puzzled Athenians eventually interpreted the oracle's riddle as meaning not a city wall, but a fleet of wooden ships. They abandoned Athens to the Persian invaders, then routed them at sea. Once the enemy was driven out, Greece's cities ceremonially relit their sacred flames from the hearth of Delphi's temple.

• *Continue up the Sacred Way and follow it as it turns left, up the hill. As you ascend, along the right-hand side you'll pass a square gray-block pedestal that once supported a big column.*

⓬ Tripod of Plataea

This monument was built to thank the oracle for victory in the Battle of Plataea (479 BC, fought near Thebes), which finally drove the Persians out of Greece. The monument's 26-foot bronze column of three intertwined snakes was carried off by the Romans to their chariot-racing track in Constantinople (today's Istanbul). A replica stands here now, based on what's left of the original column in Istanbul.

• *At the top of the path, turn left and face the six Doric columns and ramp that mark the entrance to the Temple of Apollo. In the courtyard in front of the temple are several noteworthy ruins.*

The Temple Courtyard

Take in the temple and imagine the scene 2,000 years ago as pilgrims gathered here at the culmination of their long journey. They'd come seeking guidance from the gods at a crucial juncture in their lives. Here in the courtyard they prepared themselves before entering the temple to face the awe-inspiring oracle.

Opposite the temple entrance, pilgrims and temple priests offered sacrifices at the (partially restored) gray stone ⑬ **Great Altar of Apollo.** Worshippers would enter the rectangular enclosure, originally made of black marble with white trim. Inside they'd sacrifice an animal to Apollo—goats were especially popular. One hundred bulls (a hecatomb) were sacrificed to open every Pythian Games.

To the right of the temple (as you face it) once stood several monuments that dazzled visitors. Imagine a 50-foot **Statue of Apollo Sitalkas** towering over the courtyard, where only a humble rectangular base remains today. Next to it (on the left) is the still-impressive 20-foot-tall rectangular ⑭ **Pillar of Prusias II.** Atop this was a statue of a second-century king on horseback who traveled here from Turkey to consult the oracle. To the right of the pillar are **three round column stubs** that once held ceremonial tripods. Behind them rose the tall ⑮ **Acanthus Column of Dancers,** three young women supporting a tripod (now in the museum).

• *But these sights paled in comparison to the...*

⑯ Temple of Apollo

This structure—which in its day must have towered over the rest of the site—was the centerpiece of the whole sanctuary. It was dedi-

cated to the god who ruled the hillside, and it housed the oracle who spoke in his name. This was the third and largest temple built on this site (completed 330 BC), replacing earlier versions destroyed by earthquake and fire. It was largely funded by Philip of Macedon and dedicated in the time of Alexander the Great.

The temple was gleaming white, ringed with columns, with a triangular pediment over the entrance and a roof studded with

The Oracle

The oracle was a priestess of Apollo who acted as a seer by "channeling" the god's spirit. Always female, she was usually an older empty-nester with a good reputation, but we don't know any of Delphi's oracles by name. These women were not the focus—rather, they were vessels for the words of Apollo as interpreted by priests.

Early on, there was one oracle, who prophesied only on auspicious days. At Delphi's peak, two or three oracles worked shifts every day. The oracle purified herself in the Kastalian Spring, dressed in white, and carried a laurel branch—a symbol of Apollo. Why the oracle sat on a tripod—a ritual cauldron on three legs—no one knows for sure.

The oracle presumably prophesied in a kind of trance, letting the spirit of Apollo possess her body and speaking as if she were the god himself. Many think she was high on vapors that rose from the natural chasm in the inner sanctum floor. Science has found no evidence of the supposed chasm, though ravines and springs nearby do emit psychotropic gases. The trance might also have been caused by the oracle eating or inhaling burned laurel leaves. Regardless of the source, the oracle's ultimate message was tightly controlled by the priests.

The oracle addressed all kinds of questions. Travelers came to Delphi before journeys. Rulers came to plan wars. Explorers wanted advice for getting newfound colonies off to a good start. Philosophers asked the oracle to weigh in on ethical dilemmas. Priests sought approval of new rituals and cults. Ordinary people came because their marriages were rocky or simply to have their fortunes told.

Apollo was considered a god of peace, order, and personal virtue. As the priestess of Apollo, the oracle could address moral questions and religious affairs. And because Delphi was considered the center of the world, the words of the oracle were the source of fate and the fortunes of men.

Many famous people made the pilgrimage. A young Socrates was so inspired by the phrase "Know Thyself" (inscribed on the Temple of Apollo) that he pursued the path of self-knowledge. The oracle was visited by foreign kings such as Midas (of the golden touch) and the ancient billionaire Croesus (of "rich-as" fame). The historian Plutarch served here as a priest, interpreting the oracle's utterances. Roman Emperor Nero visited, participated in the Pythian Games, and was warned about his impending assassination. Alexander the Great asked the oracle whether he'd be successful in conquering the world. When the oracle hesitated, Alexander grabbed her by the hair and wouldn't let go. The helpless oracle cried, "You're unstoppable." Alexander said, "I have my answer."

DELPHI

statues. Above the entrance, the pediment statues showed Apollo arriving in Delphi in a four-horse chariot (now in the museum). The six huge Doric columns that stand near the entrance today (reassembled in 1904) were complemented by 15 columns along each side. (Sections from a toppled column lie on the hillside below the temple's left side, near the Polygonal Wall, giving an idea of the temple's scale; to see this, backtrack down the hill.) Though the temple appeared all white, it was actually constructed with a darker local limestone. The columns were coated with a stucco of powdered marble to achieve the white color. Only the pediments and other decorations were made from costly white marble shipped in from the isle of Paros.

Imagine yourself an ancient pilgrim finally preparing to meet the oracle after the long trek to the center of the world. You've just bathed with the priests at the Kastalian Spring in the ravine east of the sanctuary. You've paraded ceremonially to the temple, up the same Sacred Way tourists walk today. At the Great Altar, you just offered a sacrifice, likely of goat (a loaf of bread was the minimum cover charge). At last, you're about to enter the temple with the priests, climbing the ramp and passing through the columns to learn your fate. Inscribed at the entrance are popular proverbs, including "Know Thyself," "Nothing in Excess," and "Stuff Happens."

Inside, the temple is cloudy with the incense of burning laurel leaves. You see the large golden statue of Apollo and the original omphalos stone, a reminder that you've arrived at the center of the world. After offering a second sacrifice on the hearth of the eternal flame, it's time to meet the oracle.

The priests lead you into the *adyton*—the farthest back, holiest chamber of the *cella*. There, amid the incense, is the oracle—an older woman, dressed in white, seated in the bowl of a tripod, perhaps with an unsettling gleam in her eye. The tripod may be balanced over a hole in the floor of the temple, exposing a natural ravine where a spring bubbles up. While you wait, the priests present your question to the oracle. She answers—perhaps crying out, perhaps muttering gibberish and foaming at the mouth. The priests step in to interpret the oracle's meaning, rendering it in a vague, haiku-like poem.

Then you're ushered out of the temple, either enlightened or confused by the riddle. For many pilgrims—like Socrates, who spent much of his life pondering the oracle's words—a visit to Delphi was only the beginning of their life's journey.

• *Uphill, to the right of the Temple of Apollo, stands Delphi's stone theater. Climb up—I'll meet you there.*

⑰ Theater

One of Greece's best-preserved theaters (fourth century BC) was built to host song contests honoring Apollo, the god of music. With

35 rows of white stone quarried from Mt. Parnassos, it could seat 5,000. The action took place on the semicircular area (60 feet across, surrounded by a drainage ditch) known as the orchestra. As at most ancient theaters, it would have been closed off along the street by a large structure that created a backdrop for the stage and served as the theater's grand entryway. The famous *Bronze Charioteer* statue (now in the museum) likely stood outside the theater's entrance, in the middle of the road, greeting playgoers. The theater was designed so that most spectators could look over the backdrop, taking in stunning views of the valley below even as they watched the onstage action.

The theater's original and main purpose was to host not plays, but song contests—a kind of "Panhellenic Idol" competition that was part of the Pythian Games. Every four years, singer-songwriters from all over the Greek-speaking world gathered here to perform hymns in honor of Apollo, the god of music. They sang accompanied by flute or by lyre—a strummed autoharp, which was Apollo's chosen instrument.

Over time, the song competition expanded into athletic contests (held at the stadium), as well as other events in dance and drama. The opening and closing ceremonies of the Pythian Games were held here. One of the games' central features was a play that reenacted the dramatic moment when Apollo slew the python and founded Delphi...not unlike the bombastic pageantry that opens and closes today's Olympic Games.

• *A steep path continues uphill to a stunning...*

⑱ View from Above the Theater

With craggy cliffs at your back, the sanctuary beneath you, and a panoramic view of the valley in the distance, it's easy to see why the ancients found this place sacred.

We're 1,800 feet above sea level on the slopes of Mt. Parnassos (8,062

Delphi's Decline and Rediscovery

After reaching a peak during the Classical Age, the oracle's importance slowly declined. In Hellenistic times, traditional religions like Apollo-worship were eclipsed by secular philosophy and foreign gods. By the third century BC, the oracle was handling more lonely-hearts advice than affairs of state. The Romans alternated between preserving Delphi (as Hadrian did) and looting its treasuries and statues. Nero famously stole 500 statues for his home in Rome (AD 66), and Constantine used Delphi's monument to decorate his new capital. As Rome crumbled, looters did their damage. Finally, in AD 394, the Christian Emperor Theodosius I closed down the sanctuary, together with all the other great pagan worship centers.

The site was covered by landslides and by the village of Kastri until 1892, when the villagers were relocated to the modern village of Delphi, about a half-mile to the west. Excavation began, the site was opened to tourists, and its remaining treasures were eventually put on display in the museum.

DELPHI

feet). The area's jagged rocks and sheer cliffs are made of gray limestone and laced with red-orange bauxite, which is mined nearby. The cliffs have striations of sedimentary rocks that have been folded upward at all angles by seismic activity. The region is crisscrossed with faults (one runs right under the temple), pocked with sinkholes, and carved with ravines.

Two large sections of rock that jut out from the cliff (to the left) are known as the Phaedriades Rocks, or "Shining Ones," because of how they reflect sunlight. At the foot of one of the rocks lies the sanctuary. Between the two rocks (east of the sanctuary) is the gaping ravine of the Kastalian Spring.

Looking down on the entire sanctuary, you can make out its shape—a rough rectangle (640 feet by 442 feet—about twice as big as a football field) enclosed by a wall, stretching from the top of the theater down to the Roman Forum. Trace the temple's floor plan: You'd enter where the columns are, pass through the lobby *(pronaos)*, walk into the main hall *(cella)*, and continue into the back portion *(adyton)*, where the oracle sat (they say) above a natural chasm.

In the distance, looking south, is the valley of the Pleistos

River, green with olive trees. Beyond that (though not visible from this spot) are the turquoise waters of the Gulf of Corinth.

• *If you're winded, you can make your way back down now. But you've come so far already—why not keep going? Hike another 10 minutes up the steep, winding path to the...*

⑲ Stadium

Every four years, athletes and spectators from across Greece gathered here to watch the same kinds of sports as at the ancient Olympics. The Pythian Games (founded at least by 582 BC) were second only to the (older, bigger) Olympic Games in prestige. They were one of four Panhellenic Games on the athletics calendar (Olympia, Corinth, Nemea, and Delphi).

The exceptionally well-preserved stadium was built in the fifth century BC. (Though you aren't allowed to walk through its center, you can still get a good look down into it from the far end.) It was remodeled in the second century AD by the wealthy Herodes Atticus, who also built a theater in Athens and a fountain in Olympia (the Nymphaeum). There was stone seating for nearly 7,000, which was cushier than Olympia's grassy-bank stadium. Among the seats on the north side, you can still make out the midfield row of judges' seats. The track—580 feet long by 84 feet wide—is slightly shorter than the one at Olympia. The main entrance was at the east end; the thick pillars once supported a three-arched entry. The starting lines (one at either end, depending on the length of the race) are still here, and you might be able to make out the postholes for the wooden starting blocks.

The Pythian Games lasted about a week and were held in the middle of a three-month truce among warring Greeks that allowed people to train and travel safely. Winners were awarded a wreath of laurel leaves (as opposed to the olive leaves at the Olympic Games) because Apollo always wore a laurel-leaf wreath. For more on the types of events held here during the games, see the Olympia chapter.

• *Wind your way back down to the exit. The museum is located 200 yards west of the Sanctuary of Apollo. Before heading in that direction, you might consider venturing a little farther out of town to reach the Kastalian Spring, gymnasium, and/or Sanctuary of Athena (all described later, under "Other Delphi Sights").*

Archaeological Museum

Delphi's compact but impressive museum houses a collection of ancient sculpture matched only by the National Archaeological and Acropolis museums in Athens.

❖ Self-Guided Tour

Follow the one-way route, looking for the following highlights. Everything is well-described in English.

• *Show your ticket and head right into the...*

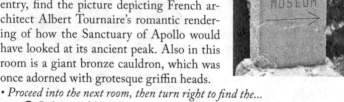

❶ **First Room:** This room holds the earliest traces of civilization at Delphi. Near the entry, find the picture depicting French architect Albert Tournaire's romantic rendering of how the Sanctuary of Apollo would have looked at its ancient peak. Also in this room is a giant bronze cauldron, which was once adorned with grotesque griffin heads.

• *Proceed into the next room, then turn right to find the...*

❷ **Sphinx of Naxos** (c. 570-560 BC): This marble beast—a winged lion with a female face and an Archaic smile—was once brightly painted, standing atop a 40-foot Ionic column in the sanctuary.

The myth of the sphinx is Egyptian in origin, but she made a splash in Greek lore when she posed a famous riddle to Oedipus at the gates of Thebes: "What walks on four legs in the morning, two at noon, and three at night?" Oedipus solved it: It's a man—who crawls in infancy, walks in adulthood, and uses a cane in old age.

• *Across the room, find the...*

❸ **Frieze from the Siphnian Treasury:** This shows how elaborate the now-ruined treasuries in the sanctuary must have been. The east frieze (left wall) shows Greeks and Trojans duking it out. The gods to the left of the battle are rooting for the Trojans, with the Greek gods to the right. The north frieze (back wall) features scenes from the epic battle between the Greek gods and the older race of giants.

• *Backtrack into the previous room, then turn right. You're face-to-face with...*

❹ **Twin Kouros Statues** (c. 600-580 BC): These statues have the typical features of the Archaic period: placid smiles, stable poses facing the front, braided dreadlocks, and geometrical anato-

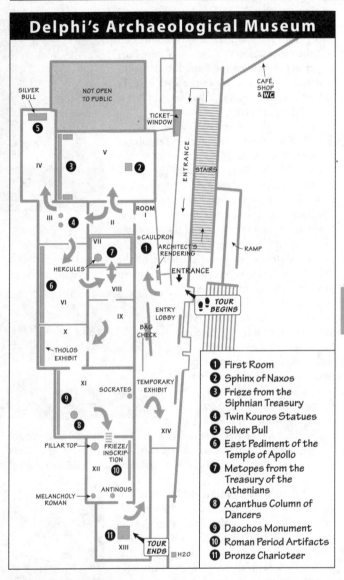

Delphi's Archaeological Museum

SILVER BULL

NOT OPEN TO PUBLIC

TICKET WINDOW

CAFÉ, SHOP & WC

ENTRANCE

STAIRS

5

IV **3** V **2**

III **4** II

ROOM I

CAULDRON **1** ARCHITECT'S RENDERING

RAMP

VII **7**

HERCULES **6**

VIII

ENTRANCE

TOUR BEGINS

VI IX

ENTRY LOBBY

X BAG CHECK

THOLOS EXHIBIT

XI SOCRATES

TEMPORARY EXHIBIT

9

8 XIV

PILLAR TOP FRIEZE/ INSCRIPTION

XII **10**

MELANCHOLY ROMAN ANTINOUS

11 XIII

TOUR ENDS

H2O

DELPHI

1 First Room
2 Sphinx of Naxos
3 Frieze from the Siphnian Treasury
4 Twin Kouros Statues
5 Silver Bull
6 East Pediment of the Temple of Apollo
7 Metopes from the Treasury of the Athenians
8 Acanthus Column of Dancers
9 Daochos Monument
10 Roman Period Artifacts
11 Bronze Charioteer

my. These sturdy seven-foot-tall athletes are the legendary twins of Argos, who yoked themselves to their mother's chariot and pulled her five miles so she wouldn't be late for the female Games (the Heraia). Upon arrival, the exhausted twins fell into a sleep so deep they never woke up.

• *In the small room behind the twins (to the right) is what's left of a...*

5 **Silver Bull:** These silver-and-gold plates are the surviving fragments that once covered a life-size bull statue from the sixth century BC. This bull and the other objects in the room were buried in ancient times (perhaps for safekeeping) and were discovered in the 20th century in a pit along the Sacred Way, near the Treasury of the Athenians.

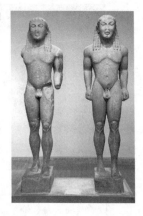

• *In the room after the twins, find the...*

❻ **East Pediment of the Temple of Apollo:** This is what greeted visitors as they stood before the temple entrance. Though it's mostly fragments today, in the center you can make out some of the four horses that pulled Apollo in his chariot. To the right, a lion jumps on an animal's back and takes it down.

• *Continue left into the next room, then turn left to find the...*

❼ **Metopes from the Treasury of the Athenians** (510-480 BC): These carvings from the sanctuary's small surviving treasury include (among other themes) six of the Twelve Labors of Hercules. In the most intact carving (directly to the left as you enter), **Hercules** is the one with the curly hair and beard, inscrutable Archaic smile, and lion skin tied preppy-style around his neck.

• *Proceed through the next three rooms (the third of which has an exhibit with some pieces from the round* tholos *monument at the Sanctuary of Athena). You'll wind up in a room with two monuments from the era of Alexander the Great, which once stood side by side in the sanctuary.*

❽ **Acanthus Column of Dancers:** This giant leafy sculpture sat atop a 40-foot column to the right of the Temple of Apollo (on the same level as the theater). The three dancing girls originally carried a bronze tripod on their shoulders. Scholars now believe that this tripod supported the **omphalos**—the gigantic pinecone-shaped stone, which represented the "navel" of the world. The omphalos, now resting next to the column, is not the original stone marking the center of the earth, but a Roman-era copy. Nearby is the bottom of the column, which appears to be sprouting out of the ground.

• *Then, as now, next to the column stand statues from the...*

❾ Daochos Monument (c. 336-332 BC): Out of the nine original statues (count the footprints), today seven survive (OK, six—one is just a sandal). They have the relaxed poses and realistic detail of Hellenism. Daochos (center, wearing a heavy cloak) was a high-ranking army commander under Alexander the Great. His family flanks him, including two of the three sons who were famous athletes, all of whom won laurel crowns at the same Pythian Games. Nude Agelaos (also in the center, armless, with sinuous *contrapposto*) won running contests in Delphi. Aghias (to the right, with two partial arms and genitals) swept all four Panhellenic Games in *pankration*, a brutal sport that combined wrestling and boxing with few holds barred.

• *Across the room and facing these gents, notice the sculpture of the bearded, balding man. Some claim that this is Socrates, who was inspired by the mystery of this place. Up the stairs, the next room features artifacts from the...*

❿ Roman Period (191 BC-AD 394): The Romans made Delphi their own in 191 BC and left their mark. On the left you'll see the **frieze** that decorated the proscenium of the theater and (high on the wall) an inscription from the proud Emperor Domitian, crowing that he had repaired the Temple of Apollo.

Across the room is the rectangular **top of a pillar,** erected by the arrogant King Perseus in anticipation of a military victory. Instead, the king was soundly defeated by Aemilius Paulus, who topped the pedestal with his own equestrian victory statue (pictured nearby) and adorned it with this frieze of scenes depicting Perseus' defeat. This sculpture is particularly exciting for historians, as it's the oldest relief work (in Western history, at least) narrating an actual event. For centuries after this, battles would be recounted in similar 3-D carvings (think of Trajan's Column in Rome or Nelson's Column in London).

Also worth noting here is the **circular altar** decorated with a graceful relief sculpture showing young women gussying up the sanctuary for a festival performance.

At the end of the room are two noteworthy sculptures. The small, lightly bearded head dubbed the **"Melancholy Roman"** (likely Titus Quinctius Flamininus, who proclaimed autonomy for the Greek state in 197 BC) demonstrates a masterful sense of emotion. Standing next to him is a full-size nude statue (minus its fore-

arms) of Emperor Hadrian's young lover, **Antinous.** The handsome curly-haired youth from Asia Minor (today's Turkey) drowned in the Nile in 130 BC. A heartbroken Hadrian declared Antinous a god and erected statues of him everywhere, making him one of the most recognizable people from the ancient world. Notice the small holes around his head, which were used to affix a bronze laurel wreath. Next to the sculpture, find the photo of excited archaeologists unearthing this strikingly intact specimen.

• *The grand finale is the museum's star exhibit, the...*

⓫ **Bronze Charioteer:** This young charioteer has just finished his victory lap, having won the Pythian Games of 474 BC. Standing ramrod straight, he holds the reins lightly in his right hand, while his (missing) left hand was raised, modestly acknowledging the crowd.

This surviving statue was part of an original 3-D ensemble that greeted playgoers at the entrance to the theater. His (missing) chariot was (probably) pulled by four (mostly missing) horses, tended by a (missing) stable boy. Nearby, a case displays scant surviving chunks of the cart, the horse, and the stable boy's arm.

The statue is life-size (5'11") and life-like. His fluted robe has straps around the waist and shoulders to keep it from ballooning out in the wind. He has a rounded face, full lips, awestruck eyes (of inset stones and enamel), and curly hair tied with the victor's headband.

The most striking thing is that—despite the charioteer having just won an intense and dangerous contest—his face and attitude are calm and humble. The statue was cast when Greece was emerging from the horrors of the Persian invasion. The victorious charioteer expresses the sense of wonderment felt as Greece finally left the battle behind, gazed into the future, and rode triumphantly into the golden age.

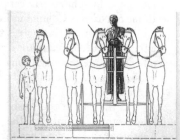

OTHER DELPHI SIGHTS

The related Sanctuary sites, especially the Temple of Athena Pronea, are worth a visit. There are also a number of hikes from Delphi—ask your hotelier for ideas.

Sanctuary of Apollo Sites

These three sites, located along the main road beyond (to the east of) the site, are associated with the Sanctuary of Apollo and free to view. You can walk to any of them, or you can view the (distant) gymnasium and the Sanctuary of Athena from the road in front of the site and museum.

Kastalian Spring: On the left side of the road, 800 yards past the archaeological site (around the jutting cliff), a spring bubbles forth from the ravine between the two Phaedriades Rocks. It was here that Apollo slew the python, taking over the area from the mother of the gods. Pilgrims washed here before consulting the oracle, and the water was used to ritually purify the oracle, the priests, and the Temple of Apollo. Inside are two ruined fountains (made of stone, with courtyards and benches to accommodate pilgrims) that tapped the ancient sacred spring, but because of rockslides, the ravine is closed to visitors (you can still see and hear the gurgling spring water).

Gymnasium: On the right side of the road, look for running tracks and a circular pool, where athletes trained for the Pythian Games.

Sanctuary of Athena Pronea: Farther along (also on the right side of the road) is a cluster of ruined temples. Because of

the area's long association with Gaia, Athena was worshipped at Delphi along with Apollo. The star attraction is the *tholos* (c. 380 BC), a round structure whose exact purpose is unknown. Although presumably less important than the Sanctuary of Apollo, its three reconstructed columns (of 20 Doric originals that once held up a conical roof) have become the most-photographed spot in all of Delphi.

Museum of Delphic Festivals

Perched high on the hill above town, this old mansion explains the quest of beloved poet and resident Angelos Sikelianos to create a new "Delphic Festivals" tradition in the 1920s. There's not much to see, aside from photos, costumes, and props of the event—which was held twice (in 1927 and 1930)—and some artifacts from Sikelianos' life. It's only worthwhile as an excuse for a strenuous hike (or quick drive) above town to grand vistas.

Cost and Hours: €3, hours vary—ask your hotelier to call ahead; generally Fri-Sun 10:00-14:00, closed Mon-Thu; +30 2265 082 175.

Sleeping in Delphi

Spending the night in Delphi is a pleasant (and much cheaper) alternative to busy Athens. The town is squeezed full of hotels, which makes competition fierce and rates soft—hoteliers don't need much of an excuse to offer a discount in slow times.

$$ Hotel Leto is a class act, with 21 smartly renovated rooms right in the heart of town (RS%, elevator, Apollonos 15, +30 2265 082 302, www.leto-delphi.gr, info@ leto-delphi.gr, Petros.

$$ Hotel Acropole is a big but welcoming group-oriented hotel along the lower road. It's quieter and has better vistas than my other listings. The 42 rooms are a little old-fashioned, but most feature view terraces for no extra charge; try to request one when you reserve (RS%, family suite with fireplace, elevator, Filellinon 13, +30 2265 082 675, www.delphi.com.gr, delphi@delphi. com.gr).

$ Nidimos Hotel is a step up style-wise from many places in Delphi, with sleek mod public spaces and an earth-tone color scheme. Some of the 34 rooms have balconies and views (breakfast extra, elevator, garage, Dimou Fragkou 10, +30 2265 082 056, www.nidimoshotel.gr, info@nidimoshotel.gr).

$ Pitho Rooms has eight good rooms above a gift shop on the main street. Your conscientious hosts, George and Vicky, pride themselves on offering a good value; they'll make you feel like part of the family (no elevator, Pavlou-Friderikis 40A, +30 2265 082 850, www.pithohotel.gr, info@pithohotel.gr).

¢ Tholos Hotel has 19 basic but comfortable rooms on the upper street, some with view balconies (breakfast extra, no elevator, Apollonos 31, +30 2265 082 268, www.tholoshotel.com, hotel_ tholos@yahoo.gr).

¢ Sibylla Hotel rents eight simple rooms at youth-hostel prices without a hint of youth-hostel grunge. No elevator, no air-conditioning...just good value. All have balconies: four with valley views, four over the street (no breakfast, ceiling fans, Pavlou-Friderikis 9, +30 2265 082 335, www.sibylla-hotel.gr, info@sibylla-hotel.gr, Christopoulos family).

Eating in Delphi

Delphi's eateries tend to cater to tour groups, with vast dining rooms and long tables stretching to distant valley-and-gulf views. The following restaurants distinguish themselves by offering high quality and good value. Look for the regional specialty, fried *formaela* cheese (spritz it with fresh lemon juice, then dig in). Most places are open daily for both lunch and dinner (around 12:00 until 22:30 or 23:00). Some close for a midafternoon siesta (roughly 16:00-18:30).

$$$ Taverna Vakhos is homey and woody, with down-home, family-run charm. The focus is on tasty traditional dishes, such as *kokoras kokkinisto* (rooster cooked in red wine) and baked lamb with lemon sauce. For dessert, try the locally produced farm-fresh yogurt with honey or ask what topping is in season (Apollonos 31, +30 2265 083 186).

$$$$ To Patriko Mas ("Our Family's Home") is more upscale, with a classy stone-and-wood interior and a striking outdoor terrace clinging to the cliff face (reservations suggested for view table, Pavlou-Friderikis 69, +30 2265 082 150, Konsta family).

$$ Taverna Dion serves standard Greek fare at reasonable prices and specializes in grilled meats. Their good-value fixed-price meals include three plates plus dessert (Apollonos 30, +30 2265 082 790).

$$ Taverna Gargadouas is proud *not* to cater to tour groups (it's too small). This simple taverna is a mix of locals and tourists, all here for affordable, unpretentious, traditional cuisine (on main drag at end of town farthest from sanctuary, +30 2265 083 074).

Picnics: There's a smattering of grocery stores along the main street. And though picnics are not allowed inside the archaeological site, you could choose a perch along the road overlooking the vast valley.

Delphi Connections

BY BUS

Delphi's one disadvantage, from a traveler's perspective, is its distance from the other places described in this book. Delphi is well-connected by bus to **Athens** (4-5/day—check times locally, 3-hour trip, €15 one-way). Connecting to the **Peloponnese** is long and complicated. For the eastern Peloponnese (such as **Nafplio**), it's best to go via Athens (see the Athens Connections chapter). To the western Peloponnese, you'll connect through **Patra** (only a few times per week, departs around 13:10; a second bus may leave Sun evening around 17:00; 3 hours, €15 one-way). From Patra you can continue on to **Olympia** (via Pyrgos) or **Kardamyli** (via Kalamata).

Either is a very long trip, and the Delphi-Kardamyli trip can't be done in one day.

For bus information, go to www.ktel-fokidas.gr (online tickets available).

ROUTE TIPS FOR DRIVERS

From Athens to Delphi: Head north (toward *Lamia/Λαμία*) on national road 1/expressway E-75 (one tollbooth). Take the second exit for Θήβα/*Theba/Thiva*, which is also marked for *Livadia/* Λιβαδειά (another tollbooth). From the turnoff, signs lead you (on road 3, then road 48) all the way to *Delphi/Δελφοί*. As you get farther up into the mountains, keep an eye out for ski resorts—Athenians come here to ski from December to March.

From Delphi to the Peloponnese: As with the bus, for sights in the eastern Peloponnese (such as **Nafplio** or **Monemvasia**), it's faster to backtrack through Athens. (See the end of the Athens Connections chapter for more driving tips.)

To reach the western Peloponnese (such as **Olympia** or **Kardamyli/Mani Peninsula**), first follow the twisting road from Delphi down toward Itea (Ιτέα) on the Gulf of Corinth, then follow signs toward *Galaxidi/*Γαλαξίδι (a charming port city worth a quick stop). Trace the gulf on a magnificently scenic, two-hour westward drive along road E-65 (toward *Nafpaktos/*Ναύπακτος). Take your time and use the pullouts to enjoy the views. In Antirrio, follow signs for *Patra/*Πάτρα across the Rio-Antirrio suspension bridge (toll) to the town of Rio. You'll enter the Peloponnese just north of the big port city of Patra (Πάτρα, described at the end of the Olympia chapter); skirt this city and head south another 1.5 hours along road E-55 toward *Pyrgos/*Πύργος—be sure to get on the faster highway, with a green sign, instead of the slower regional road. (Note that attempting to "shortcut" through the middle of the Peloponnese takes you on some very twisty, slow, and poorly signed mountain roads—avoid them unless you value scenery more than time.)

Once at Pyrgos, you can head east/inland to Ancient Olympia (Αρχαία Ολυμπία, well-marked with brown signs); or continue south to Kyparissia and Pylos, then eastward to Kalamata/ Καλαμάτα (about two hours beyond Pyrgos; note that the Kalamata turnoff, just before Kyparissia, is not well-marked). From Kalamata, continue south another hour to Kardamyli.

GREEK ISLANDS

For many people, Greece is synonymous with islands. If you need a vacation from your busy mainland Greek vacation, the islands exert an irresistible pull.

Explore a tight, twisty maze of whitewashed cubic houses with vibrant trim. Dig your toes into the hot sand while basking under a beach umbrella. Go for a dip in the crystal-clear, bathwater-warm Aegean. Sip an iced coffee along a bustling harborfront, watching fishermen clean their catch while cuddly kittens greedily beg below. Indulge in fresh seafood at a rustic seaside taverna,

and chat with the big personality whose family has owned the place for generations, all while watching the sun gradually descend into the sea. The Greek islands really do live up to their worldwide acclaim.

While I appreciate a healthy dose of restorative island time, I prefer to spend the bulk of my Greek vacation visiting the country's amazing wealth of ancient sites. That's why I've focused this book on the bustling capital of Athens and Greece's "heartland," the Peloponnese, where—compared to the islands—prices are much lower, tourism is less suffocating, and travelers have more exciting opportunities to peel back layers of history. Still, a visit to Greece isn't complete without at least one island stay. This book covers three island destinations: Hydra, Mykonos, and Santorini.

GREECE'S ISLAND GROUPS

Greece's roughly 3,000 islands and islets (227 of which are inhabited) are scattered far and wide across the eastern Mediterranean. Most are in the Aegean Sea (south and east of mainland Greece), while a few are in the Ionian Sea (west of the mainland). The islands are divided into clusters:

The **Ionian Islands,** closer to Albania and Italy than to Athens, are Greece's northwest gateway to the Adriatic and the rest of Europe—they've had more foreign invaders and rulers (from Venice, France, Britain, Russia, Austria, and so on) than anywhere else in the country. The main island is Corfu (Kerkyra in Greek), with a bustling, architecturally eclectic main town and a lush, green islandscape dotted with attractions and beaches.

The **Saronic Gulf Islands** (Argosaronikos), conveniently wedged between the Peloponnese and Athens, ooze lots of island charm and give you a chance to get away from it all without actually going very far. **Hydra,** my favorite, is in this group.

The **Sporades Islands,** due east of Athens, are dominated by the giant Evia island, which is attached to the mainland by a bridge. Thickly forested and less touristed by international visitors, the Sporades are a popular and handy weekend getaway for Athenians.

The **Cycladic Islands** (or simply Cyclades)—a bit farther south, between Athens and Crete—are the prototypical "Greek islands," boasting chalk-white houses with colorful windowsills and doorways; rocky, sun-parched landscapes; delightful beaches; old-fashioned white windmills topped with tufts of grass like unkempt hair; and an almost overwhelming crush of international visitors. **Mykonos** and **Santorini** are the two best and most famous of the Cyclades. Near Mykonos is the archaeological site of **Delos** (one of the most important locales of the ancient world).

The **Dodecanese Islands,** at the sunny, southeastern end of the Greek lands, are more rustic and less developed than the Cyclades. Their proximity to Turkey and historic ties to Venice give them a hybrid Turkish-Venetian flavor (though the population is mostly ethnic Greek, these islands merged with Greece only after World War II). Rhodes, with an appealing and very real-feeling old town, is the biggest of these islands.

The **North Aegean Islands,** relatively untrampled and remote, lie roughly between Turkey and Thessaloniki (at the northern end of mainland Greece). The southernmost of these, Samos, is a particularly handy springboard for Turkey, as it's very close to the Turkish port city of Kuşadası (near the remarkable ancient site of Ephesus).

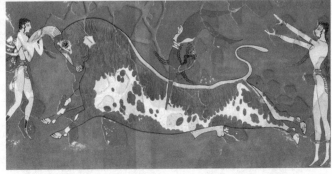

Crete is Greece's biggest island and practically a ministate (in fact, from 1897 to 1913 it was an autonomous state within the Ottoman Empire). While many of Greece's smaller islands merit a day or two of fun in the sun, Crete could occupy even a busy traveler for a week or more. Historically, Crete was home to the Minoans—the earliest advanced European civilization, peaking around 1950 BC,

GREEK ISLANDS

centuries before "the ancient Greeks" of Athens. While Crete's modern main city, Iraklio, is drab and uninviting, the rest of the island offers an engaging diversity of attractions: Minoan ruins, scenic mountains, enticing beaches, characteristic rustic villages, and dramatic caves and gorges (including the famous Samaria Gorge).

CHOOSING AN ISLAND

For this book I've chosen to cover three of the most popular escapes. **Hydra** is my favorite, thanks to its speedy connections to Athens and the Peloponnese, relaxing car-free ambience, easily reached beaches, and charming harbor that invites you to linger. Two of the most popular Greek islands are Mykonos and Santorini; both are relatively well connected to Athens. **Mykonos** boasts an adorable, windmill-topped fishing village slathered in white and thronged by a hard-partying international crowd, enjoying its many beaches and side-tripping to the ruins on nearby Delos. **Santorini** is the most geologically interesting of all the Greek islands, and arguably the most picturesque, with idyllic villages perched on the rim of a collapsed and flooded volcano crater, a handful of impressive wineries, and enough sights and activities to keep travelers occupied.

If you're choosing just one island, I'd go with Hydra. Farther-flung Mykonos and Santorini can easily be connected in a loop—they are linked to Athens' port (Piraeus), and to each other, by boat and plane (unfortunately neither connects directly with Hydra). If your travels take you to islands beyond these three, pick up another guidebook to supplement the information here.

While each Greek island has its own personality and claims to fame, most offer the same basic ingredients: a charming fishing village, once humble and poor, now a finely tuned machine for catering to (and collecting money from) a steady stream of tourists; a rugged interior and rough roads connecting coastal coves; appealing beaches with rentable umbrellas and lounge chairs, presided over by tavernas and hotels; maybe a few dusty museums collecting ancient artifacts or bits and pieces of local folklore; and occasionally a good or even great ancient site to tour.

Many islands have a main town, sometimes named for the island itself and sometimes called Chora or Hora (Χώρα), which literally means "village." This is generally the hub for transportation, both to other islands (port for passenger ferries and cruise ships) and within the island (bus station and taxi stand). Some islands—such as Rhodes, Corfu, and Crete—have sizeable cities as their capitals.

GETTING AROUND THE GREEK ISLANDS

Many passenger boats crisscross the Aegean Sea, making it quick and fairly easy to reach your island getaway. Be warned, however, that gathering ferry information takes some work, as routes can be covered by multiple companies and schedules change often. Prior to your trip, look up schedules online, then confirm the details on arrival in Greece at any travel agency (or more than one, as you may get slightly different information from different agencies). For more tips on schedules and tickets, see the Practicalities chapter; for connections from Piraeus (Athens' port), see the Athens Connections chapter. Note that boats can be canceled due to bad weather (more likely off-season).

To save time, consider flying between Athens and Mykonos or Santorini. Compared with boats, flights are less likely to be delayed or canceled, tend to offer more frequent connections, and are much faster—but often more expensive. Two major Greek carriers that offer daily flights from Athens to many Greek islands are **Olympic Airlines** (www.olympicair.com) and **Aegean Airlines** (www.aegeanair.com). Also consider **Sky Express** (www.skyexpress.gr).

The Greek islands are made to order for cruising and a major destination for cruise ships. If you're coming on a cruise, your challenge is to beat the hordes: You'll arrive in town at precisely the same time as 2,000 other visitors, all hoping to fit the maximum amount of sightseeing, shopping, or beach time in a single day. Get as early a start as possible, and explore the back lanes and beaches when the main drag gets too congested.

If you're not cruising, it's smart to be aware of when ships are scheduled to show up. Visit outlying sights or beaches when the ships are in port—by the time you return to town in the afternoon, the cruise-ship passengers will be loading up to leave again.

ISLAND ACCOMMODATIONS

Greek island accommodations range from rustic *dhomatia* to designer hotels with spectacular views. Even out-of-the-way islands get heavy tourist traffic in the summer, so options abound.

At the busiest times (July-Sept, peaking in Aug), visitors can outnumber beds; to get your choice of accommodations, book far ahead. Expect to pay (sometimes wildly) inflated prices in high season—in the most popular destinations, such as Mykonos and Santorini, prices for even budget hotels can more than double. Prices for other services—such as car rentals and restaurant meals—also increase when demand is high. For the best combination of still-good weather, fewer crowds, and more reasonable prices, visit just before or after these busy times.

Whenever you visit, enjoy your time here and simply give yourself over to the Greek islands. With a few exceptions, the "sights" (museums and ruins) are not worth going out of your way for—you're here to relax on the beach and explore the charming towns. Make the most of it.

HYDRA

Ύδρα

Hydra (pronounced EE-drah, not HIGH-drah)—less than a two-hour boat ride from Athens' port, Piraeus—is a glamorous getaway that combines practical convenience with idyllic Greek island ambience. After the noise of Athens, Hydra's traffic-free tranquility is a delight. Donkeys rather than cars, the shady awnings of well-worn cafés, and memorable seaside views all combine to make it clear...you've found your Greek isle.

The island's main town, also called Hydra, is one of Greece's prettiest. Its busy but quaint harbor—bobbing with rustic fishing boats and luxury yachts—is surrounded by a ring of rocky hills and blanketed with whitewashed homes. From the harbor, a fleet of zippy water taxis whisks you to isolated beaches and tavernas. Hydra is an easy blend of stray cats, hardworking donkeys, welcoming Hydriots (as locals are called), and lazy tourists on "island time."

One of the island's greatest features is its total absence of cars and motorbikes. Sure-footed beasts of burden—laden with every-

thing from sandbags and bathtubs to bottled water—climb stepped lanes. While Hydra is generally quiet, dawn teaches visitors the exact meaning of "cockcrow." The end of night is marked with much more than a distant cock-a-doodle-doo; it's a dissonant chorus of catfights, burro honks, and what sounds like roll call at an asylum for crazed roosters. After the animal population gets all that out of its system, the island slumbers a little longer.

Hydra's Hystory

Though it may seem tiny and low-key, overachieving Hydra holds a privileged place in Greek history. The fate of Hydriots has always been tied to the sea, which locals have harnessed to their advantage time after time.

Many Hydriot merchants became wealthy running the British blockade of French ports during the Napoleonic Wars. Hydra enjoyed its glory days in the late 18th and early 19th centuries, when the island was famous for its shipbuilders. Hydra's prosperity earned it the nickname "Little England." As rebellion swept Greece, the island flourished as a safe haven for those fleeing Ottoman oppression.

When the Greeks launched their War of Independence in 1821, Hydra emerged as a leading naval power. The harbor, with its twin forts and abundance of cannons, housed and protected the fleet of 130 ships. Hydriots of note from this period include the naval officer Andreas Miaoulis, who led the "firebrands" and their deadly "fireships," which succeeded in decimating the Ottoman navy, and Lazaros Kountouriotis, a wealthy shipping magnate who donated his fleet to the cause (more on both figures later in this chapter).

Greece won its independence, but at a great cost to Hydra, which lost many of its merchant-turned-military ships to the fighting...sending the is-land into a deep economic funk. During those lean postwar years, Hydriots again found salvation in the sea, farming the sponges that lived below the surface (sponge divers here pioneered the use of diving suits). Gathering sponges kick-started the local economy and kept Hydra afloat.

In 1956 Sophia Loren came here to play an Hydriot sponge diver in the film *Boy on a Dolphin,* propelling the little island onto the international stage. And the movie's plot—in which a precious ancient sculpture is at risk of falling into the hands of a greedy art collector instead of being returned to the Greek government—still resonates with today's Greeks, who want to reclaim their heritage for the Acropolis Museum.

Thanks largely to the film, by the 1960s Hydra had become a favorite retreat for celebrities, well-heeled tourists, and artists and writers, all drawing inspiration from the idyllic surroundings. Canadian songwriter Leonard Cohen lived here for a time—and was inspired to compose his beloved song "Bird on the Wire" after observing just that here on Hydra. Today visitors only have to count the yachts to figure out that Hydra's economy is still based on the sea.

HYDRA

Little Hydra—which has produced more than its share of military heroes, influential aristocrats, and political leaders—is packed with history. Rusted old cannons are scattered about town; black, pitted anchors decorate squares; and small museums hold engaging artifacts. But most visitors enjoy simply being on vacation here. Loiter around the harbor. Go on a photo safari for donkeys and kittens. Take a walk along the coast or up into the hills. Head for an inviting beach, near or far, to sunbathe and swim. Hang out past your bedtime in a cocktail bar. Hydra's the kind of place that makes you want to buy a bottle of ouzo and toss your itinerary into the sea.

PLANNING YOUR TIME

While Hydra can be done as a long day trip from Athens, it's better to spend at least two nights to take full advantage of the island's many dining options, and to give yourself a whole day to relax. Even if you're also visiting Mykonos, Santorini, or other Greek islands, Hydra has a totally different vibe and is still the best place I know where you can take a vacation from your Greek vacation.

To get your bearings, take my brief self-guided walk. While the walk gives you the historic context of the town, it also points out practical stops that will make your stay more efficient and enjoyable (and finishes at a wonderful little bakery). You'll still have ample time for activities: Dip into a museum that tickles your curiosity, enjoy a drink at a café, go for a hike into the hills, walk along the water to nearby villages and beaches, or catch a shuttle boat or water taxi for a spin around the island.

Orientation to Hydra

Remember, Hydra is the name of both the island and its main town (home to about 90 percent of the island's 2,000 residents). Hydra town climbs up the hill in every direction from the port.

Branching off from the broad café-lined walkway at the bottom of the harbor are four major streets. In order from the boat dock, these are called Tompazi, Oikono-

mou, Miaouli, and Lignou. Not that street names mean much in this town—residents ignore addresses, and few lanes are labeled. Though the island is small, Hydra's streets twist defiantly to and fro. If seeking a specific location, use the map in this chapter or ask a local (note that most maps of Hydra, including mine, show the

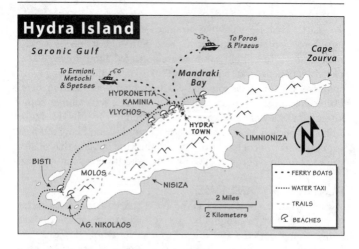

harbor—which is actually to the north—at the bottom). Expect to get lost in Hydra...and enjoy it when you do.

Consider venturing beyond Hydra town to settlements and beaches elsewhere on the island. The most accessible is the tiny seaside hamlet of Kaminia Castello, which lies just over the headland west of the harbor (with a good recommended restaurant).

Tourist Information: Hydra has no TI, but most of the hoteliers I've listed here are happy and willing to help. You can also check www.hydra.gr and the similar www.hydra.com.gr.

ARRIVAL ON HYDRA

For details on how to get to Hydra, see "Hydra Connections" at the end of this chapter. All ferry boats dock in the heart of Hydra town's harbor, along its eastern edge. Nearly all my recommended accommodations are within a 10-minute walk of the harbor. At the port you can hire a donkey to carry your bags (€10-20, establish the price up front). If you ask, better hotels will often meet you at the boat and help with your bags.

GETTING AROUND HYDRA

As there are no cars, your options are foot, donkey, or boat. You'll walk everywhere in town. You can hike to neighboring beaches, but it's fun to hop a **shuttle boat** (about €10 round-trip to the beach at Vlychos—due to Greek laws you may have to pay for a round-trip ticket even if you only use it one-way; departs about every 30 minutes in high season from in front of Hotel Sophia) or take a **water taxi** (much more expensive unless you're a small group—same rate for one person or eight). You'll see the red taxi boats stacked and waiting near the donkeys on the harborfront. Sample taxi fares: €20 to Kaminia, €25 to Vlychos. To get back to town by water taxi, call +30 2298 053 690.

HELPFUL HINTS
Summer Weather: Hydra can get extremely hot, especially in July and August. While other islands receive bursts of breezy north winds granting temporary reprieve, the entire island of Hydra is cut off from nature's air-conditioning by the Attica peninsula. Before you head out for the day, make sure you're prepared with sunscreen, a hat, and plenty of water.

Drinking Water: The island's name means "water" in ancient Greek, but that was named a long, long time ago: Today there's no natural water source on Hydra (other than private cisterns). Until recently, water was barged in daily. But with EU help, Hydra now has a seawater desalination plant, giving the island a reliable water supply and drinkable tap water.

Hydra Harbor Walk

Hydra clusters around its wide harbor, squeezed full of fishing boats, pleasure craft, luxury yachts, and the occasional Athens-bound ferry. Get the lay of the land with this lazy 30-minute self-guided stroll.

• *Begin at the tip of the port (to the right, as you face the sea). Climb the stairs (by the wall of cacti) to the cannon-studded turret. From here you have a fine...*

View of the Harbor

The harbor is the heart and soul of Hydra. Imagine it as an ancient theater: The houses are the audience, the port is the stage, the boats are the actors...and the Saronic Gulf is the scenic backdrop.

This little town has a history rich with military might, political power, and artistic sophistication. Looking at the arid, sparsely forested mountains rising up along the spine of the island, it's clear that not much grows here—so Hydriots have always turned to the sea for survival. As islanders grew

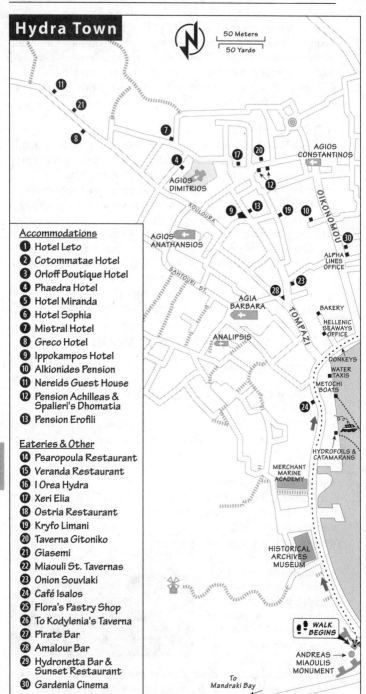

Hydra Town

50 Meters
50 Yards

Accommodations
1. Hotel Leto
2. Cotommatae Hotel
3. Orloff Boutique Hotel
4. Phaedra Hotel
5. Hotel Miranda
6. Hotel Sophia
7. Mistral Hotel
8. Greco Hotel
9. Ippokampos Hotel
10. Alkionides Pension
11. Nereids Guest House
12. Pension Achilleas & Spalieri's Dhomatia
13. Pension Erofili

Eateries & Other
14. Psaropoula Restaurant
15. Veranda Restaurant
16. I Orea Hydra
17. Xeri Elia
18. Ostria Restaurant
19. Kryfo Limani
20. Taverna Gitoniko
21. Giasemi
22. Miaouli St. Tavernas
23. Onion Souvlaki
24. Café Isalos
25. Flora's Pastry Shop
26. To Kodylenia's Taverna
27. Pirate Bar
28. Amalour Bar
29. Hydronetta Bar & Sunset Restaurant
30. Gardenia Cinema

AGIOS CONSTANTINOS

AGIOS DIMITRIOS

KOULOURA

OIKONOMOU

AGIOS ANATHANSIOS

ALPHA LINES OFFICE

SAHTOURI ST.

AGIA BARBARA

TOMPAZI

BAKERY

HELLENIC SEAWAYS OFFICE

ANALIPSIS

DONKEYS

WATER TAXIS

METOCHI BOATS

HYDROFOILS & CATAMARANS

MERCHANT MARINE ACADEMY

HISTORICAL ARCHIVES MUSEUM

WALK BEGINS

ANDREAS MIAOULIS MONUMENT

To Mandraki Bay

HYDRA

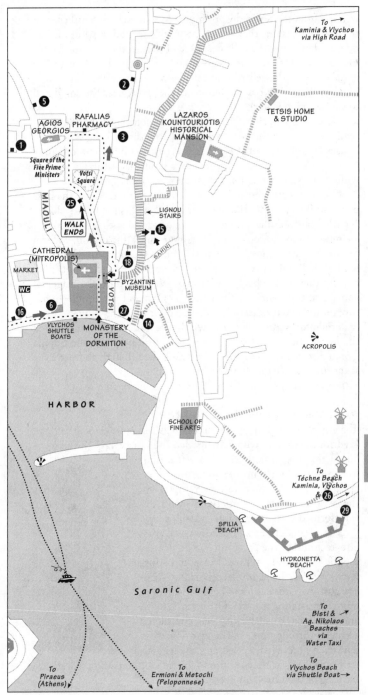

HYDRA

wealthy from the sea trade, prominent local merchant families built the grand mansions that rise up between the modest whitewashed houses blanketing the hillsides. One of these—the Lazaros Kountouriotis Historical Mansion—is open to the public (the yellow mansion with the red roof and three-column terrace facing you, high on the hill across the harbor to the right, near the small bell tower; described later).

Another mansion, the rough-stone four-story building directly across from the port (behind the imposing zigzag wall), now houses Hydra's School of Fine Arts. Artists—Greek and foreign—have long swooned over the gorgeous light that saturates Hydra's white homes, brown cliffs, and turquoise waters.

Look directly across the mouth of the harbor. Along the base of the walkway, under the seafront café tables, is the town's closest "beach," called Spilia ("Cave")—a concrete pad with ladders luring swimmers into the cool blue. For a more appealing option, you can follow the paved, mostly level path around this point to the fishing hamlet of Kaminia (with a scenic recommended restaurant) and, beyond that, to the beach at Vlychos. Visually trace the ridgeline above that trail, noticing the remains of two old windmills—a fixture on many Greek islands, once used for grinding grain and raw materials for gunpowder. The windmills' sails are long gone, but the lower one was restored for use as a film prop (for the Sophia Loren film *Boy on a Dolphin*). Crowning the hill high above are the scant ruins of Hydra's humble little acropolis.

• *Turn your attention to the centerpiece of this viewpoint, the...*

Andreas Miaoulis Monument

The guy at the helm is Admiral Andreas Miaoulis (1768-1835), an Hydriot sea captain who valiantly led the Greek navy in the revolution that began in 1821. This war sought to end nearly four centuries of Ottoman occupation. As war preparations ramped up, the wealthy merchant marines of Hydra transformed their vessels into warships. The Greeks used a clever and deadly naval warfare technique: the "fireship." (For details, see the Historical Archives Museum listing, later.) While this kamikaze-burning strategy cost the Greeks a lot of boats, it was even more devastating to the Ottoman navy—and Miaoulis' naval victory was considered a crucial turning point in the war. For three days each June, Hydra celebrates the Miaoulia Festival, when they set fire to an old ship to commemorate the burning of the Ottoman fleet.

On the monument, the cross that hangs from the steering column represents the eventual triumph of the Christian Greeks over the Muslim Ottomans. Miaoulis' bones are actually inside the stone pedestal under the statue.

• *Head back down the stairs and begin walking along the harborfront.*

Along the Harbor

About 50 yards down is the stout stone mansion that houses the **Historical Archives Museum.** This small but good collection (described later, under "Sights and Activities in Hydra") does its best to get visitors excited about Hydra's history. The gap after the museum is filled with monuments honoring Hydriot heroes. The green plaque in the pillar is a gift from Argentina to honor an Hydriot aristocrat who fought in the Argentinean war for independence. The next building is the Merchant Marine Academy, where Hydra continues to churn out sailors—many of whom often hang around out front. (During the WWII occupation of Greece, this building was used as a Nazi base.) Next, the row of covered benches along the water marks the embarkation point for the ferries ("Flying Dolphin" hydrofoils and "Flying Cat" catamarans) that connect Hydra to Athens and other Greek islands for those of us who lack yachts of our own.

Notice the three flags to the right—specifically, the **flag of Hydra.** Dating from the uprising against the Ottomans, it's loaded with symbolism: the outline of the island of Hydra topped with a flag with a warrior's helmet, a cross, and an anchor—all watched over by the protective eye of God. The inscription, Η Ταν Ή Επί Τασ, means "with it or on it" and evokes the admonition of the warlike Spartans when sending their sons into battle with their huge shields: Come back "with it," victorious and carrying your shield; or "on it," dead, with your shield serving as a stretcher to carry your body home.

When you reach the corner of the harbor, you'll likely see **donkeys and mules** shooing flies as they wait to plod into town with visitors' luggage lashed to their backs. The donkeys are more a lifestyle choice than a touristy gimmick: Hydriots have decided not to allow private motorized vehicles on their island, keeping this place quiet and tranquil and reducing pollution (now just donkey poop). Aside from a few garbage trucks and emergency vehicles, these beasts of burden are the only way to get around. It's not un-

usual to see a donkey with a major appliance strapped to its back, as it gingerly navigates the steps up to the top of town. Locals dress their burros up with rugs, beads, and charms. Behind each mule train toils a human pooper-scooper. On Hydra a traffic jam looks like a farm show. And instead of the testosterone-fueled revving of moped engines, Hydra's soundtrack features the occasional distant braying of a donkey echoing over the rooftops.

In the same corner as the donkeys is the dock for the feisty fleet of red **water taxis.** These zip constantly from here to remote points

around the island. Meanwhile, simple fishing boats squeeze between the luxury yachts to put in and unload their catch...eyed hungrily by scrawny cats.

Hang a right and continue along the bottom of the harbor. At this corner is Sahtouri street (diagonal from the water taxis), which soon becomes Tompazi and quickly devolves into a twisty warren of lanes with many hotels. Continue along the harbor, past a tiny dead-end lane leading to a good bakery. As you stroll, window shop the **cafés** and choose one to return to later. Overhead, notice the ingenious rope system the seafaring Hydriots have rigged so that they can quickly draw a canopy over the seating area—like unfurling the sails on a ship—in the event of rain...or, more commonly here, overpowering sunshine. Next, skinny Oikonomou street leads to shops and the open-air Gardenia Cinema. A few steps farther, another narrow lane leads to the public WC and Hydra's ramshackle little market hall.

Hydra is known for its **jewelry.** A few shops right here on the harbor, such as Zoe's and Elena Votsi, sell the handiwork of Hydriot designers and artists (Votsi is locally famous as the designer of the 2004 Olympic medals). Many Hydra hoteliers supplement their income by running jewelry and souvenir shops, often with the same name as their hotels (good to know if you need to find your hotelier at midday). The next street, Navarhou Miaouli, bustles with appealing **tavernas.**

Shuttle boats line up along the next stretch of the quay. They offer cheap rides to points around the island—a service much appreciated by the owners of Hydra's many remote cafés and tavernas (but which annoys the independent water-taxi drivers).

• *Near the far corner of the harbor stands a symbol of Hydra, the clock tower of the...*

Monastery of the Dormition

Hydra's ecclesiastical center is dedicated to the Dormition of the Virgin. "Dormition"—as in "sleep"—is a Greek euphemism for death. Orthodox Christians believe Mary died a human death, then (like her son) was resurrected three days later, before being assumed into heaven.

Go through the archway under the tower, and you'll emerge into what was, until 1832, an active monastery. The double-decker arcade of cells circling the courtyard was once the monks' living quarters; it now houses the offices of the city government and mayor.

The monastery's church, which doubles as Hydra's *mitropolis* (cathedral), is free to enter. Stepping inside, it's clear that this was a wealthy community—compare the marble iconostasis, silver chandelier, gorgeous Christ Pantocrator ("All Powerful") dome decoration, rich icons, and frescoes with the humbler decor you'll see at small-town churches elsewhere in Greece. Just inside the door (to the left), the icon of the Virgin and Child is believed to work miracles. Notice the many votive rings and necklaces draping it as a thank-you for prayers answered.

Back in the courtyard, you'll see war memorials and monuments to beloved Hydriots. The humble Byzantine Museum (also called the "Ecclesiastical Museum"—up the stairs across the courtyard) has a few rooms of glittering icons, vestments, and other paraphernalia from this monastery and church (€2, some English labels, Tue-Sun 10:00-14:30, closed Mon and Dec-March).

• *If the doorway's open under the museum, exit here onto Votsi street (otherwise, return to the harborfront, then hang a left up the next street). From this spot (either straight ahead or around the right side of the yellow butcher's shop) stairs head to the upper reaches of town and eventually lead over the headland and down to the village and little harbor of Kaminia. For now though, keep to the left, walking toward the orange-tree-filled square.*

Upper Town Squares

Tidy **Votsi Square** has lots of cats. Hydriots love their cats, perhaps because they share a similar temperament: tender, relaxed, but secretly vigilant and fiercely independent. At the bottom of the square (on the left) is Flora's Pastry Shop, where we'll finish our stroll.

For now, keep walking about 100 feet above the square until

the lane hits the old-time **Rafalias Pharmacy.** The pharmacy is an institution in town, and Vangelis Rafalias has kept it just as his grandfather did. Curious travelers can politely enter for a quick glimpse, or peek through the window at the old-fashioned shelves and the photo of Jackie Kennedy visiting Hydra in 1961 (on the far-right wall).

With your back to the pharmacy, one lane leads to the left, heading uphill to the site of the original town, which was positioned inland to be safely away from marauding pirates. We'll head in the other direction, right, and slightly downhill, rounding the building on the left to the little **Square of the Five Prime Ministers.** The monument, with five medallions flanked by cannons, celebrates the five Hydriots who were chosen for Greece's highest office in the nearly two centuries since independence. It's an impressive civic contribution from a little island town, perhaps due to Hydra's seafaring wealth and its proximity to the Greek capitals (Nafplio, then Athens). From here, narrow, stepped, cobblestone lanes invite exploration of Hydra's quiet side.

But for now, continue left and downhill, back to Votsi Square. The recommended **Flora's Pastry Shop** (signed Ζαχαροπλαστείο) is at the bottom of the square, on the right. Treat yourself to a homemade baklava. Or, for something more traditional, try the local favorite—*galaktoboureko* (gha-lahk-toh-boo-re-KOH), which is cinnamon-sprinkled egg custard baked between layers of phyllo.

Sights and Activities in Hydra

MUSEUMS
▲Historical Archives Museum

This fine little museum, in an old mansion right along the port, shows off a small, strangely fascinating collection of Hydra's history and has good English descriptions throughout.

Cost and Hours: €5, includes temporary art exhibits; daily 9:00-16:00, also 19:30-21:30 in June-Sept; along the eastern side of the harbor near the ferry dock, +30 2298 052 355, www.iamy.gr.

Visiting the Museum: The core of the exhibit is upstairs. At the top of the stairs, look straight ahead for a tattered, yellowed **old map** by Rigas Feraios from 1797. Depicting a hypothetical and generously defined "Hellenic Republic," it claims virtually the entire Balkan Peninsula (from the Aegean to the Danube) for Greece. The map features historical and cultural tidbits of the time (such as drawings of coins from various eras), making it a treasure trove for historians. Drawn at a time when the Greeks had been oppressed by the Ottomans for centuries, the map—with 1,200 copies printed and distributed—helped to rally support for what would become a successful revolution starting in 1821.

The stairwell is lined with portraits of **"firebrands"**—sailors (many of them Hydriots) who burned the Ottoman fleet during the war. They were considered the body and soul of the Greek navy in 1821. To learn more about their techniques, head behind the map and into the room on the left; in its center, find the **model of a "fireship"** used for these attacks. These vessels were loaded with barrels of gunpowder, with large ventilation passages cut into the deck and hull. Suspended from the masts were giant, barbed, fishing-lure-like hooks. (Two actual hooks flank the model.) After ramming an enemy ship and dropping the hooks into its deck to attach the two vessels, the Greek crew would light the fuse and escape in a little dinghy...leaving their ship behind to become a giant firetrap, engulfing the Ottoman vessel in flames. Also in this room are nautical maps and models and paintings of other Hydriot vessels.

In the biggest room (immediately behind the old map), you'll see a Greek urn in the center containing the actual, embalmed **heart** of local hero Andreas Miaoulis. On the walls are portraits of V.I.H.s (very important Hydriots). Rounding out the collection on this floor is a room filled with **weapons** and 18th- and 19th-century **Hydriot attire.**

Lazaros Kountouriotis Historical Mansion

Because of Hydra's merchant marine prosperity, the town has many fine aristocratic mansions...but only this one is open to the public. Lazaros Kountouriotis (koon-doo-ree-OH-tees, 1769-1852) was a wealthy Hydriot shipping magnate who helped fund the Greek War of Independence. He donated 120 of his commercial ships to be turned into warships, representing three-quarters

of the Greek navy. Today Kountouriotis is revered as a local and national hero, and his mansion offers visitors a glimpse into the lifestyles of the 18th-century Greek rich and famous.

Cost and Hours: €4; daily 10:00-16:00, off-season until 14:30, Nov-March by appointment only; on the hillside above town, sign-

HYDRA

posted off stepped Lignou street—turn right after Veranda Restaurant, +30 2298 052 421, www.nhmuseum.gr/en/exhibitions/lazaros-koundouriotis-historical-mansion.

Visiting the Mansion: The main building of Kountouriotis' former estate is a fine example of aristocratic Hydriot architecture of the late 18th century, combining elements of northern Greek, Saronic Gulf Island, and Italian architecture. The house has changed little since its heyday.

You'll enter on the second floor, with several period-decorated rooms. These reception rooms have beautiful wood-paneled ceilings and are furnished with all the finery of the period. Included is the statesman's favorite armchair, where you can imagine him spending many hours pondering the shape of the emerging Greek nation. Through a little garden, then down some stairs, you'll find temporary exhibits and the art of the local Byzantinos family: father Pericles (hazy Post-Impressionistic landscapes and portraits) and son Constantinos (dark sketches and bold, colorful paintings). On the top floor, which you'll reach via stairs off the house's main courtyard, you'll see a collection of traditional costumes and jewelry from throughout Greece (labeled in English).

Nearby: The nearby **Tetsis Home and Studio,** a modest 19th-century Hydriot home where the Greek artist Panagiotis Tetsis grew up, is worth a quick stop—or longer on a bad-weather day. It's particularly interesting to see the family's general store and candle manufactory on the ground floor (covered by Historical Mansion ticket, follow signs to the left as you exit the mansion grounds).

BEACHES

Although Hydra's beaches are nothing to get excited about, there's no shortage of places to swim. My first two listings are basic swimming spots in Hydra town—no beach chairs, umbrellas, or shorelines, just a place to dive in. The other three are decent beaches within a pleasant, easy walk (or shuttle-boat/water-taxi ride) of Hydra: Mandraki Bay, Kaminia Castello, and Vlychos. More-distant beaches on the southwestern tip of the island  (Bisti and Agios Nikolaos) really get you away from it all but are best reached by boat.

Spilia

The main spot to swim in town is Spilia ("Cave"), at the western entrance to Hydra harbor. There you'll find steps that lead down to a series of small concrete platforms with ladders into the sea—but no showers or changing rooms. (Spilia appears to belong to the adjacent cocktail bar, but anyone is welcome to swim here.)

Hydronetta and Téchne

You'll find two more rocky, cement "beaches" just outside the town center, on the way to Kaminia. Both are associated with name-sake restaurants, and neither has showers or changing rooms. The first, **Hydronetta,** sits just below the cannons along the ramparts stretching from the pricey **$$$$** Sunset Restaurant to the more-reasonable **$$** Hydronetta Bar. Access the beach via a stone stair-case from either eatery's terrace (no shoreline, just a series of con-crete slabs with diving terraces and ladders into the water). The bar's umbrella-shaded tables are good for between-dip refresh-ments, while couples prefer the fancier restaurant for a romantic meal. Two minutes down the same path, a zigzagging staircase leads down to **Téchne Beach,** a rocky outcrop with two rock plat-forms, a small pebble cove, and an upmarket **$$$$** restaurant fea-turing neo-Greek fare.

Mandraki Bay

This sandy beach, part of Mandraki Resort, is to the east of Hydra, along the main coastal path (30-minute walk from the eastern end of the harbor, €10 round-trip shuttle boat from Hydra). If it's sun you're after, Mandraki is best earlier in the day, as the hills around it bring shade in the late afternoon. The private beach is well-maintained, with tidy rows of lounge chairs and umbrellas. Order snacks from the resort bar, or venture to the next-door café (around €20/chair).

Kaminia Castello Beach

To the west of town is the delightful little harbor of Kaminia and the recommended Kodylenia's Taverna (15-minute walk). Just be-yond that you'll find another restaurant and bar called Castello above the small, pebbly Kaminia Castello Beach. While handy, the beach can be overwhelmed by the musical taste of the kids who run the bar, and is often crowded with lots of families. For walking directions, see "Walks," later.

Vlychos Beach

Located past Kaminia, Vlychos is my favorite. Like a little tropical colo-ny, a few dozen thatched umbrellas mark a quiet stretch of pebbly beach (€15 for two chairs and an umbrella). You'll find

other amenities here, including the **$$$ Marina Taverna,** a pleasant place for a meal (open daily for lunch and dinner, +30 2298 052 496), and showers at the beach of the nearby hotel. In peak tourist season, a shuttle boat zips from Hydra to Vlychos twice an hour until sunset (confirm last boat time, €10 round-trip). The 40-minute walk from Hydra to Vlychos is great (described next).

WALKS
Hydra to Kaminia and Vlychos
The walk from Hydra town to the cute cove of Kaminia and the excellent beach at Vlychos (both described above) is one of my favorites. While the walk leads to two beaches, it's perfectly pleasant whether or not you take a dip.

For the easy approach, simply follow the mostly level coastal path that runs west from Hydra town to the villages of Kaminia and Vlychos. As you curve out of Hydra, you'll pass the town's best-preserved windmill, which was reconstructed for the 1957 Sophia Loren film *Boy on a Dolphin.* Up the steps to the windmill is a statue honoring the film that attracted many celebrities to Hydra.

Continuing along the path, after about 15 minutes you'll find yourself at the delightful harbor in **Kaminia,** where two dozen tough little fishing boats jostle within a breakwater. With cafés, a tiny beach, and a good taverna (see "Eating in Hydra," later), this is a wonderful place to watch island life go by.

Follow the water past the harbor where the stone path hugs a hillside, passing above Kaminia Castello Beach. Soon you're all alone with great sea views. Ten minutes or so later, you round a bluff, descend across an Ottoman-style single-arched bridge, and drop into **Vlychos,** with its welcoming little beach.

From Vlychos, an inland trail leads back to upper Hydra, passing donkey-strewn terraced pastures and a small cemetery. Be aware that navigating this trail takes a good mapping app on your phone and some patience for trial and error, since paths aren't signed. Leaving Vlychos, go under the Ottoman Bridge, across the footbridge, and turn right onto the path (30 minutes to reach the top of Hydra's Lignou stairs, lit at night). You could also take this inland road the other way—starting from upper Hydra and staying inland until you finish in Vlychos.

The Hydra-Kaminia High Road: An alternate way to reach Kaminia is via an inland trail. You'll feel your way through upper Hydra town and over the headland, then descend into Kaminia.

Here shabby homes enjoy grand views, tethering off-duty burros seems unnecessary, and island life trudges on, oblivious to tourism. Along the way, look for dry, paved riverbeds, primed for the flash floods that fill village cisterns each winter. (You can also climb all the way up to the remains of Hydra's humble acropolis, topping the hill due west of the harbor.)

From Hydra, start by climbing the Lignou staircase. Near the top, take the turnoff on your right (look for two large telephone poles and an sign high overhead pointing to *Hotel* ΘEANΩ, a.k.a. Hotel Theano). About 200 yards ahead you'll see an ochre-colored grocery store on the left, Hotel Theano on the right, and the acropolis peeking out from above. Follow the road downhill, then down the staircase, staying to the left. After five minutes you'll see a large community cistern and dry riverbed that leads down (right) to Kaminia's harbor.

More Walks and Hikes

Beyond walking to a nearby beach, Hydra is popular for its network of ancient paths that link the island's outlying settlements, churches, and monasteries. Most of the paths are well-maintained and clearly marked. Review the handy signpost map of the island at the harbor (opposite the monastery) for an overview and ask your hotel for a trail map. Serious hikers should buy a detailed hiking map (sold locally), wear sturdy shoes, and carry essentials such as sunscreen, a hat, and water.

Nightlife in Hydra

Locals, proud of the extravagant yachts that flock to the island, like to tell of movie stars who make regular visits. But the island is so quiet that by midnight, all the high rollers seem to be back onboard watching movies. And yet there are plenty of options to keep visitors busy. People enjoy watching films at the town's outdoor cinema or nursing a drink along the harborfront—there are plenty of mellow cocktail bars proudly serving "Paradise in a Glass" for €10.

Pirate Bar sits on a prime spot on the water, at the little lane just past Lignou. For decades, Zeus and his family have served in-

ventive cocktails here—try the Mastiha Mist, made with *mastica*, a sweet resin liqueur. This is a mellow, trendy spot to be late at night (also homemade breakfast and lunch until 17:00, +30 2298 052 711).

Amalour Bar is "the place to fall in love" (or just enjoy wonderful music and good drinks). There's no sea view here—just cool music played at the right volume inside, and tables outside tumbling down a cobbled lane. It's mellow tunes until midnight, and then harder music (just up Tompazi street from the harbor).

Hydronetta Bar, catering to a younger crowd with younger music, offers great sea views from under the "Sofia Loren windmill," with a bunch of romantic tables nestled within the ramparts and cannons plus a small swimming hole described earlier (+30 2298 054 160). Reach it by walking along the coastline past Spilia Beach to the Sunset Restaurant. This and the neighboring Spilia cocktail bar are the most touristy of Hydra's nightlife choices.

Gardenia Cinema is part of a great Greek summer tradition: watching movies in the open air. Hydra's delightful outdoor theater, lovingly run by the local cinema club, is right in the center of town on Oikonomou street; it shows movies in the original language on summer weekends (runs in the height of summer, most nights at 21:00 and 23:00, +30 2298 053 105).

Sleeping in Hydra

Hydra has ample high-quality accommodations. But the prices are high—more expensive than anywhere on the Peloponnese and rivaling those in Athens. Prices max out in the summer (June–mid-Sept). Outside of these times, most accommodations offer discounts—always ask. Longer stays might also garner you a deal. Some cheaper hotels don't provide breakfast, in which case you can eat for about €10 at various cafés around town. Communication can be challenging at a few of the cheaper places (as noted). The only hotel with an elevator is the Leto (though no hotel has more than three stories). Because Hydra has a labyrinthine street plan and most people ignore street names, I list no addresses. To find your way, use my "Hydra Town" map (earlier), and follow signs posted around town. Most accommodations in Hydra close for the winter (typically Nov-Feb, sometimes longer).

$$$$ Hotel Leto is the island's closest thing to a business-class hotel, offering executive service and a professional vibe, 22 well-appointed rooms, and inviting public spaces (small elevator, spa treatments, closed Nov-March, +30 2298 053 385, www.letohydra.gr, info@letohydra.gr).

$$$$ Cotommatae Hotel lives up to its grand pedigree as a former mansion with elegant public areas, a restful garden, and seven carefully styled, palatial rooms. Of all the restored houses in Hydra, this one feels the most luxurious (suites available, closed Dec-Feb, +30 2998 053 873, www.cotommatae.gr, info@cotommatae.gr).

$$$$ Orloff Boutique Hotel is a lovingly maintained historic Hydriot house decorated in the traditional style. All eight rooms in this former Russian count's home have an Old-World-meets-21st-century charm (closed Nov-March, +30 2298 052 564, www.orloff.gr, hotel@orloff.gr).

$$$ Phaedra Hotel rents seven spacious and tasteful rooms in what was once a carpet factory. Helpful owner Hilda takes pride in her hotel, and it shows (family studio, 2-bed 2-bath suite with private veranda, great breakfast, open year-round, +30 2298 053 330, mobile +30 697 221 3111, www.phaedrahotel.com, info@phaedrahotel.com).

$$$ Hotel Miranda, in a sea captain's house from the early 19th century, is filled with an elegant nautical charm that feels almost New England-y—it's more atmospheric than my other listings. Its 12 simple rooms are bright with whitewashed stone  and surround a classy terrace (closed Nov-Feb, +30 2298 053 510, www.mirandahotel.gr, hydra@mirandahotel.gr).

$$$ Hotel Sophia is a quirky little boutique hotel right above the harbor restaurant strip. It's been family-run by matriarchs since 1934; today English-speaking sisters Angelika and Vasiliki, along with daughter Dorothy, are at the helm. The six thoughtfully appointed rooms, while a little tight, are stony-chic, with high ceilings, heavy exposed beams, tiny-but-posh bathrooms, and good windows that manage to block out most of the harbor noise. Three rooms come with private balconies while the others have access to a shared veranda, giving you a royal box seat overlooking all the harbor action (RS%, closed Nov-March, +30 2298 052 313, www.hotelsophia.gr, hydra@hotelsophia.gr). Ask to see the family museum filled with items from the original hotel.

$$$ Mistral Hotel is a well-run place offering 17 rooms in a comfortable, modern-equipped, ivy-covered stone building with a central lounge and a breezy courtyard. It's a fine value at the very quiet top part of town (+30 2298 052 509, www.hotelmistral.gr, info@hotelmistral.gr, Theo and Jenny serve a particularly good breakfast).

$$$ Greco Hotel rents 16 rooms set above one of the shadiest, lushest gardens in town. It's where lovely owner Maria Keramidas serves a homemade buffet breakfast...and where you'll be tempted to just relax and do nothing all afternoon (closed Nov-March, +30 2298 053 200, www.grecohotel.gr, grecohotelhydra@gmail.com; Maria speaks little English, but son Alkis is there to help).

$$ Ippokampos Hotel has 16 pleasant rooms around a cocktail-bar courtyard. The four top-floor rooms open right onto a seaview patio. The suite is a few notches up in quality and amenities, with its own private veranda (bar closes at 22:00, closed Nov-March, +30 2298 053 453, www.ippokampos.com, ippo@ippokampos.com, Sotiris and Voula).

$$ Alkionides Pension offers 10 smartly renovated rooms around a beautiful and relaxing courtyard, and is buried in Hydra's back lanes (apartment, breakfast extra, +30 2298 054 055, mobile +30 697 741 0460, www.alkionidespension.com, info@alkionidespension.com, Kofitsas family).

$$ Nereids Guest House is a bit farther from the harbor than my other listings, but the nine stony rooms offer good atmosphere and space for the price (no breakfast, two minutes past Greco Hotel, +30 2298 052 875, www.nereids-hydra.com, nereids@otenet.gr).

$$ Pension Achilleas rents 15 decent rooms in an old mansion with a relaxing courtyard terrace and a gorgeous seaview roof patio. Request one of the upstairs rooms (they're brighter), and try to land one with a balcony (apartment, no breakfast, +30 2298 052 050, www.achilleaspension.gr, kofitsas@otenet.gr, Demitris speaks only a little English, but there's usually someone else around to help).

$$ Spalieri's Dhomatia has five rooms in a cheery home with a welcoming garden courtyard. The units, though simple, are spacious. Staying with the Spalieri family provides a homier experience than at most other places in town (breakfast extra, on the corner next to Pension Achilleas, +30 2298 052 894, mobile +30 694 414 1977, mspalieri@gmail.com, minimal English).

$ Pension Erofili is a reliable budget standby in the heart of town, renting 12 basic but tasteful rooms just off (or over) a relaxing little courtyard—ask for one of the brighter rooms above the ground floor (RS%, apartment, no breakfast, +30 2298 054 049, mobile +30 697 768 8487, www.pensionerofili.gr, pensionerofili@yahoo.gr, George and Irene).

Eating in Hydra

There are dozens of places to eat, offering everything from humble gyros to slick modern-Mediterranean cuisine. Harbor views come with higher prices; places farther inland typically offer better value.

IN HYDRA TOWN

$$$$ Psaropoula Restaurant, at the southwest corner of the harbor, fills a top-floor terrace in a prime spot overlooking all the action. They specialize in seafood but also have pasta and meat dishes. Ask to see what's cooking in the kitchen, or peek inside their drawers full of fresh fish to see what looks good (daily 12:00-24:00, reservations smart in summer—especially for view tables, +30 2298 052 573, www.psaropoula.org).

$$$ Veranda Restaurant, perched on a terrace with fine views over the town and harbor, wins the best ambience award. It's great on a summer evening; enjoy a cold drink before selecting from pasta served a dozen different ways, various seafood dishes, and a creative assortment of salads (better-than-average wine list, daily 18:00-late, halfway up the steep steps on Sahini lane or along the Lignou steps, reservations smart in summer, +30 2298 052 259, Andreas and Kostas, www.hydra.com.gr/veranda-restaurant).

$$$ I Orea Hydra (Η Ωραία Ύδρα) is a serious seafood restaurant highly regarded by locals for their modern approach to Greek cuisine (daily 13:00-17:00 & 19:30-23:30, closed Nov, try to reserve one of the balcony tables for an even more romantic experience, +30 2298 052 556).

$$$ Xeri Elia (Douskos Taverna) fills a leafy courtyard just beyond the tourist zone. They serve a variety of hearty salads, simple pasta dishes, and standard taverna fare to hungry travelers (daily 12:00-16:00 & 18:00-24:00, closed Nov, +30 2298 052 886).

$$$ At Ostria Restaurant, handwritten menus in spiral-bound notebooks look more like grocery lists than dinner options, making it feel as though you're eating in a local's dining room. In this family-run taverna known for authentic food at reasonable prices, no-nonsense Tassoula runs the show while laid-back Stathis does the cooking—if you're lucky he'll be preparing freshly caught calamari, his specialty (daily 11:00-15:00 & 19:00-23:00, +30 2298 054 077).

$$$ Kryfo Limani (Κρυφό Λιμάνι—The Secret Port) is a vine-covered hideaway with a variety of typical taverna staples such as lamb stew, *keftedes* (meatballs), and souvlaki (daily 18:30-23:00, closed Nov, +30 2298 052 585).

$$ Taverna Gitoniko has a delightful rooftop garden and serves big portions of simple fare. Quality can be variable, but when it's good, it's like a home-cooked meal (daily 12:00-24:00, on Spilios Haramis street, +30 2298 053 615).

$$$$ Giasemi (Γιασεμί), across from the Greco Hotel, elegantly serves taverna-style grilled meats and seafood dishes on a covered terrace away from the main streets (daily 18:00-24:00, +30 2298 052 221).

Tavernas on Miaouli Street: This street leading up from the port (to the left of the monastery bell tower) is crammed with appealing little **$$-$$$** tavernas that jostle for your attention with outdoor seating and good food.

Souvlaki: For a quick, cheap meal, souvlaki is your best bet. For a civilized, sit-down souvlaki experience, drop by **$ Onion Souvlaki** (Και Κρεμμύδι), a cute eatery filling a charming corner up Tompazi street, across from Amalour Bar.

Cafés on the Harbor: Enjoy the scene as you nurse a drink here—drivers rolling their pushcarts, donkeys sneezing, taxi-boat drivers haggling, big boats coming and going. For a meal, try **$$$ Café Isalos** ("Waterline"), with a fun menu of light bites, including salads, sandwiches, pastas, and pizzas. In the early evening, watch for yachts trying to dock; some are driven by pros and others aren't, providing a comedic scene of naval inexperience.

Dessert: Flora's Pastry Shop is a hardworking little bakery cranking out the best pastries on the island. Flora has delightful tables that overlook Votsi Square, just behind the monastery. She sells all the traditional local sweets, including honey treats such as baklava. Many of her ingredients come from her farm on the nearby island of Dokos (daily 7:00-23:00).

EATING NEAR HYDRA, IN KAMINIA

A great way to cap your Hydra day is to follow the coastal path to the rustic and picturesque village of Kaminia, which hides behind the headland from Hydra. Kaminia's pocket-size harbor shelters the community's fishing boats. Here, with a glass of ouzo and some munchies, as the sun slowly sinks into the sea and boats become silhouettes, you can drink to the beauties of a Greek isle escape. Consider combining dinner with a late-afternoon stroll along the seafront (see "Walks—Hydra to Kaminia and Vlychos," earlier).

$$$ Kodylenia's Taverna is perched on a bluff just over the Kaminia harbor. With my favorite irresistible dinner views on Hydra, this scenic spot lets you watch the sun dip gently into the Saronic Gulf, with Kaminia's adorable port in the foreground. Owner Dimitris takes his own boat out early in the morning to buy the day's best catch directly from the fishermen. For meals, you can sit out on the shady covered side terrace above the harbor—check the chalkboard to see what's freshest today. For drinks, sit out front on the porch. Relax and take in a sea busy with water taxis, ferries that connect this oasis with Athens, old freighters—like castles of rust—lumbering slowly along the horizon, and cruise

ships anchored as if they haven't moved in weeks (visit their display case to see what's cooking, daily 12:00-23:30, may close earlier off-season, closed mid-Nov-Jan, +30 2298 053 520).

Hydra Connections

Note that there are no direct ferry routes between Hydra and Mykonos or Santorini—to reach either from Hydra you'll first backtrack to Piraeus before continuing to your final destination. For general information on Greece's ferry network, including tips on looking up schedules and buying tickets, see the Practicalities chapter.

GETTING BETWEEN ATHENS AND HYDRA

Hydra is easily reached from Athens' port at Piraeus. Your main option is to take a **Hellenic Seaways** ferry (either the "Flying Dolphin" hydrofoil or the slightly larger "Flying Cat" catamaran; 6-8/day June-Sept, 4/day Oct-May, 1.5-2 hours). **Alpha Lines'** "Speed-cat" also makes the trip (2/day June-Sept, 1/day Oct-May, 1.5-2 hours). If traveling to Hydra from Athens, then on to the Peloponnese, note that it's not necessary to return to Athens to pick up a car. You can go by ferry from Athens to Hydra, then continue by ferry from Hydra to Ermioni on the coast of the Peloponnese, where you can pick up a rental car (described later).

When to Buy Tickets: It's wise to book in advance (at least a week ahead in summer). Boats can sell out during summer weekends, when they're packed with Athenians headed to or from their Hydra getaway. Outside of summer, tickets should be available up to a day or two in advance.

Where to Buy Tickets: It's easiest to book online via **Hellenic Seaways** (www.hellenicseaways.gr) or **Alpha Lines** (www.alphalines.gr). There are a few ways to get your actual ticket. You can check in online (anytime between 30 minutes and 48 hours before departure) and have an eticket sent to you. Or, you can pick up a paper ticket at a ferry company ticket office, or at any travel agency.

It's also possible to buy a ticket in person after you arrive in Greece (tickets sold for the same price at any travel agency). Check the cancellation policy before buying your ticket.

In Hydra you can buy tickets at the **Hellenic Seaways office,** just down an alley near the harbor (long hours daily in summer, +30 2298 054 007 or +30 2298 053 812) or at the Akliros agency—affiliated with **Alpha Lines**—on Oikonomou street (daily 10:00-17:00, +30 2298 052 020).

Boat Cancellations: Boats can be delayed, or even canceled, if the weather's bad enough (mostly a concern in off-season). For more advice on navigating the Greek ferry system, see "Transportation—Boats," in the Practicalities chapter.

GETTING BETWEEN HYDRA AND THE PELOPONNESE

You have several options for connecting Hydra and the Peloponnese via several spots on the coast of the peninsula: Metochi, Ermioni, or Tolo. Drivers can leave their cars in long-term parking at either Metochi (frequent crossings to Hydra on small passenger boats, just show up) or Ermioni (larger, less-frequent ferries, can be booked in advance). You can also connect Nafplio and Ermioni by public transportation (with some effort) or pick up a rental car in Ermioni to begin a tour of the Peloponnese. Another option is to day-trip from Tolo (near Nafplio) to Hydra.

Metochi (drivers only): Metochi is the closest spot on the mainland to Hydra (under 2 hours by car from Nafplio, 3 hours from Athens). It's at the end of a dirt road with nothing there except a couple of ticket stands and a small boat pier. You can park on the road or in the small dirt lot for free, or use the pay lot (around €5/day). From Metochi, **Freedom Boats** (+30 694 732 5263, www.hydralines.gr) sail to Hydra quickly and frequently  (€7.50, about hourly in summer, less frequent in spring and fall, 20-30 minutes, no boats Jan-March). Another option is a **water taxi** (these may be waiting in Metochi, otherwise call Hydra's sea-taxi service at +30 2298 053 690, about €50 but confirm up front).

Ermioni (drivers and those without cars): Ermioni (a.k.a. Hermioni) is an actual town with some amenities, and is a little closer to Nafplio (1.5 hours). It's a 25-minute boat ride between Ermioni and Hydra on a **Hellenic Seaways** ferry (€11.50, 2-3/day in summer, fewer off-season, www.hellenicseaways.gr).

If you're visiting Hydra early in your trip and then continuing to the Peloponnese, a good plan is to ride the ferry from Athens to Hydra, then take the ferry from Hydra to Ermioni, where you can rent a car (try Pop's Car, www.popscar.gr, a five-minute walk from the ferry dock, ask about fee for dropping the car in Athens or at

HYDRA

the airport; you can also ask your Hydra hotelier to help with car rental).

Without a car, you can connect Ermioni and Nafplio by taxi and bus, though this is more complicated than it should be (see "Nafplio Connections" on page 257).

Tolo, near Nafplio (day-trippers only): **Pegasus Tours** operates an excursion boat from the port at Tolo, near Nafplio, but it runs only a few times a week, can be canceled on short notice (if not enough passengers—mainly off-season), and requires an early-morning (though short) bus ride. Stopping in both Spetses and Hydra, it's a good option only for travelers without a car who can't devote an overnight to Hydra (€38, 3-4 boats/week July-mid-Sept, 2/week May-June and mid-Sept-Oct, some sailings March-April, +30 2752 059 430, www.pegasus-cruises.gr, easiest to book through Stavropoulos Tours in central Nafplio—see the Nafplio chapter).

MYKONOS

Μύκονος

At its heart, Mykonos (MEE-koh-nohs) is the very picture of the perfect Greek island town: a seafront village crouched behind a sandy harbor, thickly layered with blinding white stucco, bright blue trim, and purple bougainvillea. (Thank goodness for all that color; otherwise, this island—one of Greece's driest—would be various shades of dull brown.) On a ridge over town stretches a trademark row of windmills, overlooking a tidy embankment so pretty they call it "Little Venice."

Mykonos' Old Town seems made for exploring. Each picture-perfect lane is slathered with a thick layer of stucco, giving the place a marshmallow-village vibe. All that white is the perfect contrast to the bright blue sky and the vivid trim. Sometimes described as "Cubist" for its irregular jostle of angular rooflines, Mykonos' townscape is a photographer's delight. Enjoy getting lost, then found again.

While Mykonos was once a sleepy, backwater fishing village, those days are a faint memory. Today's Mykonos is easily one of the most expensive, most exclusive places in Greece. Prices are stunningly high here, and the island is crammed through the summer season (especially in August). As one of the Mediterranean's premier party destinations, the entire Old Town throbs with a cacophony of nightclub beats well into the wee hours. This is fun if you're seeking late-night activity...but otherwise, it can be miserable. If you're seeking a peaceful getaway, time your visit for shoulder season—May or October—when suitable beach weather is still likely, but the town is less crowded, less

Mykonos Island

Aegean Sea

To Piraeus

MERCHIAS

AGIOS STEFANOS
TOURLOS
NEW PORT
FTELIA
OLD PORT
ANO MERA
MYKONOS TOWN
AIRPORT
KALAFATI
KAPARI
PLATIS GIALOS
AGRARI
ELIA
AGIOS IOANNIS
ORNOS
PSAROU
SUPER PARADISE
PARAGA
PARADISE

2 Kilometers
2 Miles

To Delos

To Paros,
Santorini & Crete

┄┄┄ Shuttle Boat
——— Roads
⌒ Beaches

noisy (except on weekends), and less expensive. On October 1, hotels drop their prices in half. And in winter (around Nov-March), the island essentially shuts down, as many restaurants and hotels close for the season.

Whenever you visit, find ways to enjoy the traditional soul of Mykonos. If you grow tired of fashionistas and high-end boutiques, climb just a block or two in either direction from the core of town, and you'll enter more-authentic neighborhoods relatively untrampled by tourism. Fishermen still hang out on the benches by the harbor, wearing their traditional caps (Mykonian men are famous among Greeks for their baldness).

The island's arid but idyllic terrain, with lots of hidden coves, is a favorite backdrop for filmmakers *(Shirley Valentine, Mamma Mia!, The Bourne Identity, Before Midnight).* A string of inviting beaches lines up on the sandy, pebbly coves along the jagged south coast—each with a personality of its own, and all reachable by a cheap and easy bus ride from town.

For armchair historians, the highlight here is a 30-minute boat trip to the island of Delos—one of the Greek islands' top sites, with the remains of important ancient temples honoring the birthplace of the twin gods Apollo and Artemis. Delos was a pilgrimage site for believers who came from all over to worship this "birthplace of light." Judging by the present-day sun worshippers who scramble for the best patch of sand on Mykonos each summer, things haven't changed much.

PLANNING YOUR TIME

Mykonos merits at least a full day and two overnights; more time lets you squeeze in more beaches. To avoid crowds, consider visiting outside of peak season.

On a short visit, begin with my self-guided town walk to get your bearings. Historians will want to finish the walk in time to side-trip to Delos (easy 30-minute boat trip each way, figure 3-4 hours round-trip), while vacationers can hop a bus to one of Mykonos' beaches in the afternoon. Dip into any museums that interest you, or enjoy the sunset from a beach or while sipping a cocktail near the Little Venice zone, then have a late dinner.

Orientation to Mykonos

Mykonos' main town is called Chora (or Hora, Χώρα; roughly "village"), but it's often referred to as "Mykonos town."

Mykonos town is the main point of entry for the island. The Old Town clusters around the south end of the Old Port—the harbor area bookended by two piers. To the north is the Old Port pier and bus stop, and to the southwest is the pier for boats to Delos and the Sea Bus to the New Port, where most ferries and cruise ships arrive. Squeezed between the harbor and the main road (passing above town on the gentle hill) is the Old Town's tight maze of whitewashed lanes.

To get your bearings, look at a map and notice that three "main" roads (barely wide enough for a moped) form a U-shaped circuit facing the harbor: Kouzi Georgouli, Enoplon Dinameon, and Matogianni. While some streets have names, others don't, and in any case, locals never use them—they just know where things are. If you can't find something, ask.

You'll find travel agencies, ATMs, launderettes with drop-off service, minimarkets, pharmacies, and other helpful services scattered around the Old Town. For the highest concentration of services (and tattoo parlors), head for the area around the Fabrika bus station.

Tourist Information: Mykonos doesn't have a TI. Hoteliers, travel agents, and other friendly locals can answer basic questions. Look for town maps, or consult www.mykonos.gr, the island's official website.

Private Guide: Excellent certified local guide **Antonis Pothitos** enjoys introducing visitors to the hidden nooks and crannies of Mykonos. In addition to town walks and tours of the Delos

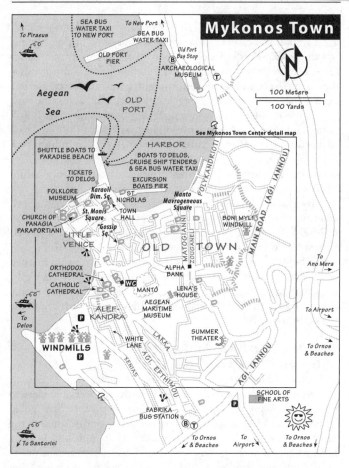

archaeological site, he enjoys leading a 2.5-hour "Food on Foot" walk with tasting stops (4-person minimum, contact Antonis for prices, +30 693 660 6640, www.delosguide.com, antonis@home-mail.com).

ARRIVAL ON MYKONOS

At the port and airport, sign-toting hotel representatives wait to transfer guests into town. To make it easy, ask your hotel in advance about this option.

By Boat: Most travelers coming by boat arrive at the **New Port,** a mile north of the Old Town, at the far end of the bay. (This serves ships from Piraeus and Santorini, as well as many cruise ships.) You have several options for getting to the Old Town: Easy and pleasant, the **Mykonos Sea Bus** runs between the New Port and Mykonos town (may stop at the Old Port pier en route; €2, 1-2/

MYKONOS

hour, runs 7:00-23:00, +30 2289 028 603, www.mykonos-seabus.gr). By land, you can take a taxi (€20-25 one-way) or ride a public bus to the Old Port bus stop (2/hour, €1.80). Cruisers may be offered a shuttle bus. In a pinch, you could walk for 25 dreary minutes along the coast into town (turn right, follow the water, and just keep going—you can see the gaggle of white houses across the bay).

A few smaller, passenger-only ferries from other islands dock at the **Old Port Pier**—just a five-minute walk from the Old Town harborfront. And if your cruise ship is tendered, you'll disembark at the pier at the opposite end of the harbor (where boats to Delos come and go). Just walk down the pier and you're at the harbor (there's a public WC on the right, along the water).

By Plane: Mykonos is well connected by air to Athens, as well as to many other European cities (airport code: JMK, +30 2289 022 327). The small airport sits just two miles outside town, easily connected by a short but pricey taxi ride (€15-20). Infrequent public buses are worthwhile only if a bus happens to be there when you arrive; ask the driver when the bus is departing. If leaving by air, note that there are separate check-in terminals for international departures (on the right) and domestic flights (on the left); both use the same arrivals area.

GETTING AROUND MYKONOS

Mykonos is a fun and easy island to explore. For bus station/stops and taxi stand locations, see the "Mykonos Town" map, earlier.

By Bus: Mykonos' bus network easily connects travelers to the island's many fine beaches (and is much cheaper than going by taxi). And because this is a party island, buses run late into the night in peak season. Schedules are posted at stops and in most hotel reception areas; tickets cost around €2—buy from the driver or (in Mykonos town) at the ticket kiosk at the Fabrika bus station (www.mykonosbus.com).

In town, the **Fabrika bus station** (serving beaches on the south side of the island) is a 10-minute walk up from the harbor, just under the main ring road. The **Old Port stop** (serving the eastern half of the island) is at the northeast edge of the Old Town, along the pier below the Archaeological Museum (look for the clearly marked ramp along the beach near the old harbor).

By Taxi: There are only about 30 cabs for the entire island, and they are extremely expensive (with fixed rather than metered prices). No cars are allowed in Mykonos town, so you'll wait for a taxi at one of two places: the stand behind the large building labeled *Remezzo* (behind the Archaeological Museum at the north end of town), or at the Fabrika bus stop (see above).

By Boat: Efficient water taxis shuttle beachgoers along the coast of the island. While most depart from outside Mykonos town, a direct boat departs from the Old Port to Paradise beach (€10, 2/hour, see "Beaches," later).

By Motorized Scooter or All-Terrain Vehicle (ATV): If I were renting a scooter or an ATV on a Greek isle, I'd do it on Mykonos—where the roads are not too heavily trafficked (you'll pass more fellow scooters and ATVs than cars), and an appealing variety of idyllic beaches are a short ride away. Travel agencies all over town rent both types of wheels for reasonable all-day rates (€30-50/day for a scooter or an ATV, some places may charge €7-10/day extra for insurance, rates depend on time of year). Two people can ride one machine, and both should ask for helmets.

Once on the road, be especially careful when turning: Tourists are notorious for renting a scooter or an ATV, overestimating their abilities, and denting someone's fender...or worse. That said, and keeping in mind the inherent risks, this can be an affordable, efficient, and memorably fun way to connect distant beaches. On a slow-moving ATV, figure 15-20 minutes from Mykonos town to most of the beaches I list (Super Paradise is the farthest). Find rental details under "Getting to the Beaches," later.

By Car: You can rent a car for as little as €40 per day; look for car-rental signs at several agencies around town—especially near the Fabrika bus station—and negotiate a good bargain if you're here outside peak season. The island is less satisfying to explore by car than Santorini—it's basically similar beaches and remote villages.

Mykonos Walk

The core of town is literally a maze, designed by Mykonians centuries ago to discourage would-be invaders from finding their way. That tactic also works on today's tourists. But I can think of few places where getting lost is so enjoyable.

This self-guided walk is designed to orient you to Mykonos' main landmarks in about 1.5 hours. Even if you follow my directions to a T and use my map, be

Mykonos Town Center

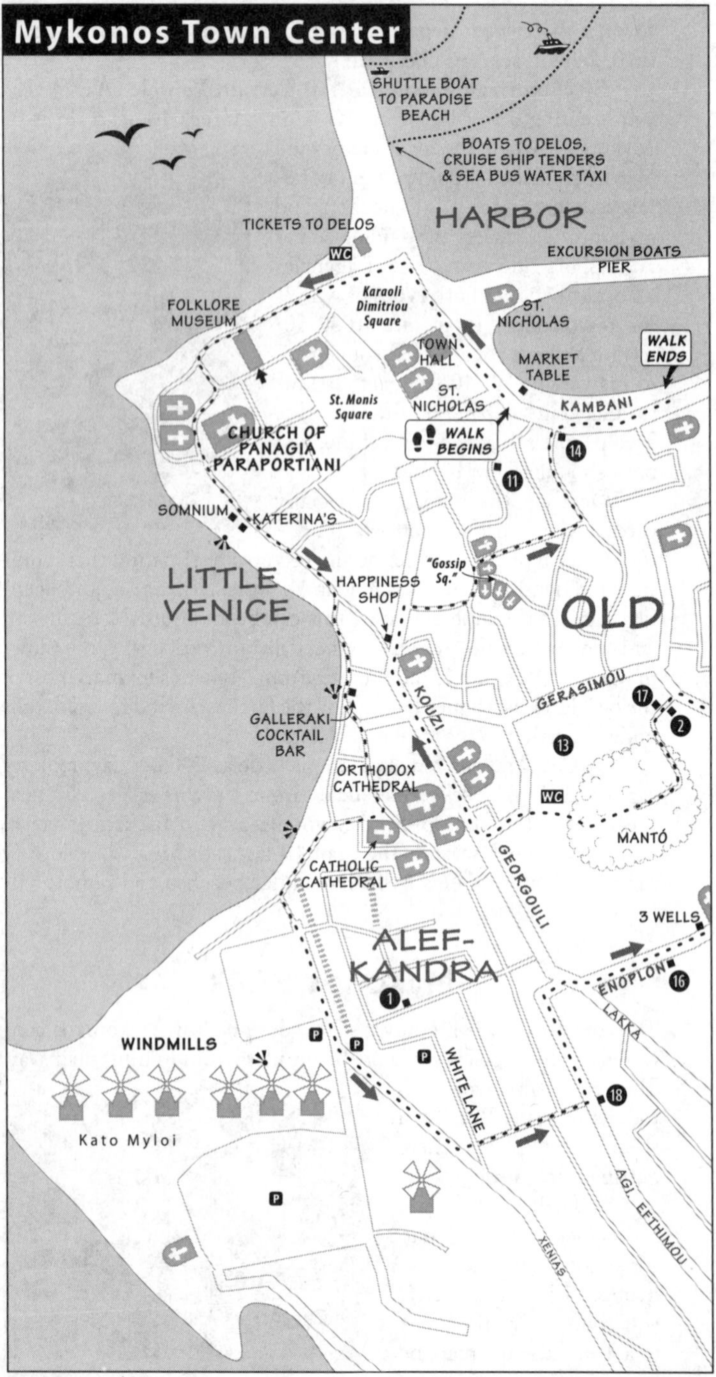

SHUTTLE BOAT
TO PARADISE
BEACH

BOATS TO DELOS,
CRUISE SHIP TENDERS
& SEA BUS WATER TAXI

HARBOR

TICKETS TO DELOS

WC

EXCURSION BOATS
PIER

Karaoli
Dimitriou
Square

WALK
ENDS

FOLKLORE
MUSEUM

TOWN
HALL

ST.
NICHOLAS

ST. Monis Square

ST.
NICHOLAS

MARKET
TABLE

KAMBANI

CHURCH OF PANAGIA
PARAPORTIANI

WALK
BEGINS

11

14

SOMNIUM

KATERINA'S

LITTLE
VENICE

HAPPINESS
SHOP

"Gossip
Sq."

OLD

KOUZ

GERASIMOU

17

2

GALLERAKI
COCKTAIL
BAR

13

ORTHODOX
CATHEDRAL

WC

MANTÓ

CATHOLIC
CATHEDRAL

GEORGOULI

ALEF-
KANDRA

3 WELLS

1

ENOPLON

16

LAKKA

WINDMILLS

P

P

P

WHITE LANE

18

Kato Myloi

AGI. EFTHIMOU

P

YENIAS

MYKONOS

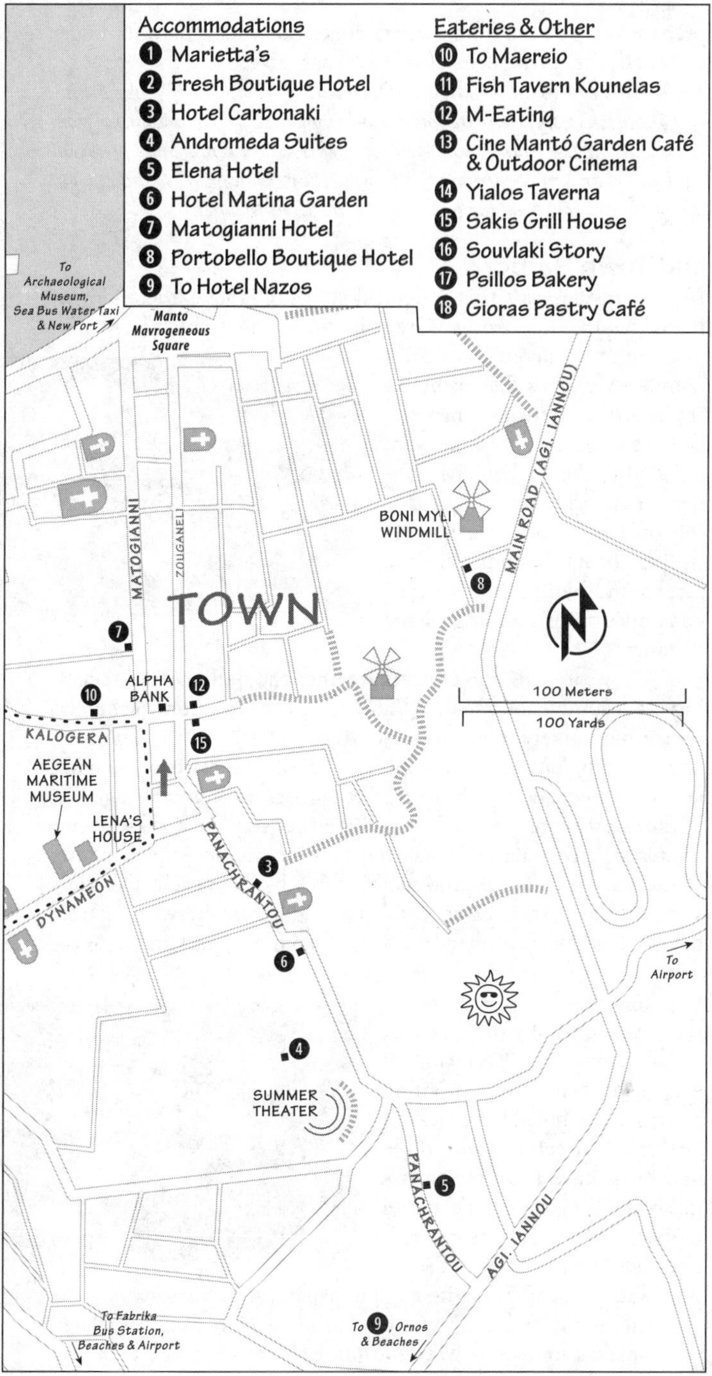

Accommodations
1. Marietta's
2. Fresh Boutique Hotel
3. Hotel Carbonaki
4. Andromeda Suites
5. Elena Hotel
6. Hotel Matina Garden
7. Matogianni Hotel
8. Portobello Boutique Hotel
9. To Hotel Nazos

Eateries & Other
10. To Maereio
11. Fish Tavern Kounelas
12. M-Eating
13. Cine Mantó Garden Café & Outdoor Cinema
14. Yialos Taverna
15. Sakis Grill House
16. Souvlaki Story
17. Psillos Bakery
18. Gioras Pastry Café

To Archaeological Museum, Sea Bus Water Taxi & New Port

Manto Mavrogeneous Square

MATOGIANNI

ZOUGANELI

TOWN

BONI MYLI WINDMILL

MAIN ROAD (AGI. IANNOU)

100 Meters

100 Yards

ALPHA BANK

KALOGERA

AEGEAN MARITIME MUSEUM

LENA'S HOUSE

DYNAMEON

PANACHRANTOU

To Airport

SUMMER THEATER

PANACHRANTOU

AGI. IANNOU

To Fabrika Bus Station, Beaches & Airport

To 9, Ornos & Beaches

MYKONOS

prepared to get lost from time to time. But with this walk under your belt, the town becomes more manageable.

• *Our walk begins at the harbor, in the heart of Mykonos. If you're arriving on a cruise-ship tender, you'll land right here; if you're coming from elsewhere on the island, you can't miss this sandy centerpiece of town. Position yourself near the marble fish-washing table/market stalls, right along the harbor, near the blue-domed church at the pier.*

Old Town Harbor

Mykonians describe this delightful swath of land as their "downtown." Unlike many other Greek island towns—which have built up bulky concrete embankments—Mykonos has kept its traditional waterfront, where the cobbles taper into a sandy beach, preserving the Mykonians' connection to the Aegean. Glancing offshore, you'll see humble fishing boats bobbing in the foreground, with 2,000-passenger cruise ships looming in the distance.

A row of cafés and restaurants lines the harborfront, including the recommended Yialos (Γιαλός; near the red-domed church). You're most likely to catch a few Mykonians (or in-the-know expats) hanging out here in the morning. Pull up a rustic table, nurse an iced coffee, and watch the tide of tourists wash over village life. Mykonians appreciate cafés like these that stay open through the winter to cater to natives (since most businesses close up shop after cruise season ends). At the marble table by the beach, fisherfolk sort and clean their catch each morning (while stray cats gather below). Nearby, old-timers and kids alike toss fishing lines into the water.

You may even see one of the resident **pelicans**—Petros, Nikolas, or Irini. Ever since a local fisherman found an ailing pelican and nursed it back to health a half-century ago, these odd birds have been the town's mascots. They hang out at the harbor, or you may see them elsewhere in town, as well—always surrounded by an entourage of paparazzi tourists.

At the far end of this sandy harbor (which we'll visit later) is the piazza known as **Manto Square.** This is marked by a bust of Manto Mavrogenous (1796-1848), a heroine of the Greek War of Independence. A wealthy aristocrat of Mykonian heritage, she spent her fortune supplying Greek forces in a battle against their Ottoman rulers. Mavrogenous—who, despite her contributions, was denied a Greek pension—ended her life destitute on the island of Paros, never regretting the sacrifices she made for Greece's freedom. Today locals still celebrate her brave spirit. Just beyond the square is the town's small, free, mostly sandy beach—but with far better options nearby, it's nothing to get excited about.

• *Turn with the water on your right, and walk about 50 yards to the little, blue-domed...*

Church of St. Nicholas (Agios Nikolakis)

This is one of an estimated 90 small churches that dot the Old Town of Mykonos (with hundreds more scattered all over the is-

land). Why so many? First, while these belong to the Greek Orthodox Church, each one was built by, and is still maintained by, a private local family—usually to honor a namesake saint. Having a chapel is a matter of familial pride. On that saint's feast day, the family invites a priest to preside over a service here, followed by a big party to which the entire community is invited. (On the day of a popular saint, many families host dueling parties.) Chapels were often built to give thanks for the safe return of a relative—and in this seafaring town, it was often necessary.

This harborfront location—which was originally on its own little island, connected by a bridge—makes sense for St. Nicholas, the patron saint of sailors and fishermen. In fact, St. Nicholas is so important that there are two churches dedicated to him in the same area: This one is officially "St. Nicholas of the Chain"—named for the chain that was once pulled across the mouth of the harbor from here in times of enemy threat. And the red-domed church just around the harbor is "St. Nicholas of the Wind," since it faces into the prevailing northerly winds.

Step inside this votive chapel to see a container of lit candles. Many local fishermen still light a candle here each morning before heading out to sea. Originally, each chapel also served as a family mausoleum, where departed relatives were interred. This unhygienic practice ended in the 18th century, when Mykonos established a cemetery just outside town. But a loophole allows locals to dig up a loved one's remains five years after burial and reinter them in the family chapel. Notice the plaques on the walls and floor marking the final resting places of several Mykonians. The one on the left wall just inside the door is significant: It marks the remains of Captain Petros I. Drakopolos, who—the plaque explains—was executed by Germans during the Nazi occupation in September 1944. (This local hero is the namesake of the first pelican mascot of Mykonos.)

• *Head back outside.*

Town Hall and Delos Pier

The big, boxy building facing St. Nicholas is the **Town Hall** (labeled in Greek and English), with the only red terra-cotta roof on the island. This was built in 1780, during a brief period of Russian occupation, when Czarina Catherine the Great sent a governor to rule over the island. (St. Nicholas was built at the same time.) The building's few marble pillars are most likely scavenged from the ancient ruins on the nearby isle of Delos, as is

the well-worn marble bench under its porch. In general, anytime you see irregular bits and pieces of marble incorporated into Mykonos buildings (thresholds, window sills, and so on), they probably came from Delos.

Now walk with the harbor on your right. Soon you'll spot the ticket kiosk for boat trips to the ancient site at Delos (more on that in a moment). Just behind that is the town dumpster and trash compactor—convenient for shipping garbage to the mainland. And just after that you'll see some handy pay WCs.

Continue along the embankment. Straight ahead, on the horizon, is the isle of **Delos**—said to be the birthplace of the god Apollo, and home of one of the ancient world's most important sites. In antiquity, this was a busy commercial port and financial center, and today it contains some fascinating ruins. Nearby, you will likely also see a cruise ship, which is fitting. In the early days of cruising—the 1920s—ships came to this area for the ruins at uninhabited Delos, and then made a pit stop on Mykonos—which slowly became a tourist destination in its own right. The town's popularity boomed in the 1950s, when celebrities discovered its allure; and again in the 1980s, when it became a mecca for gay tourists; and again in the 2000s, with the surge in cruising. Today Mykonos is arguably Greece's most popular island.

• *Reaching the end of the embankment, hook left and walk uphill to the top of the little bluff. You are in the heart of the...*

Old Venetian Quarter

This strategic spit of land, with visibility over the water in three directions, has always been an important point in Mykonos—in ancient times, this was the site of its acropolis. Like many other Greek islands, Mykonos fell under Venetian rule after the Fourth Crusade (early 13th century). The Venetians fortified this point, enclosing the entire peninsula with a stout fortress that contained some 4,000 people. While that fortress is long gone, soon we'll walk through tight lanes that make it easy to imagine those crowded conditions.

But first, turn your attention to the giant melting-marshmallow building on your right—the **Church of Panagia Paraportiani.**

This striking architectural oddity is actually a hodge-podge of five small chapels draped together in a thick layer of whitewashed stucco. The four chapels at the base are interconnected; the chapel on top is separate and gives its name to the entire complex: "Panagia" refers to St. Mary—who, according to Byzantine tradition, was often the guardian at the entrance to a town—and "Paraportiani" marks the secondary *(para)* gate *(port)* in the Venetian fortress complex. While the interior is usually closed, you may occasionally find one of the chapels open, the small space filled with the rich aroma of incense.

Now head down the tight lane just behind the church, turning left at the sign for *Kastro's Bar-Restaurant.* The houses on the right side of this street belonged to local sea captains. Here in the fickle Aegean, seafarers might be part-time merchants and traders, and part-time pirates, depending on the tenor of the times. These houses were actually the fortified outer seawall of the Venetian fortress.

A few doors down on the right, peek into the **Somnium shop,** which sells upscale medieval kitsch and offers a peek at an authentic old house interior. Notice the walls are made of heavy local granite and mica stone, with wooden beams mixed in. This wood—imported from the mainland to this nearly treeless island—gave some flex to buildings and thus made them earthquake resistant. The window at the far (seaward) end was added later; originally this was a solid chunk of the city wall, and the only opening was a small passage at the base that allowed the captain to come and go more easily.

The house next to Somnium, **Katerina's,** is named for the first female sea captain from Mykonos, Katerinas Xidaki (you can see old photos of her just inside the door...and may see her in the flesh hanging out inside).

Continue downhill on this narrow lane, keeping right at the fork. You'll pass a row of shops, bars, and restaurants. Peek through the ones on the right to see the windows overlooking the water.

When you reach the busy little intersection, turn right toward the water. When you reach the water, turn left and walk along the bar tables perched just above the

seawall. At the end of this row, look back along the waterline for a wonderful view of the area called **"Little Venice"** (Mikri Venetia). You'll see how the formerly fortified seawall is today punctuated with windows and brightly painted wooden balconies. The name, inspired by the builders of that original wall, conjures comparisons with the many fine palazzos that rise up from Venice's Grand Canal. Looking the other way, you'll enjoy fine views of the town's trademark windmills (we're heading up there soon). This scenic stretch is a favorite vantage for enjoying the sunset over a pricey cocktail; pick a spot to reserve for tonight.

• *Turn with your back to the water and, facing Galleraki Cocktail Bar, walk up past the remaining few café tables, then turn right down the little lane. Follow this until you pop out at a tiny square with a big bell tower.*

Alefkandra Neighborhood

The church on your left, with the square bell tower, is Mykonos' **Greek Orthodox cathedral** (or "metropolitan" church). And straight ahead of you is the side of the local **Catholic cathedral.** Jog to the right, around to the front door of the Catholic church (facing the water). While the Venetians left their mark with their fortress, their cultural legacy is minimal. This small chapel was built by the only Catholic family on Mykonos—and so, as the only Catholic church, it's the default cathedral.

Services are posted to the left of the door; a priest who serves the surrounding islands (especially Tinos, with a much larger Catholic population) comes here periodically to worship. Step inside to see the architectural mix of Catholic (with depictions of the Virgin Mary) and Orthodox (the candle reservoir).

Continue past the Catholic church toward the water. The small, dry channel here was once a gushing stream. It gave the Alefkandra neighborhood its name: *lefkos* means "whiten," and this stream was where locals would launder—or whiten—their textiles. Follow this channel to the waterfront, where again you enjoy views to Little Venice (right) and the windmills (left).

• *Now turn left and climb up to those windmills. You can either use the ramp (step over the parking barrier) or the grand, white staircase— where celebrities of the 1950s and 1960s famously posed, with the iconic windmills in the background, helping to put Mykonos on the map.*

Windmills

Mykonos is infamously windy, and Mykonians have special names for the different winds that blow through: "the bell ringer," "the chair thrower," and "the  unseater of horsemen." Today, locals are most concerned when the wind is bad enough to prevent cruise ships from docking or the Delos excursion boats from running.

This ridge—called **Kato Myloi**—is perfectly positioned to catch both northerly and southerly winds—which, combined, blow nine days out of ten. You'll see six intact windmills, one of which was reconstructed relatively recently. As in many Greek island towns, Mykonos' old-fashioned windmills harnessed this natural power in order to grind grain to supply its ships. Notice how the windmills are strategically located over the water, making it easy to load up ships. Traditionally, the windmills were owned not by individuals but by little committees made up of five different factions: priests, merchants, millers, bankers, and carpenters. While there's nothing to see inside these buildings, they make for a fine photo op and offer great views over town. If you'd like to enter a windmill, you'll need to head to the opposite (east) end of the Old Town, where the Boni Myli windmill is sometimes open to visitors (ask at the Folklore Museum).

• *When you're done exploring the windmills, continue up the path through the middle of the adjacent parking lot (with the mills on your right). After the base of the final, armless windmill—now a short-term rental—turn left down the narrow, unmarked street. Let's explore...*

MYKONOS

Backstreets Below the Windmills

Walk downhill on this sleepy lane, through a rare corner of Mykonos that's still predominantly residential; locals really live here (as you can tell from the laundry drying). The first side street on the left is particularly evocative, offering a rare glimpse of Mykonos before it was glitzy.

The maze of meandering, skinny lanes helped buffer the howling winds...and discouraged pirates and invaders. As you explore here, tune in to the details of Mykonos' unique architecture: Houses and public space (sidewalks and curbs) blend with little concern about who owns what. Everything is painted a blinding white, including the seams between the paving stones. Today this is decorative, but originally it was practical: By painting the lanes with lime, a natural disinfectant, locals offset the unhygienic living conditions (people living on top of each other and emptying their chamber pots in the streets). And the rooftops were painted with lime, too—they collected precious rainwater, which was carried through a network of gutters to cisterns down below. (Fresh water is hard to come by on an arid island.) Houses generally had the kitchen and living room on the main floor, a couple of bedrooms upstairs, and a tiny toilet under the stairs (exploring town, look for a few surviving under-the-stairs doors today—now mostly used for storage). Today those staircases and trim are painted bright, cheery colors, giving Mykonos its distinctive look.

Continue down the lane until you reach a T-intersection. Across the street and three steps to the right is the recommended **Gioras Pastry Café,** an old-fashioned cellar bakery selling sweet and savory pastries. For 500-some years, they used a wood oven and mainly baked breads for locals; today they focus on tourist-friendly pastries but maintain their charming and historic interior.

• *From the bakery, head downhill on the lane, past several shops. At the intersection, head right along one of the town's most bustling streets, Enoplon Dinameon.*

Enoplon Dinameon and Matogianni Streets

Strolling the lane called Enoplon Dinameon, you'll pass a school on the right. Then (just after Louis Vuitton on the left) look for **three old wells.** These were the town's main source of drinking water until the arrival of modern plumbing in the 1950s—and, as such, this was the place to see and be seen, to gossip, and to court. It was said that if a visitor was offered water from the three wells, they were really respected by a Mykonian.

Continue past the wells, between two churches. On the left you'll see the **Maritime Museum,** with a well-presented exhibit about Mykonos' seafaring history, and **Lena's House,** offering an evenings-only glimpse into a traditional old home (both described under "Sights in Mykonos").

Keep going on Enoplon Dinameon as the colors—and crowds—crescendo, and you pass under a brilliant purple bougain-

villea. (Good luck dodging all the impromptu photo shoots.) After dark, the clientele from the bars and cafés in this area all merge into one big, open-air cocktail party under purple petals. Soon you'll come to the wide cross street called **Matogianni,** nicknamed the "Catwalk of Mykonos" for its lineup of top-end boutiques. Turn left here and appreciate the traditional-architecture-meets-modern-couture vibe. After just one block, you'll run into **Alpha Bank.**

• *From here, continuing straight past the bank leads you down to the harbor. But if you're up for more exploring, stay with me a few more minutes for a look at some back lanes that many visitors miss.*

Backstreets to the Harbor

Stick with me, now: At Alpha Bank, turn left, passing the recommended To Maereio restaurant (on your right). The street curves

a bit; then, turn left immediately past Fresh Boutique Hotel. On this little lane, the red-doored house on the right is the recommended **Psillos** bakery, where locals buy sweet and savory pies. Continuing past the bakery, bear left with the street at Terra Maria Hotel, and watch on your right for the low-profile door to **Mantó Garden Café/Cine Mantó.** Step inside to a peaceful, verdant world unto itself—called the "public garden"—sheltered from the wind, filled with giant cacti and pomegranate trees, and cooled by a goldfish pond. Locals appreciate its calm, natural atmosphere—and public WCs (outside the garden near the theater entrance). Consider a drink or light meal at the café, then walk to the far end of the garden, where you'll find the screen and chairs for the delightful open-air movie theater. Exit the far end of the complex, near the theater. (If this part is closed for some reason, backtrack past the bakery, then make four successive lefts. I'll meet you there.)

Outside the garden gate is a little square with a big tree. Keep Gucci on your left and head up that lane. You'll pass the back end of the **Greek Orthodox** cathedral we saw earlier. Continue straight through this mazelike area, bearing right where the street widens. Head a couple of short blocks down this shop-lined lane. At the Happiness shop, bear right at the fork, then take the next right, up the narrow alley. Wind your way around, taking a left at the next T-intersection and continuing another 25 steps. Suddenly you find yourself alone with Mykonos, at a little square with five churches and three trees. Known locally as **"Gossip Square"** (for the way the churches seem to be gathering to swap local news), this forgotten slice of old Mykonos is entirely surrounded by today's trendy bustle.

Exit this square to the left of the three red-doored churches. From here, I'll let you find your own way down to the harbor—because you couldn't possibly follow my directions anyway. The general idea is to bear right, then listen for the surf, the horns of the ships, or the howl of the northerly wind. (*KOUNELAS* signs, to the recommended fish tavern just off the harbor, are helpful.) Enjoy getting lost in the maze, likely having some lanes to yourself.

• *You'll wind up more or less where we started, at the harbor. Your walk is finished, and you've seen a good slice of Mykonos. Circle back to any museums you'd like to see, or consider heading around the right side of the harbor for a look at the Archaeological Museum. Or, if you have time and the seas are calm, take a boat out to Delos (described later in this chapter).*

Sights in Mykonos

MUSEUMS

Mykonos Archaeological Museum

This small museum, just uphill from the Old Port, displays artifacts found on the nearby island of Rheneia, which the Athenians reserved as a burial isle for Delos in order to keep that sacred isle pure. Though the temporary exhibits can be engaging, you may find most of what's here pretty dull—vases, jewelry, and statue fragments—with limited English descriptions. One item, however, makes a visit worth considering: a large vase (in room just beyond entry, dead center along the back wall) clearly showing the Tro-

jan Horse filled with Greek soldiers sporting gleeful archaic smiles, and cartoon-like panels telling the story of the massacre that followed when they jumped out. Dating from roughly 670 BC, it's the oldest depiction of the Trojan Horse ever found. It was found right here on Mykonos, discovered in 1961 by a (surely very surprised) farmer who'd set out to dig a well. Out back you'll find a courtyard ringed with intricately carved stone grave markers.

Cost and Hours: €4, Wed-Mon 9:00-16:00, closed Tue, possibly shorter hours Nov-March, +30 2289 022 325.

Aegean Maritime Museum

This tight but endearing collection traces the story of the local mercantile shipping industry. A desert isle of history in a sea of wealthy tourism, this little place takes its subject very seriously. In its three rooms you'll find amphora jugs, model ships, portraits of great sailors, and more. The tranquil garden in back displays the actual, original lighthouse from the island's Cape Armenistis, as well as replicas of ancient sailors' gravestones. The good English descriptions offer a fine history lesson for those willing to read them.

Cost and Hours: €4, daily 10:30-13:00 & 18:30-21:00, closed Nov-March, Enoplon Dinameon 10, +30 2289 022 700.

Lena's House

This little museum (affiliated with the Mykonos Folklore Museum) shows part of a typical middle-class Mykonian house dating from the late 19th century, complete with original furnishings and artwork.

Cost and Hours: €2, Mon-Sat 18:30-21:30, Sun 19:00-21:00, closed Oct-March, Enoplon Dinameon, +30 2289 022 390.

Mykonos Folklore Museum

Housed in a typically Cycladic former sea captain's residence just up the bluff from the harbor, this museum is deceptively sprawling. Pick up a laminated info card after entering (next to the donation box). Exploring the interior, you'll peruse a random mix of traditional folk items from around the island, as well as a typical kitchen and bedroom. In the basement are fragments of the Venetian castle that once stood here, discovered only in the 1970s.

Cost and Hours: €2, Mon-Sat 10:30-14:30, closed Oct-March and Sun year-round, +30 2289 022 591.

MYKONOS

BEACHES

Mykonos' beaches rival those of any Greek island. Each beach seems to specialize in a different niche: family-friendly or party; straight, gay, or mixed; nude or clothed; and so on. (Even "family-friendly" beaches can have topless sunbathers.) Get local advice to find the one that suits your beach-bum preferences, or choose from the options below.

All these beaches have beach bars or restaurants that rent comfortable lounge chairs with umbrellas out on the sand (around €20-40 for two chairs that share an umbrella; can be much pricier at exclusive beaches). Just take a seat—someone will come by to collect money. The bars usually sell cocktails and typical Greek-island meals. You can often order from your beach chair, but heading inside can be a welcome escape from the sun. Be warned that in peak season (July and especially Aug), all beaches are very crowded, and it can be difficult to find an available seat.

Getting to the Beaches: The beaches I've recommended are all on the south coast of the island and listed here roughly in order, from west to east, as you would approach them from Mykonos town. All are within a 10- to 20-minute drive from town.

Throughout the season, **buses** run to major beaches twice hourly during the day, usually leaving from the Fabrika stop in town at :00 and :30 past each hour; most rides cost around €2. Confirm the schedule at the little ticket kiosk, then find the bus marked with your destination and hop on. As buses can be crowded at prime times, it can be smart to line up early to ensure getting a seat.

A **taxi** to the beach from town will run €20-30; some of the farther beaches can go up to €35. There are rarely taxis standing by at beaches; when you're ready to leave, call for one (+30 2289 022 400 or 22890-23700) or ask a taverna to call for you (if you've paid for chair rental or drinks, they're generally happy to do this). You may be charged a few extra euros for calling rather than hailing a taxi.

To explore a variety of beaches in one day, you can connect some of the major beaches—Platis Gialos, Paraga, Paradise, Super Paradise, Agrari, and Elia—by regular **shuttle boat** (€15 round-trip for one hop; €20 for an all-day hop-on, hop-off ticket, +30 2289 023 995). Note that these run between the beaches, starting with Platis Gialos, but do not include Mykonos town. A separate boat connects Mykonos town to Paradise beach (€10, 2/hour, departs from the same pier as Delos boats).

▲Agios Ioannis

Pronounced AY-yohs yoh-AH-nees, this appealingly remote patch of pebbly sand, tucked behind a hill, feels like a castaway isle. You'll enjoy views across to the important isle of Delos. From Mykonos town, go to Ornos, then head toward Kapari; on your way down the hill, turn off on the left at the low-profile beach signs (one directs you to ΠΥΛΗ, one of the restaurants on the beach);

this is also where buses stop, a short but steep hike above the beach. You'll drop down this road to an idyllic Robinson Crusoe spot. The two main restaurants here are the trendy, pretentious Hippy Fish (where the film *Shirley Valentine* was filmed), and the nice but more accessible Pili (ΠΥΛΗ); both rent chairs and have full food and drink menus.

For the even more secluded **Kapari** beach, continue down the road past the Agios Ioannis turnoff, then swing right at the white church.

Ornos

This easy-to-get-to, family-friendly beach is right in the middle of the sizeable town of Ornos. It's one of the more functional beaches of those I list (and has better lounge-chair values). Although it's in a built-up area, the whole place has an unpretentious charm.

Psarou and Platis Gialos

These two beaches are along the next cove east of Ornos. The main landmark here is **Platis Gialos,** a crowded, densely developed stretch of beach just below the main bus stop. You'll find a row of beach hotels, plenty of beach-chair rentals, and an array of other water activities—but it can feel a little claustrophobic (the far end from the bus stop/parking is less jammed).

I prefer to walk 10 minutes to the less developed **Psarou** (psah-ROO)—head back up the way the bus came, and watch on your left (through a little parking lot) for a fine trail that leads above the waterline down to an idyllic cove. (You can also get off the bus a stop early, but from there it's a steep hike down—along rocky, uneven steps—to the beach.) Psarou, one of the most sheltered beaches on the island, is a broad, sandy stretch with luxury yachts moored just offshore. It has an exclusive reputation, thanks to the big, fancy Mykonos Blu beach hotel and the top-end Nammos restaurant (which charges an exorbitant fee for its chair rentals). But right in the middle is the more affordable Cavo Psarou, a humbler beach bar with chair rentals priced within reach of mere mortals. This beach is relatively uncrowded, and the sand is fine—making it my favorite place for a day at the beach.

Paraga

Sometimes spelled Paranga, this stretch of coast squeezes beach chairs, bars, and high-end resorts into a compact cove, bookended at the western head by a small sandy-soft beach (free) beneath the fancy **Scorpios** luxury resort (where €140 will get you the cheapest cabana for four people, and there's a good chance you'll spot a celebrity) and to the east by a pebbly shore with a footpath to Paradise (15 minutes). Here at the eastern end is a handy **hostel**—an affordable option with mixed dorms, prefab tents, and private bungalows, all with free airport transfer (www.paragabeachhostel.com). In between, the **SantAnna** club is a hit with the 30-something crowd for its poolside lounge chairs (starting at €100).

Paradise and Super Paradise

Mykonos' famous "meat-market" party beaches are a magnet for young people in the Aegean, and more of a destination than the other beaches listed here. While a bit too rowdy for my taste, they're a little calmer in the shoulder season.

Located at the southern tip of the island, **Paradise** (a.k.a. Kalamopodi) is presided over by hotels that run party-oriented bars for young beachgoers—perfect if you want to dance in the sand all night with like-minded backpackers from around the world. By day, it's less crowded and more accessible, but still comes with thumping music. As you approach, the last stretch is through thick, high grasses, giving the place an air of secrecy; then you'll pass long rows of lockers before popping out at the party.

The next cove over hosts **Super Paradise** (Plintri) beach, which has eclipsed the original as the premier party beach on the island. Super Paradise tries to be a bit more elegant than plain old Paradise—rather than grungy backpackers, it skews slightly older, with posh thirtysomethings.

Nightlife in Mykonos

Covering the fast-changing lineup of trendy clubs is beyond the scope of this book. But here is a pair of enjoyable evening activities.

Cocktails at Sunset: The Little Venice embankment is lined with cocktail bars and cafés, crowded every night with throngs of visitors enjoying the island's best spot to watch the sunset—one of the highlights of visiting Mykonos. Plan on cocktails in the €15-20 range, with wine or beer around €10—and there may be a steep cover charge. While it's fun to window shop your options here before settling in at your pick, reputable choices include **Scarpa, Galleraki,** and **Caprice.**

Open-Air Cinema: In summer, locals and vacationers sit back and enjoy the movies under the palm trees at **Cine Mantó,** in a lovely public garden smack in the middle of town (€9, films shown in original language—usually English, June-Sept only, usually two showings a night—check signs around town for times, +30 2289 026 165, www.cinemanto.gr). You can combine this with a dinner from the adjoining, recommended café/grill for an affordable-for-Mykonos meal.

Sleeping in Mykonos

Mykonos is an extremely expensive place to overnight—especially from mid-June to mid-September (peaking in mid-July through August). During these premium times, even "budget" hotels dramatically increase their rates...which means you should lower your value-for-money expectations. If you can come outside this busy period, you can save more than half; it's worth comparison shopping in shoulder season to find the best deal. If you do come in peak season, book as far ahead as possible—most of the smaller hotels get filled up with repeat customers.

In this party town, nighttime noise—dance clubs, people carousing in the streets, and so on—is epidemic; plan to wear earplugs, and if you're a light sleeper, try requesting a hotel's quietest room. I've tried to recommend places on streets that are less raucous than the norm, but they're also very central, so no promises.

MYKONOS

IN THE OLD TOWN

$$$$ Marietta's rents four sea-breezy rooms on a quaint street near Little Venice. Rooms vary in size, but all have a balcony and/or views of the ocean or the windmills. Run by Marietta herself, the place can be hard to find: Look for the sign in the door (no breakfast, Mpaoumi street, +30 6945 225 390, www.mariettas-mykonos.com, info@mariettas.gr).

$$$$ Fresh Boutique Hotel is buried deep in the heart of Mykonos. Its 10 rooms, some with balconies, are thoroughly modern. While it has hardly any public spaces, its sleek garden restaurant (which can be noisy) serves as an ersatz lounge. With dramatic price drops outside peak season, this can be a particularly good value in slow times (breakfast extra, closed Nov-March, N. Kalogera 31, +30 2289 024 670, www.hotelfreshmykonos.com, info@hotelfreshmykonos.com).

$$$$ Hotel Carbonaki, loosely run by the welcoming Rousounelos family, rents 21 fine but faded rooms around an oasis courtyard with a hot tub. It's conveniently located a few steps above the busiest downtown streets (breakfast extra, closed Nov-Feb, Panachrantou 23, +30 2289 024 124, www.carbonaki.gr, info@carbonaki.gr, Theodore and Evi).

$$$$ Andromeda Suites feels like a little village set around its own quiet pool. The 17 units range from doubles to full-size apartments. They're slightly worn, but a decent value, and all come with a kitchenette (no breakfast, Lakka Square, +30 2289 024 712, www.andromeda-mykonos.gr, info@andromeda-mykonos.com, Jeannette and George).

$$$$ Elena Hotel, even higher up than Carbonaki (and therefore a bit more peaceful), has 32 modern rooms, helpful staff, and a pleasant veranda lounge/breakfast area with a bit of a sea view (Rochari street, +30 2289 023 457, www.elenamykonos.gr, info@elenamykonos.gr).

$$$$ Hotel Matina Garden is charming. Humble but nicely maintained, it's been family-run since 1958 (now in its third generation), with rooms surrounding a tranquil garden near the top end of town. Their 12 "hotel" rooms are priced similarly to other midrange hotels in town, but they also have seven cheaper "pension" rooms with shared bathrooms (Fournakia 3, +30 2289 022 387, www.hotelmatina-mykonos.com, info@hotelmatina-mykonos.com).

$$$$ Matogianni Hotel, with 33 rooms facing a garden in the heart of town (plus a handful under the street level), keeps its prices reasonable while offering a sense of contemporary style unusual for this price range. It has an on-site café and a long, pleasant front porch filled with wicker chairs (breakfast extra, closed

MYKONOS

Nov-Feb, Matogianni street, +30 2289 022 217, www.matogianni. gr, info@matogianni.gr).

HIGHER UP

These places get you up above the rooftops of Mykonos. This helps cut down on party noise but, as they're closer to the main road around town, can come with some traffic noise.

$$$$ Portobello Boutique Hotel is the place for well-heeled mountain goats. Perched high above town near the windmill museum (a steep 5-minute walk down, or 10-minute walk up), it has 17 rooms—some with spectacular views for higher rates—plus a popular sunset-view bar. It feels modern, fresh, and tidy (+30 2289 023 240, www.portobello-hotel.gr, info@portobello-hotel.gr).

$$$$ Hotel Nazos is up a steep street, but you're rewarded with sweeping vistas from the veranda and a warm welcome from brother-and-sister team George and Sofia. The 21 rooms are modest, but most have views and/or balconies. Stay here if you'll happily trade a hike for a low-key, family-run hideaway (breakfast extra, closed Nov-March, near the School of Fine Arts, +30 2289 0226 626, www.hotelnazos.com, info@hotelnazos.com).

Eating in Mykonos

The twisting streets of the Old Town are lined with tourist-oriented restaurants. You won't find good value here—Mykonos is expensive. Simply choose the spot with the menu and ambience that appeal to you: The harborfront has the workaday action, while the places in Little Venice are more romantic—especially at sunset. A few steps inland, tucked in the town's winding back  lanes, are countless charming restaurants filling hidden gardens under trellises of bougainvillea, some with tables out on a busy pedestrian lane. Take mental notes as you explore by day, then come back to the place that most appeals.

PRICEY DINNER RESTAURANTS

These places are open only for dinner.

$$$$ At **To Maereio** (Τό Μαερειό), in-the-know diners choose from a small but reasonably priced, inventive menu that includes some Mykonian specialties and plenty of meat options. The seating is almost entirely indoors. Out front you'll often see a long line of hopeful diners—arrive early, or be prepared to wait (daily from 19:00, Kalogera 16, +30 2289 028 825).

$$$$ Fish Tavern Kounelas, buried a few winding streets off the harbor, feels friendly and unpretentious. They offer a warm welcome, tight and atmospheric outdoor seating, a nondescript interior, and a typical taverna menu focusing on fish and seafood. Notice the little grill right out on the tiny alley where they prepare your fish (daily from 18:30, near St. Monis Square—look for blue-and-white *KOUNELAS* signs, +30 2289 028 220).

$$$$ M-Eating serves up high-end, creatively presented, modern Mediterranean cuisine with a homegrown influence. Most diners vie for their outdoor covered terrace seating; you may have better luck snagging one of the few small tables inside. Among Mykonos' posh eateries, this one distinguishes itself by delivering quality food and polished service. As it's popular, book ahead (daily from 19:00, 10 Kalogera, +30 2289 078 550, www.m-eating.gr).

MIDRANGE LOCAL OPTIONS
While these centrally located places are welcoming to tourists, they're popular with value-seeking locals and expats, too.

$$$ Cine Mantó Garden Café, filling a beautiful oasis-garden in the heart of Mykonos, is best known as an outdoor movie venue (see "Nightlife in Mykonos," earlier). But the café here—with outdoor tables under palm trees—is open all day long, and it's an ideal respite from the busy town for a drink or light meal (daily 9:00-24:00, +30 2289 026 165, www.cinemanto.gr).

Lowbrow Tavernas on the Harbor: Mykonos' harborfront has a cluster of simple tavernas that draw locals with relatively good prices and enjoyable water views (provided the wind doesn't blast you away). **$$$ Yialos** (Γιαλός), near the red-domed church, is a decent place for a straightforward meal (open long hours daily). Even if you're not up for a full meal, consider enjoying a *freddo cappuccino* or *frappé* from this comfortable perch, which offers some of Mykonos' best people-watching (and, sometimes, cat- and pelican-watching).

CHEAP EATS AND EASY LUNCHES
It's difficult to have a sit-down meal in Mykonos without dropping at least €20 per person. Here are some less expensive alternatives.

Souvlaki: A variety of **$$** souvlaki stands are scattered around town. Most cater to tourists, and Mykonos lacks a stellar souvlaki joint. But relatively reliable, central choices include the classic **Sakis Grill House** (Kalogera 7) and the slightly more up-scale **Souvlaki Story** (multiple locations, including one at Enoplon Dinameon 37).

Bakeries: Locals still shop at **Psillos,** a family-run hole-in-the-wall where they bake everything on site. Grab something from the bins of breads, cookies, and other items lining the wall, or try a cheap meat or cheese pie. It offers a bit of affordability and local flavor in the center of this pricey, touristy town (daily until 19:00, near the Fresh Boutique Hotel on Klaous street). **Gioras Pastry Café,** filling a traditional cellar on a quiet street below the windmills, also has savory and sweet pastries, and atmospheric indoor seating. It's run by a husband-and-wife team: George does the baking and Cloe is happy to help you pick out a treat (May-Oct daily 8:30-15:00, 16:00-late, Efthiniou street, +30 2289 027 784).

Mykonos Connections

BY BOAT

All bigger boats and car ferries leave from the New Port, about a mile north of town (see "Arrival on Mykonos," earlier, for information on getting there from Mykonos town). That includes most boats to Piraeus and Santorini—be sure to check locally to confirm from which port your ferry is departing. The frequency and durations listed below are approximate; schedules can change from season to season, and sailings can be canceled on short notice—confirm everything locally. For information on finding current schedules and booking tickets, see page 553 of the Practicalities chapter.

To Piraeus: Generally 3-4/day in high season (2.5 hours via fast boat, 5.5 hours on slow boat). Off-season (Nov-mid-March) there is likely one slow boat daily (confirm, especially Jan-March).

To Santorini: Generally 2-4/day in high season, none in winter, 2-3 hours, 1-2 stops en route.

Delos

As popular as Mykonos is today, it was just another island centuries ago. The main attraction was the island next door, Delos, worth ▲. In antiquity, Delos lived several lives: as one of the Mediterranean's most important religious sites, as the "Fort Knox" of Greek city-states, and as a busy commercial port for the ancient world. Its importance ranked right up there with Athens, Delphi, or Olympia. Today the island is a ghost town—but because no modern buildings were ever erected here, these ruins are nearly undisturbed. Highlights of your visit include some much-photographed lion statues (the Lion Terrace), some nice floor mosaics, the view from Mount Kynthos, and a windswept setting pockmarked with foundations that hint at Delos' rich history.

MYKONOS

GETTING THERE

Delos is a 30-minute boat ride from Mykonos. Boats depart from the pier extending straight out from the Old Town; buy the €22 round-trip ticket at the kiosk at the base of the pier (generally departing Mykonos at 9:00, 10:00, and 11:30; returning from Delos at 12:00, 13:30, and 15:00). You can take any boat back. There may also be a late-afternoon boat from Mykonos (around 17:00) that returns in the early evening (around 19:30; times differ outside peak season). Times can change depending on weather, cruise-ship arrivals and departures, and other factors, so check locally.

ORIENTATION TO DELOS

Cost and Hours: €8 for the archaeological site, €12 for site and museum (museum may be closed for renovation when you visit), open April-Oct daily from the arrival of the first boat to the departure of the last one, closed Nov-March, +30 2289 022 259, http://odysseus.culture.gr.

Planning Your Time: Most visitors find that two hours on the island is plenty to wander the site; add more time if you want to climb Mount Kynthos, or if the museum is open.

Tours: Local guides meet arriving boats (€10 for a 1- to 1.5-hour tour—you'll need more time to actually hike around the site and see the museum). Travel agencies in Mykonos town sell package excursions to Delos that include the boat, museum entry, and a guided tour (overpriced at roughly €60, though these tours last longer than those offered by on-site guides).

Services: If the museum is open, a nearby café sells coffee, juice, and basic snacks. WCs are located behind the café and near the site entrance/ticket booth.

Be Prepared: Delos has virtually no shade and minimal services. Wear good shoes, and bring sun protection and plenty of water.

MYKONOS

The Rise and Fall of Delos

Delos entered history 3,000 years ago as a sacred cult center, where gods were worshipped. Blessed with a prime location in the center of the Greek islands but cursed with no natural resources, the barren island survived as a religious destination for pilgrims.

According to myth, the philandering Zeus impregnated the mortal Leto. Zeus' furious wife, Hera, banished Leto from the earth, but Zeus implored his brother Poseidon to create a refuge for her by raising up the underwater world of "Invisible" (*Adelos*) to create an island that was "Visible" (*Delos*). Here Leto gave birth to twins—Apollo (god of the sun) and Artemis (goddess of the moon). Their human followers built temples in their honor (ninth century BC), and pilgrims flocked here with offerings.

As Athens began to assert control over the Aegean (sixth century BC), it made sure that spiritually influential Delos stayed politically neutral. The Athenians ordered a purification of the island, removing dead bodies from the cemeteries. Later, they also decreed that no one could be born or die there—there were to be no permanent residents. The Delians were relocated to an adjacent larger island called Rheneia. Ostensibly, this was to keep Delos pure for the gods, but in reality it removed any danger of rivals influencing the island's native population.

Because of its neutral status and central location, Delos was chosen in 478 BC as the natural meeting place for the powerful Delian League—an alliance of Greek city-states formed to battle the Persians and to promote trade. The combined wealth of the league was stored here in the fabulously rich bank of Delos. But all that changed in 454 BC, when Pericles moved the treasury to Athens, and Delos reverted to being a pilgrimage site.

Centuries later, under the Romans, Delos' course changed dramatically once more. Thanks to its strategic location, the island was granted the right to operate as a free port (167 BC). Almost overnight, it became one of the biggest shipping centers in the known world, complete with a town of 30,000 inhabitants.

Then, in 88 BC, soldiers from the Kingdom of Pontus, an enemy of Rome, attacked and looted the town, slaughtering 20,000 of its citizens. Delos never really recovered. Plagued by pirate attacks and shifting trade routes, Delos faded into history. Its once-great buildings were left to decay and waste away. In 1872, French archaeologists arrived (so far, scientists have excavated about one-fifth of the site), and Delos' cultural treasures were revealed to the modern world.

❂ SELF-GUIDED TOUR

• *From the boat dock, walk to the entrance, buy your ticket, pick up the helpful included map, and enter the gate.*

Pause and survey the site. The commercial harbor was to your right, and the sacred harbor to your left. Ahead and to the right

are the foundations of shops and homes that constituted one of the Aegean's finest cities in Hellenistic times. Standing above those ruins is Mount Kynthos, its hillsides littered with temple remains. The Agora of the Competaliasts—one of the main squares in town—is straight ahead (with the museum building poking up behind). The religious area (with the temples of Apollo) is ahead and to the left, at the end of the Sacred Way. And far to the left was the Sacred Lake (now a patch of trees), overlooked by the famous Terrace of the Lions.

• *Start by wandering through the long rows of foundations on your right. You can circle back to these at the end, or poke around now.*

❶ Residential and Commercial District

Most of the remains here were either homes or shops. In the second century BC (when Delos was a bustling commercial port), you

could buy just about anything from one of the many shops, and the elaborate homes of wealthy merchants and shippers covered the hillsides above. Delos was considered the most important commercial center in the known world. (One of its primary commodities was human beings—it was a major center in the ancient slave trade.) The city was cosmopolitan, with 30,000 residents and distinct ethnic groups, each with its own linguistic and cultural neighborhood (Greeks, Syrians, Beirutis, Italians, and so on). Remains of these same neighborhoods can still be seen today.

Poke into some of the **house foundations.** Homes were generally organized around a central courtyard above a giant cistern. Look for fragments of elaborate mosaic floors (intact portions are on display inside the museum), as well as marble structures that once decorated the place. The city even had a surprisingly advanced sewer system. Because wood was rare on the arid Cycladic Islands, most buildings were constructed from dry-stone walls; wood was

MYKONOS

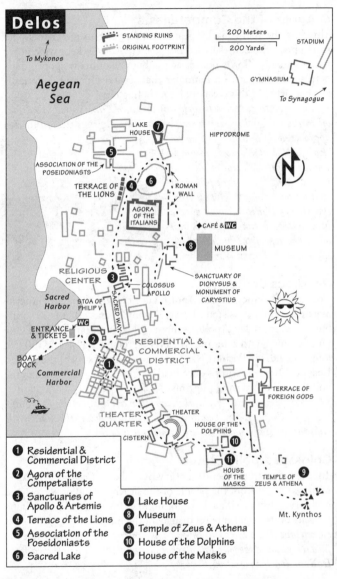

Delos

STANDING RUINS
ORIGINAL FOOTPRINT

200 Meters
200 Yards

To Mykonos

Aegean Sea

STADIUM

GYMNASIUM

To Synagogue

LAKE HOUSE ❼

HIPPODROME

❺

ASSOCIATION OF THE POSEIDONIASTS

TERRACE OF THE LIONS ❹ ❻

ROMAN WALL

AGORA OF THE ITALIANS

◆CAFÉ & WC

❽ MUSEUM

RELIGIOUS CENTER ❸

COLOSSUS APOLLO

SANCTUARY OF DIONYSUS & MONUMENT OF CARYSTIUS

Sacred Harbor

STOA OF PHILIP V

SACRED WAY

ENTRANCE & TICKETS WC

❷

BOAT DOCK

Commercial Harbor

❶

RESIDENTIAL & COMMERCIAL DISTRICT

TERRACE OF FOREIGN GODS

THEATER QUARTER

THEATER

HOUSE OF THE DOLPHINS

CISTERN

❿

⓫

HOUSE OF THE MASKS

TEMPLE OF ZEUS & ATHENA ❾

Mt. Kynthos

❶ Residential & Commercial District
❷ Agora of the Competaliasts
❸ Sanctuaries of Apollo & Artemis
❹ Terrace of the Lions
❺ Association of the Poseidoniasts
❻ Sacred Lake
❼ Lake House
❽ Museum
❾ Temple of Zeus & Athena
❿ House of the Dolphins
⓫ House of the Masks

MYKONOS

a status symbol, used only by the wealthiest to show off. Delos had some of the biggest homes of ancient Greece in part because residents could build big here without fear of the devastating earthquakes that plagued other locations in the islands. The Greeks attributed this to divine intervention, while modern seismologists have found that Delos sits away from major fault lines.

• *Now head toward the agora that's near the ticket building.*

❷ Agora of the Competaliasts

This was the main market square of the Roman merchants who worshipped the deities called *lares compitales,* who kept watch over the crossroads. This is not *the* agora, but one of many agoras (marketplaces) on Delos—a reminder that several different communities coexisted in this cosmopolitan trading city.

• Just above the upper-left corner of this agora, the Sacred Way leads off to the left. Follow the same path ancient pilgrims walked as they

approached the Sanctuary of Apollo (look for the blue arrows to guide you). Along the left side of the road runs the long ledge of the pediment (with recognizable triglyphs) from the **Stoa of Philip V** *(what we see here as the "bottom" actually ran along the top of the building). At the end of the Sacred Way is the...*

Religious Center

Both the ❸ **Sanctuary of Apollo** and, beyond that, the **Sanctuary of Artemis** consisted of several temples and other ceremonial buildings. In its day, Apollo's sanctuary had three large, stern Doric temples lined with columns. The biggest temple was nearly 100 feet long. The nearby Porinos Naos served as the treasury of the Delian League. Other treasuries once held untold riches—offerings to the gods brought by devout pilgrims.

• Follow the route to the right, then left, then left again around the Sanctuary of Apollo. Before heading off to the right down the main path, pause at the giant marble pedestal that once held the...

Colossus Apollo Statue

The 35-foot statue (seventh century BC, labeled *Colossus of the Naxians*) was a gift from the people of the nearby island of Naxos, and was carved from a single block of marble. It's long gone now, but a few bits of its fingers are on display in the museum.

• Continue down the path, beyond the Sanctuary. You'll pass more ruined temples and the foundations that surround the spacious **Agora of the Italians** *(on the right) on the way to the...*

❹ Terrace of the Lions

This row of five lion statues is the main, iconic image of this site. These are replicas, but five of the original marble statues (seventh century BC) are in the

MYKONOS

museum. One of the originals was stolen by the Venetians, "repaired" with an awkwardly too-big head, and still stands in front of Venice's Arsenal building.

• *Northwest of the lions, up a small hill, are four columns marking the* ❺ *Association of the Poseidoniasts, the religious and commercial center for a guild of ship owners and merchants from Berytus (modern Beirut), in ancient Syria. Below the columns is what was once the...*

❻ Sacred Lake

This was supposedly the source of Zeus' seed. When Leto was about to give birth to Zeus' children (according to the Homeric *Hymn to Apollo*), she cried out: "Delos, if you would be willing to be the abode of my son Apollo and make him a rich temple, your people will be well-fed by strangers bringing offerings. For truly your own soil is not rich." (French archaeologists drained the lake to prevent the spread of bacterial disease.)

• *Walk around the Sacred Lake. At the top, stop by the* ❼ *Lake House, providing a glimpse of a second-century BC Delian home. Now head up toward the museum. Just before the museum, a path detours to the left far into the distance. You can follow it to find the remains of a gymnasium, a stadium, and a Jewish synagogue.*

*Olympics-style games were held at Delos' **stadium** every five years. Like the more famous games at Olympia and Delphi, these were essentially religious festivals to the gods, particularly Dionysus. Pilgrims from across the Greek world gathered to celebrate with sports, song contests, theatrical performances, and general merrymaking.*

Make your way to the...

❽ Museum

The museum is undergoing renovation and may not be open when you visit. When it reopens, exhibits may be shuffled around (and may differ from what's described here). But in general, the collection includes statuary, vases, and other items. Look for a model of the site in its heyday. Most of the site's best pieces are in the National Archaeological Museum in Athens, but a few

highlights remain here, including a beautifully carved stone table, five of the original marble lions, the fingers of Colossus Apollo, and—perhaps the best part—several bits of striking floor mosaics.

For more body parts of other gods, exit the museum, then veer slightly left down a short downhill path to stand in front of the

MYKONOS

Monument of Carystius (once part of the Sanctuary of Dionysus), with its large (broken-off) penis-on-a-pillar statues.

• *Past the museum, the path splits. If you stay right you'll wind back to the start. Or you can go left, which starts a hike up the hill toward more remains of houses and temples all the way up to Mount Kynthos (allow about 45 minutes).*

Mount Kynthos

At 370 feet, the island's highest point feels even taller on a hot day. To ancient Greeks, this conical peak looked like the spot from which Poseidon had pulled this mysterious isle up from the deep. Up here are the remains of the ❾ **Temple of Zeus and Athena.** As you observe the chain of islands dramatically swirling around Delos, you can understand why most experts believe that the Cycladic Islands got their name from the way they circle (or cycle around) this oh-so-important islet.

• *Head back downhill, toward the theater and harbor. On your way down you'll pass the ❿ **House of the Dolphins,** with mosaics of cupids riding dolphins, and the ⓫ **House of the Masks,** with a beautiful mosaic of a tambourine-playing Dionysus riding a leopard. As you return to the boat, you'll see the remains of a giant cistern and the 5,500-seat theater...starring a 360-degree view of the Cycladic Islands.*

SANTORINI

Σαντορίνη; a.k.a. Thira (Θηρα)

Scenic, seismic Santorini is one of the world's most dramatic islands: a flooded caldera (a collapsed volcanic crater) with a long, steep, colorfully striped arc of cliffs, thrusting up a thousand feet above sea level. Sometimes called "The Devil's Isle," this unique place has captured visitors' imaginations for millennia and might have partly inspired tales of Atlantis. But the otherworldly appeal of Santorini (sahn-toh-REE-nee) doesn't end with its setting. Perched along the ridgeline is a gaggle of perfectly placed whitewashed villages punctuated with azure domes that make this, undeniably, one of Greece's most scenic spots. If this place didn't exist, some fantasy painter would have to conjure it up.

The main town, Fira (Φηρα, FEE-rah)—with Santorini's handiest services and best museum—is equal parts functional and scenic. But the village of Oia (Οια, EE-ah), on the northern tip of the island—with its chalk-white houses and vivid domes—is even more dramatic. Oia is the place you imagine first when you think "Santorini." Strolling through Oia is like spinning a postcard rack—it's tempting to see the town entirely through your camera's viewfinder. A complete visit to the island involves spending time in both towns (though Fira is, for several reasons, the more practical home base).

Santorini deserves more time than one-town islands Mykonos and Hydra. Besides the towns Fira and Oia, the rest of the island is also entertaining and fascinating—with charming villages, countryside wineries, ancient sites, unusual beaches, and a never-ending supply of

Santorini Island

To Mykonos & Piraeus

.... Excursion/ Shuttle Boat
Roads
---- Trail
Beaches

Oia
SIGALAS WINERY
Finikia
Riva
THIRASSIA
Manalos
Imerovigli
Firostefani
AGIOS THEODORI CHURCH
CABLE CAR
NEA KAMENI
Old Port
THIRA
Fira
Monolithos
Hot Springs
SEA DIAMOND SHIPWRECK
SANTO WINES
PALEA KAMENI
Athinios (New Port)
EXO GONIA VILLAGE & METAXI MAS REST.
AIRPORT
KOUTSOYANNOPOULOS WINE MUSEUM
VENETSANOS WINERY
Pyrgos
Kamari
AEGAGROS CALDERA HOUSES
Akrotiri Town
MEGALOCHORI
PETRA KOUZINA
ANCIENT THIRA
LIGHTHOUSE (FAROS)
Emporio
White Beach
Red Beach
Akrotiri Beach
AKROTIRI RUINS
Vlychada Port
Perissa
To Crete

Aegean Sea

2 Kilometers
2 Miles

stunning viewpoints (a boat trip in the caldera is a fun way to savor the area). In general, Santorini invites explorers to linger; even with several days, you won't run out of ways to enjoy yourself.

Santorini is hugely popular and can be very crowded in high season (roughly July-Sept, peaking mid-July-Aug). And it's expensive. I've done my best to find good-value accommodations and restaurants, but on a Greece-wide scale, they're still budget-busters. People coming to Santorini on a tight budget may find themselves eating lots of picnics and takeout souvlaki, and seeking accommodations with no views. Arriving via cruise ship helps control costs, even if it provides only a fleeting glimpse—but locals grumble that discount cruise lines and Airbnb attract a less wealthy clientele, who contribute less to the local economy.

They have reason to be concerned—tourism has helped make Santorini relatively affluent. It's one of the few places in Greece where young people don't have to move away to find satisfying work. Fortunately, it's not difficult to break away from the main tourist rut and discover some scenic lanes of your own. In both Fira and Oia, the cliffside streets are strewn with countless cafés, all of them touting "sunset views"...the end of the day is a main attraction here.

SANTORINI

SANTORINI OVERVIEW

The five islands that make up the Santorini archipelago are known to Greeks as Thira (Θηρα, THEE-rah). Most of the settlement is on the 15-mile-long main island, also called Thira. But most travelers call it Santorini (from the Venetian "Santa Irini," after an early Christian cathedral here)—and I do, too. The west side of Santorini (the caldera) is a sheer drop-off, while the east side (the former volcano's base) tapers more gradually to the water.

This archipelago's permanent population is officially around 15,000, but it nearly doubles with seasonal workers in the summer. Visitors to Santorini number in the millions annually. Recently, the local government has taken steps to limit the number of cruise day-trippers on the island.

The primary tourist towns perch atop cliffs on the steep western side of Santorini: **Fira** is the island's capital and transportation hub, but the main attraction is **Oia,** a village six miles to the northwest. Sprawling north from Fira, along the road toward Oia, are the even higher, hill-capping villages of **Imerovigli** and **Firostefani.** The relatively level east and south areas have the ancient sites, most of the wineries, and the best beaches.

PLANNING YOUR TIME

For a speedy visit, Santorini deserves at least two nights and a full day divided between Oia and Fira. But if you have another day or two (or longer) to spare, Santorini has plenty more to offer. Three or four nights is ideal.

If your time on Santorini is short, make a beeline (by bus or taxi) to Oia to get your fill of classic Santorini views. Then, as the midday Oia cruise crowds begin to peak, return to Fira for a little sightseeing—follow my self-guided Fira Walk, then tour the Museum of Prehistoric Thira. Be sure to catch the sunset from somewhere along the caldera ridge (see sidebar, later).

On a longer visit, rent a car or ride a bus or taxi to other points on the island, or take a boat trip in the caldera.

Don't rely on the opening hours for museums and archaeological sites given in this book; they can change at the whims of the government and the Greek economy. Check locally before planning your day.

Choosing a Home Base: Most travelers find Fira to be the handiest place to overnight. Centrally located for exploring the island, Fira has the best transportation connections. It's plenty scenic and has the best variety of accommodations, restaurants, and services. Wealthy romantics hang their hat in Oia—but it has some drawbacks. Oia feels remote (to get just about anywhere on the island, you first have to drive, taxi, or bus 25 minutes to Fira), is extraordinarily expensive (even by Santorini standards), and is un-

Santorini Sunsets

Watching the sunset from the caldera ridge is a ▲▲▲ experience that's worth planning ahead for. Find out what time the sun sets, and where (it gradually moves from north to south over the course of the summer).

Oia is the most famous place to enjoy the Santorini sunset. During July and August it provides unobstructed views, and all that whitewash beautifully captures the swirling colors of the sky. Be warned that sunset watching in Oia is hardly a

unique brainstorm—and as the shadows get long, the town's narrow streets become a tedious human traffic jam. Seriously—just before sunset, you can barely walk anywhere in the old center. If you are determined to experience an Oia sunset, arrive very early—an hour or more in peak season—and immediately stake out a spot at the prime vantage point: at or near the ruined castle at the tip of town. But, to be honest, many travelers find it simply not worth the headaches involved.

Fira is arguably just as good for enjoying the sunset, and the crowds are less concentrated. Unlike Oia, Fira affords a view over the entire caldera rather than looking out to sea (so the sun sets over land, not just water). If your hotel doesn't offer a caldera-view perch, scout a bar or restaurant during the day, and reserve a table for sunset time. If you're improvising, simply belly up to the whitewashed wall (along with every other tourist in town) along the terrace in front of the Orthodox Cathedral.

And don't forget the many **other places on the island** for sunset viewing—basically anywhere facing the caldera will work. Ask locals for tips. The villages of Firostefani and Imerovigli, just above Fira, are smaller (less crowded) and even higher up. Some of my recommended wineries on the southern part of the island (especially Venetsanos and Santo) boast spectacular sunset views, as does Selene restaurant in the village of Pyrgos. And if you're taking a cruise in the caldera, choosing one timed to coincide with sunset kills two sightseeing birds with one stone.

Remember: If you hope to watch the sunset from a particular café or winery, be sure to specifically reserve a sunset-view table well in advance.

bearably crowded around sunset...when your "private" terrace could suddenly be just steps below packs of shutterbugs. You could also look for accommodations in the smaller villages of Firostefani or Imerovigli, which adjoin Fira to the north and also have fantastic views. If you'll have a car and want to settle into island life away from the crowds, it can be somewhat cheaper to find a countryside villa on the quieter eastern side of the island.

ARRIVAL ON SANTORINI
By Boat

Boats arrive in one of two places on Santorini: Ferries from Athens and the other islands arrive at the New Port at Athinios, about five miles south of Fira; cruise ships usually tender passengers to the Old Port, directly below Fira.

By Ferry at the New Port (Athinios): The Athinios port is a hive of activity, with ferries and cruise-ship tenders coming and

going, and a row of cafés and car-rental offices facing the busy embankment. From here, a serpentine road twists up the hill. A taxi into Fira runs about €30 (more to Oia or other towns). Buses meet arriving boats to bring passengers into Fira, where you can connect to other points on the island. Going by bus is much cheaper but can take longer, as they wait to fill up before departing (there are many buses in this chaotic area—look for one marked *Local Bus*). As these buses can be very crowded in peak season, don't dawdle. You may also be accosted by transfer companies offering shared shuttle-bus rides into town (€40/2 people).

Visible from the road above Athinios, the ringed-off area in the bay just below the switchbacks is the site of the *Sea Diamond* shipwreck—a cruise ship that sank here in 2007; all but two of the 1,195 passengers were rescued. The ship rests in 450 feet of water. Concerned that it's polluting the bay, islanders are hoping to pull it up.

For boat connections from Athinios, see "Santorini Connections" at the end of this chapter.

By Cruise Ship: Cruise ships anchor in the caldera below Fira. Passengers taking excursions get the first tenders, which go to the New Port at Athinios (described earlier) and are met by tour buses; after your excursion, the bus will likely drop you off in Fira (for info on returning to your ship, see later). Independent day-trippers are tendered to the Old Port directly below Fira.

When Santorini Blew Its Top

Situated on an edgy stack of tectonic plates, Santorini was created by volcanic activity that lasted more than two million years. The island was once a neatly circular "shield volcano," with a gentle slope that was built up gradually, over a series of volcanic eruptions.

The first major eruption of Santorini took place around 21,000 years ago. The middle of the volcano collapsed and filled with about a hundred feet of water—creating the caldera we see today. For millennia, it was a mostly intact, ring-shaped island—with just a small opening at one end, and a small island in the middle...a perfect natural harbor. The island prospered as a trade port. Experts believe that the island in the middle of the ring may have been the site of a thriving city (the one that, later, may have partly inspired tales of Atlantis). It went by two names: Strongili, meaning "Circular"; and Kalliste, meaning "Beautiful."

But then came the famous "Minoan Eruption" around 1630 BC—one of the largest in human history. It blew out 24 cubic miles of volcanic material, at least four times the amount ejected by the 1883 explosion of Krakatoa in today's Indonesia. The eruption displaced enough seawater to send a tsunami screaming south toward Crete, less than 70 miles away. Archaeologists think that the tsunami (and perhaps earthquakes near the same time) caused severe hardship, eventually leading to the downfall of the Minoan civilization.

Before the full-scale eruption, the volcano likely warned Santorini's inhabitants with a major earthquake and an initial small eruption. No human skeletons and few valuable items from that

From Fira's **Old Port**, there are three ways to reach the town center on the cliff above: Take a cable car, hike up, or ride a donkey. The **cable car** is the easiest option (€6 each way, more for luggage, daily 7:00-22:00, every 20 minutes, more frequent with demand, 3-minute ride to the top). However, the cable car is small (maximum 36 people/trip)—so you might be in for a long wait if you arrive on a big ship. **Hiking** up the 588 steep steps is demanding, and you'll share them with fragrant, messy donkeys. You can

time have been found here, suggesting that islanders were able to pack up and evacuate. Good thing. Soon afterward, large amounts of ash and pumice blasted out of the crater, and super-heated pyroclastic flows swept down the island's slopes. Several walls of the ring collapsed; the island in the middle disappeared; and the caldera became much deeper—filled with more than a thousand feet of water. That's when the island took on the sunken crater shape that visitors see today.

Santorini's volcano isn't done. Two little islets emerged from the bay quite recently, by geological standards. Palea Kameni ("Old Burnt Island") rose from the deep in 197 BC, leaving island-ers awestruck. They credited the sea god Poseidon and built a temple here, which was later destroyed in further eruptions. Then, in AD 1707, Nea Kameni ("New Burnt Island") appeared beside its older brother. Both Kameni islets grew even more in the 1860s. To this day, these islets sometimes sputter and steam, and earth-quakes still wrack the entire archipelago (including a devastating one in 1956). The last small eruption (on Nea Kameni) was in 1950. Today, the geothermal springs on Palea Kameni are a popular tourist attraction.

Although the Minoan Eruption devastated the island, it also left behind a unique ecosystem and agricultural tradition (see the "Island Cuisine in a Desert" sidebar, later). And, starting in the 19th century and ramping up in the early 20th century, the volca-nic soil was also the basis for a local industry: The upper layer of pumice and volcanic ash was quarried, pulverized, and mixed with lime to create a very strong concrete (produced until recently in the blocky, abandoned building on the cliff at the southern edge of Fira). Santorini is the country's sole source of this material. But with the rise of tourism in the 1970s and 1980s, civic leaders real-ized that Santorini's pristine nature would be better in the long run than gaping quarries, most of which have halted production.

pay €10 to ride partway up on a **donkey,** but the stench and the bumpy ride make this far less romantic than it sounds. And the donkeys don't take you all the way up, leaving you a steep uphill hike of around 100 steps at the end. The cable car and donkey trail converge up top, and that point is also the start of my self-guided Fira Walk.

To **return to the Old Port,** you can take the cable car, ride a donkey, or walk down. Note that the line for the cable car can get comically long, snaking through town, as the ship's departure nears.

If, on arrival, you want to head from Fira's Old Port directly to **Oia,** shop around once on shore for local transport. A typical pack-

SANTORINI

age, costing around €30, includes a fast boat from the Old Port to Ammoudi (Oia's port), a bus ride up the hill to Oia, several hours to explore Oia and have lunch, then a 30-minute bus ride back to Fira Town.

By Plane

Santorini's sleek, modern airport sits along the flat area on the east (back) side of the island, about four miles from Fira (code: JTR, +30 2286 028 405; www.santorini-airport.com). It's about a 15-minute ride into Fira, either by taxi (around €25, cash only) or bus (around €2, roughly hourly—coordinated to meet some but not all flights).

GETTING AROUND SANTORINI

By Bus: Fira is the bus hub for the island. The bus "station" (really just a parking lot) is a block below the main street, near the south end of town (just downhill from the Orthodox cathedral and Museum of Prehistoric Thira). Schedules are posted at the kiosk at the bottom end of the lot; buy tickets from the driver (cash only). Despite the chaotic scene, buses are generally clean, much cheaper than taxis, and run on time. Buses can be extremely crowded, especially in peak season—get there early to improve your odds of claiming a seat. For bus connections, see "Fira Connections," later.

By Taxi: The main taxi stand is just uphill and around the corner from Fira's bus station, along the main street. There's often a line of people waiting for taxis, particularly when cruise ships have just arrived. If you need to head to the port or airport in the morning, book a taxi the night before through your hotel. You can also try calling for a taxi (+30 2286 022 555 or +30 2286 023 951). Distances on the island are short, but prices are high (and can be slippery): Figure €30 to Oia, Athinios port, or Perissa; €25 to Kamari's beaches or the airport; and €35 to Akrotiri. Given these prices, it's tempting for those exploring the island to simply rent their own car (typically cheaper than two or three taxi rides)—see next.

By Car: If ever there's a Greek island where it's nice to have a car, Santorini's the one. Taxis are expensive, buses are crowded, and many outlying sights and viewpoints are well worth the trip. Driving around Santorini is reasonably straightforward. Roads are winding but wide (enough), drivers are aggressive but not reckless (drive defensively), towns are well-signposted, and parking is usually free (although spots can be hard to find). Traffic, however, can be a big problem at certain times of day and in peak season.

Offices renting cars, scooters, and ATVs abound in Fira (clustering at the northern end of town, along the main street), in Oia (at the entrance to town), and at the New Port and airport. Or ask your hotel—they likely have a partnership with a company that can make things easy. A small manual-transmission car with basic insurance runs around €45-60 for 24 hours; you'll pay more for an automatic, better insurance, and during the July and August high season. You can usually rent a car on the spot, but it's smart to book ahead in July and August.

Renting an **ATV** is popular on Santorini...but I wouldn't. This island is hillier and more congested than most. Local hospitals report that, on a busy day in the summer, they treat as many as 25 injuries from ATV-related accidents. No matter how defensively you drive, you're sharing the roads with dangerous ATV novices. I'd spring a few more euros for the relative safety of a car.

By Guided Tour: Kostas and his select team of guides at **Santorini Private Tours** do an excellent job of giving meaning to your Santorini visit. They offer a variety of excursions, including "highlights" tours around the island (up to 4 people-€390/4.5 hours, €480/6 hours including Akrotiri), food and wine tours, and cooking classes. The guides work with both cruise passengers and independent travelers. Review the options and contact them through their website (www.santorini-private-guide.com).

Fira

The island's main town, Fira, is a practical hub with an extraordinary setting. Sit at a cliff-clinging café terrace, sip an iced coffee, and watch thousands of cruise-ship passengers flood into town each morning (on the cable car and donkey trail), then recede in the afternoon. This built-in business has made Fira a bit greedy; its main streets (including the aptly named "Gold Street") are lined with aggressive jewelry salespeople and restaurants with great views, high prices, and low quality.

But if you can ignore the tackiness in this part of town, you'll discover that Fira has a charm of its own—particularly in the cozy labyrinth of streets that burrow between its main traffic street and the cliff edge, and on the steep switchback lanes that zigzag down the side of the cliff toward the caldera. Fira is also home to a pair of cathedrals (Orthodox and Catholic) and the island's top museum (the excellent Museum of Prehistoric Thira).

Remember that Fira is not the setting of all those famous Santorini photos—those are taken in Oia.

Orientation to Fira

The core of Fira is squeezed between the cliff and the busy, not particularly charming main road through town, called 25 Martou. Most places of interest to visitors are in the cluster of narrow streets between here and the caldera. Even where street names exist, locals ignore them. Making navigation even more confusing, it's a very vertical town—especially along the cliff. Use a map, and don't be afraid to ask for directions.

Fira—and the island—has no real TI. For help, ask at your hotel, local travel agencies, or other businesses.

HELPFUL HINTS

Combo-Ticket: A €15 combo-ticket covers the ancient sites of Akrotiri (€12) and Ancient Thira (€6) outside of Fira, as well as the recommended Museum of Prehistoric Thira in Fira (€6)—a good value if you see all three. (Both Akrotiri and Ancient Thira often close unexpectedly, so confirm in town that they're open before you buy.)

Laundry: Most launderettes in town offer drop-off service for around €17 (generally closed Sun; ask at your hotel for the nearest location). **Penguin** offers full-service in about three hours (Mon-Sat 9:00-20:00, Sun until 17:00, on 25 Martou toward Oia side, +30 2286 023 908).

Grocery Store: Sizeable **Sklavenitis** (Σκλαβενιτης) is at the south end of town on the main road (Mon-Fri 8:00-21:00, Sat until 20:00, closed Sun).

Ferry Tickets: Three travel agencies are along Fira's main road and sell a variety of ferry tickets (and some can print your tickets, if needed): **Dakoutros Travel, Nomikos Travel,** and **Pelican Travel.**

Travel Blog: For helpful, enjoyably lowbrow local travel information, see www.santorinidave.com.

Fira Walk

This self-guided orientation walk introduces you to Santorini and its main town. It can be done in about an hour; allow more time for sightseeing, photo stops, and hiking to better views. Be warned that this walk traverses the main streets, which can be jammed

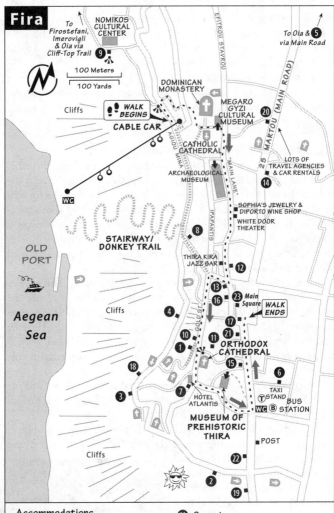

Fira

To Firostefani, Imerovigli & Ola via Cliff-Top Trail

NOMIKOS CULTURAL CENTER **9**

EFITROU STAVROU

To Ola & **5** via Main Road

100 Meters

100 Yards

DOMINICAN MONASTERY

WALK BEGINS

CABLE CAR

Cliffs

AGIOU MINA

MEGARO GYZI CULTURAL MUSEUM

MARTOU (MAIN ROAD)

20

LOTS OF TRAVEL AGENCIES & CAR RENTALS

CATHOLIC CATHEDRAL

MAIN LANE

ARCHAEOLOGICAL MUSEUM

14

WC

OLD PORT

STAIRWAY/ DONKEY TRAIL

IPAPANTIS

SOPHIA'S JEWELRY & DIPORTO WINE SHOP

WHITE DOOR THEATER

8

THIRA KIRA JAZZ BAR

12

Aegean Sea

Cliffs

OLD ST

4

13

23 Main Square

WALK ENDS

16

10

17

1

11

21

18

ORTHODOX CATHEDRAL

15

6

3

7

HOTEL ATLANTIS

TAXI STAND

BUS STATION

WC

MUSEUM OF PREHISTORIC THIRA

POST

22

2

Cliffs

19

Accommodations
1. Villa Renos
2. Kamares Apartments
3. Keti Hotel
4. Scirocco Apartments
5. To Galatia Villas
6. Villa Roussa

Eateries & Other
7. Naoussa
8. Argo
9. Volkan on the Rocks Café & Outdoor Cinema
10. Palia Kameni Cocktail Bar
11. Ouzeri
12. Nikolas
13. Parea Tavern
14. Taverna Triana
15. Lucky's
16. Obelix
17. Nick the Grill & Solo Gelato
18. Cori Rigas Art Café
19. Grocery
20. Laundry
21. Dakoutros Travel (Blue Star)
22. Nomikos Travel (SeaJets)
23. Pelican Travel (Minoan)

with tourists; it can be much more relaxing in late afternoon, or even after dark. Begin where most cruise passengers do: at the cable car station near the top of town. (The cable car is easy to find from anywhere in Fira—just look for the blue signs.)

• *With the cable car station at your back, turn right—yes, away from town—and follow the cobbled path as it curves up and to the right, toward the cliff, between scenic restaurants. Pause along the wall in front of Zafora Restaurant for a...*

Big Orientation View of Santorini

You're looking at the glorious cliff-draping town of Fira—the capital of the archipelago known internationally as Santorini and locally as Thira. This town is improbably perched along the lip of a flooded volcanic caldera—Spanish for "cauldron." And, like a cauldron indeed, Santorini bubbled over and blew its top about 3,600 years ago, obliterating what had been a tidy, ring-shaped archipelago with a busy island town in the middle (see the "When Santorini Blew Its Top" sidebar, earlier).

The crescent-shaped island you're on is called **Thira.** The next-biggest island—the smaller crescent facing Thira across the caldera—is called **Thirasia.** Its little port town, Manolas, is connected to the spine of the island by a rugged donkey path. The two chunky islands in the middle of the caldera are called **Nea ("New") Kameni** and **Palea ("Old") Kameni**—both of which remain volcanically active.

Historically, Santorini has experienced volcanic activity about every 75 years, most recently in the mid-1950s. Do the math...and keep your eyes peeled for steam venting.

Scanning the cliffs, notice the **horizontal stripes** of black, gray, and red—indicating where the original volcanic island was formed by a series of eruptions, each one building on the previous one, like the rings of a tree. The edge of the caldera was sheared off cleanly by an eruption 21,000 years ago, creating this cross-section of the striations—a unique opportunity to see eons of geology in one glance.

Now look down below, where a stepped **donkey** path twists all the way to the Old Port of Fira. You can pay €10 for the ride (almost all the way) up or down. While this seems like a tourist gimmick, beasts of burden have been hauling cargo from the port up to the cliff-capping towns for centuries. In recent years, more progressive islanders have formed the Santorini Animal Welfare

Association (SAWA) to educate the traditional donkey wranglers to treat their animals more humanely. If the cable car is totally jammed—and it usually is—you can hike down this path...but step carefully to avoid the donkey droppings.

Continue uphill past the restaurant, hiking up to better and better views. Go at least as far as the Da Costa restaurant (a 5-minute climb) and pause there. But if you have energy and want to (somewhat) escape even more crowds, you can hike all the way up to the boxy, orange Nomikos Cultural Center, which caps the trail's summit. You could continue another 10 minutes past that to the village of Firostefani with its classic blue-domed Agios Theodori Church (or even carry on a few hours farther for the rugged, unforgettably scenic—and unforgettably strenuous—hike all the way to Oia).

• *After checking the views, meet me back here at Da Costa restaurant. With your back to the water, the lane just right of its terrace leads to...*

Venetian Upper Fira

In addition to the native Greeks, people from Venice (whom locals call "Franks") have also left their mark on Santorini. While Ve-

netians have always passed through as merchants, they took notice of this archipelago after the Fourth Crusade (early 13th century)—when Byzantium was sacked and its sprawling empire fell apart, opening the door to foreign influence. Santorini was ideally located at a crossroads of the sea trade between the heart of Europe and the Middle East. Venetians also appreciated the protection its steep cliffs provided: Any would-be invader would need to stage an essentially vertical invasion. Venice fortified the island with a chain of five fortresses, including one in Imerovigli, steeply uphill from here; one in Oia; and one perched along the saddle of land to the south, just above Akrotiri. The name "Santorini" (which locals still don't entirely embrace) comes from the long-gone Venetian church of Santa Irini.

Venetian influence persists here to this day. While only a small percentage of locals are Catholic, the Catholic Church—in many ways the descendant of those original Venetian overlords—still owns lots of property. In general, beige and blocky Upper Fira—above this path—is Catholic, while the blue-and-white warren of cave houses in Lower Fira is Orthodox (including the huge, squat, blinding-white dome of the Greek Orthodox Cathedral, which you can see across the caldera).

Savor this view once more, then head up the lane next to Da Costa restaurant, hiking up the steps past the Art of the Loom gallery. The stairs dead-end at the (usually closed) doorway of the Church of the Immaculate Conception—one of many Catholic churches built in this area in the late 18th and early 19th centuries.

Turn right and follow the cobbled path to the well-marked **Catholic Cathedral**—a.k.a. the Cathedral of St. John the Baptist.

This was built in 1823, heavily damaged (like much of Santorini) by the 1956 earthquake, and reopened in 1975. Step through the gate into the courtyard, and continue inside the church itself (open long hours daily). While firmly Catholic, architecturally this feels like an eclectic hybrid of Catholic and Orthodox—with muted colors, a big chandelier, and Moorish-style arches flanking the main altar. Remember the details, which you can compare to the interior of the Orthodox Cathedral later on this walk.

Back outside, retrace your steps to the cobbled lane, where you'll turn right and head downhill, toward town. A few steps down, the wide cobbled street on your left leads to yet another Catholic institution—the **Dominican Monastery**—and good views back on the cathedral's dome and steeple. A complex of Catholic buildings sprawl from here uphill, all the way to the next town, Firostefani.

A few more steps down, displayed next to the door on the left (marked *Art and Iron Studio*), is a gnarled vine, twisted into a circular basket shape. This is how Santorini vintners cultivate their wine, to maximize retention of moisture. This door opens into a sweet little courtyard garden.

Finally, just below that—at the base of the stepped lane—is the entrance to the **Megaro Gyzi Museum,** which fills the mansion of a local parishioner who willed this property to the Church (described later, under "Sights in Fira").

• *Just below the museum, turn right onto Fira's...*

"Main Lane" (Erythrou Stavrou Street)

Locals ignore street names, but they think of this drag as the "Main Lane" of their little burg. ("Main Street," which carries car traffic, is lower down—we'll end our walk there.) One of the town's top shopping gauntlets, this lane is lined with all manner of tacky souvenir stands, posters and postcards, linens, natural sponges, seashells, and a surprising abundance of "fish pedicure" places.

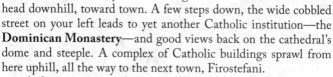

Walk down the Main Lane. After about a block, on the square on the right (toward the cable car station where we began), is the entrance to the **Archaeological Museum of Thira.** For years, it offered only dusty cases crammed with sparsely described jugs, statues, and other artifacts from ancient Thira—but after a major renovation, the museum should be refreshed and reopen by the time you visit. Either way, unless you have time to kill I recommend skipping it and saving your energy for the excellent Museum of Prehistoric Thira, which has far older and more interesting Minoan pieces from Akrotiri and is right at the end of this walk.

Continuing past the museum on Main Lane, keep straight at the fork. You'll pass **Sophia's** jewelry shop, one of many in Santorini that display the local jewelry: Finely detailed and inspired by Byzantine pieces, they feature intricate beading and filigree. Greek Orthodox priests wear simple golden cuffs for important worship services, but bishops' cuffs are more elaborately detailed—offering inspiration for some of these frilly designs. Do a little window shopping and appreciate the fine craftsmanship.

Just past Sophia's is one of two entrances to the **Diporto** ("two doors") shop, which sells local products and offers tastings of Santorini's wines in the hope you'll buy a bottle (for more on local wines, see the "Santorini Wines" sidebar).

Carry along the narrow Main Lane. After a long block, on your left is the entrance to **The White Door Theater,** which puts on a fun "village Greek wedding" folk show each night (described later, under "Nightlife in Fira"). On the next block, **Nikolas** (on the left) is a classic taverna and one of my recommended restaurants.

• *Soon the Main Lane dead-ends at the stairs to a taverna. Turn right here and walk up the blue-painted steps. This street hits a T-intersection with the street called...*

"Gold Street"

Before we head left down Santorini's most touristy strip, take a few steps to the right. Signs point downhill to the Old Port. Notice that each of the steps from here on down is painted with a number—it's exactly 588 steps to the water. If you have strong knees, returning to your cruise-ship tender down these stairs could be more appealing than joining the looooong line for the cable car that snakes through the streets of Fira shortly before call time. For now, you could head down to step #568 for some nice views over town.

From the top of the stairs, with the caldera to your back, turn right, take a deep breath, and plunge down tourist-crammed Gold Street. There was a time when the majority of vendors along here actually did specialize in golden jewelry. But many of the storefronts have been taken over by tacky souve-

nirs, ice cream parlors, resort wear, and other, less genteel goods.

Just after Classico, on the right, peer down into the ruins of a traditional Santorini cave house that collapsed after the 1956 earthquake. Rainwater was collected in the terrace out front, and the cave part of the home is under your feet. For more on this traditional style of architecture, see "Santorini's Cave Houses," later.

• *Make short work of this strip, until you pop out at the wide-open and gorgeous viewpoint I like to call...*

"Orthodox Cathedral Terrace"

This is where Fira opens up and really lets you breathe in some grand vistas. Lining the white wall, a half-dozen floating door-

ways lead down steep staircases to hotels and restaurants with big views. (For a better-value meal, without the views, Ouzeri restaurant is just before the cathedral, set back from the square on the left.)

Step up to the white wall and look down over the labyrinth of cave houses that are draped over the cliffs here. The lanes connecting these houses are far less crowded than the ones we've braved so far and come with smashing views—they're a delight to explore. Many of these are hotels, but some turn their breakfast terraces into cafés; exploring this area to find your favorite perch for a cup of coffee is a fun activity (I particularly like the **Cori Rigas Art Café,** along the lower cliffside lane—follow the stairs down at Palia Kameni Bar). The whole area is anchored, at the top of the hill, by the big, boxy Hotel Atlantis, which feels like it's keeping the steep warren of lanes from simply sliding down into the caldera. The steep lanes around the far side of the Atlantis are even quieter—it's surprisingly easy to escape most of the tourist crush.

The main feature of this terrace is the looming **Orthodox Cathedral of Candelmas** (Panagia Ypapantis). This modern ca-

thedral, which caps Fira like a white crown, has a grandly painted interior that offers a beautiful taste of the Greek Orthodox faith (free entry, open long hours daily except may close at midday). Stepping inside, appreciate the typical Greek-cross floor plan (with four equal-length arms). Flanking the entry aisle are framed icons, which some visitors reverently kiss as they enter. Farther in is the grand, golden chandelier, with a giant ostrich egg dangling from its base. Representing the body of the Church, the egg is a common symbol in Orthodox churches. The writing on the chandelier is not Greek but Cyrillic—this was a gift from the Russian patriarch (the head of the Russian Orthodox Church) to commemorate Russia's links to Santorini through the trade of a local wine used for Communion. Directly below the chandelier is a double-headed Byzantine eagle. Beyond that is the wooden iconostasis, with shimmering icons of saints. Looking up, notice the balcony overhead. Traditionally, women would worship there, while men stood on the main floor. But today, everyone fills the main hall, women on the left, men on the right. You can step through the side door into the tranquil, fenced courtyard that surrounds the cathedral, with the grave of a local bishop.

• *You could finish your walk here if you're in a rush or want to explore the meandering terraces below. Or stick with me to get a glimpse of workaday Fira and the town's top museum.*

Back outside, walk to the far end of the cathedral, and hook left between it and Hotel Atlantis. Heading downhill, you'll run into the back of the wavy-roofed Museum of Prehistoric Thira—the town's top sight. But to get inside, you'll have to circle around to the gate on its lower side: First jog right, then hook left, to walk along...

Fira's Main Street (25 Martou)

While it's not much to look at, this drag is the main artery of Fira—where the fantasyland at the cusp of the caldera meets the real world of humble island Greece.

Walk along Main Street, watching on your left for the gate to enter the excellent **Museum of Prehistoric Thira,** with a wonderful collection of artifacts (ceramics, frescoes, and a tiny golden ibex) from the Minoan-era settlement at Akrotiri. If you visit one museum on Santorini, make it this one (described later).

Now let's get practical: Across the street from the museum gate is the town's main taxi stand, where cabs fan out to the distant

SANTORINI

corners of the island. Nearby is a public WC. And around the corner is the bus station.

With the museum to your back, turn left and continue one more block—passing some cheap eats (including recommended Lucky's Souvlaki)—to where the traffic-free zone begins. This is Fira's **"Main Square,"** crammed with tourist services that cater not to high-roller Gold Street shoppers but to mere mortals and budget backpackers. You'll find lots of cheap-and-cheery eateries, ice cream stands, takeaway coffee, greasy souvlaki, and more. This is a good place to regroup, refresh, and stock up before continuing your explorations of Santorini.

• *Our orientation walk is finished. To reach other parts of the island, backtrack one block to the taxi stand and bus station. Or, rent a car or scooter at one of the rental places lining Main Street just past Main Square. To head toward the Old Port for a cruise tender, turn left up the street at the end of Main Square to return to the start of Gold Street with those 588 steps (the cable car is about a 10-minute walk to the right, along Main Lane).*

Sights in Fira

OLD TOWN
▲Megaro Gyzi Museum
Hiding in the alleys behind the Catholic cathedral, this modest local history museum celebrates Santorini life. It fills the 18th-century home of a prominent local resident, who willed it to the Catholic Church.

Cost and Hours: €3, Mon-Sat 10:00-16:00—may close later in peak season, closed Sun and Nov-April, +30 2286 023 077, www.gyzimegaron.gr.

Visiting the Museum: On the right as you enter, look for the map illustrating how the island has grown and shrunk with volcanic eruptions across the eons. Also in this main hall are evocative etchings of traditional Santorini lifestyles, and copies of old documents—some in Greek, others in Italian, still others in Arabic, emphasizing Santorini's status as a crossroads of civilizations (use the nearby laminated English handout to learn more).

In the room to the left, find the 1870 clipping from a London newspaper article about "Santorin" and, next to it, an engraving of a smoldering islet in the caldera. Nearby are photographs of the town from the early to mid–20th century (including scenes before and after the devastating 1956 earthquake), and samples of the various types of volcanic rock found on the island (some embedded with flash-fossilized palms and pistachio leaves).

Upstairs, you'll find a humble painting gallery with still lifes and landscapes donated by local families.

▲▲Museum of Prehistoric Thira

While no competition for Greece's top archaeological exhibits, this little museum is Santorini's best, presenting items found in the prehistoric city buried under ash near Akrotiri. A visit is particularly worthwhile if you plan to see the excavated ruins of that city at the southern end of the island (described under "More Sights on Santorini," later). That settlement was the largest city outside Crete in the Minoan-era world, dating back to the earliest documented civilization in the Aegean (third to second millennium BC)—ancient even to the ancients. The people who lived here fled before Santorini blew its top (likely around 1630 BC—see the sidebar, earlier), leaving behind intriguing artifacts of a civilization that disappeared from the earth not long after. Most of those artifacts have been moved off-site, either to this museum or to the biggies in Athens.

Everything in this manageable museum is described in English and well-presented in modern, air-conditioned comfort.

Cost and Hours: €6, covered by €15 combo-ticket; Wed-Mon 8:30-15:30, closed Tue; entrance across from taxi stand on the main drag, +30 2286 025 405, http://odysseus.culture.gr.

Visiting the Museum: Enter the gate below the museum, head up the stairs to buy your ticket in the freestanding white building, then hook left to the entrance. Inside, everything is displayed in one big room, which you'll visit counterclockwise.

Section C: Turning right from the entrance, look for the Early Cycladic figures and vessels, dating from 2700 to 2300 BC. The stiff figurines, with their arms crossed, perplex archaeologists, who speculate that they might represent the Mother Goddess worshipped here.

Section D: Next, the model of the Akrotiri site puts the items in context. Most of the museum's pieces date from the Late Cycladic Period (mid-17th century BC), when Akrotiri peaked just before its residents fled the erupting volcano. Although they took valuable items (such as jewelry) with them, they left behind easily replaceable everyday objects and, of course, immovable items such as wall frescoes. These left-behind items form the core of the collection.

Section D1: This section displays an intriguing assortment: Primitive cooking pots, clay ovens, and barbeque grills, along with bronze vases, daggers, tongs, and fishing hooks, offer clues to the Aegean lifestyle. The Thi-

rans were traders rather than warriors, so many items reflect their relatively comfortable lifestyle, connection with the wider world, and consumer society. One plaster cast shows the shape left by a (now-deteriorated) three-legged wooden table that could have passed for Baroque from the 17th century AD—but it's from the 17th century BC.

Section D2: Each of the three large containers in this section is marked differently to suggest its contents—for example, a vessel that held water was decorated with reeds (aquatic plants). In the nearby case, the stack of metal weights illustrates the evolution of standardization during early trading.

Wall Frescoes: The museum's highlights are several vibrantly colorful, two-dimensional wall frescoes. Local artists likely executed these wall paintings, but their naturalistic style was surely influenced by the wider Minoan culture. In keeping with the style of Crete (the home of the Minoans), men appear brown, and the women, white. (If you've been to the National Archaeological Museum in Athens, you might recognize this style of fresco from that museum's collection, which includes wall paintings of antelopes, swallows, and young men boxing, all from this same Akrotiri site.)

The wall frescoes from the House of the Ladies (section D3.5) show finely dressed women. In one, an older woman leans over and appears to be touching the arm of another (now-missing) woman and holding a dress in her right hand.

Near the House of the Ladies frescoes, notice the **vessels** (such as beautiful vases decorated with dolphins and lilies), which give us a glimpse of everyday life back then. Look for the ritual vessel shaped like a boar's head. In section D7.2, you'll see a fragment of another wall fresco showing blue monkeys. Because monkeys are not indigenous to Greece, these images offer more evidence that the Cycladic and Minoan people traveled far and wide and interacted with foreign cultures.

In a display case near the monkeys is an exquisite miniature **golden ibex**—one of the few items of great value that were left behind by fleeing islanders. Notice the delicate artistry on the skinny, twisted horns. Head downstairs for additional, impressive wall paintings; check out the youths holding fish (quite a catch).

OUTSIDE OF TOWN
▲▲▲Hike to Oia

With a few hours to spare, you can venture out on one of Greece's most scenic hikes. While the main road connecting Fira to Oia is drab and dusty, a wonderful cliff-top trail links the two towns, offering fantastic views most of the way. It's about 5 miles (plan on at least 4 hours one-way), quite strenuous (with lots of ups and downs), and offers little or no shade in hot weather—so don't attempt it unless you're in good shape and have the right gear (good shoes, water, food, sun protection). Get an early start. You can catch a bus or taxi back to Fira when you're done.

From Fira, head north through the adjoining villages of Firostefani (where you can see the church, described next) and cliff-capping Imerovigli, then continue along the lip of the caldera. You'll briefly walk along the shoulder of a busy, narrow road, along the skinny spine of the island, with Aegean views on both sides. Then you'll hike steeply up, up, up and over the bluff, then down into Oia. (Donkeys are standing by for the steepest part of the climb, for those who'd rather catch a lift.)

▲▲Agios Theodori Church in Firostefani

This Catholic church—a steep 20-minute uphill hike from the center of Fira, on the trail to Oia, in the village of Firostefani—is quintessential Santorini: With a vivid blue dome, bright-yellow bell tower, and breathtaking caldera backdrop, it's perennially ready for its close-up. This is the only classic Santorini dome where you can snap a photo of the church with only water behind it—no other buildings or townscapes—making it a magnet for photographers. Inside is a precious icon of the Virgin Mary, brought here from Russia in 1570.

Nightlife in Fira

Folk Theater

The White Door Theater puts on a faux Greek wedding in an open-air courtyard, with traditional music and dance and, of course, plate breaking. The audience, acting as guests at the wedding, is invited to participate. While this sounds tacky, it goes beyond clichés with a thoughtfully researched, well-presented program rooted in a deep respect for authentic Greek village customs.

The organizers explain that, while every other major event in Greek village life (holidays, funerals) was religious and more introspective, a traditional wedding was the one time people could cut loose and fully enjoy themselves (€65 includes tapas dinner and wine, runs May-Oct nightly at 21:00 or 21:30, 2 hours, +30 2286 021 770, www.whitedoorsantorini.com).

Outdoor Cinema

In summer, **Volkan on the Rocks Open Air Cinema** often shows crowd-pleasing classics (*Mamma Mia!*, *My Big Fat Greek Wedding*, and so on) on a small outdoor screen perched over the caldera (€20, includes a snack, June-Oct most nights at 21:00 but subject to change—call ahead or check online before making the trip, +30 2286 028 360, www.volkanontherocks.com).

Nightclubs

Fira is busy after hours. A popular venue is **Kira Thira Jazz Bar,** with good music and an artsy vibe (nightly from 20:00). For a hard-partying nightclub—open late and packed with young people—try **Enigma** or **Koo Club** (open nightly from 21:00). Both are buried deep in the town center.

Sleeping in Fira

Fira is the handier home base, but some prefer romantic Oia. All the accommodations I list have air-conditioning. Note that rates on this popular island skyrocket from July through September. While sticker shock is epidemic here, keep in mind that the spectacular views are one of the main reasons you came. Therefore, splurging on a caldera view is, in a sense, a good value at just about any price.

PLACES WITH CALDERA VIEWS

These accommodations all feature fantastic views and have peaceful terraces where you can watch the sunset. Most of these places spill down the cliffs from town and involve lots of stairs and steep climbs. For less climbing, try Kamares Apartments (a couple of minutes south of the Old Town, with parking right out front and a few stairs once you enter) or Villa Renos (some stairs, but fewer than most). Note that taxis can only take you to the top of the hill; you'll have to walk from there.

$$$$ Villa Renos, just below the Orthodox Cathedral, has nine well-appointed rooms. It's traditional (rather than trendy) and well-kept, with an inviting terrace cocktail bar and several small swimming/soaking pools. It's well-run by Vassilis Matekas, who used to live in Rhode Island (great homemade breakfast that changes daily, follow the stairs down at Palia Kameni Bar, +30 2286 022 369, www.villarenos.com, hrenos@otenet.gr).

$$$$ Kamares Apartments surround a dreamy oasis of white-on-white stucco, with eight *canava*-style rooms, most with their own hot tub, in a traditional cave home that's been in the family for generations. The service is warm and attentive, and the location—at the very south end of town—is sheltered from some of central Fira's nightlife noise. There's handy parking right in front—a rarity for places with a view (family rooms available, +30 2268 028 110, www.kamares-apartments.gr, info@kamares-apartments.gr).

$$$$ Keti Hotel is another appealing place with ten cave rooms and stupendous views. Rather than luxury, it offers stark-white, clean comfort, and the doubles are good value for this location. There's a small pool and a warm welcome from friendly Yiannis; the hotel is named after his mother (facing the caldera below the Orthodox Cathedral, +30 2286 022 324, www.hotelketi.gr, info@hotelketi.gr).

$$$$ Scirocco Apartments, run by a Greek-German couple (Eleftherios and Anja Sirigos and their daughters), rents eight straightforward, old-fashioned, but reasonably priced rooms for the location, some of them "cave houses" burrowed right into the cliffside. All rooms enjoy either a private or shared terrace and the swimming pool on the lowest level (breakfast extra, closed Nov-March, located facing the caldera below the Orthodox Cathedral, +30 2286 022 855 or +30 2286 024 811, www.scirocco-santorini.com, info@scirocco-santorini.com). For drivers, they also rent seven rooms in the countryside on the far side of the island.

CHEAPER OPTIONS WITHOUT CALDERA VIEWS

If you're willing to give something up—view, luxury, and/or in-town convenience—you'll pay lower rates. But lower your expectations: On Santorini, €150 buys a lot less comfort than it does in Athens.

Close to Town: $$ Galatia Villas is calm and out of the way of Fira's stifling crowds, with 18 tasteful rooms—including some studios—plus a small swimming pool. Technically in Kontorhori, the next village over, it's about a 10-minute walk to Fira's action along a busy road (+30 2286 024 524, www.galatiavillas.gr, info@galatiavillas.gr).

In Town: $$$ Villa Roussa offers 12 simple but comfortable, more affordable rooms tucked in a dreary modern building overlooking a parking lot, behind the taxi stand and bus station. Some rooms have balconies, but not caldera views—which are a short walk away, over the ridge (no breakfast, +30 2286 023 220, www. villaroussa.gr, villaroussa@gmail.com, Peter Pelekanos).

Eating in Fira

You'll pay dearly to dine with a caldera view. I've focused my listings on simpler tavernas with great food at better prices but less-thrilling vistas. Takeout fast-food options (grabbing a souvlaki to eat on a stool or to go) help keep costs down. Drivers note: One of my favorite places to eat on the island is **Metaxi Mas,** about a 15-minute drive into the countryside; for details, see page 489.

WITH A CALDERA VIEW

Santorini specializes in pricey restaurants with terraces facing the caldera—especially popular around sunset (reserve ahead). You'll

basically pay double, and likely compromise on quality, to eat with a caldera view—but for a memorable meal, it could still be worth it. Many Fira caldera-view restaurants are interchangeable, but the ones noted below distinguish themselves in one way or another.

Below the Orthodox Cathedral: $$$$ Naoussa is a family-friendly place that churns out big plates of sloppy Greek cooking, served on its cozy and unpretentious terrace. While pricey, it's near the bottom end of this price range and more affordable than other caldera-view eateries (daily 12:00-24:00, tucked below the big and boxy Atlantis Hotel, +30 2286 024 869).

Near the Cable Car: $$$$ Argo, also along the cliffs, serves traditional Greek food, and specializes in fish—at predictably high prices. While quite expensive, it has friendly local service and somewhat better food than its competitors. Reserve ahead for the upper deck, with the best caldera views (daily 12:00-24:00, along the donkey path just below Gold Street, +30 2286 022 594, www. argo-restaurant-santorini.com).

Microbrews at the Top of Town, above the Catholic Cathedral: Some of the most sweeping views over Santorini can be found from the high-altitude trail toward Oia, about a five-minute hike up past the Catholic Cathedral. At the crest of the trail, just under the orange cultural center, **$$$ Volkan on the Rocks Café** is an inviting, low-key spot. They produce their own craft beer ("filtered with volcanic rocks"), as well as pricey tropical cocktails and basic

Island Cuisine in a Desert

Santorini has an unusual approach to cuisine, dictated (like all facets of life here) by its volcanic geology. Most produce on the island is never watered...which is even more surprising when you consider that Santorini—and the neighboring island of Anafi—are the only places in Europe technically classified as having a desert climate. But the island's very steep cliffs trap passing clouds, so on most mornings there's a fine layer of dew covering the ground—just enough to keep plants growing. Residents claim that this approach, along with the volcanic soil, makes their produce taste particularly sweet. Santorini specialties include grapes, tomatoes, eggplant, and cucumbers.

You'll find the predictable Greek classics on most menus, but also look for some local dishes. A Santorinian salad uses the island's cherry tomatoes and cucumbers; a popular starter is *tomatokeftedes*—deep-fried tomato croquettes. *Fava* is a chickpea spread similar to hummus. Because the main settlements of Santorini are perched on the tops of cliffs—with challenging access to the sea—fish isn't as integral to the cuisine as on other islands and is quite expensive. If you want fresh seafood, it's best to descend from the cliffsides and dine by the water, such as in Akrotiri in the south or on Ammoudi Bay in the north.

meze. The lower terrace, dubbed Volkan Gardens, serves drinks only from 18:00 and is a great place to reserve for the sunset (daily 9:00-24:00, +30 2286 028 360, www.volkanontherocks.com).

Cocktails with a View: Palia Kameni Cocktail Bar (Παλιά Καμένη), with an elaborately decorated "floating doorway" just in front of the Orthodox Cathedral, has cascading terraces with magnificent caldera views, a sophisticated vibe, and a tempting menu of good—if extremely expensive—cocktails (no food, Mon-Sat 10:00-late, Sun from 17:00, reserve a few weeks ahead for sunset table, +30 2286 022 430, www.paliakameni.com).

IN THE OLD TOWN

The Old Town streets teem with better-value eateries...still expensive by Greek standards, but far more affordable than caldera-view spots.

$$$ Ouzeri (Το Ουζερι) is a big, popular, finely oiled machine of a restaurant churning out good traditional food with efficient service at the top of a shopping mall smack in the center. Their outside tables come with distant sea views—albeit ones looking east, rather than into the caldera. That means it doesn't work well at sunset (unless you're trying to avoid the crowds), but it's great for lunch or after dark. Try some of their local specialties, such as meatballs in an ouzo sauce and the *tomatokeftedes* starter—fried tomatoes with onions and herbs. They also have several vegetarian options (daily 12:00-23:00, head up the stairs next to Orthodox Cathedral, +30 2286 021 566, www.toouzerisantorini.com).

$$$ **Nikolas** oozes a family-run taverna vibe, with one big room crammed with tables overseen by a shrine-like photo of the namesake patriarch. Today his granddaughter Eleni runs the place, and while it's not quite what it used to be, they keep things traditional: stick-to-your-ribs Greek classics, specializing in casseroles and other oven-baked meals. There's no outdoor seating, but this is a good choice in bad weather or after sunset. It can get crowded—book ahead or be prepared to wait (daily 15:00-23:00, +30 2286 036 422).

$$ **Parea Tavern** is right in the thick of the tacky tourist tangle but wins plaudits for reliable quality. Its roof terrace (no sunset views) fills up quickly, so get there early or book ahead (daily 13:00-22:00, +30 2286 025 444, www.parearestaurant.gr).

$$ **Taverna Triana,** a bit out of the bustle, is unassuming; it looks like a dozen other, similar restaurants. What distinguishes it are its better-than-average takes on the Greek standards at fair prices. Hosts Spyros and Chai work hard to keep customers satisfied (daily 11:00-23:00, reservations smart, +30 2286 024 005, www.trianasantorini.com).

Souvlaki: The local favorites for $ souvlaki are the hole-in-the-wall **Lucky's,** the glitzy **Obelix** for its sizable menu (summer only), and **Nick the Grill** for its handy people-watching location right on the main square.

Ice Cream: There's lots of overpriced, garishly colored goop in Fira, but **Solo Gelato** does real-deal artisanal stuff (near recommended Nick the Grill, daily 8:00-24:00, +30 2286 036 335).

Fira Connections

From Fira by Bus to: Oia (2-3/hour, 30-40 minutes), **Athinios/ New Port** (nearly hourly—coordinated to meet boats, 20-45 minutes; for boat connections from Athinios, see "Santorini Connections" at the end of this chapter), **airport** (roughly hourly—coordinated to meet most flights, 15 minutes), **Kamari** and its nearby beaches (2-3/hour, 10 minutes), **Akrotiri** with its archaeological site and nearby red-sand beach (1-2/hour, 30 minutes), and **Perissa** with its black-sand beaches and access to the Ancient Thira archaeological site (2-3/hour, 30 minutes). A ride to virtually anywhere on the island costs about €2-3. Check schedules at the kiosk at the downhill edge of the lot and buy tickets from the driver. Bus information: +30 2286 025 404, www.ktel-santorini.gr.

Oia

Oia (pronounced EE-ah, not OY-ah; sometimes spelled "Ia" in English) is the classic, too-pretty-to-be-true place you imagine when someone says "Greek islands." This idyllic ensemble of whitewashed houses and blue domes is delicately draped over a steep slope at the top of a cliff. And in their wisdom, the locals have positioned their town just right for enjoying a sunset over the caldera. On a blue-sky day, there's no better place in Greece to go on a photo safari. Shoot the classic, blue-domed postcard views, but also wander around to find your own angle on the town. If you can't snap a postcard-quality photo here, it's time to retire your camera.

Oia wasn't always this alluring. In fact, half a century ago it was in ruins—devastated by an earthquake on July 9, 1956. When rebuilding, natives seized the opportunity to make their town even more picture-perfect than before—and it paid off. Though far from undiscovered, Oia is the kind of place that you don't mind sharing with boatloads of tourists. And if you break away from its main streets, you can find narrow, winding lanes that take you far from the crowds. This becomes more difficult at sunset, when what feels like every tourist on Santorini jams its tight streets (for strategies, see "Santorini Sunsets" sidebar, earlier). On the other hand, Oia is a delight in the early morning (before around 11:00)—before cruise excursions make their way to the town.

GETTING THERE

From Fira (the island's transport hub), it's about 7.5 miles north to Oia. You can take the bus (see "Fira Connections," earlier) or a taxi (€30 one-way), hike (several hours, see "Hike to Oia," earlier), or drive (see next).

Route Tips for Drivers: In normal traffic, it's about a 25-minute drive from Fira to Oia. The most scenic—and congested—route heads straight north out of Fira on the old road, passing the villages

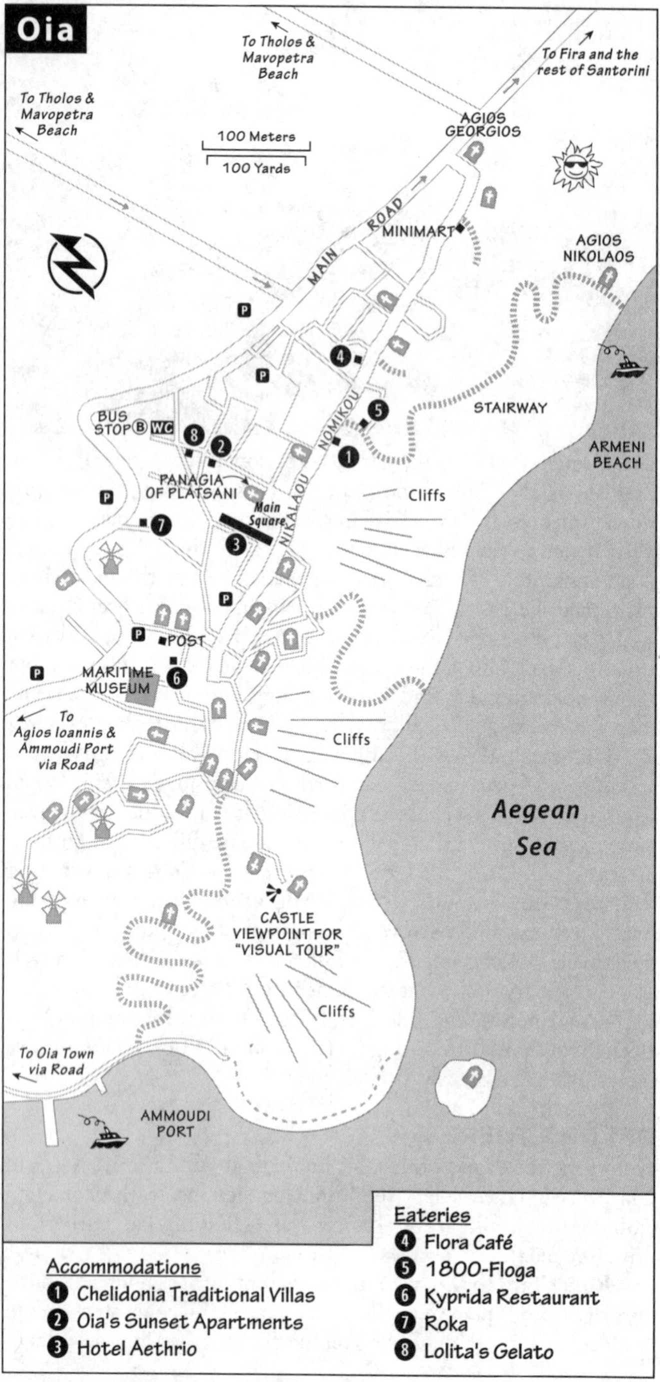

Oia

To Tholos & Mavopetra Beach

To Fira and the rest of Santorini

AGIOS GEORGIOS

To Tholos & Mavopetra Beach

100 Meters

100 Yards

MINIMART

AGIOS NIKOLAOS

STAIRWAY

ARMENI BEACH

BUS STOP

WC

MAIN ROAD

NOMIKOU

NIKALOU

PANAGIA OF PLATSANI

Main Square

Cliffs

POST

MARITIME MUSEUM

To Agios Ioannis & Ammoudi Port via Road

Cliffs

Aegean Sea

CASTLE VIEWPOINT FOR "VISUAL TOUR"

Cliffs

To Oia Town via Road

AMMOUDI PORT

SANTORINI

Accommodations
1 Chelidonia Traditional Villas
2 Oia's Sunset Apartments
3 Hotel Aethrio

Eateries
4 Flora Café
5 1800-Floga
6 Kyprida Restaurant
7 Roka
8 Lolita's Gelato

of Firostefani (consider pulling over and walking a few minutes for the classic Firostefani church view—see page 471) and Imerovigli, then driving along the spine of the island to Oia. The new road, lower down and closer to the island's east coast, is the speedier way to connect the towns (avoiding traffic on the narrow road up top). Consider taking the new road into Oia and the old (more scenic) road out (you'll be routed that direction departing Oia anyway).

If you're coming on the upper (old) road, as you approach Oia, you'll be routed down a long, one-way detour along the back side of the island, and then back up again, popping out just below the main part of town. A few parking lots are in this area, but they're often full. First, try turning right toward the port of Ammoudi; while you're still in Oia (before descending to the port), keep an eye out for parking lots that allow quick access to the scenic tip of town. If you find nothing available, go back the way you came, and continue along the one-way main road (past where you entered town) toward Fira, keeping a close eye out for additional parking lots. But don't go too far, or you'll have to loop all the way around again. (If you're here for sunset and want to enable a quick escape, it can make sense to park at the Fira end of town regardless—increasing walking but reducing traffic jams to leave town.) Some scattered spaces may be free, but most lots charge a small fee—carefully check for signs before leaving your car.

Orientation to Oia

Oia lines up along its cliff. The main pedestrian drag, which traces the rim of the cliff, is called Nikolaou Nomikou. Oia's steep seaward side is smothered with accommodations and restaurants, while the flat landward side is more functional. The town is effectively traffic-free except for the main road, which runs along the back of town, passing the town bus stop and parking lots. From here, it's a few short, nondescript blocks toward the cliff and its million-dollar views.

Sights in Oia

▲▲▲Visual Tour of Oia

You can see most of Oia with a sweep of the head from a prime vantage point: its ruined castle, at the very tip of town. Make your way there and follow this visual tour for an orientation to this picturesque little burg.

• *With your back to the water, face the homes and domes of Oia, and think of its history.*

Oia's Skyline: While today it's a posh resort, in its heyday Oia was the island's most prosperous town, located at the point

Santorini's Cave Houses

On Santorini, you'll see a unique type of building...and maybe even sleep in one: the cave house *(yposkafa)*. In addition to serving as residences or hotels, these structures house churches, *canava*s (wine-pressing rooms), and other establishments.

Cave houses were originally dug into the soft volcanic rock by poor workers who couldn't afford to build a freestanding house. High on the cliffs, they also provided security against invaders. The top of the cave is a rounded arch, rather than flat, to provide more durability in case of earthquakes. People would live and cook near the cave's front, and sleep in the back. Often the house includes a small aboveground structure; after the Venetians began to fortify the island in the 13th century—providing more safety to islanders—these became more common.

Between the inner and outer walls is a layer of pumice insulation—lighter than other  types of stone, and very effective for keeping the interiors warm in winter and cool in summer. These days, new construction looks similar but uses a synthetic Styrofoam instead of pumice. A thinner layer of Styrofoam is needed, allowing them to carve out larger interiors without violating building codes by raising the roof.

For the trim (thresholds and windowsills), look for a porous, reddish, volcanic rock; while this is often plastered over and painted, it looks sharp in its natural state.

And why all the whitewash? For one thing, white reflects (rather than absorbs) the powerful heat of the sun. White is the color of the mineral lime mixed with water, which makes a good antiseptic (islanders used it to paint their houses, so it  would naturally disinfect the rainwater that was collected on rooftops). Later, white evolved into an aesthetic choice...and a patriotic one: During the 400-year Ottoman occupation, Greeks were not allowed to fly their blue-and-white flag. But here in Oia—with its white houses, blue domes, blue sea and sky, and white clouds—the whole village was one big defiant banner for Greece. The blue-and-white color scheme also resembles the "evil eye," believed to fend off bad spirits.

where arriving ships first reached Santorini. Scan the distinctive townscape: The large, boxy buildings at the top of town were the homes of the wealthy sea captains (one of which is now a museum—see later). And the humble, whitewashed cave houses on the slopes below housed their crew, stevedores, and other laborers. These people couldn't afford to build a big, fancy house...so they dug one (see the sidebar). While the cave houses were once the poorest dwellings in town, today only millionaires can af-

ford to own them (and virtually all of them are rented out as very pricey accommodations). The few residents who live in Oia can't afford to have a view. Most "locals" live in humble villages a 10- to 20-minute drive from the caldera.

By the way, much of the Oia you see today dates back only about 60 years. Santorini is famous for its 17th-century BC eruption. But a much more recent disaster also did its part to shape the island: In the middle of the night in July 1956, a 7.7-magnitude earthquake struck the nearby island of Amorgos, followed by a tsunami. Two-thirds of the island's buildings collapsed, forcing locals to rebuild. Oia was particularly hard-hit. Today, some locals reason that perhaps this was a blessing in disguise, as it jolted notoriously conservative Santorini out of its old-fashioned ways, setting the groundwork for the tourist onslaught that was to come.

• *You're standing on the site of...*

Oia's "Castle": This stubby tower is all that remains of the Castle of Agios Nikolaos—one of the original five fortresses that the occupying Venetians built to defend against pirate invasions. The complex still belongs to the Catholic Church, which has decided to keep it a ruin. And, with its 360-degree views, it's the prime location for watching the sunset. (If you'd like to do that, you'll need to stake out a space here well before—an hour or more—and defend it jealously.) So, why is Oia so famous for its sunset? In 1982, Daryl Hannah and Peter Gallagher frolicked here in the romantic comedy *Summer Lovers,* featuring idyllic Oia (then a ghost town) and its glorious sunset. While virtually nobody remembers the movie, the buzz it created around Oia's sunset has taken on a life of its own. (For more sunset tips, see the "Santorini Sunsets" sidebar.)

• *Nearby, about 250 steps lead steeply down (immediately below town) to the port of...*

Ammoudi: Historically, this was one of the island's main

ports. Despite its desolate landscape, Santorini produced valuable exports that helped make
it wealthy—most notably the
sweet wine Vinsanto, which
was used for Communion in
Orthodox churches in Russia
and southeastern Europe. In
exchange, locals imported wood
(on this virtually unforested

island, timber was a major status symbol), barrels, kerosene, and
wheat and rye for the wealthy (the poor ate barley). Goods would
be loaded onto donkeys to be hauled to or from the port. Imagine
the steady trade—Greek grapes for Russian wood—that kept this
remote island tethered to the outside world for centuries, right up
until the Bolshevik Revolution of the early 20th century shut down
Russian Orthodox churches and shot down Santorini's main source
of export revenue. To compensate, Santorini's traders shifted to ex-
tracting and exporting pumice, a desirable building material. This
remained a big export until the 1980s; you can see an (ugly) quarry
at the right end of Thirasia, across the caldera; another abandoned
one is just south of Fira.

• *Now that you're oriented, enjoy...*

The Rest of Oia: There's not much to see or do here, other
than enjoy the commanding views. Near the castle, notice several
windmills—taking advantage of the predictably blustery Cycladic
winds. As you explore—particularly in the part of town toward
Fira—you'll notice you're walking on paving stones made of **marble,** which is not indigenous to a volcanic island. The marble came
to Santorini in the form of ballast, weighing down too-light ships
returning from Russia after delivering their heavy loads of Vinsanto. If you're determined to do some sightseeing, dip into the
Naval Maritime Museum, described next.

Naval Maritime Museum

Every Greek island seems to have its own maritime museum, and
Oia hosts Santorini's. With two floors of old nautical objects and
basic English labels, the collection includes roomfuls of old ship
paintings, letters and documents, model ships, and well-endowed
mastheads. It's nothing to jump ship for unless you're a sailor or
need a place to get out of the sun.

Cost and Hours: €5, hours can be unpredictable but generally
open Wed-Mon 10:00-14:00 & 17:00-20:00, until 19:00 in shoulder season, closed Tue and Nov-March, well-signposted a block off
the main cliff-top drag, +30 2286 071 156.

Sleeping in Oia

WITH A CALDERA VIEW

Several places rent out appealing "cave houses" just down from the main cliff-side road. They range from smaller rooms or studios for two people, to larger units sleeping four or more. Though expensive, a cave-house stay is an unforgettable experience. Of the many options, my recommendation is owned and run by locals.

$$$$ At **Chelidonia Traditional Villas,** friendly Greek-Austrian couple Triantaphyllos and Erika Pitsikali rent 13 traditional apartments surrounded by burgeoning bougainvillea and burrowed into the cliff face right in the heart of town. Triantaphyllos grew up in one of these houses, bought the others from his grandparents and cousins, and renovated them himself, retaining as much as he could of the original (large) footprint. Promising "panorama and privacy," this place lets you be a temporary troglodyte (includes breakfast, +30 2286 071 287, www.chelidonia.com, contact@chelidonia.com).

IN TOWN

It's certainly cheaper to sleep in the town center, a short walk from caldera views—but in this pricey village, you're still paying dearly for basic lodgings.

$$$$ **Oia's Sunset Apartments,** on a busy little lane at the back of town (near the bus stop), is a tight little compound with 15 relatively well-priced apartments sharing a swimming pool. While a bit loosely run, it's one of the more affordable and reliable options in town (breakfast extra, minimal soundproofing, +30 2286 071 420, www.oiasunset.com, info@oiasunset.com).

$$$$ **Hotel Aethrio** is a lovely little complex tucked deep in town (no caldera views). It feels like its own little village, with three entrances, 19 rooms scattered through several buildings, a swimming pool, a sunset deck, and even its own little church. While somewhat spartan for this swanky town, it's well-located and reasonably priced, and the grounds are inviting (+30 2286 071 040, www.aethrio.gr, info@aethrio.gr).

Eating in Oia

Oia must be the most expensive place to dine in all of Greece. Places with no view are plenty pricey—and ones with a view are even more so. Reservations at any place are wise for dinner; there's a big rush just before the sunset (for caldera-view places) and immediately after the sunset (for non-caldera-view places).

FACING THE CALDERA

The cliffside places are pretty interchangeable, but if you can't make up your mind, consider one of these (but skip the hard-to-miss Kastro restaurant, with disappointing food at terrible prices).

$$$ Flora Café is a relatively affordable alternative to the budget-busting places along the cliff, with a straightforward menu of pizzas, pastas, salads, and meat dishes. Set along the main drag (at the Fira end of town), it's essentially a classy snack bar with a pleasantly casual setting and friendly service (daily 9:00-24:00, +30 2286 071 424, Flora).

$$$$ 1800-Floga is a scenic splurge dishing up traditional Greek food with a modern spin. It's a few steps below the main drag at the Fira end of town, with dramatic caldera views—albeit not of the sunset (daily specials, daily 12:00-24:00, +30 2286 071 152).

BURIED IN TOWN, WITH DISTANT SEA VIEWS

$$$$ Kyprida Restaurant, serving traditional Cypriot cuisine, is reasonably priced by Oia standards. It's set a couple of blocks back from the cliff edge, but its top terrace still has a fine sunset view (daily 12:00-24:00, live music on Wed nights, closed Nov-March, +30 2286 071 976, www.kyprida.gr).

$$$$ Roka (Ρόκα) is a humble little *kafeneio/ouzeri* (coffee-and-ouzo taverna serving traditional dishes) but with Oia prices, tucked deep in the heart of town. It has seating on the colorful courtyard, a cozy interior, and a terrace with views over the back of the island (daily 12:30-23:00, +30 2286 071 896, www.roka.gr).

Ice Cream: Facing the bus-stop bustle, **Lolita's Gelato** has a loyal following for pricey, top-end ice cream (Mon-Sat 10:30-24:00, sometimes closed Sun, +30 2286 071 279).

More Sights on Santorini

Santorini has many worthwhile sights outside Fira and Oia, doable by bus or taxi but best by car. These include a string of beaches along its eastern side, two major archaeological sites, a lighthouse on a bluff, wineries, and boat trips around the caldera. A day or two on Santorini with a car is a delight.

▲▲BOAT TRIPS IN THE CALDERA

A variety of boat trips are designed to take tourists out into the caldera for stunning views back on the village-topped cliffs. Many of these sail from the Old Port below Fira, some depart from Ammoudi below Oia, and some can pick you up at your hotel.

A popular option takes you out to the active volcanic islets in the middle of the caldera: the crater on **Nea Kameni,** where you can hike up to the crater (exciting if you've never climbed around a lava field before); and **Palea Kameni,** known mostly for its shallow, muddy, tepid "hot" springs that's loaded with bobbing tourists. While this sounds intriguing, for most, the highlight is simply the views—not the activities on the islands themselves. Some boat trips also include a two-hour visit to **Thirasia,** the sleepy island across the caldera from Thira (with not much to see once on land). Sunset is, quite deservedly, a popular time to do these trips; cruises know where to position their passengers to be sure to see the sun swallowed up by the Aegean.

The basic choice is a crowded **tour boat,** which can cost anywhere from €25 for a 2.5-hour tour to Nea Kameni, to €40 for a five-hour sunset tour. Travel agencies all over Santorini advertise basically interchangeable options. Just drop into one, peruse your options, and book.

For something more exclusive and expensive, **catamaran cruises** are a worthwhile splurge (book ahead; these typically include a transfer from your hotel to the boat). You'll pay much more (€150-200/person for similar itineraries to those described above) but enjoy a far more relaxed and exclusive experience—with unlimited drinks and only a couple dozen people on  a small, sail-masted catamaran...plenty of room to spread out and relax. I had a memorable evening out on the sunset cruise with **Caldera Yachting,** which included pick-up and drop-off at my hotel, an excellent dinner, a top-notch and attentive crew, opportunities to swim from the catamaran, and enough caldera views to fill up my camera, all for €180 per person (www.calderayachting.gr).

BEACHES

Beaches aren't Santorini's forte. Because most towns (including Fira and Oia) cap cliffs high above the water, it's a hassle to reach an inviting spot for a dip—and they're not quite as idyllic as beaches on other islands (such as Mykonos). Perhaps the most satisfying way to go for a swim is from a boat tour in the caldera; many of these drop anchor and invite passengers to dive in from the boat deck.

If you're spending time in Oia, the easiest option is to hike or drive steeply down to the pint-sized port of **Ammoudi,** at the base

SANTORINI

of the cliffs immediately below the pinnacle of town. This is a busy working port with a few fish restaurants and just enough opportunities to get into the water. Drivers be warned that the road tethering Ammoudi to Oia is tight and extremely congested; parking is limited, so you'll likely have to squeeze in along the side of the road and hike partway. Another little cove—called **Armeni**—is just around the corner, facing the caldera below Oia, and accessible only by a very steep hike (or by yacht).

By car or bus, you can reach some beaches with unusual volcanic compositions. Two black-sand beaches flank the steep mountain, capped by Ancient Thira, at the southeastern corner of the island: near **Kamari** (tidy and more upscale-feeling) and **Perissa** (more popular with backpackers). While pleasant, these are less exotic than they sound—the black "sand" is quite coarse, and the general vibe is a typical Greek-island beach.

While these beaches look close together as the crow flies, they're separated by a mountain—it's a half-hour drive, challenging three-hour hike, or 15-minute taxi-boat ride between them.

Along the southern arc of the island, there are some famous volcanically colorful beaches near Akrotiri (facing away from the caldera). **White Beach,** with a backdrop of chalky cliffs, is accessible exclusively by boat. **Red Beach,** given its distinctive color by iron deposits, can be reached by a quite demanding hike over loose rocks and around the bluff (from the bay near the Akrotiri archaeological site, described later). Officially this is not a beach designated for swimming, and locals warn not to underestimate the danger of this hike, which is susceptible to rockslides. As this is quite close to the Akrotiri site, it's an optional add-on for hardy hikers.

▲WINERIES

Santorini, one of Greece's most high-profile wine producers, has a dozen or so wineries open to the public. If visiting during the harvest (around mid-Aug), you may even find a winery that lets you stomp some grapes. While you'll pay for tastings, and bottles are quite expensive (typically starting around €25), it's fascinating to learn about the way wine is cultivated here (see the sidebar). These places are all within about a 10-minute drive of each other, in the island's interior, roughly on the way from Fira to Kamari, Perissa, or the airport. For a meal in the area, don't miss the excellent Metaxi Mas, listed at the end of this section. See the Santorini Island map for locations.

Santorini Wines

While Greece isn't particularly acclaimed for its wines, Santorini's are well-respected. The discovery of ancient grape seeds at Akrotiri indicates that the winemaking tradition here dates back more than 3,500 years. Wine would be mixed with collected rainwater to disinfect it, making it safer to drink. Historically, the wealthier the family, the sweeter their wine; peasants basically drank vinegar. Today, the most common local grapes are assyrtiko, one of the best Greek varietals; they produce a dry white wine with minerality and acidity.

The growing vines are twisted into a round basket shape called *ampelies,* with the grapes tucked inside to protect them from the strong sunlight and fierce winds. The shape also helps retain moisture from nighttime fog on this otherwise arid isle. The pumice in the ground absorbs liquid from the atmosphere, then distributes it to the vines' roots. All of this means that, even though it can go months here without rain, local grapes typically don't require additional irrigation. Connoisseurs say that the terroir created by Santorini's unique conditions gives the wine a special flavor.

The most famous, and most expensive, Santorini-grown wine is Vinsanto (sweet dessert wine made from a blend of sun-dried grapes). Santorini's export of Vinsanto to Eastern Orthodox churches (especially in Russia), to use for the Eucharist, was historically one of its most lucrative exports. Also respected is Nykteri, a dry white wine produced in a single day (the name means "night work"). Several shops in Fira or Oia offer wine tasting, or you can visit one of the wineries on the island (I've listed a few).

Santo is the best-known option, just up the road from the New Port, on the road between Fira and Akrotiri. It's a cooperative working with all the island's wineries—the biggest operation like this in the Cyclades. Established in 1947, it produces 500,000 bottles a year, 70 percent of which are consumed in Greece. Despite the cruise-ship tour crowds that descend on this place (it can be mobbed), Santo offers a good opportunity to taste Santorini's wine while enjoying great views (if coming for sunset, call ahead to reserve a scenic table). Tastings are pricey but serious, giving you a substantial sampling of Santorini's wines (€40/6 tastes with light food pairings, €42/10 tastes focused on just the wine, daily 9:00-22:00, June-Aug until 23:00, shorter hours off-season and closed on Mon Dec-Feb). They also offer 25-minute tours of their production facility (€10/person, 25 minutes, call in the morning at 9:30 to check English tour schedule; +30 2286 022 596, www.santowines.gr).

Venetsanos, more boutique and rustic, is just a five-minute drive away and enjoys even grander views. The founder, George Venetsanos, was a real pioneer when he built this winery in 1947, using a system of interconnected equipment to turn grapes into wine, then flowing the final product from fermentation tanks through a series of pipes that ran down the hillside  and straight into barrels on ships docked at the port. To see some of the original equipment and walk through the winery's tunnels, request a tour (€12, 40 minutes). Or you can pay €26 for four tastings, served to you either on the terrace with gorgeous caldera views or in the tasting room. It's best to call a day ahead and tell them you're coming. You can also reserve a table for drinks at sunset (daily 11:00-22:00, +30 2286 021 100, www.venetsanoswinery.com).

Koutsoyannopoulos is another well-established winery, which also operates a "Cave Wine Museum." The included audioguide tells the history of the winery (which dates back to 1880); explains how grapes have been grown, transferred, and crushed through the years; and discusses the challenges facing wine producers on this hot, dry island. With its cheesy sets and fake figures, the museum is a bit old-school, though it is interesting to see the equipment that was used back in the day. Allow about an hour for the full experience (€15, includes audioguide and four tastings, daily 9:00-19:00, off-season until 17:00, last entry one hour before closing, +30 2286 031 322, www.santoriniwinemuseum.com).

Argyros, in the valley just outside of Kamari, lacks grand caldera views but makes up for it with its sleek, picturesque estate, tucked amid rolling vineyards. You can sample their wines in the modern tasting room, or call ahead to arrange a tour of the vineyards and production line (€15 tasting includes three whites and one Vinsantos with a small plate of snacks; €40 for 1.5-hour tour and tasting). While classy, Argyros has less pretense and feels a bit younger, fresher, and more personal than the others listed here (Mon-Sat 10:00-20:00, Sun from 11:00, +30 2286 031 489, www. estateargyros.com).

Beer Tasting: If your tastes skew to hops rather than grapes, stop in at **Santorini Brewing Company.** In their small production facility, they offer tastes of the beers they brew on-site and sell bottles to go. Their beers are also sold all over the island. As this is an easy walk down the road from Argyros, groups with a mix of beer and wine lovers can divide and conquer (Mon-Sat 12:00-17:00, shorter hours Oct-April, closed Sun year-round, in Mesa

Gonia about 1.5 miles out of Kamari, +30 2286 030 268, www. santorinibrewingcompany.gr).

Near Oia: For people staying in Oia, **Sigalas** is a good nearby winery (+30 2286 071 644, www.sigalas-wine.com).

Eating near the Wineries: My favorite countryside eatery on Santorini—well worth a special trip—is **$$$ Metaxi Mas** (Μεταξύ Μας), in the village of Exo Gonia, less than a 10-minute drive from most recommended wineries. Park in the big lot by the town church, then hike over the ridge into town, and you'll spot it on your right. They have ample outdoor seating, a relaxed vibe, and top-quality traditional Santorini and Greek cuisine prepared with modern techniques. Foodies love it—reserve ahead. Their outdoor terrace—across the street—comes with big views over the island and sea but lacks shade. If going for lunch, note its unusually late opening time (daily 14:30-23:00, +30 2286 031 323, www. santorini-metaximas.gr).

ANCIENT SITES

If you're hitting multiple archaeological sites on the island, invest in the great-value €14 combo-ticket, which covers Akrotiri, Ancient Thira, and the Museum of Prehistoric Thira in Fira. Both Akrotiri and Ancient Thira have a history of unexpected closures, so carefully confirm in town that they're open before you set out.

▲Akrotiri Archaeological Site

Just before Santorini's massive c. 1630 BC eruption, its inhabitants fled the island, leaving behind a city that was soon buried (and

preserved) in ash—much like Pompeii, but 1,700 years earlier. (Consider this: The Minoan-era civilization that lived here was as ancient to the Romans as the Romans are to us; many scholars think this may have been what started the legend of Atlantis.)

That city, near the modern-day town of Akrotiri, is still being excavated, with more than 30 buildings now viewable in a well-designed structure that makes it easy to explore the ruins; look for the helpful video that imagines what a high-class home might have looked like. Keep in mind that only 3 percent of the site has been unearthed—this city was huge. Visitors explore the excavation site on elevated ramps. These let you climb around and through the streets of the prehistoric city, where careful observers can pick out sidewalks, underground sewage systems, and some ceramic vases

SANTORINI

left behind. However, the most interesting items discovered here—wonderful wall frescoes, fancy furniture, painted ceramics—are on display elsewhere, mainly at Fira's Museum of Prehistoric Thira (see "Sights in Fira," earlier) and the National Archaeological Museum in Athens.

Cost and Hours: €12, €6 off-season, covered by €15 combo-ticket; Mon, Wed, Thu 8:30-15:30, Tue and Fri-Sun 8:00-20:00; Nov-March Tue-Sun 8:00-15:00, closed Mon; one-hour guided tours-€12, private guide-€120; +30 2286 081 939, http://odysseus.culture.gr.

Getting There: Without a car, Akrotiri is reachable by frequent buses from Fira (2/hour, 30 minutes, around €2) or taxi (about €25).

Eating: For some of the freshest seafood on the island, try **$$$ The Dolphins** on Akrotiri Beach, a delightful family-run fish tavern with sheltered tables on a pier and more seating along the water (daily 12:00-23:00, +30 2286 081 151; mom and sons run the place, dad fishes). To reach it, exit straight out the Akrotiri ruins, crossing the street and continuing uphill toward the left. After a few minutes you'll see signs for the restaurant on your left.

Nearby: The treacherous trail to the famous **Red Beach** is near Akrotiri (described earlier). The **lighthouse** at Faros, at the southwest tip of the island, has amazing views (and is also a good place to watch the sunset at certain times of year).

Ancient Thira

Dramatically situated on a mountaintop between Perissa and Kamari, this site dates from a more recent civilization. It was settled post-volcano by Dorians from Sparta, likely in the ninth century BC, and continued to thrive through the Hellenistic, Roman, and Byzantine periods. This place is less distinctive than the Akrotiri site and might only interest archaeology completists. If you've toured other Greek ruins from this era—in Athens, Delphi, Olympia, Epidavros, and so on—you'll see nothing new here. However, the setting could hardly be more spectacular.

Cost and Hours: €6, covered by €15 combo-ticket; Thu-Tue 8:30-15:30, closed Wed, shorter hours off-season; +30 2286 023 217, http://odysseus.culture.gr.

Getting There: Besides driving or taxi, you can take a bus to Kamari, then either walk 30 minutes or catch an hourly minibus excursion from the TI in that town. Hardy hikers can also huff up from Perissa on a very twisty serpentine path.

OTHER VILLAGES

Santorini is dotted with charming and characteristic villages, most of them easily accessible by local bus from Fira. With more time—and a rental car—consider exploring more off the beaten track. These two worthwhile options are near the recommended sights listed earlier.

Megalochori

Reachable by any local bus heading to Perissa (1-2/hour), Megalochori doesn't have sea views, but is a delight to stroll—you'll share the cobbled streets with more residents than tourists. Wander through the lanes of artisan workshops and original cave houses and enjoy.

For more official sightseeing, consider visiting the casually intimate **Gavalas Winery,** one of the oldest on Santorini (daily 10:00-19:00, tastings from €15, small snacks available, www.gavalaswines.gr), or attending a "history of sound" concert at the **Symposion** cultural center, where you'll experience Homeric spoken word, Greek bagpipes, and other ancient instrumental music (performances generally Tue-Sun at 13:00 and some evenings—check website for schedule; center open Tue-Sun 10:00-20:00, closed Mon; +30 2286 085 374, www.symposionsantorini.com; attached café serves wine, beer, and light food).

$$$ Petrino restaurant, on the main square, is popular with locals, and the **Alisachni** artists collective and wine bar is a good place to settle in.

Above town, **$$$$ Aegagros Caldera Houses** is a pleasant sleeping option with its own garden restaurant (5-minute drive from Venetsanos Winery, +30 2286 025 493, www.aegagros.eu), while slightly inland **Petra Kouzina** welcomes travelers into a traditional cave home for a cooking experience with locals (€120/4-hour class, daily at 11:00 and 17:00, +30 6981 076 655, www.petrakouzina.com).

Pyrgos

Close to Fira, and near the recommended Metaxi Mas restaurant, the village of Pyrgos (sometimes written as Pirgos on local maps and schedules) is a good alternative to Oia and Fira for watching the sun set over Santorini. Hourly buses from Fira stop in Pyrgos (direction: Perissa; note not all Perissa-bound buses stop in Pyrgos—double-check with the driver).

There are several good eating options in town, including the *meze*-style **$$$ Kantouni Taverna** (daily 9:00-23:30, +30 2286 033 474) and **$$$ Agaze,** which also has a boutique selling Greek treats (daily 9:00-24:00, +30 2286 031 003).

Santorini Connections

The New Port (Athinios) is a 20-minute bus ride from Fira, and buses can be very crowded in summer—allow enough time to make your connection. For ferry office locations in Fira, see "Helpful Hints" on page 460. The frequency and durations listed below are approximate; schedules can change from season to season, and sailings can be canceled on short notice—confirm everything locally. For information on finding current schedules and booking tickets, see page 553.

By Boat from the New Port: Santorini is connected daily to **Piraeus** in Athens (4-5/day in high season, 5 hours via fast boat, 8 hours by slow boat; off-season likely 1 slow boat daily), **Mykonos** (generally 2-4/day in high season, none in winter, 2-3 hours, 1-2 stops en route), and other Cycladic Islands, as well as to **Crete** (1-2/day in high season, 2.5 hours).

GREECE: PAST & PRESENT

Our lives today would be quite different if it weren't for a few thousand Greeks who lived in the small city of Athens about 450 years before Jesus was born. Democracy, theater, literature, mathematics, science, philosophy, and art all flourished in Athens during its 50-year "golden age"—a cultural boom time that set the tone for the rest of Western history to follow.

Greece's history since Classical times may be less familiar to most visitors, but it's fascinating nonetheless. From pagan to Christian to Muslim, to the freedom fighters of the 19th century and the refugees of the 20th and 21st centuries, Greece today is the product of many different peoples, religions, and cultures.

Greek History

THE PRE-GREEK WORLD:
THE MINOANS (2000-1450 BC)

The incredible civilization that we now call Classical Greece didn't just pop out of nowhere. Cursed with rocky soil, isolated by a rug-

ged landscape, and scattered by invasions, the Greeks took centuries to unify. The civilization of golden age Greece was built on the advances of earlier civilizations: Minoans, Mycenaeans, Dorians, and Ionians—the stew of peoples that eventually cooked up what became Greece.

A safe, isolated location on the island of Crete, combined with impressive business savvy, enabled the Minoans to dominate the pre-Greek world. Unlike most

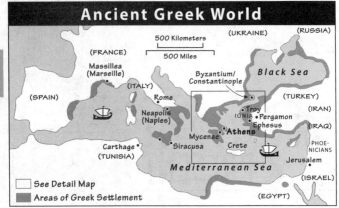

early peoples, they were traders, not fighters. With a large merchant fleet, they exported wine, olive oil, pottery, and well-crafted jewelry, then returned home with the wealth of the Mediterranean.

Today we know the Minoans by the colorful frescoes they left behind on the walls of prosperous, unfortified homes and palaces. Surviving frescoes show happy people engaged in everyday life: ladies harvesting saffron, athletes leaping over bulls, and charming landscapes with animals.

The later Greeks would inherit the Minoans' business skills, social equality, love of art for art's sake, and faith in rational thought over brute military strength. Some scholars hail the Minoans as the first truly "European" civilization.

Between about 1450 and 1150 BC, the Minoan civilization suddenly collapsed, and no one knows why (volcano? invasions?). Physically and economically weakened, they were easily overrun and absorbed by a tribe of warlike people from the mainland—the Mycenaeans.

Minoan-Era Sights

- Frescoes from Akrotiri on the island of Santorini—in the National Archaeological Museum in Athens, and the Museum of Prehistoric Thira on Santorini

MYCENAE (1600-1100 BC)

After the fall of the Minoans, the Greek mainland was dominated by the Mycenaeans (my-seh-NEE-uhns), a fusion of local tribes concentrated in the city of Mycenae (my-SEE-nee). Culturally, they were the anti-Minoans—warriors not traders, chieftains not bureaucrats. Their ruins at the capital of Mycenae (about two hours by bus southwest of Athens, or a half-hour's drive north of Naf-plio) tell the story. Buildings are fortress-like, the city has thick

Heart of Greek Ancient World

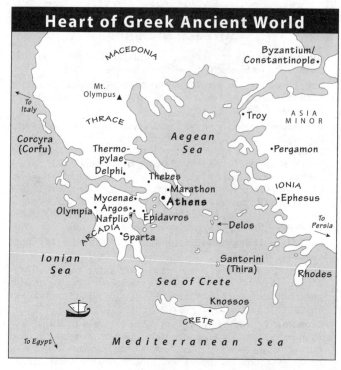

MACEDONIA

Byzantium/
Constantinople•

Mt.
Olympus ▲

To
Italy →

THRACE

•Troy

ASIA
MINOR

Corcyra
(Corfu)

*Aegean
Sea*

•Pergamon

Thermo-
pylae•

Delphi•

Thebes•
•Marathon

IONIA

Mycenae•
Olympia• •Argos•
Nafplio• •Epidavros

•Athens

•Ephesus

To
Persia →

ARCADIA

•Sparta

←Delos

*Ionian
Sea*

Santorini
(Thira)

Rhodes

Sea of Crete

Knossos

To Egypt ↘

CRETE

Mediterranean   Sea

defensive walls, and statues are stiff and crude. Early Greeks called Mycenaean architecture "cyclopean," because they believed that only giants could have built with such colossal blocks. Mycenaean kings were elaborately buried in cemeteries and tombs built like subterranean stone igloos, loaded with jewels, swords, and precious objects that fill museums today.

The Mycenaeans dominated Greece during the era of the legends of the Trojan War. Whether there's any historical truth to the legends, Mycenae has become associated with the tales of Agamemnon, Clytemnestra, and the invasion of Troy.

Around 1100 BC, the Mycenaeans—like the Minoans before them—mysteriously disappeared, plunging Greece into its next, "dark," phase.

Greece Almanac

Official Name: It's the Hellenic Republic (*Elliniki Dhimokratia* in Greek). In shorthand, that's Hellas—or Greece in English.

Size: Greece is home to 11.1 million people (similar to the state of Ohio). With 51,485 square miles, Greece is a bit smaller than Alabama.

Geography: Greece is a mountainous peninsula that extends into the Mediterranean Sea between Albania and Turkey in southern Europe. It includes the Peloponnesian Peninsula—separated from the mainland by a canal—and 3,000 rugged islands (227 are inhabited). Nearly four-fifths of the country's landscape is covered by mountains, the highest of which is Mount Olympus (9,570 feet). About 30 percent of the land is forested. Flat, arable plains are centered in Macedonia, Thrace, and Thessaly. Greece's coastline is the 10th longest in the world at 9,246 miles.

Latitude and Longitude: 39°N and 22°E. The latitude is the same as Maryland.

Biggest Cities: One in three Greeks lives in the capital of Athens (about 664,000 in the city, 3.75 million including the greater metropolitan area). Thessaloniki has 315,000 (811,000 in its urban area).

Economy: Greece has a GDP of $299 billion, with a GDP per capita of $27,000. A European Union member, Greece has used the euro as its currency since 2002. At first, its economy—based heavily on tourism, shipping, and agriculture—benefited from an

Mycenaean Sights

- The citadel at Mycenae, with its Lion Gate, Grave Circle A, palace, and *tholos* tombs
- Mask of Agamemnon and other artifacts at the National Archaeological Museum in Athens
- Dendra Panoply, a 15th-century BC suit of bronze armor in the Nafplio Archaeological Museum

THE GREEK DARK AGES
(1200-700 BC)

Whatever the reason, once-powerful Mycenaean cities became deserted, writing was lost, roads crumbled, trade decreased, and bandits preyed on helpless villagers. Dark Age graves contain little gold, jewelry, or fine pottery. Divided by mountains into pockets of isolated, warring tribes, the Greeks took centuries to unify and get their civilization back on track.

infusion of EU cash. But by the end of the decade the country was in a severe recession. In 2010, 2012, and again in 2015, Greece accepted huge bailout packages from the EU and was forced to adopt severe (and controversial) spending cuts and tax increases. They exited the bailout regime in 2018, and a new center-right government will try to guide Greece through the post-bailout era.

Government: Greece is a parliamentary republic, headed by a largely ceremonial president elected by the parliament. Power resides with the prime minister, chosen from the majority political party. The New Democracy party, headed by center-right conservative Kyriakos Mitsotakis, won Greece's 2019 election in a landslide.

Flag: A blue square bears a white cross (the symbol of Greek Orthodoxy) in the upper-left corner, against a field of horizon-

tal blue-and-white stripes. The blue is said to stand for the sky and seas, while the white represents the purity of the push for Greek independence. Each of the nine stripes is said to symbolize a syllable in the Greek motto, *Eleutheria e Thanatos,* which translates as "Freedom or Death."

It was during this time that legends passed down over generations were eventually compiled (in the ninth century BC) by a blind, talented, perhaps nonexistent man that tradition calls Homer. His long poem, the *Iliad,* describes the battles and struggles of the early Greeks (perhaps the Mycenaeans) as they conquered Troy. The *Odyssey* tells of the weary soldiers' long, torturous trip back home. The Greeks saw these epics as perfect metaphors for their own struggles to unify and build a stable homeland. The stories helped shape a collective self-image.

It was also during this time that Delphi, which was believed to be the center of the world, emerged as an important place where leaders would go to find answers and gain (divine?) inspiration.

Dark Age Sights
- The Kastalian Spring and omphalos monuments at Delphi

ARCHAIC PERIOD (700-480 BC)
Tradition holds that in 776 BC, Greek-speaking people from all over the mainland and islands halted their wars and gathered in

Olympia to compete in the first Olympic Games. Bound by a common language and religion, Greece's scattered tribes began settling down.

Living on islands and in valleys, the Greek-speaking people were divided by geography from their neighbors. They naturally formed governments around a single city (or polis) rather than as a unified empire. Petty warfare between city-states was practically a sport.

Slowly, the city-states unified, making alliances with one another, establishing colonies in what is now Italy and France, and absorbing culture from the more sophisticated Egyptians (style of statues) and Phoenicians (alphabet). Scarcely two centuries later, Greece would be an integrated community and the center of the civilized world.

Statues from Archaic times are crude, as stiff as the rock from which they're carved. Rather than individuals, they are generic people: called either kore (girl) or kouros (boy). With perfectly round heads, symmetrical pecs, and a navel in the center, these sturdy statues reflect the order and stability the troubled Greeks were striving for.

By the sixth century BC, Greece's many small city-states had coalesced around two power centers: oppressive, no-frills, and militaristic Sparta; and its polar opposite, the democratic, luxury-loving, and business-friendly Athens.

Archaic Sights

- Dipylon Vase (National Archaeological Museum in Athens) and other geometric vases in various museums
- Kouros and kore statues (National Archaeological Museum in Athens, Acropolis Museum in Athens, Archaeological Museum in Delphi)
- The Olympic Stadium and Temple of Hera in Olympia
- *Sphinx of Naxos* (Archaeological Museum in Delphi)
- *Lions of the Naxians* statues on the island of Delos

PRE-GOLDEN AGE: THE RISE OF ATHENS AND THE PERSIAN WARS (480-450 BC)

In 490 BC, an enormous army of Persians under King Darius I swept into Greece to punish the city of Athens, which had dared to challenge his authority over Greek-speaking Ionia (in today's western Turkey). A few thousand plucky Athenians raced to head off the Persians in a crucial bottleneck valley, at the Battle of

A Typical Greek Temple

Greek temples, built to house the cult image of a god, follow the same basic layout, with an inner chamber surrounded by a parade of columns. Important activities mostly took place outside, at an altar in front of the temple doors.

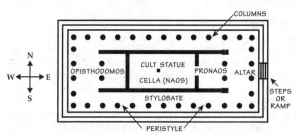

Pronaos: Small vestibule or porch, the entry to the cella

Cella (or Naos): The heart of the temple, where the cult image of the god was kept

Opisthodomos: Rear chamber, usually with no access to the cella and sometimes used as a treasury

Peristyle: Colonnade, the columns surrounding the cella

Stylobate: Platform on which the peristyle stands

Marathon. Though outnumbered three to one, the crafty Greeks lined up and made a wall of shields (a phalanx) and pushed the Persians back. An excited Greek soldier ran the 26.2 miles from the city of Marathon to Athens, gasped the good news...and died.

In 480 BC, Persia attacked again. This time all of Greece put aside its petty differences to fight the common enemy as an alliance of city-states. King Leonidas of Sparta and his 300 Spartans made an Alamo-like last stand at Thermopylae that delayed the invasion. Meanwhile, Athenians abandoned their city and fled, leaving Athens (and much of the lower mainland) to be looted. But the Athenians rallied to win a crucial naval victory at the Battle of Salamis, followed by a land victory at the Battle of Plataea, driving out the Persians.

Athens was hailed as Greece's protector and policeman, and the various city-states cemented their alliance (the Delian League)

Greek Mythology

The following were the stars among a large cast of characters—gods, beasts, and heroes—who scampered through the Greek mindscape, mingled with mortals, and inspired so much classical art and literature.

The Gods

The major Greek gods (the Olympians) lived atop Mount Olympus, presided over by Zeus, king of the gods (and father of many of them). Each god had a distinct personality, unique set of talents, and area of responsibility over the affairs of the world (they specialized). Though they were immortal and super-powerful, these gods were not remote, idealized deities; instead, like characters in a celestial soap opera, they displayed the full range of human foibles: petty jealousies, destructive passions, broken hearts, and god-sized temper tantrums. They also regularly interacted with humans—falling in love with them, seducing them, toying with them, and punishing them. The Romans were so impressed by the Greek lineup of immortals that they borrowed them, but gave them new names (shown in parentheses below).

Zeus (Jupiter): Papa Zeus liked the ladies, and often turned himself into some earthly form (a bull, a cloud, or a swan) to hustle unsuspecting mortal females. Statues depict him wearing a beard and sometimes carrying a spear. He is also symbolized by a thunderbolt or an eagle.

Hera (Juno): The beautiful queen of the gods was the long-suffering wife of philandering Zeus. She was also—whether ironically or fittingly—the goddess of marriage.

Hades (Pluto): The king of the underworld and lord of the dead is depicted as sad, with a staff.

Poseidon (Neptune): The god of the sea, he was also responsible for earthquakes, earning him the nickname "Earth Shaker." He is often shown holding a trident.

Apollo: The god of the Sun, he drives the Sun's flaming chariot across the sky each day, and represents light and truth. He is also the god of music and poetry.

Hermes (Mercury): The messenger of the gods sports a helmet and shoes with wings. He delivers a lot of flowers in his current incarnation as a corporate logo.

Ares (Mars): The god of war (and Aphrodite's boyfriend), he dresses for battle and carries a spear.

Dionysus (Bacchus): The god of wine and college frats holds grapes and wears a toga and a laurel wreath.

Athena (Minerva): The virginal goddess of wisdom was born from the head of Zeus, and is depicted carrying a spear. Athens is named for her and the Parthenon was built in her honor.

Artemis (Diana): The goddess of the Moon and hunting, she was the twin sister of Apollo. She carries a bow and arrow.

Aphrodite (Venus): The goddess of love and beauty, she was born of the sea. This good-looking lady was married to the crippled god Hephaistos, but was two-timing him with Ares.

Eros (Cupid): The god of desire is depicted as a young man or a baby with wings, wielding a bow and arrows.

Hestia (Vesta): Modestly dressed veiled goddess of the home and hearth, she oversaw domestic life.

Hephaistos (Vulcan): Poor cuckolded Hephaistos was lame and ugly, but useful. Blacksmith to the gods, he was the god of the forge, fire, and craftsmen.

Demeter (Ceres): Goddess of the seasons, the harvest, and fertility, she is shown holding a tuft of grain.

The Beasts

Pan (Faun): Happy Pan, with a body that's half man (on top) and half goat, was the god of shepherds and played a flute.

Centaur: This race of creatures, human on top and horse below, was said to be wise.

Satyr: Like Pan, satyrs were top-half man, bottom-half goat. And they were horny.

Griffin: With the head and wings of an eagle and the body of a lion, griffins were formidable.

Harpy: Creatures with the head of a woman and the body of a bird, harpies were known for stealing.

Medusa: With writhing snakes instead of hair, she had a face that turned people to stone. She was slain by Perseus.

Pegasus: The winged horse was the son of Poseidon and Medusa.

Cyclops: A race of one-eyed giants, they were known for their immense strength.

Minotaur: This beast with the head of a bull lived in the labyrinth at Knossos, the palace on Crete.

The Heroes

Hercules: This son of Zeus was born to a mortal woman. The strongest man in the world performed many feats of strength and tested negative for steroids. To make Hercules atone for killing his family in a fit of madness, the gods forced him to perform Twelve Labors, which included slaying various fierce beasts and doing other chores. He often wore a lion's skin.

Amazons: A race of powerful female warriors. Classical art often depicts them doing battle with the Greeks.

Prometheus: He defied the gods, stealing fire from them and giving it to humans. As punishment, he was chained to a rock, where an eagle feasted daily on his innards.

Jason: He sailed with his Argonauts in search of the Golden Fleece.

Perseus: He killed Medusa and rescued Andromeda from a serpent.

Theseus: He killed the Minotaur in the labyrinth on Crete.

Trojan War Heroes: This gang of greats includes Achilles, Ajax, Hector, Paris, Agamemnon, and the gorgeous Helen of Troy.

by pooling their defense funds, with Athens as the caretaker. Athens signed a 30-year peace treaty with Sparta...and the golden age began.

Pre-Golden Age Sights

- Severe-style statues, such as the *Artemision Bronze* (Athens' National Archaeological Museum) and *Bronze Charioteer* (Delphi)
- Olympia's Temple of Zeus and the bronze helmet of Miltiades

GOLDEN AGE ATHENS (450-400 BC)

Historians generally call Greece's cultural flowering the "Classical Period" (approximately 500-323 BC), with the choice cut being the two-generation span (450-400 BC) called the "golden age." After the Persian War, the Athenians set about rebuilding their city (with funds from the Delian League). Grand public buildings and temples were decorated with painting and sculpture. Ancient Athens was a typical city-state, with a population of at least  100,000 gathered around its acropolis ("high town"), which was the religious center and fort of last defense. Below was the agora, or marketplace, the economic and social center. Blessed with a harbor and good farmland, Athens prospered, exporting cash crops (wine and olive oil, pottery and other crafts) to neighboring cities and importing the best craftsmen, thinkers, and souvlaki. Amphitheaters hosted drama, music, and poetry festivals. The marketplace bustled with goods from all over the Mediterranean. Upwardly mobile Greeks flocked to Athens. The incredible advances in art, architecture, politics, science, and philosophy set the pace for all of Western civilization to follow. And all this from a Greek town smaller than Muncie, Indiana.

Athens' leader, a charismatic nobleman named Pericles, set out to democratize Athens. As with many city-states, Athens' government had morphed from rule by king, to a council of nobles, to rule by "tyrants" in troubled times, and finally to rule by the people. In golden age Athens, every landowning man had a vote in the Assembly of citizens. It was a direct democracy (not a representative democracy, where you elect others to serve), in which every man was expected to fill his duties of voting, community projects, and military service. Of course, Athens' "democracy" excluded women, slaves, freed slaves, and anyone not born in Athens.

Perhaps the greatest Greek invention was the very idea that

Greek Columns

DORIC   IONIC   CORINTHIAN

Classical Greek architecture evolved through three orders: Doric (strong-looking columns topped with simple and stocky capitals), Ionic (thinner columns with rolled capitals), and Corinthian (even thinner columns with leafy, ornate capitals). As a memory aid, remember that the orders gain syllables as they evolve: Doric, Ionic, Corinthian. The differences between the three orders point to how the Greek outlook mirrored its developing culture: Having mastered the ability to show balance and harmony in its finest Doric temples (the Parthenon being the cream of the crop), the Corinthian order caught on as architects began to prefer a more elegant look. The Corinthian order, developed to look good from all sides (Ionic columns didn't work well on corners), and to give temple interiors a foresty look, could only have come from the Hellenistic era, when Greek tastemakers preferred their art and architecture ornate and lavish.

nature is orderly and man is good—a rational creature who can solve problems. Their concept of the "Golden Mean" reveals the value they placed in balance, order, and harmony in art and in life. At school, both the mind and the body were trained.

Philosophers debated many of the questions that still occupy the human mind. Socrates questioned traditional, superstitious beliefs. His motto, "Know thyself," epitomizes Greek curiosity about who we are and what we know for sure. Branded a threat to Athens' youth, Socrates willingly obeyed a court order to drink poison rather than compromise his ideals. His follower Plato wrote down many of Socrates' words. Plato taught that the physical world is only a pale reflection of true reality (the way a shadow on the wall is a poor version of the 3-D, full-color world we see). The greater reality is the unseen mathematical orderliness that underlies the fleeting physical world. Plato's pupil Aristotle, an avid biologist, emphasized study of the physical world rather than the intangible one. Both Plato and Aristotle founded schools that would attract Europe's great minds for centuries. And their ideas would resurface much later, after Europe experienced a resurgence of humanism and critical thought.

GREEK HISTORY

Greeks worshipped a pantheon of gods, viewed as supernatural humans (with human emotions) who controlled the forces of nature. Greek temples housed a statue of a god or goddess. Because the people worshipped outside, the temple exterior was the important part and the interior was small and simple. Generally, only priests were allowed to go inside, where they'd present your offering to the god's statue in the hope that the god would grant your wish.

Most temples had similar features. They were rectangular, surrounded by rows of columns, and topped by slanted roofs. Rather than single-piece columns, the Greeks usually built them of stacked slices of stone (drums), each with a plug to keep it in line. Columns sat on a base, and were topped with a capital. The triangle-shaped roof formed a gable—typically filled with statues—called the pediment. A typical pediment might feature a sculpted gang of gods doing their divine mischief. Beneath the pediment was a line of carved reliefs called metopes. Under the eaves, a set of sculpted low-relief panels—called the frieze—decorated one or more sides of the building.

Classical art is known for its symmetry, harmony, and simplicity. It shows the Greeks' love of rationality, order, and balance. Greek art of this era featured the human body in all its naked splendor. The anatomy is accurate, and the poses are relaxed and natural. Greek sculptors learned to capture people in motion, and to show them from different angles, not just face-on. The classic Greek pose—called *contrapposto*, Italian for "counter-poise"—has a person resting weight on one leg while the other leg is relaxed or moving slightly. This pose captures a balance between timeless stability and fleeting motion that the Greeks found beautiful. It's also a balance between down-to-earth humans (with human flaws and quirks) and the idealized perfection of a Greek god.

Golden Age Sights

- The Acropolis in Athens, with the Parthenon, Erechtheion, Propylaea, Temple of Athena Nike, and Theater of Dionysus
- The Agora, Athens' main square—crossed by the Panathenaic Way and frequented by all the golden age greats
- Temple of Hephaistos, in the Agora
- Panathenaic Stadium in Athens
- Sanctuary of Apollo at Delphi
- Workshop of Pheidias at Olympia
- Museum of Cycladic Art in Athens (top-floor exhibit)

LATE CLASSICAL PERIOD: THE DECLINE OF ATHENS (400-323 BC)

Many Greek city-states came to resent the tribute money they were obliged to send to Athens, supposedly to protect them from an invasion that never came.

Rallying behind Sparta, they ganged up on Athens. The Peloponnesian War, lasting a generation, toppled Athens (404 BC), drained Greece, and ended the golden age. Still more wars followed, including struggles between Sparta and Thebes. In 338 BC, Athens, Sparta, and all the rest of the city-states were conquered by powerful Greek-speaking invaders from the north: the Macedonians.

Late Classical Sights

- Bronze statue of a youth at Athens' National Archaeological Museum
- *Statue of Hermes*, perhaps by Praxiteles, in Olympia

HELLENISM (323-100 BC)

"Hellenism," from the Greek word for "Greek," refers to the era when Greece's political importance declined but Greek culture was spread through the Mediterranean and Asia by Alexander the Great.

After King Philip of Macedonia conquered Greece, he was succeeded by his 20-year-old son, Alexander (356-323 BC). Alexander had been tutored by the Greek philosopher Aristotle, who got the future king hooked on Greek culture. According to legend, Alexander went to bed each night with two things under his pillow: a dagger and a copy of the *Iliad*. Alexander loved Greek high culture, but was also pragmatic about the importance of military power.

In 334 BC, Alexander and a well-trained army of 40,000 headed east. Their busy itinerary included conquering today's Turkey, Palestine, Egypt (where he was declared a living god), Iraq, and Iran, and moving into India. Alexander was a daring general, a benevolent conqueror, and a good administrator. As he conquered, he founded new cities on the Greek model, spread the Greek language, and opened Greek schools. After eight years on the road, an exhausted Alexander died at the age of 32, but by then he had created the largest empire ever.

Hellenistic art reflects the changes in Greek society. Rather

A Who's Who of Classical Age Greeks

Socrates (c. 469-399 BC) questioned the status quo, angered authorities, and calmly accepted his own death rather than change his teachings.

Plato (c. 424-348 BC) was Socrates' follower (and note taker), and focused on elucidating nonmaterial, timeless mathematical ideas.

Aristotle (c. 384-322 BC) was Plato's follower and championed the empirical sciences, emphasizing the importance of the physical world as a means of knowledge.

Pericles (c. 495-429 BC) was a charismatic nobleman who promoted democracy.

Pythagoras (c. 580-500 BC) gave us $a^2 + b^2 = c^2$.

Euclid (c. 335-270 BC) laid out geometry as we know it.

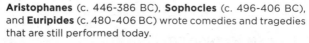

Diogenes (c. 412-323 BC) lived homeless in the Agora, turning from materialism to concentrate on ethical living.

Aristophanes (c. 446-386 BC), **Sophocles** (c. 496-406 BC), and **Euripides** (c. 480-406 BC) wrote comedies and tragedies that are still performed today.

Hippocrates (c. 460-370 BC) made medicine a hard science. He rejected superstition and considered disease a result of natural—rather than supernatural—causes.

Pheidias (c. 480-430 BC) designed the statuary of the Parthenon and several monumental statues.

Praxiteles (c. 400-330 BC) sculpted lifelike yet beautiful human figures.

than noble idealized gods, the Hellenistic artists gave us real people with real emotions, shown warts-and-all. Some are candid snapshots of everyday life, like a boy stooped over to pull a thorn from his foot. Others show people in extreme moments as they struggle to overcome life's obstacles. We see the

thrill of victory and the agony of defeat. Arms flail, muscles strain, eyes bulge. Clothes and hair are whipped by the wind. Figures are

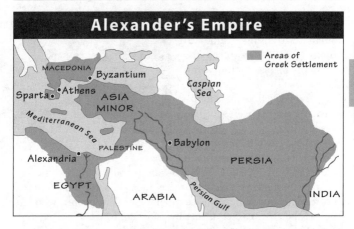

Alexander's Empire

MACEDONIA · Byzantium

Sparta · Athens · ASIA MINOR

Caspian Sea

Mediterranean Sea

PALESTINE

Alexandria

· Babylon

PERSIA

EGYPT

ARABIA

Persian Gulf

INDIA

Areas of Greek Settlement

frozen in motion, in wild, unbalanced poses that dramatize their inner thoughts.

For two centuries much of the Mediterranean and Asia—the entire known civilized world—was dominated by Greek rulers and Greek culture.

Hellenistic Sights
- Stoa of Attalos, in Athens' Agora, built by a Grecophile from Pergamon
- *Artemision Jockey, Fighting Gaul,* and other statues in Athens' National Archaeological Museum
- Head of Alexander the Great in Athens' Acropolis Museum
- Theater (and sanctuary) of Epidavros
- Philippeion temple in Olympia

ROMAN GREECE (146 BC-AD 476)
At the same time that Alexander was conquering the East, a new superpower was rising in the West: Rome. Eventually, Rome's legions conquered Greece (146 BC) and the Hellenized Mediterranean (31 BC). Culturally, however, the Greeks conquered the Romans.

Roman governors ruled cosmopolitan Greek-speaking cities, adopting the Greek gods, art styles, and fashions. Greek-style temple facades, with their columns and pediments, were pasted on the front of (Roman-arch) temples as a veneer of sophistication. Greek statues dotted Roman villas and public buildings. Pretentious Romans sprinkled their Latin conversation with Greek phrases as they enjoyed the plays of Sophocles and Aristophanes. Many a Greek slave was more cultured than his master, reduced to the role of warning his boss not to wear a plaid toga with polka-dot sandals.

Athens was a major city in the cosmopolitan Roman world.

Paul—a Jewish Christian with Roman citizenship—came to Athens (AD 49) to spread the Christian message from atop Mars Hill. The Bible makes it clear (Acts 17) that the sophisticated Athenians were not impressed.

Athens, with its prestigious monuments, was well-preserved under the Romans, but as Rome began to collapse, it became less able to protect and provide for Greece. In AD 267, Athens suffered a horrendous invasion by the Germanic Herulian people, who left much of the city in ashes. Other invasions followed.

In AD 476, even the city of Rome fell to invaders. As Christianity established itself, Greece's pagan sanctuaries were closed. For a thousand years Athens had carried the torch of pagan and secular learning. But in AD 529, the Christian/Roman/Byzantine Emperor Justinian closed Athens' famous schools of philosophy... and the "ancient" world came to an end.

Greek culture would live on, resurfacing throughout Western history and eventually influencing medieval Christians, Renaissance sculptors, and Neoclassical architects, including the ones who designed Washington, DC in the Greek style.

Roman Sights
- Roman Forum (and Tower of the Winds) in Athens
- Temple of Olympian Zeus and Arch of Hadrian in Athens
- Odeon of Agrippa and Statue of Hadrian, in Athens' Agora
- Library of Hadrian (near Monastiraki) in Athens
- Temple of Roma and Monument of Agrippa, on the Acropolis in Athens
- Odeon of Herodes Atticus (built by a wealthy ethnic-Greek/Roman-citizen) in Athens
- Mars Hill (the rock where the Christian Apostle Paul preached to the pagans) in Athens
- Nymphaeum in Olympia
- Many Greek buildings and artworks that were renovated in Roman times

BYZANTINE GREECE (AD 323-1453)
With the fall of Rome in Western Europe, Greece came under the sway of the Byzantine Empire—namely, the eastern half of the ancient Roman Empire that *didn't* "fall" in AD 476. Byzantium remained Christian and enlightened for another thousand years, with Greek (not Latin) as the common language. The empire's cap-

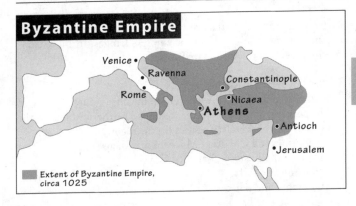

Byzantine Empire

Venice • Ravenna • Constantinople • Rome • Nicaea • **Athens** • Antioch • Jerusalem

Extent of Byzantine Empire, circa 1025

ital was Constantinople (modern Istanbul), founded in AD 330 by Roman Emperor Constantine to help manage the fading Roman Empire. For the next thousand years, Greece's cultural orientation would face east.

Though ostensibly protected by the Byzantine emperor in Constantinople, Greece suffered several centuries of invasions (AD 600-900) by vari-  ous Slavic tribes. The Orthodox Church served as a rallying point, and the invaders were eventually driven out or assimilated.

After AD 1000, Greece's economic prosperity returned—farms produced, the population grew, and cities engaged in trade—and Athens entered a second, more modest, golden age (c. 1000-1200). Greece reconnected with the rest of Western Europe during the Crusades, when Western soldiers traveled through Greek ports on their way to Jerusalem. This revived East-West trade, which was brokered by Venetian merchants who were granted trading rights to establish ports in Greek territory.

This golden age is when many of Athens' venerable Orthodox churches were built. Christian pilgrims from across the Byzantine Empire flocked to Athens to visit the famous church housed within the (still-intact) Parthenon. Byzantine mosaics, featuring realistic plants, animals, and people, were exported to the West.

The Byzantine Empire—and, by extension, Greece—was weakened by the disastrous Fourth Crusade (1204), in which greedy Crusaders looted their fellow Christian city of Constantinople. Following this, Western Crusaders occupied and ruled many parts of Greece, including Athens, and Byzantine Christians battled Crusading Christians at Monemvasia. Meanwhile, the Ottomans were whittling away at the empire's fringes. In 1453, Constantinople fell to the Ottoman Turks.

Byzantine-Era Sights
- Athens' old Orthodox churches, including the Church of Kapnikarea (on Ermou street), Agios Eleftherios (next to the cathedral), and Holy Apostles (in the Agora)
- Byzantine and Christian Museum in Athens
- Icons of the Eastern Orthodox Church
- Monemvasia fortress
- Churches and palaces at Mystras

ISLAMIC/OTTOMAN GREECE (1453-1821)

Under the Ottomans, Greece was ruled by Islamic Turks from their capital of Constantinople. Like many other temples-turned-churches, Athens' Parthenon (still intact) became a mosque, and a minaret was built alongside it.

Greek Christians had several choices for surviving the new regime. Some converted to Islam and learned Turkish, while others faked their conversion and remained closet Christians. Some moved to the boonies, outside the reach of Ottoman administrators. Many of Greece's best and brightest headed to Western Europe, helping to ignite the Renaissance (which revived the Classical achievements of ancient Athens). Most Greeks just stayed put, paid the "Christian tax," and lived in peace alongside the Ottomans. The Ottomans were (relatively) benevolent rulers, and the Greek language and Orthodox Christianity both survived.

Greece found itself between the powerful Ottomans and powerful merchants of Venice. This made Greece a center for East–West trade, but also a battleground. Venetian traders (backed by their military) occupied and fortified a number of Greek seaports in order to carry on trade throughout the Ottoman Empire. In 1687, the Venetians attacked Ottoman-controlled Athens. The Ottomans hunkered down on the Acropolis, storing their gunpowder in the Parthenon. A Venetian cannonball hit the Parthenon, destroying it and creating the ruin we see today. Venetian looters plundered the rubble and carried off statues as souvenirs.

Ottoman-Era Sights
- Benaki Museum of Islamic Art in Athens

- The Tzami, a former mosque on Monastiraki Square in Athens
- Venetian fortresses (including those in Nafplio) established in Byzantine times

GREEK INDEPENDENCE AND NEOCLASSICISM (1800s)

After centuries of neglect, Greece's Classical heritage was rediscovered, both by the Greeks and by the rest of Europe. Neoclassicism

was all the rage in Europe, where the ancient Greek style was used to decorate homes, and create paintings and statues. In 1801-1805, the British Lord Elgin plundered half of the Parthenon's statues and reliefs, carrying them home for Londoners to marvel at.

Greeks rediscovered a sense of their national heritage, and envisioned a day when they could rule themselves as a modern democracy. In 1821, the Greeks rose up against rule from Constantinople. It started with pockets of resistance by guerrilla Klepht warriors from the mountains, escalating into large-scale massacres on both sides. The Greeks' struggle became a cause célèbre in Europe, attracting Romantic liberals from England and France to take up arms. The poet Lord Byron died (of a fever) near the Gulf of Patra while fighting for Greece.

At one point the rebels gained control of the Peloponnese and declared Greek independence. The Greeks even sank the flagship of the Ottoman fleet in 1822, earning international respect for their nascent rebellion. But tribal rivalries prevented the Greeks from preserving their gains. With Egyptian reinforcements, the Ottomans successfully invaded the Peloponnese and captured several cities. An Egyptian army in Europe was too much to take for Britain, France, and Russia, who intervened with their navies and saved Greek independence.

By 1829, the Greeks had their freedom, a constitution, and—for the first time—a unified state of "Greece," based in Nafplio. But after its first president, Ioannis Kapodistrias, was assassinated in 1831, the budding democracy was forced by Europe's crowned heads to accept a monarch: 17-year-old King Otto from Bavaria (crowned in 1832). In 1834, historic Athens was chosen as the new capital, despite the fact that it was then a humble village of a few thousand inhabitants.

Over the next century, Greece achieved a constitution (or *syn-*

tagma, celebrated by Syntagma Square in Athens, as well as Nafplio and many other cities) and steered the monarchy toward modern democracy. Athens was rebuilt in the Neoclassical style. Greek engineers (along with foreigners) built the Corinth Canal. The Greek nation expanded, as Greek-speaking territories were captured from the Ottomans or ceded to Greece by European powers. In 1896, Greece celebrated its revival by hosting the first modern Olympic Games.

19th-Century Neoclassical Sights

- Syntagma Square, Parliament, and the evzone at the Tomb of the Unknown Soldier, in Athens
- National Gallery and National Garden in Athens
- Patriotic paintings in the Nafplio Annex of the National Gallery
- Zappeion exhibition hall in Athens
- Athens' Panathenaic Stadium (ancient stadium renovated for the first modern Olympics in 1896)
- Cathedral in Athens
- Museum of Greek Folk Art (17th-19th century) in Athens
- Corinth Canal

20TH CENTURY

Two world wars and the Greek Civil War caused great turmoil in Greece. During World War I, Greece remained uncommitted until the final years, when it joined the Allies (Britain, France, Italy, Russia, and the US) against Germany.

World War I scrambled the balance of power in the Balkans. Greece was given control of parts of western Turkey, where many ethnic Greeks lived. The Turks, having thrown out their Ottoman rulers, now rose up to evict the Greeks, sparking the Greco-Turkish War (1919-1922) and massacres on both sides. To settle the conflict, a million ethnic Greeks living in Turkish lands were shipped to Greece, while Greece sent hundreds of thousands of its ethnic Turks to Turkey. In 1923, hordes of desperate refugees poured into Athens, and the population doubled overnight. Many later immigrated to the US, Canada, and Australia. Today there are more than a million Greek Americans living in the US.

In World War II Greece sided firmly with the Allies, heroically repulsing Mussolini's 1940 invasion. But Adolf Hitler finished the job, invading and occupying Greece for four brutal years of repression and hunger.

Making the situation worse, the Greek Resistance movement (battling the Nazis) was itself divided. It broke out into a full-fledged civil war (1944-1949) between Western-backed patriots and Marxist patriots.

World War II and the Greek Civil War left Greece with hundreds of thousands dead, desperately poor, and bitterly divided. Thanks to America's Marshall Plan (and tourism), the economy recovered in the 1950s and '60s, and Greece joined the NATO alliance. Along with modernization came some of Europe's worst pollution, which eroded the ancient monuments.

Politically, Greece would remain split between the extreme right (the ruling monarchy, military, and the rich) and the extreme left (communists, students, and workers), without much room in the middle. The repressive royalist regime was backed heavily by the United States, which made Greece the first battleground in the Cold War (the Truman Doctrine). By the 1960s, when the rest of Europe was undergoing rapid social change, the Greek government was still trying to control its society with arrests and assassinations. When the royalists began losing control, a CIA-backed coup put the military in charge (1967-1974). They outlawed everything from long hair and miniskirts to Socrates and the theme song from *Zorba the Greek* (because its composer was accused of being a communist).

For Greece, 1974 was a watershed year. In the midst of political turmoil, Turkey invaded the Greek-friendly island of Cyprus (sparking yet more decades of bad blood between Turkey and Greece). The surprise attack caught the Greek military junta off guard, and they resigned in disgrace. A new government was elected with a new constitution. Guided by two strong (sometimes antagonistic) leaders—Andreas Papandreou and Constantine Karamanlis—Greece inched slowly from right-wing repression toward open democracy. Greece in the 1970s and '80s would suffer more than its share of assassinations and terrorist acts. But the economy grew, and Greece joined the European Union (1981) and adopted the euro (2002).

20th-Century Sights

- National War Museum in Athens
- National Gallery in Athens
- Central Market in Athens
- Greek flag atop the Acropolis in Athens (reminder of resistance leaders who flew it there during the Nazi occupation in World War II)

GREECE TODAY

After adopting the euro, the Greek economy boomed. EU subsidies flowed in for major infrastructure projects, such as highways and high-speed rail. As host of the 2004 Summer Olympics, Athens cleaned up its city and installed a new airport and Metro. But the worldwide recession that started in 2008 hit Greece hard. Three bailouts from the EU and the International Monetary Fund kept Greece afloat but required severe economic reforms, sending the economy into recession and pushing the unemployment rate over 25 percent.

Financial markets and European leaders feared a Greek exit from the euro, which could have caused a breakup of the currency. In 2019, Kyriakos Mitsotakis—a center-right conservative heading the New Democracy party—became prime minister. He pledged to lower taxes, create jobs, reduce unemployment, and reenergize the economy. Following a couple of years of GDP growth and unemployment reduction under Mitsotakis, Greeks remain cautiously optimistic and are taking a wait-and-see approach as to whether these improvements will last.

Greece is seriously hampered by widespread governmental corruption and a bloated (indeed, "Byzantine") bureaucratic system. Though recent administrations have had some success with attempts to combat the corruption, few Greeks are optimistic that the bureaucracy is headed toward efficiency.

Immigration is another hotly debated topic. The Greek people are divided over how the nation can and should accommodate the thousands of economic and political refugees who arrive here, both legally and illegally. This has bolstered support for far-right, brazenly racist extremists (about 92 percent of Greeks are citizens, while 8 percent are citizens of other countries, mainly Albania, Bulgaria, and Romania). Greeks also argue among themselves about the nation's high military spending, the draft, and excessive privileges for the Greek Orthodox church (more than 95 percent of Greeks are Orthodox, the state religion; just over 1 percent are Muslim). Meanwhile, relations with Turkey—its next-door neighbor across the Aegean pond—remain strained.

Along with these issues, Greece is dealing with the aftermath of the Covid-19 pandemic. Tourism is on the rebound, but by no means is Greece out of the economic woods. Yet, considering that the Greek language and culture have survived for more than two millennia—despite being conquered by Romans, Turks, and

Nazis—there's good reason to feel confident that they'll overcome the latest turmoil, too.

Greece Today Sights
- Ermou street pedestrian zone in Athens
- Renovated Monastiraki Square in Athens
- Acropolis Museum in Athens
- Athens' Metro and airport
- 2004 Olympic Games sights in Athens
- Athens' Psyrri neighborhood

To learn more about Greek history, consider *Europe 101: History and Art for the Traveler,* by Rick Steves and Gene Openshaw (available at RickSteves.com).

Greek Language

Even though the Greek alphabet presents challenges to foreign visitors, communication is not hard. You'll find that most people in the tourist industry—and almost all young people— speak fine English. Many signs and menus (especially in Athens and major

OUZO - TSIPOYRO GREEK LICKERS

tourist spots) use both the Greek and our more familiar Latin alphabet. Greeks realize that it's unreasonable to expect visitors to learn Greek (which has only 14 million speakers worldwide). It's essential for them to find a common language with the rest of the world—especially their European neighbors to the west—so they learn English early and well.

Of course, not everyone speaks English. You'll run into the most substantial language barrier when traveling in rural areas and/ or dealing with folks over 60, who are more likely to have learned French as a second language. Because signs and maps aren't always transliterated into our alphabet (i.e., spelled out using a Latin-letter equivalent), a passing familiarity with the basics of the Greek alphabet is helpful for navigating—especially for drivers (see "Greek Alphabet," below).

There are certain universal English words all Greeks know: hello, please, thank you, OK, pardon, stop, menu, problem, and no problem. While Greeks don't expect you to be fluent in their tongue, they definitely appreciate it when you're making an effort to pronounce Greek words correctly and use the local pleasantries.

It's nice to learn "Hello" (*"Gia sas,"* pronounced "yah sahs"), "Please" (*"Parakalo,"* "pah-rah-kah-LOH"), and "Thank you" (*"Efharisto,"* "ehf-hah-ree-STOH"). Watch out for this tricky point:

The Greek word for "yes" is *ne* (pronounced "neh"), which sounds a lot like "no" to us. What's more, the word for "no" is *ohi* (pronounced "OH-hee"), which sounds enough like "OK" to be potentially confusing. For more Greek words, see the "Greek Survival Phrases" in the appendix.

Don't be afraid to interact with locals. You'll find that doors open a little more quickly when you know a few words of the language. Give it your best shot.

Greek Alphabet

Most visitors find the Greek alphabet daunting, if not indecipherable. At first, all the signs look like...well, Greek to us. However, Greek has more in common with English than may be immediately apparent. Technically the world's oldest complete alphabet (Phoenician, its predecessor, had no vowel symbols), Greek is the parent of our own Latin alphabet—itself named for the first two Greek letters (alpha and beta). Because it's

used worldwide among mathematicians and scientists (not to mention frats and sororities), you may recognize some letters from your student days—but that doesn't help much when you're trying to read a map or a menu.

Fortunately, with a little effort the alphabet becomes a lot less baffling. Many uppercase Greek letters look just like their Latin counterparts (such as A, B, and M), and a few more look similar with a little imagination (Δ, Ξ, and Σ look a little like D, X, and S, if you squint). A few look nothing like anything in our alphabet, and a couple are particularly confusing (Greek's P is our R, and Greek's H is our I).

Getting comfortable with the lowercase letters is more challenging. Just like in our alphabet, most lowercase letters are similar to their uppercase versions, but a few bear no resemblance at all.

Once you're familiar with the letters, it's less of a challenge to learn how each is said. Nearly every letter (except P and H) is pronounced roughly like the Latin letter it most resembles. As for the handful of utterly unfamiliar characters, you'll just have to memorize those.

Most Greek words have one acute accent that marks the stressed vowel (such as ά rather than α, έ rather than ε, ί rather than ι, ό rather than ο, and ύ rather than υ). These accents are worth paying attention to, as a change in emphasis can bring a change in meaning. Also, note the list of letter combinations below—pairs of

Greek from A to Ω

Transliterating Greek to English is an inexact science, but here is the Greek alphabet, with the most common English counterparts for the Greek letters and letter combinations.

Greek	English Name	Common Transliteration	Pronounced
Α α	alpha	a	A as in father
Β β	beta	b or v	V as in volt
Γ γ	gamma	y or g	Y as in yes or G as in go*
Δ δ	delta	d or dh	TH as in then
Ε ε	epsilon	e	E as in get
Ζ ζ	zeta	z	Z as in zoo
Η η	eta	i	I as in ski
Θ θ	theta	th	TH as in theme
Ι ι	iota	i	I as in ski
Κ κ	kappa	k	K as in king
Λ λ	lambda	l	L as in lime
Μ μ	mu	m	M as in mom
Ν ν	nu	n	N as in net
Ξ ξ	xi	x	X as in ox
Ο ο	omicron	o	O as in ocean
Π π	pi	p	P as in pie
Ρ ρ	rho	r	R as in rich (slightly rolled)
Σ σ,ς	sigma	s or c	S as in sun
Τ τ	tau	t	T as in tip
Υ υ	upsilon	y	Y as in happy
Φ φ	phi	f or ph	F as in file
Χ χ	chi	ch, h, or kh	CH as in loch (gutturally)
Ψ ψ	psi	ps	PS as in lapse
Ω ω	omega	o or w	O as in ocean

*Gamma is pronounced, roughly speaking, like the English "hard" G only when it comes before consonants, or before the letters a, o, and ou.

letters that, when together, sound a little different than expected (similar to our own "th" or "ch" combinations).

Learn to recognize and pronounce each letter, and you'll be able to sound out the words you see around you: Μάνη = M-a-n-i, Mani (the peninsula, pronounced MAH-nee). Greek is phonetic—it has rules of pronunciation, and it sticks to them. As you stroll the streets, practice reading aloud—you may be surprised how quickly you'll be able to sound out words.

Certain Greek letter combinations create specific sounds. These include:

Greek		Transliteration	Pronounced
ΑΙ	αι	e	E as in get
ΑΥ	αυ	av/af	AV as in have, or AF as in after
ΕΙ	ει	i	I as in ski
ΕΥ	ευ	ev/ef	EV as in never, or EF as in left
ΟΙ	οι	i	I as in ski
ΟΥ	ου	ou/u	OU as in you
ΓΓ	γγ	ng	NG as in angle
ΓΚ	γκ	ng/g	NG as in angle, or G as in go (at start of word)
ΜΠ	μπ	mb/b	MB as in amber, or B as in bet (at start of word)
ΝΔ	νδ	nd/nt/d	ND as in land, or D as in dog (at start of word)
ΤΣ	τσ	ts	TS as in hats
ΤΖ	τζ	dz	DS as in lands, or DG as in judge

Greek Place Names

One Greek word can be transliterated into English in many different ways. For example, the town of Nafplio may appear on a map or road sign as Navplio, Naufplio, or Nauvplio. Even more confusing, there are actually two different versions of Greek: proper Greek, which was used until the 1950s (and now sounds affected to most Greeks); and popular Greek, a simplified version that is the norm today. This means that even Greeks might use different names for the same thing (for example, the city names Nafplio and Patra are popular Greek, while Nafplion and Patras are formal Greek).

The following list includes the most common English spelling and pronunciation for Greek places. If the Greeks use their own differently spelled transliteration, it's noted in parentheses.

English	Pronounced	Greek Transliteration
Greece (Ellada or Hellas)	eh-LAH-thah, eh-LAHS	Ελλάδα or Ελλάς
Athens (Athina)	ah-THEE-nah	Αθήνα
Delphi	thell-FEE (or dell-FEE)	Δελφοί
Epidavros	eh-PEE-dah-vrohs	Επίδαυρος
Hydra	EE-drah	Ύδρα
Kardamyli	kar-dah-MEE-lee	Καρδαμύλη
Mani	MAH-nee	Μάνη
Monemvasia	moh-nehm-vah-SEE-ah	Μονεμβασία
Mycenae (Mikenes)	my-SEE-nee (mee-KEE-nehs)	Μυκήνες
Mykonos	MEE-koh-nohs	Μύκονος
Nafplio	NAF-plee-oh	Ναύπλιο
Olympia	oh-leem-PEE-ah	Ολυμπία
Peloponnese (Peloponnisos)	PEL-oh-poh-neez (pel-oh-POH-nee-sohs)	Πελοπόννησος
Piraeus	pee-reh-AHS	Πειραιάς
Santorini (Thira)	sahn-toh-REE-nee (THEE-rah)	Θήρα

Note that these are the pronunciations most commonly used in English. Greeks may put the emphasis on a different syllable—for example, English-speakers call the Olympics birthplace oh-LEEM-pee-ah, while Greeks say oh-leem-PEE-ah.

PRACTICALITIES

This chapter covers the practical skills of European travel: how to get tourist information, pay for things, sightsee efficiently, find good-value accommodations, eat affordably but well, use technology wisely, and get between destinations smoothly. For more information on these topics, see RickSteves.com/travel-tips.

Travel Tips

Travel Advisories: Before traveling, check updated health and safety conditions, including restrictions for your destination, on the travel pages of the US State Department (www.travel.state. gov) and Centers for Disease Control and Prevention (www.cdc. gov/travel). The US embassy website for Greece is another good source of information (see below).

Covid Vaccine/Test Requirements: It's possible you'll need to present proof of vaccination against the coronavirus and/or a negative Covid-19 test result to board a plane to Europe or back to the US. Carefully check requirements for each country you'll visit well before you depart, and again a few days before your trip. See the websites listed above for current requirements.

ETIAS Registration: The European Union may soon require US and Canadian citizens to register online with the European Travel Information and Authorization System (ETIAS) before entering Greece and other Schengen Zone countries (quick and easy process). For the latest, check www.etiasvisa.com.

Tourist Information: The Greek **national tourist office** has a helpful website with lots of information and downloadable maps and brochures (VisitGreece.gr). Other good websites include http://odysseus.culture.gr (Greek Ministry of Culture, with information on major archaeological sites and museums), www.thisisathens.org (City of Athens Convention and Visitors Bureau), and www.athensguide.com (guide to Athens by travel writer Matt Barrett).

In Greece, tourist offices (abbreviated **TI** in this book) are often marked *EOT* (for the Greek phrase "Greek Tourism Organization"). Unfortunately, budget cuts have forced many towns to close their TIs. The offices that are still open can usually give you a free map, a few local tips, and some assistance with bus connections. In general, though, your hotelier may end up being your best source of information.

Emergency and Medical Help: For any emergency service—ambulance, police, or fire—call **112** from a mobile phone or landline (operators typically speak English). In Greece, you can also dial 171 or 1571 for the Tourist Police.

The **Tourist Police** serves as a contact point between tourists and other branches of the police and is also responsible for handling problems such as disputes with hotels, restaurants, and other tourist services (available 24 hours daily; Athens office located east of the Central Market in the Psyrri district, +30 210 322 2230).

If you get sick, do as the locals do and go to a pharmacist for advice. Or ask at your hotel for help—they'll know the nearest medical and emergency services.

Theft or Loss: To replace a passport, you'll need to go in person to an embassy (see next). If your credit and debit cards disappear, cancel and replace them (see "Damage Control for Lost Cards" on page 526). File a police report, either on the spot or within a day or two; you'll need it to submit an insurance claim for lost or stolen items, and it can help with replacing your passport or credit and debit cards. For more information, see RickSteves.com/help.

US Embassy in Athens: Dial +30 210 720 2414, after-hours emergency +30 210 729 4444; consular section open Mon-Fri 8:30-17:00, closed Sat-Sun and last Wed of month; Vasilissis Sophias 91, Metro: Megaro Moussikis, http://gr.usembassy.gov.

Canadian Embassy in Athens: Dial +30 210 727 3400, for after-hours emergency help call Canada collect at +1 613 996 8885;

PRACTICALITIES

open Mon-Fri 8:30-16:30, closed Sat-Sun; Ethnikis Antistaseos 48, www.canadainternational.gc.ca/greece-grece.

Borders: If you enter Greece from most European countries (those that are part of Europe's open-borders Schengen Agreement), you won't need to go through customs. But if you arrive on a direct flight from the US, or from the neighboring countries of Turkey, North Macedonia, Albania, or Bulgaria (which aren't part of the EU pact), you'll have to clear customs.

Time Zones: Greece, which is one hour ahead of most of continental Europe, is generally seven/ten hours ahead of the East/West Coasts of the US. The exceptions are the beginning and end of Daylight Saving Time: Europe "springs forward" the last Sunday in March (two weeks after most of North America) and "falls back" the last Sunday in October (one week before North America). For a handy time converter, use the world clock app on your phone or download one (see www.timeanddate.com).

Business Hours: Most shops catering to tourists are open long hours daily. In Athens stores are generally open weekdays from 9:00 to 20:00 or later. Afternoon breaks are common, and Saturdays are like weekdays but with earlier closing hours. Sundays have the same pros and cons as they do for travelers in the US: Sightseeing attractions are generally open, while shops and banks are closed, public transportation options are fewer, and there's no rush hour.

Watt's Up? Europe's electrical system is 220 volts, instead of North America's 110 volts. Most electronics (laptops, phones, cameras) and appliances (newer hair dryers, CPAP machines) convert automatically, so you won't need a converter, but you will need an adapter plug with two round prongs, sold inexpensively at travel stores in the US.

Bathroom Etiquette: There's a reason every bathroom in Greece has a small wastebasket next to the toilet—bad plumbing. Don't flush toilet paper; use the wastebasket instead.

Rip up this book! Turn chapters into mini guidebooks: Break the book's spine and use a utility knife to slice apart chapters, keeping gummy edges intact. Reinforce the chapter spines with clear wide tape; use a heavy-duty stapler; or make or buy a cheap cover (see the Travel Store at RickSteves.com), swapping out chapters as you travel.

Discounts: Discounts for sights are generally not listed in this book. However, seniors (age 65 and over), youths under 18, and students and teachers with proper identification cards (obtain from www.isic.org) can get discounts at many sights—always ask. Some discounts are available only to European citizens.

Online Translation Tips: Google's Chrome browser instantly translates websites; Translate.google.com and DeepL.com are also handy. The Google Translate app converts spoken or typed English into most European languages (and vice versa) and can also translate text it "reads" with your phone's camera.

Going Green: There's plenty you can do to reduce your environmental footprint when traveling. When practical, take a bus or train instead of a flight within Europe, and use public transportation within cities. In hotels, use the "Do Not Disturb" sign to avoid daily linen and towel changes (or hang up your towels to signal you'll reuse them). Bring a reusable shopping tote and refillable water bottle (Europe's tap water is safe to drink). Skip printed brochures, maps, or other materials that you don't plan to keep—get your info online instead. To find out how Rick Steves' Europe is offsetting carbon emissions with a self-imposed carbon tax, see RickSteves.com/about-us/climate-smart.

Money

Here's my basic strategy for using money wisely in Europe. I pack the following and keep it all safe in my money belt.

Credit Card: You'll use your credit card for purchases both big (hotels, advance tickets) and small (little shops, food stands). Some businesses have gone cashless, making a card your only payment option. A "tap-to-pay" or "contactless" card is the most widely accepted and simplest to use.

Debit Card: Use this at ATMs to withdraw a small amount of local cash. Wait until you arrive to get euros (European airports have plenty of ATMs); if you buy euros before your trip, you'll pay bad stateside exchange rates. You'll use cash more often in Greece than in many other European countries, especially outside big cities. Cash can help you out of a jam if your card randomly doesn't work, and can be useful to pay for things like tips and local guides.

Backup Card: Some travelers carry a third card (debit or credit; ideally from a different bank) in case one gets lost or simply doesn't work.

Stash of Cash: I carry $100-200 in US dollars as a cash backup, which comes in handy in an emergency (for example, if your debit card gets eaten by the machine).

BEFORE YOU GO
Know your cards. For credit cards, Visa and MasterCard are universal while American Express and Discover are less common. US debit cards with a Visa or MasterCard logo will work in any European ATM.

Go "contactless." Get comfortable using contactless pay options. Check to see if you already have—or can get—a tap-to-pay version of your credit card (look on the card for the tap-to-pay sym-

Exchange Rate

1 euro (€) = about $1.10

To convert prices in euros to dollars, add about 10 percent: €20 = about $22, €50 = about $55. Like the dollar, one euro is broken into 100 cents. Coins range from €0.01 to €2, and bills from €5 to €200 (bills over €50 are rarely used).

Check www.oanda.com for the latest exchange rates.

bol—four curvy lines), and consider setting up your smartphone for contactless payment (see next section for details). Both options are widely used in Europe.

Know your PIN. Make sure you know the numeric, four-digit PIN for each of your cards, both debit and credit. Request it if you don't have one, as it may be required for some purchases. Allow time to receive the information by mail—it's not always possible to obtain your PIN online or by phone.

Report your travel dates. Let your bank know that you'll be using your debit and credit cards in Europe, and when and where you're headed.

Adjust your ATM withdrawal limit. Find out how much you can withdraw daily and ask for a higher daily limit if you want to get more cash at once. Note that European ATMs will withdraw funds only from checking accounts, not savings accounts.

Find out about fees. For any purchase or withdrawal made with a card, you may be charged a currency conversion fee (1-3 percent) and/or a Visa or MasterCard international transaction fee (less than 1 percent). If you're getting a bad deal, consider getting a new card. Reputable no-fee cards include those from Capital One, as well as Charles Schwab debit cards. Most credit unions and some airline loyalty cards have low or no international transaction fees.

IN EUROPE
Using Credit Cards and Payment Apps

Tap-to-Pay or Contactless Cards: These cards have the usual chip and/or magnetic stripe, but with the addition of a contactless symbol. Simply tap your card against a contactless reader to complete a transaction—no PIN or signature is required.

Payment Apps: Just like at home, you can pay with your smartphone or smartwatch by linking a credit card to an app such as Apple Pay or Google Pay. To pay, hold your phone near a contactless reader; you may need to verify the transaction with a face scan, fingerprint scan, or passcode. If you've arrived in Europe without a tap-to-pay card, you can easily set up your phone to work in this way.

Other Card Types: Chip-and-PIN cards have a visible chip embedded in them; rather than swiping, you insert the card into the payment machine, then enter your PIN on a keypad. **Swipe-and-sign** credit cards—with a swipeable magnetic stripe, and a receipt you have to sign—are increasingly rare.

Will My US Card Work? Usually, yes. On rare occasions, at self-service payment machines (such as transit-ticket kiosks, toll-booths, or fuel pumps), some US cards may not work. Usually a tap-to-pay card does the trick in these situations. Just in case, carry cash as a backup and look for a cashier who can process your payment if your card is rejected. Drivers should be prepared to move on to the next gas station if necessary. (In some countries, gas stations sell prepaid gas cards, which you can purchase with any US card). When approaching a toll plaza or ferry ticket line, use the "cash" lane.

Using Cash

Cash Machines: European cash machines work just like they do at home—except they spit out local currency instead of dollars, calculated at the day's standard bank-to-bank rate. In most places, ATMs are easy to locate—in Greece, they are surprisingly labeled *ATM* in the Greek alphabet. When possible, withdraw cash from a bank-run ATM located just outside that bank.

If your debit card doesn't work, try a lower amount—your request may have exceeded your withdrawal limit or the ATM's limit. If you still have a problem, try a different ATM or come back later.

Avoid "independent" ATMs, such as Travelex, Euronet, Moneybox, Your Cash, Cardpoint, and Cashzone. These have high fees, can be less secure, and may try to trick users with "dynamic currency conversion" (see next).

Dynamic Currency Conversion: When withdrawing cash at an ATM or paying with a credit card, you'll often be asked whether you want the transaction processed in dollars or in the local currency. Always refuse the conversion and *choose the local currency.* While DCC offers the illusion of convenience, it comes with a poor exchange rate, and you'll wind up losing money.

Exchanging Cash: Minimize exchanging money in Europe; it's expensive (you'll generally lose 5 to 10 percent). In a pinch you can find exchange desks at airports. Banks generally do not exchange money unless you have an account with them.

Security Tips

Pickpockets target tourists. Keep your cash, credit cards, and passport secure in your money belt, and carry only a day's spending money in your front pocket or wallet.

Before inserting your card into an ATM, inspect the front. If anything looks crooked, loose, or damaged, it could be a sign of a card-skimming device. When entering your PIN, carefully block other peoples' view of the keypad.

Avoid using a debit card for purchases. Because a debit card pulls funds directly from your bank account, potential charges incurred by a thief will stay on your account while your bank investigates.

To access your accounts online while traveling, be sure to use a secure connection (see the "Tips on Internet Security" sidebar, later).

Damage Control for Lost Cards

If you lose your credit or debit card, report the loss immediately to the respective global customer-assistance centers. With a mobile phone, call these 24-hour US numbers: Visa (+1 303 967 1096), Mastercard (+1 636 722 7111), and American Express (+1 336 393 1111). From a landline, you can call these US numbers collect by going through a local operator.

You'll need to provide the primary cardholder's identification-verification details (such as birth date, mother's maiden name, or Social Security number). You can generally receive a temporary card within two or three business days in Europe (see RickSteves.com/help for more).

If you report your loss within two days, you typically won't be responsible for unauthorized transactions on your account, although many banks charge a liability fee.

TIPPING

Tipping in Greece isn't as automatic and generous as it is in the US. For special service, tips are appreciated, but not expected. As in the US, the proper amount depends on your resources, tipping philosophy, and the circumstances, but some general guidelines apply.

Restaurants: At Greek restaurants that have waitstaff, locals generally round up their bill after a good meal (usually about 10 percent). If paying with a credit card, be prepared to tip separately with cash or coins; credit card receipts often don't have a tip line. For more on tipping in restaurants, see "Eating," later.

Taxis: For a typical ride, round up your fare a bit (for instance, if the fare is €4.50, pay €5). If the cabbie hauls your bags and zips you to the airport to help you catch your flight, you might want to toss in a little more.

Services: In general, if someone in the service industry does a super job for you, a small tip of a euro or two is appropriate...but not required. If you're not sure whether (or how much) to tip for a service, ask a local for advice.

GETTING A VAT REFUND

Wrapped into the purchase price of your Greek souvenirs is a value-added tax (VAT) of about 24 percent. You're entitled to get most of that tax back if you purchase more than €50 worth of goods at a store that participates in the VAT-refund scheme. Typically, you must ring up the minimum at a single retailer—you can't add up your purchases from various shops to reach the required amount. (If the store ships the goods to your US home, VAT is not assessed on your purchase.)

Getting your refund is straightforward...and worthwhile if you spend a significant amount.

At the Merchant. Have the merchant completely fill out the refund document (they'll ask for your passport; a photo of your passport usually works). Keep track of the paperwork and your original sales receipt. Note that you're not supposed to use your purchased goods before you leave Europe.

At the Border or Airport. Process your VAT document at your last stop in the European Union (such as at the airport) with the customs agent who deals with VAT refunds (allow plenty of extra time to deal with this process). At some airports, you'll have to go to a customs office to get your documents stamped and then to a separate VAT refund service (such as Global Blue or Planet) to process the refund. At other airports, a single VAT desk handles the whole thing. (Note that refund services typically extract a 4 percent fee, but you're paying for the convenience of receiving your money in cash immediately or as a credit to your card.) Otherwise, you'll need to mail the stamped refund documents to the address given by the merchant.

CUSTOMS FOR AMERICAN SHOPPERS

You can take home $800 worth of items per person duty-free, once every 31 days. Many processed and packaged foods are allowed, including cheeses, dried herbs, jams, baked goods, candy, chocolate, oil, vinegar, condiments, and honey. Fresh fruits and vegetables and most meats are not allowed, with exceptions for some canned items. As for alcohol, you can bring home one liter duty-free (it can be packed securely in your checked luggage, along with any other liquid-containing items).

To bring alcohol (or liquid-packed foods) in your carry-on bag on your flight home, buy it at a duty-free shop at the airport. You'll increase your odds of getting it onto a connecting flight if it's packaged in a "STEB"—a secure, tamper-evident bag. But stay away from liquids in opaque, ceramic, or metallic containers, which usually cannot be successfully screened (STEB or no STEB).

For details on allowable goods, customs rules, and duty rates, visit https://help.cbp.gov.

Sightseeing

Sightseeing can be hard work. Use these tips to make your visits to Greece's finest sights meaningful, fun, efficient, and painless.

MAPS AND NAVIGATION TOOLS

A good map is essential for efficient navigation while sightseeing. The maps in this book are concise and simple, designed to help you locate recommended destinations, sights, hotels, and restaurants. In Europe, simple maps are generally free at TIs and hotels. Maps with more detail are sold at newsstands and bookstores.

You can also use a mapping app on your mobile device, which provides turn-by-turn directions for walking, driving, and taking public transit. Google Maps, Apple Maps, and CityMaps2Go allow you to download maps for offline use; ideally, download the areas you'll need before your trip. For certain features, you'll need to be online—either using Wi-Fi or an international data plan.

PLAN AHEAD

Set up an itinerary that allows you to fit in all your must-see sights. For a one-stop look at opening hours in Athens, see "Athens at a Glance" in the Sights in Athens chapter. Since the Covid-19 pandemic, hours for museums and sights have been unstable. Confirm the latest opening days and times before your visit.

Don't put off visiting a must-see sight—you never know when a place will close unexpectedly for a holiday, strike, or restoration. Many museums are closed or have reduced hours at least a few days a year, especially on holidays such as Christmas, New Year's, and Labor Day (May 1). A list of holidays is in the appendix; check for possible closures during your trip.

Most of Greece's ancient sites and archaeological museums are operated by the government. In general, hours at sights are longer during peak season (April-Oct) and on weekends, and shorter on weekdays and in the off-season. The timing of this seasonal switch can be unannounced and differs between sights. Year-round, if things are slow, places may close early with no advance notice. It's smart to arrive well in advance of listed closing times and to hit your must-see sights in the morning, especially if traveling outside of summer.

The Ministry of Greek Culture website (http://odysseus. culture.gr) lists hours for virtually all of the major sights—including Athens' Acropolis, Ancient Agora, Acropolis Museum, and the National Archaeological Museum, plus sights at Delphi, Olympia, Epidavros, and Mycenae—but you'll get more reliable, up-to-date information by asking your hotelier or calling the sights directly. These sights, including the Acropolis, are free on national holidays and every first Sunday from November through March, and children under 18 always get in free.

Going at the right time helps avoid crowds. This book offers tips on the best times to see specific sights. Try visiting popular sights very early or very late. Evening visits (when possible) are usually more peaceful, with fewer crowds. Late morning is usually the worst time to visit a popular sight.

If you plan to hire a local guide, reserve ahead by email. Popular guides can get booked up.

Study up. To get the most out of the self-guided tours and sight descriptions in this book, read them before you visit. The Acropolis is much more entertaining if you've polished up on Doric architecture the night before.

RESERVATIONS AND ADVANCE TICKETS

Many popular sights in Europe come with long lines—not to get in, but to buy a ticket. Visitors who buy tickets online in advance can skip the line and waltz right in. Advance tickets are sometimes timed-entry, meaning you're guaranteed admission on a certain date and time.

For some sights, buying ahead is required (tickets aren't sold at the sight and it's the only way to get in). At other sights, buying ahead is recommended to skip the line and save time (in some cases, you can do this even on the day you plan to visit). And for many sights, advance tickets are available but unnecessary: At these uncrowded sights you can simply arrive, buy a ticket, and go in.

Don't confuse the reservation options: available, recommended, and required. Use my advice in this book as a guide. If you do your research, you'll know the smart strategy. For Greece, consider buying tickets online for the Acropolis and Acropolis Museum to avoid a ticket-buying line at the sights.

You'll generally be emailed an eticket with a QR or bar code that you'll store on your phone to scan at the entrance (if you prefer, you can print it out). At the sight, look for the ticket-holders line rather than the ticket-buying line; you may still have to wait in a security line.

AT SIGHTS

Many of Greece's artifacts have been plunked into glass cases labeled with little more than title and date. Sights run by the Greek

Ministry of Culture provide a free information pamphlet, though usually only by request.

More than most destinations in Europe, Greece demands (and rewards) any
effort you make to really understand its treasures. If you read up on Greek history and
art, the artifacts come to life; without this
background, visiting Greece's museums can
quickly become an unforgiving slog past stiff
statues and endless ceramic vases.

It can also help to put your imagination
into overdrive. As you stroll Athens' Ancient
Agora, mentally clad the other tourists in
robes. Approach the temple at Delphi as if you were about to learn
your fate from an oracle; enter the stadium at Olympia ready to race
its length in front of a huge crowd. At museums, imagine being
the archaeologist who unearthed the intact glass vessels, intricate
golden necklaces, and vases inscribed with the faces of people who
lived four millennia ago.

Many major ancient sites have both an archaeological site and
a museum for the artifacts and models. You can choose between
visiting the museum first (to mentally reconstruct the ruins before
seeing them) or the site first (to get the lay of the ancient land before seeing the items found there). In most cases, I prefer to see the
site first, then the museum. However, crowds and weather can also
help determine your plan. If it's a blistering hot afternoon, tour the
air-conditioned museum first, then hit the ruins in the cool of evening (if opening hours allow). Or, if rain clouds are on the horizon,
do the archaeological site first, then duck into the museum when
the rain hits.

Here's what you can typically expect:

Entering: You may not be allowed to enter if you arrive too
close to closing time. And guards start ushering people out well
before the actual closing time, so don't save the best for last.

Some sights have a security check. Allow extra time for these
lines. Some sights require you to check day packs and coats. (If
you'd rather not check your day pack, try carrying it tucked under
your arm like a purse as you enter.)

At churches—which often offer interesting art (usually free)
and a cool, welcome seat—a modest dress code (no bare shoulders
or shorts) is encouraged.

Etiquette and Photography at Ancient Sites: Archaeological
sites are meticulously monitored; you're sure to hear the tweets of
many whistles aimed at visitors who've crossed a barrier or climbed
on a ruin.

PRACTICALITIES

If an attraction's photo policy isn't clearly posted, ask a guard. Generally, taking photos without a flash or tripod is allowed. Some sights ban selfie sticks; others ban photos altogether. The Greeks take their ancient artifacts very seriously. Posing with ancient statues—or even standing next to them for a photo—is strictly forbidden.

Audioguides and Apps: I've produced free, downloadable audio tours for my Athens City Walk, the Acropolis, Ancient Agora, and National Archaeological Museum; look for the 🎧 in this book. For more on my audio tours, see page 26.

In Greece, audioguides are rare, but good guidebooks are available. You can usually hire a live local guide at the entrance to major ancient sites or museums at a reasonable cost (prices are soft and negotiable; save money by splitting the guide fee with other travelers). I list recommended guides in the "Helpful Hints" section of many chapters. Two notable exceptions are Olympia, where guides are sparse, and the Acropolis, where the loitering guides are generally of poor quality.

Temporary Exhibits: Museums may show special exhibits in addition to their permanent collection. Some exhibits are included in the entry price, while others come at an extra cost (which you may have to pay even if you don't want to see the exhibit).

Expect Changes: Artwork can be on tour, on loan, out sick, or shifted at the whim of the curator. Pick up a floor plan as you enter and ask museum staff if you can't find a particular item.

Services: Important sights usually have a reasonably priced on-site café or cafeteria (handy and air-conditioned places to rejuvenate during a long visit). The WCs at sights are free and generally clean.

Before Leaving: At the gift shop, scan the postcard rack or thumb through a guidebook to be sure you haven't overlooked something that you'd like to see. Every sight or museum offers more than what is covered in this book. Use the information I provide as an introduction—not the final word.

Sleeping

Extensive and opinionated listings of good-value rooms are a major feature of this book's Sleeping sections. Rather than list accommodations scattered throughout a town, I choose hotels in my favorite neighborhoods that are convenient to your sightseeing.

My recommendations run the gamut, from dorm beds to luxurious rooms with all the comforts. I like places that are clean, central, relatively quiet at night, reasonably priced, friendly, small enough to have a hands-on owner or manager, and run with a respect for Greek traditions. I'm more impressed by a handy location and a fun-loving philosophy than oversized TVs and a fancy gym. Most of my recommendations fall short of perfection. But if I can find a place with most of these features, it's a keeper.

Book your accommodations as soon as your itinerary is set, especially if you want to stay at one of my top listings or if you'll be traveling during busy times (roughly Orthodox Easter through October). See the appendix for a list of major holidays and festivals in Greece.

Some people make reservations a few days ahead as they travel. This approach fosters spontaneity, and booking sites make it easy to find available rooms, but—especially during busy times—you run the risk of settling for lesser-value accommodations.

RATES AND DEALS

I've categorized my recommended accommodations based on price, indicated with a dollar-sign rating (see sidebar). Room prices can fluctuate significantly with demand and amenities (size, views, room class, and so on), but relative price categories remain constant. City taxes, which can vary from place to place, are generally insignificant (a few dollars per person, per night). And keep in mind that some hotels in Greece, especially smaller places, may require payment in cash.

Booking Direct: Once your dates are set, compare prices at several hotels. You can do this by checking hotel websites and booking sites such as Hotels.com or Booking.com. After you've zeroed in on your choice, book directly with the hotel itself. This increases the chances that the hotelier will be able to accommodate special needs or requests (such as shifting your reservation). And when you book on the hotel's website, by email, or by phone, the owner avoids the commission paid to booking sites, giving them wiggle room to offer you a discount, a nicer room, or a free breakfast (if it's not already included).

Getting a Discount: Some hotels extend a discount to those who pay cash or stay longer than three nights. And some accommodations offer a special discount for Rick Steves readers, indicated in this guidebook by the abbreviation "RS%." Discounts vary: Ask for details when you reserve. Generally, to qualify for this discount, you must book direct (not through a booking site), mention this book when you reserve, show this book upon arrival, and sometimes pay cash or stay a certain number of nights. In some cases, you may need to enter a discount code (which I've provided

---

Sleep Code

Hotels in this book are categorized according to the average price of a standard double room with breakfast in high season.

$$$$	**Splurge:** Most rooms over €150
$$$	**Pricier:** €110-150
$$	**Moderate:** €70-110
$	**Budget:** €50-70
¢	**Backpacker:** Under €50
RS%	**Rick Steves discount**

Unless otherwise noted, credit cards are accepted, hotel staff speak basic English, and free Wi-Fi is available. Comparison-shop by checking prices at several hotels (on each hotel's own website, on a booking site, or by email). For the best deal, *book directly with the hotel.* Ask for a discount if paying in cash; if the listing includes **RS%,** request a Rick Steves discount.

---

in the listing) in the booking form on the hotel's website. Rick Steves discounts apply to readers with either print or digital books. Understandably, discounts do not apply to promotional rates.

TYPES OF ACCOMMODATIONS
Hotels

You'll usually see the word "hotel," but you might also see the traditional Greek word *Xenonas* (ΞΕΝΩΝΑΣ/Ξενώνας). In some places, especially Nafplio, small hotels are called *pensions*.

Plan on spending €140 per hotel double in Athens and popular islands, and €85 in smaller towns. Some hotels can add an extra bed (for a small charge) to turn a double into a triple; some offer larger rooms for four or more people (I call these "family rooms" in the listings). If there's space for an extra cot, they'll cram it in for you. In general, a triple room is cheaper than the cost of a double and a single. Three or four people can economize by requesting one big room.

Arrival and Check-In: Hotels and B&Bs are sometimes located on the higher floors of a multipurpose building with a secured door. In that case, look for your hotel's name on the buttons by the main entrance. When you ring the bell, you'll be buzzed in.

Hotel elevators are common, though small, and some older buildings still lack them. You may have to climb a flight of stairs to reach the elevator (if so, you can ask the front desk for help carrying your bags up).

The EU requires hotels to collect your name, nationality, and ID number. At check-in, the receptionist will normally ask for your passport and may keep it for several hours. If you're not comfortable leaving your passport at the desk, bring a copy to give them instead.

PRACTICALITIES

Making Hotel Reservations

Reserve your rooms as soon as you've pinned down your travel dates. For busy national holidays, it's wise to reserve far in advance (see the appendix).

Requesting a Reservation: For family-run hotels, it's generally best to book your room directly via email or phone. For business-class and chain hotels, or if you'd rather book online, reserve directly through the hotel's official website (not a booking website). Almost all of my recommended hotels take reservations in English.

Here's what the hotelier wants to know:

- Type(s) of room(s) you want and number of guests
- Number of nights you'll stay
- Arrival and departure dates, written European-style as day/month/year (for example, 18/06/24 or 18 June 2024)
- Special requests (en suite bathroom, cheapest room, twin beds vs. double bed, quiet room)
- Applicable discounts (such as a Rick Steves discount, cash discount, or promotional rate)

Confirming a Reservation: Most places will request a credit-card number to hold your room. If the hotel's website doesn't have a secure form where you can enter the number directly, share this info via a phone call.

Canceling a Reservation: If you must cancel, it's courteous—and smart—to do so with as much notice as possible, especially for smaller family-run places. Cancellation policies can be strict; read

---

If you're arriving in the morning, your room probably won't be ready. Check your bag safely at the hotel and dive right into sightseeing.

In Your Room: Most hotel rooms have a TV and free Wi-Fi, which can vary in strength and quality. Simpler places rarely have a room phone.

All over Greece, including Athens, most bathrooms have ancient plumbing that clogs easily. You may see signs requesting that you discard toilet paper in the bathroom wastebasket. This may seem unusual, but it keeps the sewer system working and prevents you from getting cozy with your hotel janitor.

If visiting areas with mosquitoes (such as Kardamyli and Monemvasia), avoid opening your windows, especially at

From:	rick@ricksteves.com
Sent:	Today
To:	info@hotelcentral.com
Subject:	Reservation request for 19-22 July

Dear Hotel Central,

I would like to stay at your hotel. Please let me know if you have a room available and the price for:
• 2 people
• Double bed and en suite bathroom in a quiet room
• Arriving 19 July, departing 22 July (3 nights)

Thank you!
Rick Steves

the fine print before you book. Many discount deals require pre-payment and can be expensive to change or cancel.

Reconfirming a Reservation: Always call or email to reconfirm your room reservation a few days in advance. For *dhomatia* (privately rented rooms) or very small hotels, I call again on my arrival day to tell my host what time to expect me (especially important if arriving late—after 17:00).

Phoning: For tips on calling hotels overseas, see page 549.

night. If your hotel lacks air-conditioning, request a fan. Many hotels furnish a small plug-in bulb that helps keep the bloodsuckers at bay. If not already plugged into the electric socket, it may be on a table or nightstand. Some may have a separate scented packet that you have to unwrap and insert into the device.

Hotels in Greece are required by law to be nonsmoking, but enforcement is spotty. Hoteliers are obsessive about eliminating any odors, but if your room smells like the Marlboro man slept there, ask to be moved.

Breakfast and Meals: A satisfying Greek breakfast with cheese, ham, yogurt, fresh bread, honey, jam, fruit, juice, and coffee or tea is standard and is sometimes included in hotel prices. More expensive hotels also tend to serve eggs and cereal.

Checking Out: While it's customary to pay for your room upon departure, it can be a good idea to settle your bill the day before, when you're not in a hurry and while the manager's there.

Hotelier Help: Hoteliers can be a good source of advice. Most know their city well and can assist you with everything from public

Using Online Services to Your Advantage

From booking services to user reviews, online businesses play a greater role in travelers' planning than ever before. Take advantage of their pluses—and be wise to their downsides.

Booking Sites

Booking websites such as Booking.com and Hotels.com offer one-stop shopping for hotels. While convenient for travelers, they're both a blessing and a curse for small, independent, family-run hotels. Without a presence on these sites, small hotels become almost invisible. But to be listed, a hotel must pay a sizable commission...and promise that its own website won't undercut the price on the booking-service site.

Here's the work-around: Use the big sites to research what's out there, then book directly with the hotel by email or phone, in which case hotel owners are free to give you whatever price they like. Ask for a room without the commission markup (or ask for a free breakfast if not included, or a free upgrade). If you do book online, be sure to use the hotel's own website. The price will likely be the same as via a booking site, but your money goes to the hotel, not agency commissions.

As a savvy consumer, remember: When you book with an online service, you're adding a middleman who takes a cut. To support small, family-run hotels whose world is more difficult than ever, book direct.

Short-Term Rental Sites

Rental juggernaut Airbnb (along with other short-term rental sites) allows travelers to rent rooms and apartments, often providing more value, space, and amenities than a cookie-cutter hotel. Airbnb fans appreciate feeling part of a real neighborhood and getting into a daily routine as "temporary Europeans." Some places are run by thoughtful hosts, allowing you to get to know a local and keep your money in the community; but beware: others are impersonally managed by large, absentee agencies.

transit and airport connections to finding a good restaurant, the nearest launderette, or a late-night pharmacy.

Hotel Hassles: Even at the best places, mechanical breakdowns occur: Sinks leak, hot water turns cold, toilets may gurgle or smell, the Wi-Fi goes out, or the air-conditioning dies when you need it most. Report your concerns clearly and calmly at the front desk.

If you find that night noise is a problem (if, for instance, your room is over a nightclub or facing a busy street), ask for a quieter room in the back or on an upper floor. To guard against theft in your room, keep valuables out of sight. Some rooms come with a

Critics of Airbnb see it as a threat to "traditional Europe." Landlords can make more money renting to short-stay travelers, driving rents up—and local residents out. Traditional businesses are replaced by ones that cater to tourists. And the character and charm that made those neighborhoods desirable to tourists in the first place goes too. Some cities have cracked down, requiring owners to obtain a license and to occupy rental properties part of the year (and staging disruptive "inspections" that inconvenience guests).

As a lover of Europe, I share the worry of those who see residents nudged aside by tourists. But as an advocate for travelers, I appreciate the value Airbnb can provide in offering the chance to stay in a local building or neighborhood with potentially fewer tourists.

User Reviews

User-generated review sites and apps such as Yelp and TripAdvisor can give you a consensus of opinions about everything from hotels and restaurants to sights and nightlife. If you scan reviews of a restaurant or hotel and see several complaints about noise or a rotten location, you've gained insight that can help in your decision-making.

As a guidebook writer, my sense is that there is a big difference between the uncurated information on a review site and the vetted listings in a guidebook. A user review is based on the limited experience of one person, who stayed at just one hotel in a given city and ate at a few restaurants there. A guidebook is the work of a trained researcher who forms a well-developed basis for comparison by visiting many restaurants and hotels year after year.

Both types of information have their place, and in many ways, they're complementary. If something is well reviewed in a guidebook and it also gets good online reviews, it's likely a winner.

safe, and other hotels have safes at the front desk. I've never bothered using one and in a lifetime of travel, I've never had anything stolen from my room.

For more complicated problems, don't expect instant results. Above all, keep a positive attitude. Remember, you're on vacation. If your hotel is a disappointment, spend more time out enjoying the place you came to see.

Dhomatia (Rooms)

Rooms in private homes (similar to B&Bs, called *dhomatia*/ΔΩΜΑΤΙΑ/δωματια in Greece) offer double the cultural intimacy for a good deal less than most hotel rooms. You'll usually have air-conditioning, your own bathroom, and a mini-fridge, but expect simple, stripped-down rooms, and little or nothing in the way of a public lounge. Hosts generally speak English and are interesting conversationalists. Your stay probably won't include breakfast, but you'll have access to a kitchen.

You'll save money by booking directly with the *dhomatia* listed in this book.

Short-Term Rentals

A short-term rental—whether an apartment, a house, or a room in a private residence—is a popular alternative, especially if you plan to settle in one location for several nights. For stays longer than a few days, you can usually find a rental that's comparable to—and cheaper than—a hotel room with similar amenities. Plus, you'll get a behind-the-scenes peek into how locals live.

Many places require a minimum stay and have strict cancellation policies. And you're generally on your own: There's no reception desk, breakfast, or daily cleaning service.

Finding Accommodations: Websites such as Airbnb, FlipKey, Booking.com, and VRBO let you browse a wide range of properties. Alternatively, rental agencies such as InterhomeUSA.com and RentaVilla.com can provide more personalized service (their curated listings are also more expensive).

Before you commit, be clear on the location. I like to virtually "explore" the neighborhood using Google Street View. Also consider the proximity to public transportation, and how well connected the property is with the rest of the city. Ask about amenities (elevator, air-conditioning, laundry, Wi-Fi, parking, etc.). Reviews from previous guests can help identify trouble spots.

Think about the kind of experience you want: Just a key and an affordable bed...or a chance to get to know a local? Some hosts offer self check-in and minimal contact; others enjoy interacting with you. Read the description and reviews to help shape your decision.

Confirming and Paying: Many places require payment in full before your trip, usually through the listing site. Be wary of owners who want to take your transaction offline; this gives you no recourse if things go awry. Never agree to wire money (a key indicator of a fraudulent transaction).

Apartments or Houses: If you're staying in one place for several nights, it's worth considering an apartment or rental house (shorter stays aren't worth the hassle of arranging key pickup, buying groceries, etc.). Apartment or house rentals can be especially cost-effective for groups and families. European apartments, like hotel rooms, tend to be small by US standards. But they often come

Keep Cool

If you're visiting Greece in the summer, you'll want an air-conditioned room. Most hotel air-conditioners come with a remote control that generally has similar symbols and features: fan icon (click to toggle through wind power, from light to gale); temperature (20 degrees Celsius is comfortable); louver icon (choose steady airflow or waves); snowflake and sunshine icons (cold air or heat, depending on season); and clock ("O" setting: run X hours before turning off; "I" setting: wait X hours to start). When you leave your room for the day, do as the environmentally conscious Europeans do and turn off the air-conditioning.

with laundry facilities and small, equipped kitchens, making it easier and cheaper to dine in.

Rooms in Private Homes: Renting a room in someone's home is a good option for those traveling alone, as you're more likely to find true single rooms—with just one single bed, and a price to match. These can range from air-mattress-in-living-room basic to plush-B&B-suite posh. While you can't expect your host to also be your tour guide—or even to provide you with much info—some are interested in getting to know the travelers who pass through their home.

Other Options: Swapping homes with a local works for people with an appealing place to offer (don't assume where you live is not interesting to Europeans). Good places to start are HomeExchange.com and LoveHomeSwap.com. To sleep for free, Couchsurfing.com is a vagabond's alternative to Airbnb. It lists millions of outgoing members, who host fellow "surfers" in their homes.

Hostels

A hostel provides cheap beds in dorms where you sleep alongside strangers for about $25 per night. Travelers of any age are welcome if they don't mind dorm-style accommodations and meeting other travelers. Most hostels offer kitchen facilities, guest computers, Wi-Fi, and a self-service laundry. Hostels almost always provide bedding, but the towel's up to you (though you can usually rent one). Family and private rooms are often available.

Independent hostels tend to be easygoing, colorful, and informal (no membership required; www.hostelworld.com). You may pay slightly less by booking directly with the hostel. **Official hostels** are part of Hostelling International (HI) and share an online booking site (www.hihostels.com). HI hostels typically require that you be a member or else pay a bit more per night.

Eating

Greek food is simple...and simply delicious. Unlike the French or the Italians, who are forever experimenting to perfect an intricate cuisine, the Greeks found an easy formula and stick with it—and it rarely misses. The four Greek food groups are olives (and olive oil), salty feta cheese, ripe tomatoes, and crispy phyllo dough. Virtually every dish you'll have here is built on a foundation of these four tasty building blocks.

For listings in this guidebook, I look for restaurants that are convenient to your hotel and sightseeing. When restaurant-hunting, choose a spot filled with locals, not the place with the big neon signs boasting, "We Speak English and Accept Credit Cards." Venturing even a block or two off the main drag leads to higher-quality food for a better price.

RESTAURANT PRICING

I've categorized my recommended eateries based on the average price of a typical main course, indicated with a dollar-sign rating (see sidebar). Obviously, expensive specialties, fine wine, appetizers, and dessert can significantly increase your final bill.

The categories also indicate the personality of a place: **Budget** eateries include street food, takeaway, order-at-the-counter shops, basic cafeterias, and bakeries selling sandwiches. **Moderate** eateries are nice (but not fancy) sit-down restaurants, ideal for a pleasant meal with good-quality food. Most of my listings fall in this category—great for a good taste of local cuisine at a reasonable price.

Pricier eateries are a notch up, with more attention paid to the setting, presentation, and (often inventive) cuisine. **Splurge** eateries are dress-up-for-a-special-occasion swanky—typically with an elegant setting, polished service, and pricey and refined cuisine.

DINING TIPS

Greeks like to eat late: Dine at 18:00, and you'll be surrounded by other tourists; stick around until 21:00, and they'll all have been replaced by locals. Especially in cities, popular restaurants tend to stay open until midnight or even later.

Restaurant hours can be informal. While the opening times I've listed are reasonably reliable, closing times often depend on how busy a place is—if you arrive late on a slow day, you may find the place shuttered.

Smoking is banned in enclosed spaces, such as restaurants

Restaurant Code

Eateries in this book are categorized according to the average cost of a typical main course. Drinks, desserts, and splurge items can raise the price considerably.

$$$$	**Splurge:** Most main courses over €15
$$$	**Pricier:** €10-15
$$	**Moderate:** €5-10
$	**Budget:** Under €5

In Greece, souvlaki and other takeaway food is **$**; a basic café or sit-down restaurant is **$$**; a casual but more upscale restaurant is **$$$**; and a swanky splurge is **$$$$**.

---

and bars. As a result, many smokers occupy outdoor tables—often that's where you'll want to sit, too. Despite the law, many bars and some restaurants allow smoking inside, too.

Types of Restaurants

In addition to the traditional Greek restaurant *(estiatorio)*, you'll also encounter these places:

Taverna: Common, rustic neighborhood restaurant with a smaller menu, slinging Greek favorites. These tend to be cheaper, to cater to locals' budgets.

Mezedopolio: Eatery specializing in small plates/appetizers/ *mezedes*

Ouzerie: Bar that makes ouzo, often selling high-quality *meze*—or even meals—to go along with it

If you're looking for fast food, in addition to the usual international chains (McDonald's and Starbucks), there are some Greek versions. Gregory's is the local version of Starbucks, and Goody's is the Greek take on McDonald's. Everest is open 24/7, selling sandwiches and savory pies to go.

Ordering and Paying

When you sit down at a restaurant, you'll likely be asked if you want a basket of (generally fresh, good) bread, often with your napkins and flatware tucked inside. You'll pay a bread and cover charge of about €0.50-1 (usually noted clearly on the menu).

Menus are usually written in both Greek and English. Many tavernas will have a display case showing what they've been cooking for the day, and it's perfectly acceptable to ask for a look and point to the dish you want. This is a good way to make some friends, sample a variety of dishes, get what you want (or at least know what you're getting), and have a truly memorable meal. Be brave. *Kali orexi! (Bon appétit!)*

A small dessert (that you didn't order) may appear at the end of your restaurant meal—often a tiny pastry, candied fruit, or shot of grappa. It's included in the price of your meal. You are welcome to linger as late as you want—don't feel pressured to eat quickly and turn over the table.

Tipping: Tipping is an issue only at restaurants that have table service. If you order your food at a counter, don't tip. At Greek restaurants that have waitstaff, service is generally included, although it's common to round up the bill after a good meal (about 10 percent; so, for an €18.50 meal, pay €20). It's considered bad form to leave a single euro, though; if a bill is €10, leave a €2 tip.

GREEK CUISINE

Although the Greeks don't like to admit it, their cuisine has a lot in common with Turkish food, including many of the same dishes. (This is partly because they share a similar climate, and partly because Greece was part of the Ottoman Empire for nearly 400 years.) Some names—such as moussaka—come directly from Turkish. You'll find traces of Italian influences as well, such as *pastitsio*, the "Greek lasagna."

My favorite fast, cheap, and filling Greek snack is souvlaki pita, a tasty shish kebab wrapped in flatbread. Souvlaki stands are all over Greece (see sidebar on page 196). On the islands, eat fresh seafood. Don't miss the creamy yogurt with honey. Feta-cheese salads and flaky nut-and-honey baklava are two other tasty treats. Dunk your bread into *tzatziki* (TZAHT-zee-kee), the ubiquitous and refreshing cucumber-and-yogurt dip. (Tourists often call it *tzitziki*, which sounds like the Greek word for crickets—a mispronunciation that endlessly amuses local waiters.)

In the early 20th century, chef Nikolaos Tselementes learned international cooking techniques and used them to revolutionize Greek cuisine—codifying many recipes you'll still find all over the country. It was Tselementes who introduced non-Greek elements like béchamel sauce to local cooking, in beloved recipes such as moussaka and *pastitsio*. To this day, Greeks call a cookbook—and anyone who's really adept at using it—a "Tselementes."

Here are more flavors to seek out during your time in Greece.

Olives

As you'll quickly gather when you pass endless tranquil olive groves on your drive through the countryside, olives are a major staple of Greek food—both the olives themselves and the oil they produce. Connoisseurs can distinguish as many varieties of olives as there are grapes for wine, but they fall into two general categories: those for eating and those for making oil.

Greeks are justifiably proud of their olive oil: Their country is the third-largest producer in the European Union, and they consume more olive oil per capita than any other Mediterranean nation—almost seven gallons per person a year. Locals say that the taste is shaped both by the variety and the terrain where the olives are grown. Olive oils from the Peloponnese, for example, are supposed to be robust with grassy or herbaceous overtones. Pay attention, and you'll notice the differences as you travel. Common, edible Greek olives include the following:

Amfissa: Found in both black and green varieties, grown near Delphi. These are rounder and mellower than other varieties.

Halkithiki: Large, green olives from northern Greece, often stuffed with pimento, sun-dried tomato, feta cheese, or other delicacies

Kalamata: Purple and almond-shaped, the best-known variety. These come from the southern Peloponnese and are cured in a red-wine vinegar brine.

Throubes: Black, wrinkled olives, usually from the island of Thassos, that stay on the tree until fully ripe. Dry-cured, they have an intense, salty taste and chewy texture.

Tsakistes: Green olives grown mainly in Attica (near Athens) that are cracked with a mallet or cut with a knife before being steeped in water and then brine. After curing, they are marinated in garlic and lemon wedges or herbs.

Cheese

Feta: Protected by EU regulations, it's made with sheep's milk, although up to 30 percent of goat's milk can be added (but never cow's milk). Feta comes in many variations—some are soft, moist, and rather mild; others are sour, hard, and crumbly (it depends on how much goat milk is used, and how—and how long—it's aged).

Graviera: A hard cheese usually made in Crete from sheep's milk, it tastes sweet and nutty, almost like a fine Swiss cheese.

Kasseri: The most popular Greek cheese after feta, it's a mild, yellow cheese made from either sheep's or goat's milk.

Halloumi: A semi-hard, squeaky, brined cheese made from a mix of sheep's and goat's milk, it's often fried to a gooey crisp in the flaming dish *saganaki* (see "Salads and Starters," below).

Pies

Flaky phyllo-dough pastries (*pita,* not to be confused with pita bread) are another staple of Greek cuisine. These can be ordered as a starter in a restaurant or purchased from a bakery for a tasty bite on the run. They can be made out of just about anything, but the most common are *spanakopita* (spinach), *tiropita* (cheese), *kreato-*

pita (beef or pork), *meletzanitopita* (eggplant), and *bougatsa* (with a sweet cream filling).

Salads and Starters *(Mezedes)*

Mezedes (meh-ZEH-dehs), known internationally as *meze,* are a great way to sample several tasty Greek dishes. This "small plates" approach is common and easy—instead of ordering a starter and a main dish per person, get two or three starters and one main dish to split.

Almost anything in Greece can be served as a small-plate "starter" (including several items listed in other sections here—olives, cheeses, and main dishes), but these are most common:

Bekri meze: Literally "drunkard's snack"—chunks of chicken, pork, or beef cooked slowly with wine, cloves, cinnamon, bay leaves, and olive oil

Dolmathes: Stuffed grape (or cabbage) leaves filled with either meat or rice and served hot or cold

Gigantes (also **Gigantes plaki**): "Giant" lima beans ovenbaked until tender in a mix of tomato, peppers, dill, other herbs, and sometimes sausage or pork

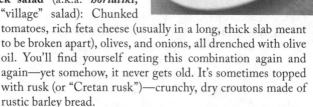

Greek salad (a.k.a. *horiatiki,* "village" salad): Chunked tomatoes, rich feta cheese (usually in a long, thick slab meant to be broken apart), olives, and onions, all drenched with olive oil. You'll find yourself eating this combination again and again—yet somehow, it never gets old. It's sometimes topped with rusk (or "Cretan rusk")—crunchy, dry croutons made of rustic barley bread.

Keftedes: Small meatballs, often seasoned with mint, onion, parsley, and sometimes ouzo

Melitzanosalata: Cooked eggplant with the consistency of mashed potatoes, usually well seasoned and delicious

Pantzarosalata: Beet salad dressed with olive oil and vinegar

Papoutsaki: Eggplant "slippers" filled with ground beef and cheese

Roasted red peppers: Soft and flavorful, often drizzled with olive oil

Saganaki: Cooked cheese, often breaded, sometimes grilled and sometimes fried, occasionally flambéed

Soutzoukakia: Meatballs with spicy tomato sauce

Taramosalata: Smoky, pink, fish-roe mixture with the consistency of mashed potatoes, used as a dip for bread or vegetables

Tirokafteri: Feta cheese that's been softened and mixed with white pepper to give it some kick, served either as a spread or stuffed inside roasted red peppers

Tzatziki: A pungent and thick sauce of yogurt, cucumber, and garlic. It seems like a condiment but is often ordered as a starter, then eaten as a salad or used to complement other foods.

Soups

Summertime visitors might be disappointed not to find much soup on the menu (including ***avgolemono,*** the delicious egg, lemon, and rice soup). Soup is considered a winter dish and is almost impossible to find in warm weather. If available, Greek chicken soup *(kotosoupa)* is very tasty, and *fasolada* (bean soup) is affectionately attributed as the country's national dish (though not as popular as *horiatiki,* a.k.a., Greek salad). ***Kremithosoupa*** is the Greek version of French onion soup, and ***kakavia*** or ***psarosoupa*** is a famous fish soup often compared to bouillabaisse.

Main Dishes

Here are some popular meat and seafood dishes you'll likely see.

Meats

Arnaki kleftiko: Slow-cooked lamb, usually wrapped in phyllo dough or parchment paper. Legend says it was created by bandits who needed to cook without the telltale signs of smoke or fire. (Baked fish, and other meats, may also be served *kleftiko.*)

Gyro: Literally "turn," a gyro is not a type of meat but a way of preparing it—stacked on a metal skewer and vertically slow-roasted on a rotisserie, then shaved off in slices. In Greece it's usually made from chicken or pork, and often served wrapped in a pita, making a handy to-go sandwich.

Moussaka: A classic casserole with layers of minced meat, eggplant, and potatoes and a topping of cheesy béchamel sauce or egg custard

Pastitsio: A layered baked dish called the "Greek lasagna." Ground meat is sandwiched between two layers of pasta with an egg-custard or béchamel topping.

Souvlaki: Pork or lamb cooked on a skewer, often wrapped in pita bread (and sometimes topped with fries); also can be served on a platter with rice

Stifado: Beef stew with onions, tomatoes, and spices such as cinnamon and cloves. It was traditionally made with rabbit *(kouneli).*

Fish and Seafood

Barbounia: Red mullet that is usually grilled or fried and is always expensive. These small fish are bony, but the flesh melts in your mouth.

Gavros: An appetizer similar to anchovies. Squeeze lemon all over them, and eat everything but the wispy little tails.

Htapothi: Octopus, often marinated and grilled, then drizzled with olive oil and lemon juice

Psari plaki: Fish baked in the oven with tomatoes and onions

Sweets

Baklava: Phyllo dough layered with nuts and honey

Bougatsa: Thin pastry filled with cream

Ekmek: A cake made of thin phyllo fibers soaked in honey, then topped with custard and a layer of whipped cream

Halva: A tahini- or sesame-based sweet confection, often with honey, chocolate, or pistachio

Karydopita: Honey-walnut cake made without flour

Kataifi: Thin fibers of phyllo (like shredded wheat) layered with nuts and honey

Loukoumades: Greek doughnut, soaked in honey or sugar syrup

Loukoumi: Similar to Turkish delight, a chewy, sweet, jelly-like candy with flavors like rose or lemon, coated in powdered sugar

Meli pita: Honey-cheese pie, traditionally served at Easter

DRINKS

Wine: There are two basic types of Greek wines—*retsina* (resin-flavored, rarely served) and nonresinated wines.

Retsina **wine,** a post-WWII rotgut with a notorious resin flavor, has long been famous as the working man's Greek wine. It makes you want to sling a patch over one eye and say, "Arghh." The first glass is like drinking wood. The third glass is dangerous: It starts to taste good. If you drink any more, you'll smell like it the entire next day. Why resin? Way back when, Greek winemakers used pine resin to seal the amphoras that held the wine, protecting the wine from the air. Discovering that they liked the taste, the winemakers began adding resin to the wine itself.

If pine sap is not your cup of tea, there are plenty of **nonresinated wine options.** With its new generation of winemakers (many of them trained abroad), Greece is receiving more recognition for its wines. More than 300 native varietals are now grown in Greece's wine regions. About two-thirds of the wine produced in Greece is white. The best known are Savatiano (the most widely grown grape used for *retsina* and other wines), Assyrtiko (a crisp white mostly from Santorini), and Moschofilero (a dry white from the Peloponnese). Red wines include Agiorgitiko (a medium red also from the

Peloponnese; one carries the name "Blood of Hercules") and Xy-nomavro (an intense red from Naoussa in Macedonia). Greeks also grow cabernet sauvignon, merlot, chardonnay, and other familiar varieties. And Santorini bottles the sweet, luxurious, expensive dessert wine called Vinsanto.

Here are a few wine terms that you may find useful: *inos* (οίνος—term for "wine" printed on bottles), *krasi* (spoken term for "wine"), *ktima* (winery or estate), *inopolio* (wine bar), *lefko* (white), *erithro* or *kokkino* (red), *xiro* (dry), *agouro* (young), *me poli soma* (full-bodied), *epitrapezio* (table wine), and O.P.A.P. (an indication of quality that tells you the wine came from one of Greece's designated wine regions).

Beer: Greeks are proud of their few local brands, including Alpha, Fix, Vergina, and Mythos.

Spirits: Beyond wine and beer, consider special Greek spirits. Cloudy, anise-flavored **ouzo,** supposedly invented by monks on Mount Athos, is worth a try even if you don't like the taste (black licorice). Similar to its Mediterranean cousins, French *pastis* and Turkish *raki*, ouzo turns from clear to milky white when you add ice or water (don't drink it straight). Greeks drink it  both as an aperitif and with food. I like to sip it slowly in the early evening while sharing a plate of several *meze* with my travel partner. Some of the best-selling brands are Ouzo 12, Plomari Ouzo, and Sans Rival Ouzo.

Even better is *tsipouro.* Similar to Italian grappa, this brandy is distilled from leftover grape skins and stems; it is sometimes flavored with anise. Stronger and purer than ouzo, it's best drunk with water on the rocks. Some of the best are Barbayanni, Tsilili, and Adolo.

Metaxa is to be savored after dinner. This rich, sweet, golden-colored liqueur has a brandy base blended with aged wine and a "secret" herbal mixture.

If you're traveling on the Peloponnese, try **Tentura,** a regional liqueur flavored with cloves, nutmeg, cinnamon, and citrus. It packs a spicy kick.

Coffee: All over Greece, Starbucks-style coffeehouses have invaded Main Street. But, while most modern Greeks drink espresso, you can still seek out traditional **Greek coffee** (similar to Turkish coffee). This unfiltered brew is prepared in a small copper pot called a *briki* or an *ibrik*, and usually served with a glass of water and a chunk of candy called *loukoumi*. While most of the world calls this candy "Turkish delight," locals boast that it was actually invented by Greek pastry chefs, then spread throughout the Ottoman Empire—so their name, "Greek delight," is more fitting.

In summer, cafés are filled with Greeks sipping **iced coffee** drinks. There are two types: *frappé* and *freddo*. Both are essentially cold coffee, whipped in a blender, and served over ice. Locals are staunchly devoted to one or the other, so what's the difference? *Frappé* is made with instant coffee that's mixed with evaporated milk and water, while *freddo* is made with coffee (from an espresso machine) and can be ordered as a *freddo espresso* (iced espresso, no milk) or *freddo cappuccino* (with cold foamed milk).

When ordering coffee, the barista will usually ask how much sugar you want in it. (They may say, "How much sugar? Normal?") You can order your coffee *pikro/sketos* (bitter/plain), *metrio* (semi-sweet—the default choice), or *gliko* (sweet).

Don't ask for a "regular coffee," as almost nobody will understand what you mean.

Water: Water is served in bottles. It's very cheap (even in otherwise expensive areas) and rarely carbonated.

Staying Connected

One of the most common questions I hear from travelers is, "How can I stay connected in Europe?" The short answer? More easily and affordably than you might think.

The simplest solution is to bring your own device—phone, tablet, or laptop—and use it much as you would at home, following the money-saving tips below, such as getting an international plan or connecting to free Wi-Fi whenever possible. Another option is to buy a European SIM card for your mobile phone. Or you can use European landlines and computers to connect.

USING YOUR PHONE IN EUROPE

Here are some budget tips and options.

Sign up for an international plan. To stay connected at a lower cost, sign up for an international service plan through your carrier. Most providers offer a simple bundle that includes calling, messaging, and data. Your normal plan may already include international coverage (for example, T-Mobile's covers data and text, but not voice calls).

Before your trip, research your provider's international rates. Activate the plan a day or two before you leave, then remember to cancel it when your trip's over.

Use free Wi-Fi whenever possible. Unless you have an unlimited-data plan, save most of your online tasks for Wi-Fi. Most

How to Dial

Here's how to dial from anywhere in the US or Europe, using the phone number of one of my recommended Athens hotels as an example (210 323 4357). If a number starts with 0, drop it when dialing internationally (except when calling Italy).

From a US Mobile Phone
Phone numbers in this book are presented exactly as you would dial them from a US mobile phone. For international access, press and hold 0 (zero) to get a + sign, then dial the country code (30 for Greece) and phone number.
▶ To call the Athens hotel from any location, dial +30 210 323 4357.

From a US Landline
Replace + with 011 (US/Canada access code), then dial the country code (30 for Greece) and phone number.
▶ To call the Athens hotel from your home landline, dial 011 30 210 323 4357.

From a European Landline
Replace + with 00 (Europe access code), then dial the country code (30 for Greece, 1 for the US) and phone number.
▶ To call the Athens hotel from a French landline, dial 00 30 210 323 4357.
▶ To call my US office from a Greek landline, dial 00 1 425 771 8303.

From One Greek Phone to Another
To place a domestic call (from a Greek landline or mobile), drop +30 and dial the phone number (including the initial 0).
▶ To call the Athens hotel from Olympia, dial 210 323 4357.

More Dialing Tips
Local Numbers: European phone numbers and area codes can vary in length and spacing, even within the same country. Mobile phones use separate prefixes (for instance, in Greece, mobile numbers begin with 69).

Toll and Toll-Free Calls: It's generally not possible to dial European toll or toll-free numbers from a US mobile or landline (although you can sometimes get through using Skype). Look for a direct-dial number instead.

Calling the US from a US Mobile Phone, While Abroad: Dial +1, area code, and number.

More Phoning Help: See HowToCallAbroad.com.

accommodations in Europe offer free Wi-Fi. Many cafés (including Starbucks and McDonald's) offer hotspots for customers; ask for the password when you buy something. You may also find Wi-Fi at TIs, city squares, major museums, public-transit hubs, and airports.

Minimize the use of your cellular network. The best way to make sure you're not accidentally burning through data is to put your device in "airplane" mode (which also disables phone calls and texts) and connect to Wi-Fi as needed. When you need to get on-

Tips on Internet Security

Make sure that your device is running the latest versions of its operating system, security software, and apps. Next, ensure that your device and key programs (like email) are password-protected. On the road, use only secure, password-protected Wi-Fi. Ask the hotel or café staff for the specific name of their network, and make sure you log on to that exact one.

If you must access your financial info online, use a banking app rather than accessing your account via a browser, and use a cellular connection, not Wi-Fi. Never log on to personal finance sites on a public computer. If you're very concerned, consider subscribing to a VPN (virtual private network).

line but can't find Wi-Fi, simply turn on your cellular network (or turn off airplane mode) just long enough for the task at hand.

Even with an international-data plan, wait until you're on Wi-Fi to Skype or FaceTime, download apps, stream videos, or do other megabyte-greedy tasks. Using a navigation app such as Google Maps over a cellular network can require lots of data, so download maps when you're on Wi-Fi, then use the app offline.

Limit automatic updates. By default, your device constantly checks for a data connection and updates app content. Check your device's settings menu for ways to turn this off, and change your email settings from "auto-retrieve" to "manual" (or from "push" to "fetch").

Use Wi-Fi calling and messaging apps. Skype, WhatsApp, FaceTime, and Google Meet are great for making free or low-cost calls or sending texts over Wi-Fi worldwide. Just log on to a Wi-Fi network, then connect with friends, family members, or local contacts who use the same service.

Buy a European SIM card. If you anticipate making a lot of local calls, need a local phone number, or your provider's international data rates are expensive, consider buying a SIM card in Europe to replace the one in your (unlocked) US phone or tablet. SIM cards are sold at department-store electronics counters and some newsstands (you may need to show your passport), and vending machines. If you need help setting it up, buy one at a mobile-phone shop.

There are generally no roaming charges when using a European SIM card in other EU countries, but confirm when you buy.

WITHOUT A MOBILE PHONE

It's less convenient but possible to travel in Europe without a mobile device. You can make calls from your hotel and check email or get online using public computers.

Most **hotels** charge a fee for placing calls. You can use a pre-paid international phone card (usually available at newsstands, and tobacco shops) to call out from your hotel.

Some hotels have **public computers** in their lobbies for guests to use; otherwise you may find them at public libraries (ask your hotelier or the TI for the nearest location). On a European keyboard, use the "Alt Gr" key to the right of the space bar to insert the extra symbol that appears on some keys. If you can't locate a special character (such as @), simply copy and paste it from a web page.

MAIL

You can mail one package per day to yourself worth up to $200 duty-free from Europe to the US (mark it "personal purchases"). If you're sending a gift to someone, mark it "unsolicited gift." For details, visit www.cbp.gov, select "Travel," and search for "Know Before You Go." The Greek postal service works fine, but for quick transatlantic delivery (in either direction), consider services such as DHL (DHL.com). Get stamps for postcards and letters at the neighborhood post office, newsstands within fancy hotels, and some minimarts and card shops.

Transportation

To connect the destinations in this book, you'll either drive, take a bus or boat, or fly (train service is minimal in Greece).

For touring around the mainland, your best options are car or bus. A **rental car** allows you to come and go on your own schedule, and make a beeline between destinations. Outside of congested Athens, roads are uncrowded, and parking is often free. However, driving in Greece can be stressful, as Greek drivers tackle the roads with a kind of anything-goes, Wild West abandon. And it's more expensive than the bus. But if you're a confident driver, the convenience of driving in Greece trumps the hassles of bus transport.

Greece's network of public **buses** is affordable and will get you most anywhere you want to go. Unfortunately, it's not user-friendly. Particularly outside of Athens, the frequency can be sparse and schedules are hard to nail down. You'll need to allow plenty of time, expect delays, and pack lots of patience to visit all of my recommended destinations.

BUSES

Greek buses are cheap, and the fleet is clean, modern, and air-conditioned, but the bus system can be frustrating. Athens has decent bus service to popular destinations such as Delphi, Nafplio, and the port town of Piraeus, but smaller destinations on the Peloponnese are connected by only one or two buses a day.

PRACTICALITIES

Transportation Costs in Greece

All buses are run by a central company (KTEL, or ΚΤΕΛ in Greek), but the local offices set their own schedules, and they often don't coordinate well. Specific bus schedules can be difficult to pin down, even for buses leaving from the town you're in. (Forget about getting bus schedules for other Greek towns.) Local TIs, where they exist, are unlikely to have the information you need. Don't hesitate to ask your hotelier for help—they're used to it.

KTEL has no helpful website or information office for the entire Greek bus system, but Greeka.com has a list of regional bus websites, which often provide more information (www.greeka.com/greece-travel/buses). The KTEL Athens site (www.ktelattikis.gr) is hard to navigate, but Matt Barrett's website has schedules for long-distance buses from and to Athens (www.athensguide.com).

Particularly on the Peloponnese, where your journeys likely will require a transfer (or multiple transfers), you frequently won't be able to get the information for the full route from the bus station at your starting point. For example, to go from Nafplio to Monemvasia, you'll change at Tripoli, then Sparta. The Nafplio bus station can give you details for the leg to Tripoli, but can't tell you anything about the rest of the journey.

Before you get on a bus, ask the ticket seller and the conductor explicitly if there are transfers—they may not volunteer these details otherwise. Then pay attention (and maybe even follow the route on a map) to be sure you don't miss your change.

BOATS

Greece has been a great seafaring nation since the days of Odysseus. Today the country's islands are connected to Athens' port (Piraeus, see the Athens Connections chapter for details) and to one another by a variety of ferries, ranging from hulking, slow-moving car ferries to sleek, speedy catamarans. While the decentralized ferry system isn't as straightforward or efficient as many travelers would like it to be, it's still fairly fast and easy to get around by boat in Greece.

Buying Tickets: In peak season (especially July-Aug), some popular connections—such as Piraeus-Hydra—can sell out early; book at least a week in advance. Advance tickets also make sense if you'll be setting sail soon after your arrival in Greece. Outside of peak season, it's generally fine to purchase your ticket a day or two before your crossing. Buying from a travel agency can be the easiest way to understand your options, and costs no more than buying online, but beware that some agencies may try to upsell you. Ferries are comfortable; there's no need to spring for business-class seats.

Greek ferry services are operated by multiple companies without a central information service. Good websites for researching connections include www.danae.gr/ferries-Greece.asp, www.greekferries.gr, and www.gtp.gr. Some ferry companies post only their current schedule—if you're looking online in January, you may not find sailing times for June. If you buy tickets online, you'll need to convert your reservation into an actual ticket. Some ferry companies let you do this through online check-in (they'll send you an eticket). Otherwise, you'll need to go to a ticket office or travel agency before the boat trip to pick up a paper ticket (you'll need your passport, and you may have to pay a small fee).

Before you buy, make sure you're clear on the ferry company's refund and exchange policies. Since schedules can flex with demand, confirm your sailing time a day ahead.

Possible Delays or Cancellations: Smaller high-speed ferries (such as the Hellenic Seaways' "Flying Cat" and SeaJets' Super-Jet or SeaJet2) can be affected by high winds and other inclement weather. Larger ferries, such as the Hellenic Seaways Highspeed,

PRACTICALITIES

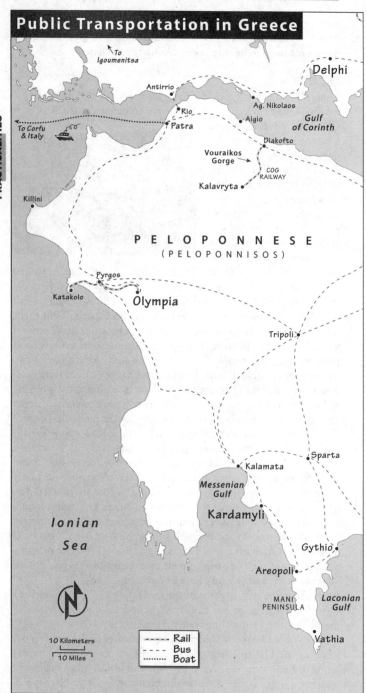

Public Transportation in Greece

To Igoumenitsa

Antirrio

Delphi

Rio

Ag. Nikolaos

Gulf of Corinth

Patra

Aigio

To Corfu & Italy

Diakofto

Vouraikos Gorge

COG RAILWAY

Kalavryta

Killini

P E L O P O N N E S E
(PELOPONNISOS)

Pyrgos

Katakolo

Olympia

Tripoli

Ionian Sea

Sparta

Kalamata

Messenian Gulf

Kardamyli

Gythio

Areopoli

MANI PENINSULA

Laconian Gulf

Vathia

10 Kilometers
10 Miles

----- Rail
- - - Bus
.... Boat

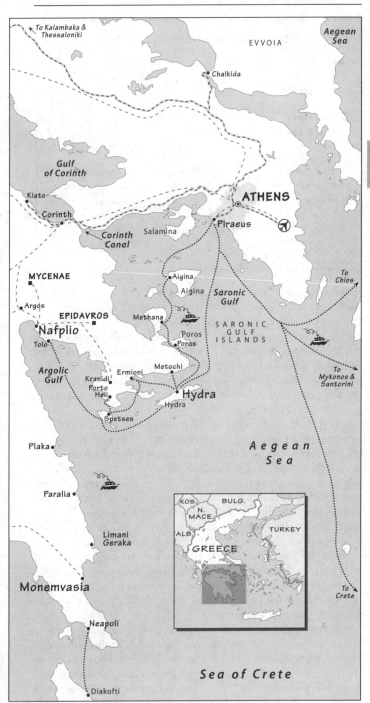

PRACTICALITIES

Ferry Companies in Greece

Hellenic Seaways	+30 210 891 9800	https://hellenicseaways.gr
Blue Star Ferries	+30 210 891 9800	www.bluestarferries.com
ANEK Lines	+30 210 419 7400	www.anek.gr
Aegean Speed	+30 210 969 0950	www.aegeanspeedlines.gr
Alpha Lines	+30 210 429 5020	www.alphalines.gr
NEL Lines	+30 281 034 6185	www.ferries.gr/nel
SeaJets	+30 210 710 7710	www.seajets.gr
Minoan Lines	+30 281 039 9899	www.minoan.gr
Kallisti Ferries	+30 281 034 6185	www.ferries.gr/kallisti-ferries

SeaJet Champion Jet, and the Blue Star ferries are slower, more stable, and less likely to be canceled. In general, cancellations are rare but possible in summer, and more common off-season. If a sailing is canceled, the ferry company will contact you to rebook (for this reason, it's essential to provide a telephone number when you book). Usually you can go later that same day, but once in a while passengers get stranded overnight. Even if the sea is rough, the ships may still run—but the ride can be very rocky. If you're prone to seasickness, be prepared.

Boarding the Ferry: If a place has several ports, make sure you know which port your boat leaves from. While ferry companies tell passengers to be at the dock 30 minutes before the boat leaves, most locals amble over to the dock about 10 minutes ahead. The sole advantage to turning up early is the chance to grab a better seat, which only makes a difference if your ferry has open seating, such as the Blue Star ferries (although even if there are assigned seats, they're often ignored). Don't be surprised if boats aren't on time—soak up some sun at the dock while you wait.

On the Ferry: Greece's ferries are very relaxing and can be a lot cheaper than flying, though they take longer. On big, slow-moving car ferries, you can sit outside and watch the islands slide by—but on the fast boats you'll be sitting inside, peering through saltwater-spattered windows.

Bigger ferries move slowly but can run in almost any weather. While the number of cars allowed onboard is limited, they can accommodate about 1,000-2,000 walk-on passengers, and tend to cost less. The smallest, fastest ferries are typically catamarans carrying only about 300-400 passengers, so they are more likely to sell out. While small boats are time-efficient, they have to slow down (or sometimes can't run at all) in bad weather. On some islands, bigger ferries arrive at a different point (usually farther from the main town) than the smaller boats (which may drop you right in the town center).

You may be able to stow your luggage on a rack on the boarding level of your boat; otherwise you'll haul it up several flights of stairs to the passenger decks. Ferries of all sizes typically are equipped with WCs and charging outlets; many offer Wi-Fi (usually for a fee and with spotty service). You can buy food and drinks on most boats. It's not too expensive, but it's usually not top quality, either. Bring your own snacks or a picnic instead.

TAXIS AND RIDE-BOOKING SERVICES

Most European taxis are reliable and cheap. In many cities, two people can travel short distances by cab for little more than the cost of bus or subway tickets. If you like ride-booking services such as Uber, their apps usually work in Europe just like they do in the US: Request a car on your mobile phone (connected to Wi-Fi or a data plan), and the fare is automatically charged to your credit card. For more about taxis and Uber (which operates as UberTaxi in Athens), see page 38.

RENTING A CAR

It's cheaper to arrange most car rentals from the US, so research and compare rates before you go. Most of the major US rental agencies (including Avis, Budget, Enterprise, Hertz, and Thrifty) have offices throughout Europe. Also consider the two major Europe-based agencies, Europcar and Sixt. For a friendly local car-rental company in Athens, consider Swift/Escape (see page 227; www.greektravel.com/swift). Consolidators such as Auto Europe (AutoEurope.com—or the sometimes cheaper AutoEurope.eu) compare rates at several companies to get you the best deal.

Wherever you book, always read the fine print. Check for add-on charges—such as one-way drop-off fees, airport surcharges, or mandatory insurance policies—that aren't included in the "total price."

Rental Costs and Considerations

If you book well in advance, expect to pay $350-500 for a one-week rental for a basic compact car. Allow extra for supplemental insurance, fuel, tolls, and parking. To save money on fuel, request a diesel car.

Manual vs. Automatic: Almost all rental cars in Europe are manual by default—and cars with a stick shift are generally cheaper. If you need an automatic, reserve one specifically. When selecting a car, don't be tempted by a larger model, as it won't be as maneuverable on narrow, winding roads or when squeezing into tight parking lots.

Age Restrictions: Some rental companies impose minimum and maximum age limits. Young drivers (25 and under) and seniors (69 and up) should check the rental policies and rules section of car rental websites. If you're considered too young or too old, look into leasing (covered later), which has less stringent age restrictions.

Choosing Pick-up/Drop-off Locations: Always check the hours of the locations you choose: Many rental offices close from midday Saturday until Monday morning and, in smaller towns, at lunchtime. When selecting an office, confirm the location on a map. A downtown site might seem more convenient than the airport but could actually be in the suburbs or buried deep in big-city streets. Pedestrianized and one-way streets can make navigation tricky when returning a car at a big-city office. Wherever you select, get precise details on the location and allow ample time to find it.

Have the Right License: If you're renting a car in Greece, bring your driver's license. You're also technically required to have an International Driving Permit—an official translation of your license (sold at AAA offices for about $20 plus the cost of two passport-type photos; see AAA.com). How this is enforced varies: I've never needed one.

Crossing Borders in a Rental Car: Be aware that international trips—say, picking up in Athens and dropping in Istanbul—can be expensive if the rental company assesses a drop-off fee for crossing a border.

Always tell your car-rental company exactly which countries you'll be entering. Some companies levy extra insurance fees for trips taken in certain countries with certain cars (such as BMWs, Mercedes, and convertibles). Double-check with your rental agent that you have all the documentation you need before you drive off (especially if you're crossing borders into non-Schengen countries, such as Turkey, where you might need to present proof of insurance).

Picking Up Your Car: Before driving off in your rental car, check it thoroughly and make sure any damage is noted on your rental agreement. Rental agencies in Europe tend to charge for even minor damage, so be sure to mark everything. In Greece, your rental car is likely to come prescratched and dented for you (which is actually a plus, in that you're unlikely to get hassled for tiny dings in the vicinity of preexisting ones). Find out how your car's gearshift, lights, turn signals, wipers, radio, and fuel cap function, and know what kind of fuel the car takes (diesel is common in Europe).

When you return the car, make sure the agent verifies its condition with you.

Car Insurance Options

When you rent a car in Europe, the price typically includes liability insurance, which covers harm to other cars or motorists—but not the rental car itself. To limit your financial risk in case of damage to the rental, choose one of these options: Buy a Collision Damage Waiver (CDW; also called "loss damage waiver" or LDW by some firms) with a low or zero deductible from the car-rental company (roughly 30-40 percent extra), get coverage through your credit card (free, but more complicated), or get collision insurance as part of a larger travel-insurance policy.

Basic **CDW** costs $15-30 a day and typically comes with a $1,000-2,000 deductible, reducing but not eliminating your financial responsibility. When you reserve or pick up the car, you'll be offered the chance to "buy down" the deductible to zero (for an additional $10-30/day; this is sometimes called "super CDW" or "zero-deductible coverage").

If you opt for **credit-card coverage,** you must decline all coverage offered by the car-rental company—which means they can place a hold on your card to cover the deductible. In case of damage, it can be time-consuming to resolve the charges. Before relying on this option, quiz your card company about how it works.

If you're already purchasing a **travel-insurance policy** for your trip, adding collision coverage can be an economical option. For example, Travel Guard (TravelGuard.com) sells affordable renter's collision insurance as an add-on to its other policies; it's valid everywhere in Europe except the Republic of Ireland, and some Italian car-rental companies refuse to honor it, as it doesn't cover you in case of theft.

For more on car-rental insurance, see RickSteves.com/cdw.

Leasing

For trips of three weeks or more, consider leasing (which automatically includes zero-deductible collision and theft insurance). By technically buying and then selling back the car, you save money on taxes and insurance. Leasing provides you a brand-new car with unlimited mileage and a 24-hour emergency assistance program. You can lease for as little as 21 days to as long as five and a half months. Car leases must be arranged from the US.

Navigation Options

If you'll be navigating using your phone or a GPS unit from home, remember to bring a car charger and device mount.

Your Mobile Phone: The mapping app on your phone works

fine for navigating Europe's roads. To save on data, most apps allow you to download maps for offline use (do this before you need them, when you have a strong Wi-Fi signal). Some apps—including Google Maps—also have offline route directions, but you'll need mobile data access for current traffic. For more on using a mapping app without burning through data, see "Using Your Phone in Europe," earlier.

GPS Devices: If you want a dedicated GPS unit, consider renting one with your car (about $20/day, or sometimes included—ask). These units offer real-time turn-by-turn directions and traffic without the data requirements of an app. The unit may come loaded only with maps for its home country; if you need additional maps, ask. Make sure you know how to use the device—and that the language is set to English—before you drive off.

Paper Maps and Atlases: Even when navigating primarily with a mobile app or GPS, I always have a paper map, ideally a big, detailed regional road map. It's invaluable for getting the big picture, understanding alternate routes, and filling in if your phone runs out of juice. The free maps you get from your car-rental company usually don't have enough detail. It's smart to buy a better map before you go, or pick one up at a local gas station, bookshop, newsstand, or tourist shop.

DRIVING IN GREECE

Statistically, Greece is one of the most dangerous European countries to drive in. Traffic regulations that are severely enforced back home are treated as mere suggestions here. Even at major intersections in large towns, you may not see stop signs or traffic lights; drivers simply help each other figure out who goes next. And yet, like so many seemingly chaotic things in Greece, somehow it works quite smoothly. Still... drive defensively. Greeks won't hesitate to pass you, if they feel you're going too slowly.

Road Rules: The speed limit, almost never posted, can be hard to ascertain on

STOP AND LEARN THESE ROAD SIGNS

Speed Limit (km/hr) · Yield · No Passing · End of No Passing Zone

One Way · Intersection · Main Road · Expressway

Danger · No Entry · Cars Prohibited · All Vehicles Prohibited

No Through Road · Restrictions No Longer Apply · Yield to Oncoming Traffic · No Stopping

Parking · No Parking · Customs or Toll Road · Peace

backcountry roads. Generally, speed limits in Greece are as follows: city—50 km/hour; open roads—90 km/hour; divided highways—110 km/hour, superhighways—130 km/hour. Making matters even more confusing, half of all Greek drivers seem to go double the speed limit, while the others go half the limit. On country roads and highways, the lanes are often a car-and-a-half wide, with wide shoulders, so passing is common—even when there's oncoming traffic in the other lane. Do as Greek drivers do on two-lane roads with wide shoulders—straddle the shoulder if someone wants to pass you.

Don't drink and drive: The legal alcohol limit is lower in Greece than in the US. It is also illegal to smoke while driving in Greece. Be aware of typical European road rules; for example, many countries require headlights to be turned on at all times, and nearly all forbid handheld mobile-phone use. In Europe, you're not allowed to turn right on a red light, unless a sign or signal specifically authorizes it, and on expressways it's illegal to pass drivers on the right. Ask your car-rental company about these rules, or check the "International Travel" section of the US State Department website (www.travel.state.gov, search for your country in the "Learn About Your Destination" box, then click "Travel and Transportation").

Road Signs: Because road numbers can be confusing and inconsistent, navigate by city names. Know the names of major cities en route to your destination. Often the signs will point only to the next major town, even if your final destination is a big city. Almost all road signs are in Greek and in English, but you should also know the name of your destination using the Greek alphabet—road sign transliteration can be confusing. Most Greek town names can be spelled a number of different ways in the Latin alphabet—don't be too worried about exact spelling, especially at the ends of town names.

Tolls: Special highways called Ethniki Odos (National Road) have tolls, which vary and must be paid in cash. This includes the road between Athens and the Peloponnese and part of the stretch between Athens and Delphi.

Fuel: Gasoline (*venzini,* βενζίνη) prices are around $6.50 a gallon for regular unleaded—labeled *95,* less for diesel, which is around $5 per gallon (*ntizel,* ντίζελ). Some pumps are color-coded: Unleaded pumps are green and labeled "E," while diesel pumps (often yellow or black) are labeled "B." Self-service gas stations are rare. Tell the attendant how much you want to spend and use cash.

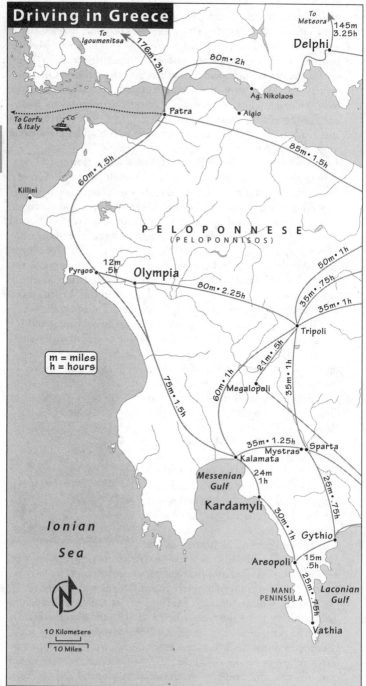

Driving in Greece

To Meteora

145m
3.25h

Delphi

To Igoumenitsa

176m • 3h

80m • 2h

Ag. Nikolaos

Patra

Aigio

To Corfu & Italy

85m • 1.5h

60m • 1.5h

Killini

PELOPONNESE
(PELOPONNISOS)

50m • 1h

35m • .75h

Pyrgos

12m
.5h

Olympia

80m • 2.25h

35m • 1h

m = miles
h = hours

Tripoli

21m • .5h

35m • 1h

75m • 1.5h

60m • 1h

Megalopoli

35m • 1.25h

Mystras

Sparta

Kalamata

24m
1h

25m • .75h

Messenian
Gulf

Kardamyli

30m • 1h

Gythio

Ionian

Sea

Areopoli

15m
.5h

MANI
PENINSULA

25m • .75h

Laconian
Gulf

N

10 Kilometers

10 Miles

Vathia

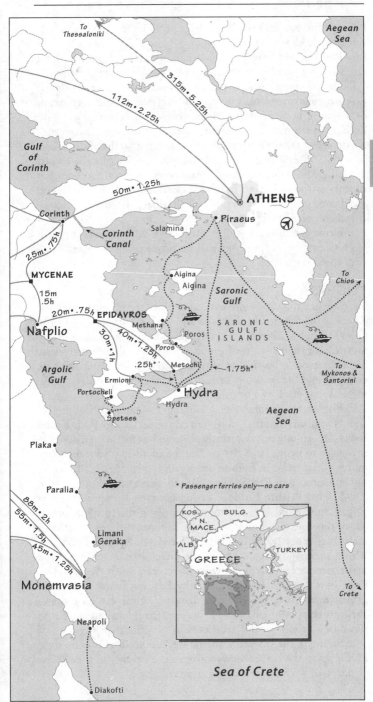

To Thessaloniki

Aegean Sea

315m • 5.25h

112m • 2.25h

Gulf of Corinth

50m • 1.25h

ATHENS

Corinth

Piraeus

Salamina

Corinth Canal

25m • .75h

MYCENAE

15m .5h

Aigina
Aigina

Saronic Gulf

To Chios

20m • .75h **EPIDAVROS**

Nafplio

30m • 1h

40m • 1.25h

Methana

S A R O N I C
G U L F
I S L A N D S

Poros
Poros

Argolic Gulf

.25h*

Metochi

1.75h*

To Mykonos & Santorini

Ermioni

Hydra

Portocheli

Hydra

Aegean Sea

Spetses

Plaka

* Passenger ferries only—no cars

Paralia

88m • 2h

55m • 1.5h

45m • 1.25h

Limani Geraka

KOS.

BULG.

N. MACE.

ALB

GREECE

TURKEY

To Crete

Monemvasia

Neapoli

Diakofti

Sea of Crete

He's just there to pump gas, so don't expect him to wash your wind-shield or check your tires.

Parking and Safety: Choose parking places carefully. You'll rarely pay for parking, and parking laws are enforced only sporadi-cally. If you're not certain, ask at your hotel (or ask another local) whether your space is legit. Keep your valuables in your hotel room, or, if you're between destinations, covered in your trunk. Leave nothing worth stealing in the car, especially overnight. If your car's a hatchback, take the trunk cover off at night so thieves can look in without breaking in. Try to make your car look locally owned by hiding the "tourist-owned" rental-company decals and putting a local newspaper in your front or back window. While you should avoid parking lots with twinkly asphalt, thieves break car windows anywhere, even at stoplights.

Drive carefully. If you're involved in an accident, expect a monumental headache—you will be blamed. Small towns come with speed traps.

FLIGHTS

To compare flights, begin with an online travel search engine: Kayak is the top site for flights to and within Europe, easy-to-use Google Flights has price alerts, and Skyscanner includes many inexpensive flights within Europe. To avoid unpleasant surprises, before you book be sure to read the small print about refunds, changes, and the costs for "extras" such as reserving a seat, check-ing a bag, or printing a boarding pass.

Flights to Europe: Start looking for international flights about four to six months before your trip, especially for peak-season travel. Depending on your itinerary, it can be efficient and no more expensive to fly into one city and out of another. If your flight re-quires a connection in Europe, see my hints on navigating Europe's top hub airports at RickSteves.com/hub-airports.

Flights Within Europe: Flying between European cities is surprisingly affordable. Before buying a long-distance bus ticket, check the cost of a flight on one of Europe's airlines, whether a major carrier or a no-frills outfit like EasyJet or Ryanair. For flights within mainland Greece and to the Greek islands, the country's main carriers are **Olympic** (www.olympicair.com), **Aegean Air-lines** (www.aegeanair.com), and **Sky Express** (www.skyexpress.gr). Be aware that flying with a discount airline can have draw-backs, such as minimal customer service, time-consuming treks to secondary airports, and a larger carbon footprint than a bus.

Flying to the US and Canada: Because security is extra tight for flights to the US, be sure to give yourself plenty of time at the airport (see www.tsa.gov for the latest rules).

Resources from Rick Steves

Begin Your Trip at RickSteves.com

My mobile-friendly **website** is *the* place to explore Europe in preparation for your trip. You'll find thousands of fun articles, videos, and radio interviews; a wealth of money-saving tips for planning your dream trip; travel news dispatches; a video library of travel talks; my travel blog; our latest guidebook updates (RickSteves.com/update); and the free Rick Steves Audio Europe app. You can also follow me on Facebook, Instagram, and Twitter.

Our **Travel Forum** is a well-groomed collection of message boards, where our travel-savvy community answers questions and shares their personal travel experiences—and our well-traveled staff chimes in when they can be helpful (RickSteves.com/forums).

Our **online Travel Store** offers bags and accessories that I've designed to help you travel smarter and lighter. These include my popular carry-on bags (which I live out of four months a year), money belts, totes, toiletries kits, adapters, guidebooks, and planning maps (RickSteves.com/shop).

Our website can also help you find the perfect **rail pass** for your itinerary and your budget, with easy, one-stop shopping for rail passes, seat reservations, and point-to-point tickets (RickSteves.com/rail).

Rick Steves' Tours, Guidebooks, TV Shows, and More

Small Group Tours: Want to travel with greater efficiency and less stress? We offer more than 40 itineraries reaching the best destinations in this book...and beyond. Each year about 30,000 travelers join us on about 1,000 Rick Steves bus tours. You'll enjoy great guides and a fun bunch of travel partners (with small groups of 24 to 28 travelers). You'll find European adventures to fit every vacation length. For all the details, and to get our tour catalog, visit RickSteves.com/tours or call us at +1 425 608 4217.

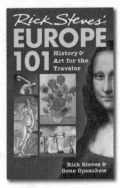

Books: This book is just one of many books in my series on European travel, which includes country and city guidebooks, Snapshots (excerpted chapters from bigger guides), Pocket Guides (full-color little books on big cities), "Best Of" guidebooks (condensed, full-color country guides), and my budget-travel skills handbook, *Rick Steves Europe Through the Back Door*. A complete list of my titles—

including phrase books, cruising guides, and travelogues on European art, history, and culture—appears near the end of this book.

TV Shows and Travel Talks: My public television series, *Rick Steves' Europe,* covers Europe from top to bottom with over 100 half-hour episodes—and we're working on new shows every year (watch full episodes at my website for free). My free online video library, Rick Steves Classroom Europe, offers a searchable database of short video clips on European history, culture, and geography (Classroom.RickSteves.com). And to raise your travel I.Q., check out the video versions of our popular classes (covering most European countries as well as travel skills, packing smart, cruising, tech for travelers, European art, and travel as a political act—RickSteves.com/travel-talks).

Audio Tours on My Free App: I've produced dozens of free, self-guided audio tours of the top sights in Europe. For those tours and other audio content, get my free **Rick Steves Audio Europe app,** an extensive online library organized by destination. For more on my app, see page 26.

Radio: My weekly public radio show, *Travel with Rick Steves,* features interviews with travel experts from around the world. It airs on 400 public radio stations across the US. An archive of programs is available at RickSteves.com/radio.

Podcasts: You can enjoy my travel content via several free podcasts. The podcast version of my radio show brings you a weekly, hour-long travel conversation. My other podcasts include a weekly selection of video clips from my public television show, my audio tours of Europe's top sights, and live recordings of my travel classes (RickSteves.com/watch-read-listen/audio/podcasts).

APPENDIX

Holidays and Festivals

This list includes selected festivals in major cities, plus national holidays observed throughout Greece. Many sights and banks close on national holidays—keep this in mind when planning your itinerary. Before planning a trip around a festival, verify the dates with the festival website, the Greek tourist office (www.visitgreece.gr), or my "Upcoming Holidays and Festivals in Greece" web page at RickSteves.com/europe/greece/festivals.

Jan 1	New Year's Day
Jan 6	Epiphany
Mid-Jan-March	Carnival season (Apokreo), famous in Patra, peaks on the last Sunday before Lent
Late Feb-Early March	"Clean Monday" (Kathari Deftera), the first day of Lent in the Orthodox church
March 25	Greek Independence Day
April	Orthodox Good Friday-Easter Monday: May 3-6 in 2024; April 18-21 in 2025
May 1	Labor Day
June	Miaoulia Festival, Hydra (falls on the weekend closest to June 21)

June	Nafplio Festival, classical music
June-Aug	Athens & Epidavros Festival (music, opera, dance, and theater at the Odeon of Herodes Atticus beneath the Acropolis in Athens; drama and music at the Theater of Epidavros; www.greekfestival.gr/en)
July-Aug	Ancient Olympia International Festival (music, dance, and theater at the site of the ancient Olympics)
Aug 15	Assumption
Sept	Athens International Film Festival
Oct 28	Ohi Day (anniversary of the "No"; commemorates rejection of Mussolini's WWII ultimatum)
Dec 25-26	Christmas and "Second Day" of Christmas

APPENDIX

Books and Films

To learn more about Greece past and present, check out a few of these books and films.

Nonfiction

Alexander the Great (Paul Anthony Cartledge, 2004). Alexander's legacy comes to life in this engaging history.

Apology (Plato, 390 BC). This is a classic for a reason, opening up a window into the Greek mind and soul.

The Cambridge Illustrated History of Ancient Greece (Paul Anthony Cartledge, 1997). Offered in large format, Cartledge's history is packed with gorgeous illustrations.

Colossus of Maroussi (Henry Miller, 1941). Miller tells a sometimes-graphic account of his down-and-out sojourn in Greece in the late 1930s.

A Concise History of Greece (Richard Clogg, 1986). For an overview of the 18th century to modern times, this history is surprisingly succinct.

Dinner with Persephone (Patricia Storace, 1996). This book is more than a memoir about living in Athens—it's one writer's critical look at modern Greek culture and family life.

Eleni (Nicholas Gage, 1983). Gage tells the riveting account of his quest to uncover the truth behind his mother's assassination during Greece's civil war.

The Greeks (H. D. F. Kitto, 1951). Considered the standard text on ancient Greece by a leading scholar, this decades-old work is still quite accessible.

The Greek Way (Edith Hamilton, 1930). Hamilton introduces the world of ancient Greece to the 20th century.

Inside Hitler's Greece (Mark Mazower, 1993). This shocking account of the Nazi occupation of Greece details the background for the country's civil war.

Lives (Plutarch, 100 AD). Written at the start of the second century, *Lives* is an epic attempt to chronicle the ancient world through biography.

Mani: Travels in the Southern Peloponnese (Patrick Leigh Fermor, 1958). This is the definitive book on the "forgotten" side of the peninsula.

Mediterranean in the Ancient World (Fernand Braudel, 1972). Braudel gives a marvelous overview of the ancient Mediterranean.

Mythology (Edith Hamilton, 1942). Along with *The Greek Way*, this is a must-read tome on classic myths and cultures.

The Nature of Alexander (Mary Renault, 1975). This biography from a famous novelist provides insight on Alexander the Great.

The Parthenon Enigma (Joan Breton Connelly, 2014). Connelly uses the temple's dramatic frieze—depicting, she says, human sacrifice—to go deep into the history of the Acropolis.

Persian Fire (Tom Holland, 2005). Holland offers an excellent history of the fifth-century BC Persian conflict.

Republic (Plato, 380 BC). In this classic, Plato captures the words of Socrates from Golden Age times.

Sailing the Wine-Dark Sea: Why the Greeks Matter (Thomas Cahill, 2003). Cahill astutely probes the relevance of ancient Greek culture to today's world.

The Spartans (Paul Anthony Cartledge, 2002). This history chronicles the rise and fall of the Spartan warriors.

The Summer of My Greek Taverna (Tom Stone, 2002). An American expat recounts his experiences in Greece while running a bar on the island of Patmos.

A Traveller's History of Greece (Timothy Boatswain and Colin Nicolson, 1990). This compact, well-written account covers the earliest times to the present.

Fiction

Corelli's Mandolin (Louis de Bernières, 1993). This novel about ill-fated lovers on a war-torn Greek island was made into a 2001 film starring Nicolas Cage and Penélope Cruz.

Deeper Shade of Blue (Paul Johnston, 2002). Detective Alex Mavros leaves Athens for the island of Trigono to find a missing woman.

Fire from Heaven (Mary Renault, 1969). The most renowned author of historical novels about Greece offers the dramatic story of Alexander the Great.

APPENDIX

The Frogs (Aristophanes, c. 405 BC). One of 11 surviving comic plays by the great playwright, it tells the story of Dionysus' journey to Hades to bring Euripides back from the dead.

Gates of Fire (Steven Pressfield, 1998). Pressfield re-creates the Battle of Thermopylae, where 300 Spartans held back the Persian army—for a while.

The Iliad/The Odyssey (Homer, 850 BC). This classic epic follows the hero Odysseus through the Trojan War and his return home.

The King Must Die (Mary Renault, 1958). Renault reimagines the Theseus legend in this exciting tale.

The Last Temptation of Christ (Nikos Kazantzakis, 1953). Kazantzakis' literary reinterpretation of the Gospels is hailed internationally as a masterpiece.

Little Infamies (Panos Karnezis, 1903). This fine collection of short stories looks at the lives of Greek villagers with magical realism.

The Magus (John Fowles, 1965). An Englishman plays psychological games with a wealthy recluse on a Greek island.

Middlesex (Jeffrey Eugenides, 2002). An American author of Greek descent explores the Greek immigrant experience in the US, as well as sexual identity.

Oedipus the King (Sophocles, c. 429 BC). The most famous of the poet Sophocles' plays along with *Antigone,* this classic Greek tragedy surrounds the prophecy that Oedipus will kill his father and marry his mother.

Stealing Athena (Karen Essex, 2008). The Parthenon plays a pivotal role in the lives of Pericles' mistress, Aspasia, and Lord Elgin's wife, Mary.

Uncle Petros and Goldbach's Conjecture (Apostolos Doxiadis, 1992). A Greek genius is obsessed with trying to prove one of mathematics' great theories.

The Walled Orchard (Tom Holt, 1990). Amusing and well-researched, this novel is the pseudo-autobiography of comic playwright Eupolis.

Zorba the Greek (Nikos Kazantzakis, 1946). A wily old rogue teaches life's lessons to a withdrawn intellectual.

TV and Film

300 (2006). Based on a graphic novel, this is a highly fictional and stylized account of the Battle of Thermopylae.

300: Rise of an Empire (2014). Also based on a graphic novel, this movie tells the tale of the final naval battle of Salamis after Thermopylae.

Alexander (2004). Colin Farrell plays the military genius who conquered the known world.

Boy on a Dolphin (1957). A beautiful sponge diver on Hydra, played by Sophia Loren, becomes aware of her cultural heritage.

Clash of the Titans (1981). Featuring an all-star cast including Laurence Olivier, Claire Bloom, and Maggie Smith, this adaptation of the Perseus myth is a classic.

The Guns of Navarone (1961). A team of English commandos tries to take out an impregnable WWII German artillery battery on a Greek island. Based on the 1957 novel by Alistair MacLean.

Mamma Mia! (2008). Filmed in the mainland region of Pelion and on the islands of Skiathos and Skopelos, this musical uses ABBA songs to tell the story of a young woman trying to find her father.

My Big Fat Greek Wedding (2002). Hilarity ensues when a Greek-American woman tries to plan her wedding while contending with her large and boisterous family (also a 2016 sequel, *My Big Fat Greek Wedding 2*).

My Family and Other Animals (2005). This film follows the adventures of an English family that relocated to Greece in 1939.

My Life in Ruins (2009). This romantic comedy stars Nia Vardalos as a struggling tour guide leading her group of misfit tourists.

Never on Sunday (1960). Melina Mercouri stars as a Greek prostitute who is pursued by an American scholar with classical ideals.

Secrets of the Parthenon (2008). This NOVA episode, available on www.pbs.org, documents the restoration of the Parthenon.

Shirley Valentine (1989). A middle-aged housewife sets off on a Greek-island holiday with a girlfriend to shake up her monotonous life.

Stella (1955). A young Greek woman must decide between falling in love and retaining her freedom.

The Trojan Women (1971). Euripides' classic tragedy of Troy's female aristocracy in chains features Katharine Hepburn, Vanessa Redgrave, and Irene Pappas.

Troy (2004). Brad Pitt stars as the petulant warrior Achilles in this adaptation of Homer's epic.

Z (1969). This thriller follows the assassination of a crusading politician—and the rise of the Greek junta—in the 1960s.

Books and Films for Kids

Ancient Civilizations: Greece (Eva Bargallo I Chaves, 2004). Kids can brush up on ancient Greece, including history, art, government, and mythology.

Ancient Greece! 40 Hands-On Activities to Experience This Wondrous Age (Avery Hart and Paul Mantell, 1999). With this book, learn how to make traditional foods, build a model temple, and put on a play.

Greece (Changing Face of...) (Tasmin Osler, 2003). This nonfiction book weaves first-person accounts from modern Greeks with a summary of today's challenges.

Greece in Spectacular Cross-Section (Stephen Biesty, 2006). Kids and grown-ups alike will enjoy these cut-away diagrams re-creating ancient sites.

Hercules (1997). This animated Disney film is loosely based on the hero of Greek legend, Hercules, son of Zeus.

If I Were a Kid in Ancient Greece (Cricket Media, 2012). Kids can put themselves in the sandals of a young Grecian in this fun series.

Percy Jackson and the Olympians (Rick Riordan, 2005). A young boy learns that he is the son of a Greek god in this clever and amusing young-adult series. Two *Percy Jackson* films bring the books to life (2010 and 2013).

The Random House Book of Greek Myths (Joan D. Vinge, 1999). Greek gods and goddesses are highlighted in this illustrated primer on Greek mythology.

This Is Greece (Miroslav Sasek, 1966). Reissued in 2009, Sasek's classic picture book captures the essence of ancient and modern Greece.

Conversions and Climate

Numbers and Stumblers

- Europeans write a few of their numbers differently than we do. 1 =1, 4 =4, 7 =7.
- In Europe, dates appear as day/month/year, so Christmas 2025 is 25/12/25.
- Commas are decimal points and decimals are commas. A dollar and a half is $1,50, one thousand is 1.000, and there are 5.280 feet in a mile.
- When counting with fingers, start with your thumb. If you hold up your first finger to request one item, you'll probably get two.
- What Americans call the second floor of a building is the first floor in Europe.
- On escalators and moving sidewalks, Europeans keep the left "lane" open for passing. Keep to the right.

Metric Conversions

A **kilogram** equals 1,000 grams (about 2.2 pounds). One hundred **grams** (a common unit at markets) is about a quarter-pound. One **liter** is about a quart, or almost four to a gallon.

A **kilometer** is six-tenths of a mile. To convert kilometers to miles, cut the kilometers in half and add back 10 percent of the original (120 km: 60 + 12 = 72 miles). One **meter** is 39 inches—just over a yard.

1 foot = 0.3 meter	1 square yard = 0.8 square meter
1 yard = 0.9 meter	1 square mile = 2.6 square kilometers
1 mile = 1.6 kilometers	1 ounce = 28 grams
1 centimeter = 0.4 inch	1 quart = 0.95 liter
1 meter = 39.4 inches	1 kilogram = 2.2 pounds
1 kilometer = 0.62 mile	32°F = 0°C

Clothing Sizes

When shopping for clothing, use these US-to-European comparisons as general guidelines (but note that no conversion is perfect).

Women: For pants and dresses, add 30 in Greece (US 10 = Greece 40). For blouses and sweaters, add 8 for most of Europe (US 32 = European 40). For shoes, add 30-31 (US 7 = European 37/38).

Men: For shirts, multiply by 2 and add about 8 (US 15 = European 38). For jackets and suits, add 10. For shoes, add 32-34.

Children: Clothing is sized by height—in centimeters (2.5 cm = 1 inch), so a US size 8 roughly equates to 132-140. For shoes up to size 13, add 16-18, and for sizes 1 and up, add 30-32.

APPENDIX

Athens' Climate

First line, average daily high; second line, average daily low; third line, average days without rain. For more detailed weather statistics for destinations in this book (as well as the rest of the world), check Wunderground.com.

J	F	M	A	M	J	J	A	S	O	N	D
56°	57°	60°	66°	75°	83°	88°	88°	82°	73°	66°	59°
44°	45°	47°	53°	60°	68°	73°	72°	67°	59°	53°	48°
24	22	26	27	28	28	30	30	28	27	24	24

Fahrenheit and Celsius Conversion

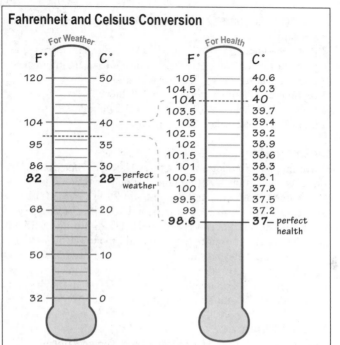

Europe takes its temperature using the Celsius scale, while we opt for Fahrenheit. For a rough conversion from Celsius to Fahrenheit, double the number and add 30. For weather, remember that 28°C is 82°F—perfect. For health, 37°C is just right. At a launderette, 30°C is cold, 40°C is warm (usually the default setting), 60°C is hot, and 95°C is boiling. Your air-conditioner should be set at about 20°C.

Packing Checklist

Whether you're traveling for five days or five weeks, you won't need more than this. Pack light to enjoy the sweet freedom of true mobility.

Clothing

- ❏ 5 shirts: long- & short-sleeve
- ❏ 2 pairs pants (or skirts/capris)
- ❏ 1 pair shorts
- ❏ 5 pairs underwear & socks
- ❏ 1 pair walking shoes
- ❏ Sweater or warm layer
- ❏ Rainproof jacket with hood
- ❏ Tie, scarf, belt, and/or hat
- ❏ Swimsuit
- ❏ Sleepwear/loungewear

Money

- ❏ Debit card(s)
- ❏ Credit card(s)
- ❏ Hard cash (US $100-200)
- ❏ Money belt

Documents

- ❏ Passport
- ❏ Other required ID: Vaccine card/Covid test, entry visa, etc.
- ❏ Driver's license, student ID, hostel card, etc.
- ❏ Tickets & confirmations: flights, hotels, trains, rail pass, car rental, sight entries
- ❏ Photocopies of important documents
- ❏ Insurance details
- ❏ Guidebooks & maps

Electronics

- ❏ Mobile phone
- ❏ Camera & related gear
- ❏ Tablet/ebook reader/laptop
- ❏ Headphones/earbuds
- ❏ Chargers & batteries
- ❏ Phone car charger & mount (or GPS device)
- ❏ Plug adapters

Toiletries

- ❏ Basics: soap, shampoo, toothbrush, toothpaste, floss, deodorant, sunscreen, brush/comb, etc.
- ❏ Medicines & vitamins
- ❏ First-aid kit
- ❏ Glasses/contacts/sunglasses
- ❏ Face masks & hand sanitizer
- ❏ Sewing kit
- ❏ Packet of tissues (for WC)
- ❏ Earplugs

Miscellaneous

- ❏ Daypack
- ❏ Sealable plastic baggies
- ❏ Laundry supplies: soap, laundry bag, clothesline, spot remover
- ❏ Small umbrella
- ❏ Travel alarm/watch
- ❏ Notepad & pen
- ❏ Journal

Optional Extras

- ❏ Second pair of shoes (flip-flops, sandals, tennis shoes, boots)
- ❏ Travel hairdryer
- ❏ Picnic supplies
- ❏ Disinfecting wipes
- ❏ Water bottle
- ❏ Fold-up tote bag
- ❏ Small flashlight
- ❏ Mini binoculars
- ❏ Small towel or washcloth
- ❏ Inflatable pillow/neck rest
- ❏ Tiny lock
- ❏ Address list (to mail postcards)
- ❏ Extra passport photos

Greek Survival Phrases

Knowing a few phrases of Greek can help if you're traveling off the beaten path. Just learning the pleasantries (such as please and thank you) will improve your connections with locals, even in the bigger cities.

Because Greek words can be transliterated differently in English, I've also included the Greek spellings. Note that in Greek, a semicolon is used the same way we use a question mark.

Hello. (formal)	Gia sas. Γειά σας.	yah sahs
Hi. / Bye. (informal)	Gia. Γειά.	yah
Good morning.	Kali mera. Καλή μέρα.	kah-**lee meh**-rah
Good afternoon.	Kali spera. Καλή σπέρα.	kah-**lee speh**-rah
Do you speak English?	Milate anglika? Μιλάτε αγγλικά;	mee-**lah**-teh ahn-glee-**kah**
Yes. / No.	Ne. / Ohi. Ναι. / Όχι.	neh / **oh**-hee
I understand.	Katalaveno. Καταλαβαίνω.	kah-tah-lah-**veh**-noh
I (don't) understand.	(Den) katalaveno. (Δεν) καταλαβαίνω.	(dehn) kah-tah-lah-**veh**-noh
Please. (Also: You're welcome.)	Parakalo. Παρακαλώ.	pah-rah-kah-**loh**
Thank you (very much).	Efharisto (poli). Ευχαριστώ (πολύ).	ehf-hah-ree-**stoh** (poh-**lee**)
Excuse me. (Also: I'm sorry.)	Sygnomi. Συγνώμη.	seeg-**noh**-mee
No problem.	Kanena problima. Κανένα πρόβλημα.	kah-**neh**-nah **prohv**-lee-mah
Good.	Orea. Ωραία.	oh-**reh**-ah
Goodbye.	Antio. Αντίο.	ahd-**yoh** (think "adieu")
Good night.	Kali nikta. Καλή νύχτα.	kah-**lee neek**-tah
one / two	ena / dio ένα / δύο	**eh**-nah / **dee**-oh
three / four	tria / tessera τρία / τέσσερα	**tree**-ah / **teh**-seh-rah
five / six	pente / exi πέντε / έξι	**pehn**-deh / **ehk**-see
seven / eight	efta / ohto εφτά / οχτώ	ehf-**tah** / oh-**toh**
nine / ten	ennia / deka εννιά / δέκα	ehn-**yah** / **deh**-kah
hundred / thousand	ekato / hilia εκατό / χίλια	eh-kah-**toh** / **heel**-yah
How much?	Poso kani? Πόσο κάνει;	**poh**-soh **kah**-nee

English	Greek (transliteration)	Pronunciation
euro	evro / ευρώ	ev-**roh**
Write it?	Grapsete to? / Γράψετε το;	**grahp**-seh-teh toh
Is it free?	Ine dorean? / Είναι δωρεάν;	ee-neh doh-reh-**ahn**
Is it included?	Perilamvanete? / Περιλαμβάνεται;	peh-ree-lahm-**vah**-neh-teh
Where can I find / buy...?	Pou boro na vro / agoraso...? / Που μπορώ να βρω / αγοράσω...;	poo boh-**roh** nah vroh / ah-goh-**rah**-soh
I'd like / We'd like...	Tha ithela / Tha thelame... / Θα ήθελα / Θα θέλαμε...	thah ee-theh-lah / thah **theh**-lah-meh
...a room.	...ena dhomatio. / ...ένα δωμάτιο.	eh-nah doh-**mah**-tee-oh
...a ticket to ___.	...ena isitirio gia ___. / ...ένα εισιτήριο για ___.	eh-nah ee-see-**tee**-ree-oh yah
Is it possible?	Ginete? / Γίνεται;	**yee**-neh-teh
Where is...?	Pou ine...? / Που είναι...;	poo **ee**-neh
...the bus station	...o stathmos ton leoforion / ...ο σταθμός των λεωφορίων	oh **stahth**-mohs tohn leh-oh-foh-**ree**-ohn
...the train station	...o stathmos tou trenou / ...ο σταθμός του τρένου	oh **stahth**-mohs too **treh**-noo
...the tourist information office	...to grafeio enimerosis touriston / ...το γραφείο ενημέρωσης τουριστών	too grah-**fee**-oh eh-nee-**meh**-roh-sis too-ree-**stohn**
toilet	toualeta / τουαλέτα	twah-**leh**-tah
men / women	andres / gynekes / άντρες / γυναικες	**ahn**-drehs / yee-**neh**-kehs
left / right	dexia / aristera / δεξιά / αριστερά	dehk-see-**ah** / ah-ree-steh-**rah**
straight	efthia / ευθεία	ehf-**thee**-ah
At what time...	Ti ora... / Τι ώρα...	tee **oh**-rah
...does this open / close?	...anigete / klinete? / ...ανοίγετε / κλείνετε;	ah-**nee**-yeh-teh / **klee**-neh-teh
Just a moment.	Ena lepto. / Ένα λεπτό.	**eh**-nah lep-**toh**
now / soon / later	tora / se ligo / argotera / τώρα / σε λίγο / αργότερα	**toh**-rah / seh **lee**-goh / ar-**goh**-teh-rah
today / tomorrow	simera / avrio / σήμερα / αύριο	**see**-meh-rah / **ahv**-ree-oh

In a Greek Restaurant

I'd like to reserve...	Tha ithela na kliso... thah **ee**-theh-lah nah **klee**-soh Θα ήθελα να κλείσω...
We'd like to reserve...	Tha thelame na klisoume... Θα θέλαμε να κλείσουμε... thah **theh**-lah-meh nah **klee**-soo-meh
...a table for one / two.	...ena trapezi gia enan / dio. ...ένα τραπέζι για έναν / δύο. **eh**-nah trah-**peh**-zee yah **eh**-nahn / **dee**-oh
nonsmoking	mi kapnizon mee kahp-**nee**-zohn μη καπνίζων
Is this table free?	Ine eleftero afto to trapezi? Είναι ελεύθερο αυτό το τραπέζι; **ee**-neh eh-**lef**-teh-roh ahf-**toh** toh trah-**peh**-zee
The menu (in English), please.	Ton katalogo (sta anglika) parakalo. Τον κατάλογο (στα αγγλικά) παρακαλώ. tohn kah-**tah**-loh-goh (stah ahn-glee-**kah**) pah-rah-kah-**loh**
service (not) included	to servis (den) perilamvanete το σέρβις (δεν) περιλαμβάνεται toh **sehr**-vees (dehn) peh-ree-lahm-**vah**-neh-teh
cover charge	kouver koo-**vehr** κουβέρ
"to go"	gia exo yah **ehk**-soh για έξω
with / without	me / horis meh / hoh-**rees** με / χωρίς
and / or	ke / I keh / ee και / ή
fixed-price meal	menu meh-**noo** μενού
specialty of the house	i specialite tou magaziou η σπεσιαλιτέ του μαγαζιού ee speh-see-ah-lee-**teh** too mah-gah-zee-**oo**
half-portion	misi merida mee-**see** meh-**ree**-dah μισή μερίδα
daily special	to piato tis meras toh pee-**ah**-toh tees meh-**rahs** το πιάτο της μέρας
breakfast / lunch / dinner	proino / mesimeriano / vradino Πρωινό / μεσημεριανό / βραδινό proy-**noh** / meh-see-meh-ree-ah-**noh** / vrah-dee-**noh**
appetizers	proto piato **proh**-toh pee-**ah**-toh πρώτο πιάτο
bread / cheese	psomi / tiri psoh-**mee** / tee-**ree** ψωμί / τυρί
sandwich	sandwich, toast "sandwich," "toast" σάντουιτς, τόστ
soup / salad	soupa / salata **soo**-pah / sah-**lah**-tah σούπα / σαλάτα
meat	kreas **kray**-ahs κρέας
poultry / chicken	poulerika / kotopoulo πουλερικά / κοτόπουλο poo-leh-ree-**kah** / koh-**toh**-poo-loh

fish / seafood	psari / psarika	**psah**-ree / psah-ree-**kah**
	ψάρι / ψαρικά	
shellfish	thalassina	thah-lah-see-**nah**
	θαλασσινά	
fruit	frouta	**froo**-tah
	φρούτα	
vegetables	lahanika	lah-hah-nee-**kah**
	λαχανικά	
dessert	gliko	glee-**koh**
	γλυκό	
(tap) water	nero (tis vrisis)	neh-**roh** (tees **vree**-sees)
	νερό (της βρύσης)	
mineral water	metalliko nero	meh-tah-lee-**koh** neh-**roh**
	μεταλλικό νερό	
milk	gala	**gah**-lah
	γάλα	
(orange) juice	himos (portokali)	hee-**mohs** (por-toh-**kah**-lee)
	χυμός (πορτοκάλι)	
coffee / tea	kafes / tsai	kah-**fehs** / **chah**-ee
	καφές / τσάι	
wine	krasi	krah-**see**
	κρασί	
wine (printed on label)	inos	**ee**-nohs
	οίνος	
red / white	kokkino / aspro	**koh**-kee-noh / **ah**-sproh
	κόκκινο / άσπρο	
sweet / dry / semi-dry	gliko / ksiro / imixiro	
	γλυκό / ξηρό / ημίξηρο	
		lee-**koh** / ksee-**roh** / ee-**meek**-see-roh
glass / bottle	potiri / boukali	poh-**tee**-ree / boo-**kah**-lee
	ποτήρι /μπουκάλι	
beer	bira	**bee**-rah
	μπύρα	
Here you are. (when given food)	Oriste.	oh-**ree**-steh
	Ορίστε.	
Enjoy your meal!	Kali orexi!	kah-**lee** oh-**rehk**-see
	Καλή όρεξη!	
(To your) health! (like "Cheers!")	(Stin i) gia mas!	(stee nee) yah mahs
	(Στην υ) γειά μας!	
Another.	Allo ena.	**ah**-loh **eh**-nah
	Άλλο ένα.	
Bill, please.	Ton logariasmo parakalo.	
	Τον λογαριασμό παρακαλώ.	
	tohn loh-gah-ree-ahs-**moh** pah-rah-kah-**loh**	
tip	bourbouar	boor-boo-**ar**
	μπουρμπουάρ	
Very good!	Poli oreo!	poh-**lee** oh-**ray**-oh
	Πολύ ωραίο!	

INDEX

INDEX

MAP INDEX

Explore Europe

At ricksteves.com you can browse through thousands of articles, videos, photos and radio interviews, plus find a wealth of money-saving travel tips for planning your dream trip. And with our mobile-friendly website, you can easily access all this great travel information anywhere you go.

TV Shows

Preview the places you'll visit by watching entire half-hour episodes of *Rick Steves' Europe* (choose from all 100 shows) on-demand, for free.

your travel dreams into affordable reality

Radio Interviews

Enjoy ready access to Rick's vast library of radio interviews covering travel tips and cultural insights that relate specifically to your Europe travel plans.

Travel Forums

Learn, ask, share! Our online community of savvy travelers is a great resource for first-time travelers to Europe, as well as seasoned pros.

Travel News

Subscribe to our free Travel News e-newsletter, and get monthly updates from Rick on what's happening in Europe.

Classroom Europe®

Check out our free resource for educators with 500 short video clips from the *Rick Steves' Europe* TV show.

Rick's Free Travel App

Get your FREE **Rick Steves Audio Europe**™ app to enjoy…

- Dozens of self-guided tours of Europe's top museums, sights and historic walks
- Hundreds of tracks filled with cultural insights and sightseeing tips from Rick's radio interviews
- All organized into handy geographic playlists
- For Apple and Android

With Rick whispering in your ear, Europe gets even better.

Find out more at ricksteves.com

Gear up for your next adventure at ricksteves.com

Light Luggage

Pack light and right with Rick Steves' affordable, custom-designed rolling carry-on bags, backpacks, day packs and shoulder bags.

Accessories

From packing cubes to moneybelts and beyond, Rick has personally selected the travel goodies that will help your trip go smoother.

Shop at ricksteves.com

Rick Steves has

Experience maximum Europe

Save time and energy

This guidebook is your independent-travel toolkit. But for all it delivers, it's still up to you to devote the time and energy it takes to manage the preparation and logistics that are essential for a happy trip. If that's a hassle, there's a solution.

Rick Steves Tours

A Rick Steves tour takes you to Europe's most interesting places with great

great tours, too!

with minimum stress

guides and small groups. We follow Rick's favorite itineraries, ride in comfy buses, stay in family-run hotels, and bring you intimately close to the Europe you've traveled so far to see. Most importantly, we take away the logistical headaches so you can focus on the fun.

Join the fun

This year we'll take thousands of free-spirited travelers—nearly half of them repeat customers—along with us on 50 different itineraries, from Athens to Istanbul. Is a Rick Steves tour the right fit for your travel dreams?

Find out at ricksteves.com, where you can also check seat availability and sign up. Europe is best experienced with happy travel partners. We hope you can join us.

See our itineraries at ricksteves.com

BEST OF GUIDES

Full-color guides in an easy-to-scan format. Focused on top sights and experiences in the most popular European destinations

Best of England
Best of Europe
Best of France
Best of Germany
Best of Ireland
Best of Italy
Best of Scotland
Best of Spain

COMPREHENSIVE GUIDES

City, country, and regional guides printed on Bible-thin paper. Packed with detailed coverage for a multi-week trip exploring iconic sights and venturing off the beaten path

Amsterdam & the Netherlands
Barcelona
Belgium: Bruges, Brussels, Antwerp & Ghent
Berlin
Budapest
Central Europe
Croatia & Slovenia
England
Florence & Tuscany
France
Germany
Great Britain
Greece: Athens & the Peloponnese
Iceland
Ireland
Istanbul
Italy
London
Paris
Portugal
Prague & the Czech Republic
Provence & the French Riviera
Rome
Scandinavia
Scotland
Sicily
Spain
Switzerland
Venice
Vienna, Salzburg & Tirol

E BEST OF ROME

, Italy's capital, is studded with
 remnants and floodlit-fountain
s. From the Vatican to the Colos-
with crazy traffic in between, Rome
erful, huge, and exhausting. The
the heat, and the weighty history

of the Eternal City where Caesars walked
can make tourists wilt. Recharge by taking siestas, gelato breaks, and after-dark
walks, strolling from one atmospheric
square to another in the refreshing evening air.

Pantheon—which
ome until the
,000 years old
ver 1,500).

athens in the Vat-
the humanistic

diators fought
her, entertaining

me ristorante.

POCKET GUIDES
Compact color guides for shorter trips

Amsterdam	Paris
Athens	Prague
Barcelona	Rome
Florence	Venice
Italy's Cinque Terre	Vienna
London	
Munich & Salzburg	

SNAPSHOT GUIDES
Focused single-destination coverage

Basque Country: Spain & France
Copenhagen & the Best of Denmark
Dublin
Dubrovnik
Edinburgh
Hill Towns of Central Italy
Krakow, Warsaw & Gdansk
Lisbon
Loire Valley
Madrid & Toledo
Milan & the Italian Lakes District
Naples & the Amalfi Coast
Nice & the French Riviera
Normandy
Northern Ireland
Norway
Reykjavík
Rothenburg & the Rhine
Sevilla, Granada & Southern Spain
St. Petersburg, Helsinki & Tallinn
Stockholm

CRUISE PORTS GUIDES
Reference for cruise ports of call

Mediterranean Cruise Ports
Scandinavian & Northern European
  Cruise Ports

Complete your library with...

TRAVEL SKILLS & CULTURE
*Study up on travel skills and gain
insight on history and culture*

Europe 101
Europe Through the Back Door
Europe's Top 100 Masterpieces
European Christmas
European Easter
European Festivals
For the Love of Europe
Italy for Food Lovers
Travel as a Political Act

PHRASE BOOKS & DICTIONARIES
French
French, Italian & German
German
Italian
Portuguese
Spanish

PLANNING MAPS
Britain, Ireland & London
Europe
France & Paris
Germany, Austria & Switzerland
Iceland
Ireland
Italy
Scotland
Spain & Portugal

Credits

RESEARCHER
For help with this edition, Rick relied on...

Ben Curtis

Ben is a native of the Pacific Northwest, but he's lived in the UK, Germany, Spain, Norway, and Hungary, too. He's worked as a university professor, a tour guide, and an advisor to the British government, and has written several books on history and politics. Nowadays home is Prague, where you might run into him at a classical concert or out wandering through the Czech mountains.

ACKNOWLEDGMENTS

Thank you to Risa Laib for her 25-plus years of dedication to the Rick Steves guidebook series. *Efharisto poli* to our tour-guide friends David Willett, Colleen Murphy, and Julie and Reid Coen for their invaluable help in shaping this book. Their travel savvy, knowledge, and understanding of Greek culture—and their never-ending quest to find the perfect ruined temple, secluded beach, bottle of ouzo, and other unique experiences—gave this book a firm foundation. Also, many thanks to Kiki Tsagkaraki-Rae for her help with the Greek survival phrases. *Stin i gia mas!*

PHOTO CREDITS

Avalon Travel
Hachette Book Group
1700 Fourth Street
Berkeley, CA 94710

Printed in Canada by Friesens
Seventh Edition. Second printing December 2023.

ISBN 978-1-64171-539-3

For the latest on Rick's talks, guidebooks, tours, public television series, and public radio show, contact Rick Steves' Europe, 130 Fourth Avenue North, Edmonds, WA 98020, +1 425 771 8303, RickSteves.com, rick@ricksteves.com.

Rick Steves' Europe

Managing Editor: Jennifer Madison Davis
Assistant Managing Editor: Cathy Lu
Editors: Glenn Eriksen, Julie Fanselow, Suzanne Kotz, Rosie Leutzinger, Teresa Nemeth, Jessica Shaw, Carrie Shepherd, Chelsea Wing
Researcher: Ben Curtis
Contributors: Cameron Hewitt, Gene Openshaw
Graphic Content Director: Sandra Hundacker
Maps & Graphics: Orin Dubrow, David C. Hoerlein, Lauren Mills, Mary Rostad

Avalon Travel

Senior Editor and Series Manager: Athena Waverley Prasher
Associate Managing Editors: Jamie Andrade, Sierra Machado
Copy Editor: Kelly Lydick
Proofreader: Maggie Ryan
Indexer: Stephen Callahan
Production & Typesetting: Lisi Baldwin, Rue Flaherty, Jane Musser
Cover Design: Kimberly Glyder Design
Maps & Graphics: Kat Bennett

COLOR MAPS

*Greece • Athens & The Peloponnese • Athens
• Central Athens • Athens Transit*

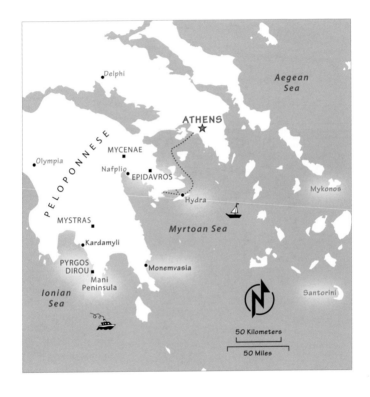

Delphi

Aegean
Sea

ATHENS

PELOPONNESE

Olympia

MYCENAE

Nafplio

EPIDAVROS

Hydra

Mykonos

MYSTRAS

Myrtoan Sea

Kardamyli

PYRGOS
DIROU

Monemvasia

Mani
Peninsula

Ionian
Sea

Santorini

50 Kilometers

50 Miles

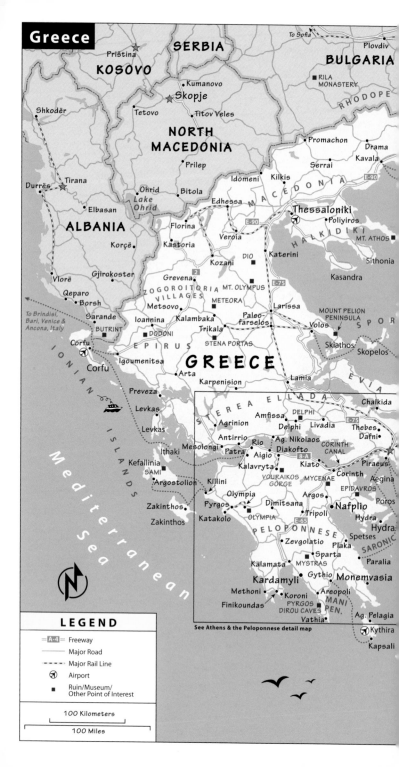

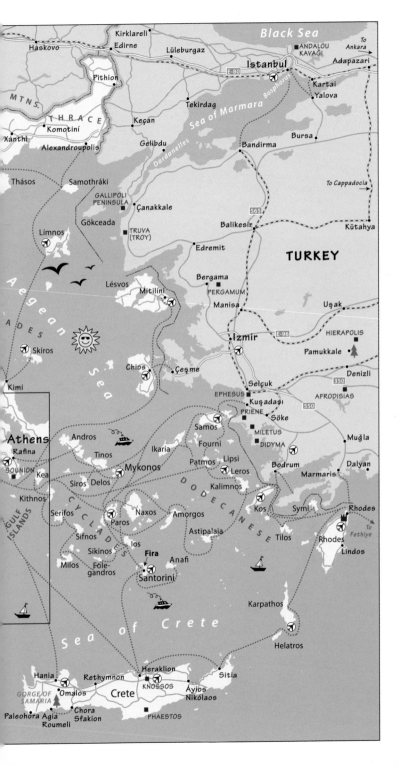

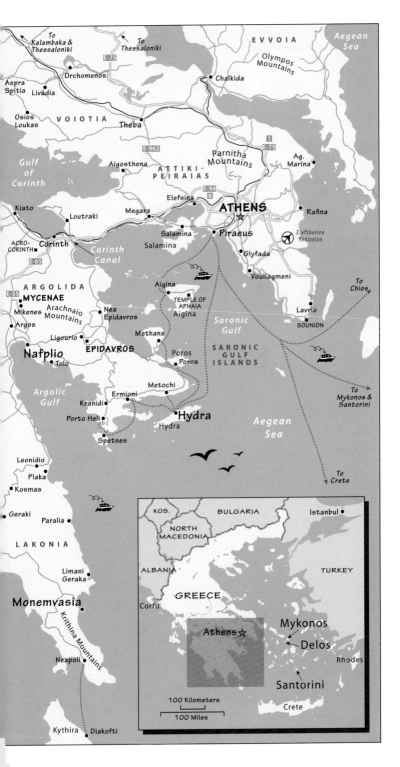

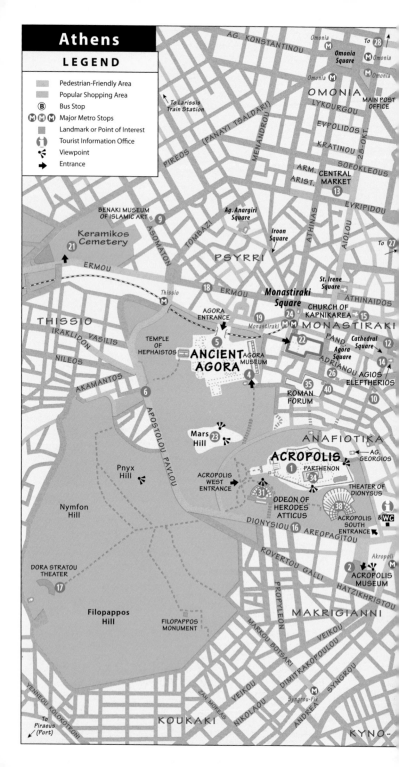

SIGHTS

1. Acropolis
2. Acropolis Museum
3. Adrianou Street
4. Agora Museum
5. Ancient Agora
6. Apostolou Pavlou Street
7. Arch of Hadrian
8. Benaki Museum of Greek History & Culture
9. Benaki Mus. of Islamic Art
10. Benizelos Mansion
11. Byzantine & Christian Museum
12. Cathedral (Mitropolis)
13. Central Market
14. Church of Agios Eleftherios
15. Church of Kapnikarea
16. Dionysiou Areopagitou St.
17. Dora Stratou Theater
18. Ermou Street
19. Flea Market
20. Jewish Museum
21. Keramikos Cemetery
22. Library of Hadrian
23. Mars Hill (Areopagus)
24. Monastiraki Square
25. Museum of Cycladic Art
26. Museum of Greek Folk Musical Instruments
27. To Mus. of the City of Athens
28. To National Archaeological Museum & Exarchia District
29. National Garden
30. To National War Museum & National Gallery
31. Odeon of Herodes Atticus
32. Panathenaic (Olympic) Stadium
33. Parliament
34. Parthenon
35. Roman Forum
36. Syntagma Square
37. Temple of Olympian Zeus
38. Theater of Dionysus
39. Tomb of the Unknown Soldier & Evzone Guards
40. Tower of the Winds
41. Zappeion

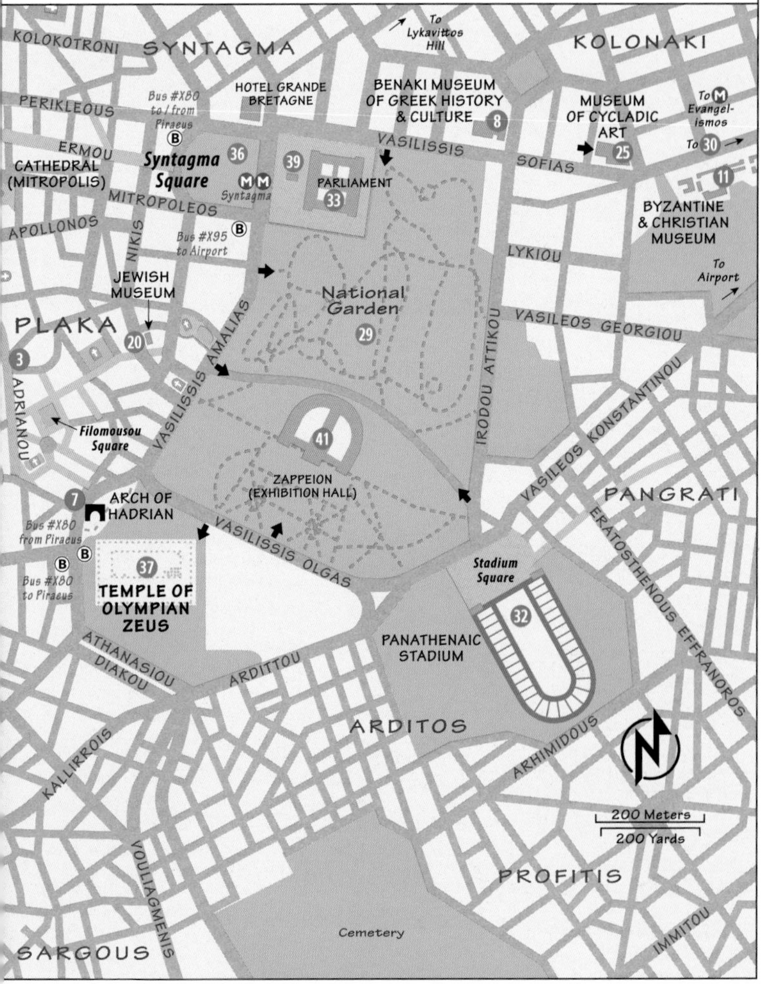

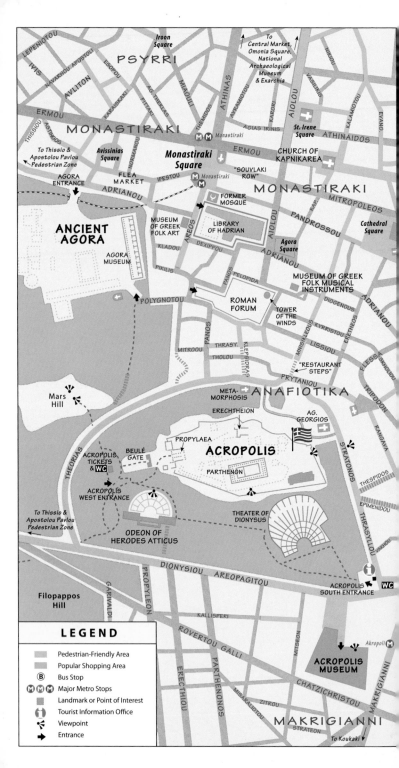

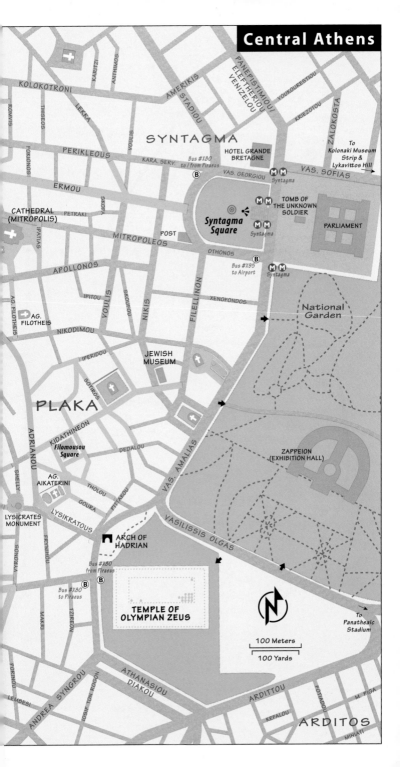

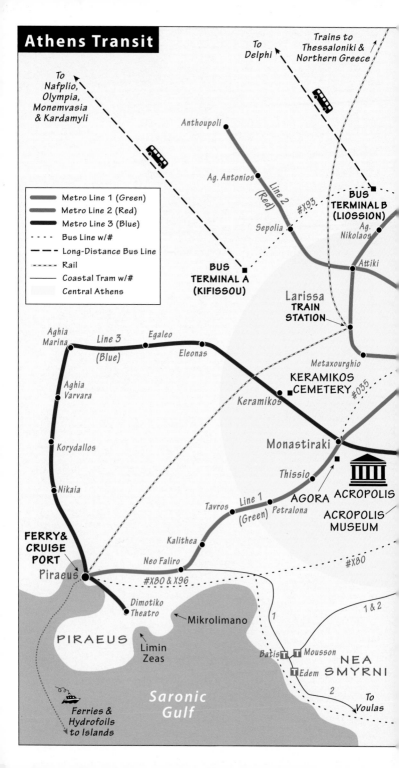

Let's Keep on Travelin'

Your trip doesn't need to end.

Follow Rick on social media!